THE LIFE AND DEATH OF STATES

The Life and Death of States

CENTRAL EUROPE AND
THE TRANSFORMATION
OF MODERN SOVEREIGNTY

Natasha Wheatley

PRINCETON UNIVERSITY PRESS
PRINCETON & OXFORD

Published by Princeton University Press
41 William Street, Princeton, New Jersey 08540
99 Banbury Road, Oxford OX2 6JX

press.princeton.edu

All Rights Reserved

Names: Wheatley, Natasha, author.
Title: The life and death of states : Central Europe and the transformation of modern
    sovereignty / Natasha Wheatley.
Description: Princeton, New Jersey : Princeton University Press, [2023] | Includes
    bibliographical references and index.
Identifiers: LCCN 2022028809 (print) | LCCN 2022028810 (ebook) | ISBN 9780691244075
    (hardback) | ISBN 9780691244082 (ebook)
Subjects: LCSH: Europe, Central—International status. | Austria—Politics and government—
    1848–1918. | Newly independent states—Europe, Central—History—20th century.
Classification: LCC KZ4160 .W44 2023 (print) | LCC KZ4160 (ebook) | DDC 341.26—
    dc23/eng/20221201
LC record available at https://lccn.loc.gov/2022028809
LC ebook record available at https://lccn.loc.gov/2022028810

British Library Cataloging-in-Publication Data is available

Editorial: Priya Nelson, Barbara Shi, and Emma Wagh
Jacket Design: Haley Chung
Production: Lauren Reese
Publicity: William Pagdatoon

Jacket image: Paul Klee, *Spiral Screw Flowers II (Spiralschraubenblüten II)*, 1932. © 2022
Artists Rights Society (ARS), New York. bpk Bildagentur / Sprengel Museum / Michael Herling |
Aline Gwose / Art Resource, NY.

This book has been composed in Miller.

10 9 8 7 6 5 4 3 2 1

For my parents
Glenda Joy Pryor and Robert Leslie Wheatley

CONTENTS

ACKNOWLEDGMENTS

THIS BOOK CONTAINS traces of many lives, continents, and communities. Something of it stretches back to the experience of coming of age in Australia in the 1990s, as Indigenous land rights movements galvanized the public sphere and first drew me to questions of rights, time, and sovereignty. But it took shape very far from home, in contexts and worlds made, not given. And it took shape slowly. I am grateful to the diverse individuals and institutions who have nourished it in Australia, Europe, and the United States over many years.

At the University of Sydney, Chris Hilliard modeled the life of the mind and first told me about something called graduate school. His support was pivotal—both in my path to the United States and when I returned to Sydney as a postdoctoral fellow—and I cannot thank him enough. The same is true of Glenda Sluga, most generous of mentors across many years. I was almost improperly happy as a PhD student at Columbia. Reading European history with Mark Mazower was a formative and humbling experience: I am grateful for his wisdom, guidance, and gracious example, including an important late intervention in the book manuscript. I owe Sam Moyn and Susan Pedersen an incalculable amount—for all they have taught me and the myriad ways they have supported me. In conversation with Sam, the world of ideas acquires a plasticity and a power that remains endlessly inspiring for me. Susan's preternatural facility with historical argument serves as model and unattainable goal. I could not have begun this project at Columbia without Debbie Coen, who gave generously of her time and insight. Her work at the intersection of Central European history and the history of science illuminates so many paths for the rest of us. In my first semester at Columbia, I stumbled into a seminar on "epistemic order/social order" taught by Matthew Jones. It turned out to be the best class I ever took, anywhere, and one that reshaped my methodological horizons. I owe thanks also to Volker Berghahn, Janaki Bakhle, Vicky de Grazia, Sheldon Pollock, and the late Fritz Stern.

The profound happiness of those years owed just as much to a world of new friendships. Simon Taylor, Tom Meaney, Jude Webre, Justin Reynolds, Simon Stevens, Liz Marcus, Maria John, Brigid von Preussen, James Chappel, Isabel Gabel, Noah Rosenblum, Kristen Loveland, Mathew Lawrence, Arthur Asseraf, Tareq Baconi, Alex Bevilacqua, and Helen Pfeifer became treasured co-conspirators in New York and beyond. So much of the road was shared with Stephen Wertheim, and I am so grateful for it. Despite its inauspicious beginnings over a cheap cheese platter at the Columbia visiting day, my friendship with Seth Anziska has grown into one of the most meaningful experiences of my life. From our shared apartment on 112th Street to much more complex lives beyond it, his existential companionship has warmed my life from the inside. Tehila Sasson, Emily Baughan, Ana Keilson, and Maja Spanu became and remain the most precious of friends. I am so lucky to have Sally Davies, soul sister, as an interlocutor in all the largest questions. As this book was going to press, we lost Philippa Hetherington, brilliant scholar, beloved friend, and irreplaceable companion along so many of these roads.

An Ernst Mach fellowship from the Österreichische Austauschdienst, and Oliver Rathkolb's gracious sponsorship, enabled a long research stay in Vienna, where Hans Peter Hye and Barbara Haider-Wilson helped me track down tricky sources and Dirk Rupnow provided social cheer and impeccable culinary guidance. Across many visits since, I am further indebted to Miloš Vec, Franz Fillafer, Johannes Feichtinger, Gerald Stourzh, and Philipp Ther. I owe particular thanks to Peter Becker, whose generosity, good temper, and insight has made our rewarding collaborations a pleasure. My dissertation research and writing were also supported by a fellowship from the Central European History Society, a yearlong traveling fellowship from the Columbia Graduate School of Arts and Sciences, a Jerrold Seigel Fellowship from the New York Consortium for Intellectual and Cultural History, and a write-up fellowship from the Doris G. Quinn Foundation. I was very lucky to move into a postdoctoral fellowship at Glenda Sluga's ARC Laureate Research Program in International History at the University of Sydney, which offered generous support for research and travel as well as much intellectual stimulation. I am grateful to the Australian Academy of the Humanities for a traveling fellowship, and to the Lauterpacht Centre for International Law at the University of Cambridge for the Brandon Research Fellowship that enabled a wonderful term at Cambridge: special thanks to Sarah Nouwen and Chris Clark. I learned a great amount at the Hurst Summer Institute in Legal History at the University of Wisconsin–Madison, expertly led by Mitra Sharafi, and at the Law and Humanities Junior Scholars Workshop at UCLA.

The Department of History at Princeton University has opened wide new horizons for intellectual growth and exploration. This is a much better book for what I have learned there, and I am grateful for the myriad ways the department has nurtured it. I am especially indebted to David Bell and Yair Mintzker for their warm support, sage advice, and thoughtful mentorship; and to Angela Creager. My thanks also to Jeremy Adelman, Michael Gordin, Dirk Hartog, Ekaterina Pravilova, Shel Garon, Margot Canaday, Ed Baring, Federico Marcon, Harold James, Gyan Prakash, Bill Jordan, Keith Wailoo, Helmut Reimitz, Janet Chen, and Judy Hanson. The friendship of Beth Lew-Williams, Casey Lew-Williams, Rosina Lozano, Peter Wirzbicki, Meg Rooney, Divya Cherian, Rob Karl, Iryna Vushko, Michael Blaakman, Barbara Nagel, Daniel Hoffman-Schwartz, and Sophie Gee has meant a great deal. Mike Laffan and Vanita Neelakanta have enabled and given so much, sharing their home and lighting a dark winter with some Pearl Bay sunshine: I am so grateful for their friendship and care. The same is true of Anurag Sinha and Lupe Tuñón, who arrived just in time and saved the day. One of the great privileges of being at Princeton is the opportunity to work with such wonderful graduate students, including Disha Jani, Nick Barone, Austen Van Burns, and Anin Luo, among so many others.

This book began to grow into its current shape during a yearlong fellowship at the Wissenschaftskolleg zu Berlin, a slice of paradise stranded in the Grunewald woods. Truly uncanny luck, especially while working on this project, to have the chance to think and learn at close quarters with Barbara Stollberg-Rilinger, Christoph Möllers, Lorraine Daston, and Franco Moretti. Conversations with Dieter Grimm were a sparkling highlight. Katharina Wiedermann, Stephan Schlak, and Dunia Najjar offered such grace and good cheer, and Stefan Gellner and Anja Brockmann in the library provided valuable assistance. Daniel Schönpflug became an interlocutor unlike any I have had.

To Sebastian Conrad and Stefan-Ludwig Hoffmann I owe much professional support, in many contexts and phases of life, as well as intellectual inspiration and friendship. I thank them both with warmth. I am so glad to have Holly Case as a co-adventurer in the world of ideas, all the way from my dissertation defense, where she served as external committee member, to the philosophy of history reading group we share with Claudia Verhoeven that provided vital intellectual sustenance this past year. Stefanos Geroulanos has given of his mind and time with incomparable generosity since the day we met. His care, encouragement, and companionship in thought and life have often made all the difference. Stef: thank you. For their friendship, spark, and warm support, I am grateful to Camille Robcis, Thomas Dodman, Dan Edelstein, Maks del Mar, Malgosia Mazurek, Tara Zahra, Stephanie McCurry, Antonio Feros, Andrew Fitzmaurice, Liz Anker, Alison Frank Johnson, Madhav Khosla, Alanna O'Malley, Hussein Omar, Harshan Kumarasingham, and Henry Moynahan Rich. Thanks also to fellow travelers, collaborators, and colleagues Jamie Martin, David Armitage, Megan Donaldson, Gerry Simpson, Rohit De, Lisa Ford, Aimee Genell, Dominique Reill, Patricia Clavin, Nick Mulder, Isabel Hull, Massimiliano Tomba, Lasse Heerten, Helen Kinsella, Cristina Florea, Miranda Johnson, Rose Parfitt, Fleur Johns, Nehal Bhuta, Benedict Kingsbury, Dan Lee, Sophie Loy-Wilson, Rebecca Sheehan, Frances Clark, Georgios Giannakopoulos, and Nathaniel Berman.

I owe particular thanks to those who have engaged closely with this manuscript. The two peer reviewers for Princeton University Press, one of whom subsequently revealed herself as Lauren Benton, read the manuscript in such a generous and constructive spirit and suggested many insightful paths forward. That sort of collegiality is a real gift, and I owe it also to Pieter Judson, Martti Koskenniemi, and Judith Surkis, conscripts for a manuscript workshop generously funded by the department. They helped me re-meet the manuscript as though from the outside, refracted through their knowledge from three very different fields: a powerful and energizing experience, and one that improved the book enormously. Sincere thanks to Pieter, Martti, and Judith for entering into the project with me in the way that they did. A writing group with Anurag Sinha and Justin Reynolds offered valuable advice and invaluable solidarity. A number of others read drafts and offered helpful comments: my thanks to David Bell, Michael Gordin (heroically, at short notice), Ekaterina Pravilova, Ed Baring, Yair Mintzker, Michael Blaakman, Peter Holquist, Peter Becker, Gábor Egry, Michael Waibel, Dirk Moses, Adil Haque, Hussein Omar, Katharina Schmidt, Austen Van Burns, Nick Barone, and most of all Stefanos Geroulanos, Sam Moyn, and Matthew Karp. You all taught me so much, even when and where I was not able to take up all your suggestions and ideas. For advice and guidance, I am also grateful to Balázs Trencsényi, Thomas Olechowski, Jeremy King, and Christian Neumeier.

I am indebted to many people for invitations to present this research, and the enlightening discussions that followed: David Armitage and Erez Manela; Lauren Benton; Sam Moyn; Antonio Feros; Nick Mulder and Cristina Florea; Chris Clark, Jean-Michel Johnston, and Celia Donert; Pieter Judson; Emily Greble and Iryna Vushko; Andrea Orzoff; Shruti Kapila; Robert Gerwath and William Mulligan; Alanna O'Malley and Anne-Isabelle Richard; Philippa Hetherington and Jan Rüger; Jana Osterkamp; Jannis Panagiotidis; Peter Becker; Franz Fillafer and Johannes Feichtinger; Chris Dietrich; Karolina Partyga and Charis Marantzidou; Georgios Giannakopoulos; and Stefan-Ludwig Hoffmann. I would like to express special thanks to the particularly engaged audiences at the Penn Annenberg Seminar and the Cornell European History Colloquium, who gave me new energy and orientation when spirits were flagging.

At Princeton University Press, I owe profound thanks to Priya Nelson, dream editor, for her many-sided help, her understanding, and her savvy insight. Thanks also to Barbara Shi and Erin Davis, and to Tobiah Waldron for assistance with the index. It was a delight to work with Kate Blackmer, mapmaker extraordinaire. I likewise extend my thanks to Kristina Poznan for her research assistance with Hungarian sources.

Elly Carroll and Claire Nakazawa, oldest of friends, anchor me in ever-new ways. I am grateful to Dirk Moses for the support he offered over many years, especially while I finished my dissertation, and to John and Ingrid Moses. Jarrod Wheatley is one of the best people I know, and my brother to boot: I feel so lucky to be sharing this life with him. The same is true of Luisa Krein, who brings such light everywhere she goes, light now doubled in little Dia. The sprawling family they have built, including Karin Krein and Vincent Krein, makes life all the richer. Warren Percy contributes so much and so thoughtfully. I thank Freddi Karp for her spirit, her company, and her loving support. As I reach the end of a long road with this book, I think of my grandfather, Colin Beevor Pryor, witness to the twentieth century, who died at age ninety-seven a few months before I submitted my dissertation, and who was always asking me if I was finished yet.

To Matthew Karp I am grateful in all the ways—and with unbridled joy.

This book is dedicated to my parents, Glenda Pryor and Robert Wheatley. I thank them for their life-shaping love and for the quietly remarkable childhood they gave my brother and me. They opened a wide, free path into the world, something neither of them had. And they showed us, by example, how to think expansively about all the forms love and family can take.

MAP 1. The Habsburg Monarchy in the late nineteenth century.

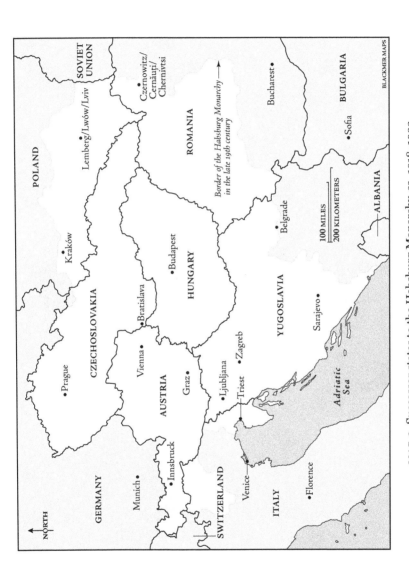

MAP 2. Successor states to the Habsburg Monarchy, ca. 1918–1923.

GERMANY

POLAND

SOVIET
UNION

• Munich

• Kraków

• Innsbruck

• Prague

Lemberg/Lwów/Lviv •

Czernowitz/
Cernăuți/
Chernivtsi •

CZECHOSLOVAKIA

• Bratislava

Vienna •

• Budapest

ROMANIA

SWITZERLAND

AUSTRIA

Graz •

HUNGARY

Border of the Habsburg Monarchy
in the late 19th century →

• Ljubljana

Venice •

• Triest

• Zagreb

Bucharest •

ITALY

YUGOSLAVIA

Belgrade
•

• Florence

Sarajevo •

Adriatic
Sea

100 MILES
200 KILOMETERS

• Sofia

BULGARIA

ALBANIA

NORTH

BLACKMER MAPS

THE LIFE AND DEATH OF STATES

Making a World of States

THE PROLIFERATION of internationally recognized, independent nation-states is one of the most striking features of modern history. Their conquest of the world map—and our political imaginaries—may be extensive, but it is also remarkably recent.[1] We only need to travel back a century and a half to grasp the magnitude of this transformation. Wildly heterogeneous political forms populated the world picture of the mid-nineteenth century, stretching from globe-spanning industrialized empires to polycentric sultanates, autonomous enclaves (in Europe as much as elsewhere), and Indigenous communities living according to their own laws. Never before, in fact—at least according to some—had the spectrum of polities ranged so widely.[2] Today, by contrast, we survey a globe almost entirely segmented into sovereign states: modular, clearly demarcated, theoretically equal under international law. The calendrical ledger of the last century kept score of this creeping transmutation of the world: in 1920, the League of Nations counted 42 member states; the United Nations had 60 in 1950, 99 in 1960, and 159 in 1990. Today there are around 200. If the state's capacity, virtue, and significance are ceaselessly in flux and up for debate, especially under the uneven integration of global capitalism, its grip on political life remains tenacious, as the populist nationalism of our own day documents all too well.

What do we know about this epochal change? "The story of how the world came to be so thickly populated with states," David Armitage wrote in 2007, "has hardly begun to be told."[3] International relations scholars, first on the scene, described it as the "expansion of international society"—as though it resembled a door slowly swung open, smoothly, benevolently, to a gradual procession of newcomers.[4] Such framing elided violent wars of national liberation and decolonization, and even the category of empire itself.[5] A new generation of research in diplomatic, international, and legal history is slowly filling in the picture.[6] Scholars have focused on the emergence of international bodies like the League of Nations and the United Nations that facilitated the state-ification of the world, and on the Anglo-American imperial order of which they formed a complex part. With the partial exception of some historians of international law, they have had less to say about its origins outside the Anglo-American world. And we have barely begun to look beneath the surface of international politics to the substratum of assumptions and preconditions that underpinned this juridical transformation. "Statehood" and "sovereignty" lock into some of the most elemental human questions about our communal life: questions about the nature and arrangement of power, and about the ultimate source of legitimate authority. Their history must also be a history of ideas—of arguments and emotions, sense and meaning, aspirations and fears. It involves—as we will see—whole philosophies of law and knowledge, visions of time and history, cosmologies of the politically possible. No part of this conversion was mechanical. Neither "state" nor "sovereignty" can be taken as fixed, pregiven things seized by premade nations.

This book uncovers a crucial piece of the larger international story in a seemingly unlikely place: the Habsburg Empire. As a result, it approaches the empire from an unaccustomed angle. A sprawling polity that dominated the heartlands of Europe for hundreds of years—extending by the nineteenth century from today's northern Italy to western Ukraine, and from southern Poland all the way to Croatia via the Czech lands, Transylvania, Hungary, Slovakia, and Slovenia—the empire lingers like a ghost over the map of Europe. Since its dissolution in 1918, historians of the Habsburg Empire have focused largely on two related issues: first, the reasons for its collapse (with shifting appraisals of its weakness and strength, modernity and backwardness); and second, the nature of the nationalisms that ostensibly brought it down (from ancient ethnic enmity to "national indifference"). This book sets both themes to one side. If it is concerned with Habsburg modernity, it is via its key role as a laboratory for juridical innovation; if it touches on questions of nationalism, it does so because these were spurs to critical questions of sovereignty. It returns to Central European history with a series of more outward-facing questions about the legal and intellectual history of empire, sovereignty, and statehood. Tying Central European history into a story of the emergence of twentieth-century international order, it also shows just how much international historians can learn from paying closer attention to a region that they have neglected.

This book uses the remaking and interwar unmaking of the Habsburg Empire to track the emergence of a world of states along three central avenues. It begins in the aftermath of the European revolutions of 1848, as the Habsburg Empire was convulsed by decades of constitutional experimentation in the face of rising provincial demands for political rights. I show, first, how these structural experiments directly confronted a set of transitions customarily deemed constitutive of the modern state: from "private" patrimonial rule to abstract "public" authority, and from pluralist, differentiated legal orders to singular, uniform, unified ones. Unlike in France, no revolution had swept away all the old rights and legalities of the ancien régime: the full complex of dynastic, patrimonial law needed to be argued over and converted manually into "modern" equivalents. Unlike in Britain, the Habsburg government had been forced into a written constitution, meaning these adaptations could not unfold backstage, gradually, fuzzily, absentmindedly: the empire's legal order had to be publicly articulated. And, unlike in Germany, the empire's rulers and thinkers could not appeal to the ostensibly organic national unity of *das Volk* to ground the unity of the state, as the dominant historical school of law did there: the Habsburg lands comprised intermixed peoples speaking some twelve different languages. Combined, these characteristics turned the Habsburg lands into a remarkably explicit workshop for the attempted production of abstract, singular sovereignty out of multinational dynastic empire. The case allows us to eavesdrop on the refashioning of the body of king into the body politic—as live, ever-unfinished history rather than static, retrospective theory—replete with its unresolved problems and inconsistencies, its myths and imaginative leaps, and its many significant consequences.

Second, I recover the place of the Habsburg Empire in that other foundational process underpinning the emergence of a world of states: the demise of (formal) empire and the rise of the nation-state in its wake. We rightly associate this story with the decolonization of Asia and Africa in the decades following World War II. Yet certain parts of the story crystallized at the end of the *previous* world war, with the dissolution of Habsburg rule in Central Europe. Under the watchful eye of the international community, assembled first at the Paris Peace Conference and then as the League of Nations, a string of newborn sovereign powers appeared in the empire's place, including Czechoslovakia, Hungary, Austria, and Yugoslavia. Important substantive differences distinguish this chapter of imperial dissolution from the one that followed the next world war—not least regarding race and economy. But the end of the Habsburg Empire raised *legal* questions about the nature of postimperial sovereignty that would remain persistent features of the subsequent global history of decolonization. Here, too, the Habsburg Monarchy occupied a distinct place in the cohort of empires—Ottoman, Russian, and German—that collapsed at the war's end, as the whole of its former territory was converted into independent, postimperial states.[7] Legal conundrums surrounding the messy end of empire and the creation of new states—especially discontinuous sovereignty and the succession of rights, obligations, and territories—were thrown onto the main stage of twentieth-century international order—in one of its most formative moments—largely by the implosion of Habsburg rule.[8] The legal stories and theories developed to make sense of that transition would echo in the subsequent decades through South Asia, Africa, and beyond.

Third, legal thinkers from this corner of the world exercised a radically outsized influence on the evolution of modern legal thought in general and theories of the state in particular. To a startling degree, the ideas that shape discourses about sovereignty to this day were born in the Habsburg lands in the decades before and after the empire's collapse. A state, according to international law's standard codification, comprises four things: an effective government, a clearly defined territory, a stable population, and the capacity to enter into relations with other states. The original architect of this (then tripartite) test was Georg Jellinek (1851–1911), son of Vienna's most famous rabbi.[9] Across a prolific career—which culminated in a chair in Heidelberg, where he was a close interlocutor of Max Weber after anti-Semitism drove him from Vienna—Jellinek forged many of the disciplinary building blocks of public and international law.[10] He also inaugurated a methodological revolution that would bear spectacular fruit in the work of his student Hans Kelsen (1881–1973). One of the twentieth century's most important legal philosophers, Kelsen was also a product of the Habsburg experience. He studied when the empire was at its apogee and taught at the University of Vienna as it came crashing down. He masterminded Austria's postwar constitution and served as judge on its constitutional court before anti-Semitism caught up with him, too. The political storms of interwar Europe tossed him first to Cologne—and a legendary confrontation with Nazi jurist Carl Schmitt—then to Geneva, and eventually to Berkeley: he escaped Europe aboard the SS *Washington* as Hitler's armies marched on Paris. Along the way, he developed an extraordinarily complete philosophy of law. Known as the pure theory of law, its analytical insight, explanatory power, and global influence are matched only by its degree of difficulty and the controversy it generated. Integral to its architecture was a radical new account of what the state *was*. It explained how law could turn a messy, contradictory material reality into a singular, unified legal entity, and it recast the relationship between sovereignty and international law. Like so many of his legendary Viennese contemporaries and interlocutors— Sigmund Freud among them—Kelsen sought a *total* theory, one that could make sense of the whole. If the logical astringency and formalism of the pure theory is now foreign to us, so is its staggering intellectual ambition.

This book explains those ideas and their significance and shows why it was not an accident that they emerged in the Habsburg lands in German-language jurisprudence.[11] The empire became such a hothouse of legal innovation—in both academic theory and constitutional practice—precisely because existing theories could not make sense of it. To confront questions of state and sovereignty in this intricately layered, prodigiously complex empire was to confront the radical limits of legal concepts *and* to be propelled toward new ones. It might be ironic that an empire saturated with historical rights and traditional law birthed the most strident apostles of legal modernism, but it is not inexplicable. On the contrary. This book shows how orders of thought evolved in dynamic tension with orders of rule, and why innovation and "anachronism" proved such intimate associates rather than each other's opposites. With imperial politics hamstrung by constitutional conflict, law and lawyers wielded an authority and significance in public life that might surprise us today. This standing persisted well into the 1920s, that heady period of state founding and constitution writing in which "the jurist was king."[12] If this book places a spotlight on Jellinek and Kelsen—both mainstays of law school histories and textbooks, but conspicuously neglected by historians—it also offers a broader contextual explanation for the many other thinkers from the Habsburg Empire who shaped twentieth-century legal history, including Eugen Ehrlich, a pioneering scholar of legal pluralism, and Hersch Lauterpacht, a giant of midcentury international law.[13] Even in this milieu, Jellinek and Kelsen stand out not just because of their fame and influence. Plugged into the main philosophical currents of the age, they shared an acute methodological self-consciousness that opens our eyes to law's place in the broader history of knowledge and epistemology. We come to understand how the challenge of making sense of statehood and sovereignty drove that history forward.

Together, these three strands—the empire's constitutional challenges, its international dissolution, and the thinkers who grappled with both—reveal a hidden story about the relationship between sovereignty and time. Foundational early modern political and legal theories of sovereignty had asserted the necessity of the state's juridical immortality. Unless the state persisted as an unchanging legal entity despite the death of a monarch or the fall of a government, it could not guarantee the intergenerational continuity of public order, rights, and duties. Some called it the doctrine of the king's "two bodies": one fleshed and mortal, the other understood as abstract and perpetual. The state's juridical agelessness—the stable continuity of its legal self within the ceaseless flow of time—remains a crucial enabling fiction for our systems of law. But that legal fiction came under extraordinary pressure in the Habsburg lands. Constitutional jurisprudence grappled with whether the empire's constituent polities like Hungary and Bohemia were still-living states, or whether their legal life had been extinguished by centuries of imperial rule; one wondered, too, about the continuity of the empire's own legal personality. The problem of how states endured and how they expired only became more charged and consequential when the empire collapsed, and representatives of the "new" states argued that, legally, they were resurrected versions of their preimperial selves. The many lives and purported deaths of these Central European states expose the visions of time and history built into sovereignty's structure. In so doing, they shed new light on the "long century of modern statehood" that, as Charles Maier has argued, began around 1850 and so integrally shaped political modernity.[14]

A Many-Bodied Problem

In 1882, Georg Jellinek—then a young adjunct lecturer at the University of Vienna angling for a permanent job—opened his new book with a provocative observation. All the major theorists of sovereignty, whether Hobbes or Bodin or Rousseau, placed the singularity of sovereignty—the notion of a single, supreme, undivided power—at the core of their definitions. Their theories, he claimed, could not make sense of sovereignty in Central Europe. Across the whole German-speaking domain—whether one looked at his home country, Austria-Hungary, or Germany or Switzerland—the "life course" of states was not leading to unitary forms. Instead, one saw different sorts of compound polities: states joined and bundled together, marked by varieties of amalgamation or disaggregation.

This discrepancy between the dominant theories and regional realities had dire consequences, he argued. Scholars manhandled such polities into these ill-fitting frames by interpreting them as "incomplete" realizations of the norm—a "transitional phase of states in a process of unification or de-unification"—and thus provisional by definition. Or they described them as "irregular" formations that were, ultimately, "juridically incomprehensible." Labels like "provisional" or "irregular" rendered them irrelevant for doctrine, so the classical definitions marched on, untroubled by the chasm between states in theory and states in fact. Scholarship suffered; the consequences for politics proved no less lamentable. These conceptions had penetrated so deeply that they structured political objectives and debate, sending state makers scurrying off to "correct" their deviant polities. "With the interpretation of a state formation as an irregular one," Jellinek observed, "politics is immediately given the task of clearing away the irregularity."[15] The dominant model had turned conglomerate states into *problems* that needed to be *solved*.

Jellinek offered his diagnosis: all these thinkers came from England and France. They reasoned from Western European experiences and presumed them universal norms. But what if the theory—not the "irregular" state—was to blame for the resulting incongruity? Why could some sorts of states generate models and be abstracted into theories, and not others? What might happen if one instead theorized *from here*, if one devised conceptions of sovereignty at home in this more complex world? Jellinek himself sensed the potential: scanning across a world of tangled empires, he concluded that nonsingular, conglomerate sovereignty in fact represented the global norm. If legal theory could find the right concepts to capture it, it might just unlock the secrets of sovereignty all around the world.[16]

The Habsburg Empire was a time capsule of European history in which different phases of state formation remained alive in the present. Its formal legal architecture preserved the logic of its medieval and early modern formation through a series of dynastic unions. On paper, it remained a concatenation of myriad distinct polities. In the era of enlightened absolutism, this legal structure had been overlaid (but not dissolved) with robust organs of centralized government, based in Vienna. The nineteenth century added yet another layer, as national movements emerged among the empire's dozen or so language communities and demanded a place of some sort in the empire's political architecture. The empire was many versions of itself at once, a layer cake of sovereign history. What was a state? *Here* was the place to find out. Or, at least—to ask.

Of course, all political orders contain inconsistencies and curiosities, traces of past political struggles and half-abandoned systems of thought. What turned this bricolage into an acute problem for politics and for thought was the revolutions of 1848. Yes, the empire survived the crisis—but only just, and only with a major concession. The emperor gave in to the liberals and nationalists barricading the burning streets and consented to an imperial constitution, that is, a constitution in the "modern" sense: a single written document, a systematic codification. Here a different sort of strife began. What is the first thing a constitution requires? It requires a legal description of the polity in question—of the name and nature of its component parts, the hierarchy and relationship of jurisdictions, the basis and logic of powers. In the Habsburg lands, no element of that description proved uncontroversial. The project of writing down, or "writing up," the empire into a single document left all the conceptual problems exposed to the cold light of day. Or, rather, it records for us the way "modern" law *produced* sovereign plurality *as* a problem.

When one tried to square the empire with the category "state," numerous plausible interpretations emerged, all of them contradictory. Only two things were certain, reflected one law professor. First, it truly was a monarchy. Second, it was "not a simple, unified polity but rather a *plural*, compound one." "Everything else," he wrote, "is doubtful or at least contested, in particular: how many states does it consist of? what are they called? what is their legal relationship to one another? do they together form a state-of-states [*Staatenstaat*] or a federal state [*Bundesstaat*]? or is their union to be considered merely as a state confederation [*Staatenbund*], so that together they don't form a state at all, but rather merely hang together in international law?"[17] Was the Habsburg Monarchy one state, two states, three states, four? In recent decades, a stream of important scholarship by Tara Zahra, Pieter Judson, Kate Brown, and others has shown how Central and Eastern Europe was gradually sorted into national communities out of a welter of more fluid, overlapping identities.[18] But this is not true only of *nations*: it had to be sorted into *states*, too.

How could the sovereign situation be so opaque? The answer lies in the nature of the empire's original legal stitching. It came into being through a series of dynastic "personal unions" in the fifteenth, sixteenth, and seventeenth centuries, in which various small polities were united through the body of a shared monarch only. The monarch acquired an additional title or ruling identity—*Herrscherpersönlichkeit*—so that the Archduke of Austria, the king of Bohemia, the Margravate of Moravia, and the king of Hungary (and so on) were one and the same physical person. But the various polities otherwise retained independent legal identities and broad autonomy, with their own provincial diets and customary laws. The most significant of these unions occurred in 1526, when a skillfully knotted net of dynastic marriages drew the crowns of Bohemia and Hungary into Habsburg hands, dramatically enlarging the latter's hitherto modest alpine holdings. Composite monarchies (as historians would later call them) were entirely unremarkable in medieval and early modern Europe.[19] But by the mid-nineteenth century, such promiscuous, sovereign-sharing state formations had lost their self-evidence: they no longer made sense in the categories and worldview of nineteenth-century European legal science and government, which saw states as clearly demarcated, singular things and distinguished sharply between domestic and international law.[20] A many-crowned emperor-king, as a literal embodiment of the distinctness *and* the unity of multiple polities, may have been natural within the frame of medieval and early modern statecraft, but how should that dynastic cosmology be transcribed into coherent, workable, respectable legal form in 1848, or 1867, or 1908? Did the king of Bohemia, for example, have international standing and international legal personality? If not—if, internationally, he disappeared into his alter ego, the emperor of Austria— then did the emperor step in and out of international law, and in and out of constitutional law, as he symbolically took off the imperial crown and put on a royal one?

The many crowns were only the most eye-catching imprints of a very different legal world. The original dynastic unions reflected a horizon of practices and imaginaries with none of the same coordinates as "modern" law. This patrimonial understanding of rule and right knew no fundamental distinction between "public" and "private," between (personal) property and (state) territory. Emperors and princes, lords and vassals, landowners and peasant laborers were all bound together in reciprocal and cascading bonds, privileges, and responsibilities, in which "juridical principles of 'scalar' or conditional property" had their correlate in "parcellized sovereignty."[21] Annunciated and renewed through oaths, coronations, and other rituals, these relationships were personal, based on tradition, and far from equal or uniform. Rule often took the shape of cyclic consensual agreements between monarchs and estates (i.e., "groups of persons who enjoyed the same rights, shared the same political obligations, and pursued their common interests in an organized manner"), often convened in territorial assemblies and diets.[22] Law, economy, and society were not distinct domains. Noble lords and large landowners administered justice and collected taxes; there was no unmediated relationship between monarchs and subjects. "Constitutions" were not written but physically enacted and performed; law was not abstract or homogeneous.[23] And, crucially, there was no expectation that law and sovereignty be logically consistent or "rational."[24] Powers and jurisdiction did not follow clear, sequential, logical chains of derivation; like rights and norms, they could overlap, coexist, cross, contradict, and reverse. Take, for example, Charles the Bold, the ambitious fifteenth-century Duke of Burgundy, who could be the vassal of the French king in some of his lands and of the (Habsburg) Holy Roman Emperor in others; while, in others still, the French king was *his* vassal.[25] If we cannot help but understand descriptions like "irrational" or "incoherent" in unambiguously pejorative terms, it is a sign of the modern valuations we all too easily take as given, as well as the inaptitude of our vocabulary for the phenomena in question.

Across the early modern period, Habsburg statecraft gradually moved out of this world. The dynasty won decisive victories over the estates that reduced the latter's power and slowly condensed governing prerogatives in Vienna, like the Battle of the White Mountain (1620) that fatally undercut the Bohemian nobility. Fundamental laws from 1713 and 1723, known as the Pragmatic Sanction, asserted the inseparability of the Habsburg lands and established a common law of succession operative across them all. The late eighteenth century witnessed the most dramatic transformation. Through wide-ranging administrative and fiscal reforms at the vanguard of European developments, Maria Theresa and her son Joseph II drew significant power away from various mediatory corporations and structures like the church and the nobility. Estate owners largely lost control of taxation and peasant labor; tariff regimes were consolidated, territories mapped, and populations counted; and new, robust organs of central government became a presence felt in the lives of ordinary people.[26]

Yet the structures, forms, and imaginaries of this older, traditional legal world did not simply wither away under the "light" of absolutism and the self-consciously modern project of centralization. Habsburg rule still differed significantly across their lands, from Tyrol to Croatia, Moravia to Galicia, bearing the marks of each one's particular (legal) history. Nowhere was this more true than in Hungary, where the nobility had resisted almost all incursions and staunchly defended its traditional rights, laws, and privileges. No one really spoke of a Habsburg "state" prior to the early nineteenth century.[27] After all, until that point, the Habsburgs also wore the crown of the Holy Roman Empire of the German Nation: a loose, patchwork polity that sprawled across the thick middle of the continent, and which encompassed some of the Habsburg hereditary lands, but not all, with Hungary and Croatia lying beyond its borders. Only in 1804, in response to Napoleon's declaration of himself as emperor of the French, and with the dissolution of the Holy Roman Empire on the horizon, did Francis I create a comparable title—emperor of Austria—that pertained to all *his* "own" lands—that is, lands he presided over not as Holy Roman Emperor but as king and archduke and all his myriad other selves.[28]

Law's Truth under Pressure

When the 1848 revolutions propelled the project of an imperial constitution to the center of political life, it immediately confronted a many-sided impasse. At the level of actual administration, the monarchy functioned as a relatively centralized state. Yet, legally, an older landscape of sovereignty persisted. Traditional rights, privileges, and obligations had in fact been continually reaffirmed through coronations and other rituals of dynastic-aristocratic rule. They all lay waiting, half lapsed but still technically legitimate, still "on the books," when representatives from across the empire gathered in a new constituent assembly tasked with thrashing out an imperial constitution. Delegates from the various kingdoms and lands were quick to insist that their traditional rights were still live, valid law, now to be enshrined in the new constitution. The first impasse, then, involved an eerie disjuncture between the factual-material reality of imperial rule—manifest in a centralized, "modern" state—and its formal legal architecture, which preserved a collage of disparate medieval and early modern polities. What did it mean if law said one thing but a world of material "facts" said something else? Had the Kingdom of Bohemia become a mere "fantasy," as one parliamentary delegate contended?[29] Either way, how could one tell? Did law have its own "reality" or truth, distinct from other sorts? How should these different genres of the real be stacked against one another?

Questions of constitutional order thus rapidly spiraled into questions about the nature of legal truth and knowledge. There was an inexorable pull toward an epistemological register: again and again, protagonists needed to make arguments about the relationship between the real and the fictional, the lapsed and the living, form and content, law and fact. That pull only gathered strength through the constitutional reconfigurations of 1849, 1860, 1861, and 1867 and the vociferous constitutional debate that continued unabated for the remainder of the empire's existence. In shifting iterations, assessments of the nature of imperial sovereignty, its underlying logic as well as its plurality or singularity, turned on accounts of the legal real.

Small wonder that as a new scholarly field emerged over the same period, it too gravitated toward problems of method and epistemology. When revolution broke out across the Danube Monarchy in 1848, the empire's constitutional law and history were not part of university curricula; there were no professorships or standard works. That lacuna makes subsequent developments all the more striking. By the early twentieth century, the empire's universities were hothouses of research in public law. The history and theory of constitutional law emerged alongside the practical task of constitutionalization. Scholars ran into the same problems as politicians. To grapple with the state "from here" was to grapple with the nature of law itself. It drove some to a radical new empiricism. Eugen Ehrlich (1862–1922), for example—a pioneering legal sociologist writing from rural, polyethnic Bukovina on the easternmost edge of the empire—was clear that the notion of a singular, encompassing state legal order could explain little about the way law actually functioned amid this tangle of traditions and practices. He developed his influential notion of "living law" from the "direct observation of life."[30] But the situation drove others in the opposite direction, pushing them toward a radical new abstraction. Faced with the jurisdictional chaos of the empire, Hans Kelsen concluded that one could only establish the coherence of sovereignty, and the formal unity of the state, by definitively cleaving off law as a material, empirical *fact*—messy, plural, riddled with inconsistencies—from law as a formal, abstract *norm*. The state's unity simply could not be established in an empirical fashion: it existed as a normative proposition only. Kelsen salvaged (or, rather, created) a logical, singular sovereignty, but only by tracking back to the deep foundations of knowing and judging, and only by abandoning the empirical world. Seen from here, it seemed, a theory of sovereignty must be a theory of knowledge, too. Across both the public sphere and the academy, arguments about *what* imperial sovereignty was or how it worked became questions of *how* one could *tell* in the first place.

Sleeping States

A disjuncture between sorts of truth was not the only impasse confronted by the constitutional project. When representatives of the kingdoms and lands invoked their traditional rights and prerogatives, looking to have them recognized in the new constitutional order(s), they were resummoning that older legal world into one that had changed materially and conceptually. They needed to convert the forms of medieval and early modern sociopolitical-legal life into "law" recognizable as such in the nineteenth century and adapted to the needs of modern constitutionalism. They scouted for terminology and ideas that could digest dynastic-feudal legal formations into those of "modern" statecraft. Their work allows us to watch a range of figures suturing the framework of modern sovereignty out of the material of orders past.

In this context, invocations of "historical rights" assumed a new importance.[31] The traditional rights and privileges of (say) Bohemian or Hungarian elites, assembled as estates in the Bohemian or Hungarian diets, were spheres of noble autonomy from princely power. They had been cyclically reaffirmed through rituals like coronations in which the monarch pledged to uphold them. Now, these traditional prerogatives were gradually reinterpreted as a form of historical *Staatsrecht*—that is, a body of public law governing a state. *Staatsrecht* has no easy English equivalent. More specific than "public law" and more general than "constitutional law" (though often used as a loose synonym for the latter), it is the law that regulates the fundamental legitimacy and nature of the state. To assert the ongoing force of one's historical *Staatsrecht* was to make a claim about the survival of old rights and also about the nature of the entity that possessed them.[32] Put succinctly, the "historical rights" of the estates became the historical rights of states. Traditional feudal prerogatives became the public law and constitution of these former polities. The Habsburg acquisition of the Holy Crown of Saint Stephen or the Crown of Saint Wenceslas in the early sixteenth century became Hungary's and Bohemia's respective loss of sovereignty, a sovereignty they had never formally renounced. "Historical rights" came to signal a genre of latent or suspended sovereignty, still normatively valid and simply awaiting renewal. To dismiss such claims as anachronisms or unserious fantasies is to overlook the fact that the anachronisms are themselves a signal feature of the story.[33] For both political actors and scholars, making sense of the empire's legal order entailed a filtering of historical formations through the paradigms of the present—a search for equivalents or matches between then and now. History, too, was "codified" into categories of state and sovereignty. These "category mistakes" mark the collision of different cosmologies of rule.

Arguments about imperial order thus contained a series of epochal transformations. They document the conceptual labor, the difficulties, and the legacies of spinning the rights of estates into the rights of states, property into territory, "private" into "public," a kaleidoscope of jurisdictions into homogeneous legal space, embodied law into abstraction, divine right into positive law and "nonderived" power. Just as "the economy," in Karl Polanyi's famous formulation, needed to become "disembedded" from a more reciprocal, integrated social order, so too did the law require active fashioning into a self-contained, coherent object.[34] As the dynastic state par excellence, the Habsburg Empire affords special visibility to the (imperfect) depersonalization of rights and rule underpinning the historical construction of public power. If there is ever-new attention to the erosion of public prerogatives and the privatization of the state in our own age, this history reminds us how recent and how fragile that construction is.[35]

In the decades after 1848, the Habsburg Empire tried out different versions of that translation in a series of constitutional orders. After a skittish cycle of short-lived constitutions between 1848 and 1851, Emperor Francis Joseph reinstated absolutism for the best part of a decade. When new fundamental laws in 1860 and 1861 reintroduced constitutional rule, the historic kingdoms and lands were affirmed as the basis of imperial order and granted robust autonomy, including wide lawmaking jurisdiction and administrative organs that ran parallel to imperial ones in an unusual dual-track structure. The most dramatic experiment, though, unfolded through the *Ausgleich*, or Settlement, of 1867, which transformed the empire into two, separate, and *equally sovereign* halves: Hungary, on one side, and the remaining "Austrian" lands, on the other. It converted the logic of composite monarchy into a new bifurcated sovereignty—a hyphenated state formation called the Austro-Hungarian Empire. Had sovereignty been doubled, or divided? How could a state be two, and somehow also always one? "The Dualist theory," historian R. W. Seton-Watson later quipped, "is almost as theological as the doctrine of the Trinity."[36]

If some class it as the last gasp of composite monarchy, the 1867 Settlement was for that reason (and not despite it) something genuinely experimental.[37] What would composite monarchy look like updated for the nineteenth-century present—a sovereignty that was aggregated and disaggregated, plural and singular at the same time? The unity, once resident exclusively in the king's body, now resided in three "common" ministries: one for war, another for foreign affairs, and a third for the finances for war and foreign affairs—that is, exclusively the outward-facing dimensions of sovereignty. Otherwise Hungary and Cisleithania, as the nameless other imperial half was sometimes known,[38] constituted separate states, with their own legislatures, their own territories, and even their own citizenship. In the subsequent unrelenting controversy over this dual structure, Hungarian politicians went so far as to claim that no overarching, "third" state—no empire—existed at all. Viennese jurists found it maddeningly hard to prove otherwise.

How *could* one prove a state existed? Where, or in what, did its "reality" reside? The right test and criteria preoccupied university seminars and parliamentary committees alike. The dual monarchy could hardly be a state, Hungarian politicians like Albert Apponyi (1846–1933) asserted, if it had no legislature or citizenship of its own. But if the empire arguably lacked the requisite features, its component polities certainly did, too. This drove political actors from Bohemia and Hungary to particular arguments about why and how their polities still counted as (quasi-sovereign) states despite the material reality of a relatively centralized empire. Valid law, they argued, could not be overridden by mere "facts." Polities could persist as legal norms—pieces of suspended legitimacy awaiting renewed recognition and the restoration of full factual life. "For centuries, Hungary has led a double existence: one in reality, another in its laws," wrote the historian Louis Eisenmann in a classic 1904 study. These laws had preserved the "legal fiction of its sovereignty. It is . . . this legal fiction which the laws of 1867 have turned into a reality."[39] In some senses, these contentions echoed and extended older arguments about the Holy Roman Empire as a mere shadow or legal fiction.[40] Only the problem of sovereignty's infirm reality now unfolded, as we will see, in a very different political and philosophical context: a late modern world of radically expanded state prerogatives; of a rapacious European imperialism trading on ideologies of stadial, graded sovereignty; of the triumph of positivist knowledge; and of intense new scholarly attention, under the sign of neo-Kantianism, to problems of the real and the true.

Sorting Self and Globe: Austria-Hungary in a World of Empires

Through the attempt to convert premodern pluralisms into modern ones, Habsburg constitutional law generated forms of quasi sovereignty. Clearly, these differed significantly from the quasi sovereignties and legal pluralisms produced by European imperialism in Africa, Asia, and the Middle East.[41] For one, their underlying logic was temporal more than spatial: they turned on the survival of rights, law, jurisdictions through time rather than the extension of rights, law, and jurisdiction through space—on history more than geography.[42] At the same time, the constitutional reformulation of the Habsburg Empire formed part of a much broader story of sovereign self-consciousness and imperial codification. A number of material and philosophical developments combined to make sovereignty a keyword of the nineteenth century. The dramatic extension of European imperialism across the globe both relied on and produced sovereignty as a central legitimating device: notions of perfect or complete European sovereignty took shape through a constitutive contrast to a nonsovereign (or imperfectly sovereign) non-European other, by definition available for conquest, occupation, and exploitation.[43] A thickening self-consciousness about sovereign status and interimperial competition, as well as the increasing complexity of imperial rule and desire for its rationalization, spurred a range of codification projects.[44] These imperatives did not affect only the blue water empires. On the contrary: with noteworthy simultaneity in the 1860s, projects of constitutional reorganization and codification seized not only the Habsburg Empire but also the Ottoman, Russian, and Japanese Empires. All these empire-states, located to a greater or lesser degree on the ambiguous peripheries of the European imperial system and "international community," felt similar pressures toward modernization, rationalization, and centralization—pressures to codify, articulate, and assert their sovereignty in mutually recognizable ways.[45]

Philosophical changes, too—and not just geopolitical ones—contributed to sovereignty's swollen nineteenth-century importance. The decline of natural law and divine right and the hydraulic rise of (legal) positivism recast the state—rather than nature, or reason, or God—as the source of law. Many jurists sought to set their discipline on new scientific, objective, empirical foundations by rejecting any metaphysical grounding and recognizing only state-made, man-made, positive law as law. Domestically, this shift heightened the significance of identifying the precise location of sovereignty and ensuring its singularity. Without recourse to a higher, transcendental principle or framework, only that singularity—as origin and end point of authority and legitimacy—could ground the unity of the legal order and prevent conflicts of law. Internationally, meanwhile, the shift went hand in hand with the rise of modern international law as a distinct discipline in the nineteenth century. Indeed, the pivot to positivism underpinned the newly sharp divide between domestic and international law, between the insides and outsides of a state, no longer both subsumed within an encompassing natural or divine order. International law was now understood as law made by sovereign states: dependent on their consent, it could not precede or exceed them. Nineteenth-century jurists, in Antony Anghie's words, "sought to reconstruct the entire system of international law as a creation of sovereign will."[46]

Sovereignty became, in short, the lens for new maps of the world—a prism for understanding, demarcating, and comparing self and other, and for constituting, analyzing, and regulating the interstate community. In their (re)articulations of Habsburg sovereignty, Central European actors located themselves on these new world maps, coding themselves into global typologies of sovereignty. Unsatisfied with the available terminology, Georg Jellinek coined the concept of "state fragments" (*Staatsfragmente*) to capture an "in-between level" between "state" and "province." Some political formations, he argued, were subordinated under a state government but not entirely "merged" with that state: "not states themselves," they presented "the rudiments of a state." This genre of quasi sovereignty captured the ambiguous status of the Austrian lands, which preserved key markers of statehood like their own, non-derived lawmaking power. It also arranged the international landscape along unfamiliar lines, grouping the Austrian lands together with the settler colonies of Australia and Canada, which likewise possessed state organs though not full independence.[47] The idiosyncrasies of Habsburg sovereignty rendered it a compelling provocation for new global taxonomies of this sort. The desire to "box states into species and types like one does with plants and animals," remarked one skeptical jurist, made Austria-Hungary an "adored object of such academic speculation."[48]

To dwell on the peculiarity and plurality of Habsburg sovereignty might seem to fly in the face of decades of Central European historiography. For at least a generation, historians have worked to overturn earlier portrayals of the Habsburg Empire as an "anachronism" on the European stage—a backward, rickety medieval relic destined to collapse. The older portrayals had their roots in polemical nationalist narratives from the interwar period that sought to shore up the legitimacy of the successor states by depicting the empire as an oppressive "prison of nationalities." In rejecting this blinkered nationalist historiography, scholars have instead asserted the fundamental modernity and robustness of the empire, tellingly taken to involve its centralization, unity, functionality, and liberalism. Thanks to this pathbreaking research, we build today from a portrait of a dynamic, participatory, progressive, and creatively multinational polity.[49] At the same time, in affirming the symbiotic connection between modernity, centralization, progress, and unity (rather than studying it as a historically situated, normative viewpoint), and in emphasizing the ways the Habsburg Empire resembled Western European states, this historiography has foreclosed an exploration of the empire's legal disaggregation as a point of connection to larger imperial and international histories. The perspectives and questions of global history bring new interpretive oxygen to continental European history. After all, rather than an automatic sign of fragility or reason for shame, legally differentiated rule remained the global norm.[50]

Moreover, a singular, linear timeline of modernity proves ill-equipped to capture the sovereign transformations at the heart of this book. As I have suggested, the "survival" of old rights and legal formations required great creativity: we can understand the persistence of historical rights and debates about residual sovereignty as movement as much as stasis.[51] Persistence is no simple phenomenon. The German historian Reinhart Koselleck was fascinated by the longer, elongated durations of legal history: as he showed in his habilitation on Prussia, the survival or stasis of law could become a dynamic historical force as it fell out of step with changing social needs and began producing new injustices, triggering new reforms and social movements.[52] History is not propelled exclusively by the arrival of "new" phenomena, though historians' eyes tend to be drawn there, as Arno Mayer observed.[53]

Just like many other dimensions of the fabled cultural and intellectual ferment of the late Habsburg Empire, it is precisely the hybridity of legal forms and ideas—eclectic and volatile compounds of the "archaic" and the hypermodern, liberal and illiberal, rational and sensual—that characterizes their power, interest, and significance.[54] Nothing about the empire's legal nature was self-evident, which conversely made so much possible or thinkable. One experimented with sovereignties stacked vertically and with dual sovereignty joined horizontally, with rights guarantees and curias for language groups and with nonterritorial jurisdictions. Small wonder this gallery of experiments echoed and traveled, especially for those dissatisfied with the unitary state and restlessly searching for wider horizons of sovereign possibility. Austro-Marxist proposals for the legal personality of national communities had afterlives in the Soviet Union as well as the League of Nations' interwar minorities regime and, later, the political theory of multiculturalism.[55] Habsburg layered sovereignty and dual-track administration shaped the thought of Austrian economists like Ludwig von Mises and Friedrich von Hayek, who transposed that schema upward when they conceived of international economic governance as a stratum lying atop and bracketed from state sovereignty.[56] The model of the 1867 Settlement, in which two states might be fully sovereign and independent yet still looped together, was discussed by Ottoman intellectuals as a model for Egypt, by Irish nationalists as a template for their autonomy, and on the subcontinent as the partition of India and Pakistan loomed.[57] Today, in the wake of new chaotic jurisdictional tangles in business and internet law, lawyers have resurrected the "living law" of Eugen Ehrlich, tellingly figured under the sign "Global Bukovina" in a nod to the far eastern reaches of the Habsburg Empire that he called home.[58] And the Habsburg Empire itself is now routinely invoked as a precedent, model, or warning for the European Union.[59]

If this book sets aside a simple modernity-backwardness dichotomy, it also offers an altered perspective on that other major theme of Central European historiography, namely, nationalism. To turn from the history of ethnic-linguistic nations to that of states is not to discount the significance of rich national histories—on the contrary. But if we now know so much about the former, the history of Habsburg sovereignty remains comparatively neglected.[60]

Sovereignty, as James Sheehan argued memorably, is not a thing but a problem and a practice, a set of claims and counterclaims "made by those seeking and wielding power, claims about the superiority and autonomy of their authority."[61] Nationalists entered into this political arena, presenting one competing vision of imperial order, but they largely failed to leave an imprint on the empire's legal structure. Despite some creative national settlements at the regional level in the last two decades of Habsburg rule, the empire remained a union of historical kingdoms and lands, not a federation of nations. These historical lands were not national entities and did not correspond to patterns of ethnolinguistic settlement. Bohemia comprised both Czech and German speakers, while Magyar speakers scarcely made out a majority in the Kingdom of Hungary, sharing space with (those who came to identify as) Slovaks, Ruthenians, Slovenes, Germans, Ukrainians, Romanians, Croats, and Serbs.

The distinction between *lands* and *nations* was fundamental to Habsburg constitutional debate and to Central and Eastern European political discourse more broadly. The historic lands—long-standing legal-political entities with a history of independence—stood in stark opposition to communities defined by common ethnicity and/or language. Nationalism in that ethnic-linguistic sense was emerging as a framework for identity and politics only over the course of the nineteenth century.[62] The significance of these contrasts transgressed political divides. Within the framework of Habsburg constitutional debate, the rights of the lands stemmed from old aristocratic privileges and estates-based law and carried that traditional-conservative imprint. But the juxtaposition of peoples who had "a history" of their own with "nonhistoric peoples" who ostensibly did not also featured in the writings of Karl Marx and Friedrich Engels, among many others. Amid the heat of the 1848 revolutions, Engels lambasted the "Southern Slavs" of the Habsburg Empire as "ethnographic relics" and "nothing but the residual fragments of peoples."[63] "Peoples which have never had a history of their own, which from the time when they achieved the first, most elementary stage of civilization already came under foreign sway," he wrote in 1849, "are not viable and will never be able to achieve any kind of independence."[64] (Half a century later, it was the Austro-Marxists who brokered a reconciliation between the Marxist tradition and ethnic nationalism.)[65] Contorted echoes of this way of categorizing the region's peoples, and judging their present rights, lingers into the twenty-first century, as we see in Vladimir Putin's assertions about the historical baselessness of Ukrainian sovereignty.[66]

This book tracks a conversation about the distribution of sovereignty between the *lands* and the empire, though chapter 3 also treats attempts to fashion ethnic nations into legal entities that could bear rights in the imperial constitutional structure. Its subject is an empire-scale contest over sovereignty that unfolded in German. Other important "internal" discussions in Czech and Hungarian and the empire's many other languages have been analyzed within particular national histories. My interest lies in arguments *directed to* the imperial government or that aimed to alter the imperial structure: rights claims that sought constitutional recognition and were articulated in German for that reason. Drawing the picture together in this way allows us to see how the imperial context shaped the nature of those claims, which often employed the same styles of historical-legal reasoning. It also allows us to see how nationalism tried to find its place within an existing landscape of legal ideas and institutions.

1919 in the History of the Austro-Hungarian Empire

The difficulties of distinguishing juridically alive states from juridically dead ones acquired new significance when the empire collapsed in 1918, exhausted from four long years of total war. The same questions of the survival, continuity, and identity of states now lurched dramatically to the center of international politics. The year 1918 was once portrayed as a Central European year zero: "Austria-Hungary sued for Peace and then vanished from history," in Margaret MacMillan's nutshell.[67] In this view, the dissolved Habsburg Monarchy became a blank terrain for a new order of nation-states.[68] This emplotment owes much to the self-presentation of nationalist state makers, who were keen to assert the naturalness of their liberation from an ostensibly unnatural imperial "prison." Tracing the history of *states* rather than *nations* reminds us just how convulsive and complicated this transition was. The wholesale rupture of sovereignty meant a rupture of the legal order itself. It raised challenging questions about the transfer of rights and obligations from old states to new ones—questions that would become key battlefields in the decolonization struggles that seized the global order after World War II. These questions arrived early to Central Europe, though the stories have not been connected before.[69] This is not to suggest that the transformation of Central Europe in 1918–19 can be meaningfully understood as "decolonization." The postimperial, as Peter Holquist reminds us, is not the same as the postcolonial.[70] Rather, I show how we can trace particular international legal problems raised by the eclipse of Habsburg rule, problems connected to the birth and death of states, along a global trajectory in the second half of the twentieth century.

Looking for ways of managing this crisis of legal legitimacy, representatives of the successor states turned to the languages of legal title they had long honed within the frame of imperial constitutional law. So much of the conceptual work had already been done. The state-ification of the empire had left them well stocked with arguments about the preexisting statehood of many of the empire's component parts. At the Paris Peace Conference and beyond, claim makers redeployed the rhetorical arsenal of imperial constitutional debate on the world stage, arguing for the survival of historic polities and their historical rights through the centuries of imperial rule and out the other side.

Legal concepts and methodologies developed to capture the particularities of imperial sovereignty ironically came to serve as intellectual tools for managing its absence—a way of sorting through the landscape of broken states, making the region legally legible to outsiders, and establishing international standing and legitimacy. The empire had died, but in a strange way, its constitution lived on: an empire turned inside out.[71]

Arguments about slumbering or residual sovereignty moved across the cusp of 1918, along with the evidentiary scaffolds—the configurations of law and fact—that supported them. Repeating old constitutional arguments almost verbatim, Czech submissions to the peace conference explained to the peacemakers that, "theoretically," the Habsburgs had always recognized, "at least implicitly, in their (official) acts, the legal existence of the Czech State and the independence of the Crown of Bohemia, the latter being considered as forming a separate State." Thus, if the Bohemian state no longer existed "practically," it still "existed legally."[72] The state had preserved its "theoretical" existence—its platonic, abstract, juridical life. Composite monarchy was a miraculous technology of state preservation. Neither the old-new Czechoslovak state nor the old-new Hungarian one needed to rely on some general justification for new states loosened from the clutches of empire, or the fraught legal logic of self-determination whereby a new international entity was conjured into being out of nothingness. According to these arguments, they only had to be reactivated, *de*-archived out of the imperial constitution and *re*introduced to the international community. Imperial rule was presented as a mere interregnum, now overturned through reversion to a preimperial status quo.

The ensuing debates over whether Czechoslovakia, Hungary, republican Austria, and Yugoslavia constituted "old" or "new" states had widespread political-legal consequences for both the succession of rights (especially to territory) and debts (especially reparations). Representatives of the new rump Austrian state used imperial constitutional law in the same way, but they used it to argue the opposite proposition: that they were *not* an old state but in fact a *new* one. The Allies' draft treaty wanted to make peace with "Austria," but a state of that name had never existed, they explained unblinkingly to the Allies, and certainly did not wage the war. Only the dualist "Austro-Hungarian" Monarchy had the legal capacity for international dealings: "De jure, an 'Austria' has never existed—thus we cannot succeed such [a state] nor represent it here."[73] Besides, the Austrian delegation continued, with its territory and population changed unrecognizably, and a revolution in the form of government, on what basis could their small republic be deemed the legal successor of the Habsburg Monarchy? The republic, they insisted, was a *new* state and could not be automatically saddled with the war debts and obligations of the former empire. The Treaty of Saint-Germain was still drafted as if a continuous Austrian legal identity could be presumed, but, behind the scenes at the conference, the Austrian arguments provoked doubt and consternation.

How could one determine if a state was legally continuous, or if it had died? What was the measure or rule? The heated memoranda war that followed in the back rooms of the peace conference revealed that no one really knew.

In the decades of decolonization that followed World War II, these same sorts of legal stories—about sovereignty suspended and resurrected, about the particular ways sovereignty worked in time—morphed into scripts for international legal politics around the globe. Jurists from India, Indonesia, Algeria, and elsewhere rejected the idea that their states were "new," with its connotations of contingency and conditionality. They too argued that their polities reverted to a sovereignty they had held prior to colonial rule. In the formulation of the prominent Indian jurist Ram Prakash Anand, colonization had "*eclipsed* rather than *extinguished* the international legal personality of the colonized countries." With suspended sovereignty now revived, postcolonial states rejoined the international legal community not as juvenile newcomers but as equals.[74]

Edges of the Knowable: States in Time

"Sovereignty" has long functioned as a limit concept. A marker of the highest and the supreme, of final things and first things, the foundation of law and yet above or before the law, sovereignty is "political theology," in Carl Schmitt's famous formulation, covered with the fingerprints of the creator God with whom it was originally associated.[75] To be "nonderived" and thus paramount—to be an original fount of law rather than something delegated from another source—relied on an ultimately mystical origin, a derivation "from nothingness."[76] "This moment of suspense," as Jacques Derrida parsed it, "this founding or revolutionary moment of law is, in law, an instance of non-law. But it is also the whole history of law. . . . It is the moment in which the foundation of law remains suspended in the void or over the abyss, suspended by a pure performative act that would not have to answer to or before anyone."[77] By pointing to origins, foundations, and sources, to the "presupposed and a priori," sovereignty represents a threshold not only for law and politics but also for knowledge.[78]

In an age dazzled by the achievements and methodological self-consciousness of the natural sciences, nineteenth-century jurists sought to modernize legal scholarship by setting it on new empirical, "scientific" foundations. Forsaking natural law and divine right in favor of legal positivism, they designated the earthbound, sovereign state as the source of law. Indeed, lawmaking power counted among its constitutive features. In so doing, they ushered in an alternate set of difficulties through the back door. If the state constituted the source of law, then anything behind or before the state became juridically invisible or incomprehensible: to be prior to the state was, by definition, to be prior to the law. The shift to positivism thus meant that there could be no such thing as legal knowledge about the creation of states (or their demise) because law could hardly regulate its own coming into being; it could not be prior to itself, there to witness and regulate its own birth. If law was grounded in the state, then the state's identity, its legal existence, was not something that could be analyzed within that same legal framework. Jellinek referred blankly to the "untenability of all attempts . . . to construe the creation of states juridically."[79] The birth and death of states was thus categorized a matter of *fact* and not *law*—made extraneous to the law and placed beyond legal cognition. It marked the vanishing point of positivist legal knowledge. Within positivist legal frameworks, dominant by the late nineteenth century, the state—as the premise of law itself—always already existed.

These formal propositions dovetailed with some much older ideas about the nature of the sovereign state. Integral to its modern incarnation was the notion of juridical immortality. Ernst Kantorowicz famously traced the medieval genealogy of this doctrine in *The King's Two Bodies*. The state did not just fasten a plurality of people into a singular legal entity: that legal entity remained the same, ageless and unchanging, despite the coming and going of a plurality of persons over time.[80] The idea also lay at the center of Thomas Hobbes's canonical account of the state as a *persona ficta*. The state, he argued, required an "artificial eternity of life." Unless it was an abstract, undying entity, it could not incur public debt or keep treaty commitments or guarantee many other facets of public order that involved time spans beyond the scale of a single generation.[81] "One reason why states are likely to remain powerful actors in the contemporary world," Quentin Skinner has written more recently, "is that they will outlive us all."[82] Undying and perpetual, states arose, Kelsen reflected a little ruefully in the 1920s, "with the claim to be valid *forever*."[83]

The end of imperial sovereignty exposed the gaping black hole surrounding the legal birth and death of states. For Central European jurists writing through and after the collapse of the Habsburg Empire, the temporal edges of sovereignty suddenly loomed out of those disciplinary shadows and bore down on the present with an existential urgency. In the early 1920s, Kelsen puzzled that legal scholars possessed endless exhaustive treatments of the state's territorial frontiers and virtually none of its temporal ones. Perhaps because the outer rim of territorial jurisdiction seemed perceptible, tangible (he used the word *fühlbar*) while any temporal limit seemed completely *im*perceptible, occluded by the doctrine of the state's *Ewigkeit*—its perpetuity, its eternity. No longer. It was now clear that states existed in time, too, and not only in space.[84] The eclipse of imperial sovereignty sensitized Kelsen and his colleagues to the fiction, the contrivance, of state immortality: the cultivated timelessness of the state's legal order, its insensibility to time, had been violently jolted into the domain of the sensible. They began to fashion states-in-time into an object of legal analysis.

For these jurists, to confront the chronological edges of sovereignty was like staring over the edge of a cliff into a terrifying zone beyond law—a legal void or vacuum completely abhorrent to modern belief in the necessary gaplessness of legal order. Some felt a colonial chill: a chronological gap between sovereignties, in the revealing analogy of Kelsen student Josef Kunz, threatened to leave Austria momentarily in the same international legal position as "so-called 'savages.'"[85] Kelsen and his circle developed a number of philosophical strategies to seal over this abyss. Strikingly, it was the conceptual innovations they had developed in response to the impasse of Habsburg sovereign plurality that now suggested ways of overcoming the impasse of sovereign mortality. They projected the "pure theory of law" upward and outward, transposing it from the jurisdictional scale of the state to that of the international legal system as a whole.

The question of time or priority had been integral to the empire's jurisdictional chaos. It had proved so hard to foreclose the stateness of the lands and establish the completeness of imperial sovereignty precisely because the lands *preceded* the empire. The original dynastic unions unfolded on the basis of *their* law: Ferdinand of Habsburg was crowned king of Bohemia on the basis of Bohemian law, and he ruled Bohemia on the basis of Bohemian law. Once divine right gave way to the notion of states as the origin of law's legitimacy, it was not easy to construe imperial sovereignty as original or nonderived— *because it was not*: the original authority to rule had been bestowed by the lands. It lingered in the lawmaking power of the lands, which was not jurisdictionally subordinate to imperial law: a law passed by the Bohemian diet was not automatically trumped by one made in the "Austrian" parliament, opening the door to chaotic legal contradictions.

In this context, it had become clear to a young Kelsen that the legal unity of the state depended on a single origin point for law, a single point of "ascription," and that that point could not be understood as a factual or historical or sociological proposition. That left one stuck in an endless mess of constitutional disputes. That singular origin point could only be *presumed* as a *logical* one. The legal order must *posit* what he came to call a *Grundnorm*—a "basic norm," or foundational norm—from which all subsequent legal norms derived. The basic norm essentially established how other norms could be made: it was a rule about rules, occupying the apex of the "pyramid of legal order."[86] In a series of exchanges through the war and in its aftermath, Vienna school jurists developed the argument that the basic norm at the apex of state sovereignty could not in fact be the final point of legal ascription. Rather, it must itself be derived from a still-higher basic norm—the basic norm at the apex of the *international* legal order. The problem of the identity and continuity of states was crucial evidence for the logical necessity of this construction. The creation and demise of states could become legally understandable only if there was a "higher" legal order outside and above the state, in existence before it and after it. That overarching order banished any legal vacuums between sovereignties. The argument constituted a radical attack on the absoluteness of state sovereignty, now construed as subordinate to international law.

Confronted with the ghostly impasse of state birth and state death, Central European jurists responded with a fit of philosophical rigor—as though it was simply a matter of thinking hard enough, of pursuing logic with enough discipline, of achieving sufficient epistemic purity. They transposed the theologically inflected problem of the origins of sovereignty into a problem of the premise of reasoning, the "point of departure" for thought and law. The argument was not that international law "came first" in a historical sense but that it came first in a logical one: as the problem of discontinuous sovereignty revealed, the world's legal order could only have theoretical coherence if international law's priority was a normative-philosophical presupposition.[87] The Viennese jurists digested the problem of sovereignty's *historical sequence* into one of *philosophical sequence*. Legal reasoning needed to begin on the premise of international law, not state sovereignty. International law—higher and prior, always already before and after—provided the continuity that breakable states could not. In making sense of the mortality of sovereignty, the jurists gifted the glow of its erstwhile immortality to international law instead.

As the geographic locus of emergent postimperial sovereignties shifted southward in the decades after World War II, jurisdictional priority remained a key thread, but with the narrative signs reversed. For many jurists from the Global South, the continuity and priority of international law were precisely the problem—and not the solution. In committing them to honor the concessions, liabilities, and obligations adopted by former imperial rulers, the postulate of legal continuity bound postimperial states into structures of economic subordination and stripped self-determination of its emancipatory potential. As they theorized and contested the law of state succession, jurists like the Algerian Mohammed Bedjaoui sought not to stitch together time to preserve order: the existing order *was* the problem. Where Kunz and his colleagues wrote transfixed by the experience and threat of state extinction, Bedjaoui and his wrote seized by the project of state birth.

Sovereignty as a Knowledge Problem (for Them and Us)

Priorness, priority, the a priori: this book probes the affinity between *jurisdictional* questions and *epistemological* ones. It is about the premises of rule, and of reasoning—about the foundations of law and ideas. It does more than explore their structural parallels: it studies their entangled history, as historical actors sought to ground and explain sovereignty after the eclipse of divine right. They had to fashion new sorts of coherence, sense, and unity if those things were no longer simply provided by God or nature. Remaking the legitimacy of sovereignty involved both styles of reasoning and styles of politics, and they evolved woven closely together. Rather than the straightforward slide from theology to law posited by Carl Schmitt, the argument structure here has more in common with the German philosopher Hans Blumenberg's book *The Legitimacy of the Modern Age*. Blumenberg depicted modern doctrines of progress "reoccupying" positions once held by religion, forced to try to answer questions about the meaning and purpose of history "left over" from Christianity.[88] This book shows what happened when positivist understandings of law tried to "answer" the "questions" left over from the divine right and many-bodied glory of kings and emperors. They were large shoes to fill, heavy crowns to wear. Ill-equipped to play that role, modern legal thought found itself in a tangle of ideas and interpretations as it tried to reground sovereignty's a priori legitimacy, its nonderivation, its singularity, and its immortality. Kelsen's pure theory of law was only the most dramatic and revealing response to a broader problem: post-God, post-emperor, logical consistency was the only form of guarantee, the only form of truth, the only proof of validity, to which law had access. The legitimacy of law and the unity of state sovereignty could only be epistemological propositions now. Legal reasoning stepped in to suffuse the whole with logic, like grace; logic *made* the whole, ordering norms harmoniously into consistent chains of norms, providing a rational unity rather than a natural one, a holism of form rather than substance. The jurist, a mini-god, conjured order out of a profoundly disordered world.

This book presents the history of modern sovereignty as an attempt to *make sense*—as a form of sense seeking.[89] It is about the *search* for coherence, rather than any fixed or finished arrival points. It approaches sovereignty as a history not only of ideas but also of knowledge and method—a history of the *reach* for ideas (and often for ideas about ideas, just as sovereignty is law about law). The method, I argue, *is* the story: one of modern law seeking to make itself rational, seeking to reconcile contradiction, seeking formal logical coherence.

In his "Prospect for a Theory of Nonconceptuality" and other essays, Blumenberg suggested that metaphors granted access to that which could not be translated back (or forward) into pure conceptuality, that which could not be reduced into abstract language—those aspects of the human lifeworld that were "conceptually irredeemable." Through them, one might excavate that buried stratum of stimulations and needs that *generated* theoretical curiosity—the lifeworld and "catalytic sphere" that sparked metaphors, the "perplexity" for which they stepped in.[90] My path here is parallel: rather than take sovereignty as a particular *idea* or *thing*, I present it as a *problem*, a stimulus, eliciting ever-new attempts to solve, to theorize, to understand, and to order. Each constitutional configuration, like each academic theory, struggled to contain or tame its object, never quite finding coherence or fixing meaning, never quite achieving political or intellectual stability. In recovering that history, I am attentive to the affective *desire* for order and logical coherence, and the *experience* of its elusiveness, treating these things not as a kind of incidental backstage to a "real" history of law or ideas but as the main stage of the story itself.[91] Precisely the "nonarrival" of the concepts gifted them their historical dynamism. *The Life and Death of States* is an intellectual history of theory *not* working, an intellectual history of an impasse—an intellectual history of not having the words.

If images of sovereignty were symptoms of perplexity, and that perplexity is my subject, *The Life and Death of States* suggests ways of reconfiguring methodological debates in intellectual and legal history. Neither an opposition between autonomous representations and social worlds nor one between theory and practice, or intellectuals and others, maps meaningfully onto the history here recovered.[92] This search, this grasping, spanned the academic and political domains: sovereignty as sense making was a shared project. The conjugation of intellectual and political order has a variety of modalities at different points of the story, but it is rarely a simple matter of one serving as the "context" for the other. The shared logics and themes across these domains— arrangements of law and fact, of priority and sequence, and of the real and the fictional—invite the language of reversibility, or multidirectionality: constitutions were modes of theory making, and, in reverse, concepts were order making. What is a constitution save a living theory of the state in question—the state distilled into abstract form, propositional form, the state on paper? Especially the iterative nature of the Habsburg constitutions (and the relentless debate about them) invites us to see them as the trying out of ideas, as rolling attempts to fix complex, shifting realities into stable forms that had a higher-order regulative and explanatory power than any individual moment (i.e., like theory!)—projects that worked to lift "the truth" out of the endless arc of historical becoming. At the same time, and confronted with the same dilemmas, legal scholars were propelled toward *constitutions for thought*, drafting and codifying rules of right knowing and right reasoning.

I thus present law as a form of what we can call public reasoning: a mode of reasoning about the public but also of reasoning publicly—of giving reasons, of laying bare the basis of a norm, of a decision, of the state; a form of argumentation in which the supporting chain of rationalization is pivotal. That image of law as public reason is internal to the history told. After the legitimacy of the state became untethered from older genres of right, reasoning itself—in the form of logical consistency and coherence—was asked to shoulder much of that burden. The longing to purify logic of contradictions and mystical leaps, and to purify jurisdiction of contradictions and gaps, came folded together and shared a common pathos in their limitations. This book, then, is a history of the "temporal life" of states in more than one sense: a history of sovereignty on this side of God, seeking legitimacy through the fallible endeavors of the human mind; of notions of sovereignty shifting in time, between a world of many-bodied emperor-kings and the advent of global decolonization; and of states-in-time as a problem, for legal epistemology and for international order. For all these stories, Central Europe has many secrets to share.

Chapter 1 opens at the dawn of the constitutional era in the Habsburg lands. It shows how the elected delegates of the empire's first parliament became the first modern theorists of its sovereignty. They debated the legal status of the empire's historical lands and weighed it against new visions of the empire restructured into a federation of nations. The chapter follows juridical argument about the lands through the constitutions of the early 1860s, before chapter 2 turns to the dramatic restructuring of the empire in the Settlement of 1867. The Settlement pioneered a new form of dual sovereignty, straining the line between constitutional and international law. In the face of heated public controversy about the location and meaning of sovereignty, a new scholarly field—Austrian constitutional law—emerged at the universities to study and teach the same questions. The codification of states tangled together with the codification of disciplines. Here we meet Georg Jellinek—young, passionate, persecuted, and certain that theories of sovereignty needed to be completely rethought. Chapter 3 tracks debate about the legal status of both lands and nations through to the empire's collapse. As Czech-speaking politicians like Karel Kramář argued that the Kingdom of Bohemia had retained its sovereignty in suspended form, others proposed turning ethnic nations into legal collectives and granting them autonomy on a nonterritorial basis. Both visions of partial and dimmed sovereignty outlived the empire that spawned them.

Chapter 4 returns to Jellinek at the century's turn and places him at the center of epochal transformations in the history of legal thought. I show how Jellinek introduced neo-Kantian philosophy into legal science and recast its epistemological foundations, shaping the departures of his student, Hans Kelsen. In conversation with Freud and others, Kelsen pursued a "pure" legal science that dissolved the state into an abstract system of norms. While he worked, states began dissolving in an all-too-concrete sense: chapter 5 analyzes the legal ends of Habsburg sovereignty and the construction of a new order in Central Europe. Ideas forged in the fight over imperial sovereignty now became resources for international claim making, with Czechs and Hungarians depicting their states as the legal heirs of their historical kingdoms. As peacemakers struggled to determine which states were new and which were old, Kelsen and his Viennese circle of collaborators thrashed out a legal theory capable of grasping the birth and death of states on a philosophical level—the subject of chapter 6. Their system, the pure theory of law, offered an explanation for the ultimate origin of law and reconfigured the relationship between sovereignty and international law. If chapters 5 and 6 explore how political actors and scholars made sense of the end of empire in Central Europe, chapter 7 follows these ideas and arguments into the era of global decolonization after World War II. A new round of claims about the resurrection of pre-imperial sovereignty echoed through the postwar international order. Again, one questioned how states live and how they die in international law. The chapter's final section shows how these problems "returned" from the Global South to Europe at the end of the Cold War, with the implosion of the USSR and a new wave of old-new states across Central, Eastern, and Southern Europe.

Readers wishing to trace the story of modern legal thought can move from the second half of chapter 2 to chapter 4 and to then chapter 6. But the book's structure, swinging back and forth between scholarly and political domains, is integral to its argument, showing how states and the ideas designed to capture them were reconfigured in parallel. Each wing reflects new light on the other: we see the worldly strains of sovereignty rippling through systems of philosophy, and we see searching questions about the real and the true playing out in public life. In smudging the line between making states and making knowledge, this book suggests new ways of writing the intellectual history of international order.

CHAPTER ONE

Constitution as Archive

DRAFTING THE EMPIRE, 1848–1860S

An empire begins to keep a diary • The people sit down to write the state • František Palacký makes a radical proposal • What is the normal-time? • Fantasy kingdoms • The emperor has no time for theory • Franz Hein fears the chaos of temporal multiplicity • An archive of archives, and a state of states

DAS PROVISORISCHE ÖSTERREICH—"provisional Austria." Franz Schuselka's 1850 title was part ironic, part accusatory. The state remained unfinished, a hesitating draft. The project of an imperial constitution was barely two years old, but several constitutions had already come and gone. The frenetic activity of the current ministry, wrote the prominent author and liberal politician, attracted more and more ridicule with each passing day. So ran the jokes: "Where then will the new Austria be made?, one asks. And the answer goes: It will be printed in the k. k. Court and State Publishing House! And in fact the occupation of our ministry is predominantly a literary one." "It seems," Schuselka quipped, "that this is also the reason one so severely suppresses the free press, so that the ministry need not fear competition for its writerly efforts. Since it has been at the helm, it has truly published a whole library of proposed, rejected, and reproposed proposals."[1] The ministry falls in love in each of its works, he complained; it sinks into theory, closes itself off from life and practical politics, "writes and writes by day and by night and believes with every printed page to have made a piece of world history."[2]

How does one write an empire? The government was trying, and failing, to set the empire into constitutional text, to produce a written description of the sprawling conglomerate polity stretched out over the continent's middle. The drafts piled up. In this unfamiliar new constitutional era, state making began to seem like a search for the right words. Schuselka's joke worked because something behind it rang true: the growing mass of legal descriptions of the empire put ever greater pressure on the relationship between words and things, between legal text and the state it ostensibly codified. The drafts revealed an unnerving truth: there was little to no agreement about what sort of thing the empire was.

One description of its constitutional reality was mooted, only for its plausibility to fade, and another sketch to take its place. The very first attempt, the so-called Pillersdorf constitution (1848), survived mere months. An elaborate new version drafted laboriously by the Kremsier parliament (1849) was never implemented, while the imposed March constitution of 1849 only partially came into effect before the government suspended all constitutional life in 1851 and returned, for a while, to absolutism. The October Diploma of 1860 barely became live law before the February Patent of 1861 succeeded it in part—and all this prior to the Settlement of 1867, which piloted an alternative approach by splitting the problem (and the empire) in two. A constitution seemingly required one to isolate and endorse a single interpretation of the "truth" from many possible versions of the empire's order. But what if the empire was many things at once?

These constitutions, and the debate they generated, together read like a diary the empire kept about itself—an evolving record of imperial self-understanding, the autofiction of a multinational dynastic state in an epoch of self-conscious modernization. Their successive quality, their restive provisionality, meant that they amassed alongside one another, overlapped, and often blended together. Many were never fully implemented, and others were not completely withdrawn. An exasperated Schuselka poked fun at this constitutional excess at the dawn of that tradition. The political philosopher Eric Voegelin pointed to something very similar from the perspective of its interwar dusk. Before the Nazis chased him from Europe to the United States, before his widely influential postwar work on religion, gnosticism, and the philosophy of history, Voegelin spent the 1930s teaching law at the University of Vienna. His study *The Authoritarian State: An Essay on the Problem of the Austrian State* (1936) was both a philosophical history of the Austrian constitutional tradition and a biting critique of its leading light, his teacher Hans Kelsen.[3] The Austrian constitutional acts, he argued, were "not unequivocal decrees" that settled issues and resolved power struggles but rather a series of documents "that can be grouped together because of their typical, recurrent cyclical nature."[4] Drafted and redrafted, they looped over and through one another. The cycles did not "repeat with total uniformity" since "each subsequent one has absorbed some of the substance of the preceding ones because of the accumulation of historical meaning." This accumulative capacity meant that "the constitution" was always much broader, more porous, and less hermetic than we might otherwise expect, existing as part of a thicker literary field. "Austrian constitutional history does not consist of individual constitutional acts, each standing by itself as a ruling decision binding for a longer or a shorter time," Voegelin wrote, "but of a series of documents in which an unsettled and uncertain situation becomes stabilized anew, and that is why it is impossible to say with certainty what the constitution of Austria was at any particular time."[5] The constitutions did not so much fix one truth in place as collectively mark out a space of unresolved uncertainty.

Gathering, amassing, accumulating: the Habsburg constitutional tradition functioned as an archive that collected and preserved different versions of the empire's legal order. That archive was not a static repository of discrete, superseded systems. As Voegelin suggested, it remained a dynamic and volatile compound. Like a time capsule that recorded successive stills of the empire's legal life but kept them all live at once, it represented an aggregative way of being in time. In this equivocation and plurality, it remained a space where rival political configurations—and rival accounts of the legally "real" and "true"—vied for supremacy.

This chapter analyzes the series of constitutions promulgated and debated between 1848 and 1861, before the Settlement of 1867 reset the game entirely. It opens with the revolutions of 1848 and the beginning of constitutional life in the Habsburg Empire. It focuses especially on the production of the so-called Kremsier constitutional draft of 1849. Authored collaboratively by a constitutional committee of the newly elected imperial parliament, the draft remained the most remarkable and influential of all the imperial descriptions, although it never became active law. The searching deliberations behind the Kremsier draft unfolded like an initial survey of the archive of constitutional order. They reflect a larger story of nineteenth-century constitutionalization: rule required reasons, ones given in a different meter to earlier periods.[6] Political claims needed explicit accounts of legitimacy, and through the debates of the first Habsburg parliament, we watch the people's representatives and the government alike figuring out what that meant for the empire's political system. In a polity deeply wedded to dynasticism and still structured (if not always administered) according to the legacies of composite monarchy, that process often unfolded like a referendum on history itself. The delegates surveyed and weighed the historical plurality of the empire's legal order, the historical rights of the estates, and the laws of dynastic succession, wondering what these institutions now signified and how they should be codified to accord with nineteenth-century ideas and realities. Often, constitutional debate unfolded as a series of disagreements about what law was still operative and valid, and what law had been drained of authority and force. The work of imperial organization required its practitioners to distinguish the timely from the untimely, the fictional from the factual, the legitimate from the lapsed, the permanent from the provisional.

Behind these distinctions lay daunting questions about sovereignty. An account of the sovereign structure of the Habsburg Monarchy required an account of the status of its component lands—the concatenation of smaller polities collected under the Habsburg rule, often with pronounced memories of their own independence and significant residual autonomy. The ambiguity surrounding their slowly fading autonomy had been a useful technique of imperial rule for the Habsburgs, but a written constitution left little room for the same gentle indeterminacy. Their status and standing needed to be codified, pushing delegates to reflect on the nature and survival of states in time.

That in turn required delegates to reckon with their own place in time. They soon realized that they lacked a historically neutral place from which to "tell" or assess imperial law. How could one codify the empire's history into law if one did not know where history started and where it stopped? The constitutional project seemed to require a vantage point outside the movement of history, a point at which the empire's shifting legal diversity could be arrested and written down. While the imperial government attempted to definitively quash the empire's legal pluralism with its neoabsolutist turn in the early 1850s, the return to constitutionalism in 1860 established the empire's historical order of kingdoms and lands, with its temporal-legal pluralism, as the foundation of the imperial constitution.

Out of Jupiter's Head

The very first imperial parliament of the Habsburg Monarchy assembled in Vienna on July 22, 1848. Among the delegates was the Bohemian František Palacký, a historian and politician and the most important Czech leader of the mid-nineteenth century. The parliament's task, in his words, amounted to "the final state formation of Austria, or the creation of a constitution."[7] The state would be completed by its people. This experiment at the popular authorship of imperial order was unprecedented and would prove unique: it remained, until the empire's collapse, the only official, representative, and open-ended debate on the normative order of the empire. For that reason, the parliament's deliberations hold a large claim on the interest of the historian of imperial sovereignty, even if they are not usually read in this way. The structure, logic, and nature of imperial rule needed to be ascertained, defended, challenged, and rewritten—often from first principles. That the delegates laboriously reached a compromise and agreed to a constitutional draft despite huge regional and political differences, and that the imperial government nevertheless decided at the last moment to discard the draft and unilaterally impose its own version, has been narrated ruefully ever since as the road not taken—the one realistic chance to disarm the empire's structural troubles (especially regarding the national question) and set it on the path of peaceful longevity. The Kremsier draft or Kremsier proposal, at it is known, became the ubiquitous ghost law haunting all subsequent constitutional debates.

The path to this parliamentary experiment had been blazed by revolution. In the six months leading up to the parliamentary opening in July, political events had followed on each other's heels at a dizzying pace. Inspired by developments in France, revolution broke out abruptly in March with students, workers, and others gathering in the capital to press the case for emphatic liberal reform. Various goals and agendas coalesced: demands for national equality blended with agitation for freedom of the press and a constitution, for civil liberties and legal equality. The weakness of the central government had been exacerbated by severe financial difficulties, and as unrest across a number of urban centers spiraled out of control, the whole empire appeared quite literally on the verge of collapse.[8] Metternich's head rolled immediately, but that seemed merely a sign of things to come. When an estates central committee met in Vienna in early April, its assessment was grave. "The old is breaking apart from all sides," observed the Viennese landholder Karl Ritter von Kleyle in the estates committee's resolution, "external and internal threats proliferate simultaneously and immeasurably, the hour of decision has struck, and if the new order does not arise rapidly and fresh with life, we will become victims of anarchy."[9]

This crisis inaugurated constitutional life in the Habsburg Empire. *Constitution* was the "magic word" and "magic wand" on everyone's lips, bundling together a broad (if vague) collection of aspirations.[10] But what kind of constitution, what kind of "new order," could juggle the uneven sovereign arrangements across the empire—especially the web of varying historic rights claims—as well as satisfy the demands for liberal reform, all the while asserting a strong centralized state? Disagreement and uncertainty raged. But most agreed that the piecemeal, accumulative nature of the empire's legal order no longer sufficed. "There is no longer time," declared Kleyle, "to advance in an organic development from municipal organization to the provincial estates and from there to the parliament; as Minerva sprang armed out of Jupiter's head, so must the constitution stride into life."[11] The jolt of revolution made codification the urgent and existential task of the state.

Attempting to regain the initiative, the government hurriedly promulgated the empire's first formal constitution on April 25, 1848. Known as the Pillersdorf constitution, it had been drafted hastily by the minister of the interior Franz von Pillersdorf using the constitutions of Baden and Belgium as models.[12] Its portrait of the empire—decidedly centralist in structure, with only a limited role for the regional diets—won scant approval. Dissatisfaction with its limited electoral laws led to their modification on May 8, but the following week, amid a radicalizing revolution, the constitution was repealed in its entirety, pending the creation of a new one.[13] Like a generic, one-size-fits-all kit, the Pillersdorf constitution was not believable as a legal articulation of the empire, appearing instead as what certain bureaucrats might have imagined a constitution to look like.

Pursuant to the drafting of a new constitution, an imperial parliament was elected on a strikingly broad basis approaching universal male suffrage—although, importantly, neither Hungary nor Lombardy-Venetia was invited to participate. The resulting parliament of the "core" Habsburg lands had a thick middle-class foundation: of the 383 possible deputies, some mere 40 were nobles. Here, for the first time, the peoples of Austria came face-to-face, with all the attendant structural questions of the monarchy clearly on display.[14] The very fact of this gathering altered the legal landscape of the empire: in calling a parliament, the emperor seemingly conceded that he was not the only source of law, and that the people(s) may have a role in lawmaking.[15] They seized the opening with both hands. Parliamentary subcommittees were already at work on draft proposals when the crown itself changed hands.

The abdication of the feebleminded emperor Ferdinand I paved the way for the coronation of an eighteen-year-old archduke on December 2. The new boy-emperor, Francis Joseph, would remain on the throne until his death more than six decades later, in a new century, with his empire-state in the deadly grip of World War I. His reign began in the midst of this very different state crisis, which he quickly tried to master. Simultaneous with his coronation, Francis Joseph issued an imperial patent that depicted the current conjuncture as one of renewal—of bringing the empire into alignment with the present. "Recognizing out of our own conviction," declared the patent, "the necessity and high value of free and timely [*zeitgemäßer*] institutions, we confidently tread the path that should lead us to a salutary reconfiguration and rejuvenation of the entire monarchy."[16]

The parliamentary deputies faced a monumental task. In the words of Anton Springer—a liberal historian who himself had been involved in the revolutions—the delegates confronted a deep "ambiguity regarding the nature of the empire."[17] They had few helpful guides or manuals. Unlike Minister Pillersdorf, they did not view Baden and Belgium as instructive models. As the jurist Ludwig Gumplowicz reflected in 1889, their task was especially difficult "because, of the numerous constitutions created since the great French Revolution, none were suitable for such a complex of lands like the Austrian."[18]

The parliament elected a special thirty-member constitutional committee, which in turn tasked a five-member subcommittee with drafting an initial proposal on the "constitution of the empire, the provinces, and municipalities" that could serve as the basis of debate.[19] But even that proved challenging. The Bohemian deputy (and leader of the Czech party) Palacký took the initiative. He penned a bold—even visionary—federalist constitutional draft that reimagined the constituent parts of the empire. His draft dissolved the traditional "members" of the empire—the historic kingdoms and lands, which were all multiethnic—and proposed in their stead a smaller number of large units formed on the basis of ethnicity alone. These units would possess the lion's share of political rights and functions and would be unified more loosely under the limited authority of the imperial center.

Murmurs of disquiet met this prescription for radical state surgery. The other members of the small constitutional subcommittee—Kajetan Mayer (from Moravia), Ferdinand Gobbi (from the Austrian Littoral, or *Küsten-lande*), Franciszek Smolka (from Galicia), and Joseph Goldmark (from Lower Austria)—remained highly skeptical of the wisdom (or the ease) of abolishing the historical lands in their entirety. Gobbi likewise prepared a draft, but neither his nor Palacký's proposal could achieve a majority in the subcommittee. Seeking to break the deadlock, Mayer then prepared a version of his own: designed to synthesize the drafts, it nevertheless left much of the historic order in place. Still they disagreed: in the end, the full constitutional committee was presented with two different constitutional descriptions of imperial order—Mayer's and Palacký's—with the former serving as the central basis for the debate. Having been dispatched to the Moravian town of Kremsier amid ongoing revolutionary flare-ups in the imperial capital, parliamentary proceedings opened on January 13, and the contest over the empire's normative order began in earnest on January 22.[20]

In 1908, the jurist and sometime minister Josef Redlich looked back in awe on the deliberations that ensued. They represented one of the most important sources for the Austrian "state problem," though they had been far from exhausted by historians—an assessment that remains true today. Reading the Kremsier debates, marveled Redlich, "one is always again astonished—and not without sadness—how most of the problems that were raised, discussed and in large part solved in the constitutional proposal there stand before us in all freshness even today, how these 60-year-old thought-paths and controversies remain in good part open questions even for us. And it is humbling to recognize how little we, in our whole repository of political thought, have moved beyond those days of the first Austrian parliament."[21] A collaboratively authored constitution for a conglomerate, multinational empire, it was a description of imperial sovereignty produced by its own citizens, a self-diagnosis from below. Though government quashed its implementation, the Kremsier draft remained hugely influential "not as a source of law, but rather as a source of legal ideas"[22]—a library of concepts and creative solutions. Remarkable as the final constitutional draft proved to be, it is the dialogical nature of its production that records most dramatically the difficulty of squaring the empire with categories of "state" and "sovereignty." The meeting protocols allow us to eavesdrop on the conversations.

The Sovereignty Diaries: What We Know about the Empire

JANUARY 22, 1849. WHERE DOES AN IMPERIAL CONSTITUTION BEGIN?

Kajetan Mayer began proceedings tentatively, conscious that the discussion could easily grow ungovernable. He suggested that the delegates first agree on the division of legislative powers and prerogatives between the center and the parts—a neutral, technical question, function or capacity rather than essence. Perhaps he was wary of opening with first principles. Out of this conversation, he explained, it might become clear how many individual parts to have and what they should be.[23] Optimism, or fear? Might a more circuitous route render the destination less challenging, through a kind of sideways crawl into constitutional life? The Bohemian delegate Adolf Maria Pinkas was not fooled for a moment. He declared the approach impossible. Surely, one must first determine the individual units of the empire, especially to know their size and scale, before powers could be rightfully distributed. For what constituent parts is the constitution proposed? This was the first question. "These constituent parts will form a state complex," Pinkas explained, "and then it will be to decide how such a state complex can stand as a whole." One reasoned from the identity of the parts toward the imperial center: in this way, they could see what prerogatives would need to be conceded to the whole, and what could remain with the individual parts.[24] The flowchart of imperial reasoning should begin in the provinces.

That is, constitutional reasoning should begin with the bearers of rights, not the rights themselves. Suspended between Mayer's cautious pragmatism and Pinkas's certainty, the very first exchanges mapped the basic structure of an unstable dialectic between rights and their subjects, one that evolved steadily throughout the subsequent history of imperial constitutional debate. Which came first, in history and in principle? Chicken and egg, subject and object. According to Mayer: the rights and legal functions will reveal the nature of their bearers. According to Pinkas: only in knowing the identity of a subject could one reason about its rights. By conceiving those rights as disembodied, as neutral functions of the law, Mayer attempted to diffuse the controversial politics of the imperial state structure. Pinkas scoffed: rights could not be uncoupled from their bearers—the latter was the very source of the former. In abstraction, rights were robbed of meaning.

The field of principles was thereby blown wide open. How did rights and law relate to the identity of their bearers? National demands loomed large for all, sharpened by the ethnic dimension of the revolutionary violence in Hungary and elsewhere. Emil Vacano, a centralist from Upper Austria, reminded those assembled of law's blindness to such questions: constitutional principles "do not depend on nationality."[25] An empire structured around the (multiethnic) historic kingdoms and lands knew no concept of nation. But was this blindness still realistic in the current age? Mathias Kautschitsch, representing Carinthia and Carniola, preemptively warned those desiring to preserve the historic provinces that Croatia, Slavonia, and Serbia would not be satisfied with that, and that Czechs and Germans in Bohemia, and Germans and Italians (*Welschen*) did not want to stay together, either. But the picture was cloudy. Anton Goriup and Ferdinand Gobbi, both from the Austrian Littoral, declared the ethnographic principle, and the breakup of the old provinces that it implied, to be impossible.[26] Palacký, meanwhile, announced himself an absolute federalist, although he had reservations about the term, because a "federation" entailed the federation of sovereign states. "But one cannot talk of such a thing in Austria," he reflected, "because the provinces do not in themselves form sovereign states."[27] With this first round of caveats already littering the terrain like mines, Mayer read aloud the proposed division of the empire from the first two sections of his draft, kicking off the list making that accompanies all constitution writing:

1) Of the state territory and its division

§1. The Austrian Empire is an indivisible constitutional hereditary monarchy formed out of the following independent crownlands.

§2. These independent indivisible crownlands are:
1. the Kingdom of Bohemia,
2. the Kingdom of Galicia with the Bukovina,
3. the Archduchy of Austria below the Enns,
4. the Archduchy of Austria above the Enns without Innviertel,
5. the Duchy of Salzburg including Innviertel,
6. the Duchy of Styria,
7. the Duchy of Carinthia,
8. the Duchy of Carniola,
9. the Duchy of Silesia,
10. the Margravate of Moravia,
11. the Princely County of Tyrol including Vorarlberg,
12. the Austrian Littoral,
13. the Kingdom of Dalmatia.

Mayer coupled this recitation with the observation "that here one proceeded from the historical perspective, because every province has independent rights, which stand as sacrosanct."[28] Pinkas declared that this question would "decide the fate of the constitution construction."[29]

Johann Kasper Ratz (from the principality of Vorarlberg within Tyrol, and formally representing the latter) tabled the first objection to Mayer's list, and its contents were telling. He did not marshal the national against the historical but rather the historical against the historical. History showed, Ratz explained, that Vorarlberg possessed an independent constitution (*selbstständige Verfassung*) when it was transferred to Austria: it never belonged to Tyrol. This history demonstrated "that Vorarlberg thus has for itself the historical right to independence."[30] Simon Turco (also from Tyrol) received this reasoning warmly: the same logic, he argued, supported the independence of the principality of Trient (in southern Tyrol), as it was only attached to German Tyrol in 1814.[31] As the atoms of the empire, the historical "lands" were not immune to their own centrifugal forces pushing for devolution into ever smaller historical particles.

This debate unmasked the historical principle—and the system it supports— as untenable, asserted Rudolf Brestel, a delegate from Vienna (representing Lower Austria). It bred endless division: "only from the national standpoint can we solve this problem." They should first fix upon the national as the highest principle.[32] The Pole Florian Ziemialkowski deemed it impossible to hold strictly to either the historical or the national framework in Austria; he sought a middle way for that reason.[33]

Amid all the back-and-forth, already riddled with a kind of unraveling, Franz Hein lamented that if this discord continued, they would never reach an agreement, and a constitution would instead be imposed. He spoke in defense of the old historical boundaries: many diverse relationships would be injured if the provinces were melted down; he opposed such "forced blending." He suggested one method of taming the historical approach, to prevent it from spiraling off into the uncontrollable pluralism of the deep past: they should take the existing situation at the moment of the outbreak of revolution "because without the revolution, the question would never have surfaced."[34] Perhaps one way of saving history was fixing its unfolding movement into a single status quo—saving its products by arresting its movement. History may be a constitutional virtue only in its own negation.

JANUARY 23, 1849. THE EMPIRE INSIDE.

Vacano (our Upper Austrian centralist) opened the second day with a grenade lobbed into the heart of the politics of representation. His comment was small, its implications explosive: for these questions of nationality, he opined, the Germans of Bohemia would need to be represented here in the committee, and they are not.[35] Bohemia had sent Czech-speaking deputies to the parliament: Could they really represent Bohemians of all ethnicities?

The Bohemians were quick to take offense. An incensed František Rieger could not agree with Vacano, not least for the mistrust he displayed, as if the Czechs of Bohemia would want to curtail the rights of their German compatriots. Were Vacano's position to be adopted, he would insist on its application to the other provinces, too. After all, one might observe that the "Bohemian" (Slavic/ Czech-speaking) element in Moravia and Carinthia was not represented in the committee either.[36] An equally incensed Palacký raised the stakes: either Vacano's proposal made no sense or it was a vote of no confidence against the Bohemians.[37] Mayer, in turn, was riled by Rieger: the latter's defense was as provocative as the initial attack. Mayer could not accept Rieger's assertion that the "Bohemian" element in Moravia was not represented "because Moravia knows no Bohemian element, only a Moravian one!"[38] Rieger, wryly: I will not get into the distinction between Czechs and Moravians, but I believe I know the "Moravian" language (he means Czech) better than my Moravian colleague Mayer. Mayer: I refuse to tolerate attacks on my Moravian "nationality"![39]

One swipe, two—if the exchange stepped quickly into the personal, it also mapped, with equal efficiency, the great difficulties of ascertaining who represented what or whom at this constitutional congress. It requires some decoding for the uninitiated. The delegates had been elected on the basis of the historical lands, which had a very uneasy relationship to ethnic identity. The Czech national revival of the preceding decades—in which Palacký's groundbreaking history of the Czechs played a central role[40]—had not yet managed to fix a stable referent. This national revival was driven by the "Czech" Slavic population of Bohemia but ostensibly encompassed the Slavic populations of all the lands of the Bohemian crown—that is, Moravia and Silesia—and perhaps the "Slovaks" of western Hungary, too. Were the Czech speakers of all these lands one and the same nation? Czech nationalists had not yet succeeded in driving through this understanding of national affiliation: "Czech"/Slavic Moravians were wont to resist Bohemian overtures (and dominance) and stress their (pan-ethnic) identity as "Moravians." This fluid equation was reflected in the awkward composition of the delegations: while Bohemia had sent three "Czechs" to the constitutional committee and not a single German Bohemian (eliciting Vacano's misgivings), all three Moravian representatives were German speakers.

This fleeting, scrappy skirmish raised to the surface the structural quagmires of the constitutional project: What did it mean to speak for a *Land*, a (multiethnic) political unit in an era of national mobilization? Was (German) Mayer as "Moravian" as his Slavic neighbors back home? Did the "Czechs" of Bohemia represent Czech interests or pan-ethnic Bohemian ones? It was effectively a transliteration, and a personalization, of the disagreements of the previous day: there was very little neutral terrain on which to speak of or for the empire without prejudicially assuming who the true legal subjects, the actual units, of the empire really were: historic lands or "nations"? The subject position of each delegate, equivocating between different kinds of political identity, expressed the difficulty of writing the empire's constitution: self-description was an unavoidable part of imperial description.

Later that day, Kautschitsch rebuked his colleagues. These squabbles missed the point entirely: we are not here to represent our provinces, but the whole of Austria![41]

JANUARY 24, 1849. FUTURE EMPIRE: THE DANGEROUS DREAMS OF HISTORY.

Rieger looked to draw a line in the sand. The previous day, a host of delegates (Josef von Lasser, Josef Halter, Anton Laufenstein) had pressed the case of various historical principalities—often in contradictory interpretations, raking over long histories, pointing to periods and shades of independence. Salzburg wanted to be independent; Carinthia, to be separate from Carniola. It never ended. At the same time, Palacký had presented his radical alternative: one should consider the health of the whole imperial polity, he argued, not merely the interests of the various lands; the strongest model consolidated the different ethnic groups into the largest possible units, federated under the crown. "A force is moving through the world," he opined; "one calls it the world spirit." This spirit found expression in the drive toward the equality of nations.[42]

Rieger, firmly in Palacký's corner, analyzed the difficulties. Granted, a consistent division of the imperial state on the basis of either history or nationality would not be possible down to the last detail. But the contradictions involved in various historical arguments were immense: "In the assessment of particular desires for separation, either one stands on the historical ground [*Boden*] of Anno 1814 or not. If one stands on that, then for example Salzburg and Innviertel have no right to the claimed autonomy. But if one does not stand on that, but rather on older ground, why would one then deny those from south Tyrol or from Vorarlberg the claimed autonomy? Where here is the limit [*Grenze*]?"[43]

To determine the empire's subpolities on the basis of historic independence, one necessarily adopted a perspective from inside history itself: history afforded no neutral vantage point on the "conclusions" of its development. Different delegates effectively "stood" on different historical "grounds"— sedimentary layers archaeologically documenting different legal domains. *Boden* and *Grenze*—ground and border—became features of time as well as space: territorial boundaries were temporal propositions, or time-relative. The difficulties of needing a "year zero" from which to think were not lost on the other delegates. Norbert Pfretzscher maintained that he did not want to "stand on historical ground, because in the end one does not know where history begins, and where it ends,"[44] while the following day Scholl disputed the idea that you could take 1814 as the "normal-time" (*die Normalzeit*).[45] By what lights could a new constitution tether itself in time? No, the historical approach made little sense to Rieger; he deemed the division of Austria on the basis of the old provinces "no longer suited to the times."[46] He affirmed his support for Palacký's proposal.

Franz Freiherr von Hein could scarcely believe his ears. A firm centralist (and future justice minister), he "awoke" over Rieger's speech "as if out of a dream," in which he saw "the emperor of Austria standing before him." An astonished emperor wondered "at the way some of the Herr Delegates as representatives of the crown want to vindicate lands for him, which he otherwise already possessed, and wished to rip other lands apart, like Slovakia from Hungary—while still others sought to found great Palacky-ian or Kautschitsch-ian empires, so that in the end little or nothing remained to his crown."[47] The delegates were behaving as sovereigns! Carving, dividing, rearranging, refounding—in Hein's opinion, they had forgotten that these territories in fact constituted possessions of the emperor. The might and majesty of the latter loomed before Hein, casting a long shadow over the debates. Rieger desired that the provinces be made the same size, recounted Hein, as though a fat man had more rights than a thin one, a tall more than a short. In fact, this rhetoric of large groupings merely allowed certain provinces to swallow up smaller ones. (Again, a Moravian looked to unmask the imperialism lurking behind grand Bohemian plans.) No, in Hein's opinion, one must retain Austria's provincial division, "and not lose oneself *forward or backward* in historical dreams."[48]

It was a clever rephrasing of the disagreement. As against the seeming unreality of various historical claims, Hein accused the Bohemians of an analogous fantasy: they were simply drunk on historical dreams of the future (a federation of nations) rather than those of the past. Both visions, stretching forward and stretching backward, were dangerously unreal: the only reliable ground was that of the present and the current provincial arrangement. Palacký's plan was not an accurate description of empire as it stood: Palacký described a future empire, an empire over the horizon and out of sight. His draft did not accord temporally with imperial reality. In Hein's own view, smaller national districts should be formed within the existing provinces: the weight of nationality could be felt at the level of district assemblies instead. Brestel proposed an alternative mediation of principles: divide only those provinces that are nationally mixed— the rest can stand as history made them.[49]

Palacký confessed his sadness upon hearing all these views. It seemed a unified Austria would not emerge, at least not through the hands of the constitutional committee. He shook his head at the opinions of his colleagues: they appealed to "the historical terrain" in order to "cloak some separatist tendencies" and took "out of history only that which currently suit[ed]" them. He understood "the historical standpoint differently" and chose to draw out the "*living* history."[50] Some history lived; other history had fallen behind life, its normative value expired. Like the "equality of nations," the emancipation of the Slavs was a principle on the rise, and it would only rise further. The delegates must take cognizance of these developments if they desired to give Austria a constitution "which will suit the present as well as the future." Otherwise, they presaged Austria's decline.[51] Synchrony needed to be established with the future rather than the past: in failing to catch the step and pace of onward movement, their stumbling constitutional efforts announced Austria's own fall out of history. The parliament should be a factory for constitutions of the future—future constitutions for the future empires lying on the cusp of coming into being.

JANUARY 25, 1849. DREAMING NOW OF METTERNICH, NOT THE EMPEROR.

The tide of opinion was slipping from Palacký, hardening in opposition. He tried one last tactic, one last play to persuade. The separatist tendencies of all the small historical lands, he regretted, were playing out of Metternich's "divide and rule" script. If the committee continued to work in this fashion, it would "build a nice house for absolutism, but not for free people."[52] The constitution was a house whose structure and dimensions would shape the lives of those who lived within. The smaller the units, the greater the central government's control, strangling the national autonomy of the peoples.

Hein was "startled to attention" by Palacký's "bid to conquer."[53] Palacký wanted big provinces to counterbalance the central administration; perhaps the former will be so big, he quipped, that no central administration will exist at all! A call broke out around the chamber: "That amounts to aspersion!" Hein did not want to suspect anyone, he insisted; he desired only that the central administration as well as the provinces be granted what they were owed.[54]

A measured Eduard Cavalcabo felt that national, historical, *and* material interests should be taken into consideration (a catalog of factors that would be repeated virtually verbatim in the debates of 1919). At home in Styria, he did not encounter much desire for separation from the Germans; social and family relationships would not allow for such a division. In his opinion, "the province is a picture of the monarchy in miniature. If one believes that the nations should be distinguished from one another in the provinces, then one demonstrates that the different nations are likewise unable to live next to one another in the monarchy."[55] The symbolic consequences of dividing the provinces along national lines snared the whole empire in their web: if the provinces were truly untimely, so, perhaps, was the empire itself. Thick threads of mutual implication knotted them together, for better or worse.

Then it was Mayer's turn to dream of Metternich, though his Metternich was different than Palacký's, and his haunting worked for different ends. While Metternich's ghost had "hovered over us" for the last four days of debate, mused Mayer, "the dragon's teeth that Metternich sowed in Austria have borne fruit."[56] It is the mistrust sown by absolutism that leads to such divergent paths: "Metternich wanted to hold the Austrian family of peoples together with an iron fist, and thereby suppressed all provincial, all national life. He [Mayer] fears that in the end he must recognize that Metternich understood better, that he was prudent, because we virtually show that we cannot otherwise stay together."[57]

Rather than crowning the victory of Metternich's demise, was the Kremsier parliament in fact proving Metternich right? Bitter irony! These days of division chipped away at the premise of the whole project, at the popular authorship of the constitution, authorship by consensus. Perhaps a multiauthored imperial order remained out of reach. The proposed plans were weighed low with practical difficulties, insisted Mayer. Kautschitsch and Palacký, he protested, "want to create new land complexes, new state individualities; but to make a new individuality out of Bohemia, Moravia, and Silesia, they must destroy existing individualities." He wondered if "that is freedom, [or] whether it would have been better if there had been no revolution, or whether one wouldn't prefer to throw Austria back into the pot of revolution, to see whether something better comes out."[58] Was the destruction of these political-legal "individualities" to be the revolution's achievement? Did this demolition really signify progress? The language of state individualities, as the legal persons of the empire, and of the improbable chemistry of melting them down and conjuring new individualities as legal and political subjects—this vocabulary and this imaginary would recur with increasing frequency in the following decades, as the old provincial estates structure was rearticulated in the idiom of statehood.

That improbable chemistry also had a human side, continued Mayer. One had created "artificial" divisions between the peoples of a province who spoke different languages, yet the general development of humankind meant that peoples who have grown together could no longer be divided. Germans and Slavs in Moravia could not be ripped apart: together they formed a "mixed people," "simultaneously German and Slavic."[59] Dividing provinces ran counter to history's course, as documented in a natural arc of ethnic intermingling. The right balance, he admitted, was hard to find. But he encouraged the delegates to return to the proposal of the subcommittee, which conceived smaller national districts within the historic provinces—a plan that took account of both history and nationality.[60]

With four days of verbal bloodletting behind them, the delegates turned to vote. They had torn through the empire, amassing a stockpile of descriptions, a political arcade that stretched both into the future and across the deep past and which taken together formed a comprehensive cross section of imperial opinion. But they needed to wrest from this catalog of possible empires a single version. Palacký's plan, which described a future empire in order to call it into being, won scant verification from his colleagues: his blueprint for a federation of nationalities received just seven of twenty-eight votes—those of the Bohemian delegates plus a couple of others such as Turco from Tyrol and Krainz from Styria. Others shied away from his radicalism; they agreed with Mayer that the division of the empire on the basis of nationality was unviable. The delegates sought instead to balance the historical and the national: the historic lands were affirmed as the empire's major subunits, the full members of the empire, but each of these would be apportioned into districts (*Kreise*) that would conform as closely as possible to the contours of national life.[61]

Naturally enough, inconsistencies and conceptual loose ends remained. In one modification of the provincial structure, the constitutional committee voted (by a vote of 20 to 7) to separate "Welschtirol" (Italian Tyrol) from German Tyrol. In protest, the German Tyroleans did not return to the next meeting, threatening to seek their own constitution from his majesty. Brestel was shocked by this stupidity and this "treason." But Hein showed more understanding: the German Tyroleans were wondering, he empathized, why their province must suffer the indignity of partition when ethnically mixed Bohemia and Galicia remained unmolested.[62]

Inconsistencies aside, the majority's position represented an extremely nimble legal solution to the empire's structural quagmires. If the delegates proved reluctant to abolish the historic lands and their rights—that is, to override the old nomos—then they simultaneously gave constitutional recognition to the rise of the nationalities as an alternative understanding of the empire's constituent parts. They preserved the continuity of the old lands but delineated new ethnic jurisdictional boundaries at the administrative level beneath them. An empire of old states and an empire of nationalities, as descriptions of the empire at different historical moments, existed simultaneously on different constitutional planes, piled atop one another and protected in public law. The Kremsier draft thus suggested that history could be accumulative rather than escalatory, stadial, or dialectic. The constitution, as written by the people's representatives in 1849, formed an archive of living empires: amassing successive historical iterations in live law, it made the "contemporaneity of the noncontemporaneous" into precept of imperial order.[63]

Shadows of Sovereignty: If These Are the Subjects, What Are Their Rights?

The lands and their subdistricts represented merely the first decision of the constitutional committee: the bones of the imperial structure still required the flesh of prerogatives and capacities—the subject Mayer had wanted to discuss on the first day. The determination of the rights of the regions proved equally revelatory of the texture and distribution of imperial sovereignty. Take the committee's deliberations over the judicial system on January 30. On this subject, the delegates returned to Palacký's plan and the broad jurisdictional domain it ascribed to the provinces (the Bohemians may have lost the fight over the identity of the lands themselves, but Palacký's proposed distribution of rights between the center and the provinces remained a live option). In advocating for the judiciary to count among the prerogatives of the lands, Pinkas insisted that this plan did not amount to "separatist longings": if anything was to be left to the lands, if anything depended on the trust of the people, surely it was the judiciary. If this ascription were not accepted, threatened Rieger, the Bohemians would appeal to the status granted to them by the "Bohemian charter" of April 1848, which ostensibly reduced the relationship of Bohemia to the other lands of the empire as one of a mere personal union.[64]

Other delegates were quick to allege the sovereign price of such plans. Vacano maintained that justice needed to be centralized, "otherwise we won't have a state, but rather a conglomerate of republics."[65] Was a single justice system a necessary component of stateness? Hein pursued the sovereign pretensions behind the Bohemian submissions yet more emphatically. "I cannot recover from the shock that different nations want a different justice [*eine andere Gerechtigkeit*]," he exclaimed. One aspect of the judicial system—the jury—would remain with the lands, but "the laws must be the same every-where, if we want to speak of a state; should justice be spoken in the name of the state or the provinces? The Bohemians may want to remain living in the fantasy that they form an independent kingdom, but they remain in fact only a province."[66] The rights of the lands reflected directly on the "stateness" of the empire as well as the "stateness" of the lands themselves; both kinds of "statehood" were in question. The Bohemians behaved as if their old statehood remained a present fact; Hein declared it illusory. It was not the last time the prospect of "fantasy" states would feature in constitutional debate.

The "stateness" of lands arose for fuller discussion on February 6. In debat-ing the powers of the central government, the delegates returned to the first section of the draft: "The Austrian Empire is an indivisible constitutional hereditary monarchy formed out of the following independent crownlands." As the foundational description of the empire, as the very first line of the projected constitution, the implications of each term in this sentence needed to be carefully considered and contained. Lasser argued that the designation "independent crownlands" itself "involved the concept of the sovereignty of the individual crownlands." To guard against "conceptual confusion," he sub-mitted that the word *independent* should be crossed out.[67] Rieger disputed that construction of the phrase: such an interpretation was prevented by the prior word *indivisible*, "in that the concept of independence is thereby suf-ficiently constricted."[68] One word worked upon the other to carefully balance and preserve imperial sovereignty.

Krainz disliked the other half of the couplet. To his mind, the term *crown-lands* depicted each land as a possession of the crown; it reminded him of the term *crown estates*. Hein suggested *imperial lands* rather than *crownlands*.[69] Kautschitsch likewise announced himself against *crownlands* because it evoked "the feudal nexus" and also against *independent* as this could lead to interpre-tations dangerous for the unity of Austria.[70] The original motion was carried, with *imperial lands* replacing *crownlands*, and *independent* struck out entirely.

Yet suspicions of, and pretensions to, provincial "stateness" could not be struck off with the simple amputation of the word *independent*. The issue gnawed away at the deliberations over many jurisdictional issues. Section 4 spoke of the lands' "right of self-government" (*Selbstregierungsrecht*). The delegates debated what precisely this term entailed. Did it mean the same as autonomy?[71] At each step, the dictionary of sovereignty was carefully worked over. Forcefully advocating the position of the German centralists, intent on a robust central government, Hein declared "that he will not concede to a single province in Austria *even a shadow of sovereignty*. Sovereignty expresses itself in the administration and in the legislature; these must stay with the center."[72]

The logic of the empire's historical structure and its rationale were con-sciously articulated by the Kremsier delegates. In affirming the empire as a conglomerate of historical lands, they codified that which had developed incrementally over centuries, translating history into clear legal propositions. It received perhaps its clearest formulation when the committee looked to "apply" its decisions to the many petitions sent to the young parliament.[73] Scholl, for example, reported on the thirty-five petitions received from both Poles and Ruthenians advocating for and against the ethnic partition of Galicia. The constitutional committee had decided against a new division of the monarchy as a postulate of the constitution, he recounted, and instead decided to retain "the territorial apportionment according to the historical principle, that is, according to the contingencies of gradual acquisition." This principle held "that every land which constitutes an independent acquisition, and had to this point a certain individual life [*Sonderleben*], namely, a particular estates constitution, should form an entity in the state in the future." Applied to the Galician case, the result seemed clear: "The part of Galicia inhabited by the Ruthenes does not constitute an independent acquisition, never had an individual life in the Austria imperial state, never a particular estates constitution."[74] If one possessed an organized legal and political life at the moment of imperial acquisition, if one formed a recognizable unit or entity at that moment, then that status carried over into ongoing rights within the empire: that independence was preserved even as it was lost. The Ruthenian nationality, though protected as a nationality in the new charter of fundamental rights, did not possess the historical prerequisites to acquire a political, territorial form within the imperial structure. The nature of the empire's gradual accumulation of freestanding units would be preserved and projected forward in law: however dimmed, sovereign shadows marked out the right to be "visible" at this level of constitutional law.

In the final draft, the German centralists, too, needed to compromise. A range of jurisdictional prerogatives—pertaining to broad social and economic domains as well as police administration—were apportioned to the lands, while the national districts were to preside over education and determine the language used in schooling, meaning that ethnic minorities would be insulated from potentially hostile majorities at the provincial level regarding cultural questions.[75] This careful balance of interests and rights came together in a formal constitutional draft that was unanimously accepted by the constitutional committee on March 2, 1849. But the hard-won compromise turned into a very different kind of historical precipice than that envisioned by the delegates.

Collapsing Pluralism:
The Legal Ambitions of Neoabsolutism

In late February, the constitutional committee had worked ever more quickly as rumors circulated and fears grew about the possibility of government intervention. The parliament and its constitution-drafting powers had been conceded at moments of acute imperial weakness. Now the new emperor, his bold new ministry, and the forces of reaction were on the offensive with the imperial army's victories in insurrectionary Hungary consolidating the government's position and bolstering its confidence one battle at a time. Sensing the shifting political equation, and having finally agreed on the draft, the constitutional committee hurriedly scheduled a plenary session of the parliament to endorse the text so that the new constitution could be proclaimed by March 15, the anniversary of the revolution. But they were too late: the army's victory in Kápolna definitively tipped the balance, and the government seized the moment.

Late on March 6, Count Franz Stadion, the minister of the interior, informed the leaders of the parliament that the emperor intended to promulgate a constitution of his own. The shock and fierce protest of the delegates proved impassioned and fruitless in equal measure—though their fervor shook even Stadion. Chastened, he wrangled a safe escape for the more radical delegates, thus saving them from arrest when imperial troops occupied the parliament the following morning.[76] The parliament's fate had already been sealed. Three imperial decrees appeared alongside the troops on March 7: an imperial manifest, a patent of political rights, and an imposed constitution; all three bore the emperor's signature and the date March 4.[77] The manifest summarily dissolved the parliament, repudiating the very idea that the people had a role in shaping the empire's fundamental laws and ensuring that the historic meeting fizzled out abruptly and ingloriously, leaving immense confusion and resentment in its wake.

The revolution must be closed, announced the manifest, constructing a narrative that signed the parliament as the author of disorder rather than of law. The reestablishment of proper order required a unified monarchy whose constituent parts were tightly woven together.[78] The first imperial parliament had been entrusted with the great task of preparing a constitution for a portion of the monarchy, but unfortunately expectations had not been fulfilled. The parliament had squandered its time on "reflections from the domain of theory" that contradicted the *real* relationships of the monarchy and undermined the return to order and legality.[79] In the meantime, military progress in Hungary had brought the goal of a unified monarchy ever closer; the people expected a constitution that would encompass the whole empire (i.e., one that applied to Hungary, too). "Thereby the work of the constitution," the emperor declared, "has stepped beyond the capacity of this meeting."[80]

The imperial manifest thus asserted that the draft constitution authored by the Kremsier parliament was already out of date, lagging behind the new imperial present. The empire needed one constitution for all its lands: without representatives from or jurisdiction over Hungary, the parliament had been superseded. The notion of explicitly subsuming Hungary under imperial law, of making it an object of Vienna's power like any other, marked a radical new development. The imperial constitution promulgated at the same time as the manifest represented the first occasion on which "Austrian" law was imposed on Hungary; until then, Hungarians had been remarkably successful at resisting such impositions.[81] The manifest thus represented an explicit repudiation of the basic legal plurality that had underwritten the imperial legal structure to that point: now the empire was ostensibly to constitute a single legal space, as constructed under the auspices of a single constitution. The previous constitutional descriptions of the empire—the Pillersdorf constitution and the Kremsier draft—had both listed the different lands for which the constitution was valid or applicable—Bohemia, Styria, and so on. They contained no statement identifying the sum of these lands as constituting the state territory of the Austrian Empire (after all, Hungary was not among them). Instead, they implicitly acknowledged that there were in fact multiple state territories: the jurisdiction of the constitution, on the one hand, and the presumed domain of the emperor's sovereignty, on the other, had not been coterminous legal spaces.[82] The imposed constitution of March 1849, in contrast, asserted the alignment of these legal markers of state and sovereignty.

The so-called March constitution or imposed constitution (*oktroyierte Verfassung*) proclaimed one free, indivisible, and indissoluble constitutional Austrian hereditary monarchy with a central imperial parliament, central administration, and a high imperial court, codifying the ambitions of German centralism.[83] Franz Stadion and his colleague Alexander von Bach, then minister of justice, had in fact begun work on it in secret already in January. Their text was influenced by the Kremsier debates, and they appropriated many of the parliament's provisions. But the main thrust of the document comprised an unmistakable reassertion of the powers of the central government. Domains like education and the church, which the Kremsier parliament had assigned to the provinces or districts, were returned to the central administration, the democratic provisions were watered down, and the emperor's absolute veto right reinstated. Stadion had little patience for the historical rights of the historical lands and had originally intended to abolish the latter altogether. He favored a division of the monarchy into districts, in the style of the French departments, to undercut the particularist politics of the lands. In the end, he was persuaded to leave the historical lands in place, but they were emptied of all real political and legal significance. Crucially, section 77 announced that new constitutions would be written for each of the lands, and that their old estates constitutions—the repository and symbol of their inherited, historical rights—were hereby rendered inoperative.[84] The Kremsier draft had made the historical lands the foundation of imperial order: stripped of this status in the March constitution, the lands gave way to the districts as the empire's significant subunits. In the representative assessment of Arnold Luschen von Ebengreuth's 1899 textbook of constitutional law, the imposed constitution asserted legal equality and a centralized bureaucracy through a "total break with the old, historical, special status and particular constitutions of the individual territorial parts."[85] This was war on the maze of historical jurisdictions. After all the possibilities and careful equations mooted in Kremsier, sovereignty was gathered back up hungrily by the central imperial government.

This proved just the first step in a more total return to centralist absolutism. The March provisions remained only partially implemented: many of the new lands constitutions, for example, were drafted but never put into effect, joining the Kremsier proposal in the growing library of unimplemented constitutional laws.[86] The shaky status of the March constitution grew more pronounced with a series of cabinet directives in August 1851, before the authoritarian Silvester (or "New Years") Patent of December 1851 definitively repealed it from the lawbooks. The New Years Patent ushered in a decade of absolute rule and centralized the empire more emphatically than ever before.[87] Across a range of fronts, imperial lawmaking looked to replace the monarchy's former legal patchwork with one uniform and consistent legal zone. This centralization and homogenization went hand in hand with great experimentation in "rational" government.

If older accounts framed the 1850s as a period of backward-looking reaction, more recent scholarship has recovered the decade as one of widespread innovation and progress, especially in the administrative and technocratic sectors. This rationalization of rule bore fruits of economic growth and social progress (including the proper end of peasant subjection), as well as dynamic development in agriculture, industry, finance, communications, and urban planning (the latter most famously in Vienna's *Ringstrasse*).[88] At the same time, questions that had dominated the revolutionary years—especially the twofold challenge to imperial sovereignty: the historic rights of the provinces and the political claims of nationalist movements—were swept off the agenda. As the liberal politician and author Joseph von Helfert would observe in 1873, the New Years Patent led to "an actual standstill of public law between 1851 and 1860."[89]

House of Cards: Facts and Theories

In the constitutional interregnum of the 1850s, a range of public figures tried to sort through the conceptual fallout of the government's actions, raking over historical rights, current "facts," and the relationship of both to legal norms. Could the government simply unilaterally dissolve the empire's historical legal diversity? Or was historical law in fact robust enough to survive the storm of neoabsolutism on some deeper level? The situation directed politicians and scholars to a series of fundamental questions concerning the real status of historical rights and historical law, and whether the empire had its own unique, "natural," or immovable constitutional structure that the government could ignore only at its own risk.

Hungarian politicians like Pál Somssich (1811–88) observed the scale of the government's repudiation of preexisting structures of legality with incredulity.

The ministry's policy since the revolution entailed "a total disregard of historical rights, a complete abolition of all contracts, guarantee decrees and laws, and so on, upon which the unified monarchy as well as the status of the individual provinces and in particular that of the Kingdom of Hungary was founded for centuries until now; in one word, a tabula rasa, upon which one wants to build anew a unitary unified monarchy from the ground up."[90] Indeed, the prominent Hungarian reformer, statesman, and author József Eötvös (1813–71) thought that the division or dissolution of the historical provinces would lead to "the confusion of all moral concepts."[91]

Liberals like Franz Schuselka advocated the retention of the historical units of the empire but *only* to the boundaries of their actual historical normativity and no farther. The historical structure must be "recognized and retained, but also only to the extent that it is a historical factum and not the speculation of separatist dreamers."[92] That historically given federalism had the tendency to slip over into historical myth and threaten the empire's integrity with separatist fantasies. Policing the line between historical fact and historical fiction was itself the work of imperial survival.

At the same time, various critiques of Palacký's national-federal proposals circulated, along with alternative invocations of fact and fictionality. Schuselka himself argued that "Austria can sustain neither a Palacký-ian federative system nor a Bach-ian centralization. Both systems are doctrinaire artificialities built in the air." Try as they might, the ethnic federation of the Bohemians and the aggressive centralization of the government both failed to capture the empire's true reality: they remained dogmatic fantasies.[93] In 1850, the historian and politician Josef Alexander von Helfert (1820–1910)—later an authority on the history of the revolution and serving at the time as under state secretary in the ministry of education—penned an open letter to Palacký. He recounted that, prior to Palacký's national-federal proposals, he had presumed the two men shared a common conviction that Austria "cannot become a Switzerland with its sovereign cantons, cannot become an ancient Greece with its independent territories."[94] The radical dispersal of sovereignty prefigured in Palacký's proposals had therefore shocked him. He argued that there were only two ways to implement such a federation of ethnicities. Either one organized a "general migration of peoples within the territory of the monarchy" until everyone was collected into nationally homogeneous groups—that is, a wholesale transfer of populations. Or one effected a "fragmentation of Austria not into seven nationality groups but rather into an innumerable mass of nationality grouplets [*Nationalitäts-Grüppchen*]."[95] If the latter, Palacký was essentially advocating a return to the chaos of the Holy Roman Empire, in which the state was divided into myriad small units of endless variation.[96] Far from sovereign progress, the Bohemian's plan marked a step backward, a return to the legal heterogeneity of the past. If this proposal were enacted, Palacký would also be the man responsible for the partition of Bohemia! What price was he willing to pay for this so-called equality of the nationalities? Palacký was playing with fire. "State structures are not just houses of cards," Helfert counseled, "that you build and then blow down again if they do not suit you."[97]

The Bohemians themselves offered their own frustrated critique of the conceptual-legal disarray sown by the government's actions. A mere fortnight after the parliament was dissolved in 1849, the Bohemian delegates dispatched a memorandum in protest that homed in directly on the government's understanding of the relationship between law and the "facts" of imperial rule. Likely authored primarily by Palacký and dated March 21, the *Denkschrift* ridiculed the government's ostensible reasons for dissolving the parliament, analyzing their implications for the nature of imperial law itself. The manifest of March 4 (promulgated March 7), we recall, had disapprovingly cited the parliament's focus on "reflections from the domain of theory" that had contradicted the "actual" relationships of the monarchy and worked against the reestablishment of an "ordered legal state of affairs in the state." "It must be a very peculiar 'legal state of affairs' that cannot tolerate 'reflections from the domain of theory'!" bristled the Bohemians. "Most likely a state of affairs that was deduced not so much from the theory of 'law' as from 'facts.'"[98] And with observations such as these, the ministry overrode a constitutive parliament! The consequences were immense: "If 'facts' in this way are stamped as the absolute sources of law, and if the government from the outset wants to reserve for itself [the ability] to determine in a biased way the meaning of these facts: then we ask whether a constitution, a parliament in general, is possible anymore in the face of such 'facts'?"[99]

To the Bohemian delegates, the relationship between "facts" and legal legitimacy posited by the government was deeply spurious: the government's appeal to a law that innocently reflected neutral "facts" hardly disguised its unilateral engineering of precisely that factual order. Far from defining and establishing an "ordered legal state of affairs," the government instead made a regular legal order impossible, collapsing the latter under the primacy of "facts" of their own authorship. The constitutional conflicts had forced the government to articulate the assumptions underlying its rule, implicitly presenting a theory of law and its relationship to material relations of rule: the Bohemians engaged them at precisely this level, debating the foundations of legitimate law and authority.

Returning to the Historical Order:
The Legal Implications of Temporal Pluralism

This knot of unresolved legal equations and suppositions lay waiting in the wings when the absolutist system unraveled on the battlefields of northern Italy in 1859. Crushing military defeats at the hands of French and Piedmontese-Sardinian forces, which culminated in the loss of Lombardy, and

severe budgetary troubles compounded growing agitation for a more participatory form of government. These strained circumstances drove a reluctant
Francis Joseph back toward the constitutional fold in search of greater domestic support.[100]

The new constitutional age began tentatively with some murmurs offstage.
Looking to gently exploit the monarchy's vulnerability, a group of Hungarian
"old conservatives" started lobbying the foreign minister, Count Rechberg, and
other members of the government in July 1859. Warning of volatile sentiment
in Hungary, they argued that absolutism and bureaucratic centralism needed
to be wound back, and a new path into constitutional life charted.[101] In mid-
August, the Hungarian magnate Count Emil Dessewffy presented a memorandum to Rechberg that spoke of the "historical foundations" of true "legality" as
against the legal confusion of absolutism. What secure route could the empire
take back toward constitutionalism? Dessewffy argued that the transition must
be effected through a "historical-legal coup" (*historisch-rechtliche Staats-
streich*).[102] The Hungarians referred back to the Pragmatic Sanction and
wrote of the moral impossibility of absolutism, even its illusory quality.[103]

The emperor met with his trusted advisers over the same period. He reluc-
tantly agreed to "enlarge" the small imperial council with a broader group of
notables and representatives from the lands, on the premise it would remain
purely consultative.[104] Announced in March 1860, the enlarged imperial council met between May and September of the same year and quickly exceeded its
formally narrow prerogatives connected to the budgetary crisis. Zooming out
to survey the predicament of the empire more generally, a majority submission or report, spearheaded by the Hungarian aristocrat Antal Szécsen and
tabled in September 1860, argued forcefully that the empire's foundations
could only be properly fortified through recognition of the historical lands
and a return to their historic laws and institutions, especially their diets—that
is, a return to the empire's historical-legal diversity. "For a number of years,"
Szécsen declared, "the true character of the monarchy was misrecognized." In
the competition for the best legal description of the empire, the architects of
absolutism had gotten it wrong. No "theoretical conception," he argued, could
replace the particular character given through "nature, history, and those relationships ripened with time."[105] Future prosperity depended on a firm tethering to "the true and the actual character of the Austrian monarchy."[106] The
lands possessed a unique historical individuality, and this "pluralism," in the
words of the Bohemian noble Heinrich Jaroslav Clam-Martinic, to the extent
that it articulated a "unity in multiplicity," bespoke the "foundational character
of the monarchy."[107]

Not everyone agreed. In fact, this sounded to some like a kind of temporal-
legal chaos. A passionate minority submission was read before the enlarged
imperial council on September 22, 1860, by none other than Franz von Hein,
the articulate centralist we encountered in the Kremsier debates. Szécsen's

majority report, Hein recounted, made the participation of the historic lands in the functions of government dependent on the resurrection of historical institutions (especially the estates diets). Yet "these institutions have very different natures, according to the different time periods [*Zeitabschnitten*] from which they are called up," and some had hardly survived or were no longer fit for life. These discrepancies would create a profoundly uneven legal landscape in which equality between the lands was impossible.[108] Clam-Martinic responded that the historical institutions would be adapted to the times, not imported from the past in frozen form. Just as much as he was against the "total misrecognition and disavowal of history," and the desire to begin "a new time calculation [*Zeitrechnung*]" with the rupture of 1848, he was equally against attempts "to hold on to some sort of time-point expired in history, to want to fetch deceased institutions out of the past," as the minority submission charged. "I cannot concede that twelve years," he said, referring to the period of centralist rule, "has cleanly swept away the work of centuries—but I also do not want to grant the past the power, nor the right, to supplant the present."[109]

Hein was not placated. The empire's legal disaggregation, according to Hein's warning, would be a sort of *historical* disaggregation, with institutions from different centuries, shaped by wildly varying assumptions, all revived simultaneously into the empire's present. Different historical eras would structure legal arrangements in different parts of the polity, making imperial law a kind of achronological display cabinet for the empire's history—not unlike a legal equivalent of the sixteenth-century painting *Die Alexanderschlacht* with which Reinhart Kosselleck opened *Futures Past*, where the whole Battle of Issus unfolds achronologically in the expansive present of a single picture.[110] In deferring so emphatically to the historical individuality of the lands, and connecting it to "autonomy in administration and internal legislation," the majority report threatened to disperse the emperor's sovereignty, Hein argued. For if "one speaks of the historical-political individualities, which are accorded complete autonomy in administration and international legislation, gentlemen!, then one speaks of 'empires,' of 'states,' not of 'crownlands'; 'states in states,' 'parallel states,' 'Austria would be a state confederation' and the sovereign would actually become a sovereign in every land."[111]

It was not only that the different regional institutions stemmed from different *Zeitabschnitten*, different time cuts: in the majority's vision, the empire's legal life would be subject to history's fluid instability. "I do not want to finger any wounds ungently, but even in Hungary there are points in time from which one would not necessarily like to call up the historical institutions," Hein cautioned. Even the Hungarians, surely, could not present history as an undifferentiated juridical virtue: "In the other lands, one might want to reach back to institutions lying far back in history, and everywhere where one asks and listens one will receive different answers, someone will want to go far back in history, someone else less far." This would frustrate equality in principle and practice.[112] Where, amid the constant movement of time, could one fix history into clear legal principles? Again, one needed a temporally fixed point from which to reason, and from which to rule. To that end, "the point of departure of the minority [report] was the present, the complete power of His Majesty and the existing institutions of the present."[113]

Amassing the Archive of Constitutional Law: "Historical Legal Consciousness" Becomes Positive Law

Hein's warning notwithstanding, the imperial council's majority report carried the day and fundamentally shaped the emperor's next move. The following month, Francis Joseph formally brought the decade of neoabsolutism to a close with a series of new fundamental laws. In this conciliatory rewriting of imperial order, the historical legal architecture of the state was formally (if belatedly) affirmed and codified in positive constitutional law.

If the new order possessed some canonical attributes of "liberal" nineteenth-century constitutionalism—including a parliament and, in the first place, a constitution—the laws of 1860 and 1861 also firmly reestablished the "rights and the standing of the individual kingdoms and lands."[114] Gone was the attempt to dissolve the state's legal "lumpiness" into the smooth, timeless, and placeless homogeneity of neoabsolutist sovereignty. In the imperial manifest of October 20, 1860, Francis Joseph spoke of connecting the "memories, legal views, and legal claims of my lands and peoples" with the needs of the monarchy, just as Eötvös and Szécsen had counseled.[115]

That connection was articulated even more clearly in the imperial diploma (known as the October Diploma) on the "regulation of the internal public law relationships of the monarchy," promulgated the same day. "It is our princely obligation to protect the predominance of the Austrian monarchy," declared the diploma, and to guarantee its security by way of unambiguous, established legal arrangements and peaceful cooperation. "Only such institutions and legal arrangements," it continued, "which accord simultaneously with the historical legal consciousness [*geschichtlichen Rechtsbewußtsein*], the existing differences of our kingdoms and lands, and the needs of their indivisible and inseparable union, can vouchsafe these pledges in full measure."[116] Austria's great power status was to be preserved by a formal resurrection of a state structure that reflected the historical "consciousness" and historical difference of the various principalities. Crucially, the diploma acknowledged the legislative rights of the diets of the kingdoms and lands: they could make law in their own right. The imperial council was enlarged again, this time into a proper parliament.[117] Another law of the same day explicitly called the historical Hungarian constitution "back to life."[118] Advocates of historical rights naturally understood the "concessions" of 1860 and 1861 not as the creation of something new but as the continuation of that which had existed before, and that in fact "legally had never ceased to exist."[119] Francis Joseph's decade of absolutism had failed to affect or override the deeper, autochthonous legality of the empire's kingdoms and lands—or so Bohemian and Hungarian statesmen claimed. In the words of Henrik Marczali, Hungary's most important historian at the turn of the century, the October Diploma "recognized Hungary's historical rights."[120]

The February Patent that followed soon thereafter in 1861 has been narrated as both a beginning and an end. Heralded as the final introduction of "proper" constitutional-parliamentary life (it established a robust bicameral system), it also represented the last attempt at a constitution for the whole of the empire, a mid-nineteenth-century project that definitively expired with the Settlement of 1867, when Hungary emphatically asserted its independence from "Austrian" law. While technically an implementation of the 1860 October Diploma, this new 1861 constitution had a more centralist bent, reflecting widespread dissatisfaction with the October Diploma's federalism among liberals and the banking community, the latter crucial to the state's budgetary crisis. Indeed, the patent's strange ideological mélange reflected the clashing power bases that the emperor was trying to balance and appease, including powerful aristocratic landholders, stubborn conservatives, the financial world, liberal constitutionalists, and constitution-wary bureaucrats.[121] It watered down the broad prerogatives granted to the lands the previous year and tied the non-Hungarian lands into a tighter union, though their autonomy remained substantial.[122] Perhaps an echo of Hein's reservations sounded in the patent's preface, which spoke of bringing the historical order of the kingdoms and lands into alignment with the present: the "rights and freedoms of the loyal estates" were to be "developed and remodeled according to the relationships and needs of the present."[123]

Especially striking was the patent's pluralist understanding of the sources of imperial public law. It enumerated the different genres of law that now composed the empire's constitutional order. Section VI spoke of the "fundaments of the public law relationships of our empire" being determined "partly through the preexisting basic laws, partly through that which has been called back to life, partly through the means of the constitution made by the new basic laws."[124] In his annotated 1911 compendium of the constitutional laws of the "Austrian" empire, the influential Viennese jurist Edmund Bernatzik (1854–1919) decoded these three different designations. The first ("preexisting basic laws") denoted, especially, the Pragmatic Sanction and the more recent October Diploma, while the second referred to Hungarian historical constitutional law, officially called back to life, and the third invoked the collection of basic laws of which the patent itself formed a part—that is, the constitutional laws of 1861.[125]

The new constitution thus wove itself into a legal tapestry that comprised early eighteenth-century dynastic contracts as well as bodies of law (the ancient Hungarian constitution) that were not of imperial origin, and that could seemingly slumber a while before being reawakened into official legitimacy. The "new" constitution thereby amassed and codified laws from different phases of the empire's history—as well as the empire's *pre*history. Rather than write the empire's constitution from scratch, or establish a singular source of law and legitimacy, it worked as the final clasp around a diverse gallery of laws and norms.[126] Hans Kelsen later termed it a "Mantelgesetz"—a jacket law.[127] The constitution archived the empire's life.

Or, rather, it made archives out of archives. If the successive constitutions recorded different versions of the empire's order, some of those constitutions— like the February Patent—were themselves containers or bundles of multiple, discrete bodies of law. More so: in preserving the historical law of the different kingdoms and lands, in retaining those lands as the units of the empire, the empire's constitution preserved those polities themselves. It was an archive of successive versions of the imperial whole, as well as an archive of the states that empire contained—an archive of self and selves. That coiled bundle of states shone through Franz Schuselka's 1861 description of Austria as "a crown made of crowns, a throne of thrones, an empire of empires."[128]

In this sense, it carried forward the logic of composite monarchy, albeit half sublimated into the form of a written constitution and modern administrative apparatus. In earlier periods, composite monarchy had been a spectacularly successful technology of state preservation: a way of keeping polities legally alive even as they were amalgamated into larger units, often for centuries. Those involved in debating the constitution after 1848 had to gauge whether the products of that technology—the legal outline of medieval polities teleported into the present—still seemed "true," whether the science still worked, and, if so, what sort of status and function these polities should have in a state framework writ new. Some dismissed them as fantasy and chaos; others thought it far less fanciful than the idea that the imperial government could rebuild the legal world from scratch. In shuttling back and forth between those interpretations of the legal real, the imperial constitutional tradition left enough space for both to be true at once.

CHAPTER TWO

The Secret Science
of Dual Sovereignty

1867 AND AFTER

Edmund Bernatzik lectures on the holes in law • Ferenc Deák and Gyula Andrássy seek something never tried before • Everything turns on the translation of a single word • Friedrich Tezner tries to prove that the empire exists • The arithmetic of witches • An empire discovers itself as an object of knowledge • Georg Jellinek resists the flight of Icarus • A global taxonomy of sovereign species • At the end of logic

WHERE LEGAL LOGIC STRUGGLED, high modernist fiction succeeded beautifully. In *The Man without Qualities*, Robert Musil (1880–1942) found a form perfectly suited to capture the late Habsburg Empire. He depicted the state—just like fin de siècle science and philosophy and art and psychology—hovering on a precipice between the rational and the absurd, the real and the fantastical. "All in all, how many amazing things might be said about this vanished Kakania!" as he called it. "Everything and every person in it, for instance, bore the label of *kaiserlich-königlich* (imperial-royal) or *kaiserlich* und *königlich* (imperial *and* royal), abbreviated as 'k.k.' or 'k.&k.'" But "to be sure which institutions and which persons were to be designated by 'k.k.' and which by 'k.&k.' required the mastery of a secret science."[1]

This spell-like sequence of *k*s was the secret science of "dualism" or "dual sovereignty," the state structure created by the Settlement of 1867. In this last major redescription of its constitutional order, the Habsburg Monarchy split into two equally sovereign halves: the Kingdom of Hungary, on one side, and, on the other, all the rest. The western imperial half had an aggregate formal designation but no name of its own: the Kingdoms and Lands Represented in the Imperial Parliament. People avoided that mouthful by referring to Cisleithania (i.e., the lands on this side of the Leitha River, as opposed to Hungary—Transleithania—on the other), or colloquially (but inaccurately) simply to Austria. The 1867 Settlement was simultaneously archaic and avant-garde. It took the logic of composite monarchy—according to which different principalities were united in the body of a shared monarch only—and translated it into the framework of modern statecraft, fitting it out with the institutional requirements and organs of a nineteenth-century great power. The unity, once resident exclusively in the king's body, now resided in three "common" ministries, all relating to a state's outward-facing prerogatives: one for war, another for foreign affairs, and a third for the finances for war and foreign affairs. Otherwise, Hungary and Cisleithania constituted separate states, with their own legislatures, their own territories, and even their own citizenship. The settlement fed early modern forms of pluralism through a sort of legal translation or time machine—with experimental results.

"We did not merely want to guarantee that the Hungarian state would have its autonomy in certain affairs, and that this autonomy would not be injured," Hungarian statesman Gyula Andrássy (the younger) reflected on the Settlement, "but rather also that it remained sovereign, in other words, we wanted to guarantee that its will would not be subject to the will of a higher state."[2] The negotiators lacked any preexisting model or vocabulary for a balancing act of this sort. They sought much more than the internal autonomy maintained by the states of the United States, for example. "For that reason we had to take refuge in an original conception," Andrássy explained. "A foreign proto-type was not at our disposal, because that which we wanted—the completely secured union of the power of two sovereign states—had never succeeded any-where." They would not tolerate "the dimming of our sovereignty even in the domain of theory." These characteristics lent dualism "its originality and chief interest in the field of constitutional [*staatsrechlichen*] theory."[3]

According to the empire's new dispensation, the two states were completely separate *and* indissolubly bound; the empire was one state and two states at the same time. Figuring out what that paradox meant for theory and how it worked in practice would dominate public life through to the empire's collapse. Every-thing from state budgets to the structure of the army turned on those algorith-mic *k*s, whose code we can now begin to unpack. In the Cisleithanian lands, Francis Joseph was emperor of Austria *as well as* king of Bohemia (and Duke of Styria and Margrave of Moravia and all his other princely selves). Accord-ingly, Cisleithanian state agencies and prerogatives were classed "imperial-royal" (*kaiserlich-königlich*), or k.k. for short. In Hungary, by contrast, he was recog-nized exclusively as the king of Hungary. Hungarians acknowledged only their "own" sovereign, and no emperor. Accordingly, a state agency in Hungary carried the descriptor *königlich*, "royal," usually abbreviated simply as *k.* or *k. ung.* But the common ministries that spanned both states were imperial *and* royal—he was emperor of Austria *and* king of Hungary—two things separated, crucially, and after significant wrangling, by an *and* rather than a hyphen. The Hungarians asserted their new independence in demanding the two *k*s be kept clearly distinct, reflecting the new schism through the body politic. *K.&k.*: joined, but not melded together. In this example and many others, tiny fragments of language—conjunctions, punctuation—carried the weight of an elaborate, old-new sovereign structure. All elements of the state were brought into alignment with this new grammar. The army, for example, as a common organ, bore the mark *k.&k.* But if you climbed into a train carriage in Budapest, bound for Vienna, your journey would proceed under the insignia *k.* until you crossed the border between Transleithania and Cisleithania: thereafter you would be traveling under the auspices of the *k.k.* railway instead.

Musil made it a language game. He dubbed the empire Kakania, or land of the two *k*s (we would render it Kaykaynia in English). But the wordplay was doubled, like the state, because *Kaka* is also the word a small child might use for feces. Musil played in that fashion all the way through, delighting in "mysteries of dualism." The state, as he put it, "did not consist of an Austrian part and a Hungarian part that, as one might expect, complemented each other, but of a whole and a part; that is, of a Hungarian and an Austro-Hungarian sense of statehood, the latter to be found in Austria." Without a separate patriotic identity, a citizen of that western half was "an Austrian plus a Hungarian minus that Hungarian"—a self defined by a negation.[4] It was almost too perfect for his purposes that no "Austria" existed in law: a modernist writer would surely have invented such a state if history had not provided it.

Across the twentieth century, Musil's bon mots have been routinely plucked to adorn arguments or throwaway lines about the "anachronism" of Austria-Hungary in the modern world—a medieval relic, a fossil or fragment of the past stranded in the present. But Musil's Kakanian humor was fueled by the same pathos that suffuses the whole novel: the pathos of the human drive to forge sense and meaning out of the chaos of sensations, ideas, and structures; the pathos, that is, of rationality's fragility. Roaming with great erudition from music and mathematics to economics and law, Musil parsed how these various modes of reasoning construct their own sensical portraits of the world, each of which remains a blinkered, fragmentary snapshot of reality.[5] Slowly, surely, *The Man without Qualities* unsettles any easy way of assessing the relative "truth" of these systems, of distinguishing sense from nonsense. Nonsense for what, for whom, on the basis of what preconditions? Far from representing modernity's opposite, the empire folds into Musil's portrait of the modern condition and its dissolving certainties with picturesque ease: "Since the world began, no creature has yet died of a language defect, and yet the Austrian and Hungarian Austro-Hungarian Dual Monarchy can nevertheless be said to have perished from its inexpressibility."[6]

This chapter enters the riddle of dual sovereignty, which was the riddle of the state itself. Had sovereignty been doubled or divided? Were those attributes even reconcilable with the concept of sovereignty? Did the Settlement create new states, or was it a codification of states already in existence? Could there really be only two states involved, or did the two singular wholes together form a third state, an empire that comprised them both? Hungarian politicians claimed that no overarching empire subsumed the two halves into a larger whole, and Viennese jurists struggled to prove them wrong. It led to surreal debates about "evidence" of the empire's "reality."[7] To the extent that the Hungarian view was technically "true," the empire's constitutional codification had had the paradoxical effect of exposing the fact that, *in law*, the empire did not actually exist.

The Settlement of 1867 stands as a pivot point in the history of sovereignty: perhaps the last gasp of an old feudal-kingly cosmology of rule, or an avant-garde subversion of the totalizing logics of singular sovereignty, it was in many senses both at once. Its *both-and* logic made it a compelling model for those in other complicated parts of the world trying to square the circle of autonomy and union. The founder of Sinn Fein took Hungary's success in 1867 as his model for Ireland; Gladstone invoked it positively in parliamentary debates over Irish home rule in the 1880s.[8] It continued to circle in discussions about federalism within the British Empire and in its wake, for example, as an alternative to the partition of India and Pakistan.[9] Ottoman intellectuals wondered if it might be a model for Egyptian autonomy, or even a broader Turkish-Arab dualist imperial reform, in which the Arab countries would "remain united with the Istanbul government, as Hungary is united with Austria."[10] With its nonunitary structure and staggered (rather than absolute) line between imperial-constitutional and international law, the Settlement opens points of connection to myriad late imperial and postimperial federalist visions, spanning the imperial world, recovered by historians as a reminder that the nation-state was not a fated or inevitable successor to imperial rule.[11]

The riddle of dual sovereignty was also the riddle of legal rationality, and this chapter shows how it spurred the creation of a whole new domain of scholarly inquiry: Habsburg/Austrian/Austro-Hungarian constitutional law. Amid so much confusion, and with the state's functioning at stake, the Settlement generated the need for new expertise—for new authorities in the "secret science" of dual sovereignty. Beginning in the 1860s and then especially in the 1870s, a steady stream of texts began appearing on the "legal nature of the Austro-Hungarian Monarchy."[12] These works emerged into an eerie disciplinary vacuum. Austrian or Austro-Hungarian constitutional law was not yet an academic field: there were no chairs, no mandatory courses, no textbooks or dictionaries. All that was about to change. The chapter traces the empire's coming-into-being as an object of legal science: something that required its own professorships, lecture courses, and state exams, as well as new scholarly tools and infrastructure like textbooks, handbooks, dictionaries, and journals. In constructing this new field, scholars reckoned with the boundaries between disciplines and their methods: they weighed the relationship between constitutional law and constitutional history, between states "in general" and the state in particular. As public debate raged about whether the empire-state formed a singular unified legal entity, the law faculties tried to stitch it into a coherent, unified object of knowledge. This intellectual history provides a crucial foundation for the scholarly departures analyzed in chapters 4 and 6.

The chapter presents these two registers as co-constitutive: an entangled process of ordering, constituting, and stabilizing the sovereignty of the state and legal knowledge about it. It shows how the constitutionalization of the state was tied together with the "scientization" or "modernization" of legal knowledge as the natural sciences became an important methodological model. Sorting the empire into states had its parallel in the sorting of disciplines and fields. The case allows us to explore the close implication of two quintessential modern myths: the possibility of unitary states defined by uniform, gapless power, and the possibility of logical, coherent, gap-free knowledge. Both remained elusive.

Representatives of the new secret science responded differently to that elusive coherence. Some, like Edmund Bernatzik (1854–1919), who edited the standard-issue compendium of Austrian constitutional law, leaned into the absurdity. He taught constitutional law to generations of Viennese students in the late nineteenth and early twentieth centuries, including Hans Kelsen and Adolf Merkl, two important characters in subsequent sections of this book. His lectures were legendary—less because of their substance than their ruthlessly sardonic style. The legal historian Friedrich Engel-Jánosi recalled with relish how Bernatzik, small and a little fleshy, "slowly putting on his pince-nez with conscious nonchalance, stepped up to the lectern and turned to face the auditorium, smiling and a little nasal: 'Yes, I am supposed to teach you Austrian constitutional law. So, do I know then, what Austria is? The *New Free Press*, of course, knows just what it is'"[13]—as though lifted from the pages of *The Man without Qualities*. Not coincidentally: Bernatzik and Musil knew each other well. They both frequented the Viennese salon of Eugenie Schwarzwald, who Musil took as a model for one of the novel's central characters, Diotima, and with whom Bernatzik collaborated on the cause of women's education.[14] Musil's law and language games ventriloquize Bernatzik's. "He was an especially critical character of great brilliance and biting irony; a cynic, basically," Kelsen recalled of Bernatzik. "He once said of himself: I am not actually teaching Austrian constitutional law, but rather the gaps in Austrian constitutional law."[15]

Faced with a state that did not logically "work" or perhaps did not even exist, Bernatzik responded with humor and unforgiving irony. But others took the provocation extremely seriously. For Georg Jellinek (1851–1911), the fact that the available theoretical models could not accommodate states like

Austria-Hungary suggested a problem with the theory, not the state. Perhaps the dominant doctrines of singular sovereignty were non-sense, rather than the pluralistic forms of statehood they failed to explain. The discrepancy between theory and practice drove him toward a new theory of sovereignty, one that involved the mapping of species of conglomerate statehood from across the whole globe. This chapter follows the first part of his career, as he experimented with different approaches from idealist philosophy to the empirical social sciences, before chapter 4 picks up the thread at the century's end, as he came to understand the state as a problem for legal epistemology at the highest level.

Thinking in Kings

Two Hungarian statesmen are known as architects of the Settlement of 1867. Ferenc Deák (1803–76) and Gyula Andrássy (1823–90) were both veterans of Hungary's 1848 revolutionary rebellion. Andrássy was in Constantinople trying to win recognition of Hungarian independence when Austrian and Russian armies crushed the insurrection. Sentenced to death in absentia and hung in effigy, the striking young aristocrat spent the neoabsolutist 1850s in exile in London and Paris, where he was known around the salons as the "handsome hanged man." Deák—older, rounder, famously principled, even puritanical— retreated from public life, took up residence in a small apartment in the Queen Elisabeth Hotel in Budapest, and became the symbol of Hungarian passive resistance. Absolutism could not last: he felt sure. When events proved him right, and military defeats propelled the Viennese government into a decade of constitutional experimentation, he reemerged into the public sphere as the sober but unwavering advocate of Hungary's autonomy inside the empire. His arguments unfolded like a legal brief: he grounded Hungary's undiminished historical right to independence in laws the Habsburgs themselves had sworn to uphold. There at his side was the eloquent and politically savvy Andrássy, back home, amnesty in hand, and soon setting tongues wagging for the palpable intimacy he developed with Empress Elisabeth (otherwise known as Sisi). In 1867, the ever-modest Deák would defer to Andrássy to become Hungary's first prime minister—the onetime "traitor" later even served as Austro-Hungarian foreign minister—but the intellectual scaffolds of Hungary's old-new sovereignty were Deák's work.[16]

Deák's case was remarkably consistent across the 1860s. After the new constitutional laws of 1860 and 1861 announced an imperial parliament, Deák took to the floor of the Hungarian diet to explain why Hungary could not countenance participation. Hungary did not need the "gift" of this new constitution: it possessed its own historical one, whose legitimacy remained intact.[17] The central condition and principle of Hungary's constitutional life was its "legal autonomy and independence." It had never assented to a centralized imperial government and parliament, presiding over all the lands; to do so now would reduce Hungary to an "Austrian province" and entail its "political obliteration."[18] At the heart of the case lay the Pragmatic Sanction. This pivotal set of Habsburg fundamental laws from the early eighteenth century established the Habsburg Monarchy's lands as an "indivisible" whole and included a uniform law of succession valid across them all, which allowed succession to pass to female members of the dynasty (paving the way for Maria Theresa to inherit the throne when her father, Emperor Charles, died without a male heir in 1740). As Deák now reminded Vienna, it also affirmed Hungary's historical autonomy by stating explicitly that nothing of the new dispensation harmed Hungary's traditional rights. Those rights were affirmed again in every coronation oath: a new monarch, crowned on the basis of Hungarian law, swore to uphold the Hungarian constitution, thereby limiting his or her power. Hungary had only ever entered into a legal relationship with the monarch, not with any of the other lands coincidentally under his or her rule. From the perspective of Hungarian law, the bond amounted to no more than a "personal union": there was "no trace" of a thicker legal amalgamation.[19] To partake in an empire-wide parliament would be to concede the opposite—that is, that delegates from Bohemia or Tyrol or Carinthia had a legitimate role in making law that applied to Hungary.

So much of what followed in the empire's constitutional history turned on the contemporary legal significance of these seemingly archaic technologies of dynastic statecraft. The problem of a many-crowned emperor-king, of multiple legal identities housed inside a single royal body: Could one really still maintain that Hungary had no legal relationship with Bohemia or Tyrol or Carinthia, despite the fact that they had shared the same physical ruler for centuries? Hungarian claims relied on the clean separation of those juridical selves. Hungarian politicians insisted they knew their monarch only as the king of Hungary: they had no connection to the king of Bohemia or even to the emperor of Austria after the title was created in 1804. Already earlier in the century, the once-natural institution of composite monarchy appeared to many a broken spell adrift in a more disenchanted age. As one observer complained apocryphally of the 1848 revolutionary wars, the king of Hungary declared war on the king of Croatia, and the emperor of Austria remained neutral, but all three monarchs were the same person.[20] Legally, though, the institution had survived, and the Deákists now invoked the legal discreteness of the "king of Hungary" and the constitution he had pledged to uphold as the autonomy of the Hungarian state itself.

To rebut the notion that the Habsburgs had, over the centuries, welded their patrimony into a tighter union—and turned a "personal union" into a "real union," in the terminology of the age—Deák pointed to a related institution: elective kingship. If the Pragmatic Sanction had not been concluded, then, upon the extinction of the male line with Charles's death in 1740, Hungary would have been free to choose a new king from whichever dynasty it pre-ferred. And if in the future the female Habsburg line also died out, then the prerogative to elect a king would again revert to Hungary, demonstrating that the only thing tying it into a common state with the other Habsburg lands was the identity of the dynasty. Deák contrasted this anemic legal bond to that between England, Ireland, and Scotland, which would not expire if the dynasty died out, because these countries existed in a real union rather than a mere personal one.[21]

Elective kingship, too, had once been commonplace. The Hungarian native dynasty—like the Bohemian one—had died out in the fourteenth century. In the period that followed, the Hungarian estates had elected a string of foreign kings; in 1526, the Habsburgs were merely one in a series. In many senses, these practices correspond to the "stranger-king" formations that anthropologists David Graeber and Marshall Sahlins have described as the dominant prototype of premodern rule. In this formation, the king's foreign ancestry anchored his authority. Set off against the autochthonous people, it gifted such polities a dual structure and implied that the people retained a "certain residual sovereignty."[22] By the nineteenth century, the Habsburgs had of course worn these crowns for hundreds of years, and they enjoyed the strong identification and affection of many of their subjects: literal strangers they were not. But in the context of constitutional debate, figures like Deák sought to reopen or reactivate that cleft between the country and its "foreign" monarch as a space for politics. By limiting legitimate succession to certain Habsburg lines, the Pragmatic Sanction provided for a potential reversion to Hungary's right to elect a new king of its choosing. Translating the politics of dynastic bloodlines into contemporary imaginaries, they emphasized that imperial law therein contained a mechanism by which Hungary might regain its independence and reemerge on the international stage entirely separate from the Habsburg lands. Hereditary time became evidence of a latent, future-conditional sovereignty: proof that the norm of independent statehood not only had survived imperial rule but in fact came built into its internal structure. Recalling pre-Habsburg pasts and opening legal space for post-Habsburg futures, the long-buried logic of elec-tive kingship was unearthed again as evidence of the imperfection of imperial sovereignty—a temporal qualification on its completeness.

These arguments caught the eye of a young legal scholar then working on his habilitation (the second dissertation required for teaching) at the Univer-sity of Vienna, only recently arrived from Prague. Wenzel Lustkandl (1832–1906) was born in Schönbach bei Eger in Bohemia, son of a craftsman who made musical instruments.[23] He responded to Deák explicitly in a text pub-lished two years later in 1863 under the title *Hungarian-Austrian Constitutional Law [Staatsrecht]: On the Solution to the Constitutional Question, Presented Historically and Dogmatically*, aimed at resolving the empire's constitu-tional problems, not least Hungary's refusal to participate in the new imperial parliament. The Hungarian protests had no legal foundation, he argued: the empire had long formed a thick and centralized real union, and Hungary a simple province within it. True, he conceded to Deák, the Pragmatic Sanction named three particular Habsburg lines capable of inheriting the crown and provided for reversion to Hungary's right of election. But he tried to outdo Deák at his own game. If the right of election represented one of Hungary's most fundamental historical rights, what was its real substance? He went digging through old Hungarian laws on succession and latched upon one from 1485 (i.e., prior to Habsburg rule). The right of election, it stated, was only triggered when no further members of the royal family existed anywhere. Using this old law to expand the right of succession beyond the limitations specified in the Pragmatic Sanction, Lustkandl twisted the Hungarian right into a dead letter. The death of every Habsburg descendant everywhere in the world was unimaginable: "Therefore what Deák claims on the contrary about the technical letter of the law, even if it were true, has absolutely no meaning."[24]

Two years later, in 1865, Deák responded in turn to Lustkandl. The Pragmatic Sanction was perfectly clear, he wrote, in anointing only the descendants of Leopold I as hereditary heirs to the Hungarian crown. Lustkandl's introduction of extraneous material and artificial arguments could hardly obscure this fact. If those particular bloodlines died out, Hungary's right of election clearly "stepped back into life."[25] Hungary had always elected its kings, and the Hungarian coronation oath and Pragmatic Sanction explicitly affirmed this right, despite Lustkandl's floundering attempts to paint all this as "mere empty word pageantry, play and deception."[26] That same year, Deák published his famous Easter Article, now seen as a blueprint for the Settlement that followed in 1867. It reiterated all these points, affirming the Pragmatic Sanction as the empire's incontrovertible legal foundation, the legal continuity of the historical Hungarian constitution, and the significance of elective kingship, while rejecting the Viennese view that Hungary had forfeited these historical rights by rebelling in 1848–49. His vision for the future built from the logic of composite monarchy and the king's separate legal selves: "The full constitutional liberty of the Cisleithanian countries can exist in parallel with the Hungarian constitution under a common sovereign and with a joint defense."[27]

The exchange between Deák and Lustkandl proved an important crucible in more ways than one. Lustkandl may not have been the most brilliant of the Habsburg constitutional jurists, but he was, in a sense, the first. His 1863 book represents perhaps the first study of the Habsburg Empire's constitutional law *as such*. The legal historian Martin Schennach has unearthed a number of eighteenth-century predecessors—Austrian jurists studying constitutional law and state theory.[28] But with some (but not all) Habsburg lands still formally part of the Holy Roman Empire, the "state" in question remained highly ambiguous and differed dramatically between the various treatments. Indeed, they often referred to the "Austrian states" in the plural. The same was true of university instruction. The imperial constitutional law on the curriculum in the eighteenth century belonged to the Holy Roman Empire. After its dissolution in 1806, the few fundamental laws that pertained to the "Austrian" lands were not considered a "whole"—were not considered a natural, complete grouping requiring a designated field of their own.[29] As sovereign formations dissolved, they took their correlate knowledge fields with them: legal history and imperial history dropped silently out of the study regulations (*Studienordnung*) in 1810.[30] Small wonder that one can scarcely speak of the academic study of Austrian constitutional or even public law prior to 1848.[31] There was no "Austrian *Staatsrecht*" because it was not entirely clear that there was an "Austrian *Staat*": legally, it was a thing in flux, still separating itself into a discrete unit from the Holy Roman Empire above and its own lands below.

To the extent that students were introduced to the legal shape of the state, it occurred through the prism of other disciplines, especially political economy and statistics as well as natural law.[32] Large statistical compendiums communicated state organization in concrete, apolitical terms; "the theory of averages" replaced any theoretical teachings on the state.[33] General questions concerning the origin and purpose of the state were addressed through the timeless, "rational" precepts of natural law, whose general tenor had shaped the great codification projects of Maria Theresa and her son Joseph II in the eighteenth century. Students learned that the legitimacy of the state leaned upon an original social contract, and its worth lay in the preservation of law, security, and well-being over and against anarchy.[34] The curriculum reflected its intended practical purpose: the goal was to produce not scholars but efficient, obedient civil servants. Later in the century, the law professor Josef Ulbrich would blame the poverty of this legal training for the "ignorance" evinced in the wildly speculative discussions of the Kremsier parliament: when Austrians began the work of constitutional construction, one could see that their "own state remained foreign to them."[35]

As we see so vividly in the exchange between Deák and Lustkandl, a new constitutional era required new forms of academic knowledge. From Lustkandl forward, the history and theory of constitutional law developed alongside the political task of writing and contesting the constitution: recovering the empire's constitutional history was not an auxiliary but a constitutive endeavor. Its origins were practical and often polemical—interventions in live questions about the arrangement of sovereignty. The exchange also established a pattern that made the dynamic interplay of politics and scholarship especially pronounced. In subsequent decades, other key articulations of the empire's legal order also took the form of debates between Hungarian statesmen and "Austrian" legal scholars, most notably Albert Apponyi and Friedrich Tezner.[36]

The (Original) Two-State Solution

In negotiations with Emperor Francis Joseph across the 1860s, the Hungarian statesmen maintained that the Pragmatic Sanction must form the "point of departure." They would not consider a settlement that began from the premise of the constitutional laws of 1860 and 1861 (let alone the absolutist 1850s), given what these implied about the empire's unity and the emperor's power. Only after the monarchy's grisly military loss to Prussia at Königgratz/Sadová in 1866—and the crisis of legitimacy, identity, and state finances it represented—did Francis Joseph concede this crucial point. On the foundation of the Pragmatic Sanction, Deák and Andrássy thrashed out the agreement's contours and tenor with the emperor and the foreign minister, Friedrich Ferdinand Beust.[37] Its many curiosities, including its method of implementation, reflected the Deákist logic of complete legal separation. It was not proclaimed by the emperor as its constitutional predecessors had been. The first and foundational legislative articulation of the Settlement appeared as "Law 1867: XII" of the Hungarian parliament, passed by the latter on March 30, 1867, and sanctioned by the emperor in June.[38] It was consecrated that same month in Budapest by the coronation of Francis Joseph and Elisabeth as king and queen of Hungary, a spectacular piece of pageantry involving the full enactment of the medieval ritual. The Settlement thus unfolded according to the very traditional logic of an agreement not between "Austria" and "Hungary" but between the monarch and the Hungarian parliament, between the crown and the *ország*.[39] Only belatedly, on December 21, 1867, was a loosely equivalent law enacted by the imperial parliament in Vienna, alongside a new, liberal constitution for the Cisleithanian lands.[40] Henceforth, two separate and equal states, sharing only those three aforementioned common ministries, would face outward as the Austro-Hungarian Empire.

The postwar Austrian legal historian Hans Lentze placed the agreement at "the end of an epoch of European constitutional history, the time of the union of estates-states [*Ständestaaten*]." The dualist settlement represented "the last interesting attempt" to transfer these traditional estates formations into the world of the second half of the nineteenth century.[41] The Habsburg jurist Hermann Bidermann was not alone in complaining that this legal syncretism produced "juridical monstrosities."[42] When the Cisleithanian imperial parliament opened in May 1867, tasked with considering the settlement with Hungary, its competence to do so was mired in uncertainty. If the imperial parliament was assembled in the sense of the February Patent of 1861, it was formally an expanded parliament that included Hungary: then it could hardly conclude an agreement with Hungary because that would entail negotiating with an entity whose interests it had been called to represent—that is, it would be dealing with itself.[43]

In 1848–49, the range of constitutional options had moved between poles of centralism and federalism. The Settlement of 1867 reimagined this set of options by creating *two* centralized states instead (or, in the words of the Hungarian jurist Gábor Máthé, a "doubly centralized state").[44] Centralization, though, was only relative. The Cisleithanian half remained robustly federal in its structure, as its formal name (the Kingdoms and Lands Represented in the Imperial Parliament) documented all too well. These historical crownlands preserved and even gradually expanded their legal and political jurisdiction, a process the historian Hans Peter Hye has described as "crownlandification," producing a noteworthy tradition of regional self-government.[45] Across the Leitha, meanwhile, Hungarian state makers fashioned a more robustly centralized state, though even here sovereignty wrinkled. The Kingdom of Hungary had long comprised a composite monarchy in its own right, with the Kingdom of Croatia and Slavonia as well as the Grand Duchy of Transylvania historically attached to the Hungarian crown—the Holy Crown of Saint Stephen.[46] Transylvania was now absorbed into Hungary proper. Not so Croatia-Slavonia. In 1868, Hungary and Croatia concluded their own "settlement" that affirmed Croatia's rights and internal autonomy within the Hungarian half of the empire. The agreement gave rise to the same sorts of debates about whether Croatia had preserved its historical "statehood." From the Croatian side, it was legally unambiguous that Croatia "existed and should still exist as an independent, autonomous state"; its "state rights, grounded in contract," were clearest of all those in the monarchy.[47] Predictably enough, Hungarian jurists refuted such interpretations with vigor, classing Croatia's status as subsidiary, provincial autonomy only.[48]

Questions of statehood and sovereignty thus cascaded downward through the whole imperial structure. As the French jurist Louis Le Fur and his collaborator Paul Posener wrote of the two "large states" of Austria-Hungary in 1902: "Both states in turn each form a higher entity of multiple states or provinces."[49] Hungary was an empire of sorts, too.[50] This took some explaining to the wider world. The prominent Hungarian statesman Albert Apponyi reacted with "mingled feelings of annoyance and amusement" when William Gladstone, supporting the first Irish Home Rule Bill before the House of Commons, elaborated a "fanciful analogy," to the effect that "there is an imperial parliament in Vienna, and a local one in Budapest." Before the second Home Rule Bill had come around, Gladstone had educated himself, Apponyi noted with satisfaction: for in fact there was an imperial parliament in *Budapest*, too, and a local one, with limited rights, in *Zagreb*.[51] Hungary was not Austria's Ireland; rather, Croatia was Hungary's Ireland. Austria-Hungary's fit in the puzzle of world empires ran a little awry, and to this day it challenges any unthinking, unipolar conception of empire. Here each of the two sovereignties (Austrian and Hungarian) housed its own collection of quasi sovereignties like two sets of Russian dolls joined at the hip.

Naturally, the Settlement reform dealt a hard blow to the monarchy's Slavs, especially Poles and Czechs, who complained that their historical rights were just as valid as the Hungarian equivalent, so why had the latter alone received such grandiose affirmation?[52] In shutting the Slavs out of government, Palacký foresaw dualism as the birthday of Pan-Slavism.[53] They now feared unchecked Germanization in the Austrian half of the Dual Monarchy, while Slovaks, Romanians, and others feared (and suffered) Magyarization in the Hungarian half. The two imperial halves diverged at this point in the treatment of national groups: a new liberal Cisleithanian constitution—dubbed the "December constitution" in keeping with the calendric eponyms of its predecessors—explicitly provided for the equality of ethnic groups and their right to the cultivation of their languages and cultures.[54]

What was dualism, and how did it work? The familiarity of the designation "dual monarchy" can numb us to the contrivance and creativity of the concept itself. In this "German-Magyar double state,"[55] "that was a duality and simultaneously a unity,"[56] the completeness of both sovereignties was taken extremely seriously. As the historian Gerald Stourzh has observed, "parity" was the Settlement's guiding principle.[57] Hungarian jurists and statesmen insisted that Hungary's sovereignty was fully formed and nonderived. Precisely for that reason, they rejected any suggestion it had been granted by the emperor as a concession. On the contrary: Hungary's sovereignty preceded Habsburg rule and had never been legally forfeited. The belief in complete sovereignty, in other words, required a doctrine of legal continuity with that earlier, pre-imperial status. If sovereignty had lapsed, it would have had to be remade, granted, conceded rather than acknowledged. According to Gyula Szekfű's classic work *The Hungarian State* (1918), the settlement worked like a hinge in a longer history of the death and birth of states: "The currently existing dualism, on the basis of the parity of both states, means nothing less from Hungary than the direct continuation of its individual statehood as it had existed before 1526."[58] The year 1867 represented the actualization or renewal of a sovereignty that had been partially suspended more than three centuries earlier. In Albert Apponyi's phrasing: "The previously merely ideal-juridical separation of the two state sovereignties was . . . actually carried out."[59] Frozen in a "merely ideal-juridical" state for recent history, Hungarian sovereignty reemerged in vital form.

Asserting nonderived, unblemished sovereignty required an elaborate legal and political edifice. Portentously, the Settlement had no single definitive legislative articulation or "location": that would have implied the existence of a single highest authority. The distinct Hungarian and Cisleithanian laws were enacted by different lawmaking organs with their own original authority: two versions of the Settlement, enacted by two different states, of seemingly equal legal weight. There existed no citizens of Austria-Hungary, only citizens of each state respectively.[60] International relations thus took on a remarkable intimacy: citizens of the Austrian half of the empire appeared as "foreigners" under Hungarian constitutional law, Henrik Marczali instructed.[61] Perhaps the most inventive aspect was a novel creation called "the delegations." Deák and Andrássy had carefully guarded against any hint of an overarching imperial parliament that would harm Hungary's total independence. How could that demand be squared with the ministerial responsibility of the three common ministers? Andrássy liked to say that he came up with the idea of delegations— deemed "crazy" by the first friends he told—while out on a long horse ride.[62] The joint ministries were responsible not to any comprehensive imperial forum but rather to "delegations" dispatched from the Cisleithanian and the Hungarian parliaments, respectively. The delegations met annually, alternating between Vienna and Budapest. The rescript that summoned them, issued by the monarch, would name the Austrian law first in even years and the Hungarian law first in odd years. The two delegations could not sit together and debate—as that could look suspiciously like a parliament—but were confined to exchanging written notes to preserve their strict separation. As the historian Éva Somogyi has observed, the "essence of the whole construction was negation": there could be no imperial government and no imperial parliament. However cumbersome or even "absurd," the delegations were a means of making the common ministries (at least somewhat) workable while also fastidiously preserving that negation.[63]

The Vanishing Empire

The situation appeared in a dramatically different light to many in Cisleithania. What else were the common ministries other than organs of a higher entity, one literally embodied in the person of the monarch shared by both states? The possibility of two plausible but radically different legal interpretations of the Dual Monarchy had deep roots in the parallel Hungarian and Cisleithanian laws that established the Settlement of 1867, which differed substantially from one another. The Hungarian law was much longer, containing elaborate exegetical discussions of constitutional theory and Hungarian history. The shorter law passed in Vienna, by contrast, appeared in standard legislative prose, sparse, colorless, and low on detail.[64] Francis Joseph had sanctioned them both, yes, but as two legally different people. As the historian Jana Osterkamp observed, he appeared in the Hungarian law as the king of Hungary and in the Cisleithanian law as an unspecified "I."[65] To cap it off, the two laws were in different languages.

The Austrian law denoted the shared domains like war and foreign affairs as *gemeinsam*, or "common." In Austria, as Edmund Bernatzik explained in his annotated 1911 compendium of Austrian constitutional law, *gemeinsam* was understood as unified or unitary (*einheitlich*): one spoke of *gemeinsamen* ministers and ambassadors as organs of a unitary polity otherwise known as the empire, that appeared alone and in the singular in foreign affairs, even if its legal existence was confined to those particular competences.[66] In Hungary, this crucial word was construed very differently. These *gemeinsamen* ministries and organs signified no more than a clasping of two equally empowered states: the word did not suggest the existence of a unified polity separate from and spanning the two. Pointing to the March Settlement laws, Hungarian actors came to dispute the continued existence of the *Reich* altogether.[67]

The trials of translation played their part in this tangle of willful misunderstandings. The Hungarian law used a word, *együttes*, that had no direct German equivalent. Arguments about the empire's legal existence came to turn on its translation. The Hungarian law, in Bernatzik's rendering, spoke of the "defense and preservation of common security with the unified ('*együttes*') force of a common and mutual obligation, which springs directly from the Pragmatic Sanction."[68] *Együttes* was an adjective formed from the stem word *együtt*, meaning "together" or "with each other" (*mitsammen, beisammen, miteinander*). As Bernatzik noted, "An adjective 'togetherly' [*mitsammenig*] or similar does not exist in the German language."[69] It was generally translated as *gemeinsam*, but the latter had a different Hungarian correlate, *közös*, with a different meaning. The jurist Ivan Žolger offered two alternative translations, one that used an awkward conglomerate ("occurring through together-force": *Zusammen-Kraft zu geschehende*),[70] and another for which he simply generated a new adjective, so that the obligation happened through "togetherly force" (*mit zusammeniger Kraft*).[71] "This translation may be exact," Bernatzik smirked, "but it is not German."[72]

As neither law "trumped" the other, this single untranslatable word ballooned into a great incommensurability at the heart of imperial law—Musil's "inexpressible" state. In the Austrian construction, *gemeinsam* implied that the two sovereign states fused—partially—into a common entity; in the Hungarian, *együttes* denoted no more than the force of two separate sovereign states working alongside one another. The distinction was subtle, but its implications were dramatic. Did the word *gemeinsam* serve as the placeholder for a supradualist imperial state, a state body over the top of the Austrian Empire and the Kingdom of Hungary, a legal space in which the two melted together? There was precious little else in the Settlement laws that documented the existence of a "third" state of this sort.

Perhaps no public figure argued the Hungarian position as insistently and with such intransigent eloquence as the Hungarian statesman Count Albert Apponyi (1846–1933). Born into the highest echelons of the Hungarian aristocracy—his father was lord chancellor of Hungary at the time of his birth—Apponyi would serve as Hungarian minister of education and later led the Hungarian delegation to the Paris Peace Conference after World War I. A lifelong devout Catholic educated by Jesuits, the polyglot Apponyi dazzled in half a dozen languages. He was known for his expansive learning and philosophical aptitude, but even more for his zealous commitment to the national

cause. That commitment represented one constant in an otherwise fickle ideological potpourri that combined political liberalism and social conservatism,
worldly pacificism and the unapologetic Magyarization of Hungary's various
nationalities. He chased popular sentiment, which in the age of dualism made
him an ideologue of Hungarian sovereignty.[73] In the years and decades following the Settlement, Hungary's legal standing vis-à-vis the Habsburg lands
became *the* determinative issue in Hungarian political party affiliation, making and breaking careers and governments as everyone competed to be the
most strident defender of Hungarian independence.[74] Before a public in the
grip of a "*Staatsrecht* psychosis," Hungary's holy crown had no more vociferous
apostle than Apponyi. He pursued "the external attributes of sovereignty 'like
a child the rainbow.'"[75]

Predictably enough, Apponyi turned interpretive pirouettes on the ambiguities of *gemeinsam*. Any argument that produced the term *gemeinsam* as
evidence of a common, singular state rested on a foundational logical error, he
argued. Conceptually, "*Gemeinsamkeit* indicates multiplicity, not unity; one
cannot have something in common [*gemeinsam*] with oneself, at least two
belong there; accordingly, common affairs are not imperial affairs, because an
empire cannot have common affairs with itself."[76] *Gemeinsamkeit*, Apponyi continued, was the category through which the laws of 1867 reconciled Hungary's full
sovereignty with the *Länder* confederation created by the Pragmatic Sanction.
This reconciliation may not have been executed elegantly, but that remained
a political question and not a legal one.[77] Everyone now poured over the awkward wording, he reported. Had this "labyrinth of laborious and contradictory
constructions," he asked incredulously, simultaneously preserved Hungary's
full sovereignty *and* "indirectly" created "a higher juridical entity standing
over this sovereignty"? Far from it. The construction of "an empire" out of the
common institutions of 1867 was "a conceptual impossibility."[78]

Apponyi surveyed the imperial structure in support of his argument. His
evidence included the "fragmentary character" and lack of independence of
the common organs and functions: "There is no autonomous imperial competence and no autonomous imperial organism." There was nothing resembling
a common legislature. "An empire without legislative capacity! Now that is
certainly awkward," he teased—especially as a legislature formed the highest public competence from which everything else flowed. An "empire" built
on these foundations, he observed, would constitute a *very* curious juridical
unit—one that remained dependent on the highest powers of its subordinate
units.[79] He went further: this supposed overarching empire "is not destroyed
now, rather, it had never existed, except in the speculations of the greater-
Austrian academic line."[80] In Apponyi's account, "the empire" amounted to
little more than a centuries-long juridical dream, now finally exposed as such.

Such provocations incited increasingly frustrated responses. One wartime pamphlet written by Paul von Fazekas expressed deep exasperation with

Apponyi's exposition of *gemeinsam*. When Apponyi, "the epicist of constitutional politics," wrote things like "*Gemeinsamkeit* indicates multiplicity, not
unity" or "one cannot have something in common with oneself, at least two
belong there," then, Fazekas protested, "it is a witch's arithmetic [*Hexeneinma-
leins*], which I characterize with the formula $1+1=1+1$, that according to the
sophism of our constitutional jurist may never become the new unit 'two.'"[81]
In Apponyi's sly arithmetic, the equation was never converted: the "answer"
simply restated the original values.[82] Only a constitutional jurist, Fazekas
complained, could argue that *Gemeinsamkeit* suggested multiplicity rather
than unity, a word game that more closely resembled a witch's trick than jurisprudence. In his own exegesis of the term, *Gemeinsamkeit* possessed a kind of
inbuilt story of development over time: "Because *Gemeinsamkeit* was once a
multiplicity. Since it became *Gemeinsamkeit*, it has naturally become a unity
there where the *Gemeinsamkeit* is, and *gemeinsame* affairs are affairs neither
of Austria nor Hungary, but rather those of the *empire*, or, if the word suits
better, of the monarchy."[83] In its own way, the term *gemeinsam* documented
the progressive formation of the empire: the unity *had been* a multiplicity, but
that plurality now lay in the past. If Fazekas criticized the pedantic and solipsistic reasoning of the jurists, he too participated in this word game or logic
puzzle—the secret science—of imperial law.

How could the empire's existence or nonexistence, legally speaking, come
to rest on the shoulders of a single term? When Austrian legal scholars, building on Lustkandl, began to publish tracts on Habsburg constitutional law in
the 1870s, they investigated precisely these foundational questions. What sort
of legal entity *was* the Habsburg Monarchy? Where—if anywhere—did sovereignty lie? In his 1877 study of the legal nature of the Dual Monarchy, the Austrian jurist Hermann Bidermann argued that the legal categorization of the
empire turned on the question of whether or not there was an independent,
overarching, paramount "central power" (*Centralgewalt*). More specifically:
Had such a thing existed before 1848, and if so, how was it affected, first, by
the events of that year, and, second, by the laws of 1867? After many pages of
laborious exposition, Bidermann thought he *had* demonstrated the historical
existence of a central power of this sort.[84] So what of the situation following
the Settlement? In all the most important competencies, such as the direction
and organization of the army, diplomatic capacity, the ability to declare war,
and so forth, a central state power still existed, he argued. But somehow that
central power, despite all those capacities, had been issued (*ausgegeben*) as if
newly founded, as if such a thing had not existed before, or as if it had legally
lapsed. It was bewildering: "Astonished the legal historian asks how the latter
happened—and with amazement he hears the denial" of the "true origin of the
current central power and the continuity of its legal efficacy."[85] In outlining
the limited common ministries, the Settlement laws had somehow allowed
the interpretation that joint organs of this sort were thereby *created in law* for

the first time. As Bidermann continued, "From the Hungarian side, it is never once admitted that one thereby had something to do with a central power, and one advances the slogan 'dualism' as justification for this."[86]

Two years later, another Austrian jurist, Josef Ulbrich, would contest Bidermann's identification of a central power: it appeared nowhere in the Settlement laws, and surely the very essence of such a power would involve its rule over subject-citizens and over a specific territory, yet Austria-Hungary had neither citizens nor territory of its own.[87] But Ulbrich conceded that Bidermann's analysis had shrewdly pinpointed continuity as the real nub of the dispute. If one simply began with the Settlement laws, as though they occurred atop a juridical tabula rasa, then legally speaking there was no central imperial state in existence. To many Austrian jurists, however, it seemed an obvious presumption that whatever the empire was, its legal identity continued over the cusp of 1867. Intuition and common sense alike understood its existence to be pre-presumed: it did not need to be made out from first principles in the Settlement laws.

This continuity thesis formed one of Friedrich Tezner's main lines of attack against Hungarian assertions of a nonexistent empire. If Apponyi was Hungary's "epicist" and "sophist" of constitutional argument, Tezner (1856–1925) was Austria's. The two locked horns directly in a series of heated exchanges.[88] Their pairing contains Habsburg worlds in miniature. Where Apponyi hailed from an illustrious family that counted as storied even among the genealogy-preoccupied aristocracy, Tezner's lineage is lost in obscurity. Tezner was born in Beraun in central Bohemia with the name Friedrich Tänzerles; his father was likely a religious teacher in the Jewish community. We know nothing of his mother, nor exactly how many siblings he had. The family moved to Vienna in 1870. Where Apponyi dispensed over castles and estates, Tezner needed to support himself from age fifteen. He began tutoring in private homes but was made to understand that a name as "laughable" (*lächerlich*) as his undermined the authority that a teacher required with children. He began introducing himself to students under a pseudonym, while their parents knew the truth. As we know from the petition he later filed to change his name to Tezner in 1882, it left him feeling like a "criminal fearing detection."[89]

He enrolled at the University of Vienna to study law in the winter semester of 1874–75, graduating in 1879. There, Lustkandl awakened his interest in public law, revealingly prompting him to investigate whether the "legal subjectivity of the monarchy" had endured through the constitutional transformation of the Settlement of 1867.[90] In some senses, Tezner never stopped answering that question—of the empire's legal existence and continuity—his whole career. He worked as a lawyer and at the Vienna *Sparkasse*; he hoped the name change would improve his prospects amid intensifying anti-Semitism. After securing the habilitation in Austrian administrative law in 1892, he began teaching at the university but never received the "call" to a full professorship, his dream.

He published feverishly, producing a corpus distinguished not only by its size but also by its idiosyncratic style: his extraordinarily complicated but logically impeccable sentences came soaked through with vivid metaphors and illusions. Assessing Tezner negatively for a faculty position, Bernatzik complained of his "florid" prolixity that called to mind a "mosaic." Combining grudging acknowledgment of Tezner's talent and industry with indictments of his personality—conceited, lacking "tact" and "taste"—Bernatzik's appraisal arguably echoes with the anti-Semitism that dogged Tezner's whole career and left him increasingly depressed and embittered.[91] Ironic, then, at first glance, that the Viennese view of the empire had no stauncher advocate than Tezner. Only "at first glance" because the story is a familiar one: with little to gain and much to lose from the increasing nationalization of political life, Jews remained disproportionately and passionately committed to the supranational Habsburg Monarchy.[92] Marked out as particular, they reached for the universal and bore its burden. Like Georg Jellinek and Hans Kelsen, Tezner experienced the exception-norm dichotomy at very close quarters.

With intellectual energy that still bounces off the page, Tezner devoted dozens of books, pamphlets, and articles to the service of his state and its sovereign integrity. He was incredulous that not only the Hungarians but even some of his own colleagues took "the whole Austro-Hungarian Monarchy and all that is attached to it" and exploded it "into thin air" in an entirely senseless "firework."[93] When they declared the monarchy "not existing, null and void" simply because it did not "fit into their catalog of formulas" for what counted as a state, it reminded him of "the conservative Englishman who declares a landscape to be wrong because it does not accord completely with the description in [the travel guide] Bädeker."[94] The conglomerate Habsburg polity may be idiosyncratic, even illogical, a sui generis entity, but that could not diminish its palpable reality.[95] Over the course of centuries, he argued, the Habsburg dynasty *had* melded its collection of lands into a thick and permanent union; the Settlement laws referenced that whole amassed history with the term *gemeinsam*. Tezner placed great emphasis on the Pragmatic Sanction and the proclamation of the Austrian imperial title in 1804. Nothing of these unions had been undone; everything carried over. The year 1867 "called forth no change in the legal subjectivity, in the state personality of the monarchy, testified a thousand times over, in the domains of either private or international law."[96] Just because the empire was not mentioned in the Settlement laws did not mean it was not there. "The fog of the Hungarian constitutional formulas," he wrote in 1909, cannot obscure the imperial state "standing behind them."[97]

Standing where exactly? Austrian jurists like Tezner had not yet produced any evidence for the legal existence of an overarching empire, Apponyi maintained. When did such a thing come into being? He ran through the history. No one doubted that Hungary was an independent sovereign state in 1526 when the Habsburgs took up the crown. According to Apponyi, "It must therefore be shown when and how this sovereignty ended or was subordinated to a higher sovereignty."[98] Taking Hungarian sovereignty as his point of departure—1526 as the starting point for reasoning—the onus fell on the other side to prove its eclipse. Where were the legitimate, lawmaking facts that could have caused such a profound change? The Pragmatic Sanction, like the 1804 proclamation, *affirmed* rather than limited all of Hungary's original rights. Indeed, the only sorts of acts that would have been capable of diminishing Hungarian sovereignty were acts of Hungarian sovereign power itself because "the empire could not possibly have been independent before its creation, before it possessed its own source of law; only a Münchhausen managed to pull himself out of the swamp by his own hair."[99] That is: in historical dynastic agreements like the Pragmatic Sanction, Hungary bound itself on the basis of its own law; how could such agreements have *also* created another separate fount of law, another original sovereign power, another state, all while never mentioning the fact?[100] He enlisted Baron Münchhausen—a popular fictional character of many impossible feats—to stage the logical-legal problem of sovereignty's origins. The empire was not "there" to legislate itself into existence. Remember Münchhausen: it was not the last time Habsburg legal thinkers would try to find their way out of his swamp.

But "by this strict measure," Tezner exclaimed, "*no* state legally exists."[101] "Apponyi asks for the formal declaration of the empire," he fumed. That was like asking for "the declaration of England, France, Spain as a state." In such matters, a "gradual development" could also fulfill the requisite "formula of a unified state [*gesamtstaatlichen Formel*]."[102] Here they were, debating how one could tell if a state had come into being, debating how to prove its very (legal) existence: more Musilesque than Musil himself. In an article titled "Apponyi's Evidence against the Reality of the Austrian Unified-State Idea," Tezner diagnosed the root of the dispute with particular acuity. It had everything to do with the relationship of history, law, and method. He argued that dynastic agreements like the Hungarian Pragmatic Sanction represented an appropriate method of centralizing "the Austrian lands into a constitutional unity" *according to the logic of their epoch*, according to the "patrimonial concept of the state." It fashioned the lands of the house into an "indivisible estate," "from which flows, if one transfers the phrase into the modern age, the constitutionally unified, indivisible function of the ruler."[103] These dynastic modes of statecraft must be assessed in their historical context. That *was* how states were made back then. Tezner consciously translated premodern vocabularies of sovereignty into modern ones, explaining the "transfer" from one to the other.

In a similar way, Tezner argued, the Hungarians had anachronistically conflated the rights of the estates with the rights of sovereignty, presuming that, because the former survived, the latter did, too. But if those dynastic laws had guaranteed Hungary's traditional rights, the guarantees "do not have the meaning of a declaration of the *sovereignty* of Hungary in the sense of the *modern* interpretation of this concept." They related to a "*constitutional* and *internal administrative independence* that does not go nearly so far as that of the *modern sovereignty* of an *isolated unified state*."[104] Tezner worked in law but thought like a historian: more clearly than his colleagues, he saw that codifying questions of statehood and sovereignty in the Habsburg lands proved so problematic because of the transformation, in the preceding centuries, of what statehood and sovereignty signified. Hungarians like Apponyi were calling up a historical genre of independence to be nested within the reality of a nineteenth-century state. And in the other direction, they applied contemporary legal methods to events in the past, seeking formal written codifications in the modern style and misunderstanding the nature of legal change. "The transition from one epoch of state development to another does not take place, as one would believe from Apponyi's amateurish demands for proof," Tezner explained, through laws that announce each respective stage "in *doctrinal* formulas." Rather, the transition unfolded "indirectly," through laws and institutions that were *rooted in* "an altered perspective on the nature of the state."[105] For example, the Austrian Civil Code of 1811 did not formally codify the essence of the absolutist police and welfare state; rather, it enshrined rules that only make sense if we grasp the doctrines of natural law lying behind them.[106] Figures like Apponyi could not simply teleport historical rights from the past into the present without translating the sovereign imaginaries that had given them meaning; similarly, one could not export present legal expectations backward and judge the past by their measure. Trying to make sense of Habsburg sovereignty brought Tezner face-to-face with the tension between history's ceaseless fluidity and law's desire for fixed, propositional certainty. Juridical formations like kingship and statehood were in flux, just like modes of legal rationality and proof, and it made "truth" and "reality" improbably relative.

Given his historical sensibilities, it is perhaps unsurprising that Tezner's own analysis of Habsburg sovereignty turned squarely on the body of the king. There may be two states, but they formed "*only one* monarchy," with a single ruling individual at the summit.[107] People neglected that simple, common-sense fact! When the Pragmatic Sanction announced the Habsburg lands as an indivisible, unified estate, the emperor subsumed all those other titles and selves into his person: one monarch presiding over one large patrimony. The "king of Hungary" disappeared in diplomatic and international affairs. Like the king of Bohemia, it became a "decorative title," significant for *internal* distributions of authority, perhaps, but not more.[108] Facing outward, the emperor and the king form an "indivisible unit, they are one, the king can never contract alone, and this indivisibility is only the expression of the indivisibility—or more correctly, the unity—of both state territories," of the "blending of both states into one subject of international law." The unified physical body of the monarch expressed—held, signified—an (externally) unified body politic. People liked to compare the Dual Monarchy to Siamese twins, Tezner reflected. Yet the analogy had a crucial defect. Siamese twins have two individual heads, two individual wills, even if they lack complete freedom of movement. "But the monarchy," Tezner protested, "has only one head."[109]

For all the transformations of modern history, that profoundly patrimonial understanding of sovereignty lingered in the legal structure of the Habsburg polity. Tezner pointed to something he called a "subsidiary absolutism" surviving into the present constitutional epoch.[110] If the two parliaments could not agree on a matter within the domain of their common affairs, the final decision fell to the monarch. He possessed the "discretionary determinative authority." His Majesty would decide. "This majesty is only one and its decision only one," even if it was subsequently *executed* twice in the two different states.[111] The fact that this "coercive, procuratorial, patriarchal function of the monarch" was indivisible proved, in the final analysis, that sovereignty lay "with the whole and not with the parts."[112] It also suggested that the "emperor of the corporatist [*ständisch*] epoch as highest organ of the monarchy, as its ultima ratio, still endures"—a piece of an older world alive in the present.[113] In this sense, the residual trace of absolutism revealed that the form of rule in both states was only "half constitutional," Tezner argued controversially.[114] The view made him unpopular with Hungarians *as well as* with German-Austrian liberals, staunch defenders of the constitutional order they had fought for and forged. "For the jurists of both imperial halves of the monarchy," Tezner wrote (ruefully? defiantly?), "I am nothing less than a byzantine, paid slave of the camarilla, crude forger, mercenary swordsman for absolutism, comrade of corpse desecrators, political poison mixer."[115]

An Empire in International Law

What are the essential characteristics of a sovereign state? Hungarians like Apponyi emphasized the Dual Monarchy's lack of its own legislature and citizenship as proof of its sovereign deficit. Tezner, conversely, stressed international law: the fact that the empire counted as *one* actor in international affairs should be determinative. Such claims reflected broader transformations in the world order. In this same period, a rapidly thickening web of global interactions—from trade and migration to violent imperial conquest— spurred the professionalization and institutionalization of international law.[116] As international lawyers tried to make their field more "scientific," they devoted intense new scrutiny to who qualified as a subject of international law. Only sovereign states, the theory went, could possess "international legal personality"—that is, be capable of possessing international rights and duties and entering into international agreements.[117] These ideas became valuable resources in debates about imperial sovereignty, where they reflected a new self-consciousness about international standing. They enabled Tezner to concede that the empire might be two states internally, but not externally:

Hungary counted as a state in *constitutional* law, but not in *international* law. As we see in his chapter topics such as "International Legal Personality of the Monarchy," international law became increasingly important to descriptions of imperial sovereignty.[118] "Legal relations in international law are an imperial monopoly," he concluded.[119] Indeed, it helped him interpret the significance of the Settlement of 1867 within the longer history of Habsburg state building. "The essence of the Settlement," he explained, was that "the emperor abandoned all claims to centralization that had been made in the earlier constitutions except for the external unity of the monarchy or its personality in international law and the preservation of the army."[120] That singular face presented to the world was all the emperor had salvaged from centuries of gradual centralization—but perhaps it was also the most important bit.

Small wonder that Hungarian politicians set out to prove this analysis wrong. If international legal personality was a central prerogative of sovereignty—now even integral to sovereignty's majesty—then Hungary must have it, too. They attacked the problem on multiple fronts. Where Tezner and other Cisleithanian jurists underlined the ultimate singularity of the monarch,[121] Hungarian actors set out to show that his multiple legal personalities had in fact remained clearly distinct. The king of Hungary had never simply melted into the emperor of Austria. In yet another instance of temporal pastiche, the priorities of modern international law drove a reinvestment of meaning in the seemingly archaic logic of composite monarchy. To be sure, there were precedents for these attempts to reassert the king of Hungary's international standing. In May 1809, Napoleon had tried to wedge the two sovereign personalities apart in an appeal to the Hungarians. "It is the emperor of Austria, not the king of Hungary, who has declared war on me. According to your institutions, he cannot do this without your assent. . . . Hungary! The moment has come to obtain your independence once more!"[122] One hundred years later, that cleft between ruling selves seemed more important than ever.

"The sovereignty in Hungary is not identical with the sovereignty in Austria, only the bearer of both crowns is the same *physical* person," the Hungarian consul Theodore Zichy explained in 1908. "The rights of the king of Hungary and those of the emperor of Austria have a different origin, they are not fused together, but rather separated from one another."[123] As evidence of the aloofness of the different legal personalities, Zichy reminded his readers of the multiple designations attached to each sovereign: Emperor Charles *VI*, for example, was king of Hungary Charles *III*. Charles's rule, in other words, was tallied according to distinct sovereign lines, and those numbers marked out the different incarnations of his ruling self. Predictably enough, Tezner was impatient with Zichy's "constitutional catechism." He recounted how Emperor Ferdinand was designated the fifth Hungarian king of that name, with both these titles preceded by his new designation as the *first* emperor of Austria of that name. The sequence distinguished the imperial title as an all-encompassing (*zussamenfassende*) one. Tezner then mapped these designations onto the structure of international law. The imperial title, he argued, was a title at the level of international law (*völkerrechtlicher Rangtitel*), one designed for international dealings, modeled on the French and Russian equivalents.[124] As Ferdinand I (of Austria), the monarch possessed an international standing or personality. As Ferdinand V (of Hungary or Bohemia), his status pertained to internal dealings within his realm only.[125] In his telling, the line between international and constitutional law threaded between the different numbers that followed the monarch's name.

But Tezner's position proved increasingly embattled. The actual practice of international affairs was in fact trending in the opposite direction. The creation of the Dual Monarchy had an immediate impact on the monarchy's external dealings. Almost before the ink had dried on the Settlement laws, the 1867–68 negotiation of a trade and customs treaty with Germany raised the uncomfortable question of what to call the old-new Habsburg polity. With whom was Germany concluding the agreement? The old designation "Austrian Empire" was not palatable to the Hungarian government: no such entity (had ever) incorporated the Hungarian lands, they insisted. As the historian Gerald Stourzh has shown, the question inaugurated several decades of struggle over the nature of the Dual Monarchy as an international actor. The Hungarian government suggested that the treaty could name the Austrian Empire and the Kingdom of Hungary as the contracting partner(s). But the "and" in this formulation raised serious objections from Imperial Chancellor Friedrich Ferdinand von Beust and others. The small word "and" suggested a radical and confronting separation of the two state parts; it also suggested that "Austrian Empire" related exclusively to the Cisleithanian lands. Yet these lands had never been constituted as a collective legal entity, let alone one under that title.[126] Such a name was, simply, legally wrong. Beust also rejected the proposal "Austria-Hungary": that sounded to him like affirming the logic of a mere personal union in front of the whole world.[127]

With the German government waiting for ratification, and the Hungarian parliament threatening to derail the whole thing, an ad hoc and very Habsburg solution was hurriedly devised. The name of the state was changed to reflect Hungarian sensitivities *only* in the Hungarian version of the treaty: the one approved by Berlin, like the one presented to the Cisleithanian parliament, still used the old title format.[128] The Dual Monarchy thereby appeared as different versions of itself in different languages—two versions of the truth existing in parallel. The pragmatic solution showed how language diversity could also be a resource, and not just a roadblock, for imperial law. Cisleithanian jurists had often accused Hungarian politicians and scholars of hiding behind their language, of exploiting the difficulties its Uralic root entailed for others. In a cheeky newspaper article, Georg Jellinek called it a "Hungarian Monroe doctrine."[129] Though Hungarians invoked their historical law incessantly ("constitutional wisdom is preached there in the laneways, in the restaurants, in the train carriage compartments"), deploying it to counter any problem or obstacle whatsoever, they also suspiciously refrained from laying bare its "secrets" in a proper scientific study published in a world language, meaning it could be endlessly elastic to their purposes.[130] (Multiple Hungarian jurists sent him protestations to the contrary).[131] Harold Steinacker similarly complained that Hungarians handled their historical law as a "secret science," writing, "One might almost think that the theoreticians and practitioners of this theory feel very comfortable behind the Chinese wall of the little-used Magyar language."[132] But the flexible truths enabled by these linguistic Chinese walls and Monroe doctrines had their own virtues as a hybrid empire-kingdom stepped hesitatingly onto the world stage.

In the end, parallel state names could only be a stopgap solution: the German trade agreement had exposed the need for formal regulation of the matter. In November 1868, Francis Joseph announced new guidelines that acceded to the Hungarian view. The monarch would henceforth sign treaties as "Emperor of Austria, King of Bohemia etc. *and* Apostolic King of Hungary," or, in abbreviated form, simply "Emperor of Austria *and* Apostolic King of Hungary."[133] The dramatic significance of that little "and" was clear to all involved: three letters that contained a whole new account of imperial sovereignty. Further, the lands over which this dual monarch ruled would be collectively known as the Austro-Hungarian Monarchy or the Austro-Hungarian Empire (though the latter aroused opposition in Hungary).[134]

In subsequent decades, Hungarians would push this dualization ever farther, inching toward the capacity to sign international agreements in their own name and thereby appear as a subject of international law in their own right. This occurred especially in fields over which they had domestic jurisdiction: not the classical questions of war and peace, but the rapidly expanding sphere of transnational technical, economic, and scientific coordination. As Peter Becker and Madeleine Herren have observed, this new international sphere often enabled the participation of various nonsovereigns and semisovereigns if they had authority over the domain in question. So Egypt was a signatory of the 1874 treaty that established the World Postal Union—a treaty also signed separately "for Austria" and "for Hungary."[135] But Habsburg practice remained inconsistent, and Cisleithanian officials continued to complain about the inaccuracy of the name "Austria."[136] Other officials responded that the Cisleithanian imperial half could hardly sign international conventions under the unwieldly designation "the Kingdoms and Lands Represented in the Imperial Parliament"! Here practice led theory: Cisleithania gradually (and arguably) became "Austria" through the international challenges of dual sovereignty.[137] Matters reached their Musilesque apogee at negotiations for the 1902 international sugar convention in Brussels, when, to the embarrassment of many, three different diplomatically accredited representatives turned up to represent Habsburg lands, each dispatched by different authorities: one representing Austria, one representing Hungary, and one representing Austria-Hungary. All three appeared as signatories on the convention.[138]

Constitutional law had slowly folded out into international law. Many scholars came to agree with the Hungarian view of dualism as a relationship located "in" international law rather than constitutional law.[139] But the difficulties of translating composite monarchy into "modern" form meant that a clear, stable line between "internal" and "external" affairs, between the inside and the outside of the state, remained elusive. It generated endless contradictions, as Harold Steinacker complained in 1910. The Settlement was intended as a legal form through which a particular political idea might continually actualize itself—closer to a political invitation than an end point. To ensure the "preservation of the empire," the Settlement established the unified treatment of military and foreign affairs. "But these constitutional, imperial-unified [reichseinheitlichen] elements are arranged in a relationship in international law that leaves both states sovereign. All real power is with them and the empire's conditions of existence depend on their unification."[140] The Settlement, he concluded, was "part international, part constitutional law and therefore a unified juridical construction is not accessible without violence [ohne Gewaltsamkeit]. What applies to theory, applies also to praxis. The constitutional and international law elements are plainly incompatible; one must yield to the other."[141] The order of 1867 institutionalized the ambiguity of a composite monarchy that had half translated the traditional autonomy of the estates into full sovereign statehood.

Austria-Hungary's extension into the Balkans exposed the costs of this tangle of imperial and international law. The Dual Monarchy walked away from the 1878 Congress of Berlin with an international mandate to "occupy and administer" Bosnia and Herzegovina, though the territories would formally remain under Ottoman sovereignty. According to many, the Habsburg empire thereby acquired its first "colony."[142] Certainly, the Habsburg state embraced a new self-understanding as civilizer of a backward east.[143] The legal status of the occupied territories remained highly obscure, suspended between the inside and the outside of both the Habsburg and the Ottoman polities.[144] Should Bosnia-Herzegovina be classified as a "protectorate," a "pseudo-protectorate," a "contractual occupation," a "dependent land," an "autonomous province"?[145] No less uncertain, though, was the identity of the occupying power. Who was governing Bosnia-Herzegovina? The "Austrian" state would not permit it to be a "Hungarian" protectorate or colony, and vice versa; and Hungary did not admit the existence of a unified empire.[146] The occupation revealed the administrative and logistical consequences of the ideology of dual sovereignty. If the Habsburg Monarchy had sometimes been called an empire without colonies, now there was a colony without an empire—at least in legal terms. Could the colony perhaps be possessed twice over—by both Hungary

and Austria separately but simultaneously, a doubled subordination? Without any clear answers, the territories were administered out of the common
finance ministry as a kind of permanently provisional stopgap arrangement.

The juridical headaches proved impossible to contain. If the Treaty of
Berlin—the origin of the right to occupy—needed to be ratified by the empire's
representative organs to become operative law (and opinion was divided here),
then which representative organ could perform such a function? The empire
did not have a parliament of its own: How could *either* the Austrian *or* the
Hungarian one ratify it in the name of the whole Dual Monarchy? Like countless other jurists, Theodor Dantscher von Kollesberg explained to his readers, almost apologetically, that occupation of Bosnia-Herzegovina forced one
to backtrack and answer the most basic, foundational questions about the
nature of the Austro-Hungarian Empire: "First it must be clear or made clear
which state form—or perhaps *state forms*—Austria-Hungary represents."[147]
One soon stumbled on a "particularly strange phenomenon." While everyone recognized the "international legal existence" of Austria-Hungary—this
was, after all, the entity that had signed the Treaty of Berlin—the "constitutional [*staatsrechtliche*] existence" of such a state was doubted from many
sides. "Austria-Hungary, *one* state outwardly, is supposed to be *two* states
inwardly."[148] "What confusion, what uncertainty in the theory about this
Austria-Hungary!" he exclaimed.[149] Little was resolved by the formal annexation of the provinces in 1908. "Bosnia Herzegovina is attached with the same
band to the one monarchy and to the other," reasoned Robert Redslob creatively.[150] Tezner was less optimistic: "A final, organic solution scarcely seems
possible on the foundation of dualism."[151]

But perhaps Bosnia-Herzegovina offered an opening. If international
affairs became an arena for staging Hungarian sovereignty, some held out
hope that this particular international venture might prove the basis for a new
work of sovereign integration. The colonial enterprise invited the expansion
of the common prerogatives and institutions, argued the law professor Karl
Lamp. The shared responsibility and shared mission of colonial rule could
galvanize new cooperation and investment. Lamp speculated that a strengthening of the power position of the monarch, an extension of the jurisdiction
of the common ministry, the creation of a new representative imperial organ,
and the organization of a bureaucratic body under the common government
would all be legal effects of the 1908 annexation of Bosnia-Herzegovina and
the 1910 promulgation of a constitution for the territories. The latter formed "a
powerful new counterweight to the tendencies toward separation that dwell to
a greater or lesser extent in all state unions" and would "direct the monarchy in
its further development on the path to federal organisation."[152]

But perhaps that reconstitution of an integrated legal self required not so
much the creation of new institutions as a change in perspective. Scholar-
turned-politician Josef Redlich certainly saw it that way. Redlich's two-volume,

nine-hundred-page epic, *Das österreichische Staats- und Reichsproblem* (The Austrian state- and imperial problem) still marks him as one of the empire's most significant legal chroniclers.[153] Well before those volumes had appeared, he headed the Austrian parliamentary commission charged with trying to "legalize" the annexation of Bosnia-Herzegovina and determine its relationship to the empire's constitutional order. Redlich's parliamentary report discussed the Hungarian argument that the act of annexation was not the act of a common monarch. This reflected the dominant Hungarian perspective that fully denied the existence of a single, unified monarchy. Such views, he asserted, rode roughshod over the fact that all Austrian and all Hungarian constitutional arrangements in relation to Bosnia had their exclusive foundation in the Treaty of Berlin that granted the mandate for occupation and administration to *the monarchy* and only to it: "Through this act neither Austria nor Hungary acquired an independent right, rather, exclusively the from-the-outside-in unified monarchy [*die nach außen hin einheitliche Monarchie*], just as the bearer of this mandate since the Berlin treaty has been exclusively the common monarch."[154] State making "from the outside in": that metajurisdictional view from international law offered a way to bypass Hungarian arguments about Hungary's undiluted sovereignty and glimpse a larger whole, a larger truth. At least there, in the Treaty of Berlin, the empire existed as a unified legal subject, Redlich insisted—even if that unity was not so easy to see closer to home.

Self-Conscious Knowledge

Legal scholars like Tezner, Lustkandl, and Bernatzik represented a new breed of expert—practitioners of an academic field that was coming into being alongside the constitutional empire-state it described and studied. It is no coincidence that the professorial council (*Professorenkollegium*) of the faculty of law at the University of Vienna first wrote to the minister for education requesting the "systematization" of a separate chair for constitutional law in November 1849—in the immediate aftermath of the empire's first steps into constitutional life. "We cannot believe," wrote the professors boldly, that the minister could want a subject as important as Austrian constitutional law merely tacked on to the long-standing chair of administrative law, especially in Vienna, the very heart of the monarchy. The failure to establish a separate chair, they concluded emphatically, would be a "political mistake!"[155]

The minister, Count von Thun-Hohenstein, rejected their proposal. By then the government was already drifting back toward absolutism, and its opinion of constitutional law remained low (though he did approve the Viennese civil jurist Moriz von Stubenrauch in a joint chair of administrative and constitutional law).[156] Thun had other agendas: in 1849–50 he had launched a systematic overhaul of higher education. Looking to the German model, the

Thun-Hohenstein Reforms sought to modernize the universities. They introduced seminars, faculty self-governance, and (in theory if not in practice)
freedom of teaching and learning. The reforms reached the legal curriculum
in 1855 with the promulgation of a new Order of Studies (*Studienordnung*),
which included no separate treatment of Austrian constitutional law.[157]

All this began to change when constitutional questions exploded back
into the center of public life in the 1860s. By the early twentieth century, the
empire's universities (especially Vienna, but also new universities on the imperial "periphery" like Czernowitz) were hothouses of research and education in
public law. Ideas and methodologies developed there would travel around the
globe, as we will see in chapters 4 and 6. In the remainder of this chapter, I show
how that intellectual history has its roots in public debates about the arrangement of sovereignty. The history and theory of constitutional law emerged
alongside the empire's constitutional reformulations in processes that were
reciprocal and entangled. As we saw so clearly in the exchanges between
Apponyi and Tezner, political and scholarly registers easily blurred. The academic field faced the same problems as the polity itself: What was the name
and nature of the state(s) involved, the parameters of the field of inquiry?
Here, too, different bodies of law needed to be sorted, arranged, and reconstituted into a cohesive unit.

When the Vienna law faculty requested a chair for the subject in 1849,
they revealingly listed the different areas of law such a professor would need
to cover. Constitutional law, they argued, "demands an independent and thoroughly exhaustive lecture course more urgently than ever" as a result of its
historical foundation "in the old-Austrian public law [*Staatsrechte*], in the
former estates constitutions, in the imperial constitution of 4. March 1849,
in the particular diet constitutions of each constituent crownland (that are
in part so highly diverse internally), and finally in the all-important vital
relationship [*Lebens-Beziehung*] of Austria to Germany."[158] They named
multiple bodies and genres of law, including law that belonged to different
sorts of polities. There were, essentially, multiple constitutional laws in play.
In their list, the imposed constitution of March 1849 coexisted alongside the
estates constitutions of the varied crownlands (often customary), as well as
legal relationships that reached beyond the state (with Germany). To stitch
them together—more: to claim and reconcile them as part of the empire's
constitution—required an intellectual empire building of its own. Like the
emergence of "scientific objects" of all sorts, the new academic field required
that scattered phenomena be "amalgamate[d] into a coherent category," as the
historian of science Lorraine Daston has argued. In such processes, "criteria of
inclusion and exclusion grow sharper," while intense investigation heightens
visibility and amplifies implications.[159]

The specificity and contingency of this arrangement of legal knowledge
is brought into sharp relief by the academic landscape that immediately

preceded it. Minister Thun's conservative recasting of the law curriculum reflected not only his deep Catholic commitments but also a shifting assessment of political danger. Where, in the Metternich era, natural law appeared pleasingly apolitical, Thun and his colleagues had come to see natural law as a nursery for revolution, with its speculative method tending dangerously toward idealism, individual rights, and the notion of (human) reason as the source of law. Indeed, the Thun-Hohenstein Reforms entailed an abasement of philosophy across the board. Instead, they looked to the influential German jurist Carl Friedrich von Savigny and the German historical school of law, with its genetic understanding of the gradual evolution of law over time, in recasting the Austrian legal curriculum along positivist, historical, and (it was hoped) traditional-conservative lines. Not for the last time, though, an uneasy friction accompanied the import of German theory into the Austrian context. The German historical school understood the ethnic community and its "spirit"—*der Volksgeist*—as the organic and ultimate source of law and order. What could such a theory mean in the Habsburg Empire, where the population was profoundly multiethnic, and the government terrified of nationalism to boot? Thun thus adopted their genetic approach but discarded their theory of law's ultimate source: not the people, *but God*, should be upheld as the origin of all law. The specter of natural law thus crept back in, with Thun's framework incoherently grafting an underlying God-given order onto a historical-positivist approach to law.[160]

Thun's curriculum notwithstanding, the empire's return to constitutional life in 1860 rippled through the law faculty. In 1861, something new appeared in the list of lectures at the University of Vienna: Stubenrauch lectured separately on Austrian constitutional law for the first time and continued to do so until his death in 1865.[161] Wenzel Lustkandl began teaching the same subject as a young adjunct lecturer (*Privatdozent*) in 1864 and then, from 1868, as an associate (*außordentlich*) professor. He spent twenty-six years as an associate because a chair in the subject still did not yet exist. The dramatic new public significance of constitutional law slowly percolated into the official schedule: a new *Rigorosenordnung* in 1872 made "General and Austrian *Staatsrecht*" into an examination subject.[162] However it was only when Thun's curriculum was fundamentally revised by a new Order of Studies in 1893 that Austrian constitutional law became a foundational part of the law degree.

The 1893 Order of Studies was the product of a consultative process. In August 1886, the minister for culture and education announced his intention to reform the law curriculum and invited the views and suggestions of the empire's law faculties. The law faculties of Vienna, Graz, Innsbruck, Prague (both the German and Bohemian universities), Krakau (Kraków), Lemberg (Lviv), and Czernowitz (Chernivtsi) sprang into action: they solicited internal reports, debated their propositions, and voted on proposals. In their detailed 1887 submissions to the minister—which read as a pulse check on legal knowledge

in transformation—opinion on one topic was unanimous: Austrian constitutional law must become a mandatory component of the degree. "It is clear,"
Lustkandl declared, "that in its importance constitutional law stands behind
no other legal discipline."[163]

How quickly things change![164] If no one now doubted the importance of the
subject, ambiguity lingered over its referent. The constitutional law of which
state, exactly? The relevant sovereign self was slippery enough that Vienna's
Theodor Dantscher von Kollesberg penned a whole memorandum on his objection to the designation "Austrian constitutional law." There was no such thing,
he exclaimed. His colleagues were using the term *österreichisches Staatsrecht*
to refer to two, quite separate things: the constitutional law of the Austro-
Hungarian Monarchy (pertaining to the limited "common affairs" that spanned
all the emperor's lands, including Hungary) and that of the Kingdoms and
Lands Represented in the Imperial Parliament (i.e., Cisleithania). These were
two separate constitutional systems valid for differing territories, and to collapse them loosely under one name was erroneous and improper.[165] What is
more, *neither* of those constitutional systems could in fact be called Austrian!
A state of that name existed nowhere in positive law. Following the Settlement
of 1867, the legal name of the empire as a whole was the Austro-Hungarian Monarchy or the Austro-Hungarian Empire, and the correct title for the constitutional
law of its shared affairs was thus Austro-Hungarian imperial-constitutional law
[*Reichs-Staatsrecht*] or constitutional law of the Austro-Hungarian Monarchy.
Similarly, the only technically correct name for the constitutional order of the
German-Slavic lands was constitutional law of the Kingdoms and Lands Represented in the Imperial Parliament. Surely the names of law courses should reflect
the actual law![166] Dantscher von Kollesberg's colleagues may have voted against
his proposed name changes,[167] but his Musilesque memorandum clearly had a
point.[168] Constitutional law was to have its own mandatory course, even if it did
not quite have its own state—or, rather, even if it had too many of them. The
challenges of stabilizing the empire's constitutional form left their trace in the
stabilization of the field devoted to its study.

Where did this new field sit in the landscape of existing and neighboring
knowledges? The law faculties grappled with the demarcation of its boundaries on a number of fronts. Most professors agreed that administrative law
should be cleaved off from constitutional law and studied separately. Some
felt that, increasingly, the internal public law of a state could hardly be understood without some grasp of international law, but their proposals to simultaneously turn international law into an obligatory course did not win majority
support.[169] The rise of the new subject made others seem redundant: Georg
Jellinek argued that constitutional law should entirely replace *Statistik* as
an exam subject. This "superficial," poorly defined field forced students to
immerse themselves in a mass of "dead numerical material" in case they were
asked in their exam about "the number of pigs in Hungary."[170] *Statistik* could

be rezoned as a *Hilfswissenschaft*, an "auxiliary science,"[171] in a welcome rearrangement of primary and secondary knowledge.

Borders needed to be drawn not only horizontally against substantively adjacent material but also vertically up and down the scale of abstraction. In a number of departments, questions arose about the relationship of Austrian constitutional law—understood as a concrete body of specific, written ("positive") laws—to something termed general constitutional law or general state law (*allgemeine Staatsrecht*). The latter comprised the theory and concept of the state in general, ideas about its nature and authority, the variety of forms it could take (federation, confederation, and so on), and the development of these over time.[172] In Lustkandl's description, it made "the interplay between the philosophical systems and positive state developments visible"; it scanned the nature and evolution of the "modern" (European) state and extracted the condensed "essence" and "internal coherence" of its order.[173] (Dantscher von Kollesberg continued his campaign against inaccurate nomenclature in complaining that it should really be called general state *theory* [*allgemeine Staatslehre*] not general state *law*, because there was no such thing as an actual body of law operative in civilized states "in general.")[174] Disagreement emerged over whether Austrian constitutional law should be taught in tandem with this more philosophical field, or whether the two needed to be kept separate. Was it conceptually and pedagogically necessary to connect the particular to the universal, the concrete to the theoretical, or in fact the reverse?

Jellinek argued forcefully that they should be bundled into one course. As in "all other legal fields," he reasoned, "only the firm ground of positive law can give general ideas scholarly purchase and practical significance." The reverse was true, too. Positive law could only be fully comprehended with "reference to the ideas that governed the course of its development as well as comparison with other legal systems." Good pedagogy in particular required the "organic fusion" of the general and the specific.[175] Others took the opposite view. "Every fusion of theory with the positive law impoverishes" either the theory or the law, maintained Franciszek Kasparek in Krakau/Kraków.[176] The state-in-general and the state-in-particular were different methodological objects: to graft them together was to create a confused, composite science.

The Austrian state: Methodologically, pedagogically, could it, should it, appear as its idiosyncratic self *and* as an instance of a generic, platonic "state" at the same time? The final 1893 Order of Studies decided yes—and enshrined general and Austrian constitutional law as a mandatory subject in the second half of the law degree.[177] Named, lectured, required: the empire's constitutional architecture took its place in the landscape of legal fields encountered by every Cisleithanian law student—took its place in the seemingly natural order of things. The 1893 reforms show the different sorts of disciplinary labor involved in its stabilization as a scholarly object. For this newly delimited object presumably had a history—or needed one, to complete and naturalize

its thingification. No surprise, then, that the reform also introduced a mandatory law course, Austrian Imperial History (History of State Formation and
Public Law).[178] During the pre-reform consultation, many of the professors
noted that a class of this sort would have been unthinkable until quite recently
because the requisite scholarship did not exist.[179] It was still now only an
"embryonic field" (*embryonalen Wissenschaft*), noted the Lemberg law faculty.[180] But the paucity of "literary aids" should not be held as a cross against
the field, inveighed Lemberg professor Józef Kaszinca, but instead taken as an
injunction to get to work assembling the fragmented contributions of special-
ists: "These are only attempts, only incomplete and separated parts, disjecta
membra, of a whole; but is it not time to systematically produce this whole?"[181]
It was hardly an unattractive job, as "perhaps no state in Europe offers such
rewarding terrain for a comparative legal history as Austria, which unites in
itself almost all important elements of European legal development."[182]

The legal history of the empire needed to be bundled up into a singular
thing—mirroring the legal amalgamation of the state itself. The connection
between state making and history writing was not lost on the government.
Already a decade earlier—in May 1876—the Ministry for Culture and Education had announced a prize "for the best textbook or handbook of Austrian
imperial and legal history," worth 2,000 Austrian gulden in silver. The work
should cover "the history of the empire with particular attention to diplomatic
and political history, that is, those public acts and events through which the
monarchy grew over the course of time into its current territorial possessions"
as well as the development of public and private law.[183] The announcement
gave instructions that not so subtly documented the imperatives of the present:
the histories of the empire's many peoples were to be covered in detail only
from the time of their incorporation, and "Hungarian imperial and legal history" was to feature only to the extent that it was "necessary for the history
of the monarchy as such."[184] Current sovereign parameters would find their
mirror in history. The book, moreover, should be oriented toward the goal of
"elevating Austrian imperial and legal history to an independent academic
discipline." Accordingly, the author should pay particular attention to the
"completeness of this field of knowledge [*die Geschlossenheit dieses Wissens-
gebietes*] and the independence of legal development inside the borders of the
monarchy."[185] To establish its reputation as a bona fide field of scholarship,
it had to be closed, coherent, self-sufficient—something like the epistemic
equivalent of sovereignty.

The 1876 prize competition failed. But the 1893 reform provided new
impetus, and in 1895 the University of Vienna historian Alfons Huber supplied
the needed textbook with his *Austrian Imperial History: History of State-
Building and Public Law*.[186] History's narrative form immediately sparked
problems. When should the story begin? From when, in legal terms, was
the Habsburg Empire itself? Its piecemeal formation over centuries offered

no clear-cut birthday. One plausible candidate was 1526—the year that the Habsburg dynasty, until then in possession of a modest assortment of alpine hereditary lands, acquired the crowns of Hungary and Bohemia. But Huber demurred. On "the question of the beginning of 'Austrian imperial history,'" he wrote, he could not restrict himself to the time since 1526 because that would mean missing the "creation and development of the most important factors in public law" like the estates, the aristocracy, the peasantry, and the estates constitutions (*ständische Verfassungen*).[187] So Huber's history stretched away into the deep past before anything recognizably like the imperial polity had emerged. More formalistically minded scholars, hewing to the letter of the law, could make plausible cases for a far more limited chronology, dating the state's sovereign completion to (for example) the final disappearance of the intertangled Holy Roman Empire in 1806.[188] The debate over the "start date" of Habsburg imperial sovereignty outlived its eventual end date, continuing in different guises into the interwar years.[189]

Making "Modern" Legal Knowledge

It was not only the new lecture course in imperial legal history that required new textbooks and official stories. Constitutional law itself was in the midst of a self-conscious formalization across Central Europe. Its consolidation in the Cisleithanian curriculum coincided with broader methodological transformations customarily summarized by the term *positivism*. The nineteenth-century rise of the natural sciences (and physics in particular) as epistemological models worth emulating spurred a widespread rejection of speculative knowledge in favor of an exclusive focus on the material, empirical ("positive") world, its causal laws, and that which could be deduced from experience. For legal scholarship, calls for a new positivist, "scientific" approach entailed not only restricting one's gaze to written, positive law but also discerning how laws formed part of an interlocked, systematic whole. The names of the German jurists Carl Friedrich von Gerber and Paul Laband became synonymous with a strictly "juristic" method—in contrast especially to the genetic approach of the historical school—that was ostensibly free from ideological or pre-positivist preconditions and that reconstructed German constitutional law as a normative-logical order.[190] Laws should not simply be collected, assembled side by side, but built into a complete and gapless *system*. Particular laws may have holes, Laband reasoned, but the notion of holes in the general legal order was an "unthinkable concept." It could tolerate holes "just as little as the order of nature itself."[191] There were no gaps in nature, only in our knowledge of it. Similarly, underdeveloped areas of law simply lay waiting to be "discovered."[192] These positivists may have severed the positive, man-made legal order from divine and natural right, but they endowed it with the perfection of God's natural one.

These disciplinary developments resonated strongly in the Austrian curriculum debates. The professorial council in Czernowitz explicitly cited Gerber's fashioning of constitutional law into "a complete and unified field" that mastered the whole as much as the tiny details.[193] The 1855 curriculum, under which individual pieces of public law were treated disjointedly and descriptively in different classes, was now inadequate, argued the Krakau/Kraków professor Józef Kleczyński. Constitutional and administrative law was to become "a genuine legal science [*eine wirkliche Rechtswissenschaft*] and not a collection of positive regulations. At the threshold of the university stand two new scientific branches and [they] claim their right of admission into the palace of sciences."[194]

That the first *textbook* of Austrian constitutional law presented the first "systematic" *treatment* of Austrian constitutional law was thus a product not only of the textbook genre but also of this broader methodological conjuncture. Published in 1883 (prior to the curriculum reforms), its author was the prolific German-Bohemian law professor and politician Josef Ulbrich (1843–1910). Ulbrich's life was tightly bound up with Charles University in Prague, where he studied then taught then served as rector, all as the institution was galvanized by Czech-German conflict and (in 1882) split in two. Unmarried and "often more than simply dressed," Ulbrich, who in earlier life "never looked very young, but in later life never very old," was a prominent Prague personality.[195] He innovated consciously. "A complete overview of Austrian constitutional law is a long-felt need," he reflected in the preface to his *Textbook of Austrian Constitutional Law*. The work was designed to meet the requirements of university study, "for which until now no handbook existed." It should equally serve as "a welcome guide and convenient reference work for practice."[196] May it be received sympathetically and its limitations excused, he entreated, for it was "the *first* attempt in an until-now undeveloped scholarly field."[197]

This field could only be transformed into a serious scholarly endeavor through the organization of dispersed pieces of law into a logical whole and the application of an exclusively juridical method. "A scientific presentation of constitutional law cannot be a cloudy mixture of philosophical, historical and statistical notes," Ulbrich sermonized. "Rather, it must handle its material juridically in a strict system."[198] Accordingly, the book did not proceed historically, tracing the evolution of constitutional organization over time, but instead proceeded logically, beginning from first principles and building outward from there. First, a definition of *Staatsrecht* itself was required. He then moved systematically through the "elements" of state (territory, population), the organs of state (the first being the emperor!), the administrative structure, the nature of government and legislature, and so on, over some eight hundred pages. Clearly, fashioning the state's law into a systematic-logical whole worked to buttress the empire's apparent unity and coherence.

Lifted outside of its jagged historical becoming, it was presented as a natural, finished fact. The consolidation and stabilization of knowledge looked a lot like the consolidation and stabilization of the state itself. That positivism thereby worked as a methodological insulation against historical-legal pluralism, nationalism, and other centrifugal forces—not to mention contradictions of more conceptual variety—echoes in the tribute Ulbrich received from his colleague Ernst Mischler after his death: "He was the jurist who taught *the* law, not *laws*."[199] Law, state, and knowledge—all in the singular.

The century's end saw the appearance of a host of new knowledge tools for the newborn field—and the state it studied. Ulbrich and Mischler collaborated on perhaps the grandest example. In 1890–92, while Mischler was Ulbrich's colleague in Prague (he subsequently moved to Graz), they hatched a wildly ambitious plan. Over the next decade they produced the monumental *Austrian State Dictionary: Handbook of All Austrian Public Law*—a complete alphabetical inventory of the state. The second edition of 1905–9, comprising contributions from some two hundred authors, stretched over four volumes and four thousand pages. The forty-three entries under "A"—including *Adelsrecht, Agrarverfassung, Arbeitsrecht, Archive, Armenpflege, Ausländer, Auslieferung, Ausnahmszustand, Auswanderung*, and *Autonomie*—consumed 383 pages.[200] Mischler explained their method: "We first constructed an exhaustive, highly detailed system of constitutional and administrative law, then divided it into monographic parts, searched for the right authors" (a difficult task, given the undeveloped nature of many subfields) and then "corresponded with them about the delimitation as against other areas, and so through our work [we] melded together"—a close and protracted collaboration that "counts among my happiest memories."[201]

By both design and necessity, many of the experts enlisted as contributors came from the world of practice: it was a manual of the state by and for scholars studying it *and* bureaucrats administering it. A standard work for both, it dissolved the distinction between knowing/analyzing and doing/governing. Mischler and Ulbrich had undertaken such a project—with its bid for a gapless mastery over the empire's public law—not without misgivings, they admitted in the preface to the first edition, especially in light of the "idiosyncratic conditions of our monarchy."[202] Indeed, the tension between dual sovereignty, on the one hand, and totalizing knowledge, on the other, could not be entirely ignored. Mischler and Ulbrich were proud of the fact that their "great unified work" encompassed not only the *Austrian* and common *Austro-Hungarian* legal material but the *Hungarian* as well.[203] Yet they felt compelled to clarify implications and soothe sensitivities, lest a unified compendium be taken as a surreptitious assertion of unified sovereignty. The dictionary included the public law of the Hungarian lands, they reassured readers, "of course with a constant emphasis on their constitutional and administrative independence."[204]

Thinking from Here:
Georg Jellinek in Search of Better Theory

Buttressed by new courses, professorships, experts, textbooks, handbooks, compendiums (and even a handy *Catechism* that condensed it all into 180 questions and answers), the legal order of the Austro-Hungarian Empire had well and truly arrived as an object of knowledge.[205] But did the arrival of this new object not affect the knowledge itself? That is, how did the empire's "idiosyncratic conditions"—which gave pause even to the most confident, centralist positivists—sit with the existing categories of legal thought and theories of state?

It rendered them nonsensical, was the clear-eyed answer given by a young Georg Jellinek. Long before he became one of the most influential jurists of the German-speaking world, back when he was an adjunct lecturer in Vienna angling for a permanent job, Jellinek published a bold, expansive work under the title *Die Lehre von den Staatenverbindungen* (literally, the theory of state "connections," of states joined together, usually translated as *The Theory of State Unions* or *The Theory of State Federations*). It appeared in 1882, the year before Ulbrich's textbook. Like Ulbrich, he thought jurisprudence needed to become more scientifically rigorous and advocated a positivist approach; like Ulbrich, he invoked a self-consciously "juridical" method that strove toward systematic knowledge, logically ordered, coherent, and unified. Yet the two works configured the interface between knowledge and state in diametric ways. Where Ulbrich looked to bed Austria-Hungary down in the familiar, authoritative genres of field making and state making (textbooks and dictionaries and manuals with their optics of gapless competence and settled knowledge), Jellinek thought "idiosyncratic" cases like Austria-Hungary ripped up the settled categories and exposed the poverty of legal theory itself. One needed new theories, even new sorts of knowledge, to make sense of such cases, which is just what Jellinek set out to create. His scholarship would transform the philosophy of law and would leave him arguably the most prominent German-speaking jurist at the century's turn—a story I follow through to its conclusion in chapter 4.

Austrian constitutional law was still in its earliest infancy when a seventeen-year-old Georg Jellinek first stepped into the Vienna law faculty, having finished his high school exams—younger than most—at Vienna's Akademische Gymnasium in 1867, the birth year of dual sovereignty. His name likely raised eyebrows. Jellinek's father, Adolf, happened to be Vienna's most famous rabbi. Just two years earlier, he had become head rabbi at the central *Stadttempel*. Born in Drslawitz (Drslavice) in Moravia in 1820, Adolf combined a wide-ranging secular education with a deep immersion in Jewish learning and philosophy. Full of the optimism of the era of emancipation, and leaving orthodoxy behind, Adolf espoused a "modern," liberal, learned Reform Judaism and made noteworthy contributions to the critical Wissenschaft des Judentums movement.[206] Georg grew up in a classic assimilated (and not terribly religious) *bildungsbürgerlich* milieu, surrounded by his parents' love of German *Kultur*. He revealingly described his mother, Rosalie—not his rabbi father—as the "most religious" person he had known, but not because of traditional observance. Under "religion" he understood a sharpened "consciousness, conveyed through feelings, of the existence and [of] the uninterrupted, unmediated workings of divine powers in the course of nature and human destinies."[207] Rosalie "overflowed" with this heightened consciousness. She was inwardly "indifferent," he claimed, to the "frozen forms and customs grown meaningless" that defined the religious practice of many. Instead, she had a "deep sense of nature, soaked through with poetry"; she was "grateful for every sun beam, every aromatic breeze that coursed down over her from the mountain forest."[208]

Georg would remain extremely close to Rosalie—just nineteen years his senior—for life. Tellingly, friends and colleagues described his own mind and personality in remarkably similar terms to those in which he paid tribute to his mother. "The formations of historical humanity stood before his mind with plastic vividness," reflected the neo-Kantian philosopher Wilhelm Windelband, with whom Jellinek's career would become intricately entwined. "There was a piece of the poet in him," and not just because he occasionally penned nice verse. "Everywhere, not only in the expositions of his books, he revealed the drive to see things in his own way and to shape them intellectually anew."[209] Jellinek had inherited Rosalie's acute responsiveness to the world: "Precisely because of the rich many-sidedness of his inner life, he had an intellectual yieldingness [*Nachgiebigkeit*], an almost feminine softness in his being, that likely also made itself felt in the assessment of academic theories."[210]

The intensity and subtlety with which he saw and felt was startling to his new wife, Camilla Wertheim, when they departed for their two-month honeymoon in Italy in 1883. Traveling with Jellinek, one could not move too quickly: his "tender brain" rebelled against so much stimulation. Everywhere his attention landed exploded into an array of implications. "What he saw in details immediately conjured up a temporal or spatial whole," she explained. "The source of a stream allowed its entire course to appear before him, so that his mind's eye saw all the lands through which it flowed."[211] Suffused with imagination, he could not bear to fix plans, appointments, or destinations in advance, which Camilla found trying. "At every train junction he had to have the reassuring feeling that he could turn left just as much as right." "This latent 'possibility,'" she reflected, "played a large role for him in general, regardless of whether he used the possibility or not."[212]

That dynamic responsiveness to the world around him made Jellinek's intellectual biography a portrait in miniature of the nineteenth-century history of knowledge. Philosophy was his first—and lifelong—passion. He possessed that "philosophical drive," as Windelband saw it, toward the unity of the whole: he wanted to understand the "ultimate coherences" that tied everything together.[213] No surprise, then, that as a student he declared allegiance to the lofty, total systems of German high idealism, penning ardent odes to the "glittering flight" of Kant and Hegel and denouncing Austria's insularity from these epochal departures and anti-intellectual focus on the practical disciplines.[214] Bored with his law lectures in Vienna, he had escaped to read philosophy in Leipzig, where he would write a dissertation on Leibniz and Schopenhauer, laud the former's "optimism" and critique the latter's "pessimism," and condemn the intellectual culture back at home for its lack of that particular "philosophical consciousness that knots all human sciences into a great web," as well as the "moral courage" to earnestly pursue the "pure truth."[215] But back in Vienna studying for his law exams, Jellinek experienced an intellectual conversion. He discovered the new discipline of sociology, and with it the intellectual revolution of positivism, then reshaping disciplines across the board. In seeking to grasp society "as a whole," sociology reminded him of philosophy's attempt to grasp nature as a whole.[216] He wrote excitedly to his best friend, Victor Ehrenberg, of his intention to contribute to this "science of the future."[217]

The book that emerged out of this conversion, *The Socio-ethical Meaning of Justice, Injustice, and Punishment*, charted a bold, progressive approach to crime and punishment focused not on individual guilt or transgression but on social objectives and social responsibility: the content of the ethical, he maintained, changed over time in connection with the evolution of the particular society in question.[218] Even more striking than the substance of the argument, though, was its methodological architecture. Jellinek had produced a strident manifesto about knowledge itself. Attempts to found a scientific (*wissenschaftlich*) rather than speculative philosophy, he now argued, had hitherto focused on the natural sciences: in contrast, the disciplines that dealt with "our psychic and social life"—including ethics, national economy, and the theory of law, state, and society—all awaited that penetrating inquiry into their deepest foundations, down to where their base elements could be "broken down no further."[219] Like the natural sciences, they must resist the temptation "to explain phenomena from abstract concepts floating above things"—must resist that "Icarus-flight into the empty space of aprioristic thinking"—and restrict themselves to what could be known from actual experience.[220] Farewell to Hegel, and hello to Comte: a positivist philosophy was the only way forward.[221]

Dramatically, at the last moment, the Vienna law faculty refused to accept Jellinek's 1878 book as a habilitation, the second dissertation required to teach.[222] Yes, the faculty were socially conservative; yes, they were skeptical about philosophical approaches to law in general.[223] But the real problem was anti-Semitism. In the precise years that Jellinek was trying to launch his academic career, a virulent new wave of anti-Semitism swept across Europe. As late as 1872, when the regulations were changed, Jews (as such) could not even complete an Austrian law degree: one had to be a Christian to sit for the exam in canon/church law (*Kirchenrecht*), and without the exam one could not graduate. Jewish law students thus tended to convert shortly before their final exams.[224] Even where the pressure was less direct, baptism had long served as a reasonably effective means to circumnavigate social and professional discrimination. But the new anti-Semitism was increasingly shaped by "scientific" discourses of race and blood, which meant that discrimination could not be circumnavigated, however imperfectly, by something like conversion.[225] With his final exams in 1873–74, Jellinek in fact numbered among the very first (nonconverted) Austrian Jews to receive a law degree. For this rabbi's son to then additionally seek the habilitation, the legal scholar Thomas Olechowski imagines, must have been almost too much for many of the Catholic-conservative professors to stomach.[226] It proved the beginning of an extremely tense relationship: they made his professional path difficult at every step of the way. If they grudgingly accepted another book (on the classification of wrongs) as his habilitation, they also blocked the extension of his teaching qualification (*venia legendi*) to include international law. The book they rejected, *The Legal Nature of State Treaties* (1880), presented a holistic new theory of international law based on the idea of "autolimitation," or the state's capacity to bind itself.[227] It was an argument, Martti Koskenniemi has written, "to which the whole subsequent theoretical discussion on the matter appears as hardly more than a footnote."[228]

This time Jellinek hardly drew breath: in response, he turned around and immediately immersed himself in a still-larger work that would become his *Theory of State Unions*. On all sides, the stakes had grown immense. He hoped it might secure not only the international law teaching qualification but also an associate (*außerordentlich*) professorship, a salaried position, which he desperately needed—because he had fallen in love. Georg and Camilla had sealed their engagement in the hills overlooking the Danube at Vienna's northern edge in May 1880, but they could not marry until he had a fixed income. He would set himself a daily quota, Camilla remembered: once three pages were full with text, "then away with paper and pens and hasten to bride."[229] It became a shared labor (of love): they spent the winter of 1881–82 joyfully working together on the manuscript corrections, which doubled, she confessed, "as a welcome occasion to gain my parents' permission for more time together."[230]

To these charged personal and professional equations, Jellinek added sky-high intellectual ambitions. In *Theory of State Unions*, he announced the inadequacy of all existing theories of state and sovereignty. He diagnosed the epistemological reasons for their impotence, and—should we be surprised?—laid out his own complete theory in their place. His book represents a pivotal point of intersection for two large stories—two stories crucial for the present book. If Jellinek was thinking "from here," trying to make sense of the curious sovereign formations in which he lived and worked, he also connected this task explicitly to problems of knowledge in general. His analysis grew out of his own intellectual journey through idealist philosophy to the empiricism of the social sciences: it was bound up with questions of induction and deduction, the general and the particular, categories and types, and the possibilities and limits of human reason.

The problem could be clearly stated. Legal theorists and philosophers defined sovereignty by its singularity. Their reasoning began with the *Einheitsstaat*—the unitary state—as model, measure, and norm. Yet across the whole domain of the "German sciences of state—in Germany, in Austria-Hungary, and Switzerland—the unitary state is not the form in which the life-course of states is being realized."[231] Theory remained blind and deaf to the compound sovereign formations in this part of the world, a disjuncture only made sharper by recent developments like the Austro-Hungarian Settlement of 1867 and the formation of the (federal) German Empire in 1871.[232] Running separate and parallel to that doctrinal literature, meanwhile, the detailed jurisprudence on questions of public law focused narrowly on the positive materials and thereby made the opposite mistake, uncritically clinging to the given and never reaching for higher concepts.[233] "Deduction from the concepts and induction from the phenomena take different paths," he complained, "so that convergence becomes impossible for both of them."[234]

As a result, legal theory possessed no means of comprehending the conglomerate states that surrounded him—it simply lacked the necessary concepts. Its inadequacy produced deformed lines of argument. Sometimes, the concrete instances were interpreted as incomplete realizations of a valid norm. So, state unions could be depicted as the "juridically incomprehensible transitional phase of states in a process of unification or deunification," on their way toward a large unitary state or breaking up into smaller unitary states. In such a view, nonunitary states were by definition *provisional* formations—and thus unimportant for theory—caught midstream in the normative arc of history that led inevitably to sovereign unity. Or, alternatively, a state union was labeled an "irregular formation," a state sui generis, whose existence could be conceded without threatening the validity of the norm. Or, on other occasions, the "logical possibility" of whichever genre of state union was flatly denied.[235]

Insulated from these "irregular, ephemeral, transitory, juridically unfathomable phenomena," legal theory continued to espouse definitions of state and sovereignty that turned on an indivisible supreme power.[236] "Because," for the theorists, "only the typical has true value; what does not carry the traits of the type is not worth serious scientific consideration." Why could some sorts of states generate models and theories, and not others? It made

Jellinek incredulous: "That not only correct formations, but also malformations are capable of scientific study, and that this knowledge is significant for the healthy life of states, like pathology is for physiology—this thought does not appear even in passing."[237] True, one could not avoid beginning an inquiry with premises and a priori categories, but these higher concepts needed to be adjusted in light of the concrete material so as to avoid the mistake of taking one particular entity, with all its contingencies, as the paradigm against which to measure all the others.[238] Far from academic games, these ways of thinking had detrimental effects on politics itself. "With the interpretation of a state formation as an irregular one," he lamented, "politics is immediately given the task of clearing away the irregularity, so that reality is eventually shaped according to the scholastic concept—the rationalism of theory inexorably entails the rationalism of fact, [and] unhistorical thinking [entails] antihistorical action."[239] The standard theory turned conglomerate states into problems that needed to be solved, into crooked deviations that needed to be corrected. Its logic seeped out into political life and structured the terms of debate, leading everyone to try and remake sovereignty in its image.

What would it look like to instead build theories from the ground up—to build typologies of statehood that began with the compound empire-states of Central Europe? Why was political life in these states forced to scramble after normative models, rather than the other way around? No—the base concepts of legal philosophy needed to be revised. To properly grasp what happened, legally, when two or more states joined together into a larger whole, one needed to reexamine the nature of sovereignty itself and build alternate state typologies on a new, factual footing—which is what Jellinek's *Theory of State Unions* set out to do. He did not doubt, at this stage, that legal theory *could* make sense of the jungle of actually existing sovereign formations—did not doubt that the world of states could be ordered into a coherent, logical whole. One just needed better theory—a philosophy more responsive to facts. As we will see in chapter 4, that epistemological confidence would not survive the century unscathed.

State Species: Taxonomies of Self and World

According to Jellinek, the first step was a new definition of sovereignty capable of encompassing and making sense of all cases. Drawing on the theory of autolimitation he had developed in his book on state treaties, he argued that the defining characteristic of a sovereign state was that it could be bound only by itself—be limited only through its own will. All other dimensions and explanations flowed from this. Precisely because a sovereign state had unlimited final authority over itself, it could decide to bind itself to another and give up some of its rights. It could decide to let another state exercise some of its prerogatives and still remain a sovereign state—because it had the (exclusive) power to make that decision. Earlier theorists had tied themselves into knots diagnosing the "doubled, divided, broken, modified, [or] fragmented sovereignty" in state unions of different sorts. In contrast, Jellinek argued that no such modifiers were necessary (or logically coherent): as long as a sovereign state had given up those rights or prerogatives through a treaty or contract—that is, by its own free will and in its own name, not coerced by a higher power—then its sovereignty remained complete and untarnished, whatever union it was part of. Suddenly one could make sense of how both halves of the Austro-Hungarian Empire could be fully sovereign despite being joined together. If one state was in a position to *impose* an obligation on another, in contrast, then the latter was *not* sovereign: it may still be a state, but it did not possess sovereignty.[240]

This definition unlocked a new world of connections and explanations. But it alone was not enough. The conceptual opacity of state unions had an additional cause. Scholars had generally tackled the problem by looking at a single case, or maybe a handful. But it was impossible to gain a properly scientific understanding from such a small sample size that inevitably cast only a particular light on the problem. To sort the essential from the incidental, one needed to examine *all* instances of the phenomenon.[241] A state could not understand itself in isolation. No one had attempted such an undertaking before, Jellinek observed. Small wonder, perhaps: the material was, of course, immense. Once one looked, it became clear that the unitary state was not actually the norm *anywhere*. Beyond the German Empire, the Swiss confederation, and the state formations united by a common ruler like Austria-Hungary and Sweden-Norway, there was the United States of America (to which he devoted extensive attention)[242] and the federations of Mexico and the Argentine republic; then there was the Ottoman Empire and "the whole Orient," rich with vassal states and conglomerate polities. "Even among the great European isolated unitary states," he observed, "there are scarce few who do not possess suzerainty or protection over more or less civilized and state-organized ethnic groups in other parts of the world."[243] Suddenly, then, one had to survey almost all of the globe: the scope of the problem stretched out across the Americas and all through the colonial world. In this way, Jellinek's approach depathologized the ornate, compound sovereignty of a state like Austria-Hungary *and* opened new connections to the rest of the world. Anticipating much contemporary scholarship, he presented conglomerate statehood as the global norm, not a problematic anomaly. His approach also implicitly exposed the cognitive dissonance involved in Western European legal philosophy, which continued to preach the gospel of unitary sovereignty even as the selfsame states amassed vast empires where sovereignty was anything but singular or unified.

Jellinek sorted this total picture into a new elaborate typology of state unions.[244] It could not be fuzzy—if law wanted to earn the mantel of a true science. The concept categories we seek, he wrote, "must be sharp, deter-mined, firm, and strictly demarcated from one another." "Confederations" could not blend into "federal states" at the fringes: proper "legal terms are always square-edged, the blurring of one into the other would be the death of science [*Wissenschaft*], the death of legal life."[245] Moreover, it would be all too easy, he warned, to sort the material according to familiar organizing princi-ples. That would be to commit the same methodological mistake of relying on a priori categories: "Only a thorough examination of each form of [state] con-nection can make it clear which category it must be classified in, and only then in conclusion can the two genera and their species be compared."[246] A global chart of sovereign species: perhaps a high point in law's nineteenth-century intoxication with the ethos, ambition, and epistemological optimism of the natural sciences.[247]

Tellingly, Austria-Hungary had to be entered into this typology *twice*. The union of Austria and Hungary clearly had a *juridical* character and not merely a historical one (one of Jellinek's key distinctions). Its shared insti-tutions, further, meant it belonged in the category of unions with their own *organs* (another categorical marker). Specifically, it constituted a "real union" in which both halves remained sovereign states: they had contracted of their own free will and in their own name, and the powers of the common organs were delegated from each state (and not the other way around).[248] But there was a *second* catalog entry for the Austrian half of the empire. Yes, the lat-ter was a sovereign state in union with Hungary, but was it not *itself* a union of multiple lands? The Kingdoms and Lands Represented in the Imperial Parliament furnished a "most excellent example," Jellinek determined, of a state union that now had a merely historical-political character rather than a juridical one. It had evolved from originally separate parts into a unitary state, however decentralized. Yes, the Austrian kingdoms and lands possessed wide-reaching autonomy and many state-like prerogatives (including their own financial organs), but they were now clearly under the authority and supervi-sion of the central state, so that one could not speak of them scientifically as "states."[249] As states, they were legally "extinct, destroyed."[250] Other authors were confused in describing Cisleithania as a "real union." The more apposite designation was a "Gradual Growing-into-One of Different States over the Course of History."[251]

A dual state, ordered twice over—Jellinek's typology may stand out for its global scope and analytical creativity, but the taxonomic imperative seized the field as a whole. Almost everyone working on Austrian constitutional law offered their own categorization of the Danube monarchy, thrashing out dif-ferent criteria and critiquing that of his colleagues.[252] Hermann Bidermann pegged the overarching empire as a *Staatenstaat*, "state of states," in which "at least two other state authorities, though imperfect, are active" (with the "at least" a charming crack in the veneer of typological certainty).[253] According to Dantscher von Kollesberg, it was a "monarchical federal state."[254] Ulbrich characterized it as a "real union of two constitutionally and administratively independent states."[255] Everyone was searching for the right legal name—as though it might work like a key that unlocked buried coherence.

In many senses, the classificatory impulse constituted a different face of the broader codification of imperial sovereignty. Like the constitutions themselves, typologies were attempts to describe, codify, and master the state form, to tame it and settle it into clear postulates and boxes. As we see so strongly in both Jellinek and Ulbrich, that conceptual codification of the particular state was closely bound up with the transformation of law as a discipline: to be a proper science, law needed to find ways of logically ordering all its material into complete pictures without gaps or contradictions. It was no coincidence that Ulbrich opened his own monograph on *The Legal Nature of the Austro-Hungarian Monarchy* by tying together the state's classification with the mission of "science" as a whole: "in the last instance, all sciences [*Wissenschaften*] have as their object the revision and purification of the concepts of the common circle of thought."[256] Defining states went hand in hand with the work of refining concepts: they were bound together in a process of mutual distillation and crystallization. Concepts and categories were to be washed clean of the nonscientific as well as the nonlegal.

The State Unboxed

Not everyone bought into this codification craze. The prominent late imperial jurist Ludwig Gumplowicz (1838–1909), a Graz-based scholar from Krakau/Kraków and an important early sociologist, doubted the fruitfulness of these quests for master concepts. "It is wasted effort," he declared, "to want to box states into species and types like one does with plants and animals, and then to want to determine in which rubric the particular state belongs." Austria, he observed skeptically, was an "adored object of such academic speculation."[257] The categorical impulse clutched at shadows: "This method is incorrect and purposeless for the reason that states are individual formations and, in the creation of the individualities, history repeats itself just as little as nature." Austria's current constitutional formation was the product of an idiosyncratic historical development that found expression in the Settlement laws of 1867. "This relationship," he counseled, "cannot be depicted with a doctrinal term"; rather, it could only be understood as a restive compromise between competing forces.[258] If one began searching for the true "legal nature" of the monarchy, the project spiraled onward ad infinitum: "In these things there is neither a court of appeal nor a mathematical proof."[259]

It was a project without an end point, a false methodology that had no reliable way of proving its conclusions. Could a state formation like Austria-Hungary in fact only be grasped in historical terms, and not by juridical logic at all? Unsurprisingly, historians made that case. The important Hungarian historian Henrik Marczali (1856–1940) argued that "the making of our constitutional law—legally just as valid as any other—has not proceeded logically or rationally in any direction. It is the existing constitutional history [*Es ist die bestehende Verfassungsgeschichte*]. As such it can only be understood and explicated genetically." He nobly offered his services: "This perspective compelled me, the historian, to enter into the solution of this difficult task."[260] The Hungarian constitution required an archaeology of the present, of the history that was not expired or properly past.

But many jurists, too, reached the same conclusion. The Budapest-born, Vienna-trained legal scholar Felix Stoerk (1851–1908) presented a thoughtful critique of the new systematic jurisprudence and its taxonomic aspirations soon after he had left Vienna for a chair in Greifswald. As products of infinitely complex social life, the formations of public law, not least the "arbitrary mosaic of our continental constitutionalism," could not be slotted into the "syllogism-chains" of private law.[261] "Every product of communal life is subject to such an abundance of forces operating concentrically but changing in their intensity, and thus becomes in so many ways dependent on historical conditions," he reasoned.[262] As a result, "the incalculable diversity of individual features here mostly makes the production of abstract formulas impossible and thereby also generally forbids the subsumption of factual forms under abstract types."[263] How could these intricate, layered objects be tamed and ordered by logical categories? He was quite sure it was impossible: "The interplay of possible permutations eludes every measurement, every approximate calculation."[264]

This conviction led Stoerk to critique the superficial way in which his law colleagues used and understood "history." Historical examination was "not some mere element of ornamentation, some external aid," useful for determining the motivations of the legislator but then safely discarded.[265] Historical complexity was not *outside* the law, a background setting for law, but rather manifestly the thing itself. The past, he wrote, was not "merely the transitory but rather the immanent root cause of the present."[266] Thus, in public law, "historical-genetic reconstruction" was the only "surrogate" for the method of "logical generalization" deployed in other domains of inquiry.[267] The development of general concepts must be secondary to historical analysis. To do the reverse, and prioritize those abstractions, was to presume that there were "fixed criteria for certainty" against which one might judge the shifting historical life of the state.[268] Did not the very notion of abstract, scientific categories for law imply a vantage point outside the flow of time? These "higher categories" represented a muddleheaded return to styles of reasoning from (now discredited) natural law.[269] Here again we see the argument that there was no historically neutral place from which to grasp and order a world of states that showed itself to be in constant flux. The quest for a science of states, Stoerk suggested, was a fruitless quest to escape the palpable historicity of state life.

Friedrich Tezner—not coincidentally a student of Stoerk's—offered a still-sharper critique of taxonomy as a knowledge tool for constitutional law. He too felt that the invocation of logical, scientific categories involved a misguided epistemological confidence. In assessing "the possibility of exactly accommodating the real phenomena of state life under the doctrinal concepts of constitutional law," he wrote, one could not forget that "firm, undisputed foundations for a constitutional *science* have not been found to this day."[270] The logical-doctrinal method simply did not work: practitioners ignored or downplayed what did not fit their crisp schemas and artificially cleared "everything lacking order and system out of the way." What is more, the taxonomic approach produced only superficial understanding, an empty sort of knowledge: "It counts stamens according to the instructions of the Linnaean system and believes thereby to have perceived the nature of plants," Tezner sniffed.[271]

The case of Austria-Hungary exposed the intellectual poverty of this method better than any. Where for Jellinek his home state proved that jurisprudence needed new categories and concepts, for Tezner, in contrast, it proved that abstract categories of that sort were a fool's gold. What type of state was it? The answer shifted depending on where in the state one looked. Chameleon-like, it appeared in different guises in different domains: if one examined the right of review for military command, for instance, the monarchy presented itself as a "monarchical unitary state"; in light of the constitutional legislature for common affairs, with its strange form of joining, it seemed like a "middle thing between monarchical state union and a federal state, which one could call dyarchy or double monarchy."[272] Clearly, "doctrinaire types form only a very raw yardstick" for the analysis of states, Tezner argued.[273] The stiffness and fixity lauded by Jellinek were precisely the problem. Among its many weaknesses, "theory has least of all a measure for degrees of mixture. It cannot determine more than the elements being mixed. It is unable to articulate degrees of difference, it has no terminology for the interaction and interlocking of the legal ideas that determine state formation."[274] In his analysis, the attempt to make legal knowledge more rigorous and more scientific had only made it useless—ever-more alienated from the realities and needs of state life: "With logical formalism one does not found states, with logical formalism one does not create institutions either. One cannot think the constitutional monarchy through *logically* to the end without arriving at anarchy and the dissolution of the state."[275]

CHAPTER THREE

Fictional States

LANDS AND NATIONS

*What do you call a state that no longer is one? • Bohemia
and Moravia claim they are still themselves • Facts are
meaningless to Karel Kramář • Sovereignty never dies • Some
newly announced rights go in search of a subject • The
Austro-Marxists find international law on the inside of the
state • At the League of Nations, Hitler's National Socialists
invoke an old-new idea*

IF A STATE DIED, would you know? Georg Jellinek was not so sure. "The demise
of an existing state can be doubtful," he warned. There were cases "where, in
the course of historical development, an independent state grows into another,
merges with another." By the time he wrote these lines in the last days of the
nineteenth century, anti-Semitism had chased him out of the Habsburg lands;
what is more, he was attempting a "general theory" of the state, an Olympian
account of the state as such. But this piece of doctrine came tied to one particular place: Austria. The slow and gradual formation of the Austrian state,
he observed, "was not accompanied by an explicit declaration of the de-state-
ification [*Entstaatlichung*] of its parts." Agreements like the Pragmatic Sanction of 1713 may have bound the lands indissolubly together, but they did not
establish a singular unified state. "The moment at which the Bohemian lands
entirely lost their state character," Jellinek observed, "cannot be determined with
complete certainty, especially since the sharp concept of the state, which strives
to remove any ambiguity, is still foreign to the eighteenth century." At some point,
Bohemia's stateness had gone missing in history—though it was impossible to
say when exactly. And maybe that was not even true? After all, "the existence of

an independent Hungarian state" looked doubtful countless times over the centuries, and only the Settlement of 1867 "secured it beyond any doubt."[1]

What a provocation for theory! It was already hard enough to square the empire as a whole with categories of state and sovereignty (as we have seen). But the same categorical fog hung over its constituent parts, too. What were these entities, the historical lands? Clearly, prior to Habsburg rule, they stood as independent kingdoms, duchies, margravates. But now? Their statehood had never been expressly abolished; perhaps—*perhaps*—it had just faded out, somehow, somewhen. It was hard to be sure because no one in the long winding history of imperial state formation had described their actions in those terms. On the contrary, the Habsburgs had studiously reiterated their deference to the lands' traditional rights and prerogatives, over and over again, adorned with all the requisite gilded solemnities. Jellinek understood the problem: the modern category of the state—with its hard edges, its gravity, and its drive toward totality—remained foreign to history's early modern protagonists. They had different logics, languages, and practices of sovereignty that had no need of the specific definitional and jurisdictional clarity that modern statecraft and modern law now demanded.

"What is a state if it is not a sovereign?" Clifford Geertz asked a century later in his "reflections on politics in complicated places." His eyes were trained on "less sorted-out polities in less shaped-up places" where the Western models did not work, where there was talk of "quasi-states," "failed states," "micro-states," "tribes with flags," and "regimes of unreality."[2] To paraphrase Sheldon Pollock, sometimes European theory does not even work for Europe.[3] What was the right legal name for these once-were-states, these maybe-still-are-states at the heart of the continent? They too strained the available categories to their breaking point. Many concluded that one needed new concepts altogether. In an earlier text, Jellinek took up the challenge. Contemporary legal theory, he argued in 1896, suffered for the lack of an "in-between level" (*Zwischenstufe*) between "state" and "province" that could capture political formations that were not states but presented the "rudiments of a state."[4] He called them "state fragments" (*Staatsfragmente*) and devoted a book to the subject. The Austrian lands fit his neologism perfectly. They possessed one especially striking characteristic: they made their own autonomous law that was not subordinate to imperial law (in contrast to the German Empire, where imperial law "trumped" law made by the component lands).[5] That sort of nonderived, nondelegated, nonsubordinate lawmaking capacity sounded very much like sovereignty.[6] Yet the lands lacked other attributes of statehood, like an "existence in international law."[7] Jellinek's new rubric of quasi sovereignty bundled the world along unfamiliar lines: the Habsburg lands found themselves classed as state fragments alongside the settler colonies Australia and Canada, which likewise possessed state organs without being completely independent states in their own right.[8]

In 1914, the prominent French-German jurist Robert Redslob composed his own globe-spanning typology of incomplete sovereignty through the moniker "dependent lands." These marginal cases had many secrets to reveal: he who grasps the nature of dependent lands, Redslob wrote, "also looks into the soul of states."[9] Alsace-Lorraine represented a dependent land, as did Bosnia-Herzegovina. "However, if we step into the double monarchy Austria-Hungary," he wrote, "our gaze will be enthralled by other formations that appear as curiosities of state theory."[10] Had "these old state formations" fallen victim to centralist strivings? "Do they still have their own life? Are they still independent organisms? Or have they all grown together into a new and singular organism?"[11] The situation could be distinguished sharply from Alsace-Lorraine, where a preexisting German empire extended its authority over the territory. Nothing of the sort occurred in Austria: "Austria never had an existence outside its lands. It lives in its lands and through its lands."[12] Austria was an empire without a metropole, or an empire that did not exist as a state prior to its "possessions," reversing the regular temporal sequence of empire building. As he put it, "The original ruling force [*Herrschergewalt*] originates in the totality of the lands."[13] They were provinces, but provinces "of a very idiosyncratic sort," as their authority was not derived from the state but constitutive of the state. They thus demanded a category of their own. Redslob called them *ursprüngliche Staatenteile*—original state parts or particles.

These scholars came late to the case. The search for the right legal name for the Habsburg lands had begun not in the university but in the public sphere. The status of the lands emerged as a pressing problem through the attempts to write an imperial constitution in 1848–49. What were these entities, and what exactly were their rights? The two questions were integrally related, and the task of codification required answers. In the decades that followed, and through to the empire's collapse, claim makers from the lands, especially Bohemia, pushed for regional autonomy on the basis of their traditional rights and laws. In developing these claims, they gradually translated their old legal entities and their privileges into the vocabulary of state and sovereignty, arguing that these polities and their rights had survived long centuries of imperial rule intact, swallowed up but not dissolved in the python of empire. Naturally, those arguments ran into serious challenges. Did a world of material evidence not contradict the notion that the lands were still-living states? Were they not mere "historical reminiscences," as one jurist later put it, with the scattered trappings of sovereignty—a coronation here, a ceremony there—now only empty symbols devoid of real content?[14]

Politicians and jurists from the lands developed creative strategies to counter this apparent reality deficit. They made a crucial distinction: the Habsburgs may have incrementally encroached on their statehood as a matter of fact, but never as a matter of legitimate law. To change the state of affairs legally would have required the participation of their own estates and diets: that is what their traditional rights required. Thus, their original legal standing, their original independence, still existed as valid law, irrespective of centuries of factual incursions to the contrary. It was a still-good norm that simply awaited renewed recognition and actualization. The discourse of "historical rights" became a means of managing the paradox of states that existed in law but not in fact: lapsed, perhaps, but still states nonetheless. Slumbering states, or residual states, ever ripe for new life. The drive to match the Habsburg lands with categories of state and sovereignty thereby generated specific styles of argumentation—ones that cleaved law away from fact and ascribed to law a sort of truth or reality that was insulated against evidence from the material world. Were states not always abstractions anyway? This configuration of the "legal real" made it very hard—if not impossible—to kill a state or to show that it had died: Jellinek was not wrong. In recent times, our interest in "paper states," "fictional states," and "juridical states" has gravitated toward Africa and other parts of the postcolonial world.[15] It can be easy to forget that modern European history is likewise littered with juridical states, clutching at a life only in law.

If the constitutional project created the need to codify forms from the past, it also raised the question of codifying what many took as the form of the future: namely, nations. Over this same period, rising national movements challenged the notion that the (multiethnic) lands should remain the empire's principal subunits. They envisaged an empire composed not of historical polities but of nations. Visions of national federation preserved the structure of a conglomerate state but recast the basis of that plurality along ethnolinguistic lines. They, too, ran into difficult questions about the relationship between law and reality. What did an empire-of-nations look like as a legal proposition, as an actual constitutional schema, not least given the empire's densely intermingled patterns of national settlement? The ethnic-linguistic nation, many observed, was not a legal category or entity: How could something as fuzzy and amorphous as "a nation" possess rights or function as an organ of government? This impasse generated its own fertile and provocative jurisprudence about the possibility of transforming territorially dispersed nations into legal "things" and granting them legal personality (i.e., making them entities capable of having rights and duties in law). Notions of "personal sovereignty," "nonterritorial autonomy," and "internal international law" all entered circulation as jurists and politicians tried to find the right legal structure for a sprawling multinational empire.

If the historical lands needed to demonstrate that old rights had been kept alive, then national communities needed to show that they could be transmuted into rights-bearing legal subjects in the first place. Actors involved in both projects thereby found themselves half-accidentally theorizing about the nature of legal truth. The former debate dwelled on the capacity of rights and state-like things to defy death, the latter on the capacity for new rights belonging to new subjects to be created out of nothingness. In both cases, we see how attempts to square the Habsburg Empire with categories of state and sovereignty filtered down to its (state-like?) subunits. What is a state that was one, what is a state that would like to be one? This chapter considers each case in turn.

In Search of a Name

Bohemia, Moravia, Silesia, Styria, Corinthia, Dalmatia. . . . The lands were commonplaces of the empire, the basic furniture of the imperial structure, the kinds of objects obvious enough to have escaped much conceptual interrogation—until 1848. Codifying the empire into constitutional law required their standing to be sorted into legal categories and cataloged according to current legal typologies. Everyone knew what they had been: hundreds of years ago, they had been states of different sorts. What language would now step in where statehood had been?

In the Kremsier draft, the delegates had settled on the terminology of "imperial lands" that were understood to possess some degree of independence or self-government.[16] They had also referred to "crownlands," "hereditary lands," "individual lands," "historical lands," and mere "provinces" in the course of their discussion; one formulation dubbed them "independent acquisitions" with a "particular life" (*Sonderleben*) of their own.[17] These terms were more compelling as political descriptions than legal categorizations and seemed to many an inadequate general shorthand for the legal standing of polities that ranged so dramatically in size, strength, and history—especially if one wanted to refer also to Hungary (which had not been included in the Kremsier draft). The more abstract and technical language of legal "persons" crept into circulation, but only on the margins.[18]

What emerged in the years after Kremsier was a kind of surrogate language of legal personality, one of "individuums" and "individualities." This terminology became a powerful method of signaling the legal distinctness of the historical lands, their collective unity as singular subjects, and the continuity of that status over time, closely mimicking the rhetorical and juridical effect of the vocabulary of personality and its operation of legal "thingification." At the same time, it carried less baggage than "personality," and, usefully, it was less precise. Under the sign of "individualities," for example, nationalities and historical lands could be discursively paired as rivals. Kajetan Mayer had complained already at Kremsier that Palacký and others wanted to "create new land complexes, new state individualities" that folded along national lines: "but to make a new individuality out of Bohemia, Moravia, and Silesia, they must destroy existing individualities."[19]

By the late 1850s, the invocation of the historical "individuality" of the lands had moved to the center of constitutional debate. The term *historical-political individualities* (*historisch-politische Individualitäten*) defied its clunky inelegance to become a key word in the dictionary of imperial self-understanding. This unlikely phrase in fact bore a substantial intellectual burden in the empire's hesitant return to constitutionalism. As we know, military defeat and fiscal crisis had led the emperor, in March 1860, to summon an "enlarged imperial council" (*verstärkten Reichsrat*) in pursuit of greater domestic support and cooperation. The preexisting *Reichsrat* had been a small advisory council of twelve appointed members; now the emperor personally selected additional notables from the church, military, and civil service, as well as thirty-eight representatives from the lands, with a clear majority of feudal aristocrats the unsurprising result.[20] While the enlarged *Reichsrat* marked the small first step in the dismantling of the neoabsolutist state, its status remained precarious. Those summoned—present at the invitation of the emperor, and lacking an electoral mandate of any sort—studiously avoided behavior that might cause the emperor to dissolve the assembly. They largely sidestepped the term *constitution* and chose their words carefully.[21] In this context, the fact that the majority submission hinged on the recognition of the so-called historical-political individuality of the lands was hardly an accident.

The majority submission had been masterminded by the conservative Hungarian statesman and aristocrat Antal Szécsen (1819–96). With diplomatic service behind him and a strong record of loyalty to the dynasty, Szécsen had long acted as a crucial path of communication between Hungarian political elites and the dynasty.[22] The tact and amenity of his conceptualization of the empire's constitutional predicament proved decisive in 1860. The report was read before a plenary meeting of the *Reichsrat* on September 22, 1860. "The strengthening and sound development of the monarchy," it declared, "demands the recognition of the historical-political individuality of each of the lands." This recognition, in turn, involved reinstating the political-legal institutions and jurisdiction of the lands: the report spoke of their "autonomy in administration and inner legislation."[23]

What the submission said was as significant as what it did not. No mention was made of constitutions, historical rights, sovereignty, or independence. Therein lay the great utility and political savvy of Szécsen's phrasing. The term *historical-political individuality* invoked the world of those concepts: it stood in for the historical independence and discreteness of the lands, nodding obliquely to their erstwhile statehood and the impossibility of dissolving them into provinces. Yet it did so without mention of any of the most inflammatory keywords, digesting the lands' residual independence into a form palatable to the dynasty. Small wonder that the historian Stefan Malfèr described the term *historical-political individuality* as "a magic word full of secrets."[24]

Szécsen did not rely on suggestiveness alone. Equally striking from a juridical perspective was his careful explication of the concept of historical-political individuality: he sought to construct a general legal category that could summarize the idiosyncratic legal identity of each of the lands. In a long speech before the *Reichsrat* elaborating the majority position, Szécsen conceded that "this concept of historical-political individuality, which is mentioned here, has received diverse interpretations from different corners."[25] But its meaning was straightforward. "The historical-political individuality of the different lands is just the expression and summary of the whole national, historical, and political development and life activity [*Lebensthätigkeit*] of the different parts of the monarchy," he explained. "It is the concept according to which there is . . . a Kingdom of Hungary rather than a Departement of the Donau and Tisza, . . . also no Departement Troppau or Salzburg, but instead a Land of Salzburg and Silesia; not a Departement of the Moldau and of the Adriatic Sea, but rather a City of Triest." It was the reason one had "a Land—a Kingdom of Bohemia."[26] With the standardized and historyless French *départements* as the counter-model, historical-political individuality was the sign under which each of the lands retained its former legal shape and identity. Whatever sort of entity or "individual" they had been, they remained. Conceptually, it made room for Bohemia to remain a "kingdom," and remain itself, without anyone mentioning statehood or sovereignty.

Such overt Hungarian authorship understandably gave rise to the impression that the majority report reflected Hungary's position and view of the empire. Szécsen worked to dilute that association. "The feeling of historical-political individuality is present, even if in various gradations, in all lands of the monarchy," he argued.[27] The leader of the Czech feudal nobility, Heinrich Jaroslaw (Jindřich Jaroslav hrabě) Clam-Martinic, another key advocate of the term and the majority's report, likewise emphasized that "this feeling and consciousness belongs to all Austrian lands, the largest as much as the smallest."[28] He defended its airy generality and lack of detail: the very sense of the report was not to posit "one singularly true theory for all lands" or to "devise uniform provisions, but rather much more to advocate the fullest consideration of the diversity of the relationships, perspectives, wishes, and needs of each particular land."[29] Historical-political individuality was a general theory that was not one: it simply made and held the space in which each mini-polity could exist as its idiosyncratic legal self.

The majority submission won the approval of the *Reichsrat* plenary (34 votes to 16) on September 27, 1860, driven by the dominant coalition of the Hungarian old conservatives and the Bohemian high nobility. The emperor's October Diploma, promulgated the following month, turned the *Reichsrat*'s sentiments into positive constitutional law: acknowledging the legal diversity of the lands and reinstating their legislative powers, it established historical legal title as the foundation of the state.[30] Szécsen's influence was obvious.[31]

The phrase "historical-political individuality" thus became a fixture of constitutional jurisprudence even if it did not formally appear in the October Diploma or subsequent constitutions. When Ludwig Gumplowicz assembled his systematic account of Austrian constitutional law for a textbook in 1891, he included a section under that title, noting the term's curious relationship

to positive constitutional law: "The concept of 'historical-political individuality' is in fact foreign to written Austro-Hungarian constitutional law, yet
because it has emerged out of history, reflecting factual relationships, positive constitutional law must in some parts accommodate this concept, it
must accept these facts for the organization of the empire."[32] In this account,
the phrase stood in for the whole evolution of the Habsburg imperial polity, signifying the historical "facts" that law could not ignore. Gumplowicz
attempted his own definition. Historical-political individuality, he wrote, "lays
claim on and incorporates a special constitutional standing in the state" and
arose from centuries-long relationships "between a complex of lands and a
state organization." It was narrower than the concept *Staatsvolk*—the state's
citizen-subjects—but broader than that of ethnicity or nationality: "Multiple
nationalities can reside in the domain of a historical-political individuality,
but one and the same nationality can also fall in multiple historical-political
individualities."[33] In distinguishing historical-political individuality from both
ethnicity and the concept of the state's citizenry in general, Gumplowicz's definition captured the ambiguity of these collective legal subjects that were neither "proper" states nor nations.

Spinning Estates into States

The notion that the lands remained "themselves" was essential if they wanted
to claim that their rights, too, had survived. Historical rights were not a species
of natural right, always again deducible in the present from the rationality of
the world. As a body of "subjective law" (in the sense of rights and other legal
properties attached to a particular subject, rather than "objective law" valid
uniformly for everyone),[34] they depended on the subject who "owned" such
law: these rights could not, as such, float freely through time and space. They
lived or died with the legal subject to which they were attached. The survival
of the Kingdom of Bohemia *as* the Kingdom of Bohemia, of the Margravate of
Moravia *as* the Margravate of Moravia (and so on) was a crucial precondition
for the survival of their historical rights into the present. Accordingly, if Czech
politicians in the 1860s wished to invoke the historical rights of the Kingdom
of Bohemia, then they (or the Bohemian diet in which they met) needed to
be the direct inheritor, legally speaking, of the Bohemian polity that had possessed those rights at the moment of imperial union in 1526. The survival of
rights and their subject was integrally bound up together.

Through the constitutional experiments of the 1860s, Czech claim makers made precisely that argument.[35] But these claims of radical continuity
involved a series of subtle conceptual transformations. To make out the case,
they translated what had been feudal prerogatives and privileges into "public
law," and estates and diets into abstract legal entities that looked much more
like a modern "state." We can watch these translations unfold in "real time"

through the string of formal constitutional protests issued by the Bohemian and Moravian diets over the course of the 1860s. These began in the wake of the February Patent of 1861.

No sooner had the October Diploma recognized the individuality of the historical lands, resurrected their diets, and granted them significant latitude over their own lawmaking than the February Patent imperiled their legal discreteness anew. As we know, the patent ostensibly enacted the diploma, but in fact it rocked the weight of legislative power away from the lands and back toward the central parliament, following widespread dissent among liberals.[36] Crucially, it foreshadowed dualism through a new distinction between the full parliament that included representatives from Hungary and a "narrower" parliament (*engerer Reichsrat*) that involved the representatives from the non-Hungarian lands only. This narrower parliament was now to command a far-reaching jurisdiction over the western half of the monarchy. This new dispensation meant that Tyroleans (for example) in the parliament would have a say in the "internal" affairs of Bohemia, and vice versa. The dilution of the legal separateness of the lands definitively contradicted the older logic of composite monarchy, in which they formed a common polity only through the shared body of the emperor, otherwise retaining distinct organs and institutions. With the neoabsolutist state disbanded, the representatives of the lands now faced a new battle to "defend" their historical right to juridical autonomy and thereby their "individuality." In this struggle, it was not only rights and privileges that were in question but also the existence of the rights subjects themselves.

This defense took a highly performative and ceremonial form, with the new diets, convening in April 1861 after hastily organized elections, issuing elaborate formal declarations of their historical rights, especially in Bohemia but also Moravia. On April 9, the estates of the Moravian diet tabled a *Rechtsverwahrung* intended to defend the constitutional "existence" of Moravia. They sought to protect the "constitutional independence" and freedoms of the Margravate of Moravia "against all provisions, clauses and resolutions" that prejudicially harmed "this independence, these rights and these freedoms." Moravia's continued existence was "constitutionally guaranteed and inviolable" thanks to a long list of state acts and rituals that the Moravian diet enumerated in turn: the "renewed Land Ordinance" of 1627, the coronation of the king of Bohemia as the margrave of Moravia down until His Majesty Ferdinand I (in Hungary and Bohemia V), the Pragmatic Sanction, the emperor-constituting patent of 1804, and not least the October Diploma of 1860.[37] The declaration thereby traced formal imperial deference to the old privileges and freedoms of Moravia, stretching back into the early modern past as an unbroken legal chain: the ritualized acknowledgment of those traditional rights secured their safe passage into the present constitutional struggle. A parallel Bohemian declaration was even more explicit on this point, declaring that their participation in the problematic new imperial order in no way interrupted the "continuity" of Bohemia's rightful constitutional standing as guaranteed "through an unbroken row of acts of state."[38]

What of the subject who carried those rights through history? The situation forced the delegates to articulate what kind of rights subject they understood a land and its diet to be. If the estates of the present day (as represented in the diet) were ostensibly the same estates that had historically held the ageless medieval privileges they claimed, the diet delegates of 1861 also renovated that legal self to accord more with an age of parliamentary constitutionalism. It was because they "viewed the estates of the Margravate of Moravia not as owners of personal prerogatives and privileges, but rather in their entirety as the defenders and bearers of the rights of the land itself," that they could not have wanted or been able to prejudice the rights and freedoms of Moravia.[39] Old feudal-social rights were thereby recast as the polity's collective public property: the "land" as such now constituted the bearer of rights. The construction of this impersonal group subject in turn meant that rights could not be damaged by the isolated actions of some delegates in the present. The Bohemian declaration included similar phrasing: "We view the estates of the kingdom not as owners of personal prerogatives and privileges, but rather as the depository of the rights of the land." For that reason, participation in the new diet could not be interpreted as a forfeiture of Bohemia's historical rights and freedoms.[40]

At a moment in which a new nineteenth-century constitutional order confronted the legal structures of an earlier patrimonial epoch, Bohemian and Moravian delegates looked to abstract and consolidate the estates-based structure of rights, with its stench of private law, into something that looked much more like a state. They constructed the lands as general, shell-like legal persons, as "depositories" of rights: a bank or storehouse in which the mass of personal rights could be deposited, depersonalized, and preserved. "We, the duly elected deputies of the Bohemian diet," announced a subsequent declaration, "proceed from the assumption that the Kingdom of Bohemia, our beloved fatherland, is undeniably a legal-individuum [*ein Rechts-Individuum*], that it has imperishable rights."[41] Finding no relief, and having failed to have the emperor crowned king of Bohemia, they decided to boycott the imperial parliament in 1863.[42] They would not return until the mid-1870s.

If Otto Brunner later complained that nineteenth-century jurists projected backward the abstract structure of the sovereign state onto a medieval order that knew only webs of far more personalized legal relationships,[43] then this projection was sometimes a conscious project. Declarations like these allow us to observe it, and the intellectual labor it required, in slow motion. A new constitutional order in the Habsburg lands prompted claim makers to construct arguments and theories about the way rights could survive despite deep, even tectonic, shifts in the legal imagination, as a plural, patrimonial social-legal order morphed into the "modern" order of states. Those with vested interests needed to explicitly articulate just how rights and rights subjects might be transferred between legal orders, with the legal "goods" of one age converted into equivalencies for a new one, without losing their core identity or continuous operation.

The Settlement of 1867 represented a catastrophe for Czech political aspirations. Hungary's claims to historical constitutional independence received grandiose affirmation in a new dualist imperial structure, while the Czech lands were to have their "existence dissolved in a 'western imperial-half,' a state formation that lacks every constitutional foundation," as they put it.[44] The Settlement provoked a landmark Bohemian declaration dated August 22, 1867, which stands as arguably the most important articulation of the Czechs' argument for their "historical state rights," as *historische Staatsrecht* is usually translated into English.[45] The specificity and multivalence of the concepts warrant emphasis: *Staatsrecht* means constitutional or public law, the law governing the fundamental structure and legitimacy of the state. Bohemians invoked their ancient constitution; in doing so, in this context, they also claimed it as a *right*—privileges and prerogatives that demanded recognition. In other words, the *Recht* in *Staatsrecht* carried its twin meanings of *law* and *right*: to defend historical constitutional law was also to claim historical state rights. In what follows, I leave *Staatsrecht* untranslated in instances when choosing between one sense and the other would strip the passage of half its meaning.

The Bohemian protest laid out a sweeping account of the empire's legal history, returning with razor-like clarity to the logic of composite monarchy with its many-bodied monarch and explaining how that structure shaped sovereign legitimacy in the present. "Until the year 1848, the lands of the house of Austria did not form a unified state, but rather particular states with varying relationships to the dynasty," argued the Bohemian representatives. These particular states were collected into an empire only through that dynasty. The crown of Bohemia had never entered into a real union with the other lands and always preserved its "particular historical and constitutional [*staatsrechtlichen*] individuality" untarnished.[46] But the new dualist order looked to melt the non-Hungarian lands down into a common but artificial state form. "Yes, the glorious historical Kingdom of Bohemia, which until now had never ceased to constitute an independent constitutional individuality, should now be robbed of this personality, it should become a mere province of the illegitimate Cisleithanian state," although it had had "no other constitutional connection with the remaining Austrian lands beyond that which existed in its common hereditary dynasty." "In this way," they protested, "all our *Staatsrecht* should be factually obliterated, the Kingdom of Bohemia and the Bohemian crown as constitutional individuals exterminated from the political world forever."[47]

In riding roughshod over old Bohemian *Staatsrecht*, the imperial government threatened a brutish political execution of the juridical "person" of

Bohemia: to rob Bohemia of its particular legal identity was to erase it from the world of states. If those rights were not respected, the legal individuum behind them expired, too. Hungarian representatives had in fact used similar constructions when they protested the 1860 October Diploma with its assertion of a unified constitution and parliament for the empire as a whole. Hungarians, declared Ferenc von Deák in a famous speech before the Hungarian diet, could not undersign "the political obliteration of the land as an independent land." If Vienna denied Hungary's right to regulate its own taxation, military service, and so on, then "Hungary may cease to be an independent, autonomous Hungary [and] become an Austrian constitutional province."[48] In both cases, the historical right preserved the existence of its bearer. Rights represented its outward-facing defenses, its emissaries in the world—messengers that referred back to a subject or source that must then be held to exist, if only by inference. Diminished by centralization, that legal person had shrunk to the size and scope of the rights it could defend, and nothing more.

Residual Sovereignty: Making Paper States

As hope faded that the empire might be reorganized from a dualist to a trialist structure in the late 1860s and early 1870s, the main discussions of historical law moved from the diets and parliaments to the academy. The struggle over Bohemian *Staatsrecht* drove an upswing in the legal sciences in the Bohemian lands in the 1860s, especially legal history, as politicians and the public alike looked to jurists for arguments and evidence.[49] A series of more scholarly studies, presenting careful and elaborate arguments about the nature of imperial law and Bohemian *Staatsrecht* within it, were published from the 1870s onward. The most important of these monographs were written by the Czech historian Josef Kalousek (1838–1915), a professor in Prague, and the lawyer Hugo Toman (1838–98).[50] At the heart of this new academic literature on Bohemian historical rights lay the reconstruction of the continuous survival of the Bohemian "state" through the long centuries of Habsburg rule. These scholars worked to find paths for rights through time.

Like German-Austrian jurists seeking to establish the field of Austrian constitutional history in the same period, Kalousek began his book *Some Foundations of Bohemian Staatsrecht* (1871) by explaining the sort of law this category comprised. "Bohemian constitutional law has developed in the first instance as customary law inherited onward from generation to generation, which gradually extended to written records in the form of princely concessions, privileges, *Majestätsbriefen*, diet resolutions, and land ordinances," he explained, "yet was never brought together in its entirety as a unified codex." The lack of codification was not fatal: "So a constitutional charter in the modern sense exists in Bohemia as little as in England."[51] One could not take any single one of the land ordinances, Kalousek argued—whether that of 1500, 1549, 1564, 1627, or so on—as the complete expression of Bohemian *Staatsrecht*, but needed rather to consider their totality. Listing the land ordinances in this way, Kalousek's survey of Bohemian constitutional law began well before Habsburg rule (1526) and posited the ongoing development of that tradition despite the Habsburg ascent to the crown. Interestingly, Kalousek argued that the first impulses toward the codification (*Fixirung*) of this customary "native public law" (*heimischen öffentlichen Rechtes*) arose when a "foreigner" was called to the Bohemian throne for the first time (Johann of Luxemburg in the fourteenth century).[52] Here, too, from the perspective of Bohemian law, the Habsburgs were implicitly just one in a line of foreign kings—stranger kings, in the terminology of Sahlins and Graeber—for whom the indigenous law needed to be translated from customary knowledge into something "readable" to an outsider.[53]

The central animating thrust of both Kalousek's and Toman's studies consisted in the demonstration of the survival of Bohemian *Recht*—as both law and rights—over the more significant "ruptures" caused by Habsburg rule. Both traced in detail the precise terms of the original transfer of the Bohemian crown to the Habsburg Archduke Ferdinand I in 1526. Ferdinand's right to the crown on the basis of his consort Anna—who was the sister of the late Jagiellonian Bohemian king—was not recognized by the Bohemian estates, Kalousek insisted. Rather, the estates chose Ferdinand in a free election, exercising their rightful capacity to elect the king of their choice. The throne was his by their grace and according to their laws.[54] Toman emphasized that although the different lands thereby entered an ongoing union under the same ruler, each was "governed in a totally independent way." The idea of a closer "amalgamation" of the lands occurred to no one.[55]

Just like the declarations of the 1860s, the survival of Bohemian law and the survival of the Kingdom of Bohemia amounted to the same question. Constructing a narrative of Bohemia's juridical continuity encountered its gravest stumbling block in the Battle of the White Mountain of 1620 and the renewed land ordinance imposed by Ferdinand II that followed on its heels in 1627. If the persistence of the Bohemian kingdom as an independent polity for the first hundred years of Habsburg rule remained generally uncontroversial, the new order of 1627 seriously altered the relationship between Bohemia and the dynasty. That Bohemia suffered a comprehensive defeat after having rebelled against the Habsburgs cleared the legal and political space for Ferdinand II to unilaterally assert new terms for his rule. The "hardest strike" of the land ordinance was its withdrawal of legislative capacities from the Bohemian diet. Henceforth, only the king would have the right to make legislation.[56] Establishing what exactly remained of traditional Bohemian *Staatsrecht* despite these blows became the key question for scholars like Kalousek.

The renewed land ordinance did defer in part—if obliquely—to preexisting traditions and conventions. By incorporating certain key traditions, especially the coronation oath (which prevented the king from alienating any part of the kingdom's patrimony) and the "Carolingen and Georgian incorporation laws," the ordinance itself testified to the fundamental juridical survival of the state. The "integrity and state individuality of the sovereign Bohemian crown" were thereby guaranteed, Kalousek argued: "A *staatsrechtliche* or administrative blending of the Bohemian state with the other states and possessions of the common ruler was neither intended nor effected by the renewed land ordinance."[57] In many respects, the ordinance marked "a violent step toward absolutism, but not to the obliteration of the state individuality of the Bohemian crown, or to its blending with other crowns and hereditary states."[58] The kingdom never went missing from history, never lost its juridical shape. In this way, the same state individuality moved forward in time through different constitutional relationships, dragging its rights and entitlements into the modern age like the long and ornate train of a ceremonial gown.

Perhaps the most famous exponent and explicator of Bohemian *Staatsrecht* was the Czech politician Karel Kramář (1860–1937), who would later become Czechoslovakia's first prime minister. Kramář's career bridged worlds. At the level of political activity, as well as through his renovation of ideas, Kramář tied the constitutional struggles of Austria-Hungary to the postimperial order, especially as a member of the Czech delegation to the Paris Peace Conference and as a founding father of the new state. A lawyer from a wealthy middle-class family, Kramář married a Russian heiress, and his financial independence, combined with political talent and prodigious command of Russian, German, French, and English, helped launch an influential political career that included leadership of the Young Czechs. While pro-Slav and pro-Russian in orientation, Kramář was considered a "realist" alongside Josef Kaizl and T. G. Masaryk—though he and Masaryk increasingly disagreed on many fronts—and had a moderate disposition toward the central government, advocating a federal settlement under the auspices of the Habsburg Monarchy until the outbreak of World War I.[59]

"For more than thirty years, the political life of Austria has been filled with the struggle over Bohemian *Staatsrecht*," he wrote in *Das böhmische Staatsrecht* (1896).[60] Kramář faced more trying circumstances than Kalousek and Toman, as Czech political work toward a new constitutional settlement or even basic concessions had come to naught, and the cross-class coalition that underpinned the original *Staatsrecht* program had fallen apart. His monograph recast Bohemian historical law for a new century, pitching its uses for a more open-ended and positive political platform than the stubborn boycott politics of the 1860s and 1870s. Most revealingly, his history looked to cleave open the tight association between the historical-constitutional tradition and the aristocracy. Bohemian *Staatsrecht*, in Kramář's telling, had nothing to do with class or any particular political ideology and everything to do with the "state" and its sovereignty.

The Czech people had always remained liberal, he argued. They had allied with the aristocracy and forgiven them their clericalism solely because the latter had fought to defend Bohemian historical rights. "But *Staatsrecht* in itself has nothing to do with the question of liberalism, of democracy. Bohemian *Staatsrecht* . . . is and remains only the question of the relationship of the lands of the Bohemian crown to the Habsburg dynasty and to its other lands."[61] Like all constitutions, it was an evolving rather than static body of law, one that would have gradually become more democratic as a natural part of its development—more democratic, even, than the Austro-Hungarian constitution of 1867!—save for the violent, centralist interventions of Maria Theresa that disrupted the natural development of this law. Thus one could not reproach it on the grounds of any social content: the democratic talents of the Czech people had been stifled by the meddling absolutism of the Habsburgs.

This line of argumentation allowed Kramář to make several key distinctions. Because historical Bohemian law could not be judged on the basis of its social content, he announced that he would not linger further on social or "internal" issues but rather "survey the history of Bohemian *Staatsrecht* from the standpoint of the outward-facing right to independence and autonomy."[62] In thereby exploring the "external" rather than the apparently internal dimensions of Bohemian *Staatsrecht*, Kramář turned the latter into a body of precedents concerning Bohemia's relations with other states and lands—that is, into a kind of international law.

Unsurprisingly, then, the nineteenth-century keyword *sovereignty* assumed a central place in his history. It lay at the heart of this genre of law: Bohemian *Staatsrecht*, most fundamentally, regulated "the relationship of the independent, sovereign lands of the Bohemian crown in their unity to the other lands of their king and to the other states."[63] As such, sovereignty was an analytical category as well as a key attribute in this history, a status that the Bohemian lands had possessed as a historical fact: "Ferdinand I took over Bohemia and Hungary as fully sovereign, independent states, he exercised the right of legislation and administration as King of Bohemia in Bohemia, as King of Hungary in Hungarian lands."[64] Bohemian *Staatsrecht*, in Kramář's telling, was a discourse on sovereignty.

The distinction between internal and external, and its elevation of the concept of sovereignty, equipped Kramář with the conceptual tools to construct a startling new history of the crisis of 1627. The basic principles of the "complete independence, the total sovereignty" of the lands of the Bohemian crown under the auspices of the Habsburg dynasty were so "self-evident," Kramář argued, that they were never questioned in the great struggle that culminated in the Battle of the White Mountain. That struggle "turned not on the independence of the lands of the Bohemian crown, but on the power of the nobility as against the dynasty."[65] It was the nobility, Kramář emphasized, that was conquered—not the polity as such. Such a defeat need not provoke sorrow or sentimentality: the nobility were oppressing the people anyway. They were destroyed, "but the kingdom, its independence and autonomy remained unaffected. It was an *internal revolution*, where the king remained the victor, as to the external standing of the state nothing was to be changed and nothing could be changed."[66] The king's own legitimacy as king of Bohemia was bound up with the preservation of the "independence and sovereignty" of the kingdom, and these he swore to protect in the renewed land ordinance of 1627.[67] For all its changes, the ordinance therefore altered only the "inner life of the state": the face Bohemia presented to the outside world was not affected in the slightest.[68] Kramář thus interpreted the struggle between the rebellious Bohemian nobility and the dynasty as a domestic struggle, virtually a class or civil war, one in which Ferdinand II acted exclusively in the guise of the king of Bohemia. The consequences of such a struggle could only register on the level of social relations and the internal distribution of power, which indeed changed dramatically, as a foreign nobility was brought in to replace the conquered Bohemian landholders.

Kramář thereby constructed a *Staatsrecht* that pertained exclusively to "the state," abstracted from the social-feudal nexus of the rights and privileges that had formed the original content of the estates constitution—precisely the sort of late nineteenth-century juridical ahistoricism to which Otto Brunner objected so caustically. Kramář's *Staatsrecht* reflected nineteenth-century preoccupations perfectly: in separating the ostensibly "internal" from the ostensibly "external," and social relations from sovereign relations, Kramář projected backward a modern understanding of law with its sharp divide between international and domestic law. This allowed him to digest the changes of 1627 into an internal social matter and enabled the external sovereign rights of the kingdom as a legal *individuum* to continue forward in time without rupture. The state lived.

Until the age of absolutism, that is. Kramář devoted many pages and much invective to the changes wrought by Maria Theresa from the mid-eighteenth century. Some centralization, he conceded, formed a normal part of the course of history: the gradual coordination of finances across the Habsburg domain, for example, appeared to him entirely natural and in no way contradictory with the rights of the lands. But Maria Theresa's absolutist program of centralization, by contrast, constituted a gross violation of the natural and just order of things. She exhibited scant regard for the delicate juridical status quo: "The old vested rights of the until-now independent states were no impediment to her." She "destroyed" the independence of the Austrian and Bohemian lands and forged them into a centralized empire, though she ran out of strength to tackle Hungary in the same way, thus laying the foundations of dualism.[69] Her centralization amounted to a grave *Rechtsbruch*, a legal rupture of great "violence and recklessness." The estates may have lost their social hegemony after 1627, but under the auspices of Maria Theresa's absolutism "the autonomy of the until-then independent, autonomous states was taken from them."[70]

These changes, however, *remained* a violation of the rightful legal order, Kramář argued. A long list of fundamental legal documents—from the "contract" of 1526 through to the renewed land ordinance of 1627 and the Pragmatic Sanction of 1713—established that the rights of the Bohemian crown could not be altered unilaterally: the participation and consent of the legal representatives of the Bohemian lands (i.e., the diet) formed a necessary component of any fundamental constitutional change. Thus, "formally and materially she was in the wrong."[71] Bohemian *Staatsrecht* could only be changed according to its own stipulations, according to its own legal mechanisms. As a result, the centralization of the era of absolutism altered the material form of the empire but never reached down to genuinely dissolve fundamental Bohemian law; the latter was effectively put on ice and preserved as it stood on the eve of these ruptures. "Bohemian *Staatsrecht*," Kramář maintained, "is today that which was the public law of Bohemia before the illegitimate and violent intervention of Maria Theresa."[72]

Kramář thus posited the deep, subterranean survival of Bohemian state law. The true legal situation of the Bohemian lands had not been altered over the last 150 years. This meant that the current constitution of 1867 was "legally invalid." "It is a piece of legislation, it has the force of a piece of legislation, one can promise to treat it as a piece of legislation, but for the Bohemian people it has only a legislative [*gesetzliche*] force, no legal [*rechtliche*] authority," he asserted, "because here representatives of other lands have decided over the fundamental rights of the Bohemian crown, which have absolutely no right to meddle in the legal sphere of the Bohemian crown."[73] With its common parliament, the constitution of 1867 fundamentally disrespected the juridical integrity and historical jurisdiction of the Bohemian lands. It was clearly a law in the sense of a legislative act promulgated by the government, but it could never command the genuine power, authority, and mystique of the rightful law.

Ten years later, in his *Notes on Bohemian Politics* (1906), Kramář restated his understanding of the survival of rightful law while expressing some distance from his earlier positions. Here again, residual legalities that had never been overridden in legitimate ways continued to shine through as the only reliable foundations of imperial law. In this early twentieth-century formulation, though, another familiar key word took its place alongside that of sovereignty: *self-determination*. Our "final goal," he asserted, was the "renewal of the legislative and administrative right of self-determination of the lands of the Bohemian crown within the framework of a federalized Austria."[74]

The campaign for the restoration of historical Bohemian law segued seamlessly into the vocabulary of self-determination, so central to the broader twentieth-century story of empire and decolonization. Yet, in Kramář's deployment, it was integrally bound up with Austro-Hungarian law and politics, and not only because self-determination found its ideal realization within an imperial union. More still, "self-determination" did not float as some freestanding abstract ideal. It had a crucial adjective: Bohemian striving and seeking, wrote Kramář, found its "idealization" in "the struggle for the *staatsrechtliche* right of self-determination of the lands of the Bohemian crown" within the imperial frame.[75] That is, this self-determination was of the *Staatsrecht* variety: it concerned the resurrection of historical rights rather than the invocation of new ones; it represented a continuity with imperial constitutional struggles rather than a departure from them. "The goal of our politics can be no other than that the Bohemian people again become the bearers of the state tradition [*Träger des Staatsgedankens*] in the lands of the Bohemian crown, that they are given back their old *staatsrechtliche* independence," though in a manner "that accords with modern requirements."[76] Kramář explicitly contrasted this kind of self-determination with that based on "mere" abstract, natural law premises, and in so doing he argued stridently for the residual force and survival of historical law. "This is no romantic historicism, as is so often charged, but rather a very realistic policy, that is, [a policy of] not forsaking the legal fundaments on which we all must stand, whether we want to or not," he warned. "Precisely because our *Staatsrecht* is a timeless, legitimate right. Every natural law theory is enough to motivate national independence—but not the right of self-determination of the lands of the Bohemian crown."[77]

Any appeal to natural law, to universal principles, could support some sort of national autonomy—so much was easy, if pedestrian, Kramář suggested diffidently. But Bohemian goals were different: they sought the self-determination of the Bohemian polity, which of course contained Germans alongside Czechs. Here, a generic or abstract legal foundation did not suffice, nor was it needed: Bohemia already possessed the deep legal foundations for an order based on self-determination—legal foundations that were more real and more resilient anyway, shining, agelessly, from the depths of the historical past. At the same time, their permanence preserved the legal identity of Bohemia: "*Staatsrecht* is nothing other than the legal content of the state sovereignty of the lands of the Bohemian crown, their indivisibility, unity, and *staatsrechtliche* individuality."[78] Bohemian state rights were not a problem "but rather an always-existing legal situation [*immer bestehender Rechtszustand*] on which the rule of the monarch in the Bohemian lands is solely based."[79]

The Legal (Un)Real: Law contra Fact

The scholarship of historical rights presents us with legal history in a fantastical key. The legal-political discourse constructed by figures like Kramář, Kalousek, and Toman sketched an otherworldly domain of ageless rights and residual statehood, one that played out in an almost metahistorical register. Yet even as claim makers peddled in mythic timescales and extraordinary tales of transtemporal survival, they devoted careful attention to the evidentiary basis of their claims. More than that: arguments about historical rights came twinned with a very conscious articulation of the sort of truth in play: it was the logic of jurisdiction, of legal reasoning itself.

In treatments of historical *Staatsrecht* spanning the empire's last five decades, we can observe the construction of a particular culture of imperial rights that relied on a clear epistemological distinction between "law" and "fact." Within this frame, the survival of old law could not be disproved or abolished by mere facts: it could only be changed or rendered obsolete by a similarly legitimate law, and law of the same sort. That distinction may sound fundamentally suspicious or spurious to pragmatic modern ears. Yet, as we will see in the following chapter, a radical distinction between law and fact also lay at the heart of the revolution in legal philosophy instigated by the empire's two most famous jurist-philosophers, Georg Jellinek and Hans Kelsen—a revolution that understood itself as the true modernization and scientization of the discipline of law. As with so many other dimensions of this story, there exists no easy line between the modern and premodern, the mythic and the true.

Kramář's 1896 account of Maria Theresa's centralist reforms exemplified this style of reasoning. "And because she was formally and materially in the wrong," he argued, "she could only produce a *fact*, but not a *law*, and for that reason the rights of the Bohemian crown, the Bohemian *Staatsrecht*, the right to the unity and inseparability of the three lands of the Bohemian crown, to their legislative and administrative independence and autonomy *is not abrogated, but rather persists wholly and completely in law.*" He explained the logic: "A law, though it may be effectively withdrawn from practice, can never ever be abrogated by a fact, even if it [the fact] is a piece of legislation. That is the immovable legal basis of Bohemian *Staatsrecht*."[80] The empress could make facts but not real law: the latter would have required the participation of the Bohemian estates. In this juridical imaginary, laws retained their force unless they had been directly overridden within their own structures of logic and legitimacy. Legitimacy could only be changed legitimately. This proposition remained true even if laws were set aside, ignored, or contradicted.

Kramář traced this subterranean stream of law running beneath a changeable world of government policy through the course of the empire's history. The patent of 1804, which established the title emperor of Austria, exhibited "precisely the discrepancy between law and the actual order of internal relations"[81] because it centralized administration and the legislature while also formally recognizing the rights of the crowns of Bohemia and Hungary that traditionally included the diets' competence across a range of domains, including taxation. "From the legal perspective of the Bohemian people," Bohemian *Staatsrecht* remained the only true law to which they owed allegiance: "Since Maria Theresa, facts and pieces of legislation may have been introduced against its legal validity, yet nothing that could abrogate the law as law, least of all the current constitution."[82] Kalousek and Toman used similar formulations, as did many Hungarians.[83]

The disjuncture between factual activity and ostensible legality was not proof of law's erroneousness, nor was it embarrassing. Far from it: the estates' protests had clearly preserved the correct legal measure and norm. This understanding of the nature of imperial law featured in more directly political representations, too. Hungarian politician Albert Apponyi recounted Hungary's original standing as an independent state within a personal union for an international audience in 1904. In various struggles since then, he argued, "the contrary tendencies of the dynasty sometimes prevailed in fact, though never in right, a protest made in due form always maintaining the legal continuity of our independence and constitutional freedom."[84] The lodged protest flagged the persistence of the underlying legitimate status quo. The Austrians had generally respected Hungarian independence, he lectured in 1911: "It was *in practice* often evaded, but never did the country recognize the juridical value of any of these evasions, and always, after a more or less protracted time of trial, we came back to the principle and the theory, *which legally had never been abandoned.*"[85]

Perhaps the most perceptive analysis of the particular temporality of this legal culture came from one of its sharpest contemporary observers, Friedrich Tezner. Tezner himself remained unconvinced of the legal plausibility of claims of historical right, and he wrote of the anachronisms involved in their construction. Such rights claims, he argued, misunderstood the legal nature of the early modern "absolutist estates state" (*ständisch-absolutistischen Staates*). The privileges acknowledged in a document like the renewed land ordinance of 1627, so central to the canon of Bohemian *Staatsrecht*, were not rights or law in the modern sense. In that kind of polity, the right of the prince "extends as far as his power": "He swears to privileges, breaks them if he can, makes temporary constitutional concessions when he needs money from the estates, in order to withdraw them in more favorable circumstances." This changeability did not entail some malevolent deception, as it would in today's world. Rather, "all this is carried out with a naive cordiality untroubled by consciousness of the injustice."[86] Resurrecting shifting legal concessions of this sort as sacred legal pacts—and expecting them to serve as the foundation of good title centuries later—transported a contemporary understanding of law back into the past.

Yet it was Tezner's observations about the "technique and spirit" of patrimonial-monarchic *Staatsrecht* that captured a fundamental characteristic of the nineteenth-century claims of historical right. In a 1901 book, Tezner parsed the nature of constitutional law in the medieval and early modern estates-based polities of continental Europe. He described a legal world that generally lacked stable and self-functioning mechanisms for the defense of formally existing rights, meaning that the legal order possessed a high degree of precarity.[87] In this world, the guarantee of a legal norm could be distinguished from a guarantee for its substantive efficacy—the horizon of legal possibilities functioned differently. The legal rhythm of this world involved constant "renovation and repetition" as the estates ritualistically and periodically appealed "for the recognition or renewal of formally existing rights."[88] Rights, then, were permanently ripe for renewal: their material absence or presence in any given moment said little about their ongoing validity, as any of those moments alone could not capture their more cyclic rhythms of renovation.

Tezner's portrayal of the nature of estates rights claims in centuries past bore more than a passing resemblance to the renovation of these (originally estates-based) rights in the second half of the nineteenth century. The sense that rights remained ever ready for reactivation, and that their loose tethering to factual observance in no way undermined their force, underpinned the logic of historical rights claims in the age of constitutionalism. Norms could survive *as norms*, irrespective of material efficacy in any given moment, constituting an entire architecture of formal legitimacy beneath the surface of things, like a platonic or hypothetical version of the empire. The statehood of the lands was a sleeping norm, a legal idea with fluctuating patterns of actualization.

Speaking before the enlarged *Reichsrat* in 1860, Szécsen presented this perspective most stridently. Neoabsolutism had misunderstood the "true character" of the monarchy. This true character instructed that "the Austrian monarchy is not a unified state [*Einheitsstaat*] in the modern sense" but rather a state formed out of "diverse elements" that all held fast to their "historical individuality." "It would be a dangerous self-deception," he warned, "to believe that the elements upon which this character rests, [the elements] out of which it [the monarchy] has developed, are obliterated or dissolved because their *staatsrechtlicher* expression is *suspended*." In fact, "*they live and function onward*, but they become delinquent and a subversive poison if one denies them recognition."[89] Those "elements," the historical legal individualities, did not disappear merely because their full force was suspended or muted. On the contrary, Szécsen warned, the government had to decide if it would allow that life force to be channeled along productive, legitimate lines or whether it would be suppressed and left to fester dangerously. The new constitution of 1860 that followed reexposed the true law, submerged but not dissolved in the absolutist and neoabsolutist eras.[90]

Thus, while Tezner disputed one sort of continuity, he is useful for the identification of a different sort. Contemporaries may have debated whether or not the rights were continuous with past entitlements, but the meaningful continuity from our perspective might lie elsewhere, namely, in the persistence of certain styles of *reasoning* about rights—in understandings of the way they worked and their relationship with time. The temporal plurality of nineteenth-century constitutionalism did not solely involve the divergent historical origins of the various rights and rights subjects in play: ways of reasoning about rights also drew older customary rights cultures into the modern fray. Modern constitution writing was thereby incorporated into longer patterns of cyclic repetition and renewal.

In the grip and then wake of World War I, a new European settlement, too, was subsumed into those longer patterns, interpellated into the reiterative sequence of historical state rights and the culture of legal truth on which they relied. In 1917, the Czech statesman Edvard Beneš would lay out the Czech case for independence in language that reproduced Kramář's formulations almost verbatim, importing the vocabulary and imaginary of imperial constitutional law into the propaganda campaigns of World War I. The Battle of the White Mountain, he recounted for an international audience, dramatically strengthened the Habsburg position, "but from the constitutional point of view the principle of the independence of the Bohemian State remained intact." He explained the logic of composite monarchies: "The King of Bohemia became a more absolute sovereign, but he always remained King of Bohemia. Legally the Czech State never ceased to exist. The Diet preserved its ancient constitutional rights, somewhat curtailed, yet in the main the same as before."[91] Like Kramář, he argued that the true, deep legality of Bohemian historical rights had been affected neither by the centralization of Maria Theresa nor by the equally illegitimate Settlement of 1867: "Up to the present day they [the Czechs] consider all the constitutional measures taken by Maria Theresa as illegal and nonexisting. They have never renounced the rights of their country." "Even when the era of the modern Constitution commenced (in 1848 and again in 1867)," he insisted, "they persisted in claiming their ancient Constitution of the kingdom of Bohemia, and with it, their independence."[92] His conclusions ventriloquized the Hungarian legal arguments that denied the legal existence of the empire itself: "Austria has never existed de jure for the Czechs."[93]

Are Nations Legal Things?
New Rights in Search of New Rights Subjects

Gleichberechtigung der Nationalitäten! National equality of rights! So ran the nationalist slogan of 1848. It expressed the aspiration that the empire's new constitutional order would involve recognition of the "rights" of the empire's "nationalities"—a claim as powerful as it was legally amorphous. How would such rights work? Who would be their subject? The great proponent of national federation, František Palacký, considered the problem at length. His first concern upon being elected to the parliament in 1848, he later reflected, had been the national equality of rights. Beginning in his famous letter to the Frankfurt parliament of April 1848, he had interpreted "each of the peoples [*Völker*], in the genetic meaning of the word, as particular personalities [*besondere Persönlichkeiten*]," with the right of association as their primary means of protection. "The ideas already existed; all difficulties concerned simply the embodiment [*Verkörperung*] and grouping of these into concrete and organic wholes."[94] How were fluid and dispersed "peoples" to be solidified into singular subjects? The consolidation of "peoples" into fixed units, capable of appearing within constitutional law, was a problem that would persistently haunt the jurisprudence of empire—and indeed that of the international minority protection that governed the new states that replaced the empire in 1918.

Palacký's thinking on the subject was characteristically articulate. In 1866, he ruminated on the "reality" of national groups as distinct from states. "Is each nation, in its totality, a moral and legal person, or not?" he asked. (In nineteenth-century jurisprudence, *moral person* was a synonym for *legal person* or *fictional person*, that is, a legal subject that was not a "natural" or physical person.) "I think that at least among thinkers there can exist no controversy about that," he wrote. "Nations such as, for example, Bohemians, Poles, Hungarians, Germans and so on are genuine realities, are particular and dynamic wholes, of which each possesses its own particular consciousness, its will, its own interests and therefore also duties; in brief, they are real moral and legal persons."[95] No one would deny, he felt, that Germans who lived in Austria, Prussia, Russia, and France had their own common national interests and friendly understanding, even as their respective governments may rage against one another.

If Palacký foreshadowed the irredentism of the interwar years, he argued—like Jellinek at the opening of this book—that one needed new legal theory to make sense of Central European realities. A local theory would capture the relationship between imperial and international law in far more fluid terms: "That the theory of international rights, in the above described sense of the different ethnicities, has not yet been developed, must obviously be attributed to the circumstance that scholars working on these rights, Englishmen, Frenchmen, Dutchmen, Italians, and Germans, live in such lands in which the concepts 'nation' and 'state' more or less coincide."[96] He mused that the intellectual energy of his countrymen had been caught up elsewhere—in Slavic philology and the exact sciences. Had they turned their minds to nationalism and legal theory instead, he speculated, there would be a far more developed jurisprudence on the international rights of nationalities—rights that transcended sovereignty and attached to human groups rather than state borders. As viewed from the multiethnic polities of Central Europe, international law would (and should) look quite different.

For now, the question of nationalities as "moral and legal persons" was enough of a challenge even within the bounds of imperial law. In the heat of revolution, the slogan of Palacký and many others—of the "national equality of rights"—had found its way into positive law. Francis Joseph used the phrase in the manifest that accompanied his rise to the throne in December 1848.[97] But the government's imposed constitution of March 1849—the constitution that superseded the Kremsier draft—had retreated from this formulation and instead declared, in article 5, "All ethnicities [*Völksstamme*] possess equal rights and each ethnicity has an inviolable right to the preservation and cultivation of its nationality and language."

The legal meaning of this provision engendered much controversy. Did it establish "ethnicities" as legal subjects capable of possessing rights? Many jurists expressed great skepticism. Ludwig Gumplowicz's critique was unforgiving. What *was* a *Volkstamm*? he asked incredulously. No piece of legislation in Austria (or elsewhere, for that matter) defined *ethnicity*. The constitution did not enumerate the ethnicities of the empire, which would presumably be a prerequisite for their rights to be made equal. Nowhere could one find an example of an ethnicity existing as "the bearer of rights," and still less was one able to construct one's own theory of how such an indefinite "ethnicity" might be made into a rights-bearing subject.[98] "We know well from the legal sciences how a corporation or an association can be a bearer of rights and exercise them, too: yet an ethnicity is neither an association nor a corporation, nor in general a 'moral person' in the sense of legal science."[99] Article 5 presented a legal riddle, Gumplowicz concluded, without providing any means for its solution. And the text only became more cryptic when it spoke further of the right of ethnicities to preserve their language and "nationality" (*Nationalität*). Can a mere ethnicity possess a nationality, he wondered? It was an empty provision with no identifiable legal content: it remained at most a proclamation.[100]

In his subsequent textbook on Austrian constitutional law, he repeated his criticisms in relation to the 1867 constitution, which again declared that all ethnicities were equal and possessed the inviolable right to cultivate their language and nationality (article 19). He classed this provision as a mere general principle that could never be implemented without further legislative elaboration, reasoning that "'ethnicities' are neither physical nor juridical persons, and therefore as such can never assert what ever rights."[101] Gumplowicz's critique was echoed by many of his colleagues in the field of public law. In his monograph on juridical persons in public law, Edmund Bernatzik argued that nationalities could not form legal persons because they did not have the necessary unified and organized will. Faced with the constitution's vague formulation, he maintained, one must immediately ask, "Who then is the subject of such a celebrated, 'inviolable' right, if it cannot be the nationality as such?"[102] He offered no solution to the problem.

So the newly announced rights were in need of a subject. They populated constitutional law like ghosts: disembodied legal signs without "persons" to carry them. Subjective rights without a legal person behind them were "unthinkable," wrote Rudolf von Herrnritt in his classic study *Nationalität und Recht* (1899), as he too puzzled over article 19.[103] Georg Jellinek could only blame the drafting. "This article has a very unlegal style [*unjuristisch stilisirt*]," he complained in 1892, "in that ethnicities that do not possess personality and languages that could never become legal subjects are granted 'rights.'" Further legislative elaboration was required "to designate the legal subjects who are to be granted an entitlement in this area."[104] Adolf Exner, a scholar of Roman law and Rudolf von Ihering's successor at (and future rector of) the University of Vienna, spoke on the subject at the Wiener Juristische Gesellschaft in 1892. "If one examines article 19, the absence of a legal subject is already apparent. Ethnicities are not juridical persons; in the first instance it is not even possible to objectively determine who belongs to an ethnicity."[105] Its "true nature," he argued, was that of a "promissory law [*Verheißungsgesetzes*]." The word *inviolable* already pointed one in that direction. "Every right can be violated. But if it says in the state fundamental law that a right is inviolable, then that is a self-limitation of the state will [*des Staatswillens*], not a guarantee of individuals against a legal injury."[106] The state was speaking to itself, not ascribing rights to others. Exner's solution to the specter of rights without subjects was to "discover" that the rights themselves did not exist in the first place: article 19 in fact housed the *duties* of the state rather than the rights of nations.

The aspiration to make nations into collective legal subjects also challenged the empire's existing legal subunits: the historical kingdoms and lands. One of the earliest proposals for a reordering of the empire along national lines came from a Romanian delegation representing Romanians living across provincial frontiers in Transylvania, Hungary, the Banat, and the Bukovina. In February and March 1849, as debate raged in the Kremsier parliament, the Romanian delegation submitted memorandums to the emperor and to the imperial government. The latter, dated March 5, laid out a detailed plan for "the amalgamation of all Romanians of the Austrian monarchy into a single independent nation, under the Austrian scepter, as an integral component of the unified monarchy."[107] While stressing their loyalty to the monarchy, they sought an "independent national administration" so that they might exercise the right to free national development, as guaranteed by the crown.[108] This independence would pertain only to internal administration as against the other nations of the monarchy. No nation should be subordinate to another. This principle meant that the realization of the national equality of rights would be possible only if "each particular nation is left to group itself into a single center over and against the remaining nations, roughly in the method of the ecclesiastical organization for the members of different confessions, without consideration of the previous provincial division, and without great consideration for territory in general."[109]

Genuine equality of national rights required the old provincial borders to be dissolved, the logic of minorities and majorities superseded, and, portentously, territory itself to fade in importance. The tyranny of geography would no longer prevent a dispersed and intermingled population from appearing as a single administrative unit. This nonterritorial model of national rights, inspired by the associational logic of confessional communities, would draw worldwide attention when it became part of the Austro-Marxist platform half a century later. But the radical reconceptualization of jurisdiction it entailed—with law attaching fluidly to human subjects, rather than to territory—had entered the bloodstream of imperial debate already in the first period of constitutional experimentation, and it had come from the eastern margins of the empire at that. Hardly surprising, perhaps: as the Hungarian statesman and reformer József Eötvös once remarked, perhaps no other people had more to gain from the national division of the empire than the Romanians.[110]

If the Romanian memorandum understood the dislocation of law from territory as progressive and liberatory, Eötvös, for his part, embedded such ideas in an alternative historical narrative. His analysis of the situation was not unlike that of the Romanian delegation: as the boundaries between language groups were far from distinct, he argued that the monarchy could only be divided up according to nationality if this was undertaken "not on the basis of territory, but rather on that of the population," with "each particular municipality exercising their political rights not in community with their neighbors, but with their kinsfolk [*Stammesgenossen*]."[111] But rather than emplot these proposals as a higher stage of legal evolution or as a sophisticated response to a complicated problem, Eötvös reversed the historical signs: forsaking territory represented a significant regression. He likened such ideas to the great migration of peoples (*Völkerwanderung*) of late antiquity and the early Middle Ages, after which, for a time, one followed the principle that the inhabitants of a land "should each be subjected to their own laws according to the diversity of their ancestry."[112] Not only private law but also the participation of individuals in public offices was determined by this principle. Eötvös deemed the full implementation of such a system impossible in today's world. His analogy invoked the archaism of the premodern, a chaotic juridical primitivism of the sort now highlighted by those who seek to establish the conceptual affinity of premodern and postmodern law.[113] For Eötvös in 1850, there was no postmodern jurisdictional pluralism on the horizon: the hegemonic model of a territorial state stretched off unendingly into the future.

Nations as Juridical Persons between Imperial and International Law

Nations never became the legal building blocks of the empire as organized legal persons. As historians like Gerald Stourzh, Tara Zahra, Börries Kuzmany, and Pieter Judson have shown, however, the provisions of article 19 still had a series of dramatic and unexpected consequences. After 1867, politicians, activists, and community representatives increasingly pitched local and regional interests as questions of language rights, with schools (as the foundational site of community reproduction) the sharpest flash point. As suffrage expanded and the empire began collecting census data on "language of everyday use," the defense of language rights served as an ever more potent lever of political mobilization. It was engagement with politics, Judson argues, that led people to understand their worlds in terms of discrete, linguistically defined nations—not the other way around.[114] Nationalist activism increasingly left its mark on legal structures, too. Various municipal organizations and voluntary associations invoked article 19 in collective claims on behalf of national interests in their particular area, giving expression to the announced rights in a piecemeal or ad hoc fashion.[115] In the empire's last decades, a small number of more ambitious constitutional experiments at the regional level—most prominently the Moravian Compromise of 1905—established national voting cadastres (where, in this case, one would vote as either a Czech or a German) with jurisdiction over areas like education and commerce.[116] The wisdom—and legal logic—of these developments remained hotly contested. In 1916, the jurist Hans von Frisch described the combination of national politics and administrative measures as the "cancer" of Austria's whole administration. The tasks of the state did not extend to national affairs: "One cannot govern with nationalities, because 'nation' is not a legal concept; one needs to finally recognize this in Austria."[117]

But visions of a wholesale legal restructuring of the empire along legal lines continued to swirl. The most famous proposals in this genre came from Otto Bauer and Karl Renner, leading lights of the widely influential Austro-Marxist movement that pursued the reconciliation of socialism and nationalism (another theoretical innovation spurred by the Habsburg condition). The legal personality of nations stood at the center of these schemes, and in precisely the way the Romanians had envisaged back in 1848: as legal entities that superseded territory altogether. In works like *The Question of Nationalities and Social Democracy* (1907) and *State and Nation* (1899), Bauer and Renner elaborated a bold federal vision for the empire built around the so-called personality principle.[118] They argued that national collectives could be constituted non-territorially among conationals, wherever they happened to live, through a curia system analogous to church membership. Their ideas would echo through subsequent Marxist, communist, and Bundist understandings of nations and nationalism and through the rising tide of appeals to self-determination around the world. The creativity and legal dexterity required to solve Austria-Hungary's constitutional conundrum emerged as a highly exportable commodity with resonance for multiethnic polities the world over: imperial constitutional law acquired a properly international stage. More than discrete unit ideas traveling between different contexts, Renner conceived the autonomy program itself as a hybrid blend of domestic and international law—a means of inviting supranational law into the imperial fold. "Incontestably, this country, despite its objectionable constitutional backwardness in all other things, has made in this area the first and most interesting attempts at an internal international law [*innerstaatlichen Völkerrechtes*]," he declared in *The Self-Determination of Nations with Particular Application to Austria*, published in 1918 (with a preface dated December 1917). The Habsburg Empire could "count as a field of experimentation for internal internationalism, and therefore has a high interest for legal research as well as political praxis."[119] It was the international law of the empire. Palacký's prophecy—that a theory of the international rights of nations would most obviously originate in a polity like Austria-Hungary—had come true.

Renner saw the problem in the same terms as many Habsburg thinkers before him: for nations to have rights, they needed to be fashioned into legal entities of some sort and made "visible" in law. "As is well known," Renner wrote, "the nations in Austria do not have juridical personality, nor any other sort of legally graspable collective presence. Current law does not know the nation, but rather only nationality as a distinctive characteristic of the individual."[120] The judge remained blind to the nation and its aspirations, otherwise he left the domain of law and entered that of politics. Yet Renner, like his colleagues, eschewed the most obvious way of making a nation visible in law— that is, through a sovereign nation-state. They viewed an "international legal order" based on "national autonomy" to be a far superior model.[121] To achieve this, he elaborated the *legal* idea of a nation within a *Nationalitätenstaat*, a state of nationalites. New legal forms and formations (*Rechtsformen*) needed to be constructed for this new "internal supranational legal order" (*innerstaatliche übernationale Rechtsordnung*).[122] The whole relationship between state and nation(s) needed to be reimagined.

Few models were available for the craftsmen of these new *juristische Formen*. Existing jurisprudence, too focused on positive law, proved little help. Scholars in the field should have been far more inquisitive about the wide variety of forms that state and nation might take. It was time, Renner announced, for a new constitutional work.[123] Crucially, this new work required moving beyond a liberal paradigm in which national characteristics belonged only to the individual.[124] Any solution based on individual rights was insufficient. "The national problem is not just and not in the first instance an economic-social or a language question," Renner maintained, "but a constitutional-political question that seizes the whole state organization."[125] Nations sought a portion of the state's functions; they wanted power. Nations must be "state legal factors [*staatliche Rechtsfaktoren*], constitutional potencies or, to utter the dreaded phrase, states within states, if peace and progress are to return to Austria."[126] Yet these states within states could not be built on territorial foundations, not only because language groups did not inhabit discrete, hermetic areas but also because such an approach misunderstood the nature of nationality. An individual did not "leave" the nation when he or she left the territory, nor did he or she "enter" it upon traversing a certain geographic domain.[127] A far more fluid solution was required, in which law attached to people rather than land—the proposition that Eötvös had viewed as reactionary and premodern. Indeed, other scholars such as Josef Lukas, who taught law in Czernowitz between 1904 and 1909, continued to liken the personality principle to a reformulated, modernized version of an original "Germanic" conception in which law attached to the *Stamm*, to ethnicity, rather than to territory.[128]

How were dispersed, mobile people to mimic the legal fixity of territory as a jurisdiction? The Austro-Marxists thus had need of the special alchemic legal fiction of collective personality, in which a plurality become a unity: individuals needed to be grouped together in such a way that the law could posit a single, unified will and intention where nature had granted none. A nation must be transformed into an "autonomous body, into a juridical person with its own actionable, judicially protected subjective rights." In other words, it was to become a "private and public law person, capable of acting in law, entitled to claim and to have claims [brought] against it."[129]

The idea had lost none of its revolutionary sting. The politician and erstwhile trade minister Joseph Maria Baernreither was quick to call the Austro-Marxists to account. Bauer and his colleagues, Baernreither observed in 1910, wanted to construe nationality as a "personal union" (*Personalverband*) rather than a "territorial body" (*Gebietskörperschaft*). If "the nation must become a legal subject" in this way, then "a relationship must be established between the individual national-comrade [*Volksgenossen*] and the nation which is like that existing today between a citizen and the state."[130] What is more, "this new legal subject, the organized nation" must then possess organs so that it could make use of the rights granted to it; one would need judges who could preside over this new area of law. Such developments would amount to "a partial transvaluation of our state law [*Staatsrecht*] into a nations-law [*Nationsrecht*]."[131] The whole basis of constitutional law would shift. They would be states within the state—if not *against* the state, Baerenreither warned.

Renner viewed such subjecthood as the only method of making national rights meaningful. Like so many other Habsburg jurists, Renner critiqued the legal construction of article 19 of the constitution that granted national rights without having organized "nations" as legal subjects. Rights without subjects were unenforceable and thus meaningless. This basic truth had been obscured in the Habsburg Monarchy, Renner explained, because of the ambiguous interaction of nationalist politics with the preexisting legal structure of the empire. It was self-evident that "national rights can only be the rights of nations. But with us one never understands the self-evident as self-evident. With a bewildering persistence, our protagonists of the national idea struggle for fifty years now for the rights of the—crownlands."[132]

He was not wrong: many Czech nationalists, for example, had focused on historical Bohemian state rights as a surrogate agenda for regional autonomy that seemed more palatable to government than naked national claim making.[133] The wires running between rights and their subject had become crossed, tangled, and ultimately misdirected. Renner understood the reasons and used a particularly striking metaphor to explain what had gone wrong. "If one wants to make a law for the nations, then one first has to make the nations," he stated. "Because that is a difficult and not at all joyful process, one used the lands . . . as the pack-carriers of national rights, and overburdened the decrepit donkey's back with rights that were meant for the nations."[134] Because of the challenges of making new legal persons, one had fallen back on the legal subjects already at hand—that is, the lands. Through an accident of history, the lands had been loaded up with rights intended for the nations, and this structural case of mistaken identity had cost the peace of the empire. In Renner's analysis, then, it was the conceptual and practical difficulties of constituting nations as juridical persons that had inadvertently kept the old historical lands at the forefront of the imperial debate about rights. The historical lands became the convenient (but lazy) mules for rights that otherwise, lacking a fixed delivery address, would have floated around indefinitely in search of a subject to embody and use them. In his words, the "question of the bearer of rights" lay at the core.[135]

Renner conceded that many feared the notion of states within states. As the interests of these legal persons diverged, would they not threaten the unity of the state? Not if the state cleverly managed their rights and took care of their common interests, Renner felt: "If Britain, Australia and Canada next to India etc. can form a political unity, should the rounded-off [*abgegrundeten*] Habsburg lands not be able to do it?"[136] Other objections pointed to the dogma of sovereignty. As he described it, his plan involved the creation of a single legal order in which sovereignty was shared with nations as well as individuals. This constituted, he admitted, an "architectonic work," resulting in an internal international law that rubbed up against old pieties: "This dogma, constructed by Bodin and Hobbes, of the indivisibility of the state force, of the absolute unity of a highest power, was abused from the beginning as the rationale and support of absolutism."[137] Having dismissed traditional doctrines of sovereignty as the handmaidens of absolutism, he cleared space for nations, as juridical persons in private and public law, to form organs of the state in their own right, with their own sphere of autonomy guaranteed within the state— that is, their "right of self-determination."[138]

Nations and Rights at Empire's End

Renner's text quickly became a classic within a constitutional tradition whose whole premise was superseded at the point of its highest creativity. Unbeknownst to Renner, that premise—the existence of the Habsburg Monarchy itself—was about to disappear out the back door of world history. Events were moving fast. As Renner deployed "self-determination" as a touchstone for keeping the Austro-Hungarian Empire together, others dispersed widely across the landscape of international politics were pinning hopes on its utility for prying other empires apart. From Woodrow Wilson's liberal internationalism to Lenin's appeal for world revolution to Sa'd Zaghlūl's anticolonial nationalism in Egypt and beyond, the catchcry of "self-determination" raced erratically between political projects and ideologies. As an intersection point between orders, it offered the semblance of convergence (and of a unified "moment," as Erez Manela famously phrased it) even as it documented their antagonism.[139] Renner's creative invocation of "international law" in his proposals for the Habsburg lands turned out to be "truer" or more literal than he could have foreseen: if the former Habsburg lands now became the prime region in which "self-determination" was ostensibly actualized, the term now served to legitimate the individual sovereignties of numerous small states rather than to distribute imperial sovereignty equitably among the monarchy's resident nations as the newborn "persons" of an empire remade.

Yet self-determination was not the only political-legal concept through which the empire's constitutional order melted messily into the "new world order." The imperial jurisprudence on the rights of nations acquired a new vocation in the postwar settlement thanks to the experimental minorities treaties forced upon the new states of Central and Eastern Europe and guaranteed by the League of Nations. If important conceptual differences distinguished the rights of "minorities" from those of "nationalities" (not least the normatively homogeneous nation-state as a conceptual prerequisite for the idea of a "minority" in the first place), the legal stakes were remarkably similar: at the heart of debates about both regimes stood the possibility (and desirability) of according nonsovereign ethnic groups a collective legal personality, and the question of how their rights and personality related to sovereignty.[140]

The projection of Habsburg nationality law onto the world stage began already during the war, when the emergence of an international system of minorities protection remained a hypothetical proposition. In 1916, the Central Organization for a Durable Peace, formed in The Hague a year earlier, produced an influential "minimum program" of nine points and established nine study commissions to further develop each of the points. The second commission, chaired by the Norwegian historian (and future Norwegian foreign minister) Halvdan Koht, tasked with exploring the question of national minorities,[141] solicited submissions from a range of international experts, which the Central Organization published progressively between 1916 and 1918.[142] Among the contributors on the question of national minorities were Rudolf Laun and Eugen Ehrlich from Austria and Oszkár Jászi from Hungary, as well as the German sociologist Franz Oppenheimer (who drew extensively and principally on the Habsburg jurisprudence, especially from Renner and Bernatzik, in his response).[143] A smaller group—Laun among them—then met in person in Christiania (Oslo), where Koht taught, in July 1917. Strikingly,

Koht's concluding report essentially presented the *Nationalitätenrecht* in place in Austria (though not Hungary) as a model that could be profitably adopted around the world.[144]

Austria had "more or less" solved the problem of nationality, Koht reported. He explicitly modeled the first of his proposals on article 19 of the Austrian constitution, guaranteeing the "inviolable" rights of ethnicities. He drew on Austrian electoral laws, the Moravian Compromise of 1905, and Karl Renner's conceptualization of national autonomy.[145] This ringing endorsement did not go unnoticed in Austria. Heinrich Lammasch (1853–1920), the Austrian jurist who would serve briefly as Cisleithania's last minister-president the following year, took the report as evidence of a slow shift in perspectives on the very nature of state legitimacy. Gradually it was dawning on people that it was impossible to replace the monarchy with nationally homogeneous states, not least without damaging the vital interests of the nationalities themselves, Lammasch wrote in 1917. Nationality may be a significant factor in the formation of states—but not the only one, nor even the most important. "In [certain] circumstances," he maintained, "the nationalities-state is just as justified as the nation-state." In fact, in the future, the former may be regarded as "a higher form for human development."[146]

Koht's high praise for the Austrian model was all the more conspicuous in the context of struggles over the representation of Austria-Hungary in the commission's preparatory work as well as more generally in wartime propaganda and claim making. In his submission for the Central Organization's commission, for example, the British politician Charles Roden Buxton had depicted Austria-Hungary according to the familiar trope of a prison of nationalities.[147] He had particularly incensed the Austrian jurists with a thought experiment intended to calculate whether a victory for the Allies or the Entente would achieve more for the oppressed nationalities of the world. An Allied victory, he reasoned, would likely satisfy the claims of Bohemians, Alsatians and Lorrainers, the Danes in north Germany, Italians in Austria, Serbo-Croats and Slovenes, as well as Romanians, Greeks, and Armenians, numbering about thirty million in total. Against this formidable multitude, a mere handful of satisfied claims (the Bulgarians of Macedonia, perhaps) could be foreseen as the likely outcome if the Entente proved victorious.[148]

Eugen Ehrlich—that pioneering Habsburg scholar of "free law" and legal pluralism—took the bait. Why did Buxton restrict himself to European nationalities? "I do not consider the Arabs, Persians and Hindus to be so very backward, as that one cannot take them into account, being peoples of ancient lineage and venerable culture," Ehrlich countered. Mr. Buxton arrived at the figure of thirty million "by fully disregarding all the nations which the Allies enslave."[149] Ehrlich's own mathematics—tallying "the Irish, Indians, Persians and Egyptians" among a long list of nationalities to be hypothetically liberated by the Entente—delivered him a figure of six hundred million souls, a "record which could hardly be beaten by the Allies." "Mr. Buxton greatly underrates the extent of generosity we too could afford at the expense of other people," Ehrlich quipped.[150]

Koht's endorsement thus filled the sails of those jurists, like a young Rudolf Laun (1882–1975), who were coming around to the view that the nationality principle could be Austria's weapon in the war of ideas rather than their Achilles' heel. Britain's propagandistic slogans—pacifism, democracy, the nationality principle—had stuck, pinning Austria as an autocratic, militaristic oppressor of nationalities. Yet Austria could be the accuser rather than the accused, Laun argued in *Das Nationalitätenrecht als internationales Problem* (1917). Austria must "turn the spear around, to reproach our opponents with their own political sins and weaknesses."[151] The world should be educated about Austrian nationality and language law: no other comparably large state had developed such ethical and practical postulates. Against their measure, others would be exposed: Austria need only adopt the claim and slogan of "the protection of national minorities."[152] After all, every large state included minorities: some in the motherland, others in colonies. Whatever political rights the oppressed majority in India possessed, Laun felt sure they fell well short of those belonging to the citizens of Austria. The question of "national minority protection . . . would therefore hand us a political weapon" that could prove more useful at the peace negotiations and in the "spiritual struggle" than various victorious battles or economic triumphs.[153] Laun's text, like Ehrlich's, documented the conceptual fluidity of the terms *nationality* and *minority* on the cusp of the new world order, especially when they served as the means for interimperial comparison. Implicit in these exchanges lurked the structural ambiguity of Austria-Hungary's place in the world of states and empires: Was it most sensibly compared with the small unitary states of Western Europe or with global empires like the British Commonwealth? Who decided on the line between "colonized," "minority," and "nationality," and with what consequences?

But Koht's report did not simply stoke debate about Austria's place in the broader wartime contest over state (and imperial) legitimacy. More substantially and, juridically speaking, most audaciously, Koht's report proposed an international treaty and international guarantee for the protection of minorities grounded in an international court of arbitration. The general skepticism about such a treaty reminds us how improbable the League of Nations' eventual minorities regime appeared even a few short years before its emergence.[154] From the outset, Laun declared that such plans for an international oversight commission (*Kontrollkommission*) and an international "court of nationalities" (*Nationalitätengerichtshof*) had little chance of success because they contradicted state sovereignty.[155] Yet this base assessment did not prevent his analysis of the proposals along one line in particular—that of legal personality.

In this area, the Austrian experience had much to offer any emergent general system, whether buttressed by an international court or not.

Laun observed that the "legal subject" appeared variously in Koht's report as the "race," the "ethnicity," and the "national minority." As a result, any community sufficiently large to open a school or a church could appeal for protection. Practical difficulties arose in Austria, he counseled, because article 19 spoke of ethnicities "as legal subjects" although "these ethnicities were not organized as juridical persons." For that reason, article 19 could not be applied directly but only indirectly "as a general principle" helpful in the interpretation of other norms. The granting of rights "without the organization of the appropriate legal subjects would thus not have the desired significance in practice."[156] Be warned of the weakness of rights without subjects: Laun offered up the empire's hard-won lessons for international consumption.

This imperial expertise hinted at further difficulties. For if one instead "wanted to explicitly propose the formation of such legal subjects, then one must expect that the proposal will encounter the greatest resistance because most states will avoid assuming an obligation according to which they had to organize their minorities as states within states."[157] Making them into legal persons—organized, unified, and with standing in public law—seemed too closely akin to making them into states. Still more fantastical was the idea of according these internal quasi states a standing in international law. "But it is entirely futile to want to make national minorities into the legal subjects not only of state law, but also of international law, who could appeal for the help of an international commission or court against their own state," Laun warned. "This would suffer the sharpest repudiation as irreconcilable with the current concept of state sovereignty and shipwreck the whole project."[158]

The migration between orders was twofold: imperial knowledge, it seemed, could be resettled from imperial into international law, but could the (potential or otherwise) juridical persons of state law cross the border into the international domain? Laun deemed it virtually impossible and instead recommended that states be obliged to incorporate provisions for the protection of minorities into their own domestic law. Extreme pacifists and others may accuse us of too great a deference to state sovereignty, Laun conceded. Yet even radical goals required slow and measured steps to achieve durable results, he argued. The longer-range, ultimate goal "is not for me the sovereign nation-state as an end in itself but rather a world state that includes the whole of humanity, in which the current individual 'sovereign' states would perhaps in some connections enjoy no more 'sovereignty' than a Swiss canton today."[159]

Laun's own career runs like a red thread through the various orders and rights regimes of the first half of the twentieth century. Born in Prague in 1882, he studied law and philosophy at the University of Vienna and had already taught for a few years as an *außerordentlicher* professor at the same university before serving in World War I, an experience that turned him into a pacifist. His interest in the empire's nationalities law segued seamlessly into the emergent international regime, and not only via the Central Organization for a Durable Peace. Having joined the foreign office as a consultant for nationalities policy in Karl Renner's new government at the end of the war, Laun attended the peace conference as a member of the Austrian delegation. His own proposal for minorities protection—that drew much from Renner and Bauer's cultural autonomy—was discussed at the Berne "League of Nations" conference in 1919.[160] Already that same year he took up a chair in the law faculty in Hamburg, launching an influential career in Germany and beyond. In the immediate aftermath of World War II, as an indefatigable advocate for the rights of the German expellees, he prominently accused the Allies of violating Germans' human rights, placing him at the center of the tussle over the legal and political significance of the new regime of international human rights.[161]

If this postwar involvement with individual rights has attracted recent scholarly attention as part of the new field of human rights history, Laun in fact spent much of the 1920s and 1930s analyzing minority rights and, more generally, the status of the "nation" or a "people" in international law. As he noted at the meeting of the German Society of International Law in 1926, the protection of national minorities and the right of self-determination formed two sides of the same coin: both addressed the status of the national question in international law. He returned repeatedly to the theme I have traced out of the womb of imperial-constitutional law, namely, the possibility of ethnic collectives coming together to form a single legal personality: group rights without sovereignty. Like so many other jurists of the period, he critiqued the formal construction of the minorities treaties that spoke of minorities not as collective wholes but only as a sum of individuals who *belonged* to a religious, racial, or linguistic minority. They were not legal subjects and not parties to their own disputes. This lack of legal status "sabotaged" the protection on offer, Laun wrote.[162]

The wording of the treaties notwithstanding, this area of law had its own dynamism, especially after minorities from across Europe took matters into their own hands through the inauguration of the "nationalities congress" that began meeting annually in 1925. At that first meeting, the delegates, with widely varying agendas, found common ground in the idea of cultural autonomy and announced as much in their resolutions. Cultural autonomy was in fact already becoming formal state law in countries like Estonia and Lithuania. This development pertained directly to the legal status of minorities, Laun reported to the German Society of International Law, "because until now the most important and decisive argument that could always be set against the claims of national minorities was that they are only a sum of private persons who coincidentally speak a different language to the majority in their state, that they are not legally organized, are not legal subjects." The granting of cultural autonomy would remedy this by equipping them with organs of self-administration, making them "comparable with the member state of a federal state." They "could then be treated as a legal subject in international law just as much as, say, Prussia or Bavaria."[163]

Here the application of cultural autonomy—itself part of the conceptual legacy of the imperial constitutional tradition—would (again) serve as the means of converting isolated individuals into corporate bodies, as it would require the establishment of formal institutions capable of legally representing the singular and unified will of the group. Strikingly, these new legal persons could then traverse the line between domestic and international law, endowed with the same ambiguous status as other nonsovereign states like Bavaria.

Habsburg Nationality Law
in the Interwar International Order

The nationality law of the empire cast a long shadow over the interwar minorities treaties. Imperial expertise found application in international law in both theory and practice. International civil servants in the minorities section at the League of Nations collected documentation from and conducted interviews with former imperial officials.[164] After a research trip to Vienna, the Swiss diplomat Edouard de Haller, then working at the league, penned a long study on Austrian nationality law intended to benefit the league's minorities work. "After completing this study," de Haller wrote, "I maintain that the legislation and jurisprudence of Austria before the war constitute useful sources for the study of minority problems in the States bound by minority treaties or declarations and especially for the successor states of Austria-Hungary."[165] At a more theoretical level, the classics of Austrian jurisprudence became the secondary literature for theories of international minority rights.[166]

Even late into the 1930s, Austrian nationality law remained an important "place" from which to analyze and critique the minorities regime, especially on the question of legal personality.[167] In his work *Völkerrecht* (1937), Alfred Verdross (whom we will encounter more closely in chapter 6) reminded his readers that the minorities treaties did not define the concept of minority and referred only to its members: "Not them, but those *belonging to* the minorities are awarded rights."[168] The treaties thus required states to guard certain individual rights.[169] Verdross argued that the premise of the treaties—that it was plausible to understand minorities as a collected mass of individuals—may be well suited to Western and Central Europe, but lacked a more general validity and applicability. Certainly, it was misconceived for the "belt of mixed peoples of the European east." To "transfer" a provision rooted in "the ideology of the nation-state" to areas of fundamentally mixed settlement appeared both irrational and contradictory.[170] His prescription was specific: "A pacification [*Befriedung*] of the European east can only be achieved if the principle of the *equal rights of ethnicities* laid down in article 19 of the old-Austrian constitution regarding the general rights of citizens (1867) is elevated to the *Magna Carta of Eastern Europe*." Peaceful coexistence could be achieved only if each group possessed an equal right to the protection and cultivation of its ethnicity and language. "But because culture is only possible in the community, mere individual rights are not sufficient," Verdross argued. One must instead "recognize *rights of the ethnic group* [*Volksgruppenrecht*]": "the rights of minorities must be rebuilt into the *rights of ethnic groups*."[171] In 1936, the nationalities congress had come to the same conclusion, declaring its impatience with individual rights and the necessity of new corporate legal bodies. "All cultural work is communal work, all national rights are communal rights," the congress declared. "For that reason, a true nationalities law that does not recognize national minorities as collective unities and legal subjects is unthinkable."[172]

On the cusp of World War II, Eastern Europe cried out for the resurrection of imperial constitutional law—at least according to Verdross. The rights languages of the empire's nationality law were far better adapted to the prose of life in this region than the misconceived platform of individual rights imposed through the new international settlement. Yet even as Verdross remembered imperial Austria, he partook in some crucial forgetting, too. For article 19 of the imperial Austrian constitution may have theoretically recognized group rights, but as we now know only too well, it had failed to formally constitute group rights *subjects* to own and defend those rights. Those rights had floated like balloons without strings, unattached to legal personalities. With some regional exceptions (such as the Moravian Compromise of 1905), nationalities had never become "states within states" in the empire—that privilege had been reserved for the historical lands.

Politicians and officials from the new states of Eastern and Central Europe, for their part, were especially keen to avoid the constitution of minorities as collective legal entities. "Care must be taken," warned a grave Edvard Beneš at the League of Nations' Sixth Committee in 1932, "not to give the impression that a minority constituted a personality in law."[173] But Adolf Hitler's National Socialists took a different view. The Nazis may have disdained the "juridification" of the interwar order, but they too shared the crucial assumption that an ethnic group, quite apart from any correlation with the borders of a state, could and should be a legal subject. For them, it was *the* legal subject. *Volkspersonlichkeit* structured the territorial map and legal imaginary; in rejecting the empty abstraction of the state, they "turned the folk-group into a collective legal entity."[174] Before Germany left the league, the German diplomat Friedrich von Keller explained its position before the league's Sixth Committee in October 1933. A nation had "a natural and moral right," he held, "to consider that all its members—even those separated from the mother country by State frontiers—constitute a moral and cultural whole."[175] (The similarity of his statements to Palacký's sentiments quoted earlier is striking.) All of a sudden, the state's containment of legal personality—previously the bugbear of progressive projects one and all—seemed to be a comforting convention.

The following day, the British statesman William Ormsby-Gore—a man with paws all over the different facets of the interwar order—passionately refuted von Keller's presentations, especially his sketch of an international relations founded on ethnic homogeneity, in which a state possessed the right and duty to concern itself with citizens of other states of the same ethnicity. "That will carry us very far," he said, aghast. "I tremble to think of the responsibilities of my Government in respect of every citizen of the United States who claims descent from those who went over in the Mayflower—and there are millions—if this idea were put into operation. We reject absolutely this conception put forward by the German delegate regarding the racial homogeneity of political units and States. How could we do otherwise?"[176] Beneš readily agreed with Ormsby-Gore: "As I see it, this theory would, if carried to the extreme, overthrow all the legal conceptions upon which not only the Minorities Treaties, but also the international relations between States composed of two or more nationalities, are based."[177] Unlike his Bohemian forebears within the Austro-Hungarian Empire, Beneš already had sovereign rights, which seemed (at least until 1938!) quite hard and real, unlike their fictional, mythic cousins in the nineteenth century. The Czechs had switched roles: his task was now to *defend* the traditional order of state relations, and the privileges of sovereignty, and certainly not to experiment with legal subjects floating fluidly beyond state and territory.

CHAPTER FOUR

Pure Theory

JELLINEK AND KELSEN REINVENT
LEGAL PHILOSOPHY

Georg Jellinek arrives in Heidelberg and departs from the material world • The state is like a symphony • What sort of thing is law? • The riddle of knowledge is the riddle of existence • Hans Kelsen's many patricides • Purity hurts • Kelsen discovers that the state does not exist • Freud and Kelsen think totems hold the key • No geometry of the irrational

HANS KELSEN STARTED at the beginning. "Like all other social groups, the state, the most significant of them all, is a specific unity of a multitude of individuals, . . . and *the inquiry into the nature of the state is fundamentally an inquiry into the nature of this unity.*" Sometimes the most basic propositions turn out to be the most confounding mysteries. "In what manner, according to what criterion," he asked, "is this multitude of individuals welded into what we are wont to assume to be a higher unity? How do the separate individuals forming the state, or their individual activities, combine into a super-individual whole?" If this question was fundamental to our public life, it was also troublingly difficult to answer. For this inquiry was thereby "identical with that concerning the peculiar 'reality' of the state, the specific nature of its being."[1] The problem of the state's unity, its status as a singular thing, slipped straight into the problem of the real.

That problem would drive Prague-born, Vienna-raised Kelsen (1881–1973) to elaborate a new epistemology for law that would shape legal philosophy around the world and through to the present.[2] As a student and then professor at the University of Vienna, Kelsen constructed what he came to call the "pure theory of law" in the years before and after World War I. Dramatic days in which to contemplate the unity—and reality—of states: as the pure theory came together, the Habsburg Empire came apart, disappearing from the world map at war's end. Kelsen did not just write *through* these epochal transformations: in a certain sense he *wrote* them, too. Serving in the war ministry at the tail end of the war, he drafted blueprints for the empire's reformation into a federation of nationalities (which the emperor accepted—but only too late); as small, rump, republican Austria emerged bruised and battered in the empire's wake, Chancellor Karl Renner invited Kelsen to draft the new state's constitution. In so doing, he created a new constitutional court—one that pioneered forms of constitutional review—and then served on its bench until 1930.[3]

The fall and rise of states, the structure and transformation of political order: these were lived, even existential questions. All the more revealing, then, that Kelsen's way of taming the chaos, the only way he found of making the state coherent, was a highly philosophical theory of legal knowledge many accused of being unforgivably removed from reality. The pure theory of law held that if legal science wanted to be able to sort law into unified, logically consistent systems, to make sense of all that we know about the legal order, it had to restrict its gaze exclusively to legal *norms* and purify its subject and its methodology of material drawn from the social-political world of *facts*. In the Kantian terminology that became its shorthand, law was a science of *Sollen* (what *ought to be*) and not *Sein* (that which *is*). This theory, as we will see, was bound up in broader transformations of fin de siècle scholarly knowledge—not least the many-sided crisis of methodology provoked by the ascendant natural sciences—but it was also the product of a very particular empire-state at the heart of the European continent.

Kelsen's first question was the state: the pure theory gradually took shape through his theorizing about the state in the last years of the Habsburg Empire. As he explained, "The decisive question in relation to the nature of the state seemed to me to be: what constitutes the unity in the plurality of individuals that constitute this community." Multiplicity into singularity: a very Austro-Hungarian conceptualization of the problem, and not one that was easy to solve. In an earlier epoch, that unity might have been anchored in the sole sovereignty of a monarch ruling by divine right. As sovereignty became a property of "the state" rather than the king, and positivism recast what it meant to know and prove, ascendant social sciences like sociology and psychology offered theories of how individuals melded into collectives like states. Kelsen immersed himself in such theories—but found no satisfaction. "And to this question I could find no other scientifically sound answer," he reported, "other than that it is a specific legal order that constitutes this unity."[4] Only a system of legal norms made the state into a unified thing—only law knew the alchemy of spinning plurality into singularity. In the world of material facts, that unity simply did not exist.

Decades later, looking out from Berkeley across San Francisco Bay to a glistening Pacific beyond, Kelsen saw how the Habsburg setting had influenced his high theorizing: "It may be that I came to this point of view not least because the state that was closest to me, and that I knew best from personal experience, the Austrian state, was obviously only a legal unity." Other theories anchored state unity in some sort of "social-psychological or social-biological connection" between people. But the Austrian state, composed of "so many groups that varied according to race, language, religion, and history," exposed these theories as "fictions."[5] One needed a different foundation: Kelsen's astringent, highly formal philosophical system salvaged coherence and unity for a political community otherwise roiled by many-sided social conflict. "Insofar as this state theory is an essential part of the Pure Theory of Law, the Pure Theory of Law can count as a specific Austrian theory."[6]

The Austro-Hungarian Empire functioned as a truth test, a fiction filter for extant theories of the state—and not only according to Kelsen. To the north in Germany, jurists invoked "organic" theories of the state that stressed its substantive unity. Famously, Friedrich Carl von Savigny and the historical school had argued that law emerged naturally from the life of the people, a product of their particular *Volksgeist*—their soul, spirit, character.[7] But such theories seemed nonsensical from the perspective of the Habsburg lands. "In Austria, with its eight peoples, was there one people's soul [*Volksseele*] or eight, or both at the same time?" the Austrian jurist Rudolf Laun later asked with ironic delight. Organicist theories of the state only seemed more absurd in light of the tumultuous political history that had followed in the empire's wake. Had Germans living in the Sudetenland changed their *Volksseele* multiple times as their region passed from the Austrian state to the Czech, and then to the German, and then back to the Czech?[8] No, if one wanted a theory that could explain how Austria-Hungary's diverse patchwork could coalesce into a single state, one would have to look elsewhere—to invent, think differently, perhaps start from scratch. "Back then in the period of national legal historicism," Kelsen's close collaborator Alfred Verdross later reflected, "a general theory of law could probably only develop in the capital of the supranational Austro-Hungarian Empire, since this structure could not be explained as the product of a particular people's spirit [*Volksgeistes*], but rather only through a supranational idea."[9]

This chapter shows how jurists from the empire came to the conclusion that they could not solve the problem of the state's unity with *more* knowledge—but only with *different* knowledge. The difficulty lay not in faulty categories or typologies (as explored in chapter 2) but in the ways of knowing themselves. To make the state make sense, one needed a new methodology, even a whole new philosophy of law. In short, the state's order and coherence became an epistemological project. If other states possessed genres of self-evidence Austria-Hungary lacked, that self-evidence had enabled lazy theorizing, Kelsen insinuated. Austria-Hungary brooked no unexamined assumptions, vague allusions, logical leaps, loose hand-waving, fictions, fudges: it made you think all the way through to the end. Political wobbliness found odd compensation in epistemic clarity. Philosophical rigor could rise to meet it—or run. One could lecture—sardonically, ruefully—on the "holes" of Austro-Hungarian constitutional law, as Bernatzik had done; or one could keep burrowing, keep digging, all the way down to the very foundations of knowledge in earnest pursuit of a solution. Taking the latter route, Kelsen recast twentieth-century legal philosophy.

The story of this epistemological departure begins not with Kelsen, though, but with his teacher Georg Jellinek. Jellinek's significance for the pure theory remains half swallowed in secondary treatments, presented through the prism of what Kelsen rejected rather than the initial formative leap Jellinek made.[10] Though scarcely recognized in our histories, it was Jellinek who first introduced the idea that legal scholarship must be a science of *Sollen* and not *Sein*—a discipline trading exclusively in *ought*, not *is*.[11] Reconstructing the origins of this enormously influential conceptualization, the chapter explains the work it did for law, and its place in the broader nineteenth-century history of knowledge, as Jellinek navigated between the natural and human sciences. No longer content with the fuzziness of natural law doctrines that appealed to God or nature or human reason, legal positivists like Jellinek desired a modern discipline based exclusively on "positive" (i.e., human-made) law and venerated the spectacular results of the new empirical sciences. But, having swooned over the energy and rigor of social sciences like sociology and psychology as a young man (as we saw in chapter 2), Jellinek gradually reached the conclusion that that sort of positivism—one based on causal reasoning and empirical observation of the material world—simply did not work for legal phenomena. And the state least of all. He forged a new path: regrounding legal epistemology on abstract-normative foundations (with neo-Kantian inspiration), while also exploring how normative and empirical knowledge fit together in a total explanation of the many "sides" of the state. Kelsen silently accepted the former departure but mercilessly critiqued the latter: there could be no synthesis between causal and normative ways of knowing. As we will see, this conviction had dramatic implications: it led Kelsen to the view that the state, as such, did not exist at all.

A Pure Thought-World

When Georg and Camilla Jellinek received the news of his appointment as professor of public law, international law, and politics in Heidelberg in 1890, they were so excited that they "could read the letter to the end only after several hours."[12] With good reason. It was a coveted chair in one of the intellectual centers of the German Empire. Fortunes had changed so rapidly. The year before had been the nadir of their lives. Anti-Semitism had hampered Jellinek's career in Vienna from the very beginning. When the professorial council recommended Jellinek be appointed associate (*außerordentlich*) professor for international law on the back of his book *Theory of State Unions* (1882), a campaign against Jellinek's appointment began to rumble through the Viennese conservative press. With cries of the "Judaization of the university," the ultramontane *Das Vaterland* led the way, explicitly noting the identity of Jellinek's rabbi father. The nature of the position aroused particular ire. "It would indeed be strange," it sneered, if, at the University of Vienna, "the international law of the *Christian* European community of states found no other interpreter than an Israelite."[13] The appointment went through, but the prejudice left its mark: Jellinek was named associate professor for *constitutional* law instead, though, in a "very Austrian solution," he would still be required to teach international law.[14]

It was a harbinger of things to come. Georg and Camilla had moved into a modest apartment at Schlickgasse 5 in Vienna's ninth district and welcomed two sons and then a daughter in quick succession.[15] As their family grew, so did the imperative to secure a full professorship (the chair in international law was still vacant)—for the increase in pay as well as a release from the subordinate position of an associate professor. Academically, the expectation was not unreasonable. Jellinek's list of publications kept expanding, alongside his fame. Promises were made in high places, but time and again they dissolved in the face of increasing counteragitation from a clerical public sphere ringing with calls for the re-Catholicization of education. In 1889, a high-profile, empire-wide conference of Catholics took place in Vienna, and the concluding resolutions expressed "deep regret" that chairs at Austrian universities were "occupied more and more with non-Catholic and faithless teachers, and that this was also the case in those chairs in law faculties that, like that for canon and international law, undoubtedly require Christian teachers."[16] The intended target of this resolution was mysterious to no one.

Despite promises to Jellinek, minister for education Paul Gautsch gave in to the pressure. In July 1889, he appointed Heinrich Lammasch, a (suitably Catholic) professor from Innsbruck, as professor not just of criminal law, as had been expected, but of international law, too.[17] Having carried the teaching of international law for six years, Jellinek had been passed over. His position undermined and his path forward blocked, he felt he had no choice but to submit his resignation. It was the only way to preserve his dignity. He half hoped Gautsch might not accept it—but in vain. It was a dizzying, heart-wrenching decision and a leap into the unknown. Hopefully he might find a position in Germany? The risky, highly unusual move caused something of a sensation.[18] The year 1889 had turned into a life caesura: just a few months earlier, Georg and Camilla had suddenly lost their eldest son, Paul, to diphtheria. From that year forward, a weaker and more illness-prone Jellinek found it harder to shake his darker moods.[19]

Mercifully, he found a position in Basel. It was far from perfect, but, "for the first time in years," Jellinek wrote to his best friend Victor Ehrenberg, he had a "feeling almost like that of happiness."[20] "I am, at any rate, grateful to destiny that I have so quickly found firm footing after the risky, but curative step of last year," he wrote to his mother from Basel in October 1890.[21] But it was only in Heidelberg—the news arrived the very next month—that the professional and financial insecurity of the Vienna years could be definitively left behind. Welcoming a new daughter named Paula after the older sibling she would never know, it proved a period of rebirth and blossoming for both Georg and Camilla.[22]

A sparkling world awaited them. Nestled on the banks of the Neckar River, Heidelberg was a small university town with a large intellectual life. The varied forms of academic sociability took Georg and Camilla by surprise. They wrote giddy reports back to Vienna of the elaborate, highly ritualized dinner parties that involved lashings of champagne and "eight to ten courses and just as much wine!"—so different from the more spartan affairs in Vienna. After such meals, Camilla reported, the men would withdraw "to the smoking room" to spend the second part of the evening immersed in intellectual exchange that resembled an academic conference.[23] It was a milieu famous for the rigor and fruitfulness of its cross-discipline conversations, and Jellinek, together with the theologian Ernst Troeltsch and the sociologist Max Weber, would become integral to its legendary golden years at the century's turn. All three scholars were members of the Eranos Circle, founded in 1904 and devoted to the study of religion, in which members took turns hosting an intimate evening lecture and discussion at their homes.[24]

Jellinek had discovered already as a student that his was a "dialogical mind": he thrived on the "nourishing proximity of healthy academic air."[25] Heidelberg intellectual life could scarcely have been better suited to someone whose learning had always roamed searchingly across multiple disciplines, especially philosophy and sociology. Far from bloodless bookishness, his curiosity looked more like desire, like an embodied drive. "He was a platonic human, suffused with eros, with the passion for knowledge," recalled the important neo-Kantian philosopher Wilhelm Windelband, whose friendship with Jellinek harked back to the latter's student days in Leipzig, when Windelband was a young private lecturer. The pair were reunited three decades later when Windelband, too, was called to a chair in Heidelberg in 1903. Even in this milieu, Jellinek's gift for intellectual exchange stood out. "In all phases of life, at the dining table of young Leipzig lecturers and in the scholarly salons of Heidelberg professors, I have watched him unfurl this virtuosity of intellectual exchange," Windelband wrote admiringly. The life of the mind was a form of sociability, an alert responsiveness, a reciprocality between both people and fields: "Jellinek was a virtuoso of that intimate interaction in which one does not give without receiving, and does not receive without giving. The richness of his intellectual interests meant that he could give and owe intellectual stimulation to the most diverse minds."[26]

It is not surprising, then, that Jellinek's thinking evolved in lockstep with the broader transformation of humanistic inquiry now surging to the fore. A year after arriving in Heidelberg, he released a startling new work that would catapult him to a new level of fame. He later described *System der subjektiven öffentlichen Rechte* (1892) as his favorite book, but even while laboring over it—across his moves from Vienna to Basel and to Heidelberg—he sensed it was special. Its intellectual demands pushed him to the limit. "I feel somewhat exhausted from the unremitting brain work of the last weeks," he wrote to a close confidant in November 1890. "Theoretical work of that sort, where I must lock one thought to the other like links in a chain, physically assaults the organism, and I will hardly have a manuscript ready for printing before the spring."[27] This conceptual labor taxed like bodily labor. With good reason, for Jellinek was not just attempting the first systematic study of rights (of both states and individuals) in public law: he was grappling with the very nature of legal truth.

Truth required new attention. For much of the nineteenth century, scholarship had unfolded under the general star of the natural sciences, with their pursuit of objective knowledge and causal laws. Dazzled by their epochmaking results and self-conscious methodological clarity, scholars in the humanistic disciplines tried to apply the insights and "scientific" ethos of the natural sciences to their own domains. They lauded objectivity, professed positivism, pursued causation, and fetishized the empirical. But in the twilight of the nineteenth century, that star slowly lost its luster. Was objective, value-free knowledge actually possible? (Or, chimed in Friedrich Nietzsche, was it even desirable?) Did not all knowledge depend on the perspective taken, the methods used? Was not every act of cognition in fact conditioned by the consciousness of the knowing subject?

Such questions rippled out across the disciplines, as scholars turned with a searching eye toward the nature of knowledge itself. Might there be more than one legitimate way of pursuing truth? History and philosophy emerged as epicenters of the new methodological self-consciousness. The philosopher Wilhelm Dilthey made perhaps the most influential case that the humanities (*Geisteswissenschaften*) should be sharply distinguished from the natural sciences: where the latter sought the observation and description of causal laws governed by strict necessity, the former sought meaning and understanding. Pursuant to these divergent goals, the humanities needed their own scholarly methodology—one that did not truncate reality into the micro-objects of positivist observation but was capable of grasping the *significance* of the whole. Building on Gustav Droysen (and pointing toward Martin Heidegger), Dilthey presented the human sciences as disciplines of interpretation that proceeded hermeneutically toward an understanding of history and culture. Every *Ich*, every knowing subject, was a mediated product of that same history, situated inside its ceaseless unfolding, inseparable from the inquiry. The placeless, timeless, untroubled objectivity held up by the natural scientists was a false god.[28] In a fluid new era of mass politics, social mobilization, and rapid modernization—in which industrial and technological change restructured lifeworlds and outpaced political theories and institutions—the older positivism felt naive and inadequate. "Rational man," as the shorthand goes, had begun to give way to "psychological man."[29]

This new methodological reflexivity did not only remake the discipline of history: it ensnared law, too (though intellectual and cultural histories of the fin de siècle ferment often overlook legal thought).[30] And although he is not generally remembered in such terms, we can trace that departure in a significant way to Georg Jellinek.[31] Immersed in these broader humanistic debates, his 1892 book announced the new epistemological frontier in unequivocal terms: "All knowledge is in its nature conditioned by the knowing subject."[32] The human protagonist of any inquiry could not be "eliminated," could never be removed from the equation, "just as every reflection appears conditioned by the nature of the mirror and disappears into it."[33] There was no way of studying the human world save through the structure of our own consciousness, determined as it was by myriad a priori assumptions: "In human things, something like absolute presuppositionlessness [Voraussetzungslosigkeit] does not exist."[34]

Where did this leave scholarship, knowledge, the noble pursuit of truth? It was easy but shallow, Jellinek cautioned, to retreat into merely negating and denying and disproving. In keeping with that optimistic spark he had always carried at the core, he instead took the new epistemological insights as an intellectual challenge, an opening tied integrally to the very experience of being human. The real task of scholarship was to build, to construct, and "recognition of the richness of human nature, which can never be completely unriddled, is its unavoidable prerequisite."[35] This meant that the first task must always be a serious analysis of the presuppositions shaping any field of inquiry. Legal scholarship, like the other humanistic disciplines, needed to properly investigate its own epistemological (erkenntnistheoretische) foundations. Without that philosophical rigor, truly fruitful scholarship was impossible.[36] He now saw that the dispute about the nature of the state, "forever new and yet so old," whirred on endlessly in part because its underlying presuppositions languished in a buried jumble, rarely raised to the surface.[37] We sense some impatience with the philosophical illiteracy of his colleagues: if they did not properly absorb the "argument about method" raging in other fields, jurists would have nothing to contribute to the most foundational questions.[38]

The implications proved dramatic. Method was not secondary but determinative: it transformed the object under investigation. "Knowledge of the object differs depending on the perspective from which it is viewed," Jellinek argued, employing the neo-Kantian insights of the age (on which, more

later).[39] The *way of knowing* fundamentally determined the *thing to be known.*
Think of a symphony, he explained. It could appear in radically different
guises as the object of physiological, psychological, or aesthetic study. The
natural scientist saw "aether or air molecules and their waves of vibration"
with no particular content. An aesthetic analysis perceived a completely different truth: a specific Beethoven piece could have the most striking reality of its
own.[40] Yet these two knowledges did not contradict one another: they simply
examined "one and the same happening" from very different points of view,
and for different purposes:

> And if, say, the "empiricist" said to the aesthetician that his works of art
> were fictions, there was no Hamlet and Faust in the world of objects,
> no Venus de Milo and no Raphaelian Madonna, no Don Juan and no
> Eroica, but only letters and paper, pieces of shaped marble and canvas
> covered with colored substances, as well as notebooks filled with curly
> drawing, which under certain circumstances provoke certain psycho-
> logical processes, then the aesthetician would quite rightly accuse the
> empiricist of a provincialism [*Bornirtheit*] that does not grasp that the
> world of beauty can be an object for psychology and the natural sci-
> ences in terms of its psychological and physical foundations, but not in
> terms of its content.[41]

Different disciplines presented radically contrasting but equally "true" faces
of the same object. The symphony analogy armed Jellinek to make a crucial
intervention. Legal inquiry was not—could not be—tasked with grasping the
entire reality of something like the state, with its many faces and forms. Rather,
its proper object was exclusively the legal dimension of the state—the state as it
appeared in law and legal thought. And here things grew especially interesting:
because, upon reflection, that legal dimension of the state did not exist in the
material world like a tree or the ocean tide. Whatever its concrete manifestations, as a *legal* proposition, "the state" was a construction of human thought—
like all law. "Property and ownership, servitude and lien, purchase and rent,
marriage and inheritance are not tangible or visible things or properties," he
wrote. Rather, they were legal *relations* that existed on an immaterial, conceptual level.[42] Obviously, material and psychological facts underpinned them,
but such facts belonged to the domain of other disciplines: "Jurisprudence
does not want and cannot perceive natural existence, cannot state natural laws
that work with irresistible power; rather its task is to grasp norms, hypothetical rules that have an Ought [*Sollen*] rather than a Must [*Müssen*] as their
content, which govern the practical life of interacting people. Its objects are
therefore not *concreta*, but rather *abstracta*."[43]

Law, Jellinek claimed, was a science of abstractions. To analyze something
legally was *not* to try to grasp the "thing in itself," an object existing independently of us in the concrete world, but rather to grasp solely the abstract
legal significance humans had assigned to it. Jurists pursued not the world

of things *as such* but rather its meaning *for us*.[44] As he would later phrase it, "Justice and injustice are never predicates attached to things themselves; they are not qualities, but relationships."[45]

Jurists therefore needed a methodology purpose-built for their particular object. To be sure, positivists of the previous generation like Paul Laband had also emphasized the need for an exclusively legal method. But they had not questioned the base suitability of a positivism modeled on the scientific investigation of the natural world; they had not stopped to wonder whether law existed in the world of facts like a chemical reaction or a pollinating bee.[46] Through this methodological intervention, Jellinek was in effect accusing his whole discipline of gross muddleheadedness about the nature of law itself. Law could not be read from the world of naturalistic facts, did not function like the inexorable causal laws governing natural processes. A legal norm did not tell us what *would* unquestionably happen, but what *should* happen—an "Ought" that did not automatically cease to be valid if, say, a particular individual did not follow its postulates as a matter of concrete fact. How could jurists and natural scientists share the same methods given these wildly divergent scholarly objects? Their inquiries had entirely different logics. The jurist could only ask the question, "How must property be thought so that all the norms relating to it can be unified into a consistent whole?" That is, Jellinek explained, the jurist could not ask, "What is property?, but rather, how should it be thought?"[47] "The juridical world," he declared, is "a pure thought-world [*eine reine Gedankenwelt*]."[48]

Lifted out of the tangible world studied by scientists, law thus analyzed and systematized society on an intangible plane where matter and material existence fell away. What use were tools like observation or empiricism in this weightless register? A deeper disciplinization was needed. But—did this view not render law a fantasy science, a make-believe world existing only in the heads of jurists? Jellinek had a response ready at hand. "It is a world of *abstractions*, not *fictions*," he explained. The distinction was crucial. "Abstraction is based on real processes in the world of external and internal events, while fiction replaces the natural with a concocted fact and equates it with the first. The abstractions rest on what has happened, the fiction on what is invented."[49] He thus presented a particular arrangement of the real and unreal: abstract, yes, but *abstracted out of* the observable world. He reinforced its reality, and the scientific legitimacy of this approach, by way of analogy with another empire of abstraction: mathematics. "Jurisprudence has its counterpart among the theoretical sciences in mathematics," Jellinek posited. Just as mathematics dealt with abstract quantities, so jurisprudence dealt with abstract relationships. And yet no one doubted the rigor or truth of mathematics. "No one has yet repudiated the point or the line, although both are imperceptible, or declared $\sqrt{2}$ a fiction because it corresponds to nothing in the tangible and visible world."[50]

The State as a Singular
Thing Exists Only for Law

How much changed once one grasped this fundamental insight about law's genre of truth! The legal nature of the state, Jellinek claimed, could now be grasped with a piercing new clarity. The state was just like the symphony. It had all kinds of material, empirical manifestations, but it could hardly be the task of jurisprudence to arrest or explain that objective totality, that world of facts. Legal theory had floundered in pursuit of this erroneous, impossible goal. Rather, jurisprudence investigated only "one side of the state concept"—the legal side. It asked, "How should the state be thought juridically?"[51]

And how should it? If the state amounted to "a unity of persons on a territorial foundation," then the crux of the matter lay in accounting for that "unity," for the state as a singular entity. It was not an entity given by nature or existing in the world "objectively," independent of human perception.[52] Rather, it was a "formal entity," meaning that its *form* preserved the individuation, even if its *content* was in constant flux. Our world was full of formal entities: we took the Rhine as always the same river despite its changing mass of water because it flowed in the same riverbed; a regiment could celebrate its hundredth birthday, although no single individual from the time of its creation still lived, because the formal characteristics of the regiment persisted despite its shifting membership.[53] Many formal entities were defined by their particular *purposes* (*Zwecken*) in the human world. A knife, for example, could "be" different sorts of entities—a weapon or a utensil—depending on the purpose ascribed to it.[54] The state, too, was a formal entity constituted by a particular human purpose. People who lived close together in a specific territory could only provide for their common needs and goals with continuing, permanent institutions. Pursuant to these constant purposes, human perception created the state as a unitary, teleological entity (*teleologische Einheit*) despite its shifting human membership.

Legal thought designated this unified collective a "legal subject"—that is, ascribed it "legal personality," the capacity to have rights and duties and function as a legal agent. To be sure, the legal personality of corporate entities was often presented as a juridical fiction par excellence. But again Jellinek resisted this characterization. Legal personality did not refer to an essence or a substance existing independently "in the world," but rather to a capacity. When human perception constructed a collective legal subject of this sort, it was not creating some spooky imaginary being. In fact, all legal subjects were created in the same way—even individuals. An individual might seem like a completely "natural," pregiven legal subject, but its constantly changing consciousness and body only became a single, continuous thing through a subjective act of "synthesis."[55] Just so with the state. As a legal phenomenon, the state was *an act of human synthesis* rather than an empirically observable "fact." "It is always conferred by law, never given by nature."[56]

For these reasons, empiricist theories of the state always failed, and would always fail. Because if one studied the state as an objective-natural-material phenomenon, then its unity simply did not exist. An empirical approach to the state could only ever see "sums of situations," an overwhelmingly complex web of human interactions that resisted clear analysis.[57] Such a method could not explain the state's formal *unity* or its *continuity*—its stable, ongoing legal identity—which were in fact its key legal features. Scholars like Emil Lingg had recently attempted a purely empirical account of the state, describing it as a "condition" or "situation" of control (*Zustand der Beherrschung*).[58] But mere "situations" or "circumstances" could not declare war or sign treaties! So how could such a theory account for the basics of international law? Nor could it explain how public institutions persisted, despite the passing of particular governments and particular rulers—indeed, despite the passing of all mortal individuals. These empirical-realistic theories might proudly proclaim their triumph over the scholastic fictions of jurisprudence, yet in truth they could not escape abstractions. When they spoke of the ruler, they meant not a specific individual but an abstract ruling personality, an office: thus they were already referring to an abstract unity constructed by human thought, not something accessible empirically.[59] If they actually meant a physical person, the state would cease to exist when the sovereign individual died— which obviously was not the case.[60] Like the state itself, "the monarch" and "the minister" were "undying": they were institutions that were continuous through time, and no factual, naturalistic empiricism could produce an adequate explanation of how that worked.[61] In this way Jellinek deployed the state's temporal characteristics—its perpetuity—as the most revealing test and measure for state theories. Indeed, if one did not first grasp that the legal world was an abstract, normative domain, then it seemed well-nigh impossible to offer a scholarly foundation for a basic premise of our political life— namely, that states persist as stable entities continuously through time.

Thus, legal thought did not seek to comprehend the state's "real essence" but rather to make it "juridically thinkable" by ordering its legal characteristics into a consistent whole, "free from contradiction."[62] Strikingly, Jellinek presented juridical thought itself as a sort of synthetic consciousness—a mirror to its synthetic subjects. Every juridical concept involved the ordering and assimilating of the juridically relevant facts into a coherent whole; juridical concepts were "nothing other than a form of synthesis of these facts."[63] Legal thought distilled complex realities into pure, nonmaterial forms *and* into logically seamless relationships. It abstracted, synthesized, congealed; and as an integral part of that same process, it made coherence, it created logical consistency. To grasp or make a legal concept—whether "the state" or any other— *was* an act of rational ordering. In pursuing a sound methodology, Jellinek had been drawn into a general account of what it meant to think juridically, of the particular sort of rationality that underpinned legal judgment. To be sure, the older positivists like Laband had also understood the construction of law into logically consistent systems as the task of jurisprudence (so-called *Begriffsjurisprudenz*).[64] But Jellinek's methodological departure made clear that the coherence, the system, existed in an abstract register only. And he re-presented that logical coherence as test or proof for the correctness of law's abstractions: "Therefore, it is from the outset a criteria of the correct juridical theory of the state that it is able to explain the state's unity."[65] Having posited the state's unity at the outset, as a necessary condition of our political world, it was law's task to make that unity *make sense*—to construct it as a coherent theory, to account for it rationally, conceptually. Legal thought thus *made* the state unified, gathered up its crumbly empirical contents into a single abstract entity buttressed by logic, even if—or especially because—that unity existed nowhere in the material world.

Facts and Norms: "Jurisprudence Has Not Yet Acquired a Kant"

This bold step away from the empiricism of the natural sciences—especially in its subsequent militant recasting by Hans Kelsen—would transform jurisprudence. Was law an *is* or an *ought*, a fact or a norm? The debate over law's status between facticity and normativity continues today.[66] All the more crucial, then, to excavate the background to Jellinek's methodological intervention. What led Jellinek to this formulation? We cannot understand the architecture of Jellinek's framework without the context of the dominant philosophical movement of the late nineteenth-century German-speaking world: namely, neo-Kantianism.

Neo-Kantian philosophy returned to Kant's distinction between "things in themselves" and our perception of them. It built on his insight that things in themselves remained fundamentally inaccessible to us: we could have direct experience only of our perception. Put differently, reason had no way of transcending the limits of experience. All knowledge of an object was conditioned by the human mind, shaped by human thinking and sensing. Accordingly, the conformity of our ideas and representations to objects "out there," existing independently of us, could not be taken as the test for truth. Quite the reverse: objects conformed to our ideas and representations of them. As a result, the object itself appeared less consequential than the *rules* according to which we constructed knowledge about it. What made knowledge true and judgments valid? Philosophy's task was to find out—to investigate the a priori rules of reasoning and judging, that is, the preconditions of knowledge.

This project gave philosophy a new vocation and lease on life. Earlier in the century, the rise of the empirical natural sciences had fatally wounded the credibility of the older speculative, metaphysical tradition of Hegel and company and left philosophy floundering. With neo-Kantianism, as Frederick

Beiser has argued, philosophy refashioned itself as epistemology (*Erkennt-nistheorie*). Pulled back from the brink of obsolescence, its questions were now relevant for every discipline. Science, too, like any act of human reasoning, had presuppositions: empiricists were naive if they thought they were simply collecting unprocessed facts. Any act of counting, or measuring, or observing presupposed concepts and principles, and philosophy could study them.[67] Neo-Kantianism thus offered a framework, a grammar of inquiry, that could be used by all other fields as they turned to analyze their internal criteria for right reasoning and right judgment, spurring further disciplinization. If, before, one might have first selected the (naturally existing) object and then the methods appropriate to studying it, it now became clear that this sequence needed to be reversed: the selection of the method determined the nature of the object studied.[68]

This was Jellinek's symphony, with its many-sided truth. In distinguishing between objects "as such" and our perception of them, in placing method at the center of the inquiry and showing how it shaped its own object, Jellinek was thinking and working with the tools and categories of neo-Kantian thought.[69] Subsequent scholarly commentary has sometimes contested Jellinek's neo-Kantianism. But Jellinek made no secret of his inspirations. In staging the methodological intervention of his 1892 book, he asserted that many controversies in legal scholarship continued endlessly "because jurisprudence has not yet acquired a Kant, whom it could thank for a critique of juridical judgment"[70]—a role he evidently hoped to play himself. Close, long-term interlocutors like Ernst Troeltsch referred to his "neo-Kantianism" unselfconsciously as a descriptive statement of fact (rather than an imputation or interpretation).[71] The confusion arises in part because legal commentators have taken their cues from Kelsen's critique of Jellinek, evaluating him against Kelsen's more astringent neo-Kantianism and deeming his "incomplete." But "neo-Kantian" seems intellectually unhelpful and historically simplistic when wielded as a checklist identity label to be *either* bestowed or withheld— especially for a movement that itself comprised a great diversity of interests and approaches.[72] Such a debate also misses the way in which Jellinek was less "receiving" neo-Kantian thought or "applying" it to law than *thinking with* it from the very beginning. Its questions and concerns were not external to his own intellectual itinerary—to be purely or impurely applied—but profoundly internal. "Those who do not know the Critique of Pure Reason are scientifically uneducated" (or intellectually unformed: *wissenschaftlich ungebildet*), he wrote in an early notebook.[73] Kant's thought formed a deep touchstone from his earliest engagement with philosophy as a student: a topic of explicit intellectual reckoning in his first essays,[74] as well as a constant reference in more informal registers, as we see in the way Kant permeates the intimate sphere he shared with his university chum and lifelong friend Victor Ehrenberg. When Ehrenberg declined a remedial trip to warmer Mediterranean climes to treat a recurring illness, to take one example, a frustrated Jellinek admonished him: "In the study of Kant you don't seem to have made it to where he speaks of *the duties towards oneself.*"[75]

Most illuminating of all, however, is his relationship with Wilhelm Windelband—an encounter more formative than any other. In 1872, during his first student spell in Leipzig, a twenty-one-year-old Jellinek stumbled into the lectures of a twenty-four-year-old Windelband, then an adjunct lecturer (*privatdozent*) in philosophy. Jellinek was dazzled, and a lifelong friendship blossomed. Jellinek's esteem proved prescient: Windelband would become one of the most prominent neo-Kantians, the figurehead of the so-called southwestern or Baden school of neo-Kantian philosophy.[76] The two kept in touch while Jellinek was back in Vienna studying for his law exams, trading letters and texts; Windelband sent a copy of his habilitation *Ueber die Gewis-sheit der Erkenntnis*, an "epistemological-psychological" study of cognition.[77] With that particular smitten attentiveness eager students can have, Jellinek and Ehrenberg discussed Windelband constantly in these early years: his career developments, his illnesses, his travels, his engagement and marriage.[78] "My first question upon arrival," Jellinek reported after he made it back to Leipzig in 1874, "was naturally of Windelband." When he managed to locate Windelband in a garrison outside of town, his "most fervent wish was finally fulfilled."[79] "The last barrier" of the formal German "you" (*Sie*), he swooned the following month, "has now fallen between us and so I possess him as a friend and brother."[80]

Jellinek's affective intensity is testament to how deeply Windelband's thought seized his imagination and influenced his intellectual development. To exchange ideas with him was to be jolted out of complacency and continually "spurred to new activity," a deep mobilization of self.[81] "Windelband's class is probably the most important currently being presented in Germany," he wrote to Ehrenberg in June 1874. "I have never heard such independence and depth of thought, such clarity and sharpness of execution, in any lecture hall. His epistemology traces the most secret beginnings of our psychic activity and follows it to the highest problems of knowledge."[82] Tracing thought from the deepest secrets to the highest problems—from root logical propositions to the pressing challenges of collective political life—would become Jellinek's aim and praxis, too. He "extracted more use" from the lectures than any other he had before, he wrote to his father, and the "necessity of thorough psychological-logical studies" grew ever clearer to him.[83] That summer he spent all his time with the circle of young lecturers Windelband had introduced him to, exhilarated—if sometimes intimidated—by their company.[84] "From the spring of pure humanity," he beamed, "I drink myself full for the life to come."[85]

The connection is all the more revealing for Windelband's particular intellectual preoccupations. Windelband built upon the basic Kantian distinction between *Sein* and *Sollen*—*is* and *ought*—to present philosophy as a "science of norms." A century earlier, Immanuel Kant had developed the *Sein-Sollen* juxtaposition in response to the pressing intellectual-moral problems of his age. If, in the wake of Newtonian physics, the natural-physical world now appeared governed by mechanistic, causal laws, what was left of human autonomy and moral agency? They must reside, Kant felt, in an ethical-rational realm completely separate from the deterministic physical one. This domain of pure reason preserved a sphere for human freedom and conscience, though arguably at the cost of divorcing morality from the material world. Windelband's teacher, the logician Hermann Lotze (1817–81), made a further distinction, contrasting matters of fact (questions of whether or not something actually existed in the world) with matters of validity—that is, truth and right reasoning. Some things—like mathematical or hypothetical propositions—could clearly be valid despite the fact that they had no factual-material existence.[86]

Windelband built from here, identifying two different forms of necessity. On the one hand, there was the *causal* necessity of natural laws that determined what would necessarily occur in the natural-physical world. But this was very different than the *logical* necessity that governed right reasoning. In the habilitation he was working on when Jellinek first attended his lectures, he explored the contrast as two different dimensions of cognition. Deterministic causal laws governed the psychological processes underpinning thought, but they produced both correct and incorrect thought, both true and false judgments. For that reason, causal laws could not serve as the test for truth. Logic, by contrast, studied only correct thought. Its laws of necessity took the form of an imperative, laying out "what we *ought* to do, or how we *should* proceed, if we are to think correctly."[87] They were the rules for producing knowledge. He called them "norms."[88]

The distinction between the normative and the natural—between the imperative *ought* and the phenomenal *is*—would remain the central terrain of Windelband's thinking.[89] As he laid out in "Norms and Natural Laws" (1882), natural laws posited what *must* be the case, while norms governed what *ought* to be the case for something to be right (or beautiful or good). Importantly, norms did not reference a metaphysical truth, something beyond themselves.[90] Rather, norms referenced the internal consistency of thinking. In the absence of some divine or naturalistic measure of correctness, logical coherence was the only way to verify or critique them: they could only be tested by their own measure.[91]

It is not hard to identify the world of common problems and thought-paths he shared with Jellinek. Jellinek's bold new account of law and legal method unfolded squarely within this framework. Law did not resemble the deterministic causal laws that governed the natural world but rather the normative-ethical imperatives that governed what humans considered to be true or beautiful or good. Method must adapt accordingly. Law's veracity or proof could not reside in causal certainty or in actual-material effectiveness in the world but rather in its own internal coherence—consistency with its own rules, consistency with itself. Because norms could not be read from or proved by natural-material facts, internal logical coherence formed the only viable basis of judgment. Rational consistency was the only truth law had. If we might otherwise assume Jellinek simply inherited his focus on logical coherence and systemic wholes from the *Begriffsjurisprudenz* of Laband and Gerber—which emerged out of the desire to construct public law as a logical, gapless system in the style of (Roman) civil law—we see here how the structure of his argument owed at least as much to philosophy, especially to the neo-Kantian waters in which he swam. The philosophical questions of the age were his questions, too. He was not "applying" the neo-Kantians but reasoning *with* them from the inside, and for the discipline of law.

"The formation of disciplines is very similar to that of the planetary system," he reflected in a letter to Ehrenberg in 1876, after reading Windelband's inaugural lecture from Zurich. "Just like the planets from the sun, so the individual disciplines detach themselves from philosophy, the only difference is that the planets shine in borrowed light, while the specialized disciplines believe they glow from their own power."[92] Philosophy was the sun, the master discipline, the original source of genuine illumination: it was false consciousness, or naive optimism, for the other disciplines to think they could solve their foundational problems without tracking back to the intellectual root. Jellinek sought that rigor for law: a jurisprudence conscious of its place in the solar system of knowledge and its ultimate anchoring in philosophy, aglow with the latter's life-giving clarity.[93] Windelband called it a "philosophical drive"—a compulsion that pushed his friend "toward a unified understanding of the world and of life." A "burning desire to gain clarity about the ultimate coherences of his own life work drove him deep into philosophy." In Windelband's reckoning, it was not simply a matter of intellectual conviction, but of Jellinek's core self. Jellinek shared with his age the necessary skepticism about scholarly metaphysics, yet no one possessed the "metaphysical need" more strongly than him. Precisely for that reason, he "immersed himself in epistemological problems," gifting his works their conceptual vividness and methodological clarity.[94] Epistemology, in this intimate appraisal, served as a surrogate for metaphysics, a point of access to ultimate things; it gratified an elemental pull toward the existential or even the divine. Perhaps Windelband saw this clearly because he felt it himself. As he wrote in the preface to his 1873 habilitation, "The question of the nature and possibility of knowledge still carries within it all the riddles of existence."[95] Troeltsch made a similar observation as a theologian. He and Jellinek "understood each other so well" because of shared intellectual concerns, though the jurist would always pull back from the theologian's eventual invocation of the realm beyond. Troeltsch recalled that if he pressed for the solution to problems "through firmer metaphysical concepts, admittedly Jellinek never wanted to agree with me there. He believed in the spirit [*Geist*] without a metaphysics of the spirit."[96]

Universal Knowledge:
The "Double Nature of the State"

Jellinek's 1892 book, experimental in both substance and method, was a sensation—and a challenge. He had been conscious of its riskiness. The value of such works, he hedged in his preface, would not lie in a "clearly veri-fied yield of absolute truth, but rather in whether they are able to become a dynamic force" in the evolution of thought, in their "mass of forward-pushing power."[97] That the risk paid off was clear immediately. Ehrenberg congratu-lated his friend: even a small way into the book, he had read "enough to gain the impression that it is the best you have written and that it is highly original and independent."[98] "My book seems to have met resounding success, more significant than my earlier ones," Jellinek wrote to his father in July 1892. "The 'cleverness' stands in second place. The basic idea is a creative one, if it is accepted then the whole theory will be placed on new foundations."[99] He may have thought he had kept his "cleverness" in check, but that did not mean it was an easy read. "Easy to fly through the book is not," reported the doyen of German administrative law, Otto Mayer, in his review. "The author brings so much that is new and unfamiliar that one has to pull oneself together to always follow him properly." "In 'forward-pushing power,'" Mayer noted dryly, alluding to Jellinek's preface, "it clearly does not lack."[100] But he left no doubt that the reader's effort would be rewarded, and he was not miserly in his praise: the book represented "a very significant event for the whole theory of public law."[101] When demand provoked a second edition of the book in 1905, many remarked how unusual it was that a legal monograph remained at the forefront of debate and required little updating thirteen years after its origi-nal publication. A long article in Vienna's *Neue Freie Presse* reflected on the standing of a work that "placed the highest demands on the reader's capacity for abstraction and mastered a theoretical problem with subtle dialectical art-istry."[102] It resisted the instrumental usefulness that characterized handbooks and textbooks (and which scholars like Ulbrich had cultivated): "The ad hoc erudition of ambitious bureau adolescents, who supply convenient quotations from constitutional law compendiums ready-made or cut to measure, can cer-tainly pass over the book. Because here there is something to learn, nothing to fetch."[103]

Across the rest of his career, Jellinek would hold firm to his understanding of legal method as a science of *ought*, not *is*. But this reformulation of legal epistemology produced new problems of its own. To draw a sharp distinction between norms and facts begged the question of their relationship. How did the realm of immaterial norms interact with the realm of material facts?[104]

What was the relationship between the state as a legal phenomenon and the state as a social-political one? If it seemed clear to Jellinek that legal scholarship was only intellectually coherent as a normative, logical endeavor, then it became equally clear that legal scholarship alone was not enough. He warned against the "scholasticism" that could result from a discipline focused exclusively on abstract norms.[105] But more than that, he craved a holistic analysis of the state that encompassed its social reality, too. In keeping with his own methodological arguments, however, legal scholarship lacked the means to study these social questions and forces. Thus any understanding of how norms related to facts would simultaneously involve an understanding of how legal knowledge related to other knowledges. The interplay of facts and norms entailed the interplay of disciplines.

An ambitious new project took shape. He set his sights on nothing less than a total theory of the state—one that encompassed both its legal *and* its social dimensions. He would spend the rest of the 1890s working on what became his magnum opus: a complete *Theory of the Modern State*. Part 1, running to seven hundred pages, appeared in 1900 under the title *General Theory of the State (Allgemeine Staatslehre)*. Jellinek never completed the projected part 2, to be titled *Particular Theory of the State* (though a fragmentary draft was published posthumously), so the work has come to be known under the title of part 1. But the overall title captures the work's self-conscious modernity.[106] It was not only that Jellinek wanted to offer a complete portrait of current knowledge about the state, a balance sheet of scholarly progress across the *Staatswissenschaften*. Still more, the modern state itself demanded a new style of analysis. The late nineteenth-century transformation of political and social life—not least through industrialization, urbanization, and the rise of democracy, mass politics, and workers' movements—required real reckoning with new political actors and social forces. What sort of scholarly framework could adequately capture this complex new reality? "The old, uncertain methods or rather the old methodlessness no longer meets the requirements of the present," he declared. "But the new methods are only just emerging."[107]

Jellinek's answer was his famous "two sides" theory. Because the state was many-sided—like the symphony—methodology must be, too. The "double nature of the state" as a legal *and* a factual object required a double epistemology.[108] On the one hand, the "causal sciences" were needed to investigate the state's concrete social and historical manifestations in the world, its actually existing *Sein*. The insights of all empirical, biological, natural, historical, and sociological research could be synthesized into a "social theory of the state" that approached it as a regime of rule, a permanent community of individuals subject to relations of will and power. But these disciplines had neither the capacity nor the inclination to investigate law's dogmatic content, to partake in the normative project of organizing its legal attributes into logical systems. Thus, on the other hand, the "norm science" of legal scholarship, which approached the state not as an empirical *is* but as a normative *ought*, was a necessary complement to the causal sciences. Research into this dogmatic content required the "art of abstraction" practiced exclusively by jurists.[109] Jellinek's general theory of the modern state thus comprised two major parts: a social theory of the state *and* a legal theory, separate but joined at the hip. Both styles of inquiry were necessary—they had contrasting methods that perceived different truths— even as they needed to be kept distinct. Their blending had been the cause of so much confusion in the past.[110] "Indeed, that there are multiple modes of cognition of the state," Jellinek wrote, "has not yet penetrated into clear consciousness."[111]

But Jellinek's curiosity—like his ambition—was not easily contained. Mere juxtaposition was not enough. He also wanted to understand the interaction of these two domains: how facts became norms and norms became facts; how they evolved and changed over time. In short: "How does nonlaw become law?"[112] A strictly legal analysis could not answer the question. Drawing on sociology and psychology, Jellinek argued that deep in human nature was a tendency to view the existing state of affairs as the legitimate one. The normal morphed into the normative.[113] (Hence "the normative power of the factual"— Jellinek's phrase so frequently quoted, often erroneously.) But that was only part of the story: humans built pathways in the opposite direction, too, when the existing factual conditions ran afoul of (changing) understandings of justice. Precisely because we tended to view current arrangements as the rightful ones, anyone who wanted to change them had to appeal to a higher law, a better right. It was no coincidence, he wrote, that all revolutions in modern history unfolded through appeals to natural law. Even today, the socialist movement has its own inventory of natural rights—to work, the working day, and so on. Natural law thus occupied a crucial place in legal change.[114] Yet it remained entirely beyond the purview of a strictly legal analysis: modern legal science had (correctly) critiqued the fuzziness of natural law and could (rightly) countenance only positive, written law as real "law." As a result, though, it could offer neither an explanation for the phenomenon of natural law (which lay at the center of many people's understanding of law and justice) nor any robust account of how positive law changed.

Hence the necessity of Jellinek's transdiscipline magnum opus: on the one hand, and in the keeping with neo-Kantian insights, different disciplines and methodologies should be sharply distinguished. On the other hand, to explain our world and answer the most crucial questions, the different branches of knowledge needed to be brought into conversation. Crucial problems unfolded precisely in their interplay, in the interstices between them, in the interface of *ought* and *is*.[115] Jellinek's tome was not just a general theory of the state that gathered together the substantive insights of law, sociology, psychology, and other fields, a repository of nineteenth-century scholarly progress; it was also a general theory of knowledge that built the disciplines into an interactive whole.[116] One student would gush that Jellinek's many-sidedness, his versatility, was unique among his colleagues, "but it was not a many-sidedness in the sense of fragmentation, but rather in the sense of complete penetration and ingenious synthesis."[117] His was a particular play of aggregation and disaggregation, dispersal and unification: he cleaved fields apart but then looked to reconnect them at a higher philosophical level, working with the neo-Kantian drive toward methodological specialization even as he sublimated it within that larger philosophical quest to understand how all knowledge hung together. If it represented a summation of nineteenth-century intellectual developments, it was also a summation of his career: the book had origins, he wrote in the preface, in "the author's urge to synthesize the yield of a scholarly life, hitherto presented in a number of monographs, into a systematic unity."[118] It wove the disparate threads of his intellectual journey into a single epic statement. One great "urge" toward unity: a reach for unified selves, unified states, and unified knowledge, all running together—before things started coming apart.

In hindsight, *Allgemeine Staatslehre* appears as a climax. First published in 1900, it crowned a century and just as crisply marked its expiration. Its very grandiosity resounds with the optimistic, liberal faith in progress—of both knowledge and the world—that was by then already in full retreat. To be sure, its short-term triumph was total. It immediately became the standard work. Translated into French, Spanish, Italian, Czech, Russian, and Japanese, it raced through three editions and countless reprintings.[119] Jellinek enjoyed genuine transcontinental fame. Students from around the world—especially Russia, Japan, and the United States—traveled to Heidelberg to partake in his legendary seminar, almost a necessary pilgrimage for ambitious young jurists.[120] So steady was the northward stream of Austrian jurists, too, that Carl Grünhut, one of Jellinek's erstwhile colleagues in Vienna, could not help note the irony of it all: having pushed Jellinek out, the Austrians now awarded bursaries for their students to travel to Heidelberg to attend his seminar![121] Students described the intense dialogue spilling out onto the street: they often accompanied him all the way to his house, still locked in conversation.[122] The luminaries wrote to pay their respects; American universities awarded him honorary degrees; newspapers begged him for articles.[123]

But that very success carried the seeds of its eclipse. Jellinek's optimistic, ecumenical synthesis became the ground from which a new generation departed.[124] A rising cohort of legal thinkers declared that synthesis unsupportable: they unpicked the "two sides" and rearranged them as a battlefront. *Is* turned on *ought* and *ought* on *is*—a front line at its sharpest in the dramatic debates of Weimar jurisprudence. Carl Schmitt took the path of *is*: law could not be separated from power, politics, factual force; it was brittle, hypocritical, arbitrary, riddled with gaps. But Schmitt's most famous opponent—Kelsen— took the opposite path, instead seizing and radicalizing the idea of law as a world of pure *ought*, pure thought, pure norm. It is to his story I now turn. If

Jellinek had thrashed out a new epistemological rationale for the separation of fact and norm, his desire to keep them somehow in conversation, to glimpse the shape of the whole, became the target of polemical critique that made the debt almost invisible.

Enter Kelsen

In the winter semester of 1907–8, one of the participants in Jellinek's Heidelberg seminar was a twenty-six-year-old student from the University of Vienna by the name of Hans Kelsen. In some senses, the two had much in common, and both their family histories read as portraits of the Habsburg Empire in miniature. Their fathers, Adolf Jellinek and Adolf Kelsen—the former born Aron, and the latter Abraham—had grown up in Jewish milieus in Moravia and Galicia, respectively, and raised their sons Georg and Hans in Vienna's assimilated middle class.[125] Where Georg Jellinek's mother, Rosalie, transfixed her young son with the Hungarian folk dances of her childhood in Pest, Kelsen's mother, Auguste, came from Bohemia. Her "mother tongue was German," Hans would recount, though she spoke "equally good Czech" and understood "herself as belonging to the Czech nation."[126]

The highly intellectual world of Rabbi Adolf Jellinek, however, contrasted with that of Adolf Kelsen, whose various business endeavors met with only checkered success. When their first son, Hans, was born in 1881, Adolf and his new bride, Auguste, had lived together in Prague for little more than a year, where his firm trading in water and gas piping was floundering amid minor scandals and some bad luck. In late 1885 they took four-year-old Hans back to Vienna—soon settling on Goldeggasse in the third district, a stone's throw from Belvedere Castle—where Adolf started afresh with a small bronze factory that made lamps and chandeliers for gas and electric lights. Fixtures from his little manufactory, tucked in a back courtyard of the Goldeggasse, would illuminate worshippers at the new synagogue built in Vienna's eighth district in 1903, later destroyed in the Kristallnacht pogrom of 1938.[127]

Recurring financial difficulties in the Kelsen household took a definitive serious turn in 1905 when a heart condition left Adolf unable to work. By that time, Hans Kelsen was approaching the final exams of his law degree at the University of Vienna. Thanks to his parents' determination to give him a humanistic education, he had finished high school at the Akademische Gymnasium in 1900, as Jellinek published his *Allgemeine Staatslehre*, and Sigmund Freud—just across town—*The Interpretation of Dreams*. There Kelsen had duly acquired Latin and Greek—and lifelong friends, like classmate Ludwig von Mises, a future giant of twentieth-century economic thought—but only average grades. By his own admission, he experienced school as a "continual injury" to his "self-confidence," which "hungered for satisfaction."[128] He immersed himself first in old German literature, but it was in idealist

philosophy that he found that deep need soothed. "Still today," he would reflect
from Berkeley in 1947, "I vividly remember the spiritual convulsion I experienced—I was then 15 or 16 years old—when I realized for the first time that the
reality of the external world was problematic."[129] He discovered Kant. "As the
core of his philosophy," Kelsen wrote, "I saw—rightly or wrongly—the idea of
the subject, which creates the object through its process of cognition." Here, in
this "subjectivist interpretation of Kant, in the notion of the *Ich* as the center
of the world," his hunger for affirmation "evidently found an adequate philosophical expression."[130]

At the university, the injuries continued—and so did the philosophy. The
old-fashioned law lectures left him cold, and he started skipping them. He
immersed himself in philosophy books instead. Here he was encouraged by
one of the most enigmatic and troubled figures of fin de siècle Vienna: Otto
Weininger.[131] It was Weininger, later described by Freud as "that highly talented and sexually disturbed young philosopher," who had first thrust Schopenhauer into Kelsen's hand while they were both still schoolboys.[132] He was
only eighteen months older than Kelsen, but at that time already radiated
the magnetism of the boy prodigy. "He was really a universally talented individual," Kelsen recalled in an interview, "full of ideas." "Only once in my life," he
said, "have I met a person of whom I had the impression, he is a genius." And it
was Weininger.[133] As a university student, Weininger devoured the natural sciences, medicine, and then psychoanalysis and seized upon Freud's theories of
sexuality as the basis for his own dissertation "Eros and Psyche: A Biological-
Psychological Study" (1902). Frustrated and disappointed, he revised it with
virulently misogynist and anti-Semitic new material (having himself just converted from Judaism to Protestantism) and published it the following year
under the title *Sex and Character*, before renting a room in the house where
Beethoven had died and shooting himself in the heart. He was twenty-three.

In the wake of Weininger's suicide, the book took Vienna by storm. Everyone read *Sex and Character*. Championed by Karl Kraus, recommended by
Ludwig Wittgenstein, and later echoing in Hitler's speeches, it raced through
thirty editions before 1940.[134] Weininger morphed into a Nietzschean martyr,
deemed to have "perished of his own philosophy."[135] We can imagine the
intensity of this episode for someone at Kelsen's proximity. "Weininger's
personality"—reaching, restless, brimming with intellectual passion—"and the
posthumous success of his book considerably influenced my decision to work
academically [*wissenschaftlich*]," Kelsen reflected.[136] Certainly, he received
scant encouragement from more traditional authority figures. When something in a law lecture finally seized his imagination—Professor Leo Strisower's
mention that Dante Alighieri had written not only poetry but also a philosophy of state—he proposed a paper on the topic, only to have Strisower dismiss
the idea incredulously. Did Kelsen not realize how much had already been
written on Dante? "But," he recalled with satisfaction, "I did not let myself

be put off." Defiant, Kelsen wrote the paper anyway (dwelling, resonantly, on Dante's ideas of universal monarchy) and could delight in some vindication when Edmund Bernatzik published it in his series.[137] Perhaps *he* might be a mentor and patron? Indeed, Bernatzik's seminar engaged his interest more than any other, as he found himself increasingly fascinated by questions of legal philosophy.[138] But here, too, lay disappointment. As his incapacitated father stopped working, and Kelsen finished the exams for his Juris Doctor in 1905, he had begun plotting a habilitation book on the "most important problems of the theory of the state."[139] When he won a scholarship that he wanted to use for a semester in Heidelberg with Georg Jellinek, "then considered the greatest authority in the area of the general theory of the state," he went to Bernatzik with his plans. But Bernatzik made it clear that Kelsen had scant chance of an academic career, telling him he would be better off becoming "a lawyer or bank official."[140] In July that same year, Kelsen lost his father. His death, at only fifty-seven years of age, compounded the family's financial stress. And so we meet Hans Kelsen in October 1907: en route to Jellinek in Heidelberg, "without the blessing" of the Vienna professor most crucial for his future prospects,[141] beset by familial and financial worries, the suicide of his most vivid intellectual model a recent memory, and under the cloud of his own father's death a mere four months earlier.

They were solitary days in Heidelberg. Kelsen did not really know anyone. And his hopes of forging a personal connection with Jellinek, whose works he had studied with great attention, faded fast. In the first instance, it proved difficult to gain any access to the great professor, then also serving as rector of the university. "He was surrounded by an almost impenetrable circle of adoring students," Kelsen recalled, "who flattered his vanity in the most unbelievable fashion." One of the favorites in this throng gave a presentation composed of "not much more than quotations from Jellinek's texts." That same day, Kelsen had the chance to accompany Jellinek on his way home, and as they walked, the professor asked his opinion of the presentation. Kelsen's reserved appraisal elicited "visible indignation. He thought it was an outstanding achievement." This fawning culture permeated the seminar itself. "He tolerated not the slightest disagreement," Kelsen complained, "which I noticed too late, and thereby lost his good favor."[142] We can picture the scene: Kelsen arriving into his field's most famous seminar, full of robust ideas and critiques and eager to debate, realizing only belatedly that he had misread the room. If this eerily self-assured and philosophically minded young Viennese jurist reminded Jellinek of himself thirty years earlier, the impression aroused no affection.

Did Jellinek sense his world was about to slip? The world of his confident nineteenth-century liberalism, of the actual states he knew most intimately, of the state theory he had forged? Seemingly not, or not yet. Kelsen did. He kept up attendance at the seminar but otherwise withdrew entirely into his own research, working feverishly on his book with growing excitement. He took only occasional breaks for walks up into the steep hills that climb directly over Heidelberg, with their dramatic views of the town and the river snaking through the valley, or sometimes finished the day with a glass of brown beer at Perkeo, one of Heidelberg's traditional hotels. For all the isolation, he was happy. "After years of financial hardship and severe anguish at the sickbed of my poor father," he explained, "I could devote myself utterly and entirely to work on the book." He felt a silent exhilaration: "I was completely intoxicated from the feeling of going a new way in my field of scholarship."

That "new way" landed on desks and in bookstores a couple of years later with a seven-hundred-page thud: Kelsen's 1911 habilitation announced nothing less than a treatment of the "main problems" in *Staatsrechtslehre*—in the theory of state law, or public law (hereafter *Main Problems*). A changing of the guard—in both theory and life. "As the last pages of this work were going to press," Kelsen wrote in the preface, "Georg Jellinek died in Heidelberg."[143] It was true: on January 12, 1911, Jellinek had lectured as usual on international law—on the heels of a semester ball he and Camilla had given the previous evening—before suffering a deadly heart attack. Reported widely in newspapers and journals, his death at fifty-nine came as a violent shock to most, unaware of the earlier heart attack he suffered while rector of the university in 1909.[144] He had always complained of his nerves, tremors, and palpitations—a motif that connected his youthful sensitivity and depression, his sensory awakeness, intellectual intensity, and the hyperextension of his relentless work ethic: the too-tight grip of life that finally seized more than his body could bear.

No one is mentioned more in Kelsen's *Main Problems* than Jellinek— and mostly in critique.[145] Following prompts of this sort, and Kelsen's dismissive attitude toward Jellinek in his later autobiography, Kelsen's thought is generally understood as a definitive overcoming of the contradictions and weaknesses in Jellinek's theories. That is, our narrative reproduces Kelsen's own emplotment of departure from—even triumph over—the great authority of the time (just as he vindicated himself against his schoolteachers, and Strisower, and Bernatzik): a grand scholarly patricide. Yet these critiques are also markers of proximity, of implication, rather than simple distance. The intensity of Kelsen's rejection mirrors the significance of what they share. That co-implication resounded through Kelsen's preface. "I had the good fortune to count among his students," he wrote of Jellinek. "Anyone who has a relationship to modern constitutional theory knows what he is to science. Almost every page of this book bears witness to the powerful influence he exerted on the development of the theory of the state. Even where I have come to different conclusions to what he taught, I have done so in large part along pathways that he opened up, along which he has advanced, a master unmatched. May my work be received as a small contribution to the memory of this great man."[146]

At the very heart of *Main Problems*, and indeed of Kelsen's entire subsequent oeuvre, lay the fundamental distinction between *Sein* and *Sollen*, *is* and *ought*, that Jellinek had introduced into legal scholarship. Kelsen completely agreed with Jellinek's seemingly avant-garde, philosophically minded position that law must be understood as a *purely* abstract domain of norms, categorically distinct from the material world of facts. He agreed with it so deeply, in fact, that he turned it against Jellinek himself.[147] He argued that Jellinek had failed to follow this insight through to its logical conclusion. If one properly absorbed the radical difference between explicative-causal and normative modes of reasoning, then there could be no general theory of the state that connected and absorbed those "two sides" into a singular whole. The divide was "unbridgeable," as he explained to the Vienna sociological society the same year. If the former epistemology studied what *must* necessarily happen, and underpinned the natural sciences, the latter focused on what *ought* to happen, facilitating disciplines like logic, ethics, and jurisprudence. What *ought* to happen could never be derived from what *did* happen, and vice versa. (For example: theft *ought* to be punished by the state, though it might not actually happen in fact; the two were not linked by inexorable causal necessity but rather by a norm; the norm persisted irrespective of factual execution.) To ask why a norm existed could only ever logically lead back to other norms, just as asking why a particular fact existed could only ever lead back to other facts.[148] He later used the concept of sovereignty to illustrate the point: the notion of a "highest" or "nonderived" power, of the ultimate or original source of law and authority—that could only ever be a normative proposition, not a factual one. There were no "highest" or "original" or "first" or "nonderived" things in nature. In the material world, chains of causation stretched on infinitely in all directions.[149]

But Kelsen did not object just to Jellinek's belief in a higher, transdisciplinary synthesis. Even the normative-juridical half of Jellinek's two-sided analysis remained impure, he argued in *Main Problems*, still reliant on a host of ideas from the factual-material world and explicative modes of cognition. Especially egregious were invocations of the state's "purpose" and its "will"—concepts with sociological and psychological referents. If one burrowed down into such notions—and burrow Kelsen did, mercilessly—they collapsed into a welter of nonsensical contradictions for jurisprudence. How could the abstract entity of the state *will* or *intend* anything?[150] No, these were category errors, "fictions" that masked theoretical problems. Such "objectionable white lies of scholarship" necessarily arose when one mixed distinct epistemologies, mixed questions and answers from different disciplines. Kelsen declared the "fight against fictions" to be "one of the goals of my work."[151]

He set out to found a new sort of "pure" jurisprudence cleansed of erroneous material from other disciplines, especially factual-causal reasoning.[152] Only an *exclusively* normative legal science could construct systems free from contradiction—and without a unified legal order, there could be no unified state. As Kelsen picked up Jellinek's notion of law as a nonmaterial normative domain, he developed it far further, grounding and explaining it more rigorously and systematically. Jurisprudence was not "normative" in the sense of a command, he explained, just as the discipline of ethics was not the legislator of morals.[153] Rather, "normative" denoted an "approach," a mode of thought, a method of hypothetical judgment, which legal science used to produce its "constructions"—its sorting and arranging of existing legal norms into logically coherent structures.[154] "Ought" represented law's way of *linking* causes and consequences. When we say that the thief is punished "because" he stole, the link is not causal in the natural science sense of inexorable necessity; instead, it captures law's imputation, its hypothetical or normative account of the link between the two.[155] Law's normative world was not, as Jellinek had described it, an "abstraction" of/from the material world: that implied that it merely simplified or condensed factual-material processes, when in fact it had an entirely different logic.[156] To the extent that these legal constructions were "abstractions," they were abstractions performed on thought itself (not on real occurrences).[157] Indeed, jurisprudence dealt with *form*—not content; it stripped away substance and body from legal norms in order to fashion them into crystalline formal systems. (The legal norm "if you steal, you ought to be punished" says nothing about any concrete instance, or whether punishment did or will in fact occur.) Jellinek's analogy was mathematics; Kelsen invoked geometry. To doubt the worth or utility of normative jurisprudence— to denounce it as brittle scholasticism—would be rebuking the definition of a sphere for neglecting the material used to give it concrete form.[158] It was not the task of geometry to actually engineer substance, just as it was not the task of jurisprudence to explain life![159] On the contrary: jurisprudence must seek a perfectly flat, perfectly pure "geometry of the totality of legal phenomena."[160]

So astringent, so uncompromising, this quest for purity! If Kelsen's intervention struck some readers (then and since) with a chill, he confessed that he had struggled, too. "To keep one's gaze fixed only on the world of *ought*," he readily conceded, "is not easy and means a sensitive restriction of intellectual freedom of movement, where the temptation arises again and again to escape into the world of real life, [the world] of *is*, and explain what actually happened."[161] But there seemed no other way. For the academic jurist was "forced into the most extreme self-restraint if he wants to have a system free of internal contradictions, if he wants to have logically tenable basic concepts."[162] Epistemological coherence extracted a personal price. To make law make sense, one had to resist the deep-set human tendency to focus on "reality rather than ideality," to find "content more accessible than form, to be more interested in the *what* than the *how*."[163] Normative jurisprudence demanded an almost ascetic self-denial, a constant, watchful vigilance directed against oneself and the gravitational pull of the real.[164] Disciplining one's more affective desires was the only means to find order amid the chaos on a "higher plane."[165] He lamented even as he lectured: his preface had a raw, confessional tone absent in the subsequent texts of the soon-to-be-superstar jurist. Working on this book "over many years and through many adversities and obstacles" had revealed to him the "painful" disjuncture between academic specialization and worldview.[166] "However unsatisfied I *feel* about a dualistic construction of the world picture," he explained, "in my *thought* I can find no path that leads away from the intolerable dichotomy between self and world, soul and body, subject and object, form and content, or in whatever other words the eternal duality might hide itself."[167] Kelsen founded the pure theory of law almost in spite of himself.

A State Theory—Without the State

A viable account of the state required a new theory of legal knowledge. That had been Jellinek's conclusion, and Kelsen's, too. But the radicalism of Kelsen's departure—the full implications of the new, "pure" philosophy of law he had begun to sketch out in *Main Problems*—became clear only in the years that followed. World war threatened, then erupted; Kelsen worked feverishly throughout. In the eye of the war that would eventually destroy his own state, he produced a study of sovereignty, that incendiary "focal point" of juridical construction: "It is precisely here, where the interrelations of the whole system emerge more clearly, that the fundamental questions of method must be decided."[168] The more he considered the problem of the state, the truer this became—with seemingly paradoxical results. By the time his book *The Sociological and Juridical Conception of the State* appeared in 1922, his conclusion was as unambiguous as it was surprising: the state, as such, did not exist. What chaotic, heady years for politics *and* philosophy: states (like Austria-Hungary) dissolved in fact; Kelsen sought to dissolve them for theory, too.[169]

His reasoning unfolded like this. Where could we locate the unity, the unitness, of the state? Kelsen surveyed the extant theories. Sociologists like Georg Simmel argued that when reciprocal exchanges and reactions between individuals reached great intensity, they could be transformed into a singular, collective entity. But if the state took shape through the mere fact of that reciprocity, where did that leave children, the insane, the sleeping, all those left out of intense associative interaction? Such theories could not explain the state's permanence (by their logic, the state would have to wax and wane, come and go, with the rise and fall of those reactions) or its human and geographic parameters. On the contrary. Psychological accounts stressed affective identification between individuals and were vulnerable to the same critique: such exchanges extended out across borders *and* broke down inside them, fractured into other internal groupings of class and nation and religion. Sociological and psychological theories of the state relied on untenable fictions that fudged the details and had no way of distinguishing the state from other collectives and affinities.[170]

In fact, the only thing that made the state the state—the only thing that compiled all those diverse members and dimensions into a singular thing—was the law. The state, Kelsen argued, emerged *only* as a system of legal norms that regulated the conditions under which coercion could be exercised by one person over another.[171] The state was a "normative order," a system of *oughts*, of imputations made by humans that did not, as such, exist in material reality. That the thief was punished "by the state" was our imputation, a normative value we assigned to an interaction that "in fact" only occurred between various individuals.[172] We imputed the state's power to one of those individuals on the basis of a legal norm. The state itself could not be accessed through empirical observation. What of "cannons and bayonets"? To think of "physically real things like the means of production, weapons, fortifications, etc." as the coercive apparatus of the state, distinct from legal norms, was "naive shortsightedness, a convenient not-thinking-through-to-the-end, that can be excused in popular perspectives but not in scholarly cognition." Such views forgot that "all those are just dead, indifferent things": only our *use* of them proved decisive.[173] State power did not reside in the mere existence of gallows and machine guns but in the fact that humans deployed them in ways they deemed valid within a larger normative order. If that system of norms lost its force and validity, the state "power" vanished too, even though "nothing has changed in the supply of gallows and machine guns."[174] In Maxim Gorky's drama *The Lower Depths*, Kelsen recounted, the actors ask a pilgrim if there is a God, and he answers: if you believe in him, then there is a God. "That applies literally to the state," Kelsen exclaimed. "If one believes in it, i.e., if the idea of the order identified as the state becomes a motive for action, [then] there 'is' a state as reality, the state becomes a reality."[175]

Thus, although people gave the state many material manifestations, that occurred only on the prior basis of a system of legal norms, not the other way around. The state did not precede the law—the state *was* the law. Without the presupposition of the law, one could "never arrive at the unity of the state."[176] It was the single "unifying bond": "The concrete desires, strivings, and purposes of individual people, which in themselves form a chaos, a senseless juxtaposition and sequence, are raised into a unity only in the legal order."[177] There was no epistemologically or logically sound way of grasping a state *prior to* or *outside* that network of norms; only in that underlying latticework of *oughts*, that formal geometry governing our relations, did the messy jumble of human life cohere into the thing we call the state. This influential thesis became known as the "identity thesis": law and the state were not two separate things but one and the same—coterminous, simultaneous, identical.

As Kelsen reflected from Berkeley, it was not a coincidence that he had reached this realization when the state "he knew best," the one that "lay closest to him," was the Austrian one. Composed of such a wild array of languages, ethnicities, and religions, it revealed all too clearly that "theories that tried to base the unity of the state on some sort of social-psychological or social-biological connection" could be no more than "fictions."[178] Could another basis be found? Rising ascetically above all the conflictual disaggregation of the factual world, Kelsen's pure theory of law tried to rescue—or really, to forge—the coherence of the state.

That new foundation for the state had dramatic consequences for legal knowledge in general. It sent Kelsen blasting through the epistemological ramparts constructed by his teacher. Jellinek's "two sides" theory had posited an object—"the state"—that could be approached from two distinct epistemological perspectives. The method shaped the object: a normative approach perceived the abstract, legal side of the state, while a causal-explicative method perceived its tangible social-political reality. Kelsen minced no words in now proclaiming this "epistemological naivete."[179] Again he turned Jellinek against himself: if method determined the object (and Kelsen agreed it did), there could be no single "state" lying beyond these two viewpoints, no common "thing" to be studied from "two sides." Despite his neo-Kantian inspirations, Jellinek had left the state *as such* intact—the state ultimately remained an object prior to cognition. Kelsen obliterated it.[180] Cheekily, he illustrated the point with Jellinek's own symphony metaphor. The physiologist and the aesthete-musicologist did not simply grasp different "sides" of the symphony: for physiology, there *was* no symphony! That particular object, the synthetic unity of tones, was the product of a musical-aesthetic approach, plucked out from the endless borderless chains of material cause and effect in the material world. In the same way, the state *as such* existed only for law: it had no identity, no thingness, in the domain of fact.[181]

But the philosophical implications billowed out much further. Drawing comparisons to other disciplines, and on contemporary philosophers like Ernst Cassirer and Hans Vaihinger, Kelsen aligned the pure theory of law with epochal transformations in the history of knowledge. Having failed to grasp the identity of state and law, legal scholars, Kelsen charged, imagined the state as some sort of powerful, "metajuridical," factually existing "force" standing "behind" and "above" the law—creating it, guaranteeing it, implementing it. "There is always the tendency to think of the state as equally real as a person," he wrote, "as some sort of 'macroanthropos' or superman," realizing its will through the law.[182] But given that all attempts to actually demonstrate that macroanthropos proved untenable, this view could only be our projection, a "personification" of the legal order itself. This personification served to "simplify and visualize a multiplicity of relations"—it was a conceptual device, a "fiction," which we enlisted to make the complex, abstract nature of the legal order more manageable for the mind.[183] Anthropomorphic fictions of this sort in fact suffused the history of human thought, as Vaihinger's *The Philosophy of As If* had illustrated so powerfully.[184] However understandable, this instinctive urge to personify led us astray. It involved a "hypostatization," a "reification," in which the fiction was confused for something real. A mere "thought tool" was "hypostatized into a 'real' entity"—a classic example of what Cassirer diagnosed as a general tendency to convert the "*means* of cognition into as many *objects* of cognition."[185] Scholars thereby "doubled" the object of their study, adding the personification to the thing itself: "In the place of one entity, two appear."[186]

Kelsen deemed the "artificially created dualism" of *state* and *law* politically suspicious as well as intellectually problematic. Politically, personification turned the state into an anonymous, mysterious power, which not only masked the domination of some people by others but fed autocratic abuse by positioning the state above and beyond the law, as though it was something separate from the constitutional-democratic order. The state became some sort of first, primal, all-powerful fact, justifying the ideology of *staatsraison*, even a "state-fetishism."[187] It was no accident, he felt, that as the worship of God declined, the ideology of the state had taken over many of its roles, fulfilling a deep-seated human need to submit to something higher and holier, something beyond full human comprehension.[188]

Intellectually, meanwhile, the dualism produced a raft of contradictions, tautologies, and "pseudo-problems."[189] As an example, Kelsen pointed to one of legal scholarship's classic topics: how could the state—the entity that ostensibly made the law—itself be bound by the law? Jellinek, we recall, had attempted to solve this quagmire with his famous theory of "autolimitation" or "self-binding."[190] But once one realized that the state and its legal order were not two separate things, but in fact one and the same, all those intractable problems just melted away. Seen from this "higher" epistemological perspective, they resolved themselves, in that "the artificial duality is reduced to the original unity, the hypostatization and with it the dualism is dissolved, the 'thing' returned back to the 'relations' from which it had been only fictionally detached."[191]

In collapsing the erroneous dualism of state and law, Kelsen positioned his pure theory within a grand evolutionary sweep of human knowledge. Across myriad domains of inquiry, modern science had turned from *substance* to *function*.[192] "The concept of the state," he explained, "plays the same role in legal science as the concept of 'force' in physics, the concept of 'soul' in psychology, generally the concept of substance in the natural sciences."[193] Scholars once pointed to powerful substances standing "behind" natural processes, invisible to the eye yet ostensibly driving them forward. But the positivist critique of knowledge—stretching through "Locke, Hume, Kant, Mach und Avenarius"—had revealed those to be human projections.[194] Now one studied *relationships* rather than *things*, *functions* rather than *substances*. Concepts like "force" and "soul" had gathered together the dynamic interplay of properties into stable, hypostatized substances; like "the state," they were simply thought tools, fictions and visualizations, conjured by the fallible, flailing human mind as it tried to make sense of a complex and mystifying world.[195] But "if modern physics has now eliminated the concept of force from its system of knowledge, just as modern psychology no longer knows a 'soul' distinct from singular psychic acts," legal science, too, needed to expel the notion of the state as an entity standing mystically "behind" the legal order, imperceptible yet apparently driving it forward. Legal scholarship must become "a state theory without the state," just as psychology was now "a theory of the soul without the soul" and physics "a theory of force without force."[196] Perhaps we should not be surprised that making sense of the state from this corner of the world required nothing less paradoxical than a stateless state theory.

"The Mythological Method": Totems and Gods

The state as a mere personifying fiction, a makeshift for thought, to be shucked off as legal science finally caught up with epistemological modernity? Could that really be right? How could so many have been so wrong? Kelsen sensed that the argument required a profound explanation of why so many had believed in a really existing, substantive state for so long—or maybe he just wanted to figure it out for himself. It propelled him into the study of "primitive" social and religious life in search of clues, traces, patterns: perhaps the earliest chapters of human social organization might reveal the elemental needs and instincts buried deep in the human psyche and imprinted on its whole development? If that notion seems strange to us, it was in the water. For, in this searching line of inquiry, he had some help from the most famous luminary of fin de siècle Vienna's cultural and intellectual effervescence—Sigmund Freud.

Dreams first led Kelsen to Freud. He was drawn early to psychoanalysis, he recounted in a 1953 interview, and to dream interpretation in particular. "The interpretation of dreams interested me very much," he reflected, "because for me, for other reasons, the dream for me is always an extremely strange thing, this double life of a person in the dream and in reality. That really occupied me." Already before he knew of Freud? Yes, "before I knew of Freud. And then, as I heard that Freud had a theory of dreams, that attracted me in particular."[197] The eeriness of our double lives, straddling the real and what lies beyond it: a reminder of how intimate these themes felt to Kelsen. We do not know what he dreamed, or what those "other reasons" were. We do know that he began attending the Wednesday evening seminars of the Vienna Psychoanalytic Association, which met in Freud's apartment on the Berggasse in Vienna's elegant ninth district, in the years before World War I. He went only infrequently, heightening the resonance of the talks he chose—among them Paul Federn on the sensation of flying in dreams, Eduard Hitschmann on Schopenhauer, and, on a spring evening in May 1912, one by Freud himself: "Über das Tabu."[198]

Sigmund Freud's *Totem and Taboo* appeared between covers the following year. The book's subtitle—*Some Points of Agreement between the Mental Lives of Savages and Neurotics*—captured its experimental premise: the "psychology of primitive peoples" could shed light on "our own" development and psychic composition—as though through a form of psychic archaeology.[199] Reading broadly in anthropology and beyond, Freud focused particularly on tribes described "as the most backward and miserable of savages, the aborigines of Australia, the youngest continent, in whose fauna, too, we can still observe much that is archaic and that has perished elsewhere."[200] Seeking psychological explanations for two central features of "primitive" social organization— totems (usually a plant or animal that stands as "the common ancestor of the clan," its "guardian spirit and helper," and the basis of "social obligations") and taboos—Freud presented a speculative reconstruction of the earliest stages of human society.[201] He expanded Darwin's hypothesis of an original "primal horde" dominated by a single powerful male who chased away the adolescent sons and denied them sexual relations with the horde's women. "One day," Freud reasoned, the brothers banded together to overpower the father, killing and then eating him. In the place of the patriarchal horde emerged a clan of brothers—founded on bonds of fellowship and kinship as well as guilt and ambivalence about the murdered father they both hated and venerated.[202] The primal father provided the prototype for the various totems and gods that later emerged ("father surrogates" all), while the totem feast—in which the tribe consumed their own totem animal, the symbol of the group itself—ritually recalled and affirmed the group's formation through the original oedipal murder, celebrated and mourned at once.[203]

On the other side of the war, on the other side of Austria-Hungary, Freud and Kelsen met again. Coincidentally holidaying in the same Tirolean lake town in 1921, they shared long walks; Kelsen's thrill in Freud's impromptu dream interpretations remained palpable in the interview thirty years later.[204] Freud now invited Kelsen to talk at the Wednesday seminar himself. Presented to the Psychoanalytic Society one November evening in 1921, Kelsen's paper, "The Conception of the State and Social Psychology: With Special Reference to Freud's Group Theory," was published in Freud's journal *Imago* the following year and then translated for the *International Journal of Psycho-analysis* in 1924—Kelsen's first publication in English.[205] It comprised a multifaceted dialogue with Freud's thought. Through the prism of his pure theory of law, he experimented with, parsed, adapted, and critiqued different ideas from Freud's oeuvre.[206] One particular dimension, though, seemed to offer unqualified illumination—and that concerned *Totem and Taboo*.

Freud's "exceptionally brilliant and far-seeing theory" of the oedipal beginnings of group life seemed so useful to Kelsen because it explained the "common root" of man's social and religious experiences in psychological terms.[207] In critiquing the personified, hypostatized state, he had become ever more aware of the uncanny parallels between dominant theories of the state, on the one hand, and doctrines of God (i.e., theology), on the other. "The agreement in the logical structure of both ideas is really amazing," he wrote. "The meta-legal state, transcending the law . . . corresponds to a hair with the supernatural deity transcending nature, who is nothing else than the grandiose anthropomorphic personification of the unity of nature itself."[208] As he laid out in a remarkable essay, "God and the State," published around the same time, the result was that both fields—theology and law—had the same epistemological structure, the same problems, and the same solutions.[209] Where law wrestled with the relationship of law and state, theology wrestled with the relationship of God and world. Both dualisms were instances of the "common pseudo-problem of the relationship between a system and its hypostatization."[210] Theology solved the problem "by means of mysticism": the "world-transcending God transforms Himself into the world," splitting himself into the God-Father and the God-Son, thereby subjecting "Himself to the world-order" he had created.[211] Law employed precisely the same solution: according to the theory of the self-limitation of the state, the supralegal state "submits herself voluntarily to her own legal code."[212] The same contortions and debates resulted. God was omnipotent and beyond the world, yet also inside it and bound by it—just like the state in the legal order.[213] God-the-Father and God-the-Son: theology, too, had its two-sides theory. "The God of the theologians was described by certain heretics as a 'minotaur,' half man half superman," Kelsen wrote, "while the critics have rejected as a 'fabulous monster' a state, which, according to the prevailing theory of the state-jurists, was supposed to be half a legal person, and half a power existing in nature."[214] Viewed from the standpoint of "the critique of knowledge," the two aligned with a striking symmetry.[215]

Where did this powerful parallel come from, and how could it remain so invisible to everyone? Here Kelsen found Freud's theories revelatory. They explained the shared architecture of our social and religious experience. Freud had "exposed the psychic root to which both the religious and social bond goes back, and this precisely by his endeavor to explain totemism on individual-psychological lines."[216] He showed that "a psychological explanation of social and religious ties, and of all that they comprise, is only forthcoming by tracing them back to a fundamental psychic experience, to the relation of children to their father."[217] The deepest common root was oedipal! "Divine and social authority," Kelsen wrote, "can only be identical because they are both but different forms of the same psychic tie that—psychologically—simply is authority itself, the authority of the father."[218] The father "intrudes into the child's mind as a giant, an overwhelming force," and all subsequent authorities (whether totems or gods or kings or heroes) aroused that same ambivalent awe. Only "as representatives of the father can these authorities release for themselves all those psychical affects which make men into children without wills or opinions of their own."[219] The monarchic state depended on this "psychic mechanism": its predominance in "political history would otherwise be incomprehensible."[220]

Freud's theory did more than explain the parallel through a common origin. In the arresting image of the totem feast—the "slaying and devouring together of a peculiarly significant animal"—Kelsen experienced a moment of light bulb recognition.[221] He glimpsed a new way of understanding—and affirming—his critique of substantive, anthropomorphic images of the state. Freud had shown how the "*participation in common substance* which entered into the body" created "a holy bond between the communicants."[222] Sharing and consuming that substance in fact *created* kinship: it forged a sacred social bond between participants and their totem god, and only in this way justifying the "holy mystery of sacrificial death."[223] These arguments had a "twofold significance" for Kelsen. "First, in that for primitive thought social *unity*, the association of a number of individuals into a unity, is expressed in the visible and palpable substance of the sacrificial animal (totem-animal) which is eaten in common."[224] And second, that social unity had a religious character from the very beginning: it was essentially created through a "union with the deity" itself. Religious and social bonds emerged together in the totem's shared flesh. Kelsen saw here a deep confirmation of his own theories. "From a position quite different to Freud's," he wrote, "I have reached conclusions strikingly parallel with these results of social-psychological investigation, results that enable the problem to be elucidated from a totally different side."[225]

Totemism, Kelsen suggested, helped explain our apparently irrepressible tendency to personify the state, to substantialize, to hypostatize it into something real looming "behind" the law and over us: "The technique of this hypostatization, with its duplication of the object of knowledge and its train of pseudo-problems, is absolutely the same as that at work in the mythological conception of nature that imagined a dryad in every tree, a god of the spring in every well, Luna in the moon and Apollo in the sun."[226] The state was a duplication of substance just like the totem god. Both were products of the dualistic "mythological method," which misinterpreted relationships as solid things and functions as substances.[227] "It seems merely a difference of degree," Kelsen asserted, "if natural science presupposes 'forces' behind phenomena where primitives still imagine gods."[228] Moderns and "primitives" created social-political collectives in the same way. If, for "primitive totemistic thought," "the combining of a multitude of individuals into a unity" could "only be expressed in the visible and palpable substance of the sacrificial (totem) animal devoured in common," it was "in principle" the "same thing" as when modern law and politics conceived of its abstract social code as a real substance, imagining a tangible, "supra-biological creature."[229] And "just as the primitive at certain times, when he dons the mask of the totem animal which is the idol of his tribe, may commit all the transgressions which are otherwise forbidden by strict social norms, so the civilized man, behind the mask of his

God, his nation or his state, may live out all those instincts which, as a simple group-member, he must carefully repress within the group."[230] The state was a "deity-idea": like nation and religion, it was a totemic "mask"—modernity's system of make-believe, a synthetic projection laid over the disaggregated facts.[231] "If we take the actors who play out the religious and social drama on the political stage, and strip the masks from their faces," Kelsen proclaimed, "then we no longer have God rewarding and punishing, or the state condemning and making war, but men putting coercion on other men, whether it be Mr. X triumphant over Mr. Y, or a wild animal slaking its reawakened thirst for blood."[232] Kelsen's conclusion was pithy and pointed: "If modern state theory is primitive in this respect, the totemic system is just the state theory of primitives."[233]

Startlingly for us, perhaps, Kelsen thus saw Freud's argument about the oedipal origins of human society as a "confirmation" of his own epistemological critique of modern state theory—and vice versa.[234] The selfsame substantializing personifications persisted. If imagining divinities and forces and souls "behind" the perceptible world was a "symptom of the mythological worldview," then "our theory of state and law is still stuck deep in that mythological stage from which the natural sciences have gradually freed themselves."[235] The state as "person" was like "the soul of the law."[236] It was time to "overthrow the theological method," Kelsen declared—to "wipe out the dualistic system," with all its hypostatized gods and souls and totems.[237] From a looming macroanthropos, the state needed to be dissolved back down into the actually existing system of positive legal norms. Only that norm system made out the unity of the state; only in the logical coherence and singularity of that system did "the state" appear as a single entity. And that was the task of legal scholarship: to sort and construe existing legal norms into logical chains and systems, into a seamless formal geometry. The "constructions" of jurists were literally constructive: they not only *made sense* of the law—in so doing, they *made* the state itself.[238]

The Unity of the Kaleidoscope: Illogical Law

Did Kelsen's engagement with psychoanalysis violate his own injunction against mixing disciplines and epistemologies?[239] What of the lodestar of purity? Indeed, Kelsen's reading and writing roamed widely. His preoccupation with the "mentality of primitives" and "primitive mythology" was longstanding and many-sided; he wrote on the idea of an immortal soul, about Greek philosophy, about justice and love and (homosexual) Eros in Plato, about Christian theology.[240] Religion and myth, self and psyche and sexuality, society and nature: all red threads through six decades of scholarly life. But these researches and writings were not part of his legal theory. Even if they offered illumination or affirmation for his legal scholarship, as with the totem feast, there was no attempt to integrate the two—on the contrary. Whatever we might think of the success of this operation, it was absolutely fundamental to Kelsen. That integration had been Jellinek's chief offense. Like Kelsen, he had been immersed not only in philosophy but also in sociology and psychology; unlike Kelsen, he sought ways of tying these domains and their insights together. If he pioneered a strictly abstract, normative understanding of law— as a domain of *ought*, not *is*—he also wanted to understand how *is* became *ought* and *ought* became *is*, how facts became norms and norms facts. Jellinek announced the existence of two sides, before heroically building bridges to traverse the gap between them. (To adopt Kelsen's framework: Jellinek took the dualism of theological method to a new degree of precision and sophistication, then cast himself as the agent of its mystical reunification.) Kelsen declared all such bridges epistemologically untenable. Legal scholarship could deal only with already-existing legal norms: everything else remained beyond its purview, including the actual creation of law, which belonged to the world of facts, politics, policy, and causal-explicative reasoning.[241]

Kelsen's pure theory may have thus salvaged solid epistemological foundations for legal scholarship and established its autonomy from other disciplines, but it did so at the cost of a sharp new compartmentalization of knowledge—and of self. Logical-legal coherence required the ascetic self-discipline of the scholar, forever warding off the pull of the real, as Kelsen had phrased it in the preface to his first major work.[242] Other intellectual drives, however thematically related, needed to be cleaved off and rechanneled: curiosity about the social role of oedipal ambivalence, about the relationship between the will to subjection and the will to power,[243] or a hunch that practices of retribution in "primitive" society unlocked modern understandings of law and causation,[244] found homes in other sorts of publications. Gone was the grand thrust toward synthesis manifest in Jellinek's *General Theory of the State*. Gone was Jellinek's nineteenth-century confidence in progress and society, in an enlightened humanistic wholeness, in the ultimate unity of knowledge. Scholarship, like the psyche, had no prospect of integration. The passage between these two Austrian philosopher-jurists offers a different perspective onto what Carl Schorske termed the transition from "rational man" to "psychological man."[245] Yes, Kelsen staked his legal philosophy on a ruthless weeding out of psychological and sociological concepts; yes, he pushed legal scholarship to new heights of cool, unforgiving rationalism; but he did so precisely because he saw this formal, objective, disembedded system as the only way to preserve order and coherence in a disordered and volatile world. The pure theory knew only hypothetical values, not absolute ones (whether national or religious or another variety); it sought foundations for democracy in a thin, agnostic formalism knowing that natural or substantive ones could not be found.[246] Its astringency and sobriety formed an inverse mirror to a world of heightened social and national conflict, of libidinal drives and oedipal ambivalence, of double lives in dreaming, of primal mythological and theological hangovers. It tried to reengineer law for a world on the other side of gods and kings, beyond nations and organic collectives, beyond natural law and moral certainty.

And, ultimately, beyond the godlike state itself. Another Musilesque pirouette: Kelsen's original driving question was the nature of the state—how could this plurality come together as a single unity?—and the inquiry led him to the conclusion that the state as such did not exist at all. The unity of the legal order was the only glue that the state had. The stakes of a gapless, seamless system of norms were thus sky high: the stakes were the state itself—the very possibility of political order, legitimacy, and authority. Only in this thin, "hypothetical," imputed, geometric way could the state be made whole. Kelsen saved the state's unity by forfeiting any "thing" or substance beyond that attribute or function: rather than a state without unity, he left us with unity without a state.

But was that logical legal geometry really even possible? If the pluralistic Habsburg world convinced Kelsen it was necessary, others thought that selfsame world proved it futile. Among them was Friedrich Tezner, thwarted veteran of the Viennese legal academy, whose dense, brilliant, voluminous scholarly work ran alongside appointments to the administrative court. His keen awareness of the exigencies of legal practice, combined with a bent of mind more historical than philosophical, convinced him that attempts to elevate legal scholarship to a "legal geometry" or "legal mathematics" could only be attempted in vain.[247] Though his high regard for Kelsen even came laced with a little pride—he had supported his younger colleague from the very beginning—it did not blunt the arrow of his critique.[248] Legal life *teemed* with inconsistences, he yelped. At every turn one encountered things that remained formally impossible according to legal logic. But that did not mean one could simply label them "metajuridical" and seal them out, declare them inexplicable, and banish them into an "external reality"![249] That was not how the world worked. Every day legal practice had to spin the legally impossible into legal reality. How could we arrive at true knowledge of the law while ignoring its realities, however soaked through with contradiction?[250] "Legal logic" was nothing like mathematical logic: it was logic squeezed by practical imperatives, and by the desires, follies, and antagonisms of humans themselves. Ambivalences and contradictions in scholarly constructions could not be written off as the scholar's methodological error: they came from the law itself![251]

After all, were humans as creatures "logical"? Tezner doubted it: "Is it not conceivable that the law, as an expression of human nature, is dominated by its duality and multiplicity, that as a manifestation of human will it suffers from all its faults and weaknesses?"[252] Had a legal order, *anywhere, ever* developed coherently? "Do we not see the highest humanitarian law encamped next to barbaric law?" Did not altruism cross with egoism, and military regimentation with anarchy, everywhere in law? Was not every law the uneasy compromise between conflicting interests? "Do not entirely disparate legal theories enter the legal order over the course of centuries, without the old ones being fully liquidated when a new one is introduced?" In this "labyrinth of ideas," he felt constitutional law in particular pushed against the construction of any logical system. If all law should in theory be logical, Tezner asked, did it really stop being law if it had internal contradictions?[253] No: the law may be an *ought-to-be*, but it also had the attributes of an *is*: "Sometimes it is clumsy, sometimes hypocritical, sometimes complete, sometimes crippled, sometimes humane, sometimes barbaric, sometimes sensible, sometimes ludicrous like witchcraft law, sometimes wise, sometimes idiotic like the formal theory of proof and the censorship law of the pre-March, sometimes everything at once."[254]

The Habsburg world pushed him toward a different scholarly agenda. Turning Kelsen upside down, Tezner declared his interest in *il*logical law—its possibility, its capacity for life, and its practical operation. A classic example of illogical law was the dualist Habsburg constitutional order of 1867, in which two states were one and one was two. Rather than trying to strip law of its fantasies, metaphors, and dogmas, as Kelsen crusaded, Tezner's approach to Austrian constitutional law dwelled precisely on its *Bilde*—its pictures and symbols—because constitutional history was inherently metaphoric (*bild-reich*) and creative. "To think juridically," he argued, "is to struggle for pictures of visualization because of the insufficiency of another expression of the legal idea, and the progress of jurisprudence exists in the progress of juridical plastics. How much legal language would be left over if the iconoclasm were unleashed against it?" Stripped of its allusions and images, legal language itself would fall apart. One needed to work *with* this literary or symbolic register if one wished to understand the development of legal thought, rather than against it. "Through and through, it is the product of creative imagination, of a desire for becoming [*Werdelust*] and transformation," Tezner held, when the jurist found a way to convert dynastic compacts into constitutional law, or the dealings of powerful states into the norms of international law.[255] Sure, these adaptations and recategorizations were messy and fallible, but so were humans—so was the world. Legal thought moved forward by leapfrogging between metaphors, genres, worlds; it crossbred images to arrive at new ones.

Kelsen's most famous opponent, Carl Schmitt, likewise smelled something otherworldly in Kelsen's ascetically pure, formal system. Hot on the heels of Kelsen's book of the same year, Schmitt's *Political Theology* (1922) famously declared that "all significant concepts of the modern theory of the state are secularized theological concepts."[256] Schmitt shared Kelsen's interest in how an omnipotent God became an omnipotent sovereign, but even more so in the theological structure of concepts themselves. He even praised the Austrian's emphasis on the methodological parallels between theology and jurisprudence.[257] But he then folded Kelsen into this broad story. A unified, gapless, normative order took over the attributes of the gapless law of nature, as though the positive order made by humans could reproduce its seamless completeness, and all exceptions and arbitrariness could be banished just as theology had banished the miracle.[258] Writing the same year, Tezner made the same point: "The unity of the legal worldview, that the Kelsenian school of law thinks it can achieve in the form of formal logic, is in truth therefore the unity of the infinite garment of the divine that shows new patterns every day, the unity of the kaleidoscope."[259] The will once attributed to the state was absorbed into the norms themselves so that they could "operate even without human assistance." The whole theory was "completely unthinkable without strong mystical influence."[260]

We were left, wrote Tezner in full flight, with two base approaches to law standing face-to-face. One of these only recognized logically perfect law, admitting no constraints on legal logic, and culminating "in a formula that is timeless, that springs from eternity and looks into eternity like the dumb and uncomprehending Sphinx in the sublime solitude of the desert and perhaps also as a preacher in the desert, the formula of the eternal, unitary categorical imperative transferred to the area of law, of the static element of law, of the stationary pole in the flight of phenomena, the formula of law in itself."[261] The other approach did the opposite. It turned its gaze to "the real, thoroughly imperfect, fragile, volatile, earthly law," understood as a human product and reflecting all the contradictions of human nature, or as "an unbroken chain of gnostic transformations in the material idea of law," that was "subject to the eternal alternation of the fall of man [*Sündenfall*] and redemption and of death and birth, and passes through the gates of hell, that always wills evil and always creates the good. The eternal law, then, may be juxtaposed with the ephemeral, the spatially and temporally in flux, which aspires toward the eternal, without ever reaching it."[262]

CHAPTER FIVE

What Is a New State?

1919 IN THE HISTORY
OF THE AUSTRO-HUNGARIAN EMPIRE

*Empty ballrooms before dawn • From Vienna to Paris •
Sleeping states awake • The Austrians say Austria never
existed • How to tell if a state is still itself • Reverting to
sovereignty—after five hundred years • Self-determination in
search of a subject • Beyond the frontiers of history • Oszkár
Jászi sees germs of war in the Danube Basin*

THE TELEPHONE RANG in the middle of the night. The minister of war summoned Hans Kelsen to his residence. The thirty-seven-year-old Kelsen had been scooped up into the minister's inner circle a year earlier. That surprising turn of events had ushered him into the inner sanctums of the state, then in the grip of total war. He sat in meetings with heads of government, even presented reform plans to the emperor himself. That night in October 1918, he moved through the darkness from his apartment behind the university to the k.&k. War Ministry, which stood on Vienna's famous *Ringstrasse* on the opposite side of the first district. The monumental building had been completed only shortly before World War I began. Comprising some thousand rooms, it had an imposing flat facade that stretched two hundred meters along the Ring. On the roof at the building's center, overlooking the entranceway, hulked a forty-ton black, double-headed eagle, the empire's symbol, set in bronze. Minister Rudolf Stöger-Steiner had an official residence in the building and received Kelsen in his private study, still in his dressing gown. He passed Kelsen a telegram. It was from the U.S. president, Woodrow Wilson.

In a last-ditch effort to save the empire, the Austro-Hungarian government had offered to grant the monarchy's nationalities self-determination, and here, now, Wilson replied. The minister wanted Kelsen's take on Wilson's words. While Kelsen read the telegram, the minister got dressed in his uniform and asked Kelsen to follow him to his office. "On the way there, we had to pass the ballroom that belonged to the minister's apartment," Kelsen recalled. "There the minister said to me that it was embarrassing to live in such sumptuous rooms at such a terrible time. 'Especially, Your Excellency, when one knows that one is the Monarchy's last Minister of War.' 'You are mad,' he retorted, 'how could you say something so awful!' 'After the response Wilson has given to our offer,' I responded, 'I see no more possibility of preserving the Monarchy.'" That nighttime exchange in the cavernous ministry, at the empire's midnight hour, remained vivid in Kelsen's mind for decades to come. "To the very last moment," Kelsen claimed, "although he had absolutely no illusions about the scale of the military defeat, the old officer could not believe it possible that an empire of many centuries could simply vanish from the stage of history."[1]

The unthinkable was already in train. National committees and councils were organizing, and authority was splintering as they spoke. The following week, even a meeting of representatives from the German-speaking parties in the imperial Chamber of Deputies declared themselves the Provisional National Assembly for German Austria. Less than a fortnight after Wilson's telegram, Kelsen was back in the same gilded room bidding the minister a personal farewell. Stöger-Steiner stood there "pale as death," Kelsen recalled. On his way to the last meeting of the empire's ministerial council, a "mob" had surrounded the minister's car, thrown stones, and smashed the windows; a shard of glass had cut his cheek. "He pressed my hand and said emotionally: you were right. I am the Monarchy's last minister of war."[2]

The tale of the Habsburg Empire's demise used to be a very simple story. What was there to explain? Figured as an absurd lump of the ancien régime stranded in the twentieth century like a beached whale, its disappearance seemed overdetermined by History itself. The naturalness of its demise mirrored the naturalness of that which replaced it. Nations, modernity, self-determination—what could be more self-evident? As Pieter Judson has argued, that emplotment owed much to the self-presentation of nationalist leaders who, in the empire's wake, sought to justify their new power through narratives of Habsburg backwardness and national liberation.[3]

As it actually unfolded, the empire's disappearance was anything but natural or self-evident, even for the nationalists. The shock of state collapse and the vacuums left in its wake required an immense intellectual mobilization in pursuit of orientation, order, sense, and legitimacy. That "unthinkability" was nowhere sharper than in the law. In our "modern," positivist understanding, law is made by the state and enforced by the state; the state anchors the legal order.[4] A state's collapse thus threatened law's collapse. The same existential problems shrouded the creation of a new state. With what authority could a state simply *start*—how did a new legal order *begin*? This chapter explores how representatives of the new states tried to make legal sense out of the fall of the empire and the rise of other states in its stead. They needed legal stories that could bridge the confronting rupture in sovereignty. As they assembled those legal arguments, they became accidental theorists of sovereignty-after-empire. As such, they stand at the head of one of the twentieth century's most dramatic transformations. In the subsequent half century, decolonization would make postimperial sovereignty a legal and political problem all around the world.

The legal stories they now told about the birth and death of states turned out to be those they had developed within the frame of imperial constitutional law. Seventy years of intense constitutional wrangling and rights claiming had generated a bank of arguments about the slumbering statehood of the empire's component parts. Those discourses of preexisting and still-living sovereignty, of historical rights ever ripe for renewed recognition, now offered a way of claiming that the sovereign ruptures of 1918 were not really ruptures at all. On the contrary: the historical states simply reawakened and resumed life, converting their paper sovereignty into the real thing. Hungary and Czechoslovakia were not "new" states, with the juridical chaos that entailed, because they inherited and carried forward the legal personality of the Kingdom of Hungary and the Kingdom of Bohemia, which the Habsburgs had never extinguished and in fact dutifully preserved. The casing of imperial sovereignty unzipped, the legal persons of Austro-Hungarian constitutional law spilled out across the face of a new Europe. Composite monarchy had proved a remarkable technology of state conservation—one with surprising twentieth-century consequences.

At the Paris Peace Conference and beyond, claim makers thus redeployed the rhetorical arsenal of imperial constitutional debate on the world stage, arguing for the survival of historic polities and their historical rights over and through the making and unmaking of empire. Legal concepts and methodologies developed to capture the particularities of imperial sovereignty ironically came to serve as intellectual tools for managing its absence—a way of sorting through the landscape of broken states, making the region legally legible to outsiders, and establishing international standing and legitimacy.[5] This chapter shows how these constitutional arguments about the way states exist in time, about the relationship between law and history, were "scaled up" from imperial to international law, redirected from Vienna to Paris.[6] The story of imperial transfers spans politics and epistemology: the next chapter traces how the new legal philosophy of Hans Kelsen and his collaborators—a theory substantially developed in response to the legal conundrum of the empire—was likewise "scaled up" at the end of the war into a philosophy of the international legal order as a whole. The final chapter follows both these methods of making sense of sovereignty-after-empire into the era of global decolonization that unfolded in the decades after World War II.

The story told in this chapter has remained obscured in part because "Habsburg constitutional law" and "the new international order of 1919"

generally occupy very different silos in the academy and its patterns of expertise, and also because of the idea that the new order emerged under the sign of
"self-determination."[7] But self-determination was not enough, as representatives of the old-new states understood all too well. While unquestionably an
important intellectual resource, it could not carry the load of legitimation alone.
There were several reasons for this. First, it clearly represented a revolutionary
challenge to the basic structure of international order and the ostensible sanc-
tity of state sovereignty. That challenge was political—in the sense that Allied
statesmen were hardly in a hurry to explicitly endorse the principle that any
rebellious national group or "minority" possessed an international right to break
away and form their own state—as well as theoretical or juridical—in the sense
that it implied the legally problematic creation of something out of nothing.[8]
Claim makers, especially the Czech leaders Beneš and Masaryk, were highly
conscious of both the theoretical and political implications of conjuring new
international legal persons. As a result, they emphasized that no such juridical magic was necessary in the case at hand. The Czech state already existed
in law—it simply needed to be revived into full factual life. It represented a
return to a deep, preimperial status quo rather than a revolutionary rupture.

Second, self-determination was inadequate because representatives of the
successor states rarely confined their aspirations to territory inhabited by their
conationals.[9] Their reasons were various, ranging from questions of industry and security to the sheer impossibility of cleanly dividing intermingled
language groups from one another. In this context, historical rights often
promised a greater utility than a claim of self-determination based on ethnic
demography or numerical precision. In the process, the idiom of "historical
rights" underwent another subtle renovation. Previously, it often (though not
always) concerned jurisdiction in the sense of the extent of rights and privileges.[10] Claim makers now recast the jurisdictional imaginary of historical
rights in emphatically territorial terms. Historical frontiers became key bones
of contention across the region. A style of reasoning developed out of formerly
feudal prerogatives and privileges acquired a very literal spatiality.

Third, it remained uncertain, to put it mildly, what self-determination
really meant. Commentators then and since have not hesitated to point out
that the peace conference "failed to define the right of self-determination, or
to provide rules for its practical application."[11] Of course, the peacemakers
implicitly offered something of an explication by way of omission: its non-
application in the extra-European world signaled clearly that it could not
be construed as a threat to the integrity of the Allies' empires. But even in
Europe, where self-determination ostensibly "happened," the yardstick for and
meaning of its application aroused endless controversy. Those caught up in
its "application" in Central Europe did not hesitate to offer their own interpretations. Hungarian claim makers in particular embraced the task of explication, demonstrating its logical affinity with their claims of historical state

rights and appropriating rather than resisting its currency. Self-determination took on the colors of its surroundings. Viewed from Central Europe rather than Paris, we see how easily self-determination was absorbed into a preexisting legal world that had been shaped by decades of imperial constitutional debate. All told, this history of claim making at the end of empire pursues Holly Case's suggestion that the salient conflicts of the period may be most fruitfully understood as contests over the legitimate grounds for statehood.[12] Two rival ways of organizing the empire—historic rights and preexisting law or national-ethnic group—became rival ways of redrawing the map of Europe.

Paper States on the World Stage

In the dying weeks of the war, the young emperor Charles I famously issued a manifesto promising his peoples an empire reborn as a federation of nations under the banner of self-determination. His very presence on the throne embodied much of the empire's fateful last years: the old emperor Francis Joseph had died in 1916 after sixty-eight long years on the throne that reached back to the very beginning of the constitutional era in the revolutions of 1848; the assassination of his nephew and heir, Franz Ferdinand, in Sarajevo in 1914 had triggered the outbreak of the great conflagration that now looked like it might swallow the empire whole. The assassination had occurred precisely over the fault line between imperial, constitutional, and international law. Bosnia-Herzegovina, we recall, had long constituted a sovereign twilight, occupied by Austria-Hungary in 1878 (while remaining formally under Ottoman sovereignty) and then annexed outright in 1908. One form of split sovereignty thereby gave way to another: the difficulties of dualism meant that it belonged neither to Austria nor to Hungary but fell under the jurisdiction of a common minister of finance in an ambiguous constitutional position that was never fully resolved.[13] Serbian nationalism only further irritated the rash of sovereign uncertainty, and the emperor risked war to pin down the fraying edges of his patrimony.

Charles's manifesto suffered from all the same ambiguities that had plagued imperial constitutional law since the Kremsier debates of 1849. Ostensibly promising a federation of nations, it also, in an attempt to secure the support of Hungarian elites, guaranteed the integrity of historic Hungary, which clearly ran counter to the national autonomy of the numerous ethnic groups long chafing under Hungarian policies of Magyarization.[14] Were the historic states or the ethnic nations the prime units of the empire? The question remained unanswered until the very end—and indeed beyond the very end. The tension between (historic) states and nations structured the legal representations of those working to properly dissolve the bonds of imperial sovereignty, not least the Czechs. By the time of the emperor's last-ditch pitch to the empire's nations, the frenetic and effective political work of Czech leaders in exile, especially Masaryk and Beneš, had already won their Paris-based national council international recognition as the provisional government of a future Czechoslovak state. International law was already playing out deep within the "internal" structure of the empire—or that was the point: it was not internal anymore.

Masaryk had left Austria-Hungary in 1914, pausing first in Switzerland before assuming a peripatetic life largely between Paris and London. As for so many others, the outbreak of the war radicalized his political agenda: full independence, rather than a brand of autonomy within the imperial frame, now constituted the goal. Beneš, an able scholar from a Bohemian peasant family and a former student of Masaryk's, followed the latter into exile in 1915.[15] Together they worked energetically to both educate and influence Allied governments and publics on the question of Czech independence, openly challenging the legitimacy of the empire—"treasonous" behavior that certainly did not go unnoticed in Vienna.[16] In London, the newly established journal *The New Europe* served as a mouthpiece, and friends like R. W. Seton-Watson and Henry Wickham Steed organized talks and introductions. Paris, meanwhile, had become a global center of nationalist agitation. Its prolific émigré press included journals peddling national independence movements everywhere from Cuba to Poland.[17] The official journal of the Czech resistance, *La Nation Tchèque* (later replaced by *L'Indépendance Tchèque*), published its first issue on May 1, 1915, announcing the Czech program as nothing less than the independence of Bohemia.[18] With Masaryk as its president and Beneš its secretary-general, a Czechoslovak "national council" was formally constituted in 1916 with Paris as its headquarters.[19]

The arguments employed by the Czech national council and its successor, the provisional government, established the framework for the legitimacy of the new Czechoslovak state at the Paris Peace Conference and beyond. Their arguments mattered, in the first instance, because the Allied governments generally favored the preservation of the Austro-Hungarian Empire right up until the end of the war. The recognition they granted to the Czech provisional government in mid-1918 was hard-won. In the circumstances, then, it is less than surprising that the Czech campaigners attached their claims to preexisting structures of legality and legitimacy rather than advocate naked revolution. They did not need to: they could rely on the world of legal concepts cultivated in imperial constitutional debate. They reasoned out of and from the logic of the imperial legal order. The establishment of an independent Czech state could in fact be construed as a particular kind of continuity with the legal framework already in existence, rather than its rupture or negation. The juridical stories they told tied the pre- and postwar worlds into one common legal tapestry.

In November 1915, *La Nation Tchèque* published an appeal to Czech "action committees" abroad that took its cues from the empire's constitutional history. Ferdinand I, it recounted, had been freely elected by the Bohemian estates and swore to preserve Bohemian law and rights. Yet the Habsburgs disrespected these commitments from day one. Bohemians rose in defense of their rights; their defeat in the Battle of the White Mountain destroyed their elites and left them exhausted for two centuries. Only once their wounds had healed did they reappear on the political stage in 1848 to resume their rights struggle.[20] Current activities were thereby subsumed within a series of legal interactions unfolding over centuries. As another 1915 declaration put it, "The Czech people are fully conscious of their historical rights."[21] For obvious reasons (Kramář was imprisoned for treason in 1915), Czech and Slovak politicians at home in the Habsburg lands professed their loyalty to the dynasty far longer. Only in January 1918, in their so-called Three Kings Declaration, did Czech *Reichsrat* delegates from Bohemia, Moravia, and Silesia announce independence as their goal, "based on our historic *Staatsrecht*."[22]

The Czechoslovak proclamation of independence of October 18, 1918, developed this mode of legal storytelling into a full-fledged account of the legitimacy of the old-new state. The Czechoslovak national council, recognized gradually by the Allied governments over the preceding summer as "the provisional government of the Czechoslovak State and Nation," declared they could not prosper under a "Habsburg mock-federation."[23] "We make this declaration on the basis of our historic and natural right," it explained:

> We have been an independent State since the seventh Century; and, in 1526, as an independent State, consisting of Bohemia, Moravia, and Silesia, we joined with Austria and Hungary in a defensive union against the Turkish danger. We have never voluntarily surrendered our rights as an independent State in this confederation. The Hapsburgs broke their compact with our nation by illegally transgressing our rights and violating the Constitution of our State, which they had pledged themselves to uphold, and we therefore refuse longer to remain a part of Austria-Hungary in any form.[24]

To understand 1918, one needed to understand 1526, or so the Czechoslovaks argued: their independence merely vindicated the rightful status quo that the Habsburgs themselves had sworn to protect. The long-term struggle over these dynastic legal contracts demonstrated the justice of the present declaration: "The world knows the history of our claims, which the Hapsburgs themselves dared not deny. Francis Joseph, in the most solemn manner repeatedly recognized the sovereign rights of our nation."[25] Only German and Magyar opposition had prevented the full flowering of this recognition. The Czechs thus claimed to be leaving the imperial union by the same legal mechanisms through which they had joined it: "Our nation elected the Habsburgs to the throne of Bohemia of its own free will, and by the same right deposes them."[26] They resurrected the trope of "stranger king" at empire's end to explain their right to *estrange* the king once more.[27] Far from washing away the legality of the old empire, Czechoslovak independence, as a legal proposition, was framed as a vindication of the juridical structures that had underpinned the empire itself.

The legalism of these declarations represented a conscious strategy. Their tone and tenor were actually at odds with Masaryk's general distaste for arguments based on historical rights (in great contrast to Kramář); the former had a resolutely democratic and liberal political vision focused on the nation rather than the state. Yet he was keenly aware of the legal and diplomatic difficulties of bringing brand-new states into being. In his memoir of the war years, Masaryk reflected candidly on his intentions. In a section titled "*de facto* and *de jure*," he examined the emergence of the Czechoslovak state "*de facto*" as well as the circumstances that "gave it *de jure*, lawful, formal existence, that is to say, how our historical and natural right to an independent State was recognized by the Allies and afterwards by the Central Powers, and how our revolution abroad and at home was legalized."[28] The new state could not be burdened with an illegitimate birth. Masaryk knew legal accounts would need to be settled at a future peace conference, and he would not be caught with a deficit of legitimacy. "In my work abroad," Masaryk explained, "I was always careful to cast our political programme into a juridical form, since I had in mind the legal and international problems that would arise at the Peace Conference." He endeavored to specify their grounds for independence "as exactly as possible." "Starting from the historical rights of the Lands of the Bohemian Crown, which entitled us to the complete restoration of our State, I explained that, de jure, our State had never ceased to exist, and I invoked also our national right to independence and unity with special reference to Slovakia."[29] This particular discourse of juridical states—a legal tradition developed in the second half of the nineteenth century to legally explain the constitutional nature of the Habsburg Empire—thus found new utility on the international stage. The legal personality of the Bohemian state may have lain dormant through the latter centuries of Habsburg rule, but it had never been formally dissolved and could be reactivated now. As he asserted in another memorandum from 1918: "Our State, in fact, has never lost its continuity of rights."[30]

The residual, juridical existence of the old Bohemian state formed a central feature of the Czechoslovak submissions to the Paris Peace Conference. In addition to Beneš and Kramář, the Czechoslovak delegation included the legal historian Jan Kapras and the international lawyer Jaroslav Kallab. The delegates submitted a series of elaborate memorandums to the conference that carefully laid out the juridical foundations of the new state.[31] Strikingly, this task essentially involved explaining the legal history of the Habsburg Empire to the world, as assembled at the conference. The Czechoslovak "Mémoire No. 2," focused on territorial claims, conceded that the Bohemian state was essentially destroyed through its grave loss to the Habsburgs in the Battle of the White Mountain in the seventeenth century. But this destruction had a major qualification: "*Theoretically, however*, the different Monarchs of the House of Habsburg immediately succeeding the Ferdinands and Marie-Thérèse were forced to recognize,—at least implicitly, in their (official) acts, *the legal existence of the Czech State and the independence of the Crown of Bohemia*, the latter being considered as forming a separate State."[32] The state had preserved its "theoretical" existence—its platonic, abstract, juridical life. Thus, the Bohemian state no longer existed "practically though it still existed legally." This juridical survival in turn meant that rights to the whole of the historical territories had survived into the present.[33] Presenting the Czechoslovak case before the Supreme Council at the Paris Peace Conference on February 5, 1919, Beneš similarly emphasized the residual theoretical statehood of the Czech lands.[34]

Through these formal presentations, a whole imperial-constitutional legal imaginary was transported into the new world order. Like the late nineteenth-century treatises of Kramář, Kalousek, and Toman, the delegation drew a clear distinction between factual survival and legal survival. We can only make sense of this set of distinctions and assumptions, laid out before the peacemakers in Paris, in light of the legal culture of the (now-fallen) empire, whose constitutional debate had driven jurists to theorize the status of the historic lands as residual, but slumbering, states. States may be invisible, but that did not mean they did not exist. Far from a juridical tabula rasa in Central Europe, the Paris system moved into a landscape already populated with the ghosts of imperial orders past. If we narrate the inauguration of the successor states purely within the tracks of nationalist history—as the self-actualization of freestanding national units—we risk obscuring the extent to which their modes of self-presentation and self-understanding might originate not with "the nation" but with the empire they ostensibly shucked off. Legacies of this sort require a less heavy-handed (and less literal) understanding of the threads of continuity that tied the world of Austria-Hungary to the new world order that followed.

Of course, invocations of historical right coexisted with other genres of right, particularly when it came to the determination of borders. Crucially, historical right claims could not support the inclusion of Slovakia alongside the lands of the Bohemian crown (Bohemia, Moravia, and Silesia), as Slovakia had long formed part of historic Hungary. Slovakia was claimed instead on the grounds of ethnic-linguistic affinity, that is, a "natural right" in the parlance of the time, leading to the bifurcated appeal to "historical and natural rights" that we see in the declaration of independence and the Masaryk quotations provided here. (The nature and implications of these twinned rights paradigms will be treated in more detail later in the chapter.) Moreover, the Czechoslovak delegation appealed to economic and security factors—as well as democratic credentials and promises of minority protection—in making out its claims for a state that included significant "minority" populations.[35]

The language of historical right performed crucial work for Czechoslovak claim makers, however, especially during the war. It had allowed them to circumnavigate what would emerge, over the course of the twentieth century, as a key theoretical quagmire concerning international law and the creation of states more generally. Positivist legal thought experienced great conceptual trouble with the creation of states, deemed to be a matter of fact and not law (as will be explored further in the next two chapters). It was precisely this leap, the murky, legally amorphous space through which would-be states pass on their way into international existence, that Masaryk and others circumnavigated with their appeal to historic rights. The new sovereignty of these successor states did not involve an extralegal entity birthed miraculously into new legal life: instead, it was the reawakening of a prior status, preserving the illusion of the uninterrupted operation of the law and flattering the law's distrust of novelty.

Old Rights and New World Orders

In imperial debates over dualism and trialism, as well as in postwar debates about rights and borders, Czechs and Hungarians faced off squarely as opponents. But in both cases, the content and style of their arguments were remarkably similar. The Hungarians, too, took their historical rights with them into the new world order. On January 16, 1920, Count Albert Apponyi appeared before the Supreme Council of the Paris Peace Conference to explain Austro-Hungarian constitutional history to the world.[36] The count was well prepared for the task: he had been explaining the idiosyncratic constitutional standing of his beloved Hungary to international audiences for years. Apponyi made his first trip to the United States in 1904, where he presented a lecture in St. Louis titled "The Juridical Nature of the Relations between Austria and Hungary."[37] In 1904, as in 1920, he stressed the anteriority and survival of Hungarian statehood. Arguments honed for rights within the imperial constitution proved just as useful in the absence of the empire itself.

It was an error to view the Habsburg Empire as the "primordial fact," he lectured in 1904, as a single polity that included Hungary and granted the latter pet concessions as a province. On the contrary: "The primordial fact is an independent kingdom of Hungary, which has allied itself for certain purposes and under certain conditions to the equally independent and distinct empire of Austria, by an act of sovereign free will, *without having ever abdicated the smallest particle of its sovereignty* as an independent nation, though it has consented to exercise a small part of its governmental functions through executive organs common with Austria."[38] In 1920, the case for rights leaned similarly on the anteriority and survival of Hungarian statehood. "We wish first of all," submitted the Hungarian delegation, "to establish the fact that Hungary is no new State born of the dismemberment of the Austro-Hungarian Monarchy, and so cannot be compared from this point of view to German-Austria, to the Czecho-Slovak, nor to the Yougoslav State. As far as public law the Hungary of to-day is the same State she has been through her past of a thousand years. She kept her position as an independent State on entering into a union with Austria and during the whole existence of this union known by the name of the Austro-Hungarian Monarchy."[39]

What *had* changed between 1904 and 1920 were the stakes of such arguments. Borders, territories, populations: there was a lot to win or, more accurately, to lose. If the anteriority of Hungarian statehood mattered then, it mattered more now, as the delegation sought the dignity—*and the rights*—of a sovereign state. After all, already-existing states had the right to territorial integrity: Had not Britain gone to war for Belgium's?[40] The legal subject did not need to be reconstituted, and only subsequently ascribed legal properties: rather, the state was a ready-made object with its rights intact, carried over from one order into another.

Making out the case required some specialized knowledge of Austro-Hungarian constitutional history, and the Hungarian delegation set about educating the Allies. Invited to join the conference only on December 1, 1919,[41] a Hungarian delegation—with Apponyi as its head and Pál Teleki and István Bethlen among its members—left Budapest for Paris on January 5 the following year.[42] Before receiving the terms of the peace, they submitted several memorandums to the conference, two of which have a special claim on our attention. The first, titled "Memorandum concerning the evolution of relations between Austria and Hungary, from the point of view of public law," carefully traced the empire's legal history and Hungary's place within it. As with the Czech submissions, the leitmotif of this history was the *legal* survival of Hungary's statehood. The second one, "The relationship of Hungary and Austria in public law till the dissolution of the Austro-Hungarian Monarchy," offered a more technical analysis of the legal nature of the empire on the cusp of its demise. It laid out all the specific forms of quasi sovereignty that had been the intellectual products of long years of constitutional debate. Lucid and rich, the two memorandums appear as classic summations of the Austro-Hungarian jurisprudence of empire.

Everyone in Hungary knew, declared the first, historical memorandum, "that Hungary had not fusioned with the Austro-Hungarian Monarchy, resigning her existence as an independent State."[43] Hungary's membership in the family of nations predated that of the fledgling Habsburg principalities: "Much before the permanent connection was formed between Hungary and the Habsburg dynasty in 1526, Hungary had taken part as an independent State in the international life of Europe, had done so, indeed, for 500 years. Her part as a sovereign State had even been an important one. . . . The State formation named Austria later on did not even exist at that time."[44] Back then, history knew only a house of Austria ruling a small feudal principality within the Holy Roman Empire. The dynasty gradually increased its holdings through pacts, marriages, purchases, and exchanges. Though its ascension to the throne of Hungary exerted "a great influence on the subsequent events of European history still, from a juridical point of view it had no effect on the independence of Hungary."[45] "From the point of view of public law," the Hungarian delegation explained, Hungarian independence survived the absolutist years intact. This account of juridical statehood thus relied, in familiar terms, on a clear distinction between political history and legal history.

Gradually "effaced" by the Pragmatic Sanction and then the creation of the imperial title in 1804, Hungary's independence was renegotiated in the Settlement of 1867, which established "a basis on which the independence of Hungary as a distinct state could be established in legal form" without harming the empire's status as a great power.[46] The delegation explained the contrasting interpretations of the 1867 Settlement. According to Austrian law, the provinces together formed a single state, with "one single, common sovereignty," within which "there could be two *parts* distinguished only." Hungarian law, on the contrary, "recognised only two autonomous states, not allowing of a common State, with a sovereignty of its own, being superposed to them."[47]

Most telling was the way in which the delegation "applied" this legal history to the situation currently before the conference. "It is apparent from the above mentioned facts," it submitted, "that now the community implied in the appellation 'Austro-Hungarian Monarchy' has ceased, Hungary cannot be considered as a new state formed upon the ruins of the Monarchy, but as a state disposing independently and without restrictions in the questions which she could not dispose of formerly without the concurrence of Austria."[48] Austria appeared here as a temporary limitation on Hungarian sovereignty, a kind of impermanent but persistent handicap that had lasted five centuries but was now at long last removed. The end of empire did not violently produce political novelties but harmoniously restored the status quo: "The severance of the bonds of the ancient Austro-Hungarian Monarchy . . . was quite a natural process."[49] The Paris Peace Conference stood at the end of a long history of sovereignty rather than at its beginning.

The second memorandum read like a "short introduction" to Austro-Hungarian constitutional law. Repeating claims voiced often by Hungarians in the years since 1867, the memorandum instructed its readers that the empire, as such, had no legal existence at all. The designation "Austro-Hungarian Monarchy," they explained patiently, was incorrect insofar as "the word monarchy denotes the rule of one person. Both the Hungarian Kingdom and the Austrian Empire were separate monarchies. But the Austro-Hungarian Monarchy was not a third political formation—comprising Austria and Hungary and rising above both. It was simply the name of the relationship between the two States." "Therefore," they continued, "it was incorrect to speak of the territory, population and citizens of the Austro-Hungarian Monarchy, because the Monarchy had neither territory, nor population, nor citizens, as only Hungary separately and Austria separately had territory, population and citizens."[50] The key characteristics of statehood belonged to each of the two states separately, with no "third state" subsuming the two into a larger whole. They thus presented the "empire as alliance" version of imperial law. The Austrians, as we will see, arrived at the conference to argue that the empire was legally dead: the Hungarians argued it did not legally exist in the first place.

These careful expositions of the peculiarities of late imperial sovereignty in Central Europe all stressed one thing: that the Hungarian state had come through the maze of imperial law untarnished, its particular state identity intact. It remained itself, "an unbroken legal continuity as Hungary."[51] Interestingly, the Sixth Committee of the League of Nations seemed to broadly agree when it considered Hungary's application for league membership in 1922. The Sixth Committee appointed a seven-member subcommittee to consider the question (that included Beneš, which must have been especially galling for the Hungarians). Members of the subcommittee unanimously recommended that Hungary be admitted, and "they concurred in the opinion expressed by one member that the Hungarian State had for a long time been a member of the 'International Family.'"[52]

What Is a New State? Paris as the Clearinghouse of Austro-Hungarian Sovereignty

In 1919, old states, like new ones, found themselves in an extremely fluid sovereign landscape. Wildly varying proposals and visions of a region reborn were concocted and pitched in all directions as states were chopped up and recombined: federations and economic unions, protectorates and mandates, zones of neutrality or demilitarization, autonomous provinces, "loose confederations of neutral republics." The South African statesman Jan Smuts, sent to Hungary by the Allied governments, deemed the region's new governments weak and inexperienced: his report recommended a "Mandatory of the Great Powers for Austria-Hungary."[53] Or perhaps Ruthenian territories should be a Czech mandate state?[54] A particularly creative Heinrich Lammasch, acting as something of a maverick in these months, sketched out proposals for an independent and neutral "Alpine Republic" that would include not only the Voralberg, Tyrol, Salzburg, the Austrian duchies, and parts of Styria and Carinthia but also certain western districts of Hungary, southern parts of Moravia and Bohemia, and even portions of southern Bavaria.[55]

In many ways, the state that would arise around the old imperial capital of Vienna remained the most formless of all. As is well known, the Allied governments vetoed attempts to have the largely German provinces of the old empire attached to Germany proper. If it was to stand alone, what was "it"? The various names in circulation included *Republik Südostdeutschland,*

Ostalpenland, and *Deutsche Alpenland*. With the name Austria—*Österreich*—so deeply bound up with the old monarchy, and no indigenous republican tradition to call upon, it was hard to reimagine the state out from behind its nomenclature.[56] Surely, the same name could not simply be reapplied to this small remaining piece of territory that seemingly bore no connection to the old grand polity? The provisional constituent assembly reached initially for *Deutschösterreich*, German Austria, which at least communicated that the new unit brought together German-speaking parts of the old monarchy. That a "Republic of Austria" eventually emerged was largely a result of the Allies, who contracted with a "Republique d'Autriche." Even the name appeared the dictate of the victors, and it was disliked all the more because of it.[57]

"German Austria," wrote Otto Bauer in 1923, "is not an organically grown formation. It is nothing but the remainder that was left over from the old empire when the other nations fell away from it. It stayed behind as a loose bundle of lands reaching away from one another," devoid of the economic foundations of their common existence.[58] No one, he reported, thought it capable of independent life; its form could only be provisional. Some sort of "connection in international law or constitutional law" would be required as a new foundation.[59] Looking back on 1919 from 1948, Renner painted a similar portrait of a historyless, unviable new polity, defined only by what it was not: "What remained of the Dual Monarchy were the German-speaking parts of the eastern Alps, a population of about 6,500,000, and the capital city of Vienna, with a population of about 2,000,000." The outlook, he wrote, was bleak: "It was a mountainous country with little arable land, without a sufficient domestic market for its industries, no outlet to the sea, and surrounded on three sides by hostile neighbors. It was, indeed, a land without a name—for this area had never been a separate state. It was treated as a vanquished enemy, and had to take over the name of Austria and the inheritance of the House of Hapsburg, with all its glory and also its ill repute."[60] No rational person, Renner maintained, thought the state could survive without aid or "withstand any shocks." Only credits from the League of Nations made it viable in the first instance. As a member of the peace delegation at Saint-Germain, he had returned to Vienna in September 1919 and recommended to parliament the acceptance of the peace treaty: "I did so in express reliance upon the League of Nations as the guarantor of our independence, and described Austria as 'an autonomous province of the League.'"[61] Like a mandated state with only the league as a mandatory, the new state was born under the care and the sign of the new order, perhaps more than any other.[62]

Representatives of the new Austria were quick to claim that no legal continuity existed between the new state and the old empire. The peace conference may have only just begun, but one of the vanquished parties had already legally disappeared, or so they argued. The "German-Austrian Government is not requesting the establishment of direct relations between the Entente Governments and the old Austro-Hungarian Monarchy but between those Governments and the German-Austrian Republic," they submitted in February 1919. The republic should not inherit the juridical identity, the legal individuality, of the latter. On what basis could this legal personality be grafted onto the new alpine republic rather than any other of the new states built atop the fallen empire? "The state of war which existed in the late Austro-Hungarian Monarchy," they asserted, "has no more devolved upon German-Austria than on Czecho-Slovakia or any other national State which has arisen on Austrian-Hungarian soil."[63] There was no reason why they would take up the old monarchy's attitudes toward or relationships with other powers. They therefore claimed "the position of a friendly Power toward all countries in the world."[64] The British Foreign Office responded skeptically. "The gist of the argument in this note is that the German-Austrian Republic is not the successor of the Austrian Empire, but one of the new states arising out of that Empire's ruins," noted A. W. A. Leeper. The question appeared to him unsettled, as it was with Hungary. "They are at present enemies," replied a cautious Sir Eyre Crowe.[65]

Responding to the peace stipulations before the Paris Peace Conference on June 2, Karl Renner, now state chancellor, made the case still more emphatically. "The Danube Monarchy," he declared, "ceased to exist on 12. November, 1918." From that day forward, there existed neither a monarch nor a great power, "nor the disastrous dualism, nor an Austrian or Hungarian government or army, nor any other kind of recognized state institution." Overnight, eight nations created their own parliaments and armies and their own state life. The young Austrian republic came into being just like the rest of them, no more the empire's successor than any other.[66] The German Austrian delegation produced a special "Note on the International Legal Personality of German Austria," drawing attention to the ambiguity of the legal subject "Austria" that appeared in the treaty drafted by the Allies.[67] The arguments had been devised by none other than Hans Kelsen.[68] Before the collapse of the monarchy, the delegation explained, such a legal subject was unimaginable, as only the dualist "Austro-Hungarian" monarchy had the legal capacity for international dealings. They offered the Allies some reading recommendations: "To appreciate more exactly the legal nature of the former state, the Peace Conference may refer to the excellent work of the French author Louis Eisenmann 'Le Compromis austro-hongrois' (Paris, 1902) and they will discover: de jure, an 'Austria' has never existed—thus we cannot succeed such [a state] nor represent it here."[69]

Austro-Hungarian constitutional jurisprudence may have emerged to analyze and codify the empire's order, but now it had a new vocation in the international management of the empire's dissolution. The postulates of the empire's life configured those of its death. "The state in question," the delegation explained further, "in its formally constituted fundamental laws, was called nothing other than 'The Kingdoms and Lands Represented in the Imperial Parliament.'" The law listed these as Bohemia, Galicia, Dalmatia, and so on. "It was these lands that—together with the lands of the Hungarian crown—waged the war, that is, de jure and de facto Bohemia, Galicia, Dalmatia etc. collectively."[70] The statehood of the historical lands had rarely been as "real" as it was right now. Legally, this collection of small medieval quasi-states—not greater than the sum of their parts—had fought a war against the Allied and Associated Powers, the delegation argued. The name "Austria" had been connected to the dynasty, not to a particular territory. While it was used more casually to refer to something more, this "something more" always included the Bohemians and the South Slavs. On what basis, then, was the empire's legal personality ascribed to this new small republic? On national grounds? This reasoning hardly made sense: those representing the empire, for example, had mostly been Hungarians, and Germans had been a minority in the parliament since 1907. Or was it the fact that Vienna was the capital? A city this large was the product of the economic power of the whole empire; now cut off from that, it would actually prove a burden to this small country.[71]

According to what logic or evidentiary basis could one establish the "newness" or the "oldness" of a state? A dense debate broke out among members of the British delegation to the peace conference on the question of whether Austria was in fact a new state or an old one. It is worth reconstructing at some length not only because it demonstrates the extent to which imperial constitutional law shaped even the Allies' thinking but also because it reveals the radical uncertainty about the legal meaning of imperial collapse and the nature of sovereignty-after-empire. The mandarins of the British Foreign Office turned the back rooms of the peace conference into a kind of clearinghouse of Austro-Hungarian sovereignty. Trust the historians: it was resident classicist James Headlam-Morley who set the cat among the pigeons with a ruminative "Note on the Draft Austrian Treaty" in May 1919. He had been looking over the draft treaty "with the object of considering the problems which come up with regard to the New States." The whole basis of the treaty seemed to him "open to very serious criticism. So far as I can understand, the theory underlying it is that what we may call the New Austria is juridically identical with the old Austria. This seems to me to be wrong in fact and dangerous in principle." What justified this imputation of state continuity? "Surely New Austria is as much a new State as Czecho-Slovakia. What happened during the course of the Revolution," he explained, "was that the Old Austro-Hungarian Monarchy completely broke up; certain portions, Bohemia, Moravia, etc. formed themselves into one State; other portions, Croatia, Dalmatia, etc. united themselves with Serbia; other portions, Upper and Lower Austria, Tyrol, Corinthia, Styria, etc. also formed themselves into a New State."[72] The atoms of the empire had broken apart, moved about, and recombined; there was no way of tracking "the empire" as a stable identity through these sovereign mutations.

Far from a dry technicality, the (dis)continuity of the empire's legal personality appeared to him a highly portentous issue. If the German-Austrian representatives had looked to discard the legal identity of the empire so as to shuck off the (negative) legal baggage it carried, Headlam-Morley was alternatively worried about the (positive) legal baggage attached to the legal person of the empire—that is, its rights. The question of the continuous legal personality of states was simultaneously the question of whether they could carry old rights through time and between orders, just as it had been within the frame of imperial constitutional debate. For this reason, Headlam-Morley thought the principle of discontinuity needed to be clearly articulated, or else a kind of platonic version of the empire could be left legally intact beneath the surface of the new states. If they adopted the principle underlying the draft treaty, then "we are driven to recognise that the New Austria, being identical with the Old Austria, inherits from the Old Austria all the rights of sovereignty and jurisdiction which the Hapsburgs exercised over the seventeen territories comprised within the Austrian half of the Dual Monarchy." True, "the Treaty provides for the renunciation of these rights, but the very fact that we ask Austria to renounce these rights means that we recognise that she has them." That was a risky path. He speculated: "Suppose now—an improbable but not impossible contingency—that owing to some unforeseen accident the Treaty was never signed, we should be left in the situation that the Allied and Associated Powers had definitely recognized the continued existence of these rights."[73]

Like Masaryk, Headlam-Morley was deeply concerned with the sound legal stitching of the new order in Europe. Old imperial rights needed to be thoroughly dissolved and prevented from lingering in a legal twilight zone, pending possible revival. For example, German-Austria presented itself as the advocate of the rights of Bohemian Germans. As a new state with clearly limited frontiers, no such status could be claimed; the threads that tied a former state to its former subjects would be cut. Yet if it constituted as the inheritor of the empire, then it would be "difficult to deny that she has now a legal right to be heard on the matter [of the German Bohemians], and even if the legal right were to be renounced, it would be very difficult to get rid of a vague moral right." The danger of residual legalities would only grow sharper if the monarchy was restored, which was "not outside the range of possibility." To properly destroy rights, one needed to destroy their subject, the legal person to which they were attached.

Disposing of the old legal architecture of Central Europe was delicate work. The liquidation of a grand old empire had fallen to the peacemakers; according to Headlam-Morley, this solemn, even world-historical task demanded both care and ceremony. The treaty with Austria could not simply be a slightly amended version of the one presented to Germany: "In the case of Austria we have not only to put an end to the state of war, but to deal with one of the greatest events which have ever taken place in European history, the dissolution of one of the oldest, the greatest and most extensive States on the Continent of Europe. I should venture to suggest that it is incumbent on us to recognise this and to find appropriate and dignified language in which we can place on record what has happened."[74] The peacemakers had their legal stories, too, writing themselves into a sweeping historical epic not unlike the claim makers they heard. Old dynastic contracts, centuries old, needed to be explicitly laid to rest. Headlam-Morley recommended an article for the treaty that not only recognized Hungary's independence but declared null and void the Pragmatic Sanction of 1723, the constitution of 1867, "and all other laws, decrees or treaties determining the relations between Hungary and other portions of the Austro-Hungarian Monarchy."[75] Left to him, the constitutional law of the empire would have become a founding feature of the international peace, even if only in its negation.

Headlam-Morley had demonstrated an impressive knowledge of Austro-Hungarian constitutional law, but other Foreign Office mandarins were not to be so easily outdone. The following week, the Polish-born historian and fellow member of the delegation, Lewis Namier, who had in fact studied in Austrian Lemberg (Lwów/Lviv) before migrating to the United Kingdom, circulated a long and erudite critique of Headlam-Morley's arguments. He took the opposite view: "If the question whether German Austria is the legal heir to the personality of the late Austrian State were to be determined on a judicial basis, there can hardly be any doubt but that it would be answered in the affirmative," he declared categorically in opening. In outlining his reasons, he set Habsburg sovereignty, and its undoing, in time:

(a) The Habsburg Monarchy has grown out of the provinces to which German Austria is now being reduced. It is returning more or less to its frontiers of 1526.

(b) The Austrian Germans were always strongly conscious of standing in a different relation to the Austrian State than did the other nationalities. . . . The Austrian Germans were invariably "die Träger des Österreichischen Staatsgedankens." . . . They cannot suddenly change their ground because it suits them to do so.

(c) It would be wrong to say that any of the new States starts an absolutely new political existence. They merely resume an existence broken by the action of the Habsburgs who had therein the support of the German Austrians. Were German Austria to be allowed to refuse the personality of the old Austrian State, it would indeed be the only one among the new States without an historical past.[76]

Namier's arguments are noteworthy for a number of reasons. In the first instance, he constructed German Austrians as an imperial people, and the original Austrian duchies as an imperial metropole, meaning "the empire" could survive even if it lost all the territories it acquired in 1526 and after.

As such, he took a position in an older legal debate[77] as well as an ongoing historiographical one.[78] Second, and crucially for our study of sovereignty and time, he painted the making and unmaking of composite monarchies as a sort of historical game of snakes and ladders. Dynastic contracts broken, constituent states—the Austrian crownlands as much as Bohemia or Hungary—simply slid back down the snake through time, "resum[ing] an existence broken by the action of the Habsburgs." Reverting to their old legal status and identity, they picked up legally where they had left off—in 1526. This was not a Central European pathology, tied to some proclivity for history. On the contrary, Namier drew an analogy to Ireland, which, if the union dissolved, "would no doubt effect a return to 1799 or to Gratton's Parliament."[79] Sovereignty could play with history, lapsing back to an old status quo, even if that involved time travel across multiple centuries. The temporal logics of sovereignty were not bound into a one-way historical progression: composite crowns contained triggers for the clock to be reset, if not reversed.

This crisscrossing of centuries had a direct bearing on the name of the old-new imperial state. Headlam-Morley had expressed doubts about the name Austria, with its historical ambiguity and multivalence. Namier saw things differently: "I do not consider the name 'German Austria' (Deutsch Österreich) an improvement on 'Austria' pure and simple. On the contrary the qualification of 'German' implies the continued existence of another, wider Austria, whereas the use of 'Austria' plain and simple would mean that it had returned to its proper national frontiers of about 1526."[80] Namier's memorandum thus tied the new order of 1919 being forged in Paris to the fateful 1526 death of Ludwig—the Jagiellonian king drowned in a swamp as he fled the Battle of Mohacs—and the passing of his two crowns into Habsburg hands. These sorts of legal stories—about the legal identity of states surviving centuries of colonization to reemerge on the other side—would become a persistent feature of the jurisprudence of decolonization, as chapter 7 shows.

So what, then, *was* a new state? Headlam-Morley identified this as the real issue when he responded to Namier in turn. If he was chastened by Namier's rebuke, it only showed in his more equivocal tone. "I think there is some confusion in regard to the meaning of the words 'New State,'" he ventured. "In using this expression I have been thinking throughout of international relations: for instance when I speak of Czecho-Slovakia as a New State, I am not in the least disputing the fact that there is an historic continuity in internal matters and that the new Republic is the direct successor of the old Bohemian Kingdom." But was that the correct vantage point to take? "On the other hand, from the international point of view," he countered, "there has been no Bohemian State for 300 years and therefore Czecho-Slovakia has to receive recognition as a new State and its whole position in international affairs has to be definitely regulated. In doing this we take the view, which I think is clearly the right one, that it starts quite afresh and in no way hampered by any of the obligations of the old Austro-Hungarian Monarchy and not inheriting any rights which the Monarchy possessed. I would treat Austria in precisely the same way."[81]

Headlam-Morley thereby suggested that the question depended on whether one viewed matters from "inside" the states concerned or from the vantage point of the international system more broadly (as Friedrich Tezner had argued about the singularity of Austro-Hungarian sovereignty). Each state, on its own terms, may be seen as continuous and thus not "new." Yet if surveyed from a higher perch, taking in the whole of international relations, its three-hundred-year absence was real. The world had changed in the meantime, and its position in the international order would necessarily differ dramatically as a result. Its standing and status needed to be reregulated: for all intents and purposes, it was a new state. International law did not have so prodigious a memory; it could not hold states in suspense for so long. The Austrian government of 1919 may well be the successor to the "old Government of Upper and Lower Austria and the other territories which go with it. But this has nothing whatever to do with its international obligations," Headlam-Morley maintained, "and my whole point is that I see no reason why, from the international point of view, Austria should be treated on different principles to Czecho-Slovakia."[82]

The question of whether republican Austria was the legal successor to the empire was never entirely resolved, despite the fact that succession was integral to a raft of postwar problems in the successor states, including state debt, citizenship, archives, pensions, and railways.[83] The treaties appeared to presume state continuity. Harold Temperley, a Cambridge historian and diplomat who served as adviser to the British delegation and who compiled a semi-official history of the peace conference, argued on the contrary that Austria and Hungary were both new states (tellingly, this helped explain why minorities treaties were imposed on them).[84] Most Austrian jurists argued for the juridical discontinuity of the new Austria with the fallen empire.[85] But many others agreed, too.[86] The question played out in a series of Austrian court cases in the 1920s.[87] Another "test case" for oldness or newness was Austria's entry into the League of Nations, considered in the league's Fifth Committee in November–December 1920, where newness seemed to hold sway.[88]

Sorting Europe's new state map into "old" and "new" did not just affect Austria, Czechoslovakia, and Hungary, even if the stakes there were especially high. The question mark also fell over the belt of small states now populating that "international frontier," to use H. Duncan Hall's memorable phrase, between the former Continental imperial centers in Germany, Russia, Turkey, and Austria.[89] It perhaps is unsurprising that the Austrian jurists took this sorting particularly seriously. Bulgaria and Austria should count as new states, Josef Kunz argued, but Hungary was identical with prewar Hungary both "legally and in the psyche."[90] Estonia, Latvia, and Lithuania were new states, Alfred Verdross explained; "in contrast it is contestable whether the Soviet Union and Yugoslavia are to be considered new subjects in international law or the continuation of Russia and Serbia."[91]

The state that became Yugoslavia proved one of the thorniest cases. It married together "nonhistorical peoples" (like the Slovenes) and suspended/ slumbering states (like Croatia) with already sovereign ones (like Serbia), producing the most diverse temporal-legal conglomerate. In this case, the categorization of old and new states mattered especially because of the minorities treaties that were fastened to the new states, broadcasting their junior status to all the world. Such indignity seemed intolerable to representatives of the Serb-Croat-Slovene government at the Paris Peace Conference. Before the war, Serbia had possessed full sovereignty. As such, there was no basis on which the Allied peacemakers could interfere in that preexisting sovereignty through the imposition of a minorities treaty. The delegation explained that, at the most, it could countenance such provisions only for those parts of the state territory that had not been sovereign before the war, for the "new" portions of the state. As Nicolas Pachitch (Nikola Pašić) wrote on behalf of the delegation on July 24, 1919, the minorities obligations presented by the peacemakers were unacceptable "because the conditions in question appear to be also applicable to the territories of the Kingdoms of Serbia and Montenegro, which would amount to our renunciation, an advance, of certain incontestable rights of sovereignty."[92] As he reaffirmed on August 1, they would only consider "proposals which do not concern the former territory of the Kingdom of Serbia and of Montenegro."[93] If the new minorities treaties were the test, then Yugoslavia could at most register as half new and half old. In the model presented by the Serb-Croat-Slovene delegation, the internal "sequence" of the state's sovereignty would have been coded into its international obligations, the history of its state formation coded into law—not unlike the old empire itself.

Self-Determination and Prefiguration

A keyword then and now, *self-determination* has accompanied the very many ends of empire for a hundred years. Part of its power lies in its chameleonlike ability to absorb an extremely broad range of agendas and political ideologies. One of the less-told chapters in its history involves its deployment by those who "lost" the Versailles settlement. In spite (or because) of losing two-thirds of their prestate territory to the new "national" states, Hungarian statesmen wrote long and careful analyses of the concept. They, too, supported it, they claimed: it simply needed to be applied in a "legal" way. In pinning down its capaciousness into clear legal principles, they drew on a preexisting horizon of legal assumptions and structures. Counterintuitively, then, the "right to self-determination" became the sign under which much of the imperial legal imaginary bled through into the new world order.

In a pamphlet dated December 1918, Apponyi declared Hungary's commitment to an "American peace" based on Wilson's ideas, citing the latter's advocacy for the "autonomy" of the nations of Austria-Hungary. How would this take effect in the case of Hungary? He surveyed the facts: on the one hand, Hungary, in its present borders, had been "a political unit for more than a thousand years"; profound geographic and economic cohesiveness underpinned its integrity. On the other hand, numerous racial communities resided in Hungary, leading to the suggestion that it should "be divided according to the racial principle, disregarding history, geography and political economy." This contrast led to a clash between "the principles upon which nations are built up"[94]—a battle for the grounds of legitimate statehood. Was one principle paramount? Could a compromise be found?

Yes, it could, Apponyi argued. "To begin with: the autonomy of the 'nations' let us even say: races, dwelling in Hungary is not synonimous [*sic*] with the annexation of their territories to a neighbouring state." The claims of neighboring states to Hungary's territory were not Wilsonian but rather imperialistic. Surely the right to self-determination did not involve a right to secession vested in every part of a nation. "America did not think so," he wrote tersely, "when she coerced in a bloody war the southern States, who had most decidedly and formally declared their will to secede from the union. Is President Wilson's meaning then to be derived from Jefferson Davis or from Abraham Lincoln?"[95] The first task, then, was conceptual clarity: the semantic field comprising "secession," "annexation," and "autonomy" needed to be carefully parsed and weighed.[96]

Apponyi presented all the statistics and tables of an inextricably intermingled population across the territory of historic Hungary, a mix that left no possibility of a clean national unmixing. Was it not then "the height of absurdity" to carve up a robust political unit, tried and tested over centuries, in order to create "national" states that would be as racially diverse as the state from which they seceded? Especially when the new states also lacked the geographic and economic advantages of the original state?[97] Apponyi suggested a compromise solution that reconciled "the laws of geographic and political economy and the deep-rooted result of history with the just demands of race." It involved "giving to every race a representation of its own elected by all the members of the race *irrespective of territorial continuity*, which cannot be obtained," and granting "to these racial representations a fair amount of self-government in every matter that concerns the race as such" within the bounds of the Hungarian state.[98] He thus embraced the kind of deterritorialized autonomy advocated most famously by Renner and Bauer. He maintained that previous Hungarian policy had not been oppressive: it had recognized "the right of the *individual* to his native language in church, school, vestry and county government. . . . *But it did not admit race as self-governing bodies.* Now we are ready to do this." As in debates of the imperial era, the constitution of national or ethnic groups into collective legal subjects represented the genuinely radical concession. These new collective subjects, he claimed "in perfect good faith," would form the basis of a new federal order.[99] Postimperial Hungary would pick up old plans out of the annals of imperial constitutional debate. And crucially, self-determination meant corporate autonomy rather than secession.

It was the jurist and politician Gyula Wlassics, though, who really attempted a systematic analysis of the term. A professor of criminal law at the University of Budapest and president of the Hungarian administrative court, Wlassics (1852–1936) had presided over widespread reform as Hungarian minister of religion and education between 1896 and 1903, championing the free exercise of religion, public schools, and the entry of women into the academy. He served as speaker of the Hungarian Upper House in 1918 and again later in the interwar years. As the new order was taking shape across the region, he turned to tackle directly "the exceedingly difficult problem of international Self-determining Right."[100] What was meant by a "people" with a right to self-determination? What qualifications must such a people possess?

Because of its importance and its capaciousness, the "laws of self-determination" must be defined with "scientific accuracy." The idea was far older than Wilson. The "political Self-determining Right," he reasoned, as a right concerned with the entitlement of a group of people to shape their political future and control their territory, has "a sovereign appearance." "If that be so, then this Right is of the same nature as hitherto was the Right of the State, which we called the Constitution."[101] Self-determination, historically understood, had been the right of states. While particular groups of peoples could also enjoy a right to self-determination within the "internal domain" of the state, this right flowed from the latter and was regulated by it. To think about self-determination *beyond* the framework of the state was very difficult, "perhaps even impossible," Wlassics warned. There were no clear international rules regulating the right of a group of people "to separate themselves from their own State, or form themselves into a new State, or join themselves to another State, or form a Union with several States."[102] But such rules would be essential to avoid arbitrariness, encroachment, and chaos.[103]

Wlassics declared that there was only one logical place to start a challenging codification project of this sort: "Beyond doubt, the very first condition for the exercise of any Right is to know who is justified in exercising it." The problem of a right led straight back to the problem of defining its correlate subject—just like the Kremsier debates in 1849, just like the uncertainty over article 19 of the 1867 constitution, and just like so many other instances in the Habsburg Empire's legal history. Self-determination, too, was in search of a subject. Wlassics argued that a set of rules was urgently required "to determine the minimum limit within which a group of peoples can dispose of their own destiny by Right."[104] Obviously, not every community was capable of independent life: "Is it possible to grant every village, every little isolated group, the Right of

Self-determination?" And even if it was, would that be desirable? As Wlassics pursued this line of argumentation, his discussion grew less abstract. And "is it possible," he continued, "on a legal basis, to sever a territory where mixed nationalities are, if these different-speaking nationalities have been welded together into one whole State through centuries, and live scattered throughout the territory in question? Is there ground for the Right of Self-determination even then," when a "rupture from the old State causes millions to come again under foreign rule?" Did nothing at all mitigate this right—not history or culture or economy or geography?[105]

Wlassics constructed his own manual for assessing the legitimacy of appeals to self-determination. History, ancestry, nationality, and ethnographical data, he wrote, "all lend a hand in settling the claim." Only "inductive research" would allow the drafting of regulations. Among "the different grounds of Right" to be considered, "historical Rights and ancestral Rights" clearly had their place.[106] Race, too, though "in science, nationality is no longer bound up with the category of Race, for then no State in the world could retain its present boundaries."[107] In fact, when it came to contemporary nationality, race really meant history rather than biology.[108] Undoubtedly, these various factors sometimes justified the creation of a new state—but only if the new state was genuinely capable of independent, unassisted existence. The new formation must actually remove the grounds of the discontent; higher cultures should not be subject to the rule of lower ones; and the claims should not be imperialistic in motivation. Otherwise, the new formation would be "just a caricature of that self-determining Right which originally floated before Wilson's eyes, and which we desire to work out in the sense of a universal rule."[109]

Unsurprisingly, he felt the case of Hungary threw "a glaring light on the rigid formula of science as it appears on paper." The large historic state at Europe's center proved the perfect test case. The politicians "who wish to carve up Hungary set up the idea of absolute and relative majority as a legal title to the counties," Wlassics complained, and "as if that were not enough, they declare quite openly that strategic principle which is incompatible with Wilson's points." Strategic considerations and raw demographics commanded only meager force within his hierarchy of norms. A settlement built on such foundations could not produce peace: "When it seeks to effect a cure it causes new wounds."[110] It might be technically possible "to cut up arbitrarily a living organism like Hungary, which forms a geographical unit, but the international right to cut it up will never be acknowledged."[111] The legal foundations were lacking. "What a logical train of thought it is," he exclaimed, "that every small territory is adapted for Self-Determination, while the historically and geographically formed Hungary, where Hungarians are in absolute majority, and where thousands and thousands of people of foreign tongue feel themselves one with the Hungarian people, is not regarded as adapted to exercise the Right of Self-Determination!"[112]

Who was adapted to the prose of self-determination? Wlassics's answer was clear. If strict racial boundaries were neither possible nor especially desirable, and if the anarchy of each tiny village lodging a separate claim was to be avoided, then the right of self-determination could only logically attach to those preexisting legal persons, that is, historic states like Hungary. The enormous difficulty of fashioning dispersed and intermingled national groups into new legal subjects led to a presumption for the already existing legal persons. The Hungarian submissions to the peace conference concurred with this interpretation entirely: "The right of self-determination was—and still is—a guarantee of the territorial integrity of our country."[113] Self-determination, in other words, was refracted through the prism of an older legal order. Surely the new order could not build all its subjects from scratch.

What is more, international law recognized no properly legitimate way of splitting those states apart. As Wlassics wrote in another text from the same period, it would offend all "international ethics, if Hungary's territory, geographically and economically a united state, were considered an [*sic*] common prey."[114] Of course, this line of argumentation about territorial integrity relied on Hungary possessing a continuous state identity—on Hungary *already being* a clearly established state in 1918. Precisely this equation—of the rights and standing of principalities emerging out of the empire—lay at the heart of the first significant international "case" on self-determination, namely, the dispute between Sweden and Finland over the Aaland Islands. In its bones, and stripped of its particular advocacy for Hungary, Wlassics's interpretation did not differ substantially from that given by the league's organs. In that dispute, the Aaland Islands sought to "leave" Finland, then in the process of gaining independence from Russia, and join Sweden. Two league commissions—one composed of jurists, another of rapporteurs—considered the question. The jurists rejected the notion of self-determination as a principle in international law, stating that "positive International Law does not recognize the right of national groups, as such, to separate themselves from the State of which they form part by the simple expression of a wish, any more than it recognizes the right of other States to claim such a separation." The right to refuse such a wish formed "an attribute of the sovereignty of every State which is definitely constituted."[115] But therein lay the catch: the jurists held that Finland was not, in fact, "definitely constituted": it remained in the process of formation. If states were *not* yet clearly established, where territorial sovereignty was lacking, self-determination could play a role in shaping the settlement. Self-determination became a factor where sovereignty was unsettled and fixed rights subjects did not yet exist.

The committee of rapporteurs, for their part, agreed that self-determination could not be viewed as a principle of international law,[116] but disagreed on the status of Finland, holding that it was *not* a new state still in the process of formation. They emphasized Soviet recognition of Finish autonomy within the bounds of the empire, and the continuity of Finland's legal personality over the cusp of 1917.[117] Whether or not Finland emerged out of the Russian Empire *as* Finland, as a hermetic and preformed legal unit, would thus determine whether it was vulnerable to its citizens' secessionist appeals to self-determination. In this sense, the application of "new" rights languages always already implied a referendum on what had survived from legal orders past. Wlassics and Apponyi understood this co-implication of world orders only too well.

The New Space of Historical Rights

The filtering of self-determination was not the only new vocation acquired by the old imperial discourses of historical sovereignty. For all the clear continuity in arguments made about historical sovereignty before and after Austria-Hungary's collapse, noteworthy shifts in emphasis occurred, too. Where the object or goal of historic rights claims had previously concerned centrally the extent of autonomy and authority as against the monarch—the *thickness* of rights, so to speak—in a post-1918 world they now became a key vocabulary for claiming extent of territory, that is, the *space* of rights. This shift reflects the broader history of jurisdiction, from a personal or relational matter to one of legally flat or legally homogeneous territory.

No state cared more about historical frontiers than Hungary—because, of course, it lost them. Hungarian statesmen argued that Hungary's historical borders were also natural borders. Hungary's many centuries of existence as a political unit confirmed the naturalness of its territory as a geographic unit: "The whole history of man and land, the surface, the geomorphological structure, . . . the course taken by the waters and the valleys of the mountains skirting the country which all widen out towards the interior, . . . the natural covering of flora . . . the fauna accommodated to the climate . . . ; in a word, every factor of the formation of life is a proof of unity."[118] The Carpathians were a climate boundary, and the history of Hungary proved this too. Apponyi was particularly lucid in his oral presentation before the Supreme Council: "You may refuse to recognize history as a principle in the building up of a juridical construction, but you cannot refuse her as a witness when she repeats the same evidence for ten centuries. It is no chance, it is the voice of nature speaking here."[119] History spoke the language of geography and gave nature voice. Even if you did not accept history as a foundation for law, it was hard to resist its power when it communicated the deep truths of the natural world. Formulations like these—and there are many of them in these years—expressed some anxiety about the receivability of historic arguments. In this context, geography gifted history a valuable scientism and universality. Apponyi had used a similar formulation in a 1919 pamphlet: "History has been the interpreter of nature, when she created and preserved the political union of Hungary's present territory."[120] History spoke, translated, and sanctified geography; history was geography at work through time.

The original set of memorandums had been drawn up before the delegates saw the terms of the peace. The shock of the Trianon borders—Hungary was to lose two thirds of its territory to neighboring states Romania, Yugoslavia, Czechoslovakia, and Austria—and the outrage they provoked would harden into a permanent feature of Hungarian politics. In the very first official responses, we see these various idioms of right being rearranged in real time. When they returned to Paris on February 12, the Hungarian delegates filed eighteen notes setting out their objections. They complained bitterly of departures from the ethnic principle and demanded plebiscites in all the territories to be separated from Hungary to assess the desires of the population and thereby respect the principles of a Wilsonian peace.[121] The language of historical right also returned with a vengeance. In their "Introduction Note," the Hungarians expressed their surprise that so many other claims of historical right had been admitted by the peacemakers: perhaps their hesitancy to rely on their tried-and-tested historical rights represented a profound tactical error. They quoted the Allies back at themselves. Faced with the Germans of Bohemia who wanted to be detached from Czechoslovakia, the Allied powers announced their decision "'to preserve as far as possible to the old Czech provinces of the Crown of Bohemia their historic frontiers.'" The Germans "'ought to remain associated with the Czech inhabitants *in order to cooperate with them in the development of the national unity to which history has rendered them jointly and severally answerable.'*" Exactly! exclaimed the Hungarians: "It could not be better put."[122] The Allies had perfectly articulated the logic of historical rights—but only (and shockingly) to the advantage of the Czechs. These words, the delegation purred, "so precisely express the confession of faith of the Allied Powers on the subject of the supremacy of historic ties binding into a political community populations of different races."

In a separate note titled "Concerning the frontiers of Hungary," the Hungarian delegation claimed their share of the widespread vindication of historical rights. The terrible injustice of partitioning Hungary on the basis of "nationality" only appeared more nonsensical in light of the principles relied on elsewhere. The delegation observed "that the decisions of the Peace Conference are influenced considerably by historical rights. The reestablishment of ancient Poland and Bohemia has been effected on the basis of historical rights." Poland was to subsume eastern Galicia with its majority of Ruthenian speakers. "This situation is absolutely analogous to Transylvania," they implored.[123] And when it came to the western frontier of Poland, the Allies stuck to the Polish frontier of 1772 rather than insisting on the language frontier. Bohemia proper had everywhere retained its historical boundaries; historical rights also found application in the de-annexation of Alsace-Lorraine. But not for Hungary: "The new frontier now placed before us is not based on historical rights—is indeed in every respect a contradiction of the same; nor is it demarcated on an ethnographical basis." No, they had felt the sharp edge of a different principle altogether: "This frontier is that of conquering peoples."[124]

They were not wrong. The frontiers of the Hungarian state were largely fixed long before any of the Hungarian submissions changed hands in Paris. They had been decided in reverse: the peace conference had appointed territorial committees for each of the smaller "Allied" states, and "Hungary" emerged as the negative space remaining between all the newly sculpted sovereigns.[125] The Hungarians were latecomers in Paris: Beneš and Kramář had appeared before the Great Powers on February 5, 1919—almost eleven months before the Hungarians had the same chance. That day, the two Czechs sought "to shape the Czecho-Slovak State."[126] Their submissions, as we know, forcefully argued for the legal survival of the "Czech" state "composed of Bohemia, Moravia, and Silesia" through the vicissitudes of imperial rule.[127] The jurisdictional imaginary of these long-standing historical rights claims now hardened around territorial borders, just like the Hungarian case. "The Czechs, therefore, in claiming as theirs the territories of Bohemia, Moravia and Silesia are only acting in accordance with a classic right, consecrated by a past History dating twelve centuries back. The frontiers of those provinces are historical frontiers," the delegates declared, and "no Czech would allow of their being changed."[128] As they summarized in conclusion, making sure no one missed the deep historical legality in play: "The Czecho-Slovaks now formulate their territorial claims—claims based on historic traditions, and consider that the Czech State (composed of their three provinces) has never ceased to exist, legally speaking. In virtue, therefore[,] of these historic traditions Bohemia, Moravia and Silesia (along with Slovakia) are considered as constituting the main basis of the national territory claimed by the Czecho-Slovak Republic."[129]

The Czechs were famously successful in virtually all the territorial claims they made, despite, equally famously, the presence of substantial "minority" populations within the bounds of these historic *Länder*.[130] Controversy raged regarding regions like Teschen (Těšín/Cieszyn)—which had a Polish majority but fell within historical Silesia—and especially regarding the fate of the large German population within historic Bohemia. The relationship of Czech and German speakers in Bohemia, we recall, had caused great agitation already in the first days of constitutional debate in Kremsier in 1849: it now became a point of sharp international contention.[131] In his verbal presentation, Beneš highlighted economic and geographic unity, too, but history certainly rang out above other languages of justification. As Masaryk reflected, "Our claim that the German minority should remain with us is based on our historical right and on the fact that the Germans of Bohemia never attached value to union with Germany while they were under Austrian rule, or even in the time of the Bohemian Kingdom."[132]

Naturally enough, these borders and the reasoning behind them provoked fierce protest and controversy. The German Bohemian politician Rudolf Lodgman von Auen (1877–1962), who had served as a representative in both the imperial parliament and the Bohemian diet, was especially vocal. In November 1918, the German Bohemian delegates to the imperial parliament had met together in Vienna and elected von Auen head of the provincial government (*Landeshauptmann*) of German Bohemia; he subsequently represented their interests as part of the Austrian delegation to the Paris Peace Conference, where his attempts to have the German areas of Bohemia included in the new Austrian republic floundered. In a December 1918 speech titled "For the Self-Determination of German Bohemia," he expressed incredulity that the Czechs could make claims in the old style: the world of those old rights, he averred, had been washed away. Now one had to refer to the will of the people![133] Outlining their case in a memorandum for the international audience in Paris, von Auen and his colleague Robert Freissler submitted that there were two different principles in play: it was a case of "historical juridical events" versus "national autonomy." The only rational path was clear. The state planned by the Czechs would "represent a deteriorated new edition of collapsed Austria." With such frontiers, it could only become a center of discontent and unrest: "A hearth of contagion will be created for the further peace of Europe."[134]

Jurists like Rudolf Laun also launched critiques. In a 1919 pamphlet titled "Czechoslovak Claims to German Land," he rehearsed the declared foundations of a Wilsonian peace. The latter ostensibly forbade conquest, annexation, and the occupation of territories inhabited by other nationalities. "It seems all the stranger," Laun wrote, "that precisely one of Europe's newly formed states, despite being introduced into the society of states as an ally of the United States of America, will only admit the validity of Wilson's principles where they are of benefit to it." At the same time, they applied entirely contradictory principles in other directions.[135] On November 14, 1918, Laun recounted, the new Czechoslovak Republic, through the mouth of its first minister-president, Dr. Kramář, insisted "firmly and steadfastly that the union of the Bohemian lands, sanctified by a history of many centuries, survives uninjured." The Germans, apparently, would not be disadvantaged if they were loyal to the Czech state, but the Czechs would never allow a "disruption to their Bohemian lands, not only because of their historical rights but also because of the right of their minority to a free national life." The Czech statesman, Laun argued, had thereby declared that "historical rights weigh more heavily than national self-determination."[136] Yet how could this be reconciled with the new world order? "Surely the Peace Conference, which should introduce a democratic age and realize the self-determination of peoples, cannot work with historical arguments."[137] Had it wanted to do that, it should not be granting Tyrol to the Italians. "German Sudetenland wants to determine its own destiny!" howled another pamphlet (or, in the wordplay of the German original—"to self determine its destiny").[138] No, the cartography of principles did not align with the new map of states, not even close. That great twentieth-century challenge of "reconciling boundaries with ideas" had begun.[139]

Fending off German claims to self-determination involved Czech statesmen in the kind of distinctions and qualifications that the Hungarians had cultivated. Germans in our state, Masaryk observed, appealed to the authority of President Wilson and the right of self-determination. "Before the war our people, too, proclaimed it; but in point of fact, it has never been clearly defined. Does it apply only to a whole people or is it valid also for sections of a people? A minority, even a big minority, is not a nation. Nor does 'self-determination' carry with it an unconditional right to political independence."[140] The subject of a right to self-determination was amorphous: it could splinter unendingly, damaging the credibility of the right itself or at least frustrating any easy presumption for its widespread application. Besides, the Czechs themselves were self-determining—they simply asserted the right to do so within their historic frontiers.

The residual legality of these historical units, and their integrity as such, sparked revealing reflections behind the scenes in Paris. Beneš reported American reservations even before the conference opened. If Bohemia's historic boundaries were recognized, would the conference not have to concede the same to the Poles? (Beneš responded, a little cattily, that the situation was entirely different, as it was necessary that order be established in these particular territories, and while the Czechs could do that, the Poles could not.)[141] But the initial terms of Allied recognition *had* referred to Czech independence in their historic frontiers, as the Czechs reminded the world in their memorandum on Silesia.[142]

Busy at work in the Political Intelligence Department, Namier reflected on this memorandum in mid-February 1919. These historic frontiers had been challenged by Germans as well as Poles, he noted. "In the case of Bohemia," he observed, "we are faced by these two extremely difficult problems: is a partition of Bohemia at all admissible? And if so, what parts are German and which of them can be separated from the Czecho-Slovak State?" If one were to disrupt the formation for the Poles, a strong presumption in favor of the German claims would be established, too. As it stood, no presumptions had been established in either direction: "We have merely accepted the existing administrative divisions because they existed."[143] If historic frontiers of the Czech provinces were abandoned in one direction, a path was opened for many more: the more neutral track—keeping the worms sealed in their can—was to leave the historical unit intact. The Czechs had thus been successful in establishing their historic state as a kind of neutral status quo, a presupposed unit whose "partition" would prove messy and unpredictable: exactly the presumption the Hungarians had fruitlessly sought for their own historic polity. Namier and Headlam-Morley seemed more of one mind on this point. Already a month earlier, the latter had written of Bohemia: "If as is to be hoped, the new State bases itself upon the historical Staatsrecht of the old Bohemian minority, the onus probandi of separating any portion of it lies with those who desire such separation."[144] Historical continuity represented the rebuttable presumption: the onus of proof and legitimation fell to those who wished to remodel history's formations. Here the old order really did prefigure the new.[145] That the Czechs were able to establish historical boundaries as the default—while their Hungarian neighbors were not—says much about their success in presenting themselves as a natural ally of the Allies rather than an integral component of the Austro-Hungarian state and its war effort.[146]

And yet, Czechoslovakia suffered from serious "rights trouble." Historical rights were not and could not be enough to justify the desired borders of the new state because those borders reached beyond Bohemia, Moravia, and Silesia and deep into historic Hungary. That is, they extended over the frontiers of history to include the Slovaks from "inside" historic Hungary. The Czech statesmen claimed a common "Czecho-Slovak" state on the basis of ethnic and linguistic kinship: or, as their peace conference memorandum had it, "in the name of the right of Nations to choose their own Government."[147] This demographic argument for national self-determination involved Czech claim makers in a permanently bifurcated discourse of legitimacy. As their declaration of independence phrased it: "We make this declaration on the basis of our historic and natural right."[148] As they had been in the imperial period, rights based on ethnicity were coded as "natural" as against the historic rights of the lands. The new state at the heart of Europe asserted the prerogative to rely on both idioms simultaneously. "Political men and theorists have long busied themselves with a constitutional definition of the union of Slovakia with our State," Masaryk reflected gingerly. "Theoretically it is a question of distinguishing more precisely between 'historical' and 'natural' right. We invoked both of them during the war; and in view of Slovakia, I had long endeavored to harmonize them."[149]

Many Czechs and Slovaks themselves remained skeptical about the union. Among the Slovak national movement, a strong consensus obtained for autonomy of some sort, but opinion then diverged as to whether this should occur under the umbrella of Czech sovereignty (or even under Hungarian sovereignty), or whether complete independence was preferable.[150] Different autonomist movements proliferated; some Slovak politicians, like Viktor Dvorčák (Dvortsák), approached the peace conference independently and complained that the nonexistent "Czecho-Slovak" nation was only the illegitimate invention of Masaryk and Kramář.[151] Many on the Czech side, too, expressed ambivalence about this bold departure from history. "I know only too well that it was no easy matter for us to provide for the inclusion of Slovakia. The Slovaks were unknown," Masaryk explained.[152] Numerous public figures, including some historians, remained tethered to a particular interpretation of the historical rights of the Bohemian lands (and their statements were "exploited" by "the pro-Austrians and the pro-Magyars"),[153] ignoring "our natural right to union with Slovakia." Masaryk mediated: "Though I admitted historical right, I always upheld natural right alongside of it."[154]

If doubts persisted on the home front, they could hardly compete with the incredulity that the union provoked elsewhere. "The Czech claim concerning the annexation of 16 Hungarian counties is founded on no historical, no legal, and no geographical basis," protested Ernő Ludwigh, Austro-Hungarian consul in Cleveland, Ohio (which was home to a large Hungarian population).[155] They had never claimed these counties. "Merely in the most recent years, however, have they worked out a new state rights theory with two applications; one for the German-Bohemian districts, based on history, and the other for the Slovak counties, based on the nationality principle."[156] It was this direct contradiction, this rights dualism, that rankled many the most.[157] While historical rights apparently trumped self-determination in the Bohemian lands, Rudolf Laun observed, in Slovakia the reverse was true: "In the east, as against Hungary, the same state claims that the right of national self-determination is stronger than historical right."[158] As the Austrian civil servant and journalist Friedrich Kleinwaechter put it in his 1920 history of the collapse of the monarchy: "For the state-forming principle of the Czechoslovak state, the historical borders are made effective as against the Germans, and the ethnic borders as against the Magyars."[159] For Kleinwaechter, this showed that no single principle, in the end, was viable across the board: "A Czech state *without* the Bohemian, Moravian and Silesian Germans is a formation incapable of life. *With* the Germans—as the future will show—actually, too."[160]

Of course, the debate as to whether territory should be carved into political units on the basis of history or of ethnicity stretched back to the Kremsier parliament of 1849. In the landmark Kremsier constitutional proposal, the delegates had agreed on a novel solution that tried to implement *both* understandings of legal-political community simultaneously: the historical units remained as the constitution's fundamental persons, but one level beneath them, the state would be carved up into smaller *Kreise* that conformed as much as possible to ethnic-linguistic settlement. Different understandings of right and jurisdiction were stacked atop one another, allowing different versions of the empire to exist simultaneously. Discarded by a militarily ascendant imperial government in March 1849, the Kremsier constitutional draft nevertheless became the semantic-legal field in which other proposals and plans circulated for the remainder of the empire's life. The old-new Czech state now imported both the natural and the historical conceptions but arranged them differently. Those jurisdictions that had been stacked atop one another in the Kremsier draft were unstacked and laid out side by side: the historical (multiethnic) conception of the political community triumphed in the state's west, while next to it, in the east, the ethnic conception did. As in the Kremsier draft, both conceptions were deemed legitimate: but unlike the Kremsier draft, they were valid separately, adjacent on the map, rather than applicable to the same territory at the same time.

These two different idioms of sovereign justification affected the legal texture and "timing" of the territories to which they applied. The bifurcated languages of legitimacy mapped onto a bifurcated timeline for the legal birth of the new Czechoslovak state. In a number of cases in the early 1920s, Czechoslovak courts were asked to determine the precise start date of Czechoslovak sovereignty. The Supreme Administrative Court held that the Czechoslovak state did not come into existence as a result of the treaties of peace but rather as a result of the revolution of October 28, 1918—"not by virtue of the international treaties which took for granted the existence of a State which was a signatory to them."[161] But what of the territorial extent of sovereignty, especially between October 28 and the final determination of the state's boundaries? The 1921 *Payment of War Tax (Czechoslovakia) Case* involved a plaintiff from Liberec (Reichenberg, Bohemia) who claimed that Austria had effectively declared the district of Liberec, as a component of "German Bohemia" (*Deutschböhmen*), to be part of the Austrian state, and that Czechoslovak sovereignty did not take effect there until the subsequent military occupation. In its decision, the Supreme Administrative Court demonstrated just how inextricably the advent of Czechoslovak sovereignty, as a legal proposition, was bound up with the imperial constitution.

According to the imperial constitution, the court recounted, the Kingdom of Bohemia had formed a distinct and autonomous unit in both administrative and constitutional law. The authority and jurisdiction of Bohemia's diet, judicial system, and administration extended over the whole kingdom. This situation persisted until the revolution of October 28, 1918. The concept of *Deutschböhmen* was entirely unknown in the empire's constitutional law and public administration alike. Thus, when the National Committee took control of all these central authorities on October 28, it also assumed power over the full extent of the territory belonging to the former Kingdom of Bohemia—including, of course, "German" areas like Liberec. As a result, the new authorities were not required to explicitly articulate the precise boundaries of the state on October 28.[162] The jurisdictional imaginary of the empire was imported wholesale from the imperial constitution into the sovereign shell of the new state: the Kingdom of Bohemia was transferred between orders as a whole unit, as an integral legal person. It did not need to be reconstituted and redescribed as the empire collapsed. For that reason, Czechoslovak sovereignty arrived instantaneously across the whole historical territory without any regard to the ethnic composition of the different regions: nations were not the basis of this sovereignty. The same transfer of old legal units and jurisdictions occurred for the other lands of the Bohemian crown—Moravia and Silesia—as well.[163]

But how did the Slovak territories fit into this origin-of-sovereignty story? Without a previous legal existence of their own (as such), their inclusion could not be construed as an unambiguous legal transfer, as an assumption that persisted over the rupture of the imperial collapse (or, if it could, this presumption would have been for their inclusion in Hungary). The Slovak territories really did require legal description—they needed to be hailed into the order of the new Czechoslovak state. On this question, the two highest Czechoslovak tribunals had different views. Consistent with the logic of the previous case, the Supreme Administrative Court held that the establishment of Czechoslovak sovereignty in Slovakia and in Subcarpathian Russia (also formally part of Hungary) required a different mechanism: it did not take effect until the Czechoslovak state actually *occupied* the region, established administration via the appointment of a *župan* (chief officer of the *župa*, or administrative district), and enabled the *župan* to assume his duties. The Supreme Court of Justice, on the contrary, held that these regions constituted part of the Czechoslovak state already at the moment of its inception on October 28[164]—perhaps by some more mystical leap of the jurisdictional imagination. Taking the former's view, the different conceptual foundations of territorial rights had resulted in a different chronology of sovereignty, with different triggers and a different onus of proof. This sequence of rights was simultaneously a sequence of their respective rights subjects: the ethnic Czechoslovak state arrived in the new order a little later than the historical one. The uneven temporality of the "beginning" of the sovereignty recorded the disjunctures of imperial law into the legal foundations of the old-new state.

Over the course of the interwar years, the conceptual duality of the Czechoslovak state became a favored explanation for and symbol of the ills of the interwar settlement in Central and Eastern Europe more broadly. The pairing of the two rights paradigms appeared to many—especially those disgruntled with the settlement—as a kind of reckless miscegenation whose results could only introduce unnatural and corrupting elements into Europe's political structure. This trope appeared simultaneously with the interwar order itself. "Too late," warned the Hungarian diplomat Szilassy in 1921, "will the Bohemian rulers arrive at the understanding that such annexations [i.e., Slovakia] in today's world mean weakness more than strength, and that they have planted all the disadvantages of the old Hungary, without its traditions and historical and geographic and economic advantages, in their hybrid body politic [*ihr hybrides Staatswesen*]."[165] In its memorandum "On Southern Hungary," the Hungarian delegation to the peace conference likewise warned that, if Slovaks were incorporated into the Czech state, they would join the string of Hungarian and German factions already undermining the new polity: "Thus even now, at the very moment of its formation, the germ of contention and ultimate dissolution is hidden in the Czech State."[166]

Hungarian revisionism never subsided, and neither did the question of Bohemia's Sudeten Germans. The trope of Czechoslovakia's juridical dualism as a kind of fatal flaw at the heart of the Versailles settlement only sharpened as the political atmosphere did the same in the 1930s. After a long study trip (supported by the Social Science Research Council) through the successor states in 1934, the Hungarian émigré scholar Oszkár Jászi collected his impressions in a series of articles under the title "War Germs in the Danube Basin." Jászi had briefly served as the first Hungarian "minister for national minorities" in the months immediately following the war's end, before migrating to the United States in 1925 and taking up a post at Oberlin College in Ohio. The tone of his 1934 reports—published across a number of issues of *The Nation*—was not upbeat. He recounted social dysfunction, economic weakness, and national strife. The Czechoslovak state received some rare praise: it represented a genuine Western democracy, he felt, and its constitution was "not a show window but a reality." "Unfortunately, however, the new state rests on unstable foundations," he wrote. "It was built on two antagonistic principles—the ethnological principle by which Hungary was dismembered, and the historical principle by which the right of the German minority to unite with Germany was denied." Under such conditions, the unity and loyalty of the population would inevitably prove difficult.[167] The conceptual friction threatened, or even promised, real-world friction. The interwar order did not have its ideas in line, did not have its ideas straight; foundational principles were not only multiple but antagonistic.

A poster child of the interwar order, Czechoslovakia was also a (partially self-appointed) bellwether for its fortunes.[168] The Germans of Bohemia emerged as the fulcrum and excuse for the messy end of the Versailles settlement. In the lead-up to the Munich agreement of 1938, in which Czechoslovakia's Sudeten German territory was fatefully ceded to Hitler's Germany, some thought that the deep roots of the crisis must be buried in the makeup of the state itself. The aforementioned Slovak campaigner Viktor Dvorčák was actively reaching toward international public opinion once more as part of the "Slovak Council." The title of its 1937 memorandum was clear enough: *Should Great Britain Go to War—for Czechoslovakia? An Appeal to British Common Sense for the Sake of World Peace.* Dvorčák and his colleagues cataloged the apparent artificiality and illegitimacy of the Czechoslovak state. Again, the Sudetenland symbolized the conceptual bankruptcy of Czechoslovakia: "By what right do the Czechs possess this territory? By historical right, they say. Yet the Czechs themselves have no respect for historical rights, since Slovakia was in the uninterrupted possession of Hungary for more than a thousand years."[169] The equally dissatisfied Ruthenians argued similarly: Czechoslovakia is about to plunge the world into another world war.[170]

The challenge of coding imperial order into constitutional law had driven the development of a number of conceptual propositions and ritualized contrasts, including the distinction between historical and natural/ethnic rights, the capacity of historical law and rights to survive in theory while not in fact, the tight co-implication of rights and their subject, the capacity of states to preserve their legal personality within imperial polities, and their capacity to carry rights with them between different legal orders. Together these components reflected a deeper set of precepts about the relationship between law, time, and sovereignty. Law recorded history, archived its path and sequence, *and* triumphed over it, preserving juridical forms and subjects through political storm after political storm. This legal imaginary remained the conceptual horizon within which many protagonists and commentators understood the cataclysm of imperial collapse in 1918. A library of usable legal stories, it allowed contemporaries to connect an extremely fluid and unfamiliar political situation to structures of legitimacy and right that stretched back across the centuries, even to 1526. It was a way of conceptually mastering the nature and magnitude of a new international order in Central Europe. Strikingly, it also furnished resources for understanding the dissolution of that order. Narratives for the building and the dismantling of interwar Europe could be sourced from the songbook of imperial law.

CHAPTER SIX

State Birth at the Frontier of Knowledge

REIMAGINING INTERNATIONAL LAW
FROM POSTIMPERIAL VIENNA

Auspicious encounters on the Wickenburggasse • Kelsen's circle try to replace God and nature with a logical hypothesis • The big bang of law's universe • Living at the edge of knowledge • The shock of sovereign mortality • Thinking like a new state • From chaos to cosmos • International law never dies • World-making as sense-making

WHAT MAKES A STATE? *Three things*. At least that would be the answer if you picked up a law textbook in the early twentieth century. A state comprised a defined *territory*, a stable *population*, and an effective *government*. This "doctrine of the three elements" was another of Georg Jellinek's inventions, and its general acceptance had been swift. But when Hans Kelsen thought about it again in 1922, he was struck by a major omission. "It is just incomprehensible," he inveighed, "why the dominant doctrine has not adopted *time* in addition to *space* as an 'element' of the state."[1] A whole dimension was missing—had no one else noticed? "State existence is limited not only in space but also in time." A state's legal order governed not just the "where" of human behaviour but also the "when."[2] True, states did not usually set temporal limits on themselves, Kelsen conceded. But surely jurists had ample reason to reckon with "the fact that historically given states have only a temporary existence." This imperative applied not just to scholars focused on the factual effectiveness of law. As Kelsen emphasized, "Also from a purely normative point of view, the aspect of temporal limitation must be taken into account."[3] Law needed a theory of states in time.

The experiences behind Kelsen's flash of insight are less than mysterious. He had just lived through the dissolution of the Austro-Hungarian Empire— that polity of many crowns, many peoples, and many centuries, and the place he called home. With a lineage snaking off into the deep past, the Habsburg dynasty had seemed a synonym for continuity and tradition, making the jolt of its sudden departure all the sharper. Apparently, states could just—*end*? Simply stop—collapse, die, disappear? Where was the theory that held that experience? The law that made sense of it?

It did not exist.[4] Kelsen mulled the reasons for that silence. By the time he revisited the point in 1925, he could place it within a larger matrix of assumptions and beliefs about the state. He was trying his hand at a textbook-style volume for the first time, a *General Theory of the State*. When he turned to enumerate the "elements" of the state, he included his innovation, listing not only the state's "spatial sphere of validity" but also its "temporal sphere of validity." There were endless exhaustive treatments of state territoriality, he observed, but hardly anyone discussed the state's dimensions in time. Why? It may be, he ventured, that for *territory*, the limits of the state's domain were palpable, perceptible, tangible (he used the term *fühlbar*). In contrast, a *temporal* limit or restriction seemed to be completely *im*perceptible. Seen from the perspective of a particular state order, Kelsen wrote, that imperceptibility was not a coincidence, because states "arise with the claim to be valid *eternally*."[5] For that reason, and especially among the older treatments, one found "eternity" or perpetuity (*Ewigkeit*) listed among the characteristics of the state, which, he noted, yielded "a further analogy between the Person of the state" and that of God.[6]

The notion of juridical immortality has long been connected to the rise of the modern state. Ernst Kantorowicz's classic *The King's Two Bodies* (1957) traced the connection back to the intertwining of medieval theological and juridical thought. Perpetuity addressed clear pragmatic ends. It enabled the continuity of public order intergenerationally: the transfer of rights and obligations (from treaty commitments to public debt) through time despite the death of a particular monarch or the fall of a particular regime. Woven into the fabric of the modern state's legal order was a structural disavowal of temporal frontiers or horizons, an open-ended projection into the future, a "quasi-infinite continuity of public institutions."[7] Sitting in Vienna in the wake of imperial collapse, Kelsen sensed the contours of that larger edifice—the almost preconscious assumption of the state's unending order— precisely because it had, for him, just crumbled. Like a myth exposed or a spell suddenly broken, he felt it sharply now that it was gone. States were in fact brittle, fallible, worldly, mortal things. And legal theory needed to catch up.

This chapter recovers legal theory's confrontation with the mortality of the state. It shows how the end of empire pushed Kelsen and his circle of collaborators toward a new theoretical framework that could make legal sense of the birth and death of states. It thereby places these thinkers at the head of one of the twentieth century's signal stories. State mortality was about to become a global mass phenomenon, remaking the map of the world and affecting the lives of tens of millions. In the decades that followed, the slow-breaking end of direct imperial rule led to an explosion of new states. The League of Nations counted 42 founding members in 1920. In 1945, the United Nations had 51; by 1965, its ranks had swollen to 117. The laws governing the emergence of these new sovereigns—especially the doctrines of succession and recognition—became battlegrounds of world order because they directly affected the economic and political standing of the new states.[8] These problems arrived "early" to Central Europe. Kelsen and his colleagues wrote on questions like succession and recognition, too—as practitioners as well as scholars. After all, the status of their own new state, the Republic of Austria, also hung in the balance. But their driving preoccupation lay with a prior question—the under-lying philosophical problem that state collapse exposed. Was it logically possible to have legal knowledge about the creation and demise of states at all?

The logical impasse they confronted had its root in the state's pivotal position in modern understandings of law. In older doctrines of natural law, law emanated quasi-automatically from God or reason or nature. For self-consciously modernizing legal positivists, in contrast, the legal order *was* the state's legal order: the state made and guaranteed the law. So how could law govern a process prior to the state itself? A process that amounted to its own conditions of possibility? The same was true for state extinction. What law could "be there," valid and operative, after the state itself was gone? Georg Jellinek had written flatly of the "untenability of all attempts . . . to construe the creation of states juridically." For these reasons, jurists had classed the creation and demise of states as matters of *fact* and not *law*.[9] Such events unfolded beyond the horizon of law; they preceded legal knowledge. As Kelsen's collaborator Alfred Verdross summarized the traditional view in 1926, "Law attaches only to the finished fact of the state."[10] The creation of states was "pre-legal data," in the words of the Belgian jurist and judge Charles de Visscher: "The international legal order does not provide foundation for the State; it presupposes the State's existence."[11]

Was it possible for legal theory to do without the presupposition of the state? In the shadow of the empire's dissolution, that was exactly what the Viennese jurists explored. The question hinged on how one understood the "beginning" of law, its source, the ultimate basis of its validity. If law's validity was anchored in the state, then state birth and death could only be an extralegal fact. So they pioneered a line of argument that rooted law's ultimate validity not in the state but in international law instead. As we will see, the only way of transforming the beginnings and ends of sovereignty into legal phenomena, banishing this anarchic legal vacuum, was to *assume* the logical-legal "primacy" of international law. The end of empire thus pushed them toward a reconceptualization of the relationship between sovereignty and international law—one that knocked state sovereignty from its position as the "highest" and "first" point in law's world.

This chapter tracks how Kelsen and his circle arrived at this theory, arguing that its genesis reveals much not only about the relationship between the end of empire and international law but also about how the Habsburg Empire shaped the history of legal philosophy.[12] It was the sovereign plurality of the Habsburg Empire that first pushed them to interrogate the ultimate source of law's validity. Prompted by the empire's constitutional tangles, they began developing a radical new theory of law's philosophical basis already during World War I. Precisely because the empire had no uncontested singular sovereignty, they gradually realized that everything turned on the jurist's opening premise. If one began the sequence of legal reasoning from the presupposition of the emperor's original unfettered sovereignty, one arrived at certain conclusions, but if one instead began from the presupposition that Hungary or Bohemia had never renounced its sovereign rights, then the results looked entirely different. This insight sparked a highly fruitful philosophical analysis of the first premises, the preconscious a priori assumptions, that underpinned all law and legal reasoning. The Viennese jurists came to call this cognitive "point of departure" the *Grundnorm*, or "basic norm." The basic norm became the capstone of the all-encompassing philosophical system they developed over the course of the war, known as the pure theory of law, which rapidly traveled all around the world.

The chapter first tracks how Kelsen and his circle collaboratively thrashed out the various elements of the pure theory. It situates their methods and modes of working in the cultural and intellectual ferment of early twentieth-century Vienna. Building on the methodological foundations first suggested by Jellinek and then developed by Kelsen in his early work (i.e., law's status as *norm* not *fact*, as explored in chapter 4), they ambitiously pursued the highest questions of legal philosophy. It then reveals how, amid the crisis of the end of empire, they "scaled up" the pure theory to the domain of international law, transferring the idea of a "basic norm" from the level of the state to that of the world. Today, the pure theory of law still counts as one of the most complete philosophies of law ever devised, a feature of any scholarly introduction to analytical jurisprudence. If its historical anchoring in Austro-Hungarian constitutional law remains underappreciated in the English-speaking world, the formative role played by the end of empire has received no focused analysis at all. This chapter shows how a theory developed to tame the legal chaos of Habsburg sovereignty was retooled to tame the legal chaos of state birth that followed in its wake. If the multitudinous Habsburg state exerted extreme pressure on the first of sovereignty's fictions, the quasi-magical transformation of a plurality into a singularity (as chapter 4 showed), its dissolution exerted similar pressure on the second fiction—its immortality.

Thinking in Circles

"We were engaged in a constant competition for new sensations." Stefan Zweig and his classmates sneaked into rehearsals at the Philharmonic Orchestra and went to all the art exhibitions; they turned up at lecture theaters in the Department of Anatomy to watch dissections and checked "booksellers' display windows every day for instant information on what had just been published." They read, and read, and read. "Our curious nostrils sniffed at everything and anything." It had seized this band of schoolboys like a "fever": the need to know the latest "in every area of the arts and sciences." And the "best cultural source for all novelty," without question, was the coffeehouse. There they would sit for hours, having exchanged "the price of a cheap cup of coffee" for a panoptic view across the landscape of culture and knowledge. For the Viennese café was an "institution of a peculiar kind, not comparable to any other in the world," Zweig explained, a "sort of democratic club" where one could meet, linger, debate, watch, play cards or chess, receive post, change clothes, attend a campaign meeting—and, above all, read. All the Viennese newspapers were on offer, but also those "of the entire German Reich, as well as the French, British, Italian and American papers, and all the major literary and artistic international magazines." Perched there, "nothing escaped us": one hunted for the new "not with just one pair of eyes but with twenty."[13]

Zweig, later one of Europe's most popular writers, was born just two months after Hans Kelsen in 1881. They came of age in a world aflame. Yes, Vienna's "fanatical love" of culture was long-standing and legendary. When "the average Viennese citizen looked at his morning paper," Zweig recounted, "his eye generally went first not to parliamentary debates or foreign affairs but to the theatrical repertory, which assumed an importance in public life hardly comprehensible in other cities." No one would look twice at the prime minister or the richest magnate strolling down the street, "but every salesgirl and every cab driver would recognise an actor at the court theatre or an operatic diva."[14] But even in this context, something unusual was irrupting at the century's turn, something a little darker, something thrilling, something young. One felt it across the city. Gustav Klimt, commissioned for a major work gracing the walls of the Faculty of Philosophy, scandalized his patrons with a knot of anguished, naked bodies suspended in some sort of underworld; Sigmund Freud published *The Interpretation of Dreams* and opened up the unconscious as a field of research with his "unorthodox science of Eros"; a gang of rebellious writers—Arthur Schnitzler and Hugo von Hofmannsthal among them—lodged themselves immovably at the Café Griensteidl and forged a new modernist front under the banner *Jung Wien*—Young Vienna.[15]

The fin de siècle explosion inaugurated some three decades of extraordinary innovation customarily figured as a central crucible of modern culture. From art history, architecture, and economics to psychology, music, literature, philosophy, and pedagogy, the Vienna of Ludwig Wittgenstein, Karl Kraus, Adolf Loos, Egon Schiele, Robert Musil, Joseph Roth, Gustav Mahler, Arnold Schönberg, Ludwig von Mises, Rudolf Carnap, Moritz Schlick, Friedrich Hayek, and Karl Popper transformed aesthetic and scientific domains alike.[16] The historian Carl Schorske famously described it as an "oedipal revolt" of the young against the legacies of the nineteenth century and a society that prized all that was measured, traditional, solid, and secure. "Young people, like certain animals, have an excellent instinct for changes in the weather," Zweig reflected, "and so our generation felt, before our teachers and our universities knew it, that with the old century some of the old artistic ideas were coming to an end, that a revolution or at least a change in values was in preparation." They sensed it everywhere: "The new century called for a new order, a new time."[17]

Various factors propelled the dynamism of this trans-field insurrection. One was rising political and social tension in the imperial capital. As national movements grew louder and larger, so too did ideological conflict. The growing strength of Victor Adler's social democratic party assumed palpable form in mass socialist May Day marches through the city center, red carnations pinned on every chest. The Christian socialists mobilized in response (white carnations on theirs), propelling Karl Lueger and his new brand of anti-Semitic politics into the mayor's office. The pan-German nationalists made their presence felt, too, in a rowdy and aggressive new style of politics. Under attack from all sides, the liberal subject withered in political and cultural spheres alike.[18]

But another pivotal factor behind the new century's creative intensity was an unusually high degree of cross-pollination between and inside these aesthetic and scholarly domains. The philosopher Wittgenstein and architect Loos took inspiration from Kraus, the newspaper satirist; the Vienna Circle of logical empiricism involved philosophers, mathematicians, logicians, and physicists. The Viennese modern blossomed dialogically, through dense and intimate exchange. Its hallmark "institutions" were the venues of those encounters: the café (as Zweig described), the salon, and, crucially, the "circle" (*Kreis*)—a semiformal constellation that often met not at the university but at the private apartment of its leading figure. The Vienna Circle of logical empiricism revolved around Moritz Schlick; the psychoanalytic society met at Freud's; and economic thought was remade—perhaps even neoliberalism invented—at the lively private seminar of Ludwig von Mises. These (often interlocking) circles blended social and intellectual life. Girded by strong personal relationships, they made thinking a collective enterprise.[19]

Hans Kelsen's revolution in legal thought crystallized in this world and bore its social-structural imprint. While still working on his habilitation, he found a job, in 1908, at the k.k. Handelsmuseum, an institution founded in 1887 to promote trade between Austria-Hungary and the wider world. The position indirectly ushered twenty-seven-year-old Kelsen into the fulcrum of a different sort of wider world—that of Viennese arts and letters. His superior there happened to be one Hermann Schwarzwald, the less-luminous half of a couple at the center of fin de siècle Viennese society. Eugenie (Genia) Schwarzwald was a legendary *salonnière*, philanthropist, and pioneering educator. Oskar Kokoschka, Freud, and Schönberg circled in and out of her open house, alongside Kelsen; Robert Musil crafted Diotima—the charismatic *salonnière* at the center of *The Man without Qualities*—in her image. Not only social intimacy developed: Kelsen also became involved in Schwarzwald's reformist projects. An indefatigable advocate for women's education, she founded pioneering schools for girls. The salon bled into the classroom. In her program of courses for university preparation, Vienna's seventeen-year-old daughters could find themselves introduced to modern architecture by Adolf Loos, to modern music by Egon Wellesz, and to sociology and political economy by Hans Kelsen.[20] Webs of life and work folded back on themselves. In May 1912, Kelsen married twenty-two-year-old Margarete (Gretl/Grete) Bondi, the third daughter of a well-to-do Jewish family, who had attended Schwarzwald's courses back in 1907–8. They both converted to the evangelical church five days before their wedding.[21] Kelsen's prodigious output over the subsequent sixty years is an index not only of his labor but also of hers: she typed thousands of manuscript pages as well as most of his correspondence. Hans, Grete, and their two daughters (Anna Renata, born 1914, and Maria Beate, born 1915) holidayed alongside the Schwarzwalds— who operated a summer guesthouse for artists and intellectuals on Lake Grundl in Styria—throughout the 1920s.[22]

Kelsen (as we have seen) attended meetings of the psychoanalytic society at Freud's apartment and drew on his theories; long-standing friendships with the Austro-Marxists underpinned perhaps the most dramatic moment of his career, when Karl Renner, soon to become the first chancellor of the newborn Republic of Austria, invited Kelsen to draft its constitution in 1918.[23] But nowhere do the structural attributes of this Viennese context shine through more strongly than in the nature of intellectual invention itself. Because Kelsen, too, had a *Kreis*. And to a significant degree, his pure theory of law was the collective product of this circle—the fruit of intense and regular exchange with a particular ring of close collaborators.

On the heels of his successful habilitation *Main Problems of the Theory of Public Law [Staatsrechtslehre]* (1911), Kelsen began teaching at the University of Vienna as a private lecturer.[24] Viennese students were notorious for their poor lecture attendance, and new professors in particular struggled to attract an audience. Apocryphally, a mere three students turned up at Kelsen's first lectures in the autumn semester 1911–12.[25] Among those three sat Adolf Merkl, a twenty-one-year-old law student who had grown up in the mountain-ringed woods seventy-five kilometers south of Vienna as the son of a forestry official.[26] Immediately gripped, he told his friend Alfred Verdross about the new lecturer. Verdross and Merkl, who had begun their law degrees together in 1908, hungered, over the course of their studies, for a more philosophical treatment of the law, something that spoke to its elemental "foundations."[27] Kelsen burst into that space. The following year, freshly minted degrees in hand, they excitedly accepted Kelsen's invitation to continue the conversation with some other recent graduates in a more intimate setting.[28] This cluster became the first iteration of Kelsen's circle. Not coincidentally, early appraisals of the burgeoning formation described it as the *jungösterreichische Schule*— the young Austrian school of legal theory.[29]

The circle met once a month on Sunday afternoons in Kelsen's apartment at Wickenburggasse 23, in Vienna's eighth district, just behind the university. Hans and Grete had moved into the apartment that same year—1912—after their honeymoon in Italy, and a mere five years after the building's construction.[30] If some later students were surprised by the modesty of the neat, bourgeois apartment—and his single-window study "neither dusty nor scattered with papers"—it was also roomy enough for the domestic help the Kelsens kept.[31] Members took turns to present papers; the intense, spirited discussion was "interrupted" only by refreshments prepared by Grete or brought in by a maid—often horn-shaped rolls, always coffee and cream (Kelsen took his with an inordinate amount of sugar).[32]

These Sunday gatherings became a pressure cooker for legal philosophy. For all their various specializations, the participants shared an overarching— even meta—project. "What united us from 1912," Verdross reflected in the 1960s, "is precisely the endeavour to systematically link the numerous subjects of positive law and give them a philosophical foundation."[33] They did not want to simply understand or theorize a subfield of law—whether constitutional or electoral or international or property law. They sought something far more elemental, and far more ambitious: a unified, logical account of the whole— the philosophical basis of all these things *as* law. Taking nothing for granted, they sought the very conditions of possibility for law as an object of inquiry. Kelsen's *Main Problems* of 1911 had in effect announced that agenda—and those in the circle were electrified by its call for a complete theory purified of contradictions and fictions—but only in rudimentary form. Over the subsequent years, this group together thrashed out what came to be known as Kelsen's pure theory of law.

Some of its key building blocks came from different members of the circle. Merkl developed the *Stufenbau* theory of law as a pyramid-like chain of creation, while Verdross constructed the first connections to international law (more on both later). But the regularity and intimacy of these exchanges meant that clear attributions could grow hazy amid the ceaseless back-and-forth. What was individual authorship or invention when thinking was done in common? Exacerbated by the speed and power of Kelsen's intellectual metabolism—his articulation of a collectively discussed problem tended to appear first and in more compelling form—tensions sometimes boiled over. In 1923, Fritz Sander, another young Viennese jurist brought into the group in 1915 who seemed for a while its rising star, accused Kelsen of plagiarism. If the ensuing university investigation cleared Kelsen of any wrongdoing, the ambiguity was not only a product of the highly strung and increasingly troubled Sander's imagination.[34] Verdross, too, felt a little sore at perceived underacknowledgment of his work.[35] This sensitivity, though, Kelsen was able to soothe without acrimony. When a second edition of *Main Problems* was published in 1923, he wrote a long preface that explicitly listed the various contributions of members of the circle and dedicated the volume to Merkl and Verdross to boot.[36]

The Very First Thing: Inventing the Origin of Law

Nothing captures the high-octane ambitions of Kelsen's circle like the *Grundnorm*. The idea of a basic norm was their version of genesis: an account of the ultimate foundations of law. Over their first decade of discussions, they came to the conclusion that one had to simply *presume* the very highest norm—an originary norm from which all others flowed. This basic norm did nothing except establish how other norms could be created: it was a norm about norms, a rule about rules. Depending on the nature of the state, it could be *do as the monarch commands*, or, alternatively, *do as the constitutive assembly determines*.[37] The monarch or the constitutive assembly then made all subsequent law or delegated the task to others. But the origin of *its* authority was the main problem, or mystery—a question of what lay *behind* the first law. In earlier eras, God or reason or nature occupied that position, serving as the ultimate anchor of legitimacy. Such unscientific, metaphysical foundations had been rejected by nineteenth-century positivist legal thought, with its self-conscious modernity. But what took their place? Legal positivists had instead anointed the state as an all-powerful, primal lawmaker. Indeed, they presented its status as the highest source of law as the essence of its sovereignty. Small wonder state sovereignty loomed so large in the nineteenth-century political imaginary: it walked in God's shoes.

The Vienna school deemed this solution inadequate because it begged the question: where did the *state's* authority come from? To simply keep repeating the mantra that sovereignty was the "highest" or "original" power did not magically make it so and could not disguise the fact that one lacked a philosophically sound explanation for why that was the case. "*That* the constitution is valid" cannot be based on a majority decision or the will of the monarch, Verdross reasoned in a 1914 essay, "because then one could in turn ask about the law-creating power of *these*, and so onward further back." The chain of authority could just spiral forth infinitely. "But one has to stop at some particular norm."[38] That point—the point at which one stopped, law's final "point of ascription"—is what Kelsen and his circle came to call the "basic norm."

Importantly, it was not something that existed in the factual-physical world. After all, there were no "highest" or "first" things in nature, nor in material relations of domination among humans: in these domains, chains of causation really did stretch on without end and offered no way of grounding legal legitimacy. Nor was the basic norm something inside the legal system itself. Rather, it was a "presupposition," a "metajuridical supposition": something that the legal scholar had to *presuppose* for the whole rest of the legal order to make sense.[39] The basic norm could not be touched or tasted or seen or heard—but only *thought*.

The basic norm became a cornerstone of the pure theory of law. It also, unsurprisingly, aroused endless controversy. Was this some sort of fantasy, the waking dream of jurists? Misunderstandings were exacerbated by Kelsen's changing formulations of the concept.[40] He sometimes referred to it as a "hypothesis," but by this he did not mean a mooted proposition awaiting verification. Similarly, when he (less frequently) described it as a "fiction," he did not mean something imagined or made up. Rather, he maintained that the basic norm emerged from an analysis of the actually existing legal system when one asked, What are the logical preconditions of this system? What must we *assume* for it all to make sense? For this whole edifice of our legal system to be valid and coherent? The basic norm was simply the "presupposed condition of all lawmaking."[41]

"In formulating the basic norm," Kelsen explained, "the Pure Theory of Law is not aiming to inaugurate a new method for jurisprudence. The Pure Theory aims simply to *raise to the level of consciousness* what all jurists are doing (for the most part unwittingly) when, in conceptualizing their object of enquiry, they reject natural law as the basis of the validity of positive law, but nevertheless understand positive law as a valid system."[42] Jurists all assumed something called law was possible despite their rejection of its metaphysical grounding. The basic norm was thus already there, rather than invented or imagined: unstated perhaps but logically implied in every legal process and statement. Only the most uncritical dogmatist, Kelsen exclaimed, could think a legal system was possible without any presuppositions at all![43] The pure theory simply dredged to the surface law's half-conscious assumptions, making visible its subterranean logical architecture. The basic norm denoted the "presupposed condition,"[44] the first "originary hypothesis" that jurists relied on routinely but rarely articulated.[45] The pure theory thus sought—and demanded—a radical new degree of disciplinary self-awareness. It absorbed the central agenda of neo-Kantian philosophy—namely, an analysis of the a priori rules that made statements true or valid—and produced a new account of law's ultimate foundations.[46]

Did this idea not repeat the sins of natural law by positing some mythical foundation story like an original social contract? Kelsen conceded a "certain degree" of commonality between the basic norm and social contract theory.

Both responded to the "same theoretical need" for a unifying presupposition.[47] But there the similarity ended. For one, Kelsen objected to the particular substance of social contract theory, especially its root "individualism," as if all normative obligation, however socially necessary, could find its ultimate justification only in the will of the individual.[48] But the real difference lay far deeper. More fundamentally, Kelsen objected to the fact that it had substance *at all*. His basic norm, in contrast, was *purely* "formal"—it was "relative" and "hypothetical."[49] It did not presume anything about human nature or the correct form of political organization, or justice, or truth, or any other content. It was a stripped-back proposition only about the possibility of lawmaking: its content would change depending on the particular legal system under investigation. One system might presuppose an autocrat as the original lawmaking organ, and another, the people. The basic norm had "no absolute content, indeed a priori no content at all."[50] It did not make natural law's mistake of positing a fact, something substantive, something fixed, as the foundation of law and legitimacy. The basic norm was morally—and politically—relative: the "rightness" or "justice" of law could only be given by the system in question.[51] It was legal philosophy loosed from the fixed truths of gods and kings.[52]

The basic norm, then, was an empty vessel. It tried to provide a philosophical basis for law that did not presume or elevate any religious, cultural, political, or national content. In so doing, it marked—even preserved—the space where God had been but left it a mere placeholder. There is a pathos to its slippery epistemological status: it captures the human search for orientation and foundations in a world cut off from older certainties. Kelsen and colleagues felt there was no way to ground law without positing *something* beyond it, something behind the first law, which established the basis of normativity itself. But they tried to make that "beyond" a purely formal, logical proposition, deduced from analysis of positive law itself rather than heaven or nature. Even so, the basic norm remained "metajuridical": it could not be *inside* the legal system because it made that system possible in the first place. To "*juridically* determine the selection of the *juridical* point of departure," Kelsen reasoned, would mean "standing on one's own shoulders, like Münchhausen's attempt to pull himself out of the swamp by his own hair."[53] The swashbuckling Baron Münchhausen became a regular cameo in the pure theory corpus.[54] A popular fictional character of many marvelous adventures and impossible feats, he rode cannonballs, fought crocodiles, traveled to the moon—and now, apparently, helped explain neo-Kantian legal philosophy. (Kelsen and colleagues were not the only twentieth-century scholars to enlist his services: his swamp predicament—a parable of the impossibility of proving truth without prior assumptions—later named a trilemma in logical philosophy.) As the precondition of law's validity, and thus of legal reasoning too, the basic norm lay beyond the horizon of actual legal investigation: it could only be *assumed*, posited, like an initial leap, or suspension of disbelief, after which everything could proceed logically, cogently, and seamlessly. It skirted along the "final frontiers" of what it is possible for law to know.[55] Not for nothing did Kelsen's student Eric Voegelin refer to his teacher's "positivistic metaphysics."[56]

Out of Austria: All about the "Point of Departure"

The basic norm, as stated abstractly in Kelsen's canonical articulations of the pure theory of law in the 1920s and 1930s, was high—even otherworldly—philosophy. Yet it had in fact emerged out of very concrete legal struggles in the Austro-Hungarian Empire. A theory that relied on the primal status of no particular nation and no particular god had obvious significance in the multinational, multiconfessional, multilingual Habsburg lands.[57] But more specific jurisdictional questions about the imperial constitution spurred the first formulations of what became the basic norm, as Robert Walter, Manfred Baldus, and Thomas Olechowski have observed.[58] It was the clash of competing sovereignties in the Habsburg lands that pushed Kelsen and other members of the circle, in a series of wartime articles, toward a new line of inquiry regarding the premises of juridical reasoning.

Over the course of the nineteenth century, we recall, a string of constitutions had tried to describe and organize the many overlapping legal domains under Habsburg rule. After the Settlement of 1867, the "Austrian" half remained vulnerable to claims that its component lands (especially Bohemia) had retained some form of statehood, too. Mainstream juridical opinion understood a law issued by the legislature of one of the lands to have the same status as a law issued by the imperial legislature. Land law and imperial law had parity: imperial law did not necessarily "trump" land law, and vice versa.[59] Each could, in theory, keep overriding the other, canceling each other out. The fact that the lands possessed this independent, nonsubordinate lawmaking capacity suggested to some—including Kelsen—the presence of a technically "sovereign" legal system in the lands.[60] It also created the danger of a conflict of norms. The different legislatures could release contradictory laws valid for the same subjects at the same time: an intolerable anarchy for those invested in the rational rule of law.[61]

In the year the world war broke out, Hans Kelsen waded into these waters. In a ninety-page article published in two parts, he tried to sort out the various theories and confusions.[62] If both land and imperial legislatures were understood as "highest sovereign" authorities, then there was simply no legal-logical way of resolving a conflict of norms between them.[63] Such a conflict could only have a legal solution if, on the contrary, one legislature was subordinate to the other, if the two were arranged hierarchically within a single legal order. The test for a unified legal order of this sort was whether they could both trace their authority back to the same ultimate source. By definition, that single "highest" authority—otherwise known as sovereignty—had the capacity to determine the distribution of powers between its subordinate organs.[64] In German jurisprudence, this attribute would become known as the "competence-competence" (*Kompetenz-kompetenz*): the competence to determine competences, or the jurisdiction to determine jurisdiction. Kelsen referred to *Kompetenzhoheit*: competence-sovereignty, or illimitable competence. So did the empire or the lands have this original unfettered jurisdiction to arrange all subsequent powers?

Here the slippery particularities of the Habsburg case assumed center stage. To the north in Germany, the answer was clear: the imperial center had competence-competence; imperial law "broke" land law. But in the Habsburg lands the answer depended on where one looked. If one took the constitutional laws of 1860 and 1861—the October Diploma and the February Patent, which had returned the empire to constitutional life after its decade of neoabsolutism—then one confronted the disquieting conclusion that *both* the lands and the empire had apparently been given *Kompetenzhoheit*. According to these laws, both legislatures had the capacity to determine their own jurisdiction, and neither was definitively made superior or subordinate. As a result, each could intervene into the other's jurisdiction, legitimately from its perspective, illegitimately from the other's.[65] The validity of a law thus was dependent on the "standpoint" one adopted: one reasoned either from the sovereign autonomy of the lands or from the sovereign autonomy of the empire. It was simply a "choice": the laws themselves offered no means of resolving this conflict.[66] The 1867 constitutional law, in contrast, more definitively granted the empire sovereignty over the competences of the lands. It thus offered a way out of the "double standpoint" that could allow a norm to "appear as valid and also invalid at the same time."[67] But why take 1867 over 1861? The later constitution had not repealed or abrogated the earlier one but simply added to it; both existed as live, valid law. And there was no legal evidence that the lands had ever been stripped of the *Kompetenzhoheit* they possessed in the 1861 patent.[68]

This led Kelsen to a key insight: everything turned on the position from which one reasoned, the legal premise with which one *began*. Proceeding logically from the 1861 law produced one account of sovereignty and jurisdiction; proceeding logically from the 1867 law produced a different one. It was the selection of the first or highest norm—he called it the *Ausgangspunkt*, the "point of departure"—that determined everything else. Crucially, the selection of that departure point was, from a *legal* perspective, "arbitrary": there could be no regular legal guidance on the question because that point itself determined the means and measure of legal judgment. "It is always a metajuridical, essentially a political question," he argued, "which norm one wants to see as the last or highest in such a way that one renounces any further juridical justification of its legitimacy. Every juridical treatment must somewhere hit one such last point on which the whole system of juridical construction rests, supported, as it were, from the outside."[69] The validity of the highest norm, as the "precondition of all juridical cognition," lay then "beyond this juridical cognition."[70] Kelsen described it, strikingly, as the "Archimedean point out of which the world of juridical cognition is set in motion."[71] It was the big bang of law's universe.

These problems, and this vocabulary, were clearly swirling freely on Sunday afternoons on the Wickenburggasse. In an article of the same year, Alfred Verdross, too, wrote of a particular norm at which "one has to stop" and accept its validity "by virtue of itself."[72] Two years later, in 1916, his article about Austria-Hungary's changed coat of arms had as its first subtitle "The Legal Construction of the Austro-Hungarian Union and the Frontiers of Juridical Cognition."[73] All details of dual sovereignty mattered far less, Verdross argued, than the position from which the analysis *departed*: "Which construction basis should be chosen, in which standpoint should one stand, which presuppositions should one assume?" Everything flowed from there. Where Kelsen had demonstrated the point in relation to competence conflicts between the lands and the imperial center in the "Austrian" half of the empire, Verdross did the same for the arrangement of sovereignty between "Austria" and Hungary. A centralist Austrian position might begin reasoning from the neoabsolutism of the 1850s, when the emperor's sovereignty appeared complete and unfettered, and track concessions to Hungary forward from the assumption of that originally perfect legal power as the source of all law. But the Hungarians did not begin reasoning from this point. They had never accepted the validity of the absolutist, unitary state. On the contrary: their point of departure was an original, perfect Hungarian sovereignty: "the sovereign principle that the Hungarian ruler can enact no legal norm without the participation of the estates and that there can be no obligations of the land without the participation of the people's representatives [*Volksvertretung*]."[74] From that original position, everything looked different: many subsequent legal developments under Habsburg rule appeared illegitimate and invalid. Austrian historians and jurists could devote endless energy to recovering myriad historical facts that contradicted the Hungarian theory, Verdross observed ruefully, but it would be of zero consequence for any legal construction that "departs from the Hungarian basic norm," according to which Hungarian sovereignty remained intact until changed in a way that the Hungarian estates, assembled in the Hungarian diet, accepted as legally legitimate.[75] The Austrian and the Hungarian arguments shared the same legal method: they arrived at different conclusions simply because they began thinking from different premises. "But this also shows," Verdross declared, "that juridical means are insufficient to solve our problem." There was "no juridical way" to establish the correctness of a point of departure. "Rather, some basic law . . . must be *assumed* as given," a "construction basis" on which the edifice could be built. "But this basic assumption is always an *extralegal* presupposition, dogmatic and unprovable vis-à-vis legal knowledge. Here, in this way, the frontiers of legal knowledge reveal themselves."[76]

Kelsen and his circle would settle on the term *basic norm* to denote that Archimedean point at the origin of law's universe. These first groping articulations of the idea expose the tight connection between problems of sovereignty and problems of legal knowledge. Legal positivists from the nineteenth century forward had pointed to the sovereign state as the origin of law: the jurist reasoned, accordingly, "from there." In determining the validity of a law, one tested it against the state's constitution. But in the Austro-Hungarian Empire, *there was no self-evident sovereign point from which to reason, measure, and judge*. Everything was in the plural: there were multiple plausibly sovereign states and multiple valid constitutions. One could inaugurate the logical sequence of law's derivation and delegation from the opening assumption of the emperor's complete sovereignty—effectively choosing the 1850s as the "start date"—or, alternatively, from a point further back, on the opening assumption of complete Hungarian sovereignty. Inside the Austrian half of the empire, meanwhile, one could reason from the constitutional laws of 1861 or those of 1867 and arrive at disparate conclusions about the sovereignty of the lands. These late Habsburg legal philosophers were confronting what the lay delegates at the Kremsier parliament had realized back in 1849: there was no neutral place outside time from which to reason, which made it very difficult to definitively determine anything. Precisely because the category "state" fit so poorly with the legal arrangements of the Habsburg Empire, Kelsen and his collaborators became more conscious than their colleagues abroad of the unexamined assumptions underpinning positivist legal thought.[77] They could not just unthinkingly reason from a supreme sovereign center point: that logical starting point—or state point—was contested and, ultimately, an "arbitrary" choice. Sovereign plurality made them relativists, even legal existentialists of a sort: it pushed them up against the edges of legal epistemology and of their own self-awareness. "It is necessary," as Verdross put it in 1916, to "become conscious of these presuppositions, these assumptions, this point of departure"[78]—as though it was a kind of disciplinary work on the self. Such was the nature of wrestling with sovereignty from here—truly a place where "the frontiers of legal knowledge reveal themselves."[79]

Practical Philosophy: Wartime Laboratory

As total war seized the Habsburg lands, the Kelsen circle was absorbed into the machinery of state. Not once, but twice, Kelsen narrowly avoided being sent to the front.[80] After a series of shorter office deployments, he ended up, through a series of coincidences, reporting directly to the minister for war, often in direct contact with the emperor himself.[81] Verdross would have had eyes trained both east and west: his father, General Ignaz Verdross, commanded elite troops on the Tyrolean front, while his brother Paul, dispatched to the Russian front, fell already in the first month of the war. Verdross remained in Vienna, writing opinions for the Supreme Military Court before joining the legal department of the Austro-Hungarian Foreign Office.[82] Merkl, too, avoided active military duty, as his father's death in 1909 had left him the sole provider for his almost-deaf mother. He worked in the Vienna city administration before a rapid rise through the civil service to the *Ministerratspräsidium*, where he worked on preparations for the Treaty of Brest-Litovsk.[83]

In these positions, they found themselves not only involved in the daily work of government but tasked with a kind of applied theorizing. State philosophy threaded into state practice, practice into philosophy. The minister first commissioned from Kelsen a blueprint for a major reform of the Austro-Hungarian military that might satisfy insistent Hungarian demands that it be split in two, in keeping with the dual empire's two sovereignties.[84] What did hyphenated, conjoined sovereignty—that adored subject of academic speculation—look like for a giant military apparatus engaged in the fight of its life? The Settlement of 1867, in its adaptation of composite monarchy, had preserved war making as one of the few "common" prerogatives: now it too fell victim to the totalizing logic of perfect sovereignty. Scholarly objects had morphed into live political projects: having lectured on Austro-Hungarian dual sovereignty at the University of Vienna in the academic years 1911–12, 1912–13, 1913–14, and 1915–16, Kelsen found himself working on its real-world development in 1917–18.[85]

The "army question" was not the only major reform project circulating through the halls of state. In the last year of the war, from their different government offices, both Kelsen and Merkl beavered away on plans to transform the empire into a federation of nations.[86] Those fabled federal schemes stand at the end of a long line of mooted constitutional redescriptions of the Habsburg lands, stretching back to 1848. The story's crescendo arrived with apposite pathos. Young Emperor Charles, not two years into his rule, finally announced constitutional plans for a national federation on October 16, 1918, in the dying days of the war, and the dying days of the state, a paper plane sent into the hurricane of history. Events raced forward unheedingly: by the time he renounced the throne weeks later, new constituent assemblies were already busy disposing over his erstwhile patrimony.[87] Back in 1849, Charles's predecessor, Francis Joseph, then in the first two years of his own rule, had declared the Kremsier constitutional draft "out of keeping with the times." Drafted and redrafted, looking both forward and back, preserving a deep past and leaping toward an avant-garde sovereign future, the Habsburg constitutions had been untimely all the way through.

Far from dulling their philosophical appetite, these crises of state only heightened the intensity of the circle's theoretical work. They largely managed to keep up the Sunday meetings at Kelsen's apartment through the war years.[88] The private seminar also migrated into more public spaces. Put in charge of building a "court-martial archive" (*Feldgerichtsarchiv*) in 1916, Kelsen secured

STATE BIRTH AT THE FRONTIER OF KNOWLEDGE [233]

employment there for three of his students, including Fritz Sander. The job apparently left enough uncommitted time for one of them, Franz Havlíček, to convert the skeptical Sander to Hermann Cohen's brand of neo-Kantianism.[89] (One imagines heated expositions of the finer points of the transcendental method as they pushed case files between desks.) Alongside the basic norm, another signal feature of the pure theory gradually took shape. This time, no one doubted authorship: it was Merkl's brainchild. His idea would remain inseparable from the spatial image he used to capture it: the *Stufenbau*. Literally "stepped construction," a structure of steps or levels, it is translated variously as the "pyramid" or the "hierarchical structure" of the legal order. This theory-image of the legal order helped explain the legal unity of the state but also offered a new way of understanding the (dis)continuity of states in time— those two recurring problems of Habsburg wrangles over sovereignty.

Merkl thought from and with the forest. The woods, mountains, and waterways that surrounded the tiny town of Naßwald an der Raxalpe were not only the companions of his childhood but also the direct object of his revered father's research and work in forestry. The younger Merkl would become an early and unstinting advocate of environmental protection and national parks.[90] The natural world left its imprint on his thinking in less literal ways, too.[91] Before the war, Kelsen had conceived of law as a flat, "static" system of norms (recall his allusion to geometry).[92] Merkl argued instead for a "dynamic" model of law. He wanted to understand the emergence and disappearance of norms, problems of their creation and their "immutability," problems of law in time and in motion.[93] He sought a theoretical account of the legal system as an integrated, dynamic, evolving, pulsing whole. His *Stufenbau* model argued that legal norms did not exist haphazardly side by side but in fact formed a single, hierarchical structure with the constitution (or, in later formulations, the basic norm) at the apex. The smallest, most specific law was thereby connected to the largest, most general one in a logical legal chain of derivation: its legitimacy could be traced back up the ladder to more foundational principles. Any given legal act had a Janus "double-faced" character in that it both implemented a higher norm and created lower norms in turn. In this way, law governed its own production (*Selbsterzeugung des Rechtes*), a kind of infinite unfolding, internal to itself. Everything was connected: a rupture to one norm affected all those farther down the chain.[94] Or downstream: in one wartime article, he argued for an image that captured "not the being, but the becoming." He invoked "a river that descends in cataracts," from one basin to the next. The "body of water, the legal becoming, does not stand still" but continues its slow fall "until the developmental sequence of legal phenomena is exhausted, until the stream flows into the sea of details."[95]

Kelsen was convinced. He adopted the *Stufenbau* theory as "an essential component" of his evolving system.[96] Outside, the geopolitical order may have been falling to pieces, but philosophically, things were coming together with an almost startling momentum. These various insights—the basic norm, the *Stufenbau* theory, alongside the fundamental separation of *is* and *ought*, laid out in his *Main Problems* (1911), and the "identity thesis" that posited the state and the legal order as one and the same thing—coalesced into a complete system of extraordinary explanatory power.[97] Kelsen called it the pure theory of law for the first time in the subtitle of the book he had been writing—about sovereignty, of course—while the war raged, published as *The Problem of Sovereignty* in 1920.[98] A theory of the state and of law in general, the pure theory explained both the former's unity and the latter's validity, two classical problems. The state formed a singular, unified entity if all its law flowed from a single basic norm—the apex of the pyramid, the mountain source of the river. And a law was valid if it was traceable back to that same single point. For example: a court decision might derive its authority from a statute, the statute from a parliament, the parliament from the constitution, all the way to a "highest norm" as the "logical origin," underpinning the authority of the constitution itself.[99]

In *The Problem of Sovereignty*, Kelsen reflected on the long history of sovereignty's shifting meanings. From Bodin to Bartolus and down to the present, one thing had remained constant: the term consistently denoted "the highest," often through a spatial image of "over" or "above." Having rejected the divine and natural metaphysics underpinning that "above," legal positivists had tried to make it an empirical proposition. They labored in vain, Kelsen asserted, because there was no such thing as the "highest" or "first" in the world of observable facts, no "completely independent" in the world of material power. Empirically, even the mightiest great state remained dependent and unfree. No, for the notion of sovereignty to make sense after God and nature and kings, one needed a completely different epistemological basis, a different sort of knowledge altogether. Here, now, at this wartime pivot point of European history, Kelsen thought he had figured it out. Sovereignty could only mean a hierarchy of *norms*—a hierarchy of law. Sovereignty's "over" and "under" denoted a *logical* or *jurisdictional* relationship rather than a material one: an ordering of norms in which one was derived from the other, logically locked into it, logically subordinate to it, in the cascading sequence of the *Stufenbau*. Only the highest norm, the basic norm, was not derived from another, unheld, unenclosed: *that* was sovereignty—the end of the logical chain, the premise that made everything else possible. Not an attribute in the world but "a presupposition in the thinking of an observer contemplating the state and law."[100]

So many things then looked different through the prism of the pure theory. Old problems disappeared or changed shape; new ones emerged. Nowhere was this clearer than in a curious, seemingly idiosyncratic article that Merkl wrote in 1918 called "The Legal Unity of the Austrian State." The topic could hardly have been more familiar. Yet it now appeared in a portentous new guise. Approached with these new philosophical tools, the question of the state's legal singularity-or-plurality morphed into one of legal continuity—or jurisdictional sequence—through time. With an eerie clairvoyance, Merkl began to hash out a problem that, a few short months later, would rock to the center of world politics: the legal birth and death of states.

Merkl began by distinguishing states in the "historical-political" sense from states in the juridical sense (just as Jellinek and Kelsen had done before him, and so many of the Hungarian and Bohemian claim makers, too). He contended that states might possess a continuous historical-political identity over many centuries (especially where they bore the same name), but a discontinuous *legal* identity, or vice versa. "*Different conditions of knowledge* exist for *jurisprudence* than for *history* or *politics*," he wrote.[101] Accordingly, the disciplines understood a state's "hour of birth and date of demise" differently.[102] Austria—of course!— provided a paradigmatic example. Where a historian or politician perceived one and the same "Austria" stretching back over hundreds of years, the jurist was forced to recognize not one entity but several. "My object of cognition, the Austrian state, has not simply altered itself in this century or even millennium—no, its juridical being has become a different one, its identity has been overturned [*aufgehoben*]."[103]

A discontinuous Austria. Why? How? This followed from the circle's new clarity about the legal nature of the state, and especially his *Stufenbau* theory. A state was a singular legal entity, a legal unity, if it could be "derived from one apex, drawn from one legal center," a role served by the constitution, as the state's highest norm.[104] That unified legal order *was* the state. Consequently, a fundamental rupture of the constitutional order meant the rupture of the state itself. Naturally, not all constitutional change affected the identity of the state. The transition from absolutism to constitutional monarchy, for example, did not necessarily disrupt the identity of the state because a monarch was perfectly entitled to divest his powers: it involved no logical-jurisdictional break. Law flowed smoothly onward: "Different constitutional forms that are logically tied together, that are conceptually derivable from one another, represent in the legal sense a *single* state *despite* their *plurality*."[105] The picture looked different if the logical chain was broken: "Only where a *conceptual leap* is required to comprehend a unity, where a hole is torn open in the legal system . . . , [only there] begins the possibility of perceiving a plurality of states."[106] The legal identity of the state was a logical problem: if different iterations could be conceptually connected without contradiction, then the state personality persisted. But where a smooth, coherent sequence of jurisdiction was derailed, state identity was, too: one state ended and another began. The stable legal identity of a state turned on continuity.

Merkl applied this theory to the constitutional history of the Habsburg Empire with surprising results. It seemed the most age-old of European states, but Austria's "bridge of legal unity" had in fact suffered repeated ruptures.[107] The empire's first formal constitution, the Pillersdorf constitution

(April 1848), did not disrupt the legal identity of the state: it was consistent with the prerogatives of the monarch in an absolutist state to relinquish some of his legislative powers, and thereby turn the state into a constitutional one. (If a revolutionary party, rather than the emperor, had declared the transition to constitutionalism, the identity of the old absolutist state would have been ruptured and a new state born. Such an act could not have been legal within the order of the old state.) Yet, when the emperor wheeled around the very next month and called a constituent assembly (that would become the Kremsier parliament), he acted unilaterally and did not respect the already-binding norms of the Pillersdorf constitution.[108] This legally inexplicable act sliced open the chain of legal logic, and juridically, a new state was born.

Merkl's counterintuitive history of state discontinuity proceeded in this vein through the years of constitutional experimentation, culminating not in 1867 but in 1865. In the latter year, the monarch again suspended a constitutional order (that of the 1860 October Diploma and the 1861 February Patent) by decree, violating the legal identity of the state. As he was once again within his (absolutist) rights to return to constitutionalism in 1867, it was 1865 that in fact marked the birth of the state that was still in existence as Merkl wrote his article in 1918. Merkl thus arranged Austro-Hungarian sovereignty differently in time. His register may have been high legal philosophy, but he nevertheless shared moves with the Bohemian and Hungarian claim makers who challenged the empire's constitutional order. Like them, he presumed legal history could be clearly distinguished from political history, and that the former possessed its own logics, rhythms, and patterns of duration.

Merkl's article recast the old problem of the empire's sovereign plurality. Again, time featured centrally in the analysis. If the political designation "Austria" indeed comprised a plurality of states, that plurality had a successive structure, as different versions of the state superseded each other in time. The year 1865 cut off the current state from those that had preceded it: "Back beyond that, extending into the past, lie (in the legal sense) foreign countries [*Ausland*]."[109] Legally, pre-1865 Austria, just like pre-1848 Austria, or France or Britain, amounted to an external state, an "abroad," with a foreign legal system.[110] The past was a foreign country—literally. Multiple states existed behind the moniker "Austria" sequentially rather than synchronously. Strikingly, the state thus acquired juridical frontiers in time as well as in space, its norms and jurisdiction extending over clearly defined territory *and* a clearly defined span of time. Beyond those temporal frontiers lay an international domain, a zone of relationships between foreign states, populated in part by previous versions of oneself, now legal strangers. Merkl thus conjured an image of international law that existed not only "above" current states but "behind" or "beneath" them historically, an international domain that, when viewed from the present, "began" in 1865 and extended backward in time. Kelsen, Verdross, Sander, and others would grab hold of these provocative ideas on the other side of the war's end as they groped for orientation in a radically changed world—one marked by a searing new sense of sovereignty's impermanence.

"This Crisis of Juridical Cognition": Confronting the Mortal Sovereign

Surely Merkl knew how prescient his argument would be? That Austria-Hungary was teetering on the edge of its own complete negation, that the question of state birth and state death was about to explode out across Europe's map? From their various corners in the halls of government, members of Kelsen's circle experienced the end of the Austro-Hungarian Empire with unmediated proximity. The state's fate felt like one's own, Merkl confessed.[111] Its demise unfolded disconcertingly in the intimate details of one's working life. In the twilight zone where the organs of imperial government still existed alongside those of the fledgling new republic, Merkl received official orders from his superiors to report to the new chancellor, Karl Renner—as though being dispatched between offices and not between states.[112] In those chaotic days of early November 1918, Renner slept in the parliament building, and Merkl served as his only assistant, managing correspondence, receiving people, developing the rudiments of government offices and a civil service—state building with bare hands.[113] Kelsen and Merkl "wrote through" the transition, or even wrote states themselves: they put down their blueprints for imperial constitutional reform and picked up drafts of a constitution for a new legal entity, the Republic of German-Austria.[114] Kelsen's appraisal of the state's juridical newness traveled in government briefcases to the Paris Peace Conference as part of the official arsenal of Austrian arguments.[115] Merkl, too, having just written academically about constitutional continuity and the identity of states, now wrestled with the theme in practice as he worked on the constitutional implications of the Treaty of Saint-Germain, which fixed Austria as the empire's legal heir.[116] Verdross, meanwhile, spent 1918–20 in Berlin as an envoy of the nascent republic, witnessing the emergence of its Weimar sibling as debate raged over an Anschluss between the two states.[117] Their words circulated through these various fronts of state making. When the Foreign Office in Berlin debated minority rights, Verdross was in the room; his report passed through Bauer's hands in Vienna before being sent onward to the Austrian peace delegation in France.[118] Academic work mixed through it all inextricably. In 1919, Merkl submitted a study of the new Austrian constitution—a constitution he had helped produce over the preceding months—as his habilitation at the University of Vienna.[119] Theory—*live*. Theory alive.

How could states just *end*—and *start*? The question shook the foundations of law itself. Where *did* law's validity come from? What lay behind the first law? Such topics—once so abstract—had become frighteningly actual. How could a small band of mortal men gather in a room, call themselves a constituent assembly, and make sounds with their mouths and scribble shapes with their pens that ostensibly carried the weight and force of binding law? There was no emperor now, clad in robes and crowns, the wearable vessels of age-old legitimacy accumulated over centuries and connected, somewhere in the deep mists of time, to divine sanction. No props or smokescreens for the majesty of sovereignty, that presumed fount of man-made law. Vienna was starving, inflation soaring, and the currency—like the existing social order—crumbling to dust. "Sovereignty" had nowhere to hide. All those questions about the ultimate basis of law, about the nature of the state, stared everyone nakedly in the face.

"Political events of the present," Fritz Sander wrote in 1919, "present various problems of legal science that, until now, were only objects of theoretical investigation, in the full light of practical actuality."[120] The full, harsh light. "Which problems does the pure legal science currently confront?" Sander asked his readers rhetorically. "We can summarize all these problems as the '*problem of revolution*.'" For the jurist, he explained, "revolution" meant "a rupture to a valid legal order caused by 'factual' (historical, social, political) events, the destruction of particular pieces of the legal order, . . . or even the state itself." It meant change that could not be assimilated into the existing legal system, change that tore it open, "brutal, metajuridical facts" that derailed the system's reproduction.[121] Did it even need mentioning that the topic had "eminent 'practical' significance"? That all the pressing issues connected to state succession could only be solved from here? So much so, Sander reflected, that any distinction between practice and theory dissolved. "Especially in this area of law, 'praxis' means nothing other than a particular sort of theory"—a theory with the power and opportunity to be executed in the world. One could not speak meaningfully of a conflict between theory and practice but only "between theory and theory."[122]

It was like experiencing the edge of knowledge. Because, "until now," Sander reminded his readers, public law theory unequivocally held that the state's "emergence and demise lay beyond juridical construction." Wherever scholarship broached the theme, it wandered helplessly into "the 'enigma' of the emergence of 'law' from 'not-law'"; lost itself in the "dogma of spontaneous creation."[123] In the Vienna of 1918–19, they were living through that murky, miraculous zone of genesis, the rationally confounding generation of a new state legal order out of nothingness. How intolerable, even unconscionable, for law to lack an explanation—for this ostensibly modern science to stand neutered and powerless before the problem of state creation! Just like the diplomatic representatives of the successor states, these theorists groped for ways to avoid the anarchic cliff of complete legal rupture. Where the former invoked the survival of actual *states* over the precipice of the empire's collapse, the latter searched for a method of stringing together the survival of legal *order* across that same precipice. "This problem of revolution," Sander reasoned, "holds at its logical core the *problem of the continuity of the legal order*."[124]

But if legal order *was* the state's legal order, if the state was the origin and guarantor of law, there could be no continuity. A state collapsed and took its order down with it. Cut off from its mountaintop source, the river ran dry. The stability of the nineteenth-century European state system had dulled awareness of the challenge this represented for legal thought. Josef Kunz, one of the newer additions to Kelsen's circle, pitched the problem via the most dramatic revolution of them all. How can we explain, he wondered, that both the czar's order *and* the Bolshevik order are law, when they stand next to one another entirely separate and unrelated, with no legal bridge from one to the other, so that, from the perspective of consistent legal reasoning, either one *or* the other can be law—but not both? Without any thread of continuity, without any residual "law" persisting across the two, there was no conceptually coherent means of understanding them both as valid legal orders.[125]

In his 1919 article, Sander briefly—almost haphazardly—hit upon a basis for the sought-after continuity, one that proved enormously influential for all the thinkers of the pure theory. He picked up Merkl's 1918 account of the (dis)continuity of the Habsburg state. He argued that Merkl failed to follow his own idea of the *Stufenbau* of the legal order through to its logical conclusion: because above the *Stufenbau* of state law rose the *Stufenbau* of *international* law.[126] Perhaps the state was not the apex of the pyramid, the final source of the river? And law stepped onward, upward, beyond it? Only from the perspective of a logically higher "level," Sander suggested, could one gain any epistemological purchase on the legal continuity of the state. "Whether continuity prevails between two (empirical) constitutions cannot be determined through a comparison of both constitutions, but rather only through seeking out a higher rung [*Stufe*]."[127] Analyzing the legal identity of the state required a position outside the state's own order. It was international law that could judge and record such continuities and discontinuities; it was international law that held and archived the lives of states (just as the imperial constitution had done before). Worlds may have separated Fritz Sander in war-shattered Vienna and Headlam-Morley in Britain's peace conference delegation, but at the same moment they both argued the same point, namely, that the obscurity of state birth and state death could only be clarified from afar—from the hilltop of international law.[128]

"Pure legal science releases international law from its former isolation and sets it as the highest level [*Stufe*] in the world legal system," Sander declared.[129] Legal theory must reach out beyond and above the individual state legal systems to international law, "in which all state law is rooted."[130] In a time and place where states had been dramatically exposed as fragile, extinguishable things, legal order tout court needed a new anchor. "It is international law," Sander wrote, "that guarantees continuity."[131] The integration of international and state law into a single system became one of the pure theory's signal features. Traditionally, they had been understood as two distinct sorts of law (the "dualist" theory). Verdross had first suggested their integration in 1914. In place of the dualist theory, he proposed a "monist" one, which understood them both as different components of a single legal order. A monist construction raised the problem of the relationship and hierarchy of the two bodies of law: Was international law part of a legal order grounded in the state, or was the state part of a legal order grounded in international law? Which was the highest, the root, the source? Which housed the basic norm? In 1914, it seemed clear to Verdross that one could not contemplate the primacy of international law, "insofar as one remains committed to the sovereignty of state will."[132] And that commitment appeared self-evident. Axiomatically, the state counted as the highest, the first, the supreme. Accordingly, international law must be its product, delegate, and subordinate. But in the wake of the war and state collapse, the self-evidence of sovereignty's supremacy, its stranglehold on the legal imagination, slipped. Verdross changed his mind.

How little the old theory could explain! Postwar predicaments exposed its inadequacy at every turn. In texts from 1920 and 1921, Verdross advocated for a monist theory of law based on the primacy of international law instead of state sovereignty. His evidence for this new hierarchy could have been lifted straight from the daily newspapers. Everyone, he observed, accepted the norm that treaties continued to be binding on a state despite a rupture in its constitution, despite the discontinuity of its own legal order. Buried in this supposedly innocuous principle lay "the seed of a different systematization."[133] That a state could persist as an entity—an entity capable of carrying forward those treaty obligations—despite its utter and radical transformation, *that* was a proposition that could only be anchored in *international* law. Such continuity could not be based on the state's constitution, the state's will, because that had just been broken. The principle presupposed some form of law that "stood *above* the state constitutions," untouched by their worldly rise and fall.[134] And therein lay the rub. Because, on that basis, international law could not be wholly dependent on states as its "creators," its authors; at least some of it must exist independent of their will and consent.[135] His 1921 formulations grew clearer and more emphatic. If international law had its basis in state constitutions, it could have no greater power than the constitutions themselves: it would collapse when states collapsed. Yet it clearly did no such thing! On the contrary, international law forged "connections" between two discontinuous constitutions, carrying over rights and duties from a fallen state to the new one.[136] The old theory failed to explain the given world: it must make way for a new construction.[137]

Reasoning directly from their experience of state collapse, the jurists of Kelsen's circle thus moved toward a radical reappraisal of the relationship between sovereignty and international law. They transferred their theories of the *Stufenbau* and the basic norm—theories originally developed to make sense of the empire's legal plurality—to the domain of international law. The two problems in fact possessed a structural similarity: both involved the relationship of different sources of law. Again they asked the question: What must we *presume* for the whole legal order to make sense? Which source must we *presume* to be the highest? Only now the question produced dramatically different results. Historical events had forcibly widened their field of vision. The crisis of state extinction suggested that one must in fact presume the primacy of international law. Otherwise, without some form of continuous law, without a "legal bridge," one stood helpless before the lawless anarchy of state extinction and those mysteries of spontaneous creation.[138] International law took sovereignty's place at the apex of the legal pyramid and reoccupied the position of the basic norm, becoming the point of departure for legal reasoning. It amounted to "an alteration in the original standpoint," Verdross observed in 1923.[139]

Verdross and Kunz emerged as the most impassioned advocates of this view. Kunz, born in Vienna in 1890, was the same age as Verdross and Merkl but brought a swath of international experience to his first encounters with Kelsen's circle in the immediate aftermath of the war. He had spent the last peace years studying abroad, at the Sorbonne in Paris and University College in London, before four long years at the front. In October 1924, he was back in London, this time standing in front of the Grotius Society as an apostle for the new theories from Vienna.[140] It proved the beginning of a long career explaining the pure theory to English-speaking audiences.

In these early arguments, Verdross and Kunz advanced two key pieces of evidence, taken from the existing legal world, in support of the necessary primacy of international law. Both principles related to the death and birth of states, and both would become legal flash points of the era of global decolonization following World War II. The first, as already mentioned, involved the persistence of rights and duties (like debts and treaty obligations) across a revolutionary rupture in the state's own legal order.[141] The second was the related fact that international law bound new states. The standard theory, they now saw, suffered from a major logical inconsistency. On the one hand, it held that states were only bound by international laws to which they themselves had consented. On the other, it also presumed that new states were immediately liable to the general principles of international law, whether or not they had consented to them. A blatant contradiction! If the state-centric theorists wanted to maintain the latter, they would have to give up the former, that is, their beloved doctrine of state supremacy. Or did they really want to concede, Verdross asked incredulously, that "a new, not-yet recognized state commits no international law wrong if it kills foreigners in its territory, seizes their property, when it raids foreign areas"? Equally, did an existing state commit no international legal wrong if it acted in a similar way against the new state?[142]

Hardly. The hypothesis of untrammeled state sovereignty could not explain how new states arrived into an existing legal world, already subject to laws they had had no role in creating.[143]

Kelsen's students blazed a trail. He himself remained somewhat more equivocal. As he grappled with international law for the first time during the war and in its immediate aftermath, he had likewise come to the conclusion that state law and international law must form a singular unity.[144] They could not be completely separate and, at the same time, equally valid: that would produce the sort of logical contradictions and jurisdictional conflicts that had plagued the empire's multiple legal orders. If they remained separate, the jurist could regard only one—and not both—as valid law.[145] And the goal of all cognition, all science, must be the forging of logically coherent systems capable of accounting for the given world, for all that we know.[146] So international and state law must cohere somehow in a singular, monist order. This meant that one must be superior and the other subordinate, based on a singular source of validity, a singular originary hypothesis or basic norm, that would allow conflicts to be resolved: that much he shared with Verdross and Kunz.[147] Differences emerged, however, regarding the direction of that hierarchy. In his 1920 book, Kelsen presented *both* possible constructions—that international law was subordinate and subsumed within the state's legal order, and, alternatively, that state law was subordinate and subsumed within the international legal order—and refused to definitively endorse one or the other. They represented "two different presuppositions for legal knowledge," two different "*epistemological hypotheses*."[148] Just like the predicament of imperial constitutional law, everything turned on the selection of the initial premise, the point from which one reasoned. And, again like imperial constitutional law, both premises were possible as a strict matter of logic—though they produced radically different accounts of the world—so he dutifully presented them both.[149] But he left no doubt about his preference. And he had both legal and political reasons for it.

Legally, his preference for the primacy of international law was based on the same factors given by Verdross and Kunz. Only this hypothesis could explain the continuity of international obligations despite constitutional rupture and why international law was already valid for new states at the moment of their emergence.[150] One liked to say that a new state "finds" preexisting international law, he recounted. But if it existed before them, then it existed as law independently of them: it was not delegated or reliant on their consent for its validity.[151] To these reasons he added the doctrine of sovereign equality: that, too, was a principle only possible on the premise of an overarching legal order coordinating the coexistence of states.[152] Like his collaborators in the circle, he was thinking like a new state. They inhabited a different perspective to their colleagues on the winning side of the war whose states had survived unscathed. As he noted explicitly in his discussion of the theory of recognition, such principles served the interests of *old* states, even if unconsciously.[153] To reason unthinkingly from the premise of preexisting sovereignty was a privilege those living amid the wreckage of empire could no longer afford.

But his preference for the premise of international law's primacy had political foundations, too. In the closing sections of *The Problem of Sovereignty*, Kelsen took an uncharacteristic swerve into a highly emotional register. The intensity of the historical moment shone through undimmed. The choice of premise had "ethical-political" as well as "epistemological" significance, he wrote searchingly.[154] The opening hypothesis of supreme sovereignty entailed a radically "subjective" perspective on the world. Followed through to its logical conclusions, it involved the denial of all other legal systems (both other states and international law) because they existed only so far as the sovereign state in question (voluntarily) recognized them.[155] This "subjectivist epistemology," he maintained, "proceeds from its own 'I' [*vom eigenen Ich*] and thereby can never get beyond the own 'I,' in that it can only understand . . . the whole world of values as the will of this own 'I,' so that the own sovereign 'I' stretches over the universe, thereby incapable of grasping the other subject, the Not-'I' appearing with the same claim to sovereignty, the 'You' that also wants to be an 'I,' as a center of the universe in its own way, because incapable of honoring its own claim to sovereignty."[156] Kelsen's sentences riffed and ran on; vivid and undisciplined, their propulsive form carried the affect of their author. "The exclusivity of sovereignty, the uniqueness of the sovereign State-'I,' is only the analogy, is more than the analogy, of the inescapable solipsistic consequence of subjectivism."[157]

The alternate premise, that of the primacy of international law, reversed the signs, replacing subjectivism with objectivism. In order to "arrive at the 'I,'" Kelsen wrote, "it proceeds from the world." It "presupposes an objective world reason, a world spirit, whose subjectivizations or concretizations, whose only-very-ephemeral and provisional manifestations are knowing and willing individuals whose spirits are only integral parts of the world spirit, . . . whose 'I' is only the fief of the singly sovereign World-'I,' coordinated and similar to one another, but not—as in subjectivism—the You alien and incomprehensible to the 'I.'"[158] By adopting international law as the point of departure, the jurist grasped states as mere components or subsections of a higher, all-encompassing order. This viewpoint made their "sovereignty" relative rather than absolute: it signified a jurisdiction over a particular part of that larger legal order, a power delegated from international law and ultimately limited by it.[159]

To look from the self toward the world, or from the world toward the self—from sovereignty to international law, or from international law to sovereignty: how much turned on the point of departure! Kelsen emotively raised the stakes of the choice, even as he refused to definitively make it. Subjectivism aligned with the unconstrained egoism of imperialism, he warned. With sovereignty as the original premise, there were no objective limits on the state's preferences and territory.[160] Worse still: the solipsism of the subjective view ultimately led to the negation of law itself because law's essence and existence depended on the "*objectivity* of its validity." To give that up meant a slide into the perspective of brute power.[161]

He made the opposition so stark, and yet he upheld the formal viability of both viewpoints: Kelsen performed his scholarly restraint and seriousness almost ostentatiously. But it left him pensive and unsettled. How could one make sense of the entanglement of epistemology and ethics, scholarship and politics, world and self? "The connection between theoretical and practical cognition," he reflected, "is not logically systematically verifiable, but it is established *factually* through the *character*-unity of the knowing and willing subject." Logic could not prove it, but all these spheres of thinking and feeling coincided experientially in the same human consciousness. "A certain *world-view* links to a specific *life-view*, an epistemology [links to] an ethical-political conviction," because they were "ultimately rooted in the nature of one and the same character." "It is the same person," he seemed to be almost affirming— or puzzling?—to himself, "who chooses, on the basis of a final and uncontrollable determination, between the world- and life-views presented to him, and thus makes a decision for himself that remains denied to objective science."[162] Another leap, then—another encounter with what we cannot formally explain, but have to keep living anyway. Even as he deferred so unequivocally to the demands of logic and reason, he confessed here that he *experienced* their limits. That epistemological existentialism gripped the whole Vienna circle: political events had made their philosophical interrogation of the ultimate source of law's validity into a literal concern in their working lives. States had collapsed, and so had—by their lights at least—the viability of traditional legal theory. It only intensified their drive to find ways of making the whole make sense.

Sealing Over the Abyss:
Making State Creation a Legally Knowable Thing

How could legal scholarship lack an account of the birth and death of states? If the experience of living through the end of imperial sovereignty made that blind spot intolerable, it also made the reason for it crystal clear. So Kelsen: "The numerous, continually repeated attempts to understand the emergence of states juridically, to legally ground the state, i.e., the legal order, must of course fail—as an attempt to pull oneself out of the swamp by one's own hair— so long as one retains the dogma of the sovereignty of the state."[163] Baron Münchhausen conscripted to the cause again! In the same 1920 text, Kelsen invoked the baron's swamp predicament to explain both the problem of the basic norm and that of the creation of states. Not coincidentally: they were different instances of the same quagmire—the same epistemological problem of beginnings.[164] "If one presupposes the individual state legal order as sovereign," he wrote, "then the question of its first emergence must necessarily fall beyond the domain" of legal analysis, must remain "metajuridical in nature."[165] Logically, law could not be present to govern its own creation and the state could not be present to govern its own emergence, just as a constitutional rupture could not be regulated by the constitution itself.[166] One could not pull oneself out of the swamp from inside the swamp. Jurists attempting a theory of state creation, Kelsen wrote, left the parameters of the state's legal order and its sovereign supremacy without fully realizing or acknowledging the implications of what they were doing. Though they "took care to overlook" it, one could not in fact "go beyond the narrow limits of the state without constructing a world law [*Weltrecht*] that encompasses states and stands over them." Yet the same jurists still resisted sovereignty's subordination to an overarching "world law." If they truly wanted to uphold an image of the state as the highest, primal source of law, then prior to the state could only be a legal void. Kelsen was pithy and pointed: "There is no legal cognition in legally empty space."[167] There could be no legal knowledge of—or in—a legal vacuum.

The postwar crisis had left the Viennese jurists staring blankly into that vacuum. With their new theory of the primacy of international law, they could seal over that void. The price was sovereignty's supremacy. "Only recourse to an international legal order that rises above states or constitutions standing next to each other territorially as much as following each other temporally" resolved the problem, Kelsen wrote. Only that could "thrust the bridge of law over the abyss that revolution has laid between two constitutions."[168] We hear the echo of Merkl's original 1918 article on the empire, with his image of the international sphere standing over states that coexisted in space *as well as* followed each other sequentially in time. It had to be *above* but also *before* and *after* the state. Only this sort of all-encompassing international legal order, existing prior to the consent of states, could transform the creation and demise of states from a matter of fact to one of law because such events now unfolded *inside* a (higher) legal order, not beyond it. Viewed from this perspective, Kelsen wrote, "the rise and fall of the state . . . show themselves to be legal phenomena." International law "determines not only juxtaposition in space, it also determines succession in time, that is, the temporal sphere of validity of the state legal systems."[169] Applying the pure theory to international affairs, he made the same point to the Permanent Court of International Justice when asked for an expert opinion on the birth of Czechoslovakia.[170] As on so many other occasions in this history, grappling with sovereignty meant redrawing the line between law and fact. "The origin, the formation, of a new state is therefore, by no means, as many writers believe, 'a pure fact,' something going on outside the domain of law, in the realm of nature," Kunz concurred, "but a condition determined by a rule of international law. The same is true of the 'extinction' of a state." The principle made "the 'revolution' in a state *juridically understandable*."[171]

Kelsen, Kunz, and Verdross were growing the empire of law. They pushed out its frontiers to encompass a formerly external, metajuridical realm of raw fact. In this way they could seal over the "abyss," banish "legally empty space," foreclose the vacuum. A "supraordinated" international law forged the "bridge of law" through time in an age where states had shown they could not serve that function.[172] Kunz rejected traditional rules about the recognition of new states for parallel reasons. There, too, one could hardly rely on an international law dependent on the arbitrary consent of existing states. He offered the new Republic of Austria as an example: created on October 30, 1918, it was recognized by the Allied powers only at the end of May 1919. Surely it was not the case that Austria lay outside the boundaries of international law for those intervening seven months, an "international law Nothing," incapable of legal relations? A state of affairs in which "no legal norms" applied to an interaction between, say, France and Austria, their relationship instead like that between "states of the international legal community and so-called 'savages'?"[173] Kunz's association was revealing. Modern international law had often figured the colonial world as extralegal space: unsovereign or semisovereign, legally unpossessed, even unoccupied. Some (though clearly not all) European jurists imagined it a zone devoid of valid legal actors or relations, a domain where the rules of "civilized" states did not apply, paving the way not only for colonial domination but also for unrestrained warfare and violence.[174] Small wonder Kunz found the thought of a legal void so insufferable. If state birth and death could only be construed as an irruption of facts beyond the pale of law, then imperial collapse threatened to leave Central Europe in a state of analogous legal indignity and defenselessness. With the protective mantel of sovereignty ripped off, the specter of the extralegal boomeranged back to Europe.

Most fundamentally, the Vienna circle's monist vision of law—according to which law must form an integrated, unified whole—spoke to their deepest convictions about the nature of knowledge itself. They were engaged in *Wissenschaft*—in science (not to be confused with the natural sciences)—and treated that vocation with a deadly seriousness, even a quasi-religious devotion. *Wissenschaft*, on the Kantian foundations of the age, entailed a particular sort of scholarly agenda. "*Wissenschaft ist System*," in Kunz's programmatic phrasing.[175] To count as science, knowledge had to be systematic. Not a mere collection of materials, a conglomerate, an aggregate—but a system. By definition, the jurist searched for ways of integrating existing law into a singular, coherent unity, not one pockmarked with contradictions, exceptions, or vacuums. In seeking to comprehend law, Kelsen explained, "legal cognition sets the very same task for itself that natural science sets for itself: to represent its object as a unity. The negative criterion of this unity is non-contradiction."[176] Logic was the lodestar of all legal reasoning, and system its permanent goal. More pragmatically, this "scientific" approach guarded against conflicts of norms (like the contradictory, overlapping jurisdictions of the empire). But it also stemmed from the deeper reckoning—spearheaded by Jellinek and then Kelsen on either side of the century's turn—with law's place among the disciplines. As explored in chapter 4, the two Austrian philosopher-jurists realized law could not rely on the empirical methodology of the natural sciences. It did not unfold according to inexorable causal laws like processes in the natural world. It was a science of *Ought*, not *Is*, of norm, not fact. As such, the only truth or proof to which it had access was an *internal* coherence, a logical consistency. When, in the immediate aftermath of the war, Kelsen and his circle tackled state creation and the relationship between sovereignty and international law, they did so in precisely this framework. The monist integration of state law and international law reflected, in Kelsen's words, "the epistemological requirement that all law be considered in one system, that it be considered from one and the same standpoint as an integral whole in itself."[177] And to answer the next question of whether state or international law had primacy, the jurist needed to ask, pace Kunz, which of these two hypotheses was better able to "guarantee the connection of the material of all the positive rules of international law, given by experience, into one system."[178] They may have rejected the empiricism of the natural sciences, but in a certain sense, law's normative world was to mimic the perfect holism of the natural world: an integrated, gapless universe composed of pure logic.

And like the natural sciences, they wanted—needed—to explain their integrated universe without God or even the trace of him. When the dominant legal theories presented state creation as a mere fact "lying beyond juridical construction," Sander heard the echo of a divine "act of creation."[179] Like a catastrophe or cataclysm, these legal caesuras apparently irrupted like a *Stoß von Außen*—a jolt from the outside, a surge from the beyond, unexplained and unexplainable. Only now the "creator of law is no longer God but rather the materials of other—historical, sociological, political—sciences."[180] These legal theories languished in a prescientific phase, reliant on magical acts of creation beyond the grasp of their methods. "The causa efficiens of the constitution always remains an inexplicable miracle," Sander complained. "The emergence of 'islands of law' in the river of social events must simply be accepted as a fact."[181] Contradictions and enigmas riddled this "murky picture" of the "transition from legally empty to legally filled space."[182] "A matter of fact in legally empty space"—that is, the birth of a state—"that has legal consequences in legally filled space is the mystery of generatio aequivoca," of spontaneous creation.[183] No more. No more legal vacuums or black holes, no more legally inexplicable facts. By adopting the hypothesis of the primacy of international law, and thus transforming state creation from a matter of fact to a matter of law, the Viennese jurists looked to banish these embarrassing miracles from legal theory.[184]

If true legal *Wissenschaft* must absorb all legally relevant facts into its unified system, that unity was something made, not found. The jurist produced it by construing and ordering existing legal norms. "It is precisely the task, the only task of science," Sander declared, "to shape the confused multiplicity of experiences into unified systems."[185] But precisely in its totality, its holism, its purity, and its perfect order, this hyperscientism sounded its own echoes of the divine. In his book *The Unity of the Legal Worldview on the Basis of the Constitution of International Law* (1923), Verdross—whose Catholic investment in natural law would come to the fore over the course of the 1920s—set out to determine if existing law was "a chaos" or whether it formed "a cosmos."[186] Those formulations resonated with Merkl, too, who wrote of the configuration of "pre-scientific chaos into a cosmos" as "real meaning" of scientific work.[187] Legal science could *make* its own cosmos. If Kelsen was first driven to develop a purely normative, purely formal, unforgivingly logical theory of law in order to tame the legal chaos of the Habsburg Empire, he and his colleagues now deployed the same tools to tame the chaos of state birth that followed in its wake.

Could one just declare a cosmos? Did these images of a unified world law amount to more than wishful thinking? The Viennese arguments about the primacy of international law met with all the same skeptical objections as the notion of the basic norm. An invented fantasy! How could it be plausible that international law "preceded" the state? The notion flew in the face of common-sense understandings of international law as a body of rules and practices created *by* states. The criticism drove Kelsen and his circle to lay out very explicitly the sort of reality or "truth" involved in their propositions. A critique along such lines, Verdross explained, "confuses a historical relationship with a legal one."[188] "The *logical* and *legal* supraordination of international to municipal law," Kunz concurred, "is not to be confused or identified with the quite different problem of *historical priority*."[189] They were not saying that international law preceded state law as a matter of historical fact. International law was superior, "but this superiority, this sovereignty, of International Law is not a political, but a theoretical one."[190] The thinkers of the pure theory arranged law into the most logically coherent sequences of authority, not into sequences of material causation. The aim was to understand law, not history.

Kelsen led readers through this argument step by step. "Although general international customary law is more recent in origin than the state legal systems," he explained, "this does not stand in the way of it serving as the basis of their validity." Tellingly, he invoked the analogy of a federal state: "Similarly for a federation: the validity of a member state's system derives from the constitution of the federation, even though the system antedates the federation of once independent individual states. One must not confuse historical sequence with the logical relation between norms."[191] It was just like it had been in the erstwhile Habsburg Empire. The lands may have preceded the empire, but at a certain point (well, at least according to some!) the empire had overtaken their role as the logical-legal source of validity, the highest jurisdiction and fount of law. Verdross made the same analogy, invoking Germany instead: "Just as Bavaria or Prussia existed before the German empire historically, yet are currently subordinated to the empire, and derive their competence from the imperial constitution, so states are subordinated to the international law constitution."[192] Oldest did not necessarily mean highest. These jurists were thinking from the experience of conglomerate statehood, transferring hard-won insights about plural sovereignty and overlapping legal orders from the imperial to the international sphere.

In this way, they replaced historical priority with logical priority. The pyramid of jurisdiction, the cascade of the *Stufenbau*, was not pegged to the sequence of historical events. On the contrary: its direction could be reversed. They sought the "point of departure" for *reasoning*—a point of departure that could make sense of the whole and assemble it into a unity—not a point of departure in the ceaseless flow of historical events. The theory exhibited so many of the recurring features of the Central European wrestle with sovereignty: the cleaving of law from fact, the tense relationship between historical time and legal time, the juxtaposition of different sorts of truth, the inexorable pull into an epistemological register. The problem of sovereignty in (post-) Habsburg Central Europe—its mortality as much as its plurality—could scarcely be addressed without an inbuilt theory of the nature of knowing itself.

Noteworthy here is the curious fate of the state's erstwhile immortality. Kelsen and his circle had learned through bitter experience that states were mortal entities, that legal science could not take them for granted as its first premise, that they could not provide the continuity required for conceptual coherence and political stability. They turned instead to international law to serve that role. "The domain of the *temporal* validity of international law," Kunz wrote, "is unlimited in principle."[193] In positing an international law that existed both *before* and *after* states, even as a matter of logic rather than history, they transferred the gloss of immortality from the state to international law. As though law could not quite do without some scaffold of timelessness; as though logic might now provide the transtemporal authority once proffered by gods and kings. Fritz Sander may have been the most troubled member of the circle: having repeatedly burned bridges with Kelsen and even supported National Socialist demonstrations at the Prague lectures of his former teacher in 1936, his death three years later was widely suspected a suicide.[194] But his more erratic brilliance often hit upon the crackling insight or revelatory phrase amid more muddled passages. In that programmatic article "On the Fact of Revolution and the Continuity of the Legal Order" (1919), so generative for other members of the circle, he already saw that the dissolution of imperial sovereignty entailed a "crisis of juridical cognition."[195] In suggesting that international law must scale above state law to overcome this crisis, he borrowed words from Constantin Franz in calling international law "the crown of all law, from which all other law first receives its full light."[196] The king's body had been exposed as mortal: the Viennese jurists passed his crown to international law instead.

World Making by Logic

In 1934, Kelsen compiled the pure theory of law into a succinct, manifesto-like overview.[197] Streamlined and muscular, the book bore scant trace of the collaborative, dialogic nature of the theory's production. It also bore scant trace of the experiences that had sparked and shaped its philosophical questing: the legal complexity of the Austro-Hungarian Empire, followed by the legal problems attending its collapse. That whole "catalytic sphere," the "perplexity" that propelled theoretical curiosity, had been stripped away to leave an astringent, highly abstract philosophy of law in propositional form.[198] One would not know from its pages, for example, that the "necessary" monism of international and state law had appeared to the Viennese jurists as such only amid the state-breaking crisis of World War I. Unburdened by markers of time and place, the book's crystalline propositions could travel—and did. By 1946, the book or shorter versions of it had appeared in French, Swedish, Italian, Spanish, Czech, Polish, English, Portuguese, Japanese, Bulgarian, and Chinese.[199] Critics and converts responded with comparable passion.

Yet, in light of the history recovered in the present book, we might say that no attribute of the pure theory reflected the Habsburg context *more* than its abstraction.[200] The pure theory's sky-high philosophy existed in inverse proportion to the detailed complexity of what needed to be solved: one had to rise so far above ground to order that chaos into cosmos. Abstraction stands as an unmarked archive of what it meant to wrestle with sovereignty in Central Europe. This applies not just to the theory's formalism and its thesis of the identity of state and law, which Kelsen himself connected to the empire's diversity in his autobiography.[201] Along other vectors, too, the predicament of the Habsburg lands (both before and after 1918) pushed the circle's jurists up against "outsides" of legal order and drove them to reflect on law in meta terms. The empire's multiple plausibly sovereign legal orders generated the realization that everything turned on the initial premise of reasoning, on the so-called point of departure that they later conceptualized as the "basic norm." It was a confronting insight because the selection of that point of departure could not be determined from inside a legal system. It lay beyond the legal order as its external premise, the "Archimedean point out of which the world of juridical cognition is set in motion."[202] And they argued that it must be singular: one could not reason from multiple a priori positions—*could not, apparently, reason from multiple states*—at once. Imperial dissolution then taught them the hard way that one could not reason from states *at all.* State sovereignty could not be the highest and first premise of law's world. That way lay anarchy. States came and went and law must stay. This Central European setting, in which nothing at all about sovereignty was self-evident, forced the scholar to peer into the hidden recesses of the legal imaginary, to excavate the preconditions of legal reasoning, and rework its founding assumptions in a way that enabled coherent results. The case at hand brooked no half-baked ideas or fudged transitions; it demanded unsparing self-interrogation and self-reflexivity. This book opened with Jellinek's lament that British and French theories of sovereignty were exported for supposed universal application, and his question: why could the more complex, conglomerate states of Central Europe not produce their own abstract theories? It closes with precisely that: an autochthonous theorization, an abstract record of regional experiences and imperatives, now, ironically, launched on its own path of global dissemination.

But the pure theory did not just travel the world: it offered a new legal account of the world. "The Pure Theory of Law relativizes the state," proclaimed Kelsen's manifesto.[203] It left the state "freed of the ossifying absolutism of the dogma of sovereignty." The state instead settled modestly into its place in a "continuous sequence of legal structures, gradually merging into one another"—the whole world now reimagined through the image of Merkl's watery cascade.[204] Kelsen rarely sounded so proud: "The theoretical dissolution of the dogma of sovereignty, the principal instrument of imperialistic ideology directed against international law, is one of the most substantial achievements of the Pure Theory of Law." Though science, apparently, should take the credit for this happy result: "Although it was certainly not arrived at by political design, it is an achievement that may nevertheless have political import."[205] A beautiful coincidence. However disingenuously, Kelsen not only disavowed intention here but presented sovereignty's diminution as a straightforward product of the scientific method.[206] And his hopes for it were high, "For it eliminates a nearly insurmountable barrier confronting every technical improvement in international law." No longer could the doctrine of sovereignty be wielded against those crucial improvements. Epistemological system melded with world system: "The Pure Theory of Law, because it secures the cognitive unity of all law by relativizing the concept of the state, creates a presupposition not without significance for the organizational unity of a centralized system of world law."[207]

World making as sense making, world making as a methodological practice. This chapter concludes with three different ways of situating this endeavor, both synchronously in the years after World War I and diachronically with an eye toward subsequent twentieth-century developments. First: in demoting state sovereignty to a subsidiary component of the international legal order, Kelsen and his circle moved in step with a transnational cohort of jurists critiquing the dogma of sovereignty in the immediate wake of World War I. This cohort judged the doctrine of unfettered state sovereignty culpable for the catastrophe of the war and sought to strengthen international law at its expense. But where French jurists like Léon Duguit and Georges Scelle worked with sociological tools—deploying a Durkheimian vision of organic solidarity to puncture the state's "metaphysical fictions"—the Viennese jurists pursued the same effect through (what they took to be) logic alone.[208] They shrank the state against a larger systemic coherence of their own construction. By their lights, and at least in the domain of legal theory, a methodologically pure logical analysis could humble the state into that mere "fief of the singly sovereign World-'I.'"

The devotion to logic, the pursuit of systems, the astringent formalism: these qualities contrast sharply to the piecemeal, pragmatic legal cultures of other imperial formations (especially the British)[209] and direct our attention to a second setting, namely, the Viennese intellectual context and its constellation of other "circles" thinking in strikingly parallel ways. They included the Vienna Circle of logical empiricism, Wittgenstein's philosophy of language, and the Austrian school of economics. Connections to the latter seem particularly arresting in light of Quinn Slobodian's argument that the collapse of the Habsburg Empire drove the economists to turn from the state to the globe as the relevant scale for economic theory. They, too, reached for systemic integration of the whole, a "spaceless" world economy that shrank the significance of sovereign independence and operated like "an enormous clock or factory apparatus."[210] Certainly, the circles intersected in very personal ways, stretching back to childhood. Classmates at Vienna's Akademische Gymnasium, Kelsen and Ludwig von Mises remained friends for life.[211] Kelsen served as an examiner for Friedrich von Hayek's dissertation at the University of Vienna in 1923.[212] After anti-Semitism pushed Kelsen out of Austria and then Germany, he found a position in Geneva in 1933, not long before Mises did the same. The Austrian economists clustered there—becoming the "Geneva School," in Slobodian's account—and Hans and Greta Kelsen found a natural social world among this community of exiles. When Mises, surprising everybody, decided to marry in 1938, he asked Kelsen to be one of the witnesses.[213]

For all that, the politics behind their "systems" diverged widely. Slobodian has shown how the progenitors of neoliberal economic thought sought to "inoculate" the market against democratic publics, horrified by Red Vienna's marching workers as much as the profusion of new tariff walls erected by the successor states.[214] Kelsen, by contrast, remained politically close to the Austro-Marxists, whose key figures he had known since his student days. "From the very beginning," Kelsen recalled in his autobiography, "I was in unreserved agreement" with the "democratic program of the Austrian party." He confessed some initial skepticism about its economic program. But later, "especially under the impression of the economic convulsions brought by the war, I was more and more inclined to recognize that the system of economic liberalism . . . provided absolutely no guarantee for the economic security of the property-less masses and that economic security—under the given circumstances—can only be achieved through planned economy, and in the end that means nationalization of production."[215] Yes, he was well aware of the difficulty of reconciling nationalization with the political freedom of the individual. "But," he wrote, "I believe I must be objective enough to recognize that economic security for the great majority is more important than anything else." And that he "had no right" to fight for an economic system that benefited people like him and against a system "in the interest of the great majority," one to which, he believed, "the future belong[ed]."[216] Kelsen held to the clear separation of politics and academic work and never joined the Social Democratic Party for that reason.[217] But he understood the pure theory's formalist system as an ally—not an enemy—of that social democratic economic agenda. For example, the pure theory dissolved all "subjective" rights—like property rights—into an "objective" system of norms. This meant that one could not conceive of things like property rights as "prior to" the legal order.[218] Nothing was outside that order, and everything could be determined (nationalized?) by it. The precise opposite, that is, of the economists' efforts to insulate the world of *dominium* (private ownership) from that of *imperium* (political rule).[219] Indeed, Kelsen's extensive but long-neglected writings on democracy are now being recovered as a significant contribution to democratic theory.[220]

For our purposes, the most illuminating parallel between Vienna's trailblazing jurists and economists might instead lie in the connection between imperial dissolution, on the one hand, and the scale of theory, on the other. For both groups, the traumatic collapse of the Habsburg Empire and its replacement by a string of new "national" states—the teetering Austrian republic not least among them—spurred a rescaling of their theories to the plane of the whole world. To "start out" as a new state, especially a small, economically vulnerable one so structurally dependent on others, directed attention to the relationship between state sovereignty and world order, to the relationship between the whole and the parts. This rescaling suggests a third "setting" that we can call "world making after empire," with a nod to Adom Getachew's landmark book. Getachew has shown how the thinkers and state makers of decolonization in the Global South understood that the promise of their hard-won sovereignty could only be fulfilled through changes to the international order. The fight for true independence required not only an understanding of interdependence but an agenda for its reconfiguration.[221] For all the myriad differences between these historical moments—not least race, material inequality, and the violent wars of national liberation that structured decolonization in Asia and Africa—together they illustrate how the bracing experience of new statehood made questions of international order existential and drove new theories and projects at the scale of the world.

Indeed, the collapse of the Habsburg Empire turned Central and Eastern Europe into a key crucible for the interwar international order.[222] Seeking to overcome the same "world of walls" as the economists, actors in the region drove some of those new schemes, including the founding of what became Interpol and the organized field of international public health.[223] Others were imposed on the new states by the "international community," including the coercive restructuring of national economies in Austria and Hungary in exchange for loans, and the minorities treaties that qualified the state sovereignty in the name of international oversight.[224] International jurisdiction and authority grew exponentially precisely where sovereignty was new or fragile.[225] This pattern only thickened as the century aged and postcolonial states around the world became the objects of international development, trusteeship, peacekeeping, humanitarian intervention, and coercive loans.

The legal dimensions of new statehood suggest particular, hitherto unobserved lines of connection running between the end of empire after World War I and the decades of global decolonization that followed World War II. The juridical problem of sovereign beginnings that had so gripped Kelsen and his colleagues would prove no less crucial to the founding of postcolonial states around the world. New sovereignty necessarily raised questions about the relationship of law and time: about legal continuity and discontinuity, revolution and rupture, priority and sequence. As this and the preceding chapter have shown, Central European actors developed two key strategies to manage these problems: state makers experimented with claims that new states were not new at all but rather old ones resurrecting a sovereignty wrongfully interrupted by imperial rule; while scholars experimented with the idea that international law "preceded" (all) sovereignty and provided the legal continuity that fallible states could not. As the following chapter shows, both these arguments would feature in the legal battles of decolonization, though with some curious twists and reconfigurations.

CHAPTER SEVEN

Sovereignty in Sequence

LAW, TIME, AND DECOLONIZATION

Leaving eternity behind • Another new world order • Charles Henry Alexandrowicz departs for Tamil Nadu and gets busy in the archives • Shrinking colonialism in time • Upendra Baxi finds Hans Kelsen in the garden • Living and dying in international law • James Crawford wonders if his book can exist • Krystyna Marek helps Baron Münchhausen out of the swamp • Mohammed Bedjaoui summons the future • Martti Koskenniemi at the end of history

THE STATE HAD FRONTIERS IN TIME. Such was Kelsen's 1922 insight from shell-shocked Vienna in the aftermath of imperial collapse.[1] As we recall, when he reprised the idea a couple of years later, in 1925, he speculated about the reasons for legal theory's blindness to these temporal edges. *States appeared with the presumption to be valid eternally—to be valid forever.* Legal theory had, in effect, accepted that presumption of temporal limitlessness with its echo of the divine.[2] In 1952, he returned to the point once again. So much had changed in those dense intervening decades. Kelsen now sat some six thousand miles away from Vienna, under the California sun, on the rim of the Pacific Ocean, and wrote in English. Behind him lay the personal and geopolitical upheavals of another world war. He and his wife, Greta, had escaped Europe at the last minute: as German troops took Paris in 1940, Kelsen and Greta were afloat aboard the SS *Washington,* bound for the new world. Precarious, itinerant years followed, before a permanent berth at Berkeley. The wider world looked different, too, and those changes echoed in his work. When he reproduced his account of the state's temporal frontiers for the book *Principles of International Law,* gone was the invocation of the state's presumption to be valid forever. In a section titled "Determination of the Temporal Sphere of Validity of the National Legal Order (Existence of the State in Time) by International Law," he wrote that it was (still) "characteristic of traditional theory that it considers space—the territory—but not time as an 'element' of the state. A state exists, however, not only in space but also in time; and if we regard territory as an element of the state, then we have to regard the period of its existence as an element of the state, too."[3] In fact, he underscored, "both spheres are limited. Just as the state is spatially not infinite, it is temporally not eternal."[4] Eternity must be abandoned: states had finite life spans.

Coming from Central Europe, such lessons were hard to forget. The rise and fall of the Nazi empire had led to a second round of uncertainty about whether Austria, Czechoslovakia, and other states of the region were new or old—whether their sovereign personality had persisted, in some suspended form, through years of German occupation and annexation or whether it had been extinguished. For the second time in a generation, Kelsen as well as statesmen like Edvard Beneš wrote briefs and argued theories about the continuity and discontinuity of states.[5] But gradually, then rather suddenly, these questions stopped seeming like particularly Central European pathologies. World order lay on the cusp of a new era. State birth and death was about to explode as a political event and legal problem all around the globe.

Three years later, Josef Kunz tried to take stock of the rapidly evolving situation. He, too, was now in the United States—though on Lake Erie rather than the Pacific. He had found a position at the University of Toledo in Ohio in 1934 and would teach there until he retired in 1960, having established himself as a well-known figure in U.S. international law circles and developed new expertise on Latin America through long, roving travels to the south.[6] Writing in 1955, it seemed to him that the era of the two world wars now melded together into general crisis with the unresolved question of state identity at its heart. When he tried to sort all the cases into some form of order, it read like a typology of all the ways sovereignty could be set in time: "These troubled times since 1914 have seen the *coming into existence, transformation, extinction,* and *resurrection* of many states. Whereas in many cases no difficulty has arisen in determining whether a certain state is a *new state* or *identical with a pre-existing state*, there are many doubtful cases. They all have significantly to do with cases of *fusion* or *dismemberment* of states or with so-called *'resurrected' states* and, in one particularly important case, with *conquest not followed by annexation*."[7] Within the category of unambiguously "new" states he named "Poland, Czechoslovakia, the Baltic republics, Finland, Iraq after the First World War, and Syria, Lebanon, Libya, Israel, Burma, Ceylon, Indonesia, Pakistan after the Second World War." As "identical with a pre-existing state" he understood the Turkish republic and the Soviet Union. Yugoslavia represented a "doubtful" case of "fusion," while Austria-Hungary was a similarly "doubtful" one of "dismemberment." Under "resurrected" states he pointed to Czechoslovakia (the second time around), Albania, and Ethiopia, as well as the unresolved question of whether the Austria of 1945 was somehow the same state as Austria of 1918, with Nazi Germany's (internationally recognized) annexation in between, breaking the continuity of state identity (again). Had the twentieth century, barely halfway through, known one Austria, two, three, or four? From a permanent fixture of the European balance of power, it had fractured into states old, new, fused, and resurrected, sometimes more than once: an archive of sovereignties infected by time.

Now a new global era of state mortality and natality had begun. The same year that Kunz compiled his typology, sixteen states gained admission to the United Nations, among them Cambodia, Laos, Libya, and Nepal— alongside Austria, Albania, and Romania. By 1960, another twenty-four had done the same, including Ghana, Tunisia, Sudan, Cameroun, Nigeria, Somalia, and Togo. This left UN membership at ninety-nine, virtually double the number at its founding just fifteen years earlier. Contemporaries spoke of an "explosion" of new states. "There have occurred vast, almost revolutionary changes in the composition and structure of the international society during the past few years," the Indian jurist Ram Prakash Anand wrote in 1972. "With the crumbling of colonialism, scores of new nations with their teeming millions, which had hitherto been considered as no more than *objects* of international law, have emerged as independent sovereign states." He liked to say that the "active participation" of the new Asian-African countries had made international society, "for the first time in history, a true world society."[8]

The transformation generated something we might call a jurisprudence of sequentialized sovereignty: that is, of sovereignty set unmistakably in time. The sovereignties that emerged in empire's wake were placed in sequence: they were old states, new states, resurrected states; they *came before* or they *came after*; they were recovered, or perhaps old and new at once. They did not have access to the unmarked, rimless present of European imperial sovereignty—to sovereignty untouched by time, the sort of presumptively eternal sovereignty taken as the norm in European textbooks (and the target of Kelsen's critique). Their sovereignty existed in chrono-logical relationship to other sovereignties, to things beyond itself.

That sequential structure shaped the status of the postimperial states. Kunz's variegated set of options—resurrected, transformed, extinct, fused— settled into an overwhelming focus on two stark categories: *old states* and *new states*. Especially in the 1960s and 1970s, jurists from states both old and new picked up their pens, producing scores of analyses of the "new states," debating their significance for international order and their standing within it.[9] The seemingly banal, descriptive designations "old" and "new" became semantic fields of immense ambivalence—conceptual, political, and legal. "New" sovereignty, many sensed, bore the mark of the contingent and conditional: the recent and the juvenile, limited already at birth by myriad obligations and problems inherited from the imperial "past." Time-qualified sovereignty tracked as qualified sovereignty tout court. The international law scholar Gerry Simpson has written of "a tenacious division between states that were put on earth by God and others that are here quite by chance," a division that maps all too closely onto that between the ostensibly normal and abnormal, the rich and the poor.[10]

New statehood, that is, carried the indignity of all-too-known origins. Classically, as we recall, sovereignty was by definition a *nonderived* power: if it was derived or delegated from something else, it could not be the highest, the first, the supreme. The political theorist Wendy Brown parses sovereignty as "ontologically a priori, presupposed, original. Even practically, as Jean Bodin notes, sovereignty cannot be conferred. The presupposed or a priori nature of political sovereignty is both drawn from theology and is part of what gives sovereignty religious dimensions. It is a reminder that all political sovereignty is modeled on that religiously attributed to God."[11] Made messily—*made recently*—in front of the eyes of the world, the twentieth century's postcolonial states had no access to the majesty of the a priori and presupposed. They were worldly things, temporal twice over: lodged incontrovertibly in time, and located incontrovertibly in the mortal world, without recourse to the godly gloss of the nonderived and eternal. Once constituted on a conditional basis, Rose Parfitt has argued, the rights of states remain conditional, dependent on performance and vulnerable to intervention. Conditional, partial sovereignty, she suggests, has become the new norm—"with the possible exception of those (very few, exclusively Western European) states which international law considers to have been members of the so-called family of nations 'since time immemorial.'"[12]

In the jurisprudence of decolonization, the content of the categories "old" and "new" thus hovered unstably between law and history. If these classifications referred to the "facts" of recent historical chronology, they also possessed legal content. As on so many other occasions in this book, *historical* sequence and *jurisdictional* sequence—priority in time and priority in law—tangled together ambiguously. In 1972, the Indonesian jurist J. J. G. Syatauw referred candidly to the "emotional overtones of the word 'new.'"[13] He wanted a different name for these states. "New" was all "too easily equated with inexperience and/or irresponsibility in the practices of international law." It stigmatized and entrapped. "New states," he observed, were understood axiomatically as Asian and African ones, which gave "a character of permanency to a temporary and fluid situation." Exit paths remained troublingly unclear: "When and how does a new state become an old state?"[14]

Sovereignty after empire was sequential sovereignty, sovereignty without eternity, as Kelsen had learned. This experience connects the collapse of empire at the end of World War I to the era of global decolonization that followed World War II. To the extent that histories of international law have connected these two processes, they have focused on the mandates system operating over the wreckage of the Ottoman and German empires in the Middle East, Africa, and the Pacific. As Antony Anghie's foundational work documents most prominently, thinking from the mandates system toward postwar decolonization highlights particular (and crucial) connections and genealogies, especially in relation to the history of development. The mandates system proved a powerful device for spinning the "standard of civilization" into international development and, subsequently, into a global governance of indicators and the Responsibility to Protect doctrine.[15] To draw the Habsburg Empire into this story exposes different red threads. One is the inception of international economic governance and intervention, as Quinn Slobodian and Jamie Martin have argued.[16] Another is the legal problem of "old" states and "new" states—the juridical-philosophical problem of state birth and death itself.

As we saw in chapters 5 and 6, the collapse of the Habsburg Empire produced two noteworthy methods of taming the legal problem of "new" states and ruptured sovereignty. They both tackled sequence and priority, but along contrasting tracks. The first approached sequence as a matter of *historical* priority: many statesmen and diplomats appealed to the preexisting, preimperial statehood of their old-new polities. "Hungary is no new State born of the dismemberment of the Austro-Hungarian Monarchy," in the argument of the Hungarian delegation to the Paris Peace Conference. Independent Hungary, and not the Habsburg Empire, was the real "primordial fact."[17] The second approached sequence as a matter of *epistemological* priority: Vienna's philosopher-jurists reframed historical sequence as a question of the logical sequence of legal reasoning. To construct a theory of law that was free of contradictions and capable of accounting for the birth and death of states, international law must be presumed to be *prior* (and thus superior) to sovereignty. The remainder of this chapter tracks forward these two strategies into the era of global decolonization. Each case features a bridge figure traveling with us from Central Europe into the postwar world: Charles Alexandrowicz and Krystyna Marek, two Poles born Habsburg citizens—the former in 1902, the latter in 1914—with itinerant careers in front of them.

Sovereignty and Historical Priority

State succession—defined most simply as the replacement of one state by another—was named as an area ripe for codification by the International Law Commission at its very first meeting in 1949. But it took the storm of decolonization and its myriad legal ambiguities to make it an urgent priority. In the late 1960s, the Commission sought clearer consensus about what happened to the juridical entrails of erstwhile imperial states—to the treaties signed, concessions granted, property owned, investments made. When its reports were tabled before the UN's Sixth Committee, the representative from Ceylon, Naina Marikar, raised a formal objection to the designations "old" and "new." Why were "ancient" states like Ceylon designated as "new" states, he asked, when they had long, proud traditions as independent polities prior to European colonization? Should they not be called "old" or "original" states instead?[18] Such states, he argued, were not acquiring sovereignty for the first time but in fact were *reverting* to the sovereignty they had enjoyed prior to colonial rule.

He was far from the first to reject the category "new." If the invocation of prior sovereignty suggested a way around the hierarchy implied by youth and the rightslessness of new birth, it was also used to strip from established states some of the power of recognition, to circumnavigate the logic of permission. The Algerian jurist Mohammed Bedjaoui, son of a cobbler born in 1929 in Sidi Bel-Abbès, would become one of the leading participant-analysts of decolonization, "trailblazer of combative diplomacy in the service of the Third World."[19] Orphaned at four, Bedjaoui worked with his uncle and guardian in Tlemcen's fruit and vegetable markets before departing to study in Grenoble at the age of nineteen.[20] Across a long and prodigious career—he was Minister of Justice "at an age when others are still in the throes of writing some anonymous thesis"[21]—Bedjaoui served as a diplomat, arbitrator, ambassador, and scholar as well as judge at the International Court of Justice.[22] In *Law and the Algerian Revolution*, published in 1961, he documented and analyzed the liberation movement from very close quarters: he had worked as legal adviser to the National Liberation Front (FLN) and the Provisional Government of the Algerian Republic. The Provisional Government's request for recognition, sent "to all the Chancellories" in September 1958, had declared that the Algerian state and government "were not new legal entities but ancient institutions which had been resuscitated. It was less a question of recognising a new State than of confirming the legal resurrection of a pre-existing State."[23] In Bedjaoui's own gloss, the "restoration of the Algerian State" was "in accordance with international law": the "sovereign rights of the Algerian people" could not "be regarded as extinguished in law on the grounds of French conquest and occupation since 1830."[24]

Around the same time, another version of the argument was also being made in the halls of the International Court of Justice. In a much-cited dissenting opinion for a case involving Portuguese rights of passage through Indian territory, heard in 1960, the Argentine judge Lucio Moreno Quintana parsed the nature of India's sovereign independence in analogous terms. "We must not forget," he held, "that India, as the territorial successor, was not acquiring the territory for the first time, but was recovering an independence (sovereignty) lost long since. Its legal position at once reverted to what it had been more than a hundred years before, as though British occupation had made no difference."[25] Resuscitation, resurrection, restoration, recovery. In ways now familiar to us, these arguments posited a sovereignty that *came before* empire and *returned after* it: the new states were not subsequent to the Great Powers, but (at least) coterminous with them, interruptions notwithstanding. It was a way of repackaging change as return—a structurally conservative appeal to law's preference for precedent and its distrust of novelty. As such, legal thinkers like Bedjaoui strategically deployed such arguments without signing over all legitimacy to them, using this historical-juridical framework alongside the natural/national right to independence (as, in fact, Czech politicians had done in 1918–19, too).[26]

Marikar's 1968 comments at the UN, though, caught the ever-curious eye of Charles Henry Alexandrowicz. They resonated with his own research, and he seized on them as an opportunity to programmatically lay out a new doctrine he saw emerging. He called it "reversion to sovereignty." Born Karol Aleksandrowicz in Habsburg Lemberg (Lviv/Lwów), Alexandrowicz had traveled a long way to this argument—or perhaps not so far at all. Schooled first at Vienna's Schottengymnasium, he studied law at the Jagiellonian University in Kraków, in newborn Poland, after World War I.[27] After Poland fell in 1939, he escaped to Romania, where, as head of the Polish army's research commission, he became involved with the project of preserving the Polish state's continuity. Work on Poland's suspended sovereignty remained his brief with the Polish government-in-exile in London, which he reached in 1941 via Istanbul and Cairo.[28] He lectured in London after the war before his career took a sharp sideways swerve. The vice chancellor of the University of Madras, A. L. Mudalair, wondered if Alexandrowicz might be interested in setting up a Department of Constitutional and International Law.[29] Alexandrowicz departed for Tamil Nadu in 1951. There, in the fresh aftermath of Indian independence, something new and special took shape. He created a circle—that characteristic form of Central European intellectual life. (Indeed, as Alexandrowicz sat in classes at the Schottengymnasium in the years before World War I, Kelsen's circle was beginning its weekly meetings on the Wickenburggasse, just a few blocks from the school.) Vibrant and interdisciplinary, Alexandrowicz's Madras *Kreis* called itself the India Study Group of International Affairs. Its journal, the *Indian Yearbook for International Affairs*, became India's leading forum for international law in the 1950s.[30] If his "Madras School of Law" left its imprint on the history of law and legal education in India more broadly, India also left a deep imprint on Alexandrowicz.

The Madras libraries did not have the sorts of European books he would normally use, so he turned to the archives instead.[31] A vast new set of materials and problems opened up. Immersing himself in the latticework of treaties governing trade and relations between South Asian and European actors in the sixteenth, seventeenth, and eighteenth centuries, he came face-to-face with a past that, according to the prevailing European views, did not as such exist. He began to rethink all the received truths about the history of international law, which ostensibly emerged from the relations of an exclusive circle of European sovereigns. He suddenly saw the whole history differently—he saw it from South Asia. And the present-day implications seemed to him immense. His conversion was swift: already in 1954, in an article titled "Grotius and India," he staked out a new intellectual agenda and critique of the contemporary conversation. "The Family of Nations of the XX century opened its doors to newcomers from the continent of Asia," he wrote, "but their admission has been not infrequently treated as the opening chapter of their international career as if Asia had been a political vacuum in past centuries."[32] In fact, international law took shape through a globe-spanning history of legal interactions, in which—as the treaty evidence showed—South Asian states were understood and respected as sovereigns, too. That truth, and that past, had been erased from European thought with the rise of positivism in the nineteenth century, he argued. At this point, now beholden to a more parochial understanding of "civilization," European actors reimagined both sovereignty and international law as unique products of Christian Europe.[33] Treaty by treaty, text by text, Alexandrowicz set out dismantling this highly ideological act of forgetting, firing shots at the myopic narcissism of European doctrine from the archives of India. Articles like "Mogul Sovereignty and the Law of Nations" (1955) and "'Jus Gentium' and the Law of Nature in Asia" (1956) followed in quick succession.[34] This attempt to reverse the perspectival orientation of international legal thought made him one of the forerunners of the Third World Approaches to International Law movement, as members of the next generation such as B. S. Chimni and Upendra Baxi have noted.[35]

Alexandrowicz's research proved useful to the new cohort of South Asian jurists (like Baxi) who would become pivotal protagonists of the jurisprudence of decolonization. Ram Prakash Anand, born in 1933, took his first degrees in Delhi before departing for graduate work at Yale. In programmatic early articles from 1962 and 1966, he pointed to Alexandrowicz's work to establish that "when European Powers arrived in India," "they did not find themselves in an area of lawlessness, but rather were confronted with a *sui generis* family of nations extending all over Asia."[36] Their "mutual dealings took place on the reciprocal acknowledgement of sovereignty."[37] How preposterous, then, that those same European states would later appropriate to themselves "the authority to admit new member States" to their international club! As though the prerogative was theirs to "issue, or deny, a certificate of birth to States or governments irrespective of their existence."[38] He quoted Alexandrowicz: "Asian States, who for centuries had been considered members of the family of nations, found themselves in an ad hoc created legal vacuum which reduced them from the status of international personality to the status of candidates competing for such personality."[39] Small wonder that, in the 1962 article, Anand placed the "new" of "new states" in quotation marks throughout the text. In the 1966 one, he avoided the term altogether, referring to "the Asian-African" states or countries instead.[40]

In 1967, Anand convened a six-part "All-India Seminar" at the Indian School of International Studies in Delhi to discuss the major transformation of international order and the place of Asian states in it. In the third and fourth sessions, the participants picked up Alexandrowicz's challenge to the traditional European understanding of international law's history. "It was suggested," Anand reported in the seminar's published proceedings, "that Alexandrowicz's thesis that colonization during the 18th and 19th centuries *eclipsed* rather than *extinguished* the international legal personality of the colonized countries was salutary since it removed the emotional overtones implicit in the term 'colonization.'" To recall earlier sovereignty was to relativize colonialism in time: "In international law, the term 'colonization' merely meant temporary legal incapacity of the once sovereign actors."[41]

In his own contribution to the seminar, Upendra Baxi doubled down on the political usefulness of this larger timescale in the fight against Eurocentrism. "From the perspective of human history," he wrote, "the colonial epoch can be regarded as being no more than a brief interlude in the historical life of the colonized nations." Viewed in this light, the vocabulary of "old" and "new" did "not make much sense," he explained. "The nations which have now joined international, political and economic organizations are 'new' only from the limited perspective of mid-twentieth century history." "History," he declared, "is the great equalizer." Though he then added, a little wistfully: "In any case, to the realities and perplexities of the mid-twentieth century, *all* nations come as relative strangers."[42]

Alexandrowicz was not at the 1967 seminar. After a decade in Madras, he had continued his idiosyncratic itinerary to another corner of the former British Empire, accepting Julius Stone's offer of a job in Sydney in 1961.[43] But the conversation continued—in the flesh and in footnotes. Upendra Baxi's own trajectory documents the interlocked circuits of people and ideas. Born in Rajkot, Gujarat, in 1938, he studied in Bombay before leaving for Berkeley in 1964 in search of—Hans Kelsen. The elderly Kelsen, no longer seeing students, had no time for the Indian student who introduced himself in the library. "Very curt and very German," was Baxi's glum summation. Undeterred, he tried a more creative tack. "I rang up Mrs Kelsen." She invited him to come for tea on Saturday when Kelsen would be gardening and "in a good mood."[44] In October 1964, Baxi could write to his father in Bombay of the happy results of Greta Kelsen's lithe intercession. "I met Prof. Hans Kelsen, now 83, and one of the world's greatest jurists. His mind is as sharp and clear as sunrays—and it burns me!"[45] Their first conversations about relativism spiraled. Thereafter, Baxi would return to the Kelsens' fortnightly for the next three years.[46]

With his Berkeley LL.M. then in hand, Baxi, too, found a job in the Faculty of Law at the University of Sydney. He departed for Australia from Berkeley in 1967, already eager to meet Alexandrowicz, whose work he had followed closely while studying in both India and the United States. "I learned my international law from his various writings on the subject," he recalled. Their first encounter remained vivid decades later: "Tall, upright, and gracious personage, with a dash of silver-grey hair, he extended his hand upon introduction by Jules (Julius Stone) which I grasped too greedily!"[47] They began meeting regularly, too. In some conversational ticks, Baxi sensed the world of experiences Kelsen and Alexandrowicz shared. "Like Hans Kelsen," he reported, "Charles used to ask me about the possibility of a third world war. It was much later I realized how that prospect always seemed imminent to some European emigres who had suffered immeasurably" through Europe's midcentury descent into war.[48]

Alexandrowicz's programmatic article "New and Original States: The Issue of Reversion to Sovereignty" (1969) can thus be seen as a cumulative product: of deep and sustained dialogue with colleagues in South Asia and beyond, of immersion in the Indian archives and the non-European pasts of international law, of state practice in the heady decades of decolonization, and of the lived experience of states clinging desperately to life (like Poland) as well as those in the first flush of postcolonial independence (like India). He argued that, if states like Ceylon already existed as international actors in the past—and the archival record showed they did—then it was "correct to assume that they reverted to sovereignty and that they are not newcomers to the Family of Nations."[49] They should be classed "original states" instead.

The present-day legal stakes were clear. The new doctrine produced "a legal presumption that a State which lost its sovereignty but reverted to it (before the dust of history had settled), recovers a full and unencumbered sovereignty. The interpretation of rights and obligations connected with such sovereignty would therefore be in favour of the reverting State."[50] Old or original states could not be considered outsiders, coming cap in hand, and admitted only by the grace of the existing powers, often obliged to accept disadvantageous terms in exchange for recognition of their fledgling new sovereignty. The state reverted "to the same quantum and degree of sovereignty which it lost at the time of elimination from the Family of Nations."[51] "The orthodox view," he continued in his article "The New States and International Law" (1974), "is that New States have no choice as to the law which shall apply to them since they are born into the existing international order and must accept its tenets."[52] Reversion undid that assumption, reversed the onus. Though it required an elastic understanding of time: the "dust of history," apparently, had never settled on colonialism.

In this rendering, the global equality of states, sovereign parity between north and south, turned on a temporal or chronological equation, almost a legal magic trick, whereby the juridical effects of imperial rule were to be undone and reversed—empire erased from the sequential ledger of legal transactions as if it had never happened. Postcolonial states picked up international legal standing again exactly where it had left off centuries earlier.

It was precisely the same strategy, the same legal story or script, that the Hungarians and Czechs had marshaled in 1918–19. Seeking to circumnavigate the power differentials of sovereignty-after-empire, they all argued that it was not *after* empire at all, but rather *before*: "eclipsed," maybe, as Anand said, but not "extinguished" by the colonial epoch that followed. The timescale of empire shrank—a "brief interlude," in Baxi's phrasing—as the timescale of their sovereignty extended out in inverse proportion. The shakiness of the new made way for the majesty of the old and original. Indeed, to claim the mantel "original state" was to claim precisely the quality of the nonderived and nonconferred—the a priori and presupposed—that the classical notion of sovereignty emphasized.

Sovereignty in sequence was, or became, sovereignty *as* sequence: to be fully sovereign, one needed to be the first, the original, the prior. The ends of imperial rule made contemporaries conscious of the connection between time and sovereignty that might otherwise remain submerged below the sight lines of daily politics. Alexandrowicz cast that problem of sovereign sequence as one of literal history, literal chronology, a problem of facts and events that could be solved in the dusty corner of an archive. If sovereignty involved assumptions about the "point of departure" from which law and legal thought began, he indexed that point to historical dates and periods. Why reason from colonialism as the unexamined norm, from the assumptions of nineteenth-century European positivism, from the "limited perspective" (so Baxi) of the mid-twentieth century? Amid the heady transformations of the 1960s, when real change in the structure of international affairs seemed possible and proximate, that shift in temporal perspective felt electric. As Alexandrowicz's student and collaborator T. S. Rama Rao recalled, "I remember the thrill with which I read his following words: 'The new Asian democracies are by no means newcomers to the Family of Nations. They had to come back sooner or later. . . . [C]olonialism cannot be considered as a starting point but as an interlude only."[53] Pre-empire was the norm and "start point"—postempire the future.

In Alexandrowicz's life and thought, we can see how the *from-when* of reasoning tangled together with the *from-where*. The geography of perspective shaped his theorizing—twofold. He needed ideas that could capture what he saw from and learned in both Poland *and* Madras, two different (semi) peripheral vantage points on a world order in violent flux, local theory but doubled. That lived trajectory from Central Europe to the subcontinent generated its own connections. He made no effort to cover over his tracks. "In the search for precedents in the field of reversion to sovereignty," he wrote in "New and Original States," it was "only logical to look to the case of Poland" after World War I. If Poland was no "victim of colonialism," he thought the principles involved were the same.[54] Among the group of states whose recovered sovereignty could clearly be tethered to a legal entity survived from the past, he counted Ceylon, Madagascar, Algeria, and Poland.[55] Like those of the legal scholars from the empire-state of his birth, his categories and typologies produced unfamiliar maps of the world.

These images and theories of prior sovereignty lost-and-found echo today in ongoing struggles over Indigenous rights especially in settler colonies, a current frontier in debates about decolonization and self-determination.[56] "We continue to challenge the idea that somewhere we have 'lost' our international juridical status as nations and peoples," writes the Indigenous Australian law professor and activist Irene Watson. "Aboriginal peoples' status as sovereign and independent is not a claim to be given but one that seeks a re-affirmation of who we have always been." Aboriginal peoples were not "created out of international law" but "come to international law as pre-existing, already formed and arrived entities."[57] Why should the burden fall on Aboriginal peoples to "prove our continuing sovereignty?" Watson asked. That burden should be reversed.[58] In its work on Indigenous rights in the 1990s, the UN's Commission on Human Rights agreed. Of those Indigenous people seeking the juridical status of nations, "it must be presumed until proven otherwise that they continue to enjoy such status."[59] "Uluru Statement from the Heart" (2017), a major Indigenous submission for Australian constitutional reform, holds that the "ancient sovereignty" of Aboriginal and Torres Strait Islander Peoples "was never ceded or extinguished, and co-exists with the sovereignty of the Crown." The time shrinking of imperial rule and the time expansion of original sovereignty take on monumental new proportions. "How could it be otherwise?" asks the Uluru statement. "That peoples possessed a land for sixty millennia and this sacred link disappears from world history in merely the last two hundred years?"[60]

Sovereignty and Logical Priority

In 1967, Alexandrowicz retired from Sydney to London. That same year saw the publication of his major work *An Introduction to the History of the Law of Nations in the East Indies (16th, 17th, and 18th Centuries)*, a summative statement of the research sparked by his arrival in Madras. He returned to Europe with the preoccupations and questions of his wide circuit through the British postempire. "While I continue to explore the problems of the entry of the Afro-Asian countries into the Family of Nations, I also carried out more research on Australia in the Public Record Office and other archives," he wrote in 1971 to his friend Hedley Bull, who was shuttling between Australia and London on his way to becoming a canonical figure in the young discipline of international relations. Four years prior to his death, Alexandrowicz was still neck-deep in the archives and buzzing with questions. He told Bull, "I think it would be interesting to . . . write something on the evolution of Australian external sovereignty. What I have in mind is an examination of the antecedents of Australian independence in the period before World War I and immediately afterwards."[61] Another front of the ambiguous ends of empire. Alexandrowicz died in London in 1975 with his Australian project unfinished. At that moment, some fifty miles to the northwest, a student from Adelaide called James Crawford was formulating his own major project on the birth and death of states that he hoped to submit for an Oxford doctorate. The resulting book—*The Creation of States in International Law* (1979)—would become the standard work on the topic, and its author "the outstanding public international lawyer of our age."[62]

If Alexandrowicz researched and reasoned historically, Crawford's approach was squarely doctrinal. But therein lay the problem—and the suspense. As he explained in his opening pages, "This then is an investigation of the question whether, and to what extent, the formation and existence of States is regulated by international law, and is not simply a 'matter of fact.'"[63] That is: Does my topic even exist? Read on to find out! Behind Crawford's cliffhanger opening lay a century of answers in the negative—an epoch of self-imposed ignorance. As we recall from chapter 6, modern international law had disavowed knowledge of the creation and demise of states. Within the dominant positivist, voluntarist paradigm, international law's binding force rested on the will and consent of states. And if international law was *made by* states and depended on them, then it always came *after* them in the logical-legal chain. States were its precondition. How could it possibly regulate that which *preceded* the state, that which preceded its own operation and own conditions of possibility?[64] The murky processes whereby states came into being were "prelegal" matters of fact of no consequence to international law. Debate focused on the question of state recognition instead.[65] The "figure of the sovereign state occupied such a central position within the discipline of international law," reflects the legal scholar Matthew Craven, "that its presence or absence was not something that could be adequately conceptualized internally within the same framework": "their existence or demise could only be presupposed, or appreciated at some distance from the everyday discourse of an otherwise relational conception of law."[66]

We can see the logical-legal impasse of state birth especially clearly in debates about the existence of a "right to self-determination." Self-determination was a signal feature of the political vocabulary of decolonization after both world wars, but attempts to construe it as an international right tripped into the same quagmire. From a formal perspective, one could not have an international legal right to self-determination (or anything) if one was not yet an international legal person: there was not yet a legal personality to whom such a right could attach. As Nathaniel Berman explained, "the process of determination, the attainment of the indica of statehood, has always already occurred; if it has not, the entity in question does not exist in the eyes of the law."[67] It was a self-canceling loop: How could one stake a claim to statehood when the legal platform for doing so required that you already had it? The disappearance and succession of states proved just as legally ambiguous as their birth. What happened to the rights and obligations acquired by imperial governments, especially in relation to economic concessions and rights to resources? Did international law really bind the "new" states before they had consented to it? The legal uncertainty around all these questions exposed the "contagion of sovereignty" as an intellectual or philosophical problem as much as a geopolitical one:[68] law lacked a language adapted to the new liquidity of the world of states.

As a result, the birth and death of states arrived only very belatedly as a topic for international legal inquiry. Decolonization forced the issue. Or rather, it drove others to the same conclusion that Kelsen's circle had reached after the collapse of Austria-Hungary: the creation of states could not remain metajuridical. The spectacular, complicated, and conflict-ridden arrival of scores of postimperial states made that structural blindness untenable. Crawford's opening page did not dissemble: "The emergence of so many new States represents one of the major political developments of this century." Yet, "that a problem is of great, even very great, importance in international relations does not entail that it is regulated by international law."[69] It was embarrassing. To Crawford's mind, the coherence of international law itself was at stake. If the emergence of states remained a matter of fact rather than law, if international law foreswore all say in the making of its own subjects, then it could never be a complete or coherent system.[70] He innovated consciously, pausing in his preface to note the remarkable paucity of scholarship on the subject. "Apart from Marek's study on identity and continuity of States (published in 1954 and reissued in 1968), and various accounts of recognition of States in books on recognition generally, there is, to the writer's knowledge, no monograph dealing with the topic of statehood as such."[71]

Apart from what? Apart from a now-forgotten book by a now-forgotten Polish exile by the name of Krystyna Marek. Her Geneva dissertation-turned-monograph, *The Identity and Continuity of States in Public International Law*, was published more than twenty years before Crawford's. It was long, lucid, thorough, careful, sprawling. The problem at the heart of the book—the legal identity of states, and the continuity and discontinuity of that identity over changes in sovereignty—was the problem of their "very existence," Marek wrote in opening. It concerned the foundational question of how international law might even know if one state had ended and another started.[72] As perhaps the first international legal monograph on "the topic of statehood as such," its obscurity is itself compelling. Crawford was not alone in identifying Marek's book as a disciplinary departure: when it first appeared, Alfred Verdross wrote a review that hailed it as "the first comprehensive monograph on that so topical problem, the international law identity and continuity of states"—and called it learned, keen-witted, and original to boot.[73] Her work may sit astride an epochal shift in the history of legal knowledge about sovereignty, but Marek remains absent from histories of the field.[74] We can recover her study as a hinge moment in the epistemological history of international law—a moment in which international law was explicitly reconceiving its boundaries of the knowable.

Marek was born in Habsburg Krakau/Kraków in the first year of World War I.[75] The threads of her life run in parallel to those of Alexandrowicz, so closely that they must have touched. Alexandrowicz's father, Franciszek, was a general in the Austro-Hungarian army; Marek's father, Zygmut, was a Polish politician and socialist delegate to the imperial parliament in Vienna. She studied law at the Jagiellonian University a decade after Alexandrowicz had done the same. She too fled to Romania in 1939 and would eventually land in London, though her route passed though France, Spain, French Morocco, Tangiers, and Gibraltar. And she, too, spent the rest of the war working for the Polish government-in-exile there.[76] She quickly progressed from secretarial and editorial work, passing the diplomatic and consular examination of the Polish Ministry of Foreign Affairs in 1943 before being formally appointed attaché of the Polish embassy in London, where she worked closely with the ambassador Count Edward Raczyński, who would remain a friend for life.[77] The unorthodoxy of a female diplomat did not pass unnoticed. When the British Foreign Office wrote to the count to confirm that Marek's name had been duly added to the Diplomatic List, he noted that she would however be unable to attend the king's levées, since attendance at such functions was "rigidly confined to men."[78]

A question mark hovered not only over the woman diplomat but also over the state she represented. Divided up, occupied, and annexed by the Nazi and Soviet behemoths in succession, prewar Poland clung to legal life only through its government-in-exile. The pulse was faint and artificial. Suspended extraterritorially in London, the exilic government was excised from its own territory like a heart in a laboratory vat, showing only a technical sign of life. Marek's own fate was tied to that tenuous thread. As the Soviets consolidated control over Polish territory, Britain withdrew recognition from the Polish government-in-exile at midnight between July 5 and July 6, 1945, making legal exiles of its erstwhile representatives like Marek. That date is scattered throughout her papers, in both her academic notes and her legal status and documentation. State and self switched over on that same midnight stroke: if it left her a refugee for much of her life,[79] it also meant the legal death of her home state. Or did it?

The narrow searchlight of the curriculum vitae picks up Marek again only in 1949, as she lands in Geneva to begin a doctoral dissertation at the Graduate Institute of International Studies under the supervision of Paul Guggenheim. Working sporadically as a bilingual secretary, translator, and editor at various international organizations to support herself, she threw herself into a wildly ambitious project.[80] Her questions hardly require contextualizing. How could one tell if a state's international personality was extinguished? What was the legal effect of belligerent occupation? What was the legal meaning of independence, the legal status of a puppet state? The "identity" and "continuity" of a state, she wrote, were "another aspect of the problem of State extinction": "To ask whether a State is identical with a State which has preceded it in time . . . is to enquire whether one State has died and another has been born in its place, or whether the old State continues its unchanged legal personality."[81]

Sovereignty in an existential key. What of international law's much-protested ignorance of such matters? The traditional characterization of state birth and state death as beyond the pale of law's operation was incontrovertibly correct, she wrote, if the problem was approached from the perspective of state-based, domestic law:

> But it is clear that this problem can be investigated only from "outside" States themselves, since the norms of municipal law are valid only "within" the State and cannot serve as a legal criterion of external happenings. Moreover, the creation of municipal norms does not precede the birth of a State, but coincides with it,—just as the end of their validity coincides with the State's extinction. Hence, the time factor alone prevents the application of municipal norms to the question of the birth and death of States. For those who regard State law as the summit of the legal pyramid, the birth, extinction and transformation of States are thus metajuridical matters, not capable of legal appraisal. Any attempt to solve these problems within the framework of municipal law fully deserves Kelsen's picturesque analogy with Baron Münchhausen's efforts to drag himself out of the mud by his own hair.[82]

Münchhausen returns![83] And with him, the whole philosophical framework thrashed out by Kelsen's circle in his Vienna apartment in the years during and after World War I. Confronted with the same problems of state birth and state death, she reached the same conclusion: those problems could only be tackled through an epistemological change—by shifting the point of departure for legal cognition. One could not begin with the states themselves, could not reason out of and through their own legal systems, for they had no capacity to comprehend (let alone regulate) their own nonexistence. There was no continuous "I" that could consciously comprehend its own death or "remember" a time before it was born.[84] States, in the end, could know so little about themselves, and only international law could remedy that lack of self-knowledge.

"When, however, the problem is seen in its proper perspective," Marek wrote, "all such artificial difficulties disappear. Since they break the framework of municipal law, the birth, extinction and transformation of States can be made the subject of legal enquiry only by reference to a legal order which is both higher than State law and yet belongs to the same system of norms, on the basis of monism and the primacy of international law."[85] Marek explicitly took over the monist framework of Kelsen, Merkl, Verdross, Kunz, and Sander: international law and state law were one order, and international law stood at the peak of the pyramid.[86] Her footnotes stage a conversation between their moment of state rupture and her own, a conversation between the aftermath of World War I and the aftermath of World War II, unfolding with a three-decade time lag. As Marek reasoned: "On this clearly correct assumption, a legal evaluation of the birth, death and transformation of States can easily be undertaken from 'without' and from 'above,' by means of a higher legal system whose norms have existed before the formation, and continue to exist after the extinction, of the State in question."[87] For the topic to come into (legal) view, international law needed to be not only *above* and *outside* states, but also *before* and *after* them, too. International law had to exist "prior to" and "post" the state so that there was an existing legal order continuously in place that could witness and regulate the emergence of a new state or the demise of an old one.

And she clung to that continuity. It was the only way in which her Poland might still exist, somewhere, somehow. In the last pages of *Identity and Continuity of States*, a streak of emotion rips the otherwise smooth and controlled surface of the text. International law, Marek had earlier explained, had a general interest in avoiding discontinuities of rights and obligations. It was "basically reluctant lightly to admit the extinction of a State" and could preserve the particular "international delimitation" of a state through substantial changes of territory and population, or periods of anarchy and revolution.[88] What about occupied and dominated states? Belligerent occupations did not in themselves affect the continuity of a state's identity. While they remained temporary and unrecognized, occupations created facts but not law, thus leaving the original state legal personality intact. An occupied state could thus reemerge "as itself" on the other side of illegal domination. But if the occupation persisted for a considerable period, and commanded a relative stability, then the state would count as "new" should it rise again. The question of a state's continued existence—or its eclipse—thus pivoted on the point at which a temporary and provisional occupation sank into the permanent.[89] The point at which, we might say, the "dust of history" settled.

On this basis, she wrote passionately in the book's conclusion, "There *can still be* a relation of identity and continuity between the independent Baltic States of 1940 and such Baltic States as will recover their effective freedom before an overwhelming normative pressure of facts will have brought about their final extinction; *and there can still be* a relation of identity between the independent Polish Republic of 1939 and a Polish Republic *which will have re-established herself on Polish territory in time to forestall her final extinction by those same overwhelming, law-creating illegal facts.*"[90] International law might just have the power to forestall and prevent the juridical death of her homeland. As the American jurist Philip Jessup put it in his (very complimentary) review of Marek's book, "Has the villain really killed the hero or will the latter emerge triumphant in the end?"⁹¹

Like Alexandrowicz, then, Marek did not hide her tracks. Though it was not only Poland. For her (and for others in this period), all the key examples for these questions—that is, for the birth and death of states—unfolded in Central Europe. When Austria-Hungary collapsed, as we know, the status of its successor states raised myriad questions about state identity, continuity, and succession. The bellwether case was always Republican Austria and its relationship to the empire, but there was also Czechoslovakia, and Yugoslavia, whose legal relationship to Serbia proved thorny. After World War II, Nazi occupations and annexations meant Austria and Czechoslovakia were bellwether cases for a second time in thirty years, joined now by Ethiopia and Albania and the divided and occupied Germany. So if the Vienna school shaped Marek's theoretical perspective, at the level of state practice and empirical test cases, her argument was developed through the lives and deaths of the seam of states between the Habsburg and the National Socialist empires.⁹² And in the moment in which she wrote, it was of course a third Continental empire, the Soviet Union, whose power across the states of Eastern Europe pressed legal categories to the edges of their plausibility and into the public discussion. At its foundational moment, this jurisprudence of state identity and continuity was "thinking with the cases" of the Central European states.⁹³

The parallel with Alexandrowicz is arresting: their direct, wartime experience of a Poland suspended ambiguously between life and death drove a searching preoccupation with the capacity of the identity of states to survive imperial rule of different sorts. Under what conditions did it buckle and crumble, what was the prose of its survival? A sense of the brittleness of sovereign identity hangs low and heavy in their texts, even as they attribute to the state fantastical powers of duration and persistence. Telling are the different disciplinary guises in which Marek and Alexandrowicz anchored that sovereign longevity. They both appealed to an international law that existed before and after states. But he understood this literally, as a matter of historical fact. He invoked an early modern, prepositivist international law that had already recognized states the world over—including those "new" states now (re)emerging into full life in the postcolonial world. Marek performed a parallel move in an abstract, normative register. Just like members of Kelsen's circle, she understood international law's priority as a normative or philosophical proposition rather than a literal historical one. International law preceded sovereignty as a matter of legal logic. Legal knowledge about state birth and state death thus required formal-theoretical time travel to a point always prior to sovereignty (and always subsequent to it). To reason from international law, in this formal guise, was to reason from an *everywhen*. And that epistemological decision about sequence—about the a priori premise of the inquiry—made a jurisprudence of state creation and extinction possible. Epistemology held the key.

That highly philosophical approach, and the aspiration for complete theories of knowledge it entailed, was in transition as Marek wrote. A cohort of Weimar intellectuals-turned-refugee-scholars translated their interwar experience of the fragility of (Central European) states into a strident antiformalism, which they injected deep into the (American) discipline of international relations.[94] As they turned from law and textualism to power and interests, Marek doubled down on a certain sort of formalism and an unabashedly philosophical methodology. Here, perhaps, the Central European experience fractures into those (like Hans Morgenthau) thinking "from" large, powerful states such as Germany and those thinking from the beltway of smaller polities (such as Poland) long wedged on all sides by hungry empires. In Marek we taste the "culture of formalism" that, in Martti Koskenniemi's account, looks to counter brute power by dragging the particularism of individual interests toward the horizon of universality.[95]

The 1950s are perhaps the last moment in which state precarity seemed like a particularly Central European problem. As the gravity point of the jurisprudence on old and new states rapidly shifted south in the years after Marek published her book, the work of these two exiled Poles constitutes one refraction of the nexus between the "second world" and the "third"—one of mobile knowledges moving between, co-constructing, and contesting the world's "peripheries."[96] Through that movement, though, so much looked different. If the legal-philosophical problems surrounding state creation remained the same, the political implications diverged sharply. Put simplistically: for Europeans like Kelsen and Marek, the transtemporal continuity of international law appeared as the solution. For many in the Global South, it was the problem— though the reasons varied.

"The newly independent states do not easily forget," wrote the Egyptian jurist Georges M. Abi-Saab in 1962, "that the same body of international law that they are now asked to abide by, sanctioned their previous subjugation and exploitation and stood as a bar to their emancipation."[97] Debate swirled about whether they should accept it—and if they had the choice. "Is it actually possible to compel new states to submit to rules which admittedly were established without their help or consent?" asked J. J. G. Syatauw a few years later.[98] The question cut sharpest over the laws of state succession. Central to the emerging agenda of the postimperial states of the Global South was a revision of the structures of economic subordination that condemned them to dependency and undermined their autonomy. "The newly independent states," in Abi-Saab's words, "prefer to start with a *tabula rasa*, a clean slate."[99] But the laws of succession developed by (European, imperial) international law prevented that. It ostensibly committed them to the concessions, liabilities, and obligations adopted by erstwhile imperial rulers, stripping self-determination of its genuinely emancipatory potential.[100] The continuity of legal and economic structures from the colonial era had produced what Bedjaoui called "phantom sovereignties": "In this version of the infancy of decolonization, fictitious independence triumphs and the sovereignty of the new State takes the form of a mirage."[101] It was sovereignty already hollowed out by imperialism, sovereignty with wholesale autonomy already foreclosed. In this sense, the new states were not new enough. On the one hand, they were denied the radical newness of real beginnings; on the other, they were still stained with newness and youth in the sense of being juvenile latecomers arriving *after* international law, with the structures and rules already set in place. They were always-already subject to a legal system not of their own making. Too new and not new enough: time only hurt.

In this loaded context, the ILC named Mohammed Bedjaoui as a special rapporteur in their long-standing attempts to codify the laws of succession. A perfect tinderbox: perhaps the most creative of all the jurists of decolonization, tasked with a report on one of decolonization's sharpest battlefronts. He tabled some thirteen reports connected to the subject between the late 1960s and early 1980s.[102] Unsurprisingly, they rarely looked like a conventional attempt at "codification." He signaled this explicitly. A choice "must be made between the technique of codification and the technique of progressive development of international law," he announced unblushingly under "Methods of work" in his 1968 report. Of course he chose the latter. Why should they codify a traditional body of law "in whose formation most existing states took no part"?[103] No: he would reach for a new law. His report thus "codified" a law that did not yet exist, a law he was summoning into being. He would later defend this approach against more conservative critics who accused him of riding roughshod over established principles and undermining the very existence of law. "A norm is not necessarily better because it has been accepted by numerous generations and has stood the test of time."[104] On the contrary: the opposite assumption may be required to repair the outrages of colonialism. Law needed to respond to new realities or else "lawyers end by mummifying law and worshipping it for its own sake," a form of "legal paganism" that bordered on "totem worship."[105] He associated this excessive formalism with Kelsen (who had, we recall, once appealed to totemism and early religion to critique his own methodological adversaries).[106] Bedjaoui announced the "denunciation of legal chronolatry," the worship of time. Old idols would be smashed: "the developing countries are schismatics of chronolatry."[107]

He wrote to make the future. And he needed a new method to do it. As on so many other occasions in his career, Bedjaoui reinvented genres as he went along, rarely chaining his brilliance to received forms. He argued here that succession in the context of decolonization was something different than succession in any other previous context, and that the law must reflect that. The "origins" of a particular succession should determine the rules in play. Succession needed to be "classified according to type," and priority must be "given to succession resulting from the elimination of colonialism."[108]

He set about building a classificatory typology for succession, but of a very idiosyncratic sort. His ILC report presented a quasi-hypothetical schema that not only condensed cases into composite general profiles but also spanned the past, present, *and future*. Here, too, he was disarmingly explicit: "The classification which we are trying to establish here does not have the virtues of absolute rigour, and is not even completely orthodox. It is designed only to bring out—by magnifying or even caricaturing the facts—the marked differences between traditional succession and modern succession."[109] His loose, heuristic, futuristic typology posited three general types of succession: "dismemberment," "decolonization," and "merger." They were "hypothetical" categories that rearranged the past and foresaw the future. As he explained, "Schematically, it could be said that the first refers to the past, the second covers the present and the third looks to the future."[110] Embedded in the structure of this schema was Bedjaoui's argument that the old rules and laws should not apply: postcolonial states must be set free.

Type One—The Past: Dismemberment. Bedjaoui's first category covered "all the hypothetical cases of *traditional State succession*."[111] Usually in such cases, the region affected was "relatively 'homogenous' in levels of living and civilization (as in the case of the succession of States in Europe, for instance)." The legal orders of the states concerned did not differ dramatically; the people involved went from being citizens of one state to citizens of another. Though cases of this sort may still occur "from time to time," the category nevertheless related "to the *past*, when State succession, although regulated in some areas by the principle of *tabula rasa*, was governed mainly by the principle of legal continuity and stability."[112]

Type Two—The Present: Decolonization. "The hypothetical cases related to the present, on the other hand," Bedjaoui declared, "are regulated by the opposite principle of *rupture and change*."[113] They resulted from decolonization and entailed the creation of a state. He enumerated the characteristics of this composite type: "The new entity is under-developed; its level of living and degree of civilization differ from those of the former metropolitan country, and it seeks to become stronger." The people involved had been subjects; now, they became citizens. This sort of succession undid colonialism: "The relationship based on domination is dissolved, and the principle of succession does not apply to those components of the former juridical order which reflect that relationship." As he explained it, "Since emancipation *ex hypothesi* involves a change in political, economic and social aims within the territory, it normally constitutes a hiatus, a break in continuity."[114]

Unremarked, Bedjaoui's typology had slid into a different sort of truthiness because he was not describing what the law actually was. On the contrary: actors from the Global North insisted repeatedly that all their economic rights and privileges remained hard law. No, Bedjaoui was describing the law as it should be. This was his "codification" as "progressive development." Even here, in his entry for "the present," he was describing an international law that did not yet exist, one he was willing into being as he wrote. Rather than protecting the economic interests of (neo)colonialism, the law of succession would, pace Bedjaoui, be transformed into a means of shucking it off, as the new state refused "to grant any indemnity or assume responsibility for any liabilities." The rationale was clear: "Having been subjected to a period of domination during which its own property and that of its nationals were not consistently or completely protected, but were, on the contrary, often confiscated at the time of conquest by the colonial Power and its nationals, the new State tries to translate into legal terms its need to recover fully everything it considers it lost through colonization."[115]

Type Three—The Future: Merger. Bedjaoui came to the third and final entry in his schema. It involved "what might be called a kind of 'legal futurism.'"[116] Some mergers had occurred in the past; he saw it above all as "the form of the future, of the era of groupings and large political aggregations." The age of nationalism, he foretold, was making way for an "age of integration." He argued that "it is probably not so much the dying phenomenon of decolonization as the emerging phenomenon of integration which will characterize the future of our planet and pose problems of State succession."[117] Under the signs of nationalism and decolonization, political entities had broken down into ever-smaller units. They stood before a new epoch in which they would be put back together again, only this time, on an entirely different basis. "A merger generally takes place," wrote Bedjaoui descriptively of this future world as though he already saw it, "between two political entities at approximately the same level of political and social development (otherwise it would be but another manifestation of colonialism)." Gone was any trace of "subordination or domination." Of their own free will, the merging states "have decided to join forces in the future" and "pursue a common destiny."[118]

Here we hear the echo of "worldmaking after empire"—of the myriad schemes for federation and for new forms of international solidarity pursued by the thinkers and activists from the Global South in the decades of decolonization.[119] In the 1970s, Bedjaoui would become one of the most articulate and influential advocates of the New International Economic Order, proposed by a broad coalition from the Third World, that sought the systemic revision of global inequality and a new "welfare world."[120] In his 1968 report, he looked to cleave off the past, redefine the terms of the present, and clear space for that solidarist future. In constructing that meta map of states breaking apart and coming together, extending outward into the future, his ILC report read like its own philosophy of history. Tasked with codifying the rules for state succession, Bedjaoui answered: it depends *when* the succession occurs, and it depends what sort of state it is. The rules governing the temporal frontiers of sovereignty should be relative to time and place. Indeed, his typology was temporalized in both form and content: he categorized types of states in motion and transformation—dismemberment, decolonization, merger—and set those categories themselves in time—past, present, and future: a sequential map of sequentialized sovereignty. International law needed to be local theory: local to place, *and* local to time.

Eternal Returns

"We, the republic of Byelorussia, the Russian Federation and the Ukraine, . . . state that the U.S.S.R., as a subject of international law and a geopolitical reality, is ceasing its existence."[121] The declaration of December 9, 1991, made headlines around the world. "Declaring Death of Soviet Union, Russia and 2 Republics Form New Commonwealth," broadcast the front page of the *New York Times*.[122] Among the signatories was Boris Yeltsin, representing the Russian Federation, the largest and most populous of the USSR's fifteen constituent republics. Mikhail Gorbachev, president of the sum, clung to power for three more weeks before his resignation confirmed the prognosis.[123] December 31, 1991, is a date often given for the death of what had been, for the whole of its existence, the biggest state in the world.

The end of the Cold War exploded the map of Europe. Old certainties and old sovereignties liquified with vertiginous speed. The Soviet Union dissolved into fifteen republics as the two Germanies merged together; Yugoslavia began slowly, violently, breaking into pieces while Czechs and Slovaks concluded a "velvet divorce," consigning their compound Czechoslovak state, quintessential heir to the Habsburg legacy, to history. Commentators foresaw the coming of a "new Versailles Treaty": "The 1990s, like the 1920s, will accentuate the agonies of the small states of Central and Eastern Europe."[124] Amid the chaos and uncertainty, some reached for old schemes—perhaps "a new Austria/Hungary, made up of Austria, Hungary, Czechoslovakia, Croatia and Slovenia"—or heard "the dream of the 1930s whispered from the lips of angels—a United States of Central Europe."[125] Once again, historical claims and ethnic claims clashed violently.[126] "This spontaneous redrawing of the map of Europe has not merely put a final end to the European order established at Yalta in 1945," opined the Austrian foreign ministry in 1992. "It has also largely eliminated the geopolitical traces of the 1939 Hitler-Stalin pact, and has even destroyed significant results of the 1919/20 Paris peace treaties after the First World War."[127]

Among those watching events very closely was the Finnish international lawyer Martti Koskenniemi. "Rarely has territorial authority been reconceived and reallocated in as spectacular a fashion as in Europe since 1989," he later reflected. "Old political structures disappeared, new ones were being proclaimed and communities whose political identity had been held in abeyance during the long years of the Cold War were reasserting themselves."[128] Koskenniemi was not watching from the sidelines. The long-serving Finnish diplomat would later establish a new standard for the history of international law with his groundbreaking book *The Gentle Civilizer of Nations* (2001). But the "end of history"—as Francis Fukuyama notoriously dubbed it—found Koskenniemi in the Finnish Foreign Ministry with much law and history to make.

The eerie passing of the Soviet behemoth left countless questions and "dumbfounded analysts" in its wake.[129] Transfixed by what he described as "world history's ultimate vanishing act," the historian Norman Davies, for example, went in search of history's other "vanished kingdoms" and a synthetic understanding of "how states die."[130] "Everything was forever," in Alexei Yurchak's phrase, "until it was no more."[131] But this enigmatic cessation represented a very concrete and urgent sort of problem for international law. Had the Soviet state truly legally vanished? The consequences would be enormous. The USSR was party to some 16,000 treaties; it was a nuclear power with a permanent seat on the UN Security Council.[132] Uncertainty about its legal identity— and thus about the continuity or discontinuity of its international rights and obligations—cast doubt over myriad institutions of international order.

"One day I woke up," Koskenniemi recalled, and had to write a memo for "my president about, what is the country that lies east from our border?"[133] No one was sure, not even the "people in St. Petersburg." State continuity and succession became a formative problem "not just for me but for a whole generation of professionals in Europe trying to figure out" the status of "this large thing around St. Petersburg" and the many other successor states of the USSR, Yugoslavia, and Czechoslovakia. They all began reading and writing in the area; they "became very familiar" with Marek and others.[134] Policy memorandums, law journal articles, and document compendiums began flying off the press. Most thought the first problem to resolve was "whether an entity has become altogether 'new' or whether it continues the existence of an 'old' State." With that question clarified, one could begin to determine its rights and obligations. "Identity, continuity and succession," Koskenniemi wrote, "haunt legal imagination."[135] Contrary to everyone's expectations, the major locus of questions about the life and death of states had "returned" from the Global South to Eastern Europe.

That transit between world regions was far from smooth. The codification efforts of the 1960s and 1970s had unfolded under the sign of decolonization, with protagonists like Bedjaoui pursuing justice for postimperial states in Africa and Asia. The resulting conventions posited a fundamental distinction between "normal" succession and succession for "newly independent states." In the former case, the presumption would be for the continuity of rights and obligations, but in the latter, the presumption would be the reverse: a "clean slate," a sovereignty unburdened by the undertakings of former imperial governments. The distinction aroused much dissent—especially from conservative jurists in the Global North—and remained highly controversial.[136] What is more, the conventions failed to win widespread assent from state governments. The 1978 Vienna Convention on Succession of States in Respect of

Treaties took nineteen years to attract the fifteen signatories necessary for it to enter into force; its counterpart, the 1983 Vienna Convention on Succession of States in Respect of State Property, Archives and Debts, is still not in force, with a mere seven states signed on.

As a result, the law of succession remained profoundly uncertain in the 1990s, and many jurists expressed serious skepticism that the conventions, so consciously shaped by the imperatives of decolonization, could be applied to the new wave of cases in Central, Eastern, and Southern Europe.[137] If Bedjaoui had questioned whether the traditional law of succession made sense in the decolonizing world, others now asked the same question in the reverse direction. Regional experiences translated into law retranslated into regions retranslated into law retranslated into regions: local theory codified into abstract form and decoded once again. What was the relationship between specific geopolitical contexts and general international rules? Could the successive waves of emerging new states—Europe after World War I, decolonization in the 1960s, and then Europe in the wake of Soviet collapse—be folded into universal categories? What was the norm, and what the exception? And how could one tell without measuring from a particular location and a particular time?

As they played out over the 1990s, the post-Soviet transformations spanned the full gambit of legal positions—from continuous states to discontinuous ones, with many permutations in between. Already on December 24, 1991, Yeltsin wrote to the UN Secretary General that the USSR's membership in the UN, inclusive of its seat on the Security Council, was "being continued by the Russian Federation," with the latter maintaining "full responsibility for all the rights and obligations of the USSR."[138] He requested the appropriate name change on documents and name plates, those trappings of sovereign self-presentation. Eager for stability, no one protested. The exchange set the tone for the international community's general acceptance of Russia as the "continuator" of the legal personality of the USSR.[139] But unresolved contradictions abounded. What to make of the fact that many of the USSR's constituent republics had declared its extinction? And what of the significant changes in territory, population, and form of government between the USSR and the Russian Federation? In the census of 1989, for example, the population of Russia amounted to little more than 50 percent of the whole USSR.[140] It was not enough, moreover, for the Russian Federation to be a mere "successor state" of the USSR: a successor state can inherit rights and obligations from a preceding state, but it must still apply for UN membership in the regular way, as UN membership cannot be conferred through succession. Russia's claim to continuous identity avoided the process of reapplication and the dangerous uncertainty it would have involved, especially regarding its all-important permanent seat on the Security Council. Small wonder that these murky legal transitions would resurface in 2022. As Russia's invasion of Ukraine loomed,

Ukraine's Permanent Representative to the UN, Sergiy Kyslytsy, asserted that Russia had never been legally admitted to the UN. "For over 30 years, people have been sitting in the UN Security Council with a sign that reads 'Russian Federation' and pretending to be a legitimate member"[141]—pretending to be a state they were not, like a game of sovereign charades. The UN Charter named the USSR as a permanent member of the Security Council, and Russia alone could not reoccupy that voided position. The move remained illegitimate: "There is nothing in the UN Charter about continuity as an insidious way to get to the members of the Organization."[142]

Yugoslavia's fate contrasted sharply. Here, too, the question applied: Was its breakdown a full dissolution in which none of the new states continued the old state's legal life? Or, on the contrary, did some parts simply detach themselves from a state that otherwise continued its legal existence? Yugoslavia's implosion unfolded in slow motion: Slovenia and Croatia declared independence in June 1991, Macedonia followed in September, and Bosnia and Herzegovina passed a resolution on sovereignty in October.[143] In April 1992, Serbia and Montenegro declared themselves a dual state called "The Federal Republic of Yugoslavia (Serbia and Montenegro)" (FRY) and insisted that it continued forward the legal personality of the Socialist Federal Republic of Yugoslavia. That continuity was contested by other constituent republics and, unlike Russia, not accepted by the international community.[144] In September 1992 the UN Security Council held that "the state formerly known as the Socialist Federal Republic of Yugoslavia has ceased to exist" and that, accordingly, "the Federal Republic of Yugoslavia (Serbia and Montenegro) cannot continue automatically the membership of the former Socialist Federal Republic of Yugoslavia in the United Nations."[145] The FRY was invited to apply for membership anew, which it refused to do. Only in 2000, after the overthrow of Slobodan Milošević, did FRY relent and rejoin the UN as a new member state.

If the Russian Federation claimed to "continue" the USSR, most of the remaining Soviet Socialist Republics became successor states of various sorts—with three notable exceptions.[146] The Baltic states of Estonia, Latvia, and Lithuania rejected all inheritance from the USSR and claimed instead to be resurrecting the sovereignty they had possessed as independent states in the interwar years, before their forcible annexation by the USSR in 1940. In a style of reasoning that we will now find familiar, they argued that because the annexation was illegal, their residual legal personality had never been destroyed. Already in early 1990, the Supreme Soviet of the Estonian SSR asserted that "the occupation of the Republic of Estonia by the Soviet Union on June 17, 1940 has not suspended the existence of the Republic of Estonia de jure. The territory of the Republic of Estonia is occupied to this day."[147] Smallest of the Soviet Republics, it appealed to the international community to "support our self-evident right to regain our place in the community of independent states, taken from us by force, where we have belonged for 70 years both spiritually and de jure."[148] The Resolution on the National Independence of Estonia (August 1991) assumed "the continuity of the Republic of Estonia as a subject of international law."[149] Their sovereignty had persisted, in some form of shadowy abeyance, through fifty years of Soviet rule. In the image of legal scholar Lauri Mälksoo, they now awakened from a deep sleep like Snow White.[150]

The international community largely accepted these claims of "suspended" sovereignty resurrected.[151] "The Community and its Member States warmly welcome the restoration of the sovereignty and independence of the Baltic States which they lost in 1940," announced the European Community.[152] Some explicitly cited Alexandrowicz, Crawford, and Marek in positing that they seemingly "reverted to sovereignty."[153] Again scholars pondered the way in which a state's legal life might detach from its material reality. Because the annexation was illegal in international law, the Baltic states "did not lose their international personality, even if they were not able to realize its attributes," wrote Polish scholar Lech Antonowicz. "It should be asked, however, how long such a difference between theory and practice can exist."[154] How long could personality persist in an "unrealized" state? If there were "no rules of international law establishing the time limit for restoring a statehood illegally abolished," it also seemed clear to Antonowicz "that such a status cannot exist ad infinitum."[155] That dust of history must settle at some point—or perhaps not. The Baltic claim to resurrected sovereignty "is a claim that has reality particularly in legal terms," Koskenniemi maintained.[156] For some purposes, it involved a kind of time travel to the legal situation "that existed 50 years ago."[157] Treaties from the USSR period were shucked off while some from the interwar period stepped back into force; the UK allowed the Baltic states to collect gold deposited by the Central Banks before 1940.[158]

Old states, new states, extinct states, reverting states, dismembered states, continuator states, states playing charades: another end of empire, another round of controversy about who was who and how one could tell. Koskenniemi was given the unenviable task of trying to sort this chaotic landscape of claim and practice into some conclusions about the law of succession. Spurred by "the extraordinary political events in Eastern Europe," The Hague Academy devoted its 1996 session to the topic and asked Koskenniemi and Pierre Michel Eisenmann to direct it. Their report appeared in 2000.[159] There was voluminous material to collate and myriad case studies to cover, but larger, more difficult questions about international law itself permeated the whole undertaking. Did the kaleidoscope of varying results not challenge the idea that international law offered much guidance in this area? Did it not call into question the extent to which international law was capable of regulating the creation and extinction of states at all?

In Koskenniemi's hands, the ad hoc and pragmatic legal responses to the region's transformations yielded their own theoretical insights. It had, for example, become possible to think of a state's identity as continuing in some dimensions and not in others—as still living in relation to some treaties, say, but dead in relation to others. Such a perspective, he suggested, "avoids the anthropomorphism implied in thinking about status in material terms, as an inalienable 'soul' of a State."[160] Still, the moment had touched a nerve. It exposed something brittle, something delicate and fallible, about what international lawyers were doing in trying to make sovereignty make sense, something he felt compelled to probe and try to explain. Simplistic juxtapositions of law and "reality" misunderstood the processes in question: "The right metaphor for the relations of texts and practices is not that of one 'reflecting' or 'not reflecting' the other," Koskenniemi argued. "Rather it is that of diplomatic bricolage, the collecting of bits and pieces from normative materials, however open-ended or otherwise obscure, lying around in treaties, doctrinal writings and diplomatic discourse and constructing from them whatever it takes to get from one day to the next. This is not to belittle the importance of that activity but, on the contrary, to take seriously the imaginative efforts that have enabled lawyers simultaneously to construct and seek to understand and control the social world of international change."[161]

The Temporal Life of States

WE RARELY PAUSE to notice all the things our order of states presumes about time. We are born into a state that precedes us and that will, generally speaking, outlive us. As a legal entity, it continues smoothly onward, untroubled by our passing, unaltered by time. We take this perpetuity for granted in myriad institutions and transactions, like state treaties or public debt, whose validity extends beyond individual governments and biological life spans. The state is an "inter-generational transition mechanism"—as though a portal connecting us to those long dead and those still unborn.[1] Enduring collective legal entities like states and corporations are sometimes called "fictional persons" or "artificial persons." In the gloss of one philosopher, they "are fictional only in the sense of being formed and indeed *granted*, that is, of having historical origin." If they are potentially immortal, they are not outside history altogether: they are bodies we have *made* rather than ones naturally given; they are "potentially eternal *products*, indeed one of the very few eternal productions possible."[2] As legal persons of this sort, states exist in time yet also repel it—immutable things inside time's flow.[3] In that sense, something like a philosophy of history is sedimented into the legal form of the state: a particular configuration of stasis and movement, fixity and fluidity, change and changelessness. That configuration has made it easy to posit states as history's prime agents—stable protagonists acting in dynamic time like "history machines."[4]

The Life and Death of States is a history of these ahistorical things. It pursues the historical life of entities that claim to be immune to time's passing. It presents legal continuity as something actively made, desired, and doubted by historical actors, and analyzes the intellectual scaffolding such continuity required. At the center of this book, then, lies an interest in the historical production of abstraction. It explores ways of situating abstractions in time—ways of doing contextual histories of continuity. As such, I engage methodological questions about the nature of contextual knowledge that all historians share, but I explicate these contradictions historically, as features of the history itself.

Many of the problems encountered by the actors in this book—for example, the lack of a vantage point outside time from which to reason and judge—are our problems, too. The disciplinary resonances are sharper still for law, where the evacuation of context is a key component of the claim to be general, not local, universal rather than particular: a key component, that is, of law's authority.

Bids for perpetuity reveal that dynamic of abstraction with powerful clarity. Such bids were closely connected to claims about sovereignty: they spoke to the relationship between highest things and first things and to the origins of public power. The desire to be outside time was another face of the desire for perfect independence, for a clean inception in which nothing is owed to any other epoch or anybody else. Western states in continuous existence over the last two centuries have often had the luxury of taking that sovereign ideology for granted and acting as if it were true. The situation is different for "newer" states, for postimperial states. With their sovereignty saddled with strings and commitments and debts from the beginning, there could be no illusion of rule without priors, of autonomy from history itself. The tension between time and sovereignty, or between historical sequence and jurisdictional sequence, remains laced into the structure of international law. Such are the "contradictions implicit in the idea of statehood," as international legal scholar Matthew Craven puts it: "that it be both antecedent and a product of international law."[5] It is a familiar problem—*who comes first?*—that still hovers uneasily between being a historical determination and a legal one, just as it did when Hans Kelsen and his colleagues diagnosed the problem in the midst of the dissolution of their own empire-state at the end of World War I.

Historians of legal and political thought have explored the idea of state immortality as it emerged in the medieval and early modern periods. Here I have traced its fate and meaning in the modern period, in an era of imperial upheaval and collapse. I show who needed it, when, and why, and analyze the work it performed in managing and taming historical change.[6] In Habsburg Central Europe, we see how it acquired a visibility, even urgency, in moments when the legitimacy of state power needed to be renegotiated: first in the waning of traditional patrimonial understandings of sovereignty and the dawning of a new constitutional era, and then as the empire dissolved and a new order of nation-states rose in its wake. That history opens up new ways of situating Austria-Hungary in a world of empires.[7] The survival of various forms of slumbering and suspended sovereignty within empire and the path of these semisovereign entities into a postimperial age allow us to connect Central European history to parallel processes elsewhere, whether we look to the Indian princely states (once dubbed "hollow crowns" and "theatre states" by Nicholas Dirks), to the autonomous provinces of the Ottoman Empire, or to myriad other cases.[8] Those dynamics remain with us: images of submerged sovereignty, as well as recurring issues of continuous and discontinuous law, accompany Indigenous movements for rights and land in many settler colonies.[9]

If this book proposes a new framework for thinking about the Habsburg Empire in global imperial history, it also shows how we can locate Central Europe in histories of the relationship between empire and international order. Pioneering work by scholars like Duncan Bell, Mark Mazower, and Susan Pedersen traced the deep imprint of the British Empire on the structures and imaginaries of international organizations like the League of Nations.[10] More recently, historians have begun to explore similar linkages for the continental empires, including powerful research on Russia and international law.[11] The Habsburg path here is particular. As Peter Becker has argued, the Habsburg Empire kept a relatively low profile in internationalist endeavors in the late nineteenth and early twentieth centuries.[12] *The Life and Death of States* suggests that the interface between imperial and international governance played out along alternate vectors: central features of imperial constitutional law circulated into the international peacemaking of 1919 and the new European order it consecrated.

To understand the legal afterlives of the Danube Monarchy, I suggest, it is not enough to look at the years immediately preceding its collapse. By returning to the dawn of Habsburg constitutional government in 1848, I show the emergence of a particular culture of claim making and a framework for thinking about sovereignty, one that juxtaposed the historical rights of erstwhile states with the presumptive (but indeterminate) rights of ethnic-linguistic nations. That juxtaposition was not inevitable. It was shaped by the particularities of Habsburg empire building as well as the polity's political culture and its class and ethnic composition. The successive constitutions that followed, and the debate about them, developed this schema into a detailed body of thought and doctrine about the relationship of state sovereignty to different sorts of political community. That tradition persisted as the framework for establishing state legitimacy and claiming territory in the wake of the empire's collapse in 1918, as peacemakers, government delegations, jurists, and propagandists argued over the continuity and discontinuity of historical states, the geographic dispersal of conationals, the rationale for state borders, minority rights, and the status of postimperial sovereignty. The tension between these rival historical and ethnic foundations for state legitimacy continued to rile Europe's interwar order and shaped key moments of its undoing. In the Munich Agreement of 1938, Adolf Hitler seized the German-speaking Sudetenland, included in Czechoslovakia according to the historical borders of the Kingdom of Bohemia, at a critical juncture in his violent march into World War II.

Even before 1918, though, the line between imperial and international law was porous in ways that parallel Lauren Benton and Lisa Ford's insights about British imperial law.[13] As we saw in chapter 2, the Kingdom of Hungary increasingly performed its sovereignty on the world stage after the Settlement of 1867: subimperial polities asserted an independent international life. If constitutional law was projected outward, international law was also

projected inward. Proposed legal solutions to the "national problem," especially those developed by the Austro-Marxists Karl Renner and Otto Bauer,
invoked images of an "internal international law," a new sort of supranational
framework under the aegis of empire, as detailed in chapter 3. These and other
instances document how the vocabulary of international law and sovereignty
had become a ubiquitous way of conceptualizing imperial politics in an era of
heightened inter-imperial competition and self-consciousness.

By recovering the legal scripts that accompanied the dissolution of the
Habsburg Empire, this book charts pathways from the end of empire in
Europe to that across the wider world. The same structures of argument
would be used time and again as postcolonial states won independence in the
decades after World War II. Especially in South Asia, jurists like Ram Prakash
Anand and Upendra Baxi invoked a preimperial sovereignty that had merely
been interrupted, not extinguished, by centuries of colonial rule. Shrinking
colonialism in time, such constructions framed postcolonial sovereignty as
something original and recovered rather than new and precarious. The story
comes full circle at the end of the Cold War. As the USSR, Czechoslovakia,
and Yugoslavia came apart, and as the two Germanies merged back together,
the question of the birth, death, and continuity of states roared back into the
center of European politics. Once again, one asked if states were old or if they
were new. One asked if states had "ceased" or if they had survived; one asked if
sovereignty, once lapsed, could be resurrected. Once again, one wondered how
legal time related to historical time, and about international law's capacity to
make sense of these ruptures in the fabric of world order.

As *The Life and Death of States* stitches the Habsburg Empire into the
larger tapestry of international history, it also draws our attention back to
some of the features that made it unusual. The empire constituted a crucial
site for the history of modern legal thought. There were many reasons for
this. The first was the intense ambiguity surrounding the empire's fit with
categories of state and sovereignty. An improbably large set of legally plausible
interpretations meant that everything had to be made out from first principles: sovereignty and statehood needed to be investigated all the way down.
As constitutional questions came to dominate political life—leading to parliamentary boycotts and budgetary crises—those determinations assumed
an outsized public importance. Not only scholars but also parliamentarians
and journalists debated the relevant criteria. Where did sovereignty lie in this
dual state, this empire of empires with its crown of crowns? Could Austria-
Hungary count as a state if it lacked its own legislature and its own citizens?
What entity had annexed Bosnia-Herzegovina? How could one prove—*or
disprove*—that a polity like Bohemia was still a state? What did it mean if
"facts" said one thing and law something else? The nature of law mattered
here. Amid polemics about "fantasy kingdoms" and nonexisting empires, the
problem of the "reality" of the state ricocheted through the political sphere

even before it became the subject of one of the most significant philosophical departures in modern legal theory.

Arguments about sovereignty and state continuity unfolded in two important contexts. The first was the destabilization of traditional, patrimonial understandings of sovereignty and state legitimacy. Though monarchies still predominated, one could no longer rely on kingship and other institutions of patrimonial rule to establish the coherence and legitimacy of the state, at least not in any simple, unthinking way. But in the Habsburg lands, it remained unclear what could fill the vacuum left in their wake. One could not point to a revolutionary refounding grounded in natural law and its "self-evident" truths ("we the people . . ."); nor could one invoke the (ethnic) nation as the state's ultimate foundation—two favored lodestars in our usual stories about modern statehood. The Habsburg Monarchy would have to chart an alternate path into sovereign modernity, to think its way toward different theories capable of anchoring public order in an age disenchanted with gods and kings.

The second major context was the philosophical revolution wrought by the rise of positivism and the spectacular success of the natural sciences. Jurists turned from natural to positive law and set out to construct gapless, "scientific" systems of knowledge comparable to those of their colleagues in the empirical sciences. But new awareness about how methods determined results—even created the object of inquiry—generated uncertainty about the method appropriate to the study of law. "The state," Georg Jellinek observed, did not exist in the empirical world like a tree or an ocean, determined by natural laws of cause and effect. So what sort of object *was* the state, and law in general? If the foundations of state legitimacy were in flux and under pressure, so were the foundations of legal knowledge.

Those two structural problems combusted together for Habsburg jurists. First in Jellinek's work and then especially in the pure theory of law developed by Hans Kelsen and his circle, we see the emergence of a philosophy of law that addressed both dilemmas, simultaneously accounting for the coherence and cohesiveness of the state and the coherence and validity of law and legal knowledge. The state, as we saw Kelsen argue in chapter 4, consisted *only* in a unified system of law, only as a pyramid of norms. The state's unity could not be established through appeals to some sort of social, psychological, or national collective. Nor could one point to material entities like "gallows and machine guns" as the hard reality of the state because they remained the same inanimate matter even if the state in question vanished. What was determinative was the way *we ascribed* the force of gallows and machine guns *to* "the state." To ask whether the state existed was like asking whether God existed, Kelsen explained. If you believed in it, then it existed; if you act on that basis, then "there 'is' a state as reality, the state becomes a reality."[14]

The state as a crystalline geometry of abstract norms: the pure theory stands as a backhanded testimony to the challenges of making sovereignty make sense in Habsburg Central Europe. Kelsen sought coherence in a sky-high philosophical system when none was to be found closer to the ground. Of course, abstraction was not the only possible response. On the contrary: Kelsen had many critics. Law's chaotic pluralism could not be wished away, maintained Eugen Ehrlich in Czernowitz; nor could its endless contradictions and fantasies, insisted Friedrich Tezner in Vienna.[15] Even these apostles of law as *fact*, not *norm*, delivered passionate methodological justifications for their positions—and this reveals much about the intellectual culture that shaped them all. Together with Kelsen, they document how a pervasive deficit of self-evidence about the natures of law and state pushed them all to articulate the deepest foundations of their arguments and, in so doing, turned the empire into a powerhouse for legal thought.

For all the richness of this landscape, it was Kelsen's theory that traveled rapidly all around the world and into the canons of legal philosophy. It stands as a (if not the) high-water mark of legal modernism. In its tenets, we see modernity trying to ground itself, anchor itself, without access to the balustrades of centuries past. It no longer seemed plausible to imagine God, or nature, or the divine right of kings as the ultimate source of law's authority. In their stead, as we saw in chapter 6, Kelsen proposed the "basic norm": a hypothetical presupposition from which all other norms flowed. The basic norm tried to fill the hole left by the passing of more theologically inflected images of sovereignty—tried to answer questions about highest things, first things, and ultimate coherence. It says much about the predicament of modernity that Kelsen could do so only in an abstract, formal way: the pure theory knew no substantive values or absolute truths, only relative, hypothetical ones. The political community had to choose how to fill the empty placeholder of the basic norm and could not rely on any extrahuman authorities to provide answers. We were alone in making meaning, sense, and law. The pure theory grasped at foundations in a world without any.

As the usual story goes, the power of the pure theory withered and died on the other side of Europe's midcentury apocalypse. The devastations of World War II drove people away from positivism and back toward natural law in search of moral orientation and certainty. Many of the leading lights of European intellectual life—Kelsen among them—washed up in the United States, as though from the shipwreck of a whole continent, and scavenged for work. There in the power-flush halls of a new world hegemon, politics and scholarship took a definitive pragmatic turn. One lauded policy, process, and technocratic solutions; the young discipline of international relations had the answers that international law did not. In the harsh light of Cold War realism, Kelsen appeared to many the relic of a superseded world—a "leftover European philosophizer," as David Kennedy imagines it, "who could never quite get with the program in the United States after the war, . . . remembered as much for his

tin ear toward specific international legal issues as for his old worldly philosophical arguments."[16]

The limits of his formal, normative system were never more apparent. Did
he not realize, Harvard political theorist Judith Shklar wondered incredulously,
that formalism was a political choice? That there was no such thing as an objective geometry of laws, cleaved off cleanly from politics? More than naive, it
smacked of self-deception: proponents of legalism should own their liberalism
(which she shared) and defend it explicitly. Not least in Kelsen's case, where the
price of his formalism "in terms of extreme abstractness and remoteness from
law as a social phenomenon seems particularly exorbitant."[17] In other quarters, meanwhile, Kelsen's thought conversely appeared far too concrete. When
a string of coups d'état ripped through several postcolonial states, courts in
those countries faced a series of challenging questions: Had the constitutional
order survived the coup? Were the perpetrators guilty of treason? On what
foundations could the legitimacy of the new regime be based? First in Pakistan
in 1958 and then in Uganda, Seychelles, Grenada, Lesotho, and Transkei over
subsequent decades, courts validated the usurpers and explicitly based their
arguments on the theories of Hans Kelsen. A successful coup changed the basic
norm, the courts held: it inaugurated a new fount of legitimacy and legality. As
Tayyab Mahmud has argued, these cases took Kelsen's hypothetical proposition and turned it into a concrete rule of decision, treating the basic norm like
something in the world rather than a presupposition of reasoning.[18]

Way too abstract or way too concrete, too high or too low: it was as though
the pure theory's pitch—the register or frequency on which it sounded—no
longer existed. The theory limped on and never lacked true believers, but it
no longer seemed convincing or desirable or powerful in the way it had.[19]
Historians of science like Lorraine Daston have observed that what makes
something appear plausible or true often has less to do with the proposition in question than with its underlying conditions of possibility. It is that
deeper grammar or architecture, a framework of prior assumptions, that gifts
something its persuasiveness—and that can take it away again.[20] Returning
to pivotal departures in modern legal thought, this book offers a genealogical
reanimation of ideas. It reconstructs the lifeworlds that made them seem sensical and urgent—the questions that drove them and the needs that they met.
The Habsburg Empire emerges as the ghost in the machine. The problems it
faced—sovereign multiplicity and then sovereign mortality—strained law's production of abstraction: they drew attention to the leaps and fictions involved
in theories of sovereignty and at the same time made those abstractions all the
more critical. The ideas made there chased the sense in sovereignty through the
remaking and unmaking of multinational empire. In so doing, they tell one
story of the modern world, albeit until now written in invisible ink.

Introduction

1. As Jane Burbank and Frederick Cooper have reminded us in *Empires in World History: Power and the Politics of Difference* (Princeton, NJ: Princeton University Press, 2010).

2. Jürgen Osterhammel, *The Transformation of the World: A Global History of the Nineteenth Century* (Princeton, NJ: Princeton University Press, 2014), 572–73.

3. David Armitage, *The Declaration of Independence: A Global History* (Cambridge, MA: Harvard University Press, 2007), 20.

4. Canonically: Hedley Bull and Adam Watson, eds., *The Expansion of International Society* (Oxford: Clarendon Press, 1984).

5. For subsequent reckoning with empire and with race in international relations and international political theory, see, for example, Tarak Barkawi and Mark Laffey, "Retrieving the Imperial: Empire and International Relations," *Millennium* 31, no. 1 (2002): 109–27; Duncan Bell, ed., *Empire, Race, and Global Justice* (Cambridge: Cambridge University Press, 2019).

6. Matthew Connelly, *A Diplomatic Revolution: Algeria's Fight for Independence and the Origins of the Post-Cold War Era* (Oxford: Oxford University Press, 2003); Todd Shepard, *The Invention of Decolonization: The Algerian War and the Remaking of France* (Ithaca, NY: Cornell University Press, 2006); Erez Manela, *The Wilsonian Moment: Self-Determination and the International Origins of Anticolonial Nationalism* (Oxford: Oxford University Press, 2007); Susan Pedersen, *The Guardians: The League of Nations and the Crisis of Empire* (New York: Oxford University Press, 2015); Adom Getachew, *Worldmaking after Empire: The Rise and Fall of Self-Determination* (Princeton, NJ: Princeton University Press, 2019); Lydia Walker, "Decolonization in the 1960s: On Legitimate and Illegitimate Claims-Making," *Past and Present* 242, no. 1 (2019): 227–64; Andrew Fitzmaurice, *King Leopold's Ghostwriter: The Creation of Persons and States in the Nineteenth Century* (Princeton, NJ: Princeton University Press, 2021); Eva-Maria Muschik, *Building States: The United Nations, Development, and Decolonization* (New York: Columbia University Press, 2022). Note, too, pivotal work by legal scholars, including Antony Anghie, *Imperialism, Sovereignty and the Making of International Law* (Cambridge: Cambridge University Press, 2005); Rose Parfitt, *The Process of International Legal Reproduction: Inequality, Historiography, Resistance* (Cambridge: Cambridge University Press, 2019); and the special issue "Technologies of Stateness" edited by Nehal Bhuta and Guy Fiti Sinclair in *Humanity* 11, no. 1 (2020): 1–144, including Megan Donaldson, "The League of Nations, Ethiopia, and the Making of States," 6–31.

7. This development contrasted with the fate of Ottoman and German territories in the Middle East, Africa, and the Pacific that were taken by the Allied powers under the aegis of a new form of internationalized empire known as the mandate system, and to the fate of some of czarist Russia's western territories that the Soviets reabsorbed into their federal-imperial fold. These settlements contained their own important prehistories of postwar global decolonization: see especially Antony Anghie's pioneering account of how the mandate system laundered the imperial civilizing mission into the international prerogative of development and Susan Pedersen's on the mandate system and the production of "normative statehood." Anghie, *Imperialism, Sovereignty*; Pedersen, *The Guardians*. On the entangled collapse of the continental empires, see also Aviel Roshwald, *Ethnic Nationalism*

and the Fall of Empires: Central Europe, Russia and the Middle East, 1914–1923 (London: Routledge, 2001); Michael A. Reynolds, *Shattering Empires: The Clash and Collapse of the Ottoman and Russian Empires, 1908–1918* (Cambridge: Cambridge University Press, 2011).

8. The nineteenth century had seen the birth of postimperial states in Latin America as well as in the Ottoman Empire's European territories (Greece first in the 1820s before Romania, Bulgaria, Serbia, and Montenegro after 1878). These events unfolded in a different philosophical and legal context: the creation of states was not the same sort of problem within the framework of natural law—which held law to be derived from God or nature or reason, and to encompass all states and peoples—as it would be for jurists by the end of the century, who had rejected natural law in favor of legal positivism and now saw law as the product of the state rather than something that could exist without it, meaning that the birth and death of states represented a new sort of crisis. By the time of the Habsburg Empire's collapse, international lawyers were also trying to shed old doctrines of the "standard of civilization" in favor of more "objective" and "scientific" ways of regulating the legal recognition of new states (with mixed results, needless to say).

9. Jellinek developed the doctrine of the "three elements" of the state (government, territory, population); the expanded "four elements" were codified in the 1933 Montevideo Convention on the Rights and Duties of States.

10. In 1880, for example, Jellinek constructed a new account of why international law was real law, arguing that it was based on "auto-limitation," that is, the capacity of sovereign states to bind themselves. Georg Jellinek, *Die rechtliche Natur der Staatenverträge: Ein Beitrag zur juristischen Construction des Völkerrechts* (Vienna: Alfred Hölder, 1880). The "whole subsequent theoretical discussion on the matter," Martti Koskenniemi has written, "appears as hardly more than a footnote." Martti Koskenniemi, "Between Coordination and Constitution: International Law as a German Discipline," *Redescriptions* 15 (2011): 53; see also Koskenniemi, *The Gentle Civilizer of Nations: The Rise and Fall of International Law, 1870–1960* (Cambridge: Cambridge University Press, 2001), 200–206.

11. For other recent work highlighting legal innovation in the Habsburg lands, see Thomas R. Prendergast, "The Sociological Idea of the State: Legal Education, Austrian Multinationalism, and the Future of Continental Empire," *Comparative Studies in Society and History* 62, no. 2 (2020): 327–58; Franz Leander Fillafer, "Imperial Diversity, Fractured Sovereignty, and Legal Universals: Hans Kelsen and Eugen Ehrlich in Their Habsburg Context," *Modern Intellectual History* 19, no. 2 (2022): 421–43.

12. Mark Mazower, *Dark Continent: Europe's Twentieth Century* (New York: Vintage Books, 2000), 7.

13. For an evocative recent work that places Lemberg/Lwów/Lviv at the center of twentieth-century international legal history, though without any deeper contextualization in Habsburg history, see Philippe Sands, *East West Street: On the Origins of "Genocide" and "Crimes against Humanity"* (New York: Vintage Books, 2017).

14. Charles S. Maier, *Leviathan 2.0: Inventing Modern Statehood* (Cambridge, MA: Belknap Press of Harvard University Press, 2012), 8.

15. Georg Jellinek, *Die Lehre von den Staatenverbindungen* (Berlin: O. Haering, 1882), iii, 3, 12, 13–14.

16. From the United States, Mexico, and Argentina to Sweden-Norway, the Ottoman Empire, and "the whole Orient." Jellinek, 4.

17. Hermann Bidermann, *Die rechtliche Natur der österreichisch-ungarischen Monarchie* (Vienna: Carl Fromme, 1877), 4.

18. Tara Zahra, *Kidnapped Souls: National Indifference and the Battle for Children in the Bohemian Lands, 1900–1948* (Ithaca, NY: Cornell University Press, 2008); Zahra, "Imagined Non-communities: National Indifference as a Category of Analysis," *Slavic Review* 69, no. 1 (2010): 93–119; Pieter Judson, *Guardians of the Nation: Activists on*

the Language Frontiers of Imperial Austria (Cambridge, MA: Harvard University Press, 2007); Jeremy King, *Budweisers into Czechs and Germans: A Local History of Bohemian Politics, 1848–1948* (Princeton, NJ: Princeton University Press, 2005); Kate Brown, *A Biography of No Place: From Ethnic Borderland to Soviet Heartland* (Cambridge, MA: Harvard University Press, 2004); Francine Hirsch, *Empire of Nations: Ethnographic Knowledge and the Making of the Soviet Union* (Ithaca, NY: Cornell University Press, 2005).

19. See, for example, J. H. Elliot, "A Europe of Composite Monarchies," *Past and Present* 137 (1992): 48–71; H. G. Koenigsberger, "Composite States, Representative Institutions and the American Revolution," *Historical Research* 62, no. 148 (1989): 135–53; Koenigsberger, "Monarchies and Parliaments in Early Modern Europe: Dominium Regale or Dominium Politicum et Regale," *Theory and Society* 5, no. 2 (1978): 191–217; Albert Kiralfy, "Independent Legal Systems under Common Dynastic Rule: The Examples of England and Hungary," *Journal of Legal History* 11, no. 1 (1990): 118–28. For a sociological analysis in the context of European state building, see Thomas Ertman, *Birth of the Leviathan: Building States and Regimes in Medieval and Early Modern Europe* (Cambridge: Cambridge University Press, 1997), esp. 19ff.

20. This is not to say that such images necessarily captured the reality: after all, states like Britain and France presided over global empires characterized by highly varied and ambiguous legal arrangements. See further the subsection "Sorting Self and Globe" later in this introduction.

21. Perry Anderson, *Lineages of the Absolutist State* (London: Verso, 1979), 25; see also Rafe Blaufarb, *The Great Demarcation: The French Revolution and the Invention of Modern Property* (New York: Oxford University Press, 2016); Nicolas Barreyre and Clare Lemercier, "The Unexceptional State: Rethinking the State in the Nineteenth Century (France, United States)," *American Historical Review* 126, no. 2 (2021): 481–503.

22. This definition of estates is taken from Barbara Stollberg-Rilinger, *The Holy Roman Empire: A Short History*, trans. Yair Mintzker (Princeton, NJ: Princeton University Press, 2018), 143.

23. See, for example, Barbara Stollberg-Rilinger, *The Emperor's Old Clothes: Constitutional History and the Symbolic Language of the Holy Roman Empire*, trans. Thomas Dunlap (New York: Berghahn, 2015); Tamar Herzog, *A Short History of European Law: The Last Two and a Half Millennia* (Cambridge, MA: Harvard University Press, 2018).

24. On "systematization" as a feature of "late" systems of legal thought, see, for example, Max Weber: "According to present modes of thought it represents an integration of all analytically derived legal propositions in such a way that they constitute a logically clear, internally consistent, and, at least in theory, gapless system of rules, under which, it is implied, all conceivable fact situations must be capable of being logically subsumed lest their order lack an effective guaranty." Max Weber, *Economy and Society: An Outline of Interpretive Sociology* (New York: Bedminster Press, 1968), 2:656.

25. Engels invoked this example, subsequently picked up by Perry Anderson: Friedrich Engels, "Über den Verfall des Feudalismus und das Aufkommen der Bourgeoisie" (1884), in Karl Max and Friedrich Engels, *Werke* (Berlin: Dietz Verlag, 1975), 21:396; Anderson, *Lineages of the Absolutist State*, 38.

26. These reforms introduced mandatory schooling well in advance of most European states. Also of particular note in this context is the first universal permanent tax (1760), the Codex Theresianus of 1766, and the new criminal code (Allgemeines Gesetzbuch) of 1787. For powerful accounts of this Enlightenment-era state building, see Pieter Judson, *The Habsburg Empire: A New History* (Cambridge, MA: Harvard University Press, 2016); John Deak, *Forging a Multinational State: State Making in Imperial Austria from the Enlightenment to the First World War* (Stanford, CA: Stanford University Press, 2015). For an overview of varying conceptions and projects to create a supranational Austrian citizenry,

see Jiří Kořalka, *Tschechen im Habsburgerreich und in Europa, 1815-1914: Sozialgeschichtliche Zusammenhänge der neuzeitlichen Nationsbildung und der Nationalitätenfrage in den böhmischen Ländern* (Vienna: Verlag für Geschichte und Politik, 1991), 27-37.

27. As against the Habsburg dynasty, or House of Austria, or the Hereditary Kingdoms and Lands, and so on. See Arnold Luschin von Ebengreuth, *Handbuch der österreichischen Reichsgeschichte: Geschichte der Staatsbildung, der Rechtsquellen und des öffentlichen Rechts*, vol. 1, *Österreichiche Reichsgeschichte des Mittelalters*, 2nd ed. (Bamberg: C. C. Buchners Verlag, 1914), 3.

28. He held both imperial titles—a double emperor—for two years before effecting the dissolution of the Holy Roman Empire by abdicating its throne in 1806, after the disastrous Battle of Austerlitz in December 1805.

29. *Protokolle des Verfassungs-Ausschusses im österreichischen Reichstag 1848-1849*, ed. Anton Springer (Leipzig: G. Hirzel, 1885), 68 (per Franz Hein).

30. Eugen Ehrlich, *Grundlegung der Soziologie des Rechts* (Munich: Duncker & Humblot, 1913); Ehrlich, "The Sociology of Law," trans. Nathan Isaacs, *Harvard Law Review* 36, no. 2 (1922): 130-45. As Sally Engle Merry recounted, the legal pluralism subfield developed through an interest in the imposition of Western legal systems onto Indigenous cultures in the non-European world before scholars reimported the theoretical apparatus and ethnographic method developed in the study of colonial situations to study legal pluralism in industrialized societies, too. She cited Eugen Ehrlich's research as an exception to this trajectory, an account of "nonstate forms of normative ordering" that was curiously indigenous to Europe. Sally Engle Merry, "Legal Pluralism," *Law and Society Review* (1988): 874 and passim. See also Marc Hertogh, ed., *Living Law: Reconsidering Eugen Ehrlich* (Oxford: Hart, 2008). On Ehrlich, see also importantly Fillafer, "Imperial Diversity, Fractured Sovereignty," 421-43.

31. See Jana Osterkamp, "Geschichte als Argument: Das Böhmische Staatsrecht als politischer Leitbegriff im 19. Jahrhundert," *Střed* 1 (2016): 9-27.

32. That is, uses of the term in this context involved the dual meaning of *Recht* as both *law* and *right*: they were referencing a body of historical-constitutional law as well as their right to its recognition. English-language historiography usually translates this claim-making program as the "historical state rights" argument, but thereby downplays the significance of the framing of these rights as a genre of constitutional law.

33. This projection backward of nineteenth-century understandings of statehood and sovereignty onto medieval polities did not, of course, occur only in Habsburg constitutional law. Jellinek observed that in the constitution of the old German Empire, the territories (*Territorien*) were not states, and dominion (*Landeshoheit*) was a complex of internally inconsistent components that blended together public and private law. "In the last period of the empire, however, the territories were declared by imperial jurists [*Reichspublizisten*] to be states." Georg Jellinek, *Allgemeine Staatslehre*, 3rd ed. (Berlin: O. Häring, 1914), 345-47. For a recent study of related issues in the German Empire, see Bardo Fassbender, *Der offene Bundesstaat: Studien zu auswärtigen Gewalt und zur Völkerrechtssubjektivität bundesstaatlicher Teilstaaten in Europa* (Tübingen: Mohr Siebeck, 2007). In the mid-twentieth century, Otto Brunner would become famous for his critique of the ahistorical nineteenth-century construction of the "sovereignty," "statehood," and "public law" of the medieval Austrian *Länder*: the Middle Ages, he wrote, knew no concept of sovereignty in the modern sense: Otto Brunner, *Land und Herrschaft: Grundlagen der Territorialen Verfassungsgeschichte Südostdeutschlands im Mittelalter* (Baden bei Wien: Rudolf M. Rohrer, 1939), esp. 132-94. This debate continues to the present day. Fear of anachronism has cut both ways: if scholars like Brunner rejected the backward projection of a modern concept, others have resisted the idea that early modern polities lacked a conception of something like "the state" just because they did not conform to modern definitions. For a survey, see Susan Reynolds,

"The Historiography of the Medieval State," in *Companion to Historiography*, ed. Michael Bentley (London: Routledge, 1997), 117–38; and Stuart Airlie, Walter Pohl, and Helmut Reimitz, eds., *Staat im frühen Mittelalter* (Vienna: Verlag der österreichischen Akademie der Wissenschaften, 2006).

34. On Austro-Hungarian scholar Karl Polanyi's influential account of a transition from economic life "embedded" in reciprocal social relationships to one increasingly framed as an autonomous, self-contained sphere, see Karl Polanyi, *The Great Transformation: The Political and Economic Origins of Our Time* (New York: Farrar and Reinhart, 1944); Timothy Mitchell, *Carbon Democracy: Political Power in the Age of Oil* (New York: Verso, 2011); Mitchell, "Fixing the Economy," *Cultural Studies* 12, no. 1 (1998): 82–101.

35. If recent work on the British, French, and German empires has explored the private-commercial/public entanglements involved in the extension of colonial rule, this book reminds us of the instability and historicity of the public-private divide in European sovereignty *in Europe*, too—here in a (post)feudal rather than mercantile guise. On some of these themes in Russia and France, see Ekaterina Pravilova, *A Public Empire: Property and the Quest for the Common Good in Imperial Russia* (Princeton, NJ: Princeton University Press, 2014); and Blaufarb, *Great Demarcation.* On the blue water empires, see Philip Stern, *The Company State: Corporate Sovereignty and the Early Modern Foundations of the British Empire in India* (Oxford: Oxford University Press, 2012); Steven Press, *Rogue Empires: Contracts and Conmen in the Scramble for Africa* (Cambridge, MA: Harvard University Press, 2017); Andrew Phillips and J. C. Sharman, *Outsourcing Empire: How Company-States Made the Modern World* (Princeton, NJ: Princeton University Press, 2020). For political theory on more recent public-private recalibrations, see Chiara Cordelli, *The Privatized State* (Princeton, NJ: Princeton University Press, 2020).

36. R. W. Seton-Watson, "The Austro-Hungarian Ausgleich of 1867," *Slavonic and East European Review* 19, no. 53/54 (1939–40): 134.

37. On the 1867 Settlement as the "last interesting attempt to transfer the forms of the estates-state into the world of the second half of the 19th century," see Hans Lentze's brief but programmatic conference paper "Die Ständischen Grundlagen des Dualismus," in *Die Freiheitsrechte und die Staatstheorien im Zeitalter des Dualismus: Materialien der VII. Ungarisch-tschechoslowakischen Rechtshistorikerkonferenz in Pécs (23–25 September, 1965)*, ed. Andor Csizmadia (Budapest: Tankönyvkiadó, 1966), 88.

38. The formal designation of the western half of the empire was the Kingdoms and Lands Represented in the Imperial Parliament, known colloquially as Austria or Cisleithania (the latter paired with Hungary as Transleithania, on the far side of the Leitha River).

39. Louis Eisenmann, *Le Compromis Austro-Hongrois de 1867: Étude sur le Dualisme* (Paris: Société Nouvelle de Librarie et d'Édition, 1904), 639.

40. In 1802, Hegel famously argued that the empire had become a mere external form devoid of any internal substance: G. W. F. Hegel, "The German Constitution," in *Political Writings*, ed. Laurence Dickey and H. B. Nisbet, trans. H. B. Nisbet (Cambridge: Cambridge University Press, 1999), 6–101. Josef Ulbrich, a minor character in this book, described the suzerainty of the Holy Roman Empire as having become a mere "apparitional silhouette" (*einem wesenlosen Schattenbilde*): Josef Ulbrich, *Die rechtliche Natur der österreichisch-ungarischen Monarchie* (Prague: H. Dominicus, 1879), 38–39. See also Stollberg-Rilinger, *Emperor's Old Clothes*; and, along a different track, Walter Ullmann, "The Development of the Medieval Idea of Sovereignty," *English Historical Review* 64, no. 250 (1949): 1–33.

41. For a sample of recent works, see Lauren Benton, *Law and Colonial Cultures: Legal Regimes in World History* (New York: Cambridge University Press, 2002); Lauren Benton and Richard J. Ross, eds., *Legal Pluralism and Empires, 1500–1850* (New York: New York University Press, 2013); Mary Lewis, *Divided Rule: Sovereignty and Empire in French*

Tunisia, 1881-1938 (Berkeley: University of California Press, 2013); Paolo Sartori and Ido Shahar, "Legal Pluralism in Muslim Majority Colonies: Mapping the Terrain," *Journal of the Economic and Social History of the Orient* 55, nos. 4–5 (2002): 637–63; Judith Surkis, *Sex, Law, and Sovereignty in French Algeria, 1830–1930* (Ithaca, NY: Cornell University Press, 2020).

42. Benton has made an especially strong case for the close imbrication of legal and geographic "lumpiness": see Lauren Benton, *A Search for Sovereignty: Law and Geography in European Empires, 1400–1900* (New York: Cambridge University Press, 2010). On legal pluralisms of this temporal variety, see Natasha Wheatley, "Legal Pluralism as Temporal Pluralism: Historical Rights, Legal Vitalism, and Non-synchronous Sovereignty," in *Power and Time: Temporalities in Conflict and the Making of History*, ed. Dan Edelstein, Stefanos Geroulanos, and Natasha Wheatley (Chicago: University of Chicago Press, 2020), 53–79.

43. Anghie, *Imperialism, Sovereignty*; Jennifer Pitts, *Boundaries of the International: Law and Empire* (Cambridge, MA: Harvard University Press, 2018).

44. Lauren Benton and Lisa Ford, *Rage for Order: The British Empire and the Origins of International Law* (Cambridge, MA: Harvard University Press, 2016); Lauren Benton, "From International Law to Imperial Constitutions: The Problem of Quasi-sovereignty, 1870–1900," *Law and History Review* 26, no. 3 (2008): 595–619; Benton, "Introduction to AHR Forum: Law and Empire in Global Perspective," *American Historical Review* 117 (2012): 1094. These codification projects played out in surprising ways. British imperial constitutional codification in India, for example, worked as a stimulus and model for codification in the metropole. Elizabeth Kolsky, "Codification and the Rule of Colonial Difference: Criminal Procedure in British India," *Law and History Review* 23, no. 3 (2005): 631–83.

45. Burbank and Cooper, *Empires in World History*; Pitts, *Boundaries of the International*; Gerrit Gong, *The Standard of "Civilization" in International Society* (New York: Oxford University Press, 1984); Karen Barkey, *Empire of Difference: The Ottomans in Comparative Perspective* (New York: Cambridge University Press, 2008). On the 1860s as a global moment of the territorialization and reconstruction of states, see Maier, *Leviathan 2.0*, chap. 2; and Charles S. Maier, "Consigning the Twentieth Century to History: Alternative Narratives for the Modern Era," *American Historical Review* 105, no. 3 (2000): 807–31; Linda Colley, *The Gun, the Ship, and the Pen: Warfare, Constitutions, and the Making of the Modern World* (New York: Liveright, 2021), chap. 7; Michael Geyer and Charles Bright, "Global Violence and Nationalizing Wars in Eurasia and America: The Geopolitics of War in the Mid-Nineteenth Century," *Comparative Studies in Society and History* 38, no. 4 (1996): 619–57; and on integration, comparison, connectivity, and temporality, see Vanessa Ogle, *The Global Transformation of Time, 1870–1950* (Cambridge, MA: Harvard University Press, 2015); Sebastian Conrad, " 'Nothing Is the Way It Should Be': Global Transformations of the Time Regime in the Nineteenth Century," *Modern Intellectual History* 15, no. 3 (2018): 821–48. For new research on Austria-Hungary in a world of empires, see Alison Frank, "The Children of the Desert and the Laws of the Sea: Austria, Great Britain, the Ottoman Empire, and the Mediterranean Slave Trade in the Nineteenth Century," *American Historical Review* 117, no. 2 (2012): 410–44.

46. Anghie, *Imperialism, Sovereignty*, 33. Koskenniemi, *Gentle Civilizer of Nations*; Mónica García-Salmones Rovira, *The Project of Positivism in International Law* (Oxford: Oxford University Press, 2013). For an overview of these method debates focused on Germany in this period, see Michael Stolleis, *Public Law in Germany, 1800–1914* (New York: Berghahn Books, 2001), 315–53. As part of these transitions, international lawyers were also increasingly employed in the service of the state, often taking over as diplomatic practitioners and wielding significant influence in the halls of government. See Marcus Payk, *Frieden durch Recht? Der Aufstieg des modernen Völkerrechts und der Friedenschluss*

nach dem Ersten Weltkrieg (Oldenbourg: De Gruyter, 2018); Isabel Hull, *A Scrap of Paper: Breaking and Making International Law during the Great War* (Ithaca, NY: Cornell University Press, 2014). Though this book largely focuses on jurists working as scholars, many of them (for example, Hans Kelsen, Josef Redlich, and Heinrich Lammasch) also served in government roles at different moments, especially during the war.

47. Georg Jellinek, *Ueber Staatsfragmente* (Heidelberg: Gustav Koester, 1896), 11, 25, 29–30.

48. Ludwig Gumplowicz, *Das Oesterreichische Staatsrecht (Verfassungs- und Verwaltungsrecht): Ein Lehr- und Handbuch* (Vienna: Manz'sche, 1891), 48.

49. Judson, *Habsburg Empire*; Deak, *Forging a Multinational State*; Gary B. Cohen, "Nationalist Politics and the Dynamics of State and Civil Society in the Habsburg Monarchy, 1867–1914," *Central European History* 40 (2007): 241–78; Laurence Cole and Daniel Unowsky, eds., *The Limits of Loyalty: Imperial Symbolism, Popular Allegiances, and State Patriotism in the Late Habsburg Monarchy* (New York: Berghahn Books, 2007); Tamara Scheer, "Language Diversity and Loyalty in the Habsburg Army, 1868–1918" (habil., University of Vienna, 2020). For studies of the backwardness paradigm, see Maria Todorova, *Imagining the Balkans* (New York: Oxford University Press, 2009); Larry Wolff, *Inventing Eastern Europe: The Map of Civilization on the Mind of the Enlightenment* (Stanford, CA: Stanford University Press, 1994).

50. Burbank and Cooper, *Empires in World History*, 16–17 and passim. Moreover, as Sheldon Pollock has written about related interpretive problems, "There is no shame in premodernity." Sheldon Pollock, "Pretextures of Time," *History and Theory* 46 (2007): 366–83. On the modernity of multinational empire, see also Prendergast, "Sociological Idea of the State"; Benno Gammerl, *Subjects, Citizens and Others: Administering Ethnic Heterogeneity in the British and Habsburg Empires, 1867–1918*, trans. Jennifer Walcoff Neuheiser (New York: Berghahn, 2018).

51. For a related but revealingly contrasting example of scrambled tradition-modernity timelines, see Christopher Clark's brilliant analysis of consciously artificial coronation rituals in chapter 1 of *Time and Power: Visions of History in German Politics, from the Thirty Years' War to the Third Reich* (Princeton, NJ: Princeton University Press, 2019).

52. Reinhart Koselleck, *Preußen zwischen Reform und Revolution: Allgemeines Landrecht, Verwaltung und soziale Bewegung von 1791 bis 1848* (Stuttgart: Ernst Klett, 1967). Koselleck developed this theme over the course of his whole career, preoccupied with how all novelty depended on "structures of repetition" that made it possible and visible. Law and language constituted perhaps his two favorite examples of these structures of repetition. Reinhart Koselleck, "Wiederholungsstrukturen in Sprache und Geschichte," in *Vom Sinn und Unsinn der Geschichte: Aufsätze und Vorträge aus vier Jahrzehnten*, ed. Carsten Dutt (Berlin: Suhrkamp Verlag, 2010); Koselleck, "Was sich wiederholt," *Frankfurter Allgemeine Zeitung*, July 21, 2005, 6; Koselleck, "History, Law, and Justice," in *Sediments of Time: On Possible Histories*, trans. and ed. Sean Franzel and Stefan-Ludwig Hoffmann (Stanford, CA: Stanford University Press, 2018), 117–36. On the things law does with time, see Natasha Wheatley, "Law and the Time of Angels: International Law's Method Wars and the Affective Life of Disciplines," *History and Theory* 60, no. 2 (2021): 311–30.

53. Arno Mayer, *The Persistence of the Old Regime: Europe to the Great War* (London: Verso, 1981).

54. Law has featured only marginally, if at all, in the rich literature on fin de siècle Vienna despite its emphasis on cross-field fertilization and exchange. For significant exceptions, see Johannes Feichtinger's *Wissenschaft als reflexives Projekt. Von Bolzano über Freud zu Kelsen: Österreichische Wissenschaftsgeschichte 1848–1938* (Bielefeld: Transcript Verlag, 2010); Clemens Jabloner, "Kelsen and His Circle: The Viennese Years," *European Journal of International Law* 9 (1998): 368–85. See further chapter 6 of this book. There

is an especially riveting comparison to be made between law and climate science, which, as Deborah Coen shows, was a way of thinking unity and diversity at once. Deborah R. Coen, *Climate in Motion: Science, Empire, and the Problem of Scale* (Chicago: University of Chicago Press, 2018).

55. For example, Börries Kuzmany, "Non-territorial Autonomy in Interwar European Minority Protection and Its Habsburg Legacies," in *Remaking Central Europe: The League of Nations and the Former Habsburg Lands*, ed. Peter Becker and Natasha Wheatley (Oxford: Oxford University Press, 2020); Ephraim Nimni, "Nationalist Multiculturalism in Late Imperial Austria as a Critique of Contemporary Liberalism: The Case of Bauer and Renner," *Journal of Political Ideologies* 4, no. 3 (1999): 289–314.

56. In his memoirs, Mises reflected that the fact that "state and nation did not coincide in Austria pushed one to study problems that one could not so easily observe in the nation-states." Ludwig von Mises, *Erinnerungen* (Stuttgart: Fischer, 1978), 16. It was in the context of Austria-Hungary's structural questions that Friedrich von Hayek first "played with constitutional reform," wondering if a "double government, a cultural and an economic government," would solve "the conflict between nationalities." See "Nobel Prize–Winning Economist," oral history interview with Friedrich A. von Hayek, Oral History Program, UCLA, 1983, 46, https://archive.org/details/nobelprizewinnin00haye/page/n7/mode/2up. Quinn Slobodian unearthed this rich contextualization for neoliberal thought in *Globalists: The End of Empire and the Birth of Neoliberalism* (Cambridge, MA: Harvard University Press, 2018), esp. 104–12.

57. See, for example, Adam Mestyan, "A Muslim Dualism? Inter-imperial History and Austria-Hungary in Ottoman Thought, 1867–1921," *Contemporary European History* 30, no. 4 (2021): 478–96; Kavita Saraswathi Datla, "Sovereignty and the End of Empire: The Transition to Independence in Colonial Hyderabad," *Ab Imperio* 3 (2018): 76; Arthur Griffith, *The Resurrection of Hungary: A Parallel for Ireland*, 3rd ed. (1904; Dublin: Whelan and Son, 1918). Griffith was the founder of Sinn Fein.

58. Gunther Teubner, "Globale Bukowina: Zur Emergenz eines transnationalen Rechtspluralismus," *Rechtshistorisches Journal* 15 (1996): 255–90; Teubner, "Global Bukovina: Legal Pluralism in the World Society," in *Global Law without a State*, ed. Gunther Teubner (Aldershot: Dartmouth, 1997), 3–28. For other contemporary deployments of Ehrlich's thought, see David Nelken, "Eugen Ehrlich, Living Law, and Plural Legalities," *Theoretical Inquiries into Law* 9 (2008): 443–71; Ralf Michaels, "The Re-state-ment of Non-state Law: The State, Choice of Law, and the Challenge from Global Legal Pluralism," *Wayne Law Review* 51 (2005): 1209–59; Brian Z. Tamanaha, "A Non-essentialist Version of Legal Pluralism," *Journal of Law and Society* 27, no. 2 (2000): 296–321.

59. For but a few examples, see Larry Wolff, "How to Save the European Union," *Washington Post*, July 6, 2018, https://www.washingtonpost.com/news/made-by-history/wp/2018/07/06/how-to-save-the-european-union/; Helen Thompson, "The Habsburg Myth and the European Union," in *Europe's Malaise: The Long View*, ed. Francesco Duina and Frederic Merand (Bingley, UK: Emerald Group Publishing, 2020), 45–66; Stephen G. Gross and S. Chase Gummer, "Ghosts of the Habsburg Empire: Collapsing Currency Unions and Lessions for the Eurozone," *East European Politics and Societies* 28, no. 1 (2014): 252–65.

60. This is not true in the same way for German-language scholarship. See Jana Osterkamp, *Vielfalt ordnen: Das föderale Europea der Habsburgermonarchie (Vormärz bis 1918)* (Göttingen: Vandenhoeck & Ruprecht, 2020); Peter Becker, "Der Staat: Eine österreichische Geschichte?," *Mitteilungen des Instituts für Österreichische Geschichtsforschung* 126, no. 2 (2018): 317–40; Martin P. Schennach, ed., *Rechtshistorische Aspekte des österreichischen Föderalismus* (Vienna: Verlag Österreich, 2015); Gerald Stourzh, *Der Umfang der österreichischen Geschichte* (Vienna: Böhlau Verlag, 2011); *Die Habsburgermonarchie 1848–1918*, vol. 7, *Verfassung und Parlamentarismus*, ed. Helmut Rumpler and Peter

Urbanitsch (Vienna: Verlag der österreichischen Akademie der Wissenschaften, 2000), especially the contributions by Stourzh and Hans Peter Hye. For related research on the fate and afterlives of the Polish-Lithuanian Commonwealth, see Timothy Snyder, *The Reconstruction of Nations: Poland, Ukraine, Lithuania, Belarus, 1569–1999* (New Haven, CT: Yale University Press, 2003): "States, no less than nations, exist in time" (4).

61. James Sheehan, "The Problem of Sovereignty in European History," *American Historical Review* 111, no. 1 (2006): 3, 4 (and generally).

62. For a sweeping new history of East-Central European nationalisms, see John Connelly, *Peoples into Nations: A History of Eastern Europe* (Princeton, NJ: Princeton University Press, 2020). On the historical and methodological significance of those who remained "indifferent" to nationalism, see works by Tara Zahra, Pieter Judson, and Jeremy King, cited above.

63. Friedrich Engels, *Po and Rhine* (Berlin: Franz Dunder, 1859), in *Karl Marx, Friedrich Engels: Collected Works*, trans. Richard Dixon and others (New York: International Publishers, 1975), 16:254; Friedrich Engels, "The Magyar Struggle," *Neue Rheinische Zeitung*, no. 194 (January 13, 1849), in *Collected Works*, 8:235.

64. Friedrich Engels, "Democratic Panslavism," *Neue Rheinische Zeitung*, nos. 222 and 223, February 15 and 16, 1849, in *Collected Works*, 8:367. This string of *NRZ* articles rebuking *geschichtslosen Völker* were penned by Engels at Marx's request and published under Marx's name. The Ukrainian Marxist Roman Rosdolsky wrote perhaps the most systematic treatment of this topic: *Engels and the "Nonhistoric" Peoples: The National Question in the Revolution of 1848*, trans. and ed. John-Paul Himka (Glasgow: Critique Books, 1986).

65. Rosa Luxemburg softened but largely agreed with Engels's views: "The idea of insuring all 'nations' the possibility of self-determination is equivalent to reverting from Great-Capitalist development to the small medieval states." Rosa Luxemburg, *The National Question: Selected Writings by Rosa Luxemburg*, ed. Horace B. Davis (New York: Monthly Review Press, 1976), 130. The Austro-Marxists, while still referring to historical and nonhistorical people, pioneered a different approach; see Otto Bauer, *The Question of Nationalities and Social Democracy*, trans. Joseph O'Donnell (1907; Minneapolis: University of Minnesota Press, 2000), as well as chapter 3 of this book. For Karl Renner's analysis of how these legal and national formations related to the history of class, see Rudolf Springer [Karl Renner], *Grundlagen und Entwicklungsziele der Österreichisch-Ungarischen Monarchie* (Vienna: Franz Deuticke, 1906), 47–55.

66. In his preinvasion statement, Putin emphasized that Ukraine was "entirely created by Russia" after the communist revolution in 1917, a policy he now saw as "worse than a mistake": "Why was it necessary to appease the nationalists, to satisfy the ceaselessly growing nationalist ambitions on the outskirts of the former empire?" "In reality, the union republics did not have any sovereign rights" in the USSR; through to today, "Ukraine actually never had stable traditions of real statehood. And, therefore, in 1991 it opted for mindlessly emulating foreign models, which have no relation to history or Ukrainian realities." Vladimir Putin, "Address of the President of the Russian Federation," February 21, 2022, http://en.kremlin.ru/events/president/news/67828.

67. Margaret MacMillan, *Paris 1919: Six Months That Changed the World* (New York: Random House, 2001), 121.

68. A new generation of scholars are busy undoing that story. For studies that explore Habsburg afterlives and legacies in the successor states, see Judson, *Habsburg Empire*, especially the epilogue; Dominique Kirchner Reill, *The Fiume Crisis: Life in the Wake of the Habsburg Empire* (Cambridge, MA: Harvard University Press, 2020); Paul Miller and Clare Morelon, eds., *Embers of Empire: Continuity and Rupture in the Habsburg Successor States after 1918* (New York: Berghahn Books, 2018); Gábor Egry, "The Empire's New Clothes: How Austria-Hungary's Legacy Kept the Successor States Running," Foundation for Austrian Studies, Leiden, Annual Lecture 2020, http://real.mtak.hu/id/eprint/141411;

Dominique Kirchner Reill, Ivan Jeličić, and Francesca Rolandi, "Redefining Citizenship after Empire: The Rights to Welfare, to Work, and to Remain in a Post-Habsburg World," *Journal of Modern History* 94, no. 2 (2022): 326–62; Franz Adlgasser and Fredrik Lindström, eds., *The Habsburg Civil Service and Beyond: Bureaucracy and Civil Servants from the Vormärz to the Inter-war Years* (Vienna: Verlag der Österriechischen Akadamie der Wissenschaften, 2018); Tomasz Pudłocki and Kamil Ruszała, eds., *Postwar Continuity and New Challenges in Central and Eastern Europe, 1918–1923: The War That Never Ended* (Abingdon: Routledge, 2022); Iryna Vushko, *The Lost Fatherland: Europeans between Empire and Nation States, 1867–1939* (New Haven, CT: Yale University Press, forthcoming). For explorations of the implications and afterlives for *international* order, see Patricia Clavin, "The Austrian Hunger Crisis and the Genesis of International Organization after the First World War," *International Affairs* 90, no. 2 (2014): 265–78; Natasha Wheatley, "Central Europe as Ground Zero of the New International Order," *Slavic Review* 78, no. 4 (2019): 900–911; Peter Becker and Natasha Wheatley, eds., *Remaking Central Europe: The League of Nations and the Former Habsburg Lands* (Oxford: Oxford University Press, 2020).

69. New ways of connecting stories of the ends of empire in Europe and in the wider world are now emerging into view. For parallel inquiries, focused on different themes, see James Mark and Quinn Slobodian, "Eastern Europe in the Global History of Decolonization," in *The Oxford Handbook of the Ends of Empire*, ed. Martin Thomas and Andrew Thompson (Oxford: Oxford University Press, 2018), 351–72; Slobodian, *Globalists*; James Mark and Paul Betts, coordinators, *Socialism Goes Global: The Soviet Union and Eastern Europe in the Age of Decolonization* (Oxford: Oxford University Press, 2022); Ntina Tzouvala, "'These Ancient Arenas of Racial Struggles': International Law and the Balkans, 1878–1949," *European Journal of International Law* 29, no. 4 (2018): 1149–71; Jamie Martin, *The Meddlers: Sovereignty, Empire, and the Birth of Global Economic Governance* (Cambridge, MA: Harvard University Press, 2022); Malgorzata Mazurek, *Economics of Hereness: The Polish Origins of Developmentalism (1918–1968)* (Ithaca, NY: Cornell University Press, under contract).

70. See Peter Holquist, Review of *Imperial Apocalypse: The Great War and the Destruction of the Russian Empire* by Joshua A. Sanborn, *Slavic Review* 74, no. 3 (2015): 602; cf. Sanborn's portrayal of the Russian experience of war and revolution as one of decolonization: Joshua A. Sanborn, *Imperial Apocalypse: The Great War and the Destruction of the Russian Empire* (Oxford: Oxford University Press, 2014).

71. Holly Case writes memorably of sovereignty turned "inside out" in a different sense in "The Quiet Revolution: Consuls and the International System in the Nineteenth Century," in *The Balkans as Europe, 1821–1914*, ed. Timothy Snyder and Katherine Younger (Rochester, NY: University of Rochester Press, 2018), 110–38.

72. Czechoslovak Delegation, Peace Conference, *Mémoires*, Mémoire No. 2: Territorial Claims of the Czecho-Slovak Republic [1919].

73. Deutschösterreichiche Delegation, Note über die internationale Rechtspersönlichkeit Deutschösterreichs, June 16, 1919, Beilage 29, in *Bericht über die Tätigkeit der Deutsch-österreichischen Friedensdelegation in St. Germain-en-Laye* (Vienna: Deutschösterreichische Staatsdruckerei, 1919).

74. R. P. Anand, "Editor's Introduction," in *Asian States and the Development of Universal International Law*, ed. R. P. Anand (Delhi: Vikas Publications, 1972), xvii (emphasis in original).

75. Carl Schmitt, *Political Theology: Four Chapters on the Concept of Sovereignty*, trans. George Schwab (1922, 1934; Cambridge, MA: MIT Press, 1985). For a cogent and succinct introduction to the history of the concept of sovereignty, see Dieter Grimm, *Sovereignty: The Origin and Future of a Political and Legal Concept* (New York: Columbia University Press, 2015).

76. The phrase here is from Schmitt, *Political Theology*, 32.

77. Jacques Derrida, "Force of Law: The 'Mystical Foundation of Authority,'" trans. Mary Quaintance, *Cardozo Law Review* 11 (1989–90): 911–93.

78. Wendy Brown, *Walled States, Waning Sovereignty* (New York: Zone Books, 2010), 66 (and see chap. 2). On the deep entangling of sovereignty and colonialism with questions of historical periodization, see Kathleen Davis, *Periodization and Sovereignty: How Ideas of Feudalism and Secularization Govern the Politics of Time* (Philadelphia: University of Pennsylvania Press, 2008).

79. Jellinek, *Allgemeine Staatslehre*, 270.

80. Ernst Kantorowicz, *The King's Two Bodies: A Study in Mediaeval Political Theology* (1957; Princeton, NJ: Princeton University Press, 1997), 284.

81. For Hobbes, see Quentin Skinner, *From Hobbes to Humanism: Studies in Rhetoric and Politics* (Cambridge: Cambridge University Press, 2018), 365.

82. Quentin Skinner, "The Sovereign State: A Genealogy," in *Sovereignty in Fragments: The Past, Present and Future of a Contested Concept*, ed. Hent Kalmo and Quentin Skinner (Cambridge: Cambridge University Press, 2010), 46; see also 34–37.

83. "Sie tritt mit dem Anspruch auf, *ewig* zu gelten." Kelsen, *Allgemeine Staatslehre*, 148 (emphasis in original).

84. Kelsen, 148; and see earlier Hans Kelsen, *Der soziologische und der juristische Staatsbegriff: Kritische Untersuchungen des Verhältnisses von Staat und Recht* (Tübingen: J. C. B. Mohr, 1922), 85.

85. "sogenannten 'Wilden.'" In this passage Kunz was critiquing theories of recognition that would leave Austria as an "international-law Nothing" between the end of Habsburg sovereignty and the Allied recognition of the Republic of Austria. Josef Kunz, *Die Anerkennung von Staaten und Regierungen im Völkerrecht* (Stuttgart: Kohlkammer, 1928), 89.

86. Kelsen's first exposition of what would become the *Grundnorm* occurred in his analysis of the competing priority of land law and imperial law: Kelsen, "Reichsgesetz und Landesgesetz nach österreichischer Verfassung," *Archiv des öffentlichen Rechts* 32 (1914): 202–45, 390–438. Other scholars have highlighted this direct imperial-constitutional derivation: Manfred Baldus, "Hapsburgian Multiethnicity and the 'Unity of the State'—On the Structural Setting of Kelsen's Legal Thought," in *Hans Kelsen and Carl Schmitt: A Juxtaposition*, ed. Dan Diner and Michael Stolleis (Gerlingen: Bleicher, 1999), 13–25; Thomas Olechowski, *Hans Kelsen: Biographie eines Rechtswissenschftlers* (Tübingen: Mohr Siebeck, 2020). See chapter 6 of this book.

87. Josef L. Kunz, "On the Theoretical Basis of the Law of Nations," *Transactions of the Grotius Society* 10 (1924): 140.

88. Hans Blumenberg, *The Legitimacy of the Modern Age*, trans. Robert M. Wallace (Cambridge, MA: MIT Press, 1985).

89. This approach aligns with, but also extends or makes more specific, framings of sovereignty as a *claim* or an *argument*. For the former, see Sheehan, "The Problem of Sovereignty in European History"; and the latter, Hent Kalmo and Quentin Skinner, "Introduction: A Concept in Fragments," in *Sovereignty in Fragments: The Past, Present and Future of a Contested Concept*, ed. Hent Kalmo and Quentin Skinner (Cambridge: Cambridge University Press, 2010), 1–25, as well as Christoph Möllers, *Der Staat als Argument* (Munich: C. H. Beck, 2000). See also Jeremy Adelman, *Sovereignty and Revolution in the Iberian Atlantic* (Princeton, NJ: Princeton University Press, 2009), 2n2: "The quest to define it [sovereignty] has been a motor force of international and infranational conflict."

90. Hans Blumenberg, *Paradigms for a Metaphorology*, trans. Robert Savage (1960; Ithaca, NY: Cornell University Press, 2010), 3, 4 ("metaphorology seeks to burrow down to the substructure of thought, the underground, the nutrient solution of systematic crystallizations," 5); Blumenberg, "Prospect for a Theory of Nonconceptuality," included in Hans

Blumenberg, *Shipwreck with Spectator: Paradigm of a Metaphor for Existence*, trans. Steven Rendall (1979; Cambridge, MA: MIT Press, 1997), 81–102.

91. I thus take the opposite methodological approach to Jana Osterkamp's wonderful book: having likewise observed that existing nineteenth-century categories of state did not fit Habsburg realities, she argues that *we* should understand it as federalism, even if her historical protagonists did not. Rather than try to "correct" or improve on the theorizations of the historical figures, my interest lies precisely in their difficulty finding an adequate conceptualization of state and sovereignty in the Habsburg lands. See Osterkamp, *Vielfalt ordnen*. For pioneering work (influential for my own approach) on the emotions, needs, and desires shaping the history of international law, see Nathaniel Berman, *Passion and Ambivalence: Colonialism, Nationalism, and International Law* (Leiden: Martinus Nijhoff, 2012); Sundhya Pahuja, *Decolonising International Law: Development, Economic Growth and the Politics of Universality* (Cambridge: Cambridge University Press, 2011); Samuel Moyn, *The Last Utopia: Human Rights in History* (Cambridge, MA: Harvard University Press, 2010); Lori Allen, *A History of False Hope: Investigative Commissions in Palestine* (Stanford, CA: Stanford University Press, 2020). In a parallel vein, note creative new work on sovereignty's aesthetic and affective underpinnings: Zvi Ben-Dor Benite, Stefanos Geroulanos, and Nicole Jerr, ed., *The Scaffolding of Sovereignty: Global and Aesthetic Perspectives on the History of a Concept* (New York: Columbia University Press, 2017).

92. See Samuel Moyn, "Imaginary Intellectual History," in *Rethinking Modern European Intellectual History*, ed. Darrin McMahon and Samuel Moyn (New York: Oxford University Press, 2014), 112–30; and for a recent discussion of theory and practice in international legal history, Benton and Ford, *Rage for Order*.

Chapter One: Constitution as Archive

1. Franz Schuselka, *Das provisorische Österreich* (Leipzig: Grunow, 1850), 17.

2. Schuselka, 18.

3. Eric Voegelin, *The Collected Works of Eric Voegelin*, vol. 4, *The Authoritarian State: An Essay on the Problem of the Austrian State*, trans. Ruth Hein, ed. Gilbert Weiss (Columbia: University of Missouri Press, 1999). First published as *Der autoritäre Staat: Ein Versuch über das österreichische Staatsproblem* (Vienna: Springer, 1936).

4. Voegelin, *The Authoritarian State*, 141.

5. Voegelin, 142.

6. On older forms of legitimization and political communication, often articulated through ritual and symbol, see famously Barbara Stollberg-Rilinger, *The Emperor's Old Clothes: Constitutional History and the Symbolic Language of the Holy Roman Empire*, trans. Thomas Dunlap (New York: Berghahn, 2015). For a sweeping survey of the region-wide "proliferation of theories regarding the reorganization of empires" in this period, see Balázs Trencsényi, Maciej Janowski, Monika Baár, Maria Falina, and Michal Kopeček, *A History of Modern Political Thought in East Central Europe* (Oxford: Oxford University Press, 2016), 1:281–317.

7. František Palacký, *Politisches Vermächtniss*, 2nd ed. (Prague: Theodor Mourek, 1872), 15. On Palacký, see Jiří Kořalka, *František Palacký (1798–1876): Der Historiker der Tschechen im österreichischen Vielvölkerstaat* (Vienna: Verlag der Österreichischen Akademie der Wissenschaften, 2007); Monika Baár, *Historians and Nationalism: East-Central Europe in the Nineteenth Century* (Oxford: Oxford University Press, 2010).

8. On unrest and reform movements leading up to and driving the revolution, see Pieter Judson, *Exclusive Revolutionaries: Liberal Politics, Social Experience, and National Identity in the Austrian Empire, 1848-1914* (Ann Arbor: University of Michigan

Press, 1996), 25ff. In a helpful summary of the revolution's major events, R. J. W. Evans argues that the revolutions were not only longer but also more disruptive in the Habsburg lands than in any other European state: R. J. W. Evans, "1848–1849 in the Habsburg Monarchy," in *The Revolutions in Europe, 1848–1849: From Reform to Reaction*, ed. R. J. W. Evans and Hartmut Pogge von Strandmann (Oxford: Oxford University Press, 2000), 181–206. For a thorough exploration of the social conditions and questions at the heart of the revolution, see Wolfgang Häusler, *Von der Massenartmut zur Arbeiterbewegung: Demokratie und soziale Frage in der Wiener Revolution von 1848* (Vienna: Jugend und Volk, 1979). Heinrich Reschauer provides a detailed account of the revolutionary "March days" in *Das Jahr 1848: Geschichte der Wiener Revolution* (Vienna: Verlag von R. v. Waldheim, 1872) while Anton Springer's classic work extends beyond the capitals to cover the revolutionary movement in the regions and smaller cities as well: *Geschichte Österreichs seit dem Wiener Frieden 1809* (Leipzig: G. Hirzel, 1865), 2:135ff. (and for regional developments, especially 365ff.). On the development of the revolution in the Bohemian lands, see Stanley Z. Pech, *The Czech Revolution of 1848* (Chapel Hill: University of North Carolina Press, 1969); for the quite separate unfolding of the revolution in Hungary, see Istvan Deak, *The Lawful Revolution: Louis Kossuth and the Hungarians, 1848–1948* (New York: Columbia University Press, 1979).

9. The estates central committee met between April 10 and 17 and adopted Kleyle's constitutional proposal as a resolution; it is reproduced as "Beilage V" in Karl Hugelmann, "Der ständische Zentralausschuß in Österreich im April 1848," *Jahrbuch für Landeskunde von Niederösterreich* 12 (1913): 229.

10. Hugo Hantsch, *Die Geschichte Österreichs*, 2nd ed. (Graz: Verlag Styria, 1952), 2:343 (*Zauberwort, Zauberstab*).

11. Kleyle in "Beilage V" of Hugelmann, "Der ständische Zentralausschuß," 229.

12. Österreichische Verfassung vom 25. April 1848, Politische Gesetzsammlung LXXVI, Nr. 49, in Edmund Bernatzik, *Die österreichischen Verfassungsgesetze mit Erläuterung*, 2nd ed. (Vienna: Manzsche, 1911), 102–9. This centralist constitution did not apply to Hungary, affirming its separateness; the other lands were treated merely as "provinces" and denied participation in lawmaking. On the Pillersdorf constitution, see Karl Hugelmann, "Die Entwicklung der Aprilverfassung von 1848," *Jahrbuch für Landeskunde von Niederösterreich* 17–18 (1918–1919): 235–78.

13. See Kaiserl. Proklamation vom 8 Mai 1848, PGS. Nr. 57, and Kaiserl. Proklamation vom 16 Mai 1848, PGS. Nr. 65, text of both proclamations in Bernatzik, *Die österreichischen Verfassungsgesetze*, 110 and 111, respectively.

14. Hantsch, *Geschichte Österreichs*, 352.

15. On the ambiguous legal status of the new parliament, viz., royal power, see Ronald Bacher, "Volkssouveränität oder monarchisches Prinzip? Zur rechtlichen Grundlage des österreichischen Reichstages von 1848/49," *Innsbrucker Historische Studien* 10/11 (1988): 201–22.

16. Kaiserl. Patent vom 2. Dezember 1848, RGBl. Nr. 1 ex 1849, in Bernatzik, *Die österreichischen Verfassungsgesetze*, 113–14 (here 113).

17. Springer, *Geschichte Österreichs seit dem Wiener Frieden*, 614.

18. Ludwig Gumplowicz, *Einleitung in das Staatsrecht* (Berlin: Carl Heymanns Verlag, 1889), 208.

19. A second subcommittee was tasked with preparing an initial proposal on fundamental civil rights. For its deliberations, see Alfred von Fischel, *Die Protokolle des Verfassungsausschusses über die Grundrechte: Ein Beitrag zur Geschichte des österreichischen Reichstags vom Jahre 1848* (Vienna: Gerlach und Wiedling, 1912).

20. Anton Springer, "Vorbericht," in *Protokolle des Verfassungs-Ausschusses im Österreichischen Reichstag 1848–1849*, ed. Anton Springer (Leipzig: G. Hirzel, 1885), 3–8;

Andreas Gottsmann, *Der Reichstag von Kremsier und die Regierung Schwarzenberg: Die Verfassungsdiskussion des Jahres 1848 im Spannungsfeld zwischen Reaktion und nationaler Frage* (Vienna: Verlag für Geschichte und Politik, 1995), 48–49; Paula Geist-Lányi, *Das Nationalitätenproblem auf dem Reichstag zu Kremsier, 1848/1849: Ein Beitrag zur Geschichte der Nationalitäten in Österreich* (Munich: Drei Masken Verlag, 1920), 144 and passim.

21. Josef Redlich, "Die Originalprotokolle des Verfassungsausschusses im Kremsier Reichstag," *Österreichische Rundschau* 17 (1908): 163.

22. "Nicht als Rechtquelle, wohl aber als Quelle von Rechtsideen," as the constitutional historian Franz Hauke phrased it in his text: "Verfassungsgeschichte," in *Österreichisches Staatswörterbuch: Handbuch des gesamten österreichischen öffentlichen Rechtes*, ed. Ernst Mischler and Josef Ulbrich, 2nd ed. (Vienna: Alfred Hölder, 1909), 4:725.

23. *Protokolle des Verfassungs-Ausschusses im Österreichischen Reichstag 1848–1849*, ed. Anton Springer (Leipzig: G. Hirzel, 1885), 12.

24. *Protokolle des Verfassungs-Ausschusses*, 13.

25. *Protokolle des Verfassungs-Ausschusses*, 12.

26. *Protokolle des Verfassungs-Ausschusses*, 13, 14.

27. *Protokolle des Verfassungs-Ausschusses*, 15.

28. *Protokolle des Verfassungs-Ausschusses*, 15–16.

29. "*Constitutionswerks.*" *Protokolle des Verfassungs-Ausschusses*, 16.

30. *Protokolle des Verfassungs-Ausschusses*, 17.

31. *Protokolle des Verfassungs-Ausschusses*, 19. Turco stated further that those from Trient could only then be loyal Austrians, when they were granted independence (within the empire).

32. *Protokolle des Verfassungs-Ausschusses*, 19–20 (quotation on 19).

33. *Protokolle des Verfassungs-Ausschusses*, 20.

34. *Protokolle des Verfassungs-Ausschusses*, 21.

35. *Protokolle des Verfassungs-Ausschusses*, 21.

36. *Protokolle des Verfassungs-Ausschusses*, 21.

37. *Protokolle des Verfassungs-Ausschusses*, 22.

38. *Protokolle des Verfassungs-Ausschusses*, 22.

39. *Protokolle des Verfassungs-Ausschusses*, 22.

40. Franz [František] Palacký, *Geschichte von Böhmen*, 5 vols. (Prague: In Commission bei Kronberger und Weber, 1836ff.).

41. *Protokolle des Verfassungs-Ausschusses*, 23.

42. "Es geht ein Kraft durch die Welt, man nennt sie den Weltgeist." *Protokolle des Verfassungs-Ausschusses*, 26.

43. *Protokolle des Verfassungs-Ausschusses*, 29.

44. "Er wolle sich übrigens gar nicht erst auf den historischen Boden stellen, denn man wisse am Ende nicht, wo die Historie anfange, und wo sie aufhöre—vielleicht bei Pilatus, der zu Folge einer alten Sage einmal in den Bodensee gesprungen sein soll?" When Josef Redlich uncovered the original Kremsier minutes in the early twentieth century, he identified a few short passages that were not included in Springer's published 1885 edition of the *Protokolle*. This quotation, from the committee meeting of January 24, is one such passage, reproduced in Redlich, "Die Originalprotokolle des Verfassungsausschusses im Kremsier Reichstag," 175.

45. *Protokolle des Verfassungs-Ausschusses*, 36.

46. *Protokolle des Verfassungs-Ausschusses*, 30.

47. *Protokolle des Verfassungs-Ausschusses*, 32.

48. *Protokolle des Verfassungs-Ausschusses*, 32 (emphasis added).

49. *Protokolle des Verfassungs-Ausschusses*, 33.

50. *Protokolle des Verfassungs-Ausschusses*, 34 (emphasis added).

51. *Protokolle des Verfassungs-Ausschusses*, 35.

52. *Protokolle des Verfassungs-Ausschusses*, 37.

53. *Protokolle des Verfassungs-Ausschusses*, 38.

54. *Protokolle des Verfassungs-Ausschusses*, 38.

55. *Protokolle des Verfassungs-Ausschusses*, 39.

56. *Protokolle des Verfassungs-Ausschusses*, 42.

57. *Protokolle des Verfassungs-Ausschusses*, 42.

58. *Protokolle des Verfassungs-Ausschusses*, 42.

59. *Protokolle des Verfassungs-Ausschusses*, 42.

60. *Protokolle des Verfassungs-Ausschusses*, 43.

61. See C. A. Macartney, *National States and National Minorities* (Oxford: Oxford University Press, 1934), 144–45.

62. *Protokolle des Verfassungs-Ausschusses*, 45–46.

63. Made famous by Reinhart Koselleck, "Gleichzeitigkeit des Ungleichzeitigens" was first coined by the German Marxist philosopher Ernst Bloch in 1932 in an attempt to capture the temporal complexity of Nazism, looking both forward and back in time. See Ernst Bloch, "Nonsynchronism and the Obligation to Its Dialectics," *New German Critique* 11 (1977): 22–38. The essay was originally written in 1932 and published in his book *Erbshaft dieser Zeit* in 1935. In Koselleck's hands, it captured the heterogeneity of modern time, moving beyond either synchrony or diachrony to allow for the various temporal extensions and the "diversity of temporal strata" of "varying duration" that can exist in the same chronological moment. See Reinhart Koselleck, *Futures Past: On the Semantics of Historical Time*, trans. Keith Tribe (Cambridge, MA: MIT Press, 1985).

64. *Protokolle des Verfassungs-Ausschusses*, 67.

65. *Protokolle des Verfassungs-Ausschusses*, 67.

66. *Protokolle des Verfassungs-Ausschusses*, 68.

67. *Protokolle des Verfassungs-Ausschusses*, 117.

68. *Protokolle des Verfassungs-Ausschusses*, 117.

69. *Protokolle des Verfassungs-Ausschusses*, 117.

70. *Protokolle des Verfassungs-Ausschusses*, 118.

71. *Protokolle des Verfassungs-Ausschusses*, 124.

72. *Protokolle des Verfassungs-Ausschusses*, 303 (emphasis added).

73. On the petitions more broadly, see Otto Hörhan, "Die Petitionen an den Kremsierer Reichstag 1848/49" (PhD diss., University of Vienna, 1966).

74. *Protokolle des Verfassungs-Ausschusses*, 347.

75. Rudolf Schlesinger, *Federalism in Central and Eastern Europe* (London: K. Paul, Trench, Truber, 1945), 174–76.

76. Karl Tschuppik, *The Reign of the Emperor Francis Joseph, 1848–1916*, trans. C. J. S. Sprigge (London: G. Bell and Sons, 1930), 21.

77. On Stadion and the March constitution, see John Deak, *Forging a Multinational State: State Making in Imperial Austria from the Enlightenment to the First World War* (Stanford, CA: Stanford University Press, 2015), chap. 2.

78. Kaiserl. Manifest vom 4. März 1849, RGBl. Nr. 149, in Bernatzik, *Die österreichischen Verfassungsgesetze*, 147–50 (here 147).

79. "Erörterungen aus dem Gebiete der Theorie." The government had been especially aggrieved by the proposition—first presented by the subcommittee on fundamental rights and later discarded—that sovereignty proceeded from the people. Stadion insisted that hereditary dynastic right, not Volkssouveränität, was the inalienable source of state power.

80. Kaiserl. Manifest vom 4. März 1849, RGBl. Nr. 149, in Bernatzik, *Die österreichischen Verfassungsgesetze*, 148–49.

81. There had been sporadic attempts to do so; Joseph II had, for example, looked to extend Austrian judicial law over Hungary. See Christian Neschwara, "Gescheiterte Modernisierung durch Transfer: Die österreichische Rechtsfamilie und die ungarische Rechtskultur im 19. Jahrhundert," in *Dny Práva—2009—Days of Law: The Conference Proceedings*, ed. David Sehnálek, Jiří Valdhans, Radovan Dávid, and Libor Kyncl (Brno: Masaryk University, 2009), n.p.

82. In Brauneder's terms, "Staatsgbiet und Geltungsbereich" were not identical: Wilhelm Brauneder, "Der Österreich-Begriff der Pillersdorf'schen Verfassung und des Kremsierer Entwurfs," in *Bericht über den dreizehnten österreichischen Historikertag in Klagenfurt 1976*, ed. Verband Österreichische Geschichtsvereine (Vienna: Verband Österreichische Geschichtsvereine, 1977), 207.

83. Gottsmann, *Der Reichstag von Kremsier und die Regierung Schwarzenberg*, 100–102. For the constitution itself, see Reichsverfassung für das Kaiserthum Österreich (Kaiserl. Manifest vom 4. March 1849), RGBl. Nr. 150, in Bernatzik, *Die österreichischen Verfassungsgesetze*, 150–66.

84. §77, Reichsverfassung für das Kaiserthum Österreich (Kaiserl. Manifest vom 4. March 1849), RGBl. Nr. 150, in Bernatzik, *Die österreichischen Verfassungsgesetze*, 160.

85. Arnold Luschen von Ebengreuth, *Grundriss der österreichischen Reichsgeschichte: Eine Bearbeitung seines Lehrbuches der "Österreichischen Reichsgeschichte"* (Bamberg: C. C. Buchner Verlag, 1899), 341–42.

86. Gerald Stourzh, *Die Gleichberechtigung der Nationalitäten in der Verfassung und Verwaltung Österreichs, 1848–1918* (Vienna: Verlag der Österreichischen Akademie der Wissenschaften, 1985), 41.

87. On Austrian neoabsolutism, see especially Harm-Hinrich Brandt, *Der österreichische Neoabsolutismus: Staatsfinanzen und Politik, 1848–1860*, 2 vols. (Göttingen: Vandenhoeck und Ruprecht, 1978).

88. Pieter Judson, *The Habsburg Empire: A New History* (Cambridge, MA: Harvard University Press, 2016), 218–68; Judson, *Exclusive Revolutionaries*, 69ff.; Deak, *Forging a Multinational State*, chap. 3; R. J. W. Evans, "From Confederation to Compromise: The Austrian Experiment, 1849–1867," *Proceedings of the British Academy* 87 (1995): 135–67. Christopher Clark draws on Evans's work to make an analogous argument for postrevolutionary European regimes more broadly in "After 1848: The European Revolution in Government," *Transactions of the Royal Historical Society* 22 (2012): 171–97.

89. Joseph Alexander von Helfert, *Die Böhmische Frage in ihrer jüngsten Phase* (Prague: F. Tempsky, 1873), 21.

90. Paul [Pál] von Somssich, *Das legitime Recht Ungarns und seines Königs* (Vienna: Jasper, Hügel & Manz, 1850), 22.

91. N. N. [József Eötvös], *Über die Gleichberechtigung der Nationalitäten in Oesterreich* (Pest: Hartleben's Verlag, 1850), 103.

92. Schuselka, *Das provisorische Österreich*, 34.

93. Schuselka, 34–35.

94. Josef Alexander Helfert, *Oesterreich und die Nationalitäten: Ein offenes Wort an Herrn Franz Palacky* (Vienna: Carl Gerold & Sohn, 1850), 8.

95. Helfert, 19.

96. Helfert, 19.

97. Helfert, 36.

98. Denkschrift der böhmischen Abgeordneten über die von ihnen auf dem constituirenden Reichstag zu Wien und Kremsier befolgten politischen Grundsätze (1849), reproduced in Franz [František] Palacký, *Gedenkblätter: Auswahl von Denkschriften, Aufsätzen und Briefen aus den letzten fünfzig Jahren, als Beitrag zur Zeitgeschichte* (Prague: F. Tempsky, 1874), 189–205 (here 204).

99. From the Denkschrift in Palacký, *Gedenkblätter*, 204.

100. On Emperor Francis Joseph's deep ambivalence about any kind of constitution, see Fritz Fellner's important article "Das 'Februarpatent' von 1861: Entstehung und Bedeutung," *Mitteilungen des Instituts für Österreichische Geschichtsforschung* 63 (1955): 549–51.

101. See Stefan Malfèr, "Einleitung," in *Die Protokolle des Österreichischen Minister-rates, 1848–1867*, Abteilung IV, Das Ministerium Rechberg, vol. 1, 19. Mai 1859-2/3 März 1860 (Vienna: öbv & hpt, 2003), xxxvi.

102. Dessewffy to Rechberg, August 14, 1859, Haus-, Hof- und Staatsarchiv, Vienna (hereafter HHStA), Nachlaß Rechberg, Karton 527, Mappe Ungarn, fol. 1078ff.

103. See Szecsen to Rechberg, September 25, 1859, HHStA, Nachlaß Rechberg, Karton 527, Mappe Ungarn, fol. 1104–53.

104. For a succinct overview of the unfolding of these events, see Stefan Malfèr, "Der Kampf um eine Verfassung 1859–1861," in *Der österreichische Neoabsolutismus als Verfas-sungs- und Verwaltungsproblem: Diskussionen über einen strittigen Epochenbegriff*, ed. Harm-Hinrich Brandt (Vienna: Böhlau Verlag, 2014), 425–47.

105. *Verhandlungen des österreichischen verstärkten Reichsrates 1860, nach den stenog-raphischen Berichten* (Vienna: Friedrich Manz, 1860), 2:45–46.

106. *Verhandlungen des österreichischen verstärkten Reichsrates 1860*, 2:46.

107. *Verhandlungen des österreichischen verstärkten Reichsrates 1860*, 2:68.

108. *Verhandlungen des österreichischen verstärkten Reichsrates 1860*, 2:41–42.

109. *Verhandlungen des österreichischen verstärkten Reichsrates 1860*, 2:71.

110. See Koselleck, *Futures Past*, 9ff. Albrecht Altdorfer's *Die Alexanderschlacht* (1529) is reproduced as a frontispiece in the book.

111. *Verhandlungen des österreichischen verstärkten Reichsrates 1860*, 2:74.

112. *Verhandlungen des österreichischen verstärkten Reichsrates 1860*, 2:76.

113. *Verhandlungen des österreichischen verstärkten Reichsrates 1860*, 2:79.

114. Kais. Manifest vom 20. Oktober 1860, RGBl. Nr. 225, in Bernatzik, *Die öster-reichischen Verfassungsgesetze*, 222–23.

115. Kais. Manifest vom 20. Oktober 1860, RGBl. Nr. 225, in Bernatzik, *Die öster-reichischen Verfassungsgesetze*, 222–23.

116. Kais. Diplom vom 20. Oktober 1860, RGBl. Nr. 226, zur Reglung der inneren staatsrechtlichen Verhältnisse der Monarchie, in Bernatzik, *Die österreichischen Verfas-sungsgesetze*, 228.

117. See Hauke, "Verfassungsgeschichte," 4:728.

118. "die verfassungsmäßigen Institutionen Meines Königreiches Ungarn wieder ins Leben rufe." Ah. Handschreiben vom 20. Oktober 1860 an den zum ungarischen Hofkan-zler ernannten Freiherrn v. Vay, in Bernatzik, *Die österreichischen Verfassungsgesetze*, 230–32 (here 231).

119. In Helfert's assessment, "Die Vertheidiger des einheimischen Landrechts" under-stood the throne's concessions here not as a new formation but rather as "der Weiterfüh-rung dessen, was früher und in seinen ersten Anfängen seit langen Jahrhunderten zu Recht bestanden und von Rechtswegen zu bestehen nie aufgehört hate [*sic*]." Helfert, *Die Böhmische Frage in ihrer jüngsten Phase*, 21.

120. Heinrich [Henrik] Marczali, *Ungarisches Verfassungsrecht* (Tübingen: J. C. B. Mohr, 1911), 24.

121. On the relationship of the October Diploma and the February Patent, see Hans Kelsen, *Österreichisches Staatsrecht: Ein Grundriss Entwicklungsgeschichtlich Dargestellt* (Tübingen: J. C. B. Mohr, 1923), 13–14, and Fellner's rebuttal: Fellner, "Das 'Februarpatent' von 1861," 555–56. On the liberal agenda, the nature and achievements of the February Patent, and the important role of liberal finance minister Ignaz von Plener, see Judson, *Exclusive Revolutionaries*, 73–84.

122. See Josef Redlich, *Das Österreichische Staats- und Reichsproblem: Geschichtliche Darstellung der inneren Politik der habsburgischen Monarchie von 1848 bis zum Untergang des Reiches* (Leipzig: Der Neue Geist Verlag, 1920), 1:793ff.; Fellner, "Das 'Februarpatent' von 1861," 561.

123. "Finden Wir, um die Rechte und Freiheiten der getreuen Stände dieser Königreiche und Länder nach den Verhältnissen und Bedürfnissen der Gegenwart zu entwickeln, umzubilden, und mit den Interessen der Gesammtmonarchie in Einklang zu bringen."

124. Kais. Patent vom. 26. Februar 1861, RGBl. Nr. 20, text in Bernatzik, *Die österreichischen Verfassungsgesetze*, 255–59, here 258.

125. Bernatzik, *Die österreichischen Verfassungsgesetze*, 258.

126. Thus Fellner described the February Patent as "just the last step." Fellner, "Das 'Februarpatent' von 1861," 556. For other contemporary accounts of the February Patent as an amalgamation of different kinds of law, see Ludwig Gumplowicz, *Das Oesterreichische Staatsrecht (Verfassungs- und Verwaltungsrecht): Ein Lehr- und Handbuch* (Vienna: Manz'sche, 1891), 23; Wenzel Lustkandl, *Das Wesen der österreichischen Reichsverfassung: Ein akademische Antrittsrede* (Vienna: Wilhelm Braumüller, 1864), 4.

127. Kelsen, *Österreichisches Staatsrecht*, 14.

128. Franz Schuselka, *An Franz Deák* (Vienna: Friedr. Förster & Brüder, 1861), 11.

Chapter Two: The Secret Science of Dual Sovereignty

1. Robert Musil, *The Man without Qualities*, trans. Sophie Wilkins (1930; New York: Vintage International, 1996), 29.

2. Julius [Gyula] Andrássy, *Ungarns Ausgleich mit Österreich vom Jahre 1867* (Leipzig: Duncker & Humblot, 1897), 184–85. Andrássy's homonymous father was one of the key architects and negotiators of the settlement. See further below.

3. Andrássy, 185.

4. Musil, *Man without Qualities*, 180. "Mysteries of dualism" on 181.

5. As we see especially clearly in Musil's delusional character Moosbrugger, whose (ir) rationality is understood differently by the law, by psychiatry, and by Moosbrugger himself. Musil's deep interest in these different ways of understanding the world reflects the neo-Kantian debates of the day (and Kant's *Critique of Pure Reason* makes a number of appearances in the novel). In entering into multiple knowledge and aesthetic systems, and presenting them agnostically as valid ways of understanding reality, *The Man without Qualities* might be considered the literary twin of Ernst Cassirer's *Philosophy of Symbolic Forms*, which was being written over the course of the 1920s, just like Musil's novel.

6. Musil, *Man without Qualities*, 491.

7. For example, Friedrich Tezner, "Apponyis Beweise gegen die Realität der österreichischen Gesamtstaatsidee," *Österreichische Rundschau* 29 (1911): 259–71, 352–62, 429–439. See further below.

8. See Arthur Griffith, *The Resurrection of Hungary: A Parallel for Ireland*, 3rd ed. (1904; Dublin: Whelan and Son, 1918); William Ewart Gladstone in the government of Ireland debate, April 8, 1886, House of Commons, Hansard's Parliamentary Debates, 1886, vol. 304, col. 1047 (https://api.parliament.uk/historic-hansard/commons/1886/apr/08/motion-for-leave-first-night).

9. For an example of its general circulation, see R. W. Seton-Watson to Josef Redlich, 6 October 1911, Autogr. 1457/1(1–17) Han, Nachlass Josef Redlich, Sammlung von Handschrifren und alten Drucken, Österreichische Nationalbibliothek; and for the subcontinent

at midcentury: Kavita Saraswathi Datla, "Sovereignty and the End of Empire: The Transition to Independence in Colonial Hyderabad," *Ab Imperio* 3 (2018): 76; T. G. Fraser, *Partition in Ireland, India and Palestine: Theory and Practice* (London: Macmillan, 1984), 5–7.

10. 'Aziz 'Ali al-Misri, quoted in Eliezer Tauber, *The Emergence of the Arab Movements* (Abingdon: Routledge, 1993), at both 221 and 250; see also 285. For a full treatment of this topic, see Adam Mestyan, "A Muslim Dualism? Inter-imperial History and Austria-Hungary in Ottoman Thought, 1867–1921," *Contemporary European History* 30, no. 4 (2021): 478–96.

11. For a sample of this literature, see Adom Getachew, *Worldmaking after Empire: The Rise and Fall of Self-Determination* (Princeton, NJ: Princeton University Press, 2019); Manu Goswami, "Imagined Futures and Colonial Internationalisms," *American Historical Review* 117, no. 5 (2012): 1416–85; Frederick Cooper, *Citizenship between Empire and Nation: Remaking France and French Africa, 1945–1960* (Princeton, NJ: Princeton University Press, 2014); Gary Wilder, *Freedom Time: Negritude, Decolonization, and the Future of the World* (Durham, NC: Duke University Press, 2015). But see, too, important critiques of the revisionist view: Samuel Moyn, "Fantasies of Federalism," *Dissent* 62, no. 1 (2015): 145–51; Michael Goebel, "After Empire Must Come Nation?," September 8, 2016, https://medium.com/afro-asian-visions/after-empire-must-come-nation-cd220f1977c.

12. For two of the earlier ones, see Hermann Bidermann, *Die rechtliche Natur der österreichisch-ungarischen Monarchie* (Vienna: Carl Fromme, 1877); Josef Ulbrich, *Die rechtliche Natur der österreichisch-ungarischen Monarchie* (Prague: H. Dominicus, 1879). In Hungary, handbooks of Hungarian public law can be dated a little earlier but likewise pick up in the 1860s; for example, with the work of Emil Récsi (who also taught Austrian law): Emil Récsi, *Magyarország közjoga* (1861; Budapest: Kiadja Pfeifer Ferdinánd, 1869). Perhaps a stronger parallel to this German-language jurisprudence, though, in terms of approach and questions, arrives with the jurist Ernő Nagy and his 1887 book, *Magyarország közjoga (államjog)* (1887; Budapest: Eggenberger-féle könyvkeres kedés, 1891). For an introduction to its themes and method, see László Péter, "The Holy Crown of Hungary, Visible and Invisible," *Slavonic and East European Review* 81, no. 3 (2003): 478–80.

13. Friedrich Engel-Jánosi, *. . . aber ein stolzer Bettler: Erinnerungen au seiner verlorenen Generation* (Graz: Verlag Styria, 1974), 39.

14. On Schwarzwald and the salon, see further in chapter 6, as well as Deborah Holmes, *Langeweile ist Gift: Das Leben der Eugenie Schwarzwald* (St. Pölten: Residenz Verlag, 2012).

15. Hans Kelsen, "Autobiographie (1947)," in Hans Kelsen, *Werke*, ed. Matthias Jestaedt (Tübingen: Mohr Siebeck, 2007), 1:37.

16. Note, though, the important foundation of József Eötvös's thought. See Balázs Trencsényi, Maciej Janowski, Mónika Maár, Maria Falina, and Michal Kopeček, *A History of Modern Political Thought in East Central Europe* (Oxford: Oxford University Press, 2016), 1:277–94. For introductions to this period and these characters, see Paul Lendvai, *The Hungarians: A Thousand Years of Victory in Defeat*, trans. Ann Major (Princeton, NJ: Princeton University Press, 2021), chaps. 24 and 25 ("le beau pendu" on 274); István Fazekas, Stefan Malfèr, and Péter Tusor, eds., *Széchenyi, Kossuth, Batthyány, Deák: Studien zu den ungarischen Reformpolitikern des 19. Jahrhunderts und ihren Beziehung zu Österreich* (Vienna: Institut für ungarische Geschichtsforschung in Wien, 2011), pt. 4; C. A. Macartney, *The Habsburg Empire, 1790–1918* (London: Weidenfeld and Nicolson, 1969), 544–68. On the romance between Andrássy and Elisabeth, see Brigitte Hamann, *The Reluctant Empress* (New York: Knopf, 1989), 179.

17. Hungary's historical constitution was a body of customary, mostly unwritten laws that Hungarian noblemen had preserved through the years of Ottoman occupation. Many

of these laws and customs were famously collected by the Hungarian scholar and states-man István Werbőczy and published in Vienna as *Tripartitum Opus Iuris Consuetudinarii Inclyti Regni Hungariae* in 1517. For an introduction, see Martyn Rady, "The Prologue to Werbőczy's Tripartitum and Its Sources," *English Historical Review* 121, no. 490 (2006): 104-45. For an overview of the place of the Tripartitum (and constitutional law more generally) in the development of the Hungarian state, see Thomas Ertman, *Birth of the Leviathan: Building States and Regimes in Medieval and Early Modern Europe* (Cambridge: Cambridge University Press, 1997), 290-303 and passim.

18. [Ferenc Deák], *Die Rede Franz Deak's bei Gelegenheit der Adreßdebatte im Unter-hause des ungarischen Landtages* (Vienna: Friedrich Förster & Brüder, n.d. [1861]), 1, 8.

19. [Deák], 2-3.

20. There are multiple versions of and attributions for this complaint, often with long and ambiguous footnote chains; see, as a sample, István Deák, *Beyond Nationalism: A Social and Political History of the Habsburg Officer Corps, 1848-1918* (New York: Oxford University Press, 1990), 40.

21. [Deák], *Die Rede Franz Deak's bei Gelegenheit der Adreßdebatte*, 3.

22. David Graeber and Marshall Sahlins, *On Kings* (Chicago: HAU Books, 2017), 5, 7, and generally; see also Marshall Sahlins, "Stranger-Kings in General: The Cosmo-logics of Power," in *Framing Cosmologies: The Anthropology of Worlds*, ed. Allen Abramson and Martin Holbraad (Manchester: Manchester University Press, 2014), 137-63.

23. "Wenzel Lustkandl †," *Zeitschrift für das Privat- und Öffentliche Recht der Gegen-wart* (1907): 269-72.

24. Wenzel Lustkandl, *Das ungarisch-österreichische Staatsrecht: Zur Lösung der Verfassungsfrage, historisch-dogmatisch dargestellt* (Vienna: Wilhelm Braumüller, 1863), 249-50.

25. Franz von Deák, *Ein Beitrag zum ungarischen Staatsrecht: Bemerkungen über Wen-zel Lustkandl's "Ungarisch-österreichisches Staatsrecht"; Vom Standpunkte der Geschichte des ungarischen Staatsrechts* (Pest: Gustav Emich, 1865), 78.

26. Deák, 82.

27. Ferenc Deák, "A húsvéti cikk," *Pesti Napló*, April 16, 1865, available as "The Easter Article," trans. Dávid Oláh, in *Discourses of Collective Identity in Central and Southeast Europe (1770-1945)*, vol. 3, *Modernism: The Creation of Nation-States*, pt. 1, ed. Ahmet Ersoy, Maciej Górny, and Vangelis Kechriotis (Budapest: Central European University Press, 2010), 74-83.

28. Martin P. Schennach, *Austria Inventa? Zu den Anfängen der österreichischen Staatsrechtslehre* (Frankfurt am Main: Vittorio Klostermann, 2020); Martin P. Schenn-ach, "Die 'österreichische Gesamtstaatsidee': Das Verhältnis zwischen 'Gesamtstaat' und Ländern als Gegenstand rechtshistorischer Forschung," in *Rechtshistorische Aspekte des österreichischen Föderalismus*, ed. Martin P. Schennach (Vienna: Verlag Österreich, 2015), 1-29. See also Hans Peter Hye, "Die Länder im Gefüge der Habsburgermonarchie," in *Die Habsburgermonarchie 1848-1918*, vol. 7, *Verfassung und Parlamentarismus*, ed. Helmut Rumpler und Peter Urbanitsch, pt. 2, *Die regionalen und Repräsentativkörperschaften* (Vienna: Verlag der österreichischen Akademie der Wissenschaften, 2000), 2435.

29. Friedrich Engel-Jánosi, "Die Theorie vom Staat im deutschen Österreich, 1815-1848," *Zeitschrift für öffentliches Recht* 2 (1921): 360-61.

30. Gerhard Oberkofler, *Studien zur Geschichte der österreichischen Rechtswissenschaft* (Frankfurt am Main: Peter Lang, 1984), 408.

31. The few existing monographs that treated aspects of constitutional law could be counted on one hand. Michael Stolleis, *Public Law in Germany, 1800-1914* (New York: Berghahn Books, 2001), 185-87; Oberkofler, *Studien zur Geschichte der österreichischen*

Rechtswissenschaft, 395; Franz Zeilner, *Verfassung, Verfassungsrecht und Lehre des Öffentlichen Rechts in Österreich bis 1848* (Frankfurt am Main: Peter Lang, 2008), 57.

32. *Statistik* in this context denotes a now deceased disciplinary formation only indirectly related to the current mathematical meaning of statistics. Sometimes called *Staatenkunde*, it sought to provide an objective, aggregate description of the state in the present, covering geography, population, economy, politics, and law. Its methodological looseness and substantive ambiguity attracted critiques even at the time. See Robert Walter, "Die Lehre des Verfassungs- und Verwaltungsrechtes an der Universität Wien von 1810–1938," *Juristische Blätter* 110, no. 10 (1988): 610–11.

33. Zeilner, *Verfassung, Verfassungsrecht*, 51–53; Engel-Jánosi, "Die Theorie vom Staat," 360–62; Stolleis, *Public Law in Germany*, 185–87.

34. Maria Theresa had appointed the University of Vienna's first professor of natural law, Karl Anton von Martini, in 1754. See Engel-Jánosi, "Die Theorie vom Staat," 362–67.

35. Josef Ulbrich, "Universitäten: Rechts- und staatswissenschaftliche Studien," in *Oesterreichisches Staatswörterbuch: Handbuch des gesammten österreichischen öffentlichen Rechtes*, ed. Ernst Mischler and Josef Ulbrich (Vienna: Alfred Hölder, 1897), vol. 2, pt. 2, 1394.

36. For an overview of exchanges with politicians and the different positions taken by the Austrian jurists, see Peter Berger, "Der österreichisch-ungarische Dualismus 1867–1918 und die österreichische Rechtswissenschaft," *Der Donauraum* 13, no. 3 (1968): 156–70.

37. On the negotiations, see Karin Olechowski-Hrdlicka, *Die gemeinsamen Angelegenheiten der Österreichisch-Ungarischen Monarchie: Vorgeschichte—Ausgleich 1867—Staatsrechtliche Kontroversen* (Frankfurt am Main: Peter Lang, 2001), 80–124.

38. XII Gesetzartikel 1867, text in Edmund Bernatzik, *Die österreichischen Verfassungsgesetze mit Erläuterung*, 2nd ed. (Vienna: Manzsche, 1911), 329–50. See also Žolger's rendering, which places the Hungarian and German texts side by side, with *extensive* annotation (including some fifty pages on §69 alone): Ivan Žolger, *Der staatsrechtliche Ausgleich zwischen Österreich und Ungarn* (Leipzig: Duncker & Humblot, 1911), 43–297.

39. A basic dualism between the crown and the *ország* (the "country" or "land," in this case meaning the qualified community of nobles) was fundamental to the historical Hungarian constitution. See Péter, "The Holy Crown of Hungary," 447 and passim; Péter, "Die Verfassungsentwicklung in Ungarn," in *Die Habsburgermonarchie 1848–1918*, vol. 7, *Verfassung und Parlamentarismus*, pt. 1, *Verfassungsrecht, Verfassungswirklichkeit, Zentrale Repräsentativkörperschaften*, ed. Helmut Rumpler and Peter Urbanitsch (Vienna: Verlag der Österreichischen Akademie der Wissenschaften, 2000), 240–41. The continuity of the constitution in this regard, it should be remembered, also entailed the continued dominance of the landholding feudal elite. See Péter, "The Aristocracy, the Gentry, and Their Parliamentary Tradition in Nineteenth-Century Hungary," *Slavonic and East European Review* 70, no. 1 (1992): 77–110.

40. Gesetz vom 21. Dezember 1867, RGBl. Nr. 146, text in Bernatzik, *Die österreichischen Verfassungsgesetze*, 439–51.

41. Hans Lentze, "Die Ständischen Grundlagen des Dualismus," in *Die Freiheitsrechte und die Staatstheorien im Zeitalter des Dualismus: Materialien der VII. Ungarisch-tschechoslowakischen Rechtshistorikerkonferenz in Pécs (23–25 September, 1965)*, ed. Andor Csizmadia (Budapest: Tankönyvkiadó, 1966), 88.

42. Bidermann, *Die rechtliche Natur der österreichisch-ungarischen Monarchie*, 44.

43. See also Franz Hauke, "Verfassungsgeschichte," in *Österreichisches Staatswörterbuch: Handbuch des gesamten österreichischen öffentlichen Rechtes*, 2nd ed., ed. Ernst Mischler and Josef Ulbrich (Vienna: Alfred Hölder, 1909), 4:731.

44. Gábor Máthé, "Gesamtmonarchie oder selbstständiger ungarischer Staat? Gedan-ken zur Diskussion Lustkandl-Deák," in *Der österreichisch-ungarische Ausgleich 1867*, ed. Barna Mezey (Budapest: Rechtsgeschichtlichen Forschungsgruppe der Ungarischen Akademie der Wissenschaften an dem Lehrstuhl für Ungarische Rechtsgeschichte Eötvös Loránd Universität, 2008), 65.

45. Hye, "Die Länder im Gefüge der Habsburgermonarchie." See further Gerald Stourz, "Länderautonomie und Gesamtstaat in Österreich 1848–1918," in *Der Umfang der österreichischen Geschichte: Ausgewählte Studien 1990–2010* (Vienna: Böhlau Verlag, 2011); Martin P. Schennach, ed., *Rechtshistorische Aspekte des österreichischen Föderal-ismus: Beiträge zur Tagung an der Universität Innsbruck am 28. und 29. November 2013* (Vienna: Verlag Österreich, 2015); Jana Osterkamp, "Cooperative Empires: Provincial Ini-tiatives in Imperial Austria," trans. Jaime Hyland, *Austrian History Yearbook* 47 (2016): 128–46; Christian Neschwara, "Länder und Gesamtstaat—Landtage und Gesamtparla-ment: Ein Überblick der Entwicklung seit 1861," in *Februarpatent 1861: Zur Geschichte und Zukunft der österreichischen Landtage*, ed. Robert Kriechbaumer and Peter Beßjäger (Vienna: Böhlau Verlag, 2011), 145–162. On the significance of local government and the dual track administrative system, see Pieter Judson, *Habsburg Empire: A New History* (Cambridge, MA: Harvard University Press, 2016); John Deak, *Forging a Multinational State: State Making in Imperial Austria from the Enlightenment to the First World War* (Stanford, CA: Stanford University Press, 2015), especially 146–64; Jeremy King, "The Municipal and the National in the Bohemian Lands, 1848–1914," *Austrian History Yearbook* 42 (2011): 89–109.

46. Péter, "Holy Crown of Hungary," 447–59; Ernst [Ernő] Nagy, "Ungarn: A. Staatsrecht," in *Österreichisches Staatswörterbuch: Handbuch des gesamten österreichischen öffentli-chen Rechtes*, 2nd ed., ed. Ernst Mischler and Josef Ulbrich (Vienna: Alfred Hölder, 1909), 4:587–89; Ulbrich, *Die rechtliche Natur der österreichisch-ungarischen Monarchie*, 67; Heinrich [Henrik] Marczali, *Ungarisches Verfassungsrecht* (Tübingen: J. C. B. Mohr, 1911), 32; Martyn Rady, *Customary Law in Hungary: Courts, Texts, and the Tripartium* (Oxford: Oxford University Press, 2015), 6.

47. Ivan Andrović, *Das Verhältnis zwischen Kroatien und Ungarn* (Vienna: Verlag der politischen Zeitschrift "Ujedinjena Hrvatska," 1904), 20, 11.

48. See, for example, Marczali, *Ungarisches Verfassungsrecht*, 159–60.

49. Louis Le Fur and Paul Posener, *Bundesstaat und Staatenbund* (Breslau: J. U. Kern's Verlag, 1902), 301–2.

50. See Bálint Varga, "The Two Faces of the Hungarian Empire," *Austrian History Yearbook* 52 (2021): 118–30.

51. Albert Apponyi, "The Army Question in Austria and Hungary," *Monthly Review* 16 (July 1904): 1–2.

52. See Gustav Kolmer, *Parlament und Verfassung in Österreich*, vol. 1, *1848–1869* (Vienna: Carl Fromme, 1902), 271.

53. For a discussion of this and other reactions, see, for example, Leslie C. Tihany, "The Austro-Hungarian Compromise, 1867–1918: A Half Century of Diagnosis; Fifty Years of Post-Mortem," *Central European History* 2, no. 2 (1969): 114–38; Tibor Frank, "The Austro-Hungarian Compromise of 1867 and Its Contemporary Critics," *Hungarian Studies* 14, no. 2 (2000): 196–99.

54. See Gerald Stourzh, *Die Gleichberechtigung der Nationalitäten in der Verfassung und Verwaltung Österreichs, 1848–1918* (Vienna: Verlag der Österreichischen Akademie der Wissenschaften, 1985), 8–9 and passim. On the December constitution of 1867, see Barbara Haider, *Die Protokolle des Verfassungsausschusses des Reichsrates vom Jahre 1867* (Vienna: Verlag der Österreichischen Akademie der Wissenschaften, 1997); Pieter Judson, "The Lost Heroes of Austria's Fundamental Laws," in *150 Jahre Staatsgrundgesetz: Über*

die allgemeinen Rechte der Staatsbürger, ed. Franz Merli, Magdalena Pöschl, and Ewald Wiederin (Vienna: Manz, 2018), 1–15.

55. Rudolf Springer [Karl Renner], *Grundlagen und Entwicklungsziele der Österreichisch-Ungarischen Monarchie: Politische Studie über den Zusammenbruch der Privilegienparlamente und die Wahlreform in beiden Staaten, über die Reichsidee und ihre Zukunft* (Vienna: Franz Deuticke, 1906), 48.

56. Heinrich von Srbik, "Franz Joseph I: Charakter und Regierungsgrundsätze," *Historische Zeitschrift* 144, no. 3 (1931): 509.

57. Gerald Stourzh, "Der Dualismus 1867 bis 1918: Zur staatsrechtlichen und völkerrechtlichen Problematik der Doppelmonarchie," in *Die Habsburgermonarchie 1848–1918*, vol. 7, *Verfassung und Parlamentarismus*, part 1, *Verfassungsrecht, Verfassungswirklichkeit, Zentrale Repräsentativkörperschaften*, ed. Helmut Rumpler and Peter Urbanitsch (Vienna: Verlag der Österreichischen Akademie der Wissenschaften, 2000), 1177–83.

58. Gyula Szekfű, *Der Staat Ungarn: Eine Geschichtsstudie* (Stuttgart: Deutsche Verlags-Anstalt, 1918), 191.

59. Albert Apponyi, *Die rechtliche Natur der Beziehung zwischen Österreich und Ungarn: Eine Entgegnung* (Vienna: Carl Fromme, 1911), 46.

60. Ludwig Gumplowicz, *Das Oesterreichische Staatsrecht (Verfassungs- und Verwaltungsrecht): Ein Lehr- und Handbuch* (Vienna: Manzsche, 1891), 56.

61. Marczali, *Ungarisches Verfassungsrecht*, 39. The entry for *Ausländer* in the landmark compendium *Austrian State Dictionary* treated the subject of foreigners a little more equivocally: Georg Pražák, "Ausländer," in *Österreichisches Staatswörterbuch: Handbuch des gesamten österreichischen öffentlichen Rechtes*, 2nd ed., ed. Ernst Mischler and Josef Ulbrich (Vienna: Alfred Hölder, 1905), 1:365.

62. Éva Somogyi, "Die Delegation als Verbindungsinstitution zwischen Cis- und Transleithanien," in *Die Habsburgermonarchie 1848–1918*, vol. 7, *Verfassung und Parlamentarismus*, pt. 1, *Verfassungsrecht, Verfassungswirklichkeit, Zentrale Repräsentativkörperschaften*, ed. Helmut Rumpler and Peter Urbanitsch (Vienna: Verlag der Österreichischen Akademie der Wissenschaften, 2000), 1107. As Somogyi shows, Andrássy's self-aggrandizing narrative overlooks precursors in earlier Hungarian proposals from the 1860s. On the creativity of the delegations, see also Macartney, *Habsburg Empire*, 537.

63. Somogyi, "Die Delegation als Verbindungsinstitution," 1122 (quotation here), 1134; "absurd" in the eyes of some Austrian centralists: 1119.

64. Theodor Zichy, "Österreich und Ungarn," *Deutsche Rundschau* 137 (1908): 85; Seton-Watson, "Austro-Hungarian Ausgleich of 1867," 133.

65. Jana Osterkamp, *Vielfalt ordnen: Das föderale Europea der Habsburgermonarchie (Vormärz bis 1918)* (Göttingen: Vandenhoeck & Ruprecht, 2020), 206.

66. See Bernatzik, *Die österreichischen Verfassungsgesetze*, 451.

67. See Bernatzik, 452.

68. XII Gesetzartikel 1867, text in Bernatzik, 331.

69. Bernatzik, 332n7.

70. Žolger, *Der staatsrechtliche Ausgleich zwischen Österreich und Ungarn*, 59. For his remarks on translation and interpretation of this section, see also 67–72.

71. Žolger, 70.

72. Bernatzik, *Die österreichischen Verfassungsgesetze*, 332n7.

73. Julius Miskolczy, *Ungarn in der Habsburger-Monarchie* (Vienna: Verlag Herold, 1959), 164–65; Harold Steinacker, "Graf Albert Apponyi," *Jahrbücher für Geschichte Osteuropas* 2, no. 2 (1937): 274, 275, 279. Steinacker's biographical essay doubled as a review of *Apponyi világnézete* (Budapest 1935) by Gyula Kornis.

74. Miskolczy, *Ungarn in der Habsburger-Monarchie*, 151, 164–65; Stourzh, "Der Dualismus 1867 bis 1918," 1181; D. Kosáry, "Ungarische politische Bestrebungen und die

Probleme der Monarchie im Zeitalter des Dualismus," *Acta Historica Academiae Scietiarum Hungaricae* 17, no. 1–2 (1971): 27–52.

75. Steinacker, "Graf Albert Apponyi," 274, 275. On Apponyi's role in the constitutional crisis of 1905, see also Péter, "Holy Crown of Hungary," 491.

76. "Weil Gemeinsamkeit nicht auf Einheit, sondern auf Vielheit hinweist; einer kann nichts mit sich selbst gemeinsam haben, dazu gehören mindestens zwei; gemeinsame Angelegenheiten sind demnach nicht Reichsangelegenheiten, denn ein Reich kann keine mit sich selbst gemeinsame Angelegenheiten haben." Apponyi, *Die rechtliche Natur der Beziehung zwischen Österreich und Ungarn*, 47.

77. Apponyi, 47.

78. Apponyi, 49.

79. Apponyi, 49.

80. Apponyi, 58.

81. Paul von Fazekas, *Das Staatsrecht des Weltkrieges*, Flugschriften für Österreich-Ungarns Erwachen, no. 27/28 (Warnsdorf: Strache, Kunst- und Verlagsanstalt, 1917), 31.

82. Apponyi also employed mathematical equations; see the elaborate numerical play at Apponyi, *Die rechtliche Natur der Beziehung zwischen Österreich und Ungarn*, 51.

83. Fazekas, *Das Staatsrecht des Weltkrieges*, 31 (emphasis in original).

84. Bidermann, *Die rechtliche Natur der österreichisch-ungarischen Monarchie*, 34.

85. Bidermann, 35.

86. Bidermann, 35.

87. Ulbrich, *Die rechtliche Natur der österreichisch-ungarischen Monarchie*, 51–52.

88. For a survey of their debates, see József Buzás, "Zur Geschichte des österreichisch-ungarischen öffentlich-rechtlichen Verhältnisses: Friedrich Tezner über die Rechtsnatur der dualistischen Staatsverbindung," *Zeitschrift der Savigny-Stiftung für Rechtsgeschichte* 102, no. 1 (1985): 269–82; on Tezner, see Friedrich Wilhelm Kremzow, "Friedrich Tezner: Ein Beitrag zur Geschichte der österreichischen Verwaltungswissenschaft," *Acta Universitatum: Zeitschrift für Hochschulforschung Kultur- und Geistesgeschichte* 1, no. 2–3 (1971): 23–41; Johannes Feichtinger, *Wissenschaft als reflexives Projekt. Von Bolzano über Freud zu Kelsen: Österreichische Wissenschaftsgeschichte 1848–1938* (Bielefeld: Transcript Verlag, 2010), 348–54.

89. His appeal to change his name provides one of the few biographical sources. It is preserved in the Niederösterreichische Statthalterei (Zl. 40.345/882) but is quoted here from Kremzow's article, which reproduces it at length: Kremzow, "Friedrich Tezner," 27n43.

90. Kremzow, "Friedrich Tezner," 27–28, 31 (quotation on 31).

91. Bernatzik's biting 1902 report weighed candidates for positions prompted by Lustkandl's retirement; while Tezner had his advocates, Bernatzik's view won out. Kremzow reproduces his internal faculty report at length: Kremzow, here 37–38 (note 109, carrying over).

92. See, generally, Marsha L. Rozenblit, "The Jews of the Dual Monarchy," *Austrian History Yearbook* 23 (1992): 160–80; Rozenblit, *Reconstructing a National Identity: The Jews of Habsburg Austria during World War I* (Oxford: Oxford University Press, 2001); Steven Beller, *Vienna and the Jews, 1867–1938: A Cultural History* (Cambridge: Cambridge University Press, 1989); Malachi Hacohen, "Nation and Empire in Modern Jewish European History," *Leo Baeck Institute Yearbook* 62 (2017): 53–65; Hacohen, *Jacob & Esau: Jewish European History between Nation and Empire* (Cambridge: Cambridge University Press, 2019), especially chap. 7. On anti-Semitism in the Austrian legal academy and legal practice, see Ilse Reiter-Zatloukal, "Antisemitismus und Juristenstand: Wiener Rechts- und Staatswissenschaftliche Fakultät und Rechtspraxis vom ausgehenden 19. Jahrhundern bis zum 'Anschluss' 1938," in *Der lange Schatten des Antisemitismus: Kritische Auseinandersetzungen mit der Geschichte der Universität Wien im 19. und 20. Jahrhundert*

(Vienna: Vienna University Press, 2013), 183–205 (also discussing Tezner at 200 in relation to his work as a judge).

93. "in die Luft . . . verpuffen": Friedrich Tezner, *Ausgleichsrecht und Ausgleichspolitik: Ein Appell an das Parlament des allgemeinen gleichen Wahlrechts* (Vienna: Manzsche, 1907), 9.

94. Tezner, 9.

95. Friedrich Tezner, "Das ständisch-monarchische Staatsrecht und die österreichische Gesamt- oder Länderstaatsidee," *Zeitschrift für das privat- und öffentliche Recht der Gegenwart* 42 (1916): 135.

96. Friedrich Tezner, *Der österreichische Kaisertitel, das ungarische Staatsrecht und die ungarische Publicistik* (Vienna: Alfred Hölder, 1899), 192.

97. Friedrich Tezner, *Das österreichisch-ungarische Staatsrecht des Grafen Theodor Zichy*, Sonderabdruck of *Deutsche Rundschau* (Berlin: Verlag von Gebrüder Paetel, 1909), 141.

98. Albert Apponyi, "Die rechtliche Natur der Beziehung zwischen Österreich und Ungarn," *Österreichische Rundschau* 28 (1911): 168.

99. Apponyi, 168.

100. Apponyi, 169–71.

101. Friedrich Tezner, "Das staatsrechtliche und politische Problem der österreichisch-ungarischen Monarchie," *Archiv des öffentlichen Rechts* 30 (1913): 120 (emphasis added).

102. Friedrich Tezner, "Apponyis Beweise gegen die Realität der österreichischen Gesamtstaatsidee," 352.

103. Tezner, 353. See also Tezner, "Das staatsrechtliche und politische Problem der österreichisch-ungarischen Monarchie," 129–30.

104. Tezner, "Das staatsrechtliche und politische Problem der österreichisch-ungarischen Monarchie," 126 (emphasis in original).

105. Tezner, 129 (emphasis in original).

106. Tezner, 129.

107. Friedrich Tezner, *Der Kaiser: Österreichisches Staatsrecht in Einzeldarstellungen für den praktischen Gebrauch* (Vienna: Manzsche, 1909), 245.

108. Friedrich Tezner, *Die Wandlungen der österreichisch-ungarischen Reichsidee: Ihr Inhalt und ihre politische Notwendigkeit* (Vienna: Manzsche, 1905), 5.

109. Tezner, 57.

110. Tezner, "Das ständisch-monarchische Staatsrecht und die österreichische Gesamt- oder Länderstaatsidee," 135.

111. Tezner, "Apponyis Beweise gegen die Realität der österreichischen Gesamtstaatsidee," 431.

112. Tezner, "Das ständisch-monarchische Staatsrecht und die österreichische Gesamt- oder Länderstaatsidee," 136.

113. Tezner, 136.

114. Tezner, "Apponyis Beweise gegen die Realität der österreichischen Gesamtstaatsidee," 431.

115. Tezner, "Das ständisch-monarchische Staatsrecht und die österreichische Gesamt- oder Länderstaatsidee," 136, footnote 280.

116. See, generally, Martti Koseknniemi, *The Gentle Civilizer of Nations: The Rise and Fall of International Law, 1870–1960* (Cambridge: Cambridge University Press, 2001); and, for the context, Martin H. Geyer and Johannes Paulmann, eds., *The Mechanics of Internationalism: Culture, Society, and Politics from the 1840s to the First World War* (Oxford: Oxford University Press, 2001).

117. On the interwar unraveling of this consensus, see Natasha Wheatley, "Spectral Legal Personality in Interwar International Law: On New Ways of Not Being a State," *Law*

and History Review 35, no. 3 (2017): 753–87; Wheatley, "New Subjects in International Law and Order," in *Internationalisms: A Twentieth-Century History*, ed. Patricia Clavin and Glenda Sluga (Cambridge: Cambridge University Press, 2017), 265–86.

118. Tezner, *Die Wandlungen der österreichisch-ungarischen Reichsidee*, chap. 6.

119. Tezner, *Der österreichische Kaisertitel*, 217; see also 197.

120. Tezner, *Das österreichisch-ungarische Staatsrecht des Grafen Theodor Zichy*, 130.

121. For other examples, see Ulbrich, *Die rechtliche Natur der österreichisch-ungarischen Monarchie*, 53–54; Gumplowicz, *Das Oesterreichische Staatsrecht*, 57; Springer [Renner], *Grundlagen und Entwicklungsziele der Österreichisch-Ungarischen Monarchie*, 23.

122. Quoted at length in Paul von Somssich, *Das legitime Recht Ungarns und seines Königs* (Vienna: Jasper, Hügel & Manz, 1850), 13.

123. Zichy, "Österreich und Ungarn," 89 (emphasis in original).

124. Tezner, *Das österreichisch-ungarische Staatsrecht des Grafen Theodor Zichy*, 128–29.

125. Tezner, 131, 132.

126. Stourzh, "Der Dualismus 1867 bis 1918," 1183–84, 1186.

127. Stourzh, 1184–85.

128. Stourzh, 1185.

129. Georg Jellinek, "Ungarisches Staatsrecht: Eine politische Reisebetrachtung," *Neue Freie Presse*, no. 14655, June 11, 1905, Morgenblatt, 2.

130. Jellinek, 1, 2. Jellinek wrote partly out of frustration: as one of the editors of Marquardsen's *Handbuch des öffentliches Rechtes*, he had been trying to procure a definitive German-language treatment of Hungarian public law for years. For his efforts in this regard, see, for example, Paul Siebeck (Verlagsbuchhandlung J. C. B. Mohr) to Georg Jellinek, 27 September 1909 and 15 October 1909, Nachlass Georg Jellinek, Bundesarchiv Koblenz (hereafter NGJ, BArch), N 1136/27.

131. Gejza von Fernandy to Georg Jellinek, 18 June 1905, NGJ, BArch, N 1136/7; Elemér Hantos to Georg Jellinek, 13 June 1905, NGJ, BArch, N 1136/10.

132. Harold Steinacker, *Zur Frage nach der rechtlichen Natur der österreichisch-ungarischen Gesamtmonarchie: Ein Beitrag zur Kritik der magyarischen Auslegung des Ausgleichs von 1867* (Vienna: Carl Fromme, n.d. [1910]), 1.

133. Allerhöchsten Handschreiben vom 14. November 1868 (with emphasis added), quoted in Stourzh, "Der Dualismus 1867 bis 1918," 1190.

134. Stourzh, 1191.

135. The logic trickled down beyond Hungary: in 1911, representatives from the Kingdom of Bohemia participated in the Stockholm conference of the International Women's Suffrage Alliance in their own name, to the chagrin of the Austrian ambassador. See Peter Becker, "Von *Listen* und anderen Stolpersteinen auf dem Weg zur Globalisierung: Die Habsburgermonarchie und der Internationalismus des 'langen' 19. Jahrhunderts," in *Internationale Geschichte in Theorie und Praxis*, ed. Barbara Haider-Wilson, William D. Godsey, Wolfgang Mueller (Vienna: Verlag der Österreichischen Akademie der Wissenschaften, 2017), 665–93. Becker builds on the argument of Madeleine Herren, *Hintertüren zur Macht: Internationalismus und modernisierungsorientierte Außenpolitik in Belgien, der Schweiz und den USA, 1865–1914* (Munich: Oldenbourg Verlag, 2000).

136. Stourzh, "Der Dualismus 1867 bis 1918," 1200–1201.

137. Stourzh, 1202, 1212.

138. Stourzh, 1201–02, 1206, 1208, 1213.

139. For the Hungarian interpretation, see for example Andrássy, *Ungarns Ausgleich mit Österreich*, 171–72; Apponyi, *Die rechtliche Natur der Beziehung zwischen Österreich und Ungarn*, 46, 57–58.

140. Steinacker, *Zur Frage nach der rechtlichen Natur der österreichisch-ungarischen Gesamtmonarchie*, 8.

141. Steinacker, 8–9.

142. See especially Clemens Ruthner and Tamara Scheer, eds., *Bosnien-Herzegowina und Österreich-Ungarn, 1878–1918: Annäherungen an eine Kolonie* (Tübingen: Francke, 2018). On the occupation and annexation of Bosnia-Herzegovina as an opening for the application of postcolonial theory to the Habsburg lands, see also Johannes Feichtinger, Ursula Prutsch, and Moritz Csaky, eds., *Habsburg Postcolonial: Machtstrukturen und Kollektives Gedächtnis* (Innsbruck: StudienVerlag, 2003); Clemens Ruthner, "Central Europe Goes Post-colonial: New Approaches to the Habsburg Empire around 1900," *Cultural Studies* 16, no. 6 (2002): 877–83; Clemens Ruthner, Diana Reynolds Cordileone, Ursula Reber, and Raymond Detrez, eds., *WechselWirkungen: Austria-Hungary, Bosnia-Herzegovina, and the Western Balkans, 1878–1918* (New York: Peter Lang, 2015). For skepticism about the usefulness of a toolbox of racialized "othering" and hegemony in a state that otherwise had citizenship, legal equality, and very fluid national identification—a skepticism that Edward Said himself shared—see Pieter Judson, "L'Autriche-Hongrie était-elle un empire?," *Annales* 63, no. 3 (2008): 563–96; Tara Zahra, "Looking East: East Central European 'Borderlands' in German History and Historiography," *History Compass* 3 (2005): 1–23; Edward W. Said, *Culture and Imperialism* (New York: Vintage Books, 1993), xxii; see also xxiii.

143. On the Habsburg civilizing mission in Bosnia-Herzegovina, see further Judson, *Habsburg Empire*, 319–32; Robin Okey, *Taming Balkan Nationalism: The Habsburg "Civilizing Mission" in Bosnia 1878–1914* (Oxford: Oxford University Press, 2007). For Bosnian intellectuals' own view of the modernization efforts of both empires and their creation of a European Islamic intellectual tradition, see importantly Leyla Amzi-Erdogdular, "Alternative Muslim Modernities: Bosnian Intellectuals in the Ottoman and Habsburg Empires," *Comparative Studies in Society and History* 59, no. 4 (2017): 912–43.

144. On the entangled (legal) history of the Habsburg and Ottoman Empires, see Emily Greble, *Muslims and the Making of Modern Europe* (Oxford: Oxford University Press, 2021); Jared Manasek, "Refugee Return and State Legitimation: Habsburgs, Ottomans, and the Case of Bosnia and Herzegovina, 1875–1878," *Journal of Modern European History* 19, no. 1 (2020): 63–79; Ruthner and Scheer, *Bosnien-Herzegowina und Österreich-Ungarn*; Mestyan, "A Muslim Dualism?"; Larry Wolff, *Woodrow Wilson and the Reimagining of Eastern Europe* (Stanford, CA: Stanford University Press, 2020).

145. For a survey, see Josef L. Kunz, *Die Staatenverbindungen*, Handbuch des Völkerrechts (Stuttgart: W. Kohlhammer, 1929), vol. 2, pt. 4, 224–27. In our own day, the historian John Deak terms it an "internal colony." Deak, *Forging a Multinational State*, 261.

146. At the same time, neither "state" wanted it especially, for it would entail a dramatic increase in the number of "Slavs" and potentially upset the already tense ethnonational situation.

147. Theodor Dantscher von Kollesberg, *Der Monarchische Bundesstaat Oesterreich-Ungarn und der Berliner Vertrag nebst der Bosnischen Vorlage* (Vienna: Alfred Hölder, 1880), 2 (emphasis in original).

148. Dantscher von Kollesberg, 4.

149. Dantscher von Kollesberg, 5.

150. Robert Redslob, *Abhängige Länder. Eine Analyse des Begriffs von der ursprünglichen Herrschergewalt: Zugleich eine staatsrechtliche und politische Studie über Elsaß-Lothringen, die österreichischen Königreiche und Länder, Kroatien-Slavonien, Bosnien-Herzegowina, Finnland, Island, die Territorien der nordamerikanischen Union, Kanada, Australien, Südafrika* (Leipzig: Veit & Comp., 1914), 202.

151. Tezner, "Das staatsrechtliche und politische Problem der österreichisch-ungarischen Monarchie," 183.

152. Karl Lamp, "Die Verfassung von Bosnien und der Herzegowina vom 17. Februar 1910," *Jahrbuch des öffentlichen Rechts der Gegenwart* 5 (1911): 229. Lamp is highlighted in Judson, *Habsburg Empire*, 380–81.

153. Josef Redlich, *Das österreichische Staats- und Reichsproblem: Geschichtliche Darstellung der inneren Politik der habsburgischen Monarchie von 1848 bis zum Untergang des Reiches*, 2 vols. (Leipzig: Der Neue Geist Verlag, 1920, 1926).

154. "Bericht des Referenten im Ausschusse für bosnische Angelegenheiten, Reichsratsabgeordneten Professor Dr. Josef Redlich," 1912, Österreichische Nationalbibliothek, Sammlung für Alte Handschriften und Drucke, Nachlass Josef Redlich, Cod. Ser. n. 53589 Han.

155. Dekan Joseph von Kudler erstattet im Namen des Professorenkollegiums der rechts- und staatswissenschaftlichen Fakultät der Universität Wien einen Vorschlag betreffend die Besetzung mehrerer an dieser Fakultät vakanter Lehrkanzeln, 8 November 1849, Allgemeines Verwaltungsarchiv Wien, Akten des Ministeriums für Kultus und Unterricht, Zahl 2319/1850. Oberkofler reproduces the whole memorandum in *Studien zur Geschichte der österreichischen Rechtswissenschaft*, 128–43 (here 141).

156. Oberkofler, *Studien zur Geschichte der österreichischen Rechtswissenschaft*, 123–24; Stolleis, *Public Law in Germany*, 284.

157. Erlaß des Ministeriums für Cultus und Unterricht, 2 October 1855, RGBL 172, and then Verordnung des Ministeriums für Cultus und Unterricht, 16 April 1856, RGBL 54. Elements of Austrian constitutional law were once again bundled into *Statistik*. In the first year one read *German* "imperial and legal history." See Walter, "Die Lehre des Verfassungs- und Verwaltungsrechtes an der Universität Wien," 614.

158. Dekan Joseph von Kudler memorandum in Oberkofler, *Studien zur Geschichte der österreichischen Rechtswissenschaft*, 141.

159. As Lorraine Daston observes in "Introduction: The Coming into Being of Scientific Objects," in *Biographies of Scientific Objects*, ed. Lorraine Daston (Chicago: University of Chicago Press, 2000), 6.

160. As observed brilliantly by Johannes Feichtinger in *Wissenschaft als reflexives Projekt*, 132–39.

161. *Öffentliche Vorlesungen an der K. K. Universität zu Wien im Sommer-Semester 1861* (Vienna: Aus der kaiserlich-königlichen Hof- und Staatsdruckerei, 1861), 7.

162. Verordnung des Ministers für Cultus und Unterricht, 15 April 1972, RGBL 57. See Walter, "Die Lehre des Verfassungs- und Verwaltungsrechtes an der Universität Wien," 614; Stolleis, *Public Law in Germany*, 284; Thomas Olechowski and Kamila Staudigl-Ciechowicz, "Allgemeines und österreichisches Staatsrecht, Verwaltungslehre und österreichisches Verwaltungsrecht," in *Die Wiener Rechts- und Staatswissenschaftliche Fakultät 1918–1938*, ed. Thomas Olechowski, Tamara Ehs, and Kamila Staudigl-Ciechowicz (Vienna: Vienna University Press, 2014), 467.

163. "Gutachten des Professors Dr. Lustkandl betreffend die Stellung der Staatswissenschaften," in *Gutachten und Anträge zur Reform der juristischen Studien: Erstattet von den rechts- und staatswissenschaftlichen Facultäten der österreichischen Universitäten* (Vienna: Karl Gorischek, 1887), 18–19.

164. Many reflected on the reasons underlying the complete reversal between Thun's curriculum and current views. The 1855 regulations were a product of their epoch, noted Krakau/Kraków professor Józef Kleczyński: "The teaching of operative public law could not exist in a country that possessed neither a constitution nor an institution for the defense of public law." "Gutachten des Professors Dr. Kleczyński," in *Gutachten und Anträge zur Reform der juristischen Studien: Erstattet von den rechts- und staatswissenschaftlichen Facultäten der österreichischen Universitäten* (Vienna: Karl Gorischek, 1887), 277.

165. "Separatvotum des Professors Dr. Dantscher betreffend die Bezeichnung 'österreichisches Staatsrecht,'" in *Gutachten und Anträge zur Reform der juristischen Studien: Erstattet von den rechts- und staatswissenschaftlichen Facultäten der österreichischen Universitäten* (Vienna: Karl Gorischek, 1887), 61–62.

166. "Separatvotum des Professors Dr. Dantscher," 61–64.

167. See Sitzung vom 14. December 1886, "Protokoll der Sitzungen des Professoren-Collegiums betreffend die Vehandlung über die von der Commission gestellten Anträge," in *Gutachten und Anträge zur Reform der juristischen Studien: Erstattet von den rechts- und staatswissenschaftlichen Facultäten der österreichischen Universitäten* (Vienna: Karl Gorischek, 1887), 53.

168. A different version of the point surfaced in Lustkandl's report when he noted that, in contrast to Germany, the concept "empire" (*Reich*) had a threefold meaning in the Habsburg lands: it was relevant for the empire as a whole, for the Kingdoms and Lands Represented in the Imperial Parliament, and the Lands of the Hungarian crown—all three were imperial composites of multiple lands. "Gutachten des Professors Dr. Lustkandl," 22.

169. See, for example, the submission "Gutachten des Professors Dr. Jellinek betreffend die Stellung der Staatswissenschaften, der Rechtsphilosophie und des Völkerrechts," in *Gutachten und Anträge zur Reform der juristischen Studien: Erstattet von den rechts- und staatswissenschaftlichen Facultäten der österreichischen Universitäten* (Vienna: Karl Gorischek, 1887), 27–28. (The proposal was rejected by the Vienna faculty at their meeting of November 28, 1886: see the meeting minutes at page 47 of the same volume.) The Krakau/Kraków faculty, however, did submit that international law should be mandatory: "Bericht des Decanates vom 20. Jänner 1887," in *Gutachten und Anträge zur Reform der juristischen Studien: Erstattet von den rechts- und staatswissenschaftlichen Facultäten der österreichischen Universitäten* (Vienna: Karl Gorischek, 1887), 242.

170. "Gutachten des Professors Dr. Jellinek," 27.

171. "Gutachten des Professors Dr. Jellinek," 27.

172. See, for example, the description of its contents in "Gutachten des Professors Dr. Dantscher betreffend das Studium der Staatswissenschaften und der Rechtsphilosophie," in *Gutachten und Anträge zur Reform der juristischen Studien: Erstattet von den rechts- und staatswissenschaftlichen Facultäten der österreichischen Universitäten* (Vienna: Karl Gorischek, 1887), 29.

173. "Gutachten des Professors Dr. Lustkandl," 19–20.

174. "Separatvotum des Professors Dr. Dantscher," 62.

175. "Gutachten des Professors Dr. Jellinek," 26. Lustkandl agreed they should be taught together.

176. "Gutachten des Professors Dr. Kasparek," in *Gutachten und Anträge zur Reform der juristischen Studien: Erstattet von den rechts- und staatswissenschaftlichen Facultäten der österreichischen Universitäten* (Vienna: Karl Gorischek, 1887), 273–74. See also: "Gutachten des Professors Dr. Dantscher," 30.

177. For the *Studienordnung* itself, see Gesetz, betreffend die rechts- und staatswissenschaftlichen Studien und Staatsprüfungen, 20 April 1893, RGBl 68; for the detailed subject breakdown, see the subsequent Verordnung des Ministers für Cultus und Unterricht, betreffend die Regelung der rechts- und staatswissenschaftlichen Studien und der theoretischen Staatsprüfungen, 24 December 1893, RGBl 204.

178. "Österreichische Reichsgeschichte (Geschichte der Staatsbildung und des öffentlichen Rechtes)." Under Thun's 1855 *Studienordnung*, law students took a class on Austrian history but in the philosophy faculty and taught by historians (and it was not an exam subject). Under the 1893 curriculum reform, the new class on imperial and legal history would be taught by law professors as an integral component of legal training. On the emergence of legal history as an academic field in Hungary, see Barna Mezey, "Rechtsgeschichte an der

Juristischen Fakultät in Budapest," *Journal on European History of Law* 2, no. 1 (2011): 21–28.

179. "Bericht der zur Berathung der Studienreformfrage eingesetzten Commission" (Graz), in *Gutachten und Anträge zur Reform der juristischen Studien: Erstattet von den rechts- und staatswissenschaftlichen Facultäten der österreichischen Universitäten* (Vienna: Karl Gorischek, 1887), 144.

180. "Bericht des Professoren-Collegiums vom 18. Jänner 1887" (Lemberg), in *Gutachten und Anträge zur Reform der juristischen Studien: Erstattet von den rechts- und staatswissenschaftlichen Facultäten der österreichischen Universitäten* (Vienna: Karl Gorischek, 1887), 318.

181. "Separatvotum des Professors Dr. Kasznica," in *Gutachten und Anträge zur Reform der juristischen Studien: Erstattet von den rechts- und staatswissenschaftlichen Facultäten der österreichischen Universitäten* (Vienna: Karl Gorischek, 1887), 357.

182. "Separatvotum des Professors Dr. Kasznica," 357.

183. The prize was announced in the *Wiener Zeitung*; see "Preisausschreibung," *Wiener Zeitung*, no. 103 (May 5, 1876): 1–2.

184. "Preisausschreibung," 1.

185. "Preisausschreibung," 1.

186. Alfons Huber, *Österreichische Reichsgeschichte: Geschichte der Staatsbildung und des öffentlichen Rechts* (Vienna: F. Tempsky, 1895).

187. Huber, *Österreichische Reichsgeschichte*, iii–iv.

188. Ulbrich, *Die rechtliche Natur der österreichisch-ungarischen Monarchie*, 38–39. The proclamation of the Austrian imperial title in 1804 was another candidate. The Hungarian historian János Mailáth would call it the "capstone" crowning and sealing the Austrian state: Johann Mailáth [János Nepomuck Jozsek Mailáth], *Geschichte des österreichischen Kaiserstaates* (Hamburg: Friedrich Perthes, 1850), 5:249. The Pragmatic Sanction of 1713 was another obvious candidate. Josef Redlich termed the sanction "the first positive formal affirmation of the Austrian-Bohemian-Hungarian [tradition of] imperial thought." Redlich, *Das österreichische Staats- und Reichsproblem*, 1:6.

189. A heated interwar debate about medieval *Landeshoheit*, and the territorial supremacy and *Reichsunmittelbarkeit* of a range of Markgrafschaften and Herrschaften, contested the point at which one could identify the emergence of an "einheitliche landesherrliche Gewalt." See the debate between Otto Stowasser and Alfons Dopsch: Otto H. Stowasser, "Die Entwicklung des Landes Oesterreich," *Vierteljahrschrift für Sozial- und Wirtschaftsgeschichte* 19, no. 4 (1926): 413–30; Alfons Dopsch, "Landesherrlichkeit in Österreich," *Vierteljahrschrift für Sozial- und Wirtschaftsgeschichte* 20, no. 3–4 (1928): 460–74.

190. See Stolleis, *Public Law in Germany*, 315–28; Walter Pauly, *Der Methodenwandel im deutschen Spätkonstitutionalismus: Ein Beitrag zu Entwicklung und Gestalt der Wissenschaft vom Öffentlichen Recht im 19. Jahrhundert* (Tübingen: J. C. B. Mohr, 1993); Peter von Oertzen, *Die soziale Funktion des staatsrechtlichen Positivismus: Eine wissenssoziologische Studie über die Entstehung des formalistischen Positivismus in der deutschen Staatsrechtswissenschaft* (Frankfurt am Main: Suhrkamp, 1974).

191. Paul Laband, *Das Budgetrecht nach dem Bestimmungen der preußischen Verfassungs-Urkunde unter Berücksichtigung der Verfassung des Norddeutschen Bundes* (Berlin: J. Guttentag, 1871), 75.

192. See the perceptive discussion in Stefan Korioth, "Erschütterung des staatsrechtlichen Positivismus im ausgehenden Kaiserreich: Anmerkungen zu frühen Arbeiten von Carl Schmitt, Rudolf Smend und Erich Kaufmann," *Archiv des öffentlichen Rechts* 117, no. 2 (1992): 216, as well as Christoph Schönberger, "Ein Liberaler zwischen Staatswille und Volkswille: Georg Jellinek und die Krise des staatsrechtlichen Positivismus um die

---

Jahrhundertwende," in *Georg Jellinek: Beiträge zu Leben und Werk*, ed. Stanley L. Paulson and Martin Schulte (Tübingen: Mohr Siebeck, 2000), 1–32.

193. In the context of advocating the separate treatment of constitutional and administrative law. "Bericht des Professoren-Collegiums vom 17. Jänner 1887" (Czernowitz), in *Gutachten und Anträge zur Reform der juristischen Studien: Erstattet von den rechts- und staatswissenschaftlichen Facultäten der österreichischen Universitäten* (Vienna: Karl Gorischek, 1887), 389.

194. "Gutachten des Professors Dr. Kleczyński," 277–78.

195. Alongside his activities at the university, Ulbrich had a notable political career, culminating in his appointment to the Upper House (Herrenhaus) in 1905. The quotations here are from the tribute by his close colleague: Ernst Mischler, "Josef Ulbrich: Ein Lebensbild," *Sammlung Gemeinnütziger Vorträge*, ed. Deutschen Vereine zur Verbreitung gemeinnütziger Kenntnisse in Prag, no. 400 (1912): 4. I am grateful to Johannes Feichtinger for sharing this source.

196. Joseph Ulbrich, *Lehrbuch des Oesterreichischen Staatsrechts: Für den akademischen Gebrauch und die Bedürfnisse der Praxis* (Vienna: Verlag von Carl Konegen, 1883), v.

197. Ulbrich, vi (emphasis in original).

198. Ulbrich, v.

199. Mischler, "Josef Ulbrich: Ein Lebensbild," 13 (emphasis in original). As Mischler recounts, Ulbrich was a staunch opponent of Bohemian historical rights/*Staatsrecht* (12). On legal positivism as a state-friendly science of the status quo, see Feichtinger, *Wissenschaft als reflexives Projekt*, 344–48; as well as Johannes Feichtinger, "'Staatsnation,' 'Kulturnation,' 'Nationalstaat': The Role of National Politics in the Advancement of Science and Scholarship in Austria from 1848 to 1938," in *The Nationalization of Scientific Knowledge in the Habsburg Empire, 1848–1918*, ed. Mitchell Ash and Jan Surman (Basingstoke: Palgrave Macmillan, 2012), 57–82; drawing on Peter von Oertzen's discussion of the same function in the German context: Oertzen, *Die soziale Funktion des staatsrechtlichen Positivismus*.

200. Ernst Mischler and Josef Ulbrich, eds., *Österreichisches Staatswörterbuch: Handbuch des gesamten österreichischen öffentlichen Rechtes*, 2nd ed. (Vienna: Alfred Hölder, 1905), 1:1–383.

201. Mischler, "Josef Ulbrich: Ein Lebensbild," 10.

202. Ernst Mischler and Josef Ulbrich, "Vorwort zur I. Auflage," in *Österreichisches Staatswörterbuch: Handbuch des gesamten österreichischen öffentlichen Rechtes*, 2nd ed., ed. Ernst Mischler and Josef Ulbrich (Vienna: Alfred Hölder, 1905), 1:iii.

203. Mischler, "Josef Ulbrich: Ein Lebensbild," 10.

204. Mischler and Ulbrich, "Vorwort zur I. Auflage," 1:iv.

205. Bernatzik's compendium of the Austrian constitutional laws was another noteworthy product of this new set of knowledge tools, likewise intended for academic and professional use. The popular *Catechism of the Austrian State Constitution*, already in its eighth edition by 1912, was published anonymously; Mischler suspected it must have been authored by Ulbrich. *Katechismus der österreichischen Staatsverfassung* (Vienna: G. J. Manz'schen Buchhandlung, 1874); Mischler, "Josef Ulbrich: Ein Lebensbild," 12.

206. See especially Klaus Kempter's marvelous multigenerational family biography of the Jellineks: Klaus Kempter, *Die Jellineks 1820–1955: Eine familienbiographischen Studie zum deutschjüdischen Bildungsbürgertum* (Düsseldorf: Droste, 1998), as well as Marsha L. Rozenblit, "Jewish Identity and the Modern Rabbi: The Cases of Isak Noa Mannheimer, Adolf Jellinek, and Moritz Güdemann in Nineteenth-Century Vienna," *Leo Baeck Institute Year Book* 35 (1990): 103–31.

207. Georg Jellinek, "Unsere Mutter: Ein Familiengedenkblatt" (1893), NGJ, BArch, N 1136/36.

208. Jellinek, "Unsere Mutter: Ein Familiengedenkblatt."

209. Wilhelm Windelband, "Zum Geleit," in Georg Jellinek, *Ausgewählte Schriften und Reden* (Aalen: Scientia Verlag, 1970 [1911]), 1:viii.

210. Windelband, vix.

211. Camilla Jellinek, "Georg Jellinek: Ein Lebensbild," in Georg Jellinek, *Ausgewählte Schriften und Reden* (Aalen: Scientia Verlag, 1970), 1:37*. The original 1911 edition of this posthumous collection was republished in 1970 to include a personal biographical sketch by Georg's widow, Camilla, that she did not want published during her lifetime. The asterisks result from the book's multiple paginations.

212. C. Jellinek, "Georg Jellinek: Ein Lebensbild," 1:37*–38*.

213. Windelband, "Zum Geleit," vii.

214. Georg Jellinek, "Die deutsche Philosophie in Österreich," *Im neuen Reich* 4, no. 2 (1874): 328.

215. Jellinek, 333–34.

216. Georg Jellinek to Victor Ehrenberg, 25 September 1873, in *Victor Ehrenberg und Georg Jellinek: Briefwechsel 1872–1911*, ed. Christian Ketter (Frankfurt: Vittorio Klostermann, 2005) (hereafter *Briefwechsel*), 201.

217. See Georg Jellinek to Victor Ehrenberg, 26 July 1878, in *Briefwechsel*, 278, where he describes his intention to contribute to the foundation of sociology, that "*Zukunftswissenschaft*."

218. Georg Jellinek, *Die Socialethische Bedeutung von Recht, Unrecht und Strafe* (Vienna: Alfred Hölder, 1878). The book later became especially famous for Jellinek's definition of law as "nothing other than the *ethical minimum*" (4). See Kempter, *Die Jellineks 1820–1955*, 191–95, and C. Jellinek, "Georg Jellinek: Ein Lebensbild," 21*–23*, for reception and significance.

219. Jellinek, *Die Socialethische Bedeutung von Recht, Unrecht und Strafe*, iii, 3, 4.

220. Jellinek, 3, 4.

221. Jellinek, 1–14; Jellinek critiques Hegel, and builds on Comte, at 5 and 4, respectively.

222. Jellinek wrote to Ehrenberg that the date for his trial lecture had already been set when he received the bad news. Jellinek to Ehrenberg, 26 July 1878, in *Briefwechsel*, 278.

223. Kempter, *Die Jellineks 1820–1955*, 195–97.

224. See Thomas Olechowski, "Von Georg Jellinek zu Hans Kelsen: Ein Beitrag zur Geschichte der Staatsrechtslehre an der Universität Wien um 1900," in *Migration und Innovation um 1900: Perspektiven auf das Wien der Jahrhundertwende*, ed. Elisabeth Röhrlich (Vienna: Böhlau, 2016), 379; Anna L. Staudacher, "Zwischen Emanzipation und Assimilation: Jüdische Juristen im Wien des Fin-de-Siècle," in *Hans Kelsen: Leben—Werk—Wirksamkeit*, ed. Robert Walter, Werner Ogris, and Thomas Olechowski (Vienna: Manzsche, 2009), 4–53.

225. For a rich exploration of the Jellinek family in the fulcrum of this "new Jewish question," see Kempter, *Die Jellineks 1820–1955*, 207–60. Conversion, in any case, was not an option for Jellinek: though he himself felt religiously indifferent, it would have meant a violent break with (and humiliation for) his prominent father, whom he respected enormously. Only in 1892, the year before his father's death, did Jellinek, by then a professor in Heidelberg and far away from the politics of Vienna, quietly leave the Jewish community. (And only in 1910, a year before his own death, did he convert to Lutheranism.) See the *Zeittafel* in *Victor Ehrenberg und Georg Jellinek: Briefwechsel 1872–1911*, ed. Christian Keller (Frankfurt: Vittorio Klostermann, 2005), 454, 456.

226. See Olechowski, "Von Georg Jellinek zu Hans Kelsen," 380.

227. Georg Jellinek, *Die rechtliche Natur der Staatenverträge: Ein Beirag zur juristischen Construction des Völkerrechts* (Vienna: Alfred Hölder, 1880).

228. Martti Koskenniemi, "Between Coordination and Constitution: International Law as a German Discipline," *Redescriptions* 15 (2011): 53; see also Koskenniemi, *Gentle Civilizer of Nations*, 200–206.

229. C. Jellinek, "Georg Jellinek: Ein Lebensbild," 31*.

230. C. Jellinek, 32*.

231. Georg Jellinek, *Die Lehre von den Staatenverbindungen* (Berlin: O. Haering, 1882), iii.

232. Jellinek, 12–14.

233. Jellinek, 5–6.

234. Jellinek, 7.

235. Jellinek, 3, 6, 12, 232–33 (quotation on 3).

236. Jellinek, 13.

237. Jellinek, 12.

238. Jellinek, 14.

239. Jellinek, 12.

240. Jellinek, 19, 26, 34–36, 42–44, 53–57 (quotation on 35).

241. Jellinek, iii, 11.

242. The interest was returned: the extensive correspondence in Jellinek's *Nachlass* reveals the extent of his North American readership. He had unriddled the United States, David K. Goss wrote in 1893: "Your work on the Staatenverbindungen has been received in America by scholars as finally settling the most difficult as well as momentous question of our Public Law." David K. Goss to Georg Jellinek, 22 November 1893, NGJ, BArch, N 1136/9. See notably Albert Bushnell Hart to Georg Jellinek, 19 April 1891, NGJ, BArch, N 1136/10; and Roscoe Pound to Georg Jellinek, 17 January 1907, NGJ, BArch, N 1136/23, in which Roscoe Pound could not resist correcting Jellinek's account of a case before the Supreme Court of Nebraska. On Jellinek's engagement with America, see also Duncan Kelly, "Revisiting the Rights of Man: Georg Jellinek on Right and the State," *Law and History Review* 22, no. 3 (2004): 493–529.

243. Jellinek, *Die Lehre von den Staatenverbindungen*, 4.

244. Jellinek would subsequently develop his thinking about types as a heuristic tool: see the influential *Typenlehre* in his masterwork *Allegemeine Staatslehre*, first published 1900.

245. Jellinek, *Die Lehre von den Staatenverbindungen*, 15.

246. Jellinek, 58. For the language of species and genus, see also 315.

247. Here we see borrowing from biology in practices and concepts of organizing knowledge, and not only in more substantive metaphors like that of the organism. On the latter, see Helmut Coing, "Bemerkung zur Verwendung des Organismusbegriffs in der Rechtswissenschaft des 19. Jahrhunderts," in *Biologismus im 19. Jahrhundert: Vorträge eines Symposiums vom 30. bis 31. Oktober 1970 in Frankfurt am Main*, ed. Gunter Mann (Stuttgart: Enke, 1973), 147–57; and Hubert Rottleuthner, "Biological Metaphors in Legal Thought," in *Autopoietic Law: A New Approach to Law and Society*, ed. Gunther Teubner (Berlin: Walter de Gruyter, 1988), 97–127.

248. Jellinek, *Die Lehre von den Staatenverbindungen*, 226–53.

249. Jellinek, 76–78.

250. Jellinek, 78.

251. "Allmäliges Ineinswachsen [*sic*] verschiedener Staaten im Laufe der Geschichte." Jellinek, 81.

252. For example: Jellinek devoted some eight pages to a critique of the analysis of his Vienna colleague Theodor Dantscher von Kollesberg: Jellinek, 227–34.

253. Bidermann, *Die rechtliche Natur der österreichisch-ungarischen Monarchie*, 47 (emphasis in original).

254. Dantscher von Kollesberg, *Der Monarchische Bundesstaat* (see title and generally).

255. Ulbrich, *Die rechtliche Natur der österreichisch-ungarischen Monarchie*, 53.

256. Ulbrich, 1.

257. Gumplowicz, *Das Oesterreichische Staatsrecht*, 48.

258. Gumplowicz, 49.

259. Gumplowicz, 49n47.

260. Marczali, *Ungarisches Verfassungsrecht*, iv.

261. Felix Stoerk, *Zur Methodik des öffentlichen Rechts* (Vienna: Alfred Hölder, 1885), 32, 34. On Stoerk and his critique of typological Begriffsjurisprudenz, see also Feichtinger, *Wissenschaft als reflexives Projekt*, 348–50; and in the context of the development of German imperial jurisprudence, Stolleis, *Public Law in Germany*, 326.

262. Stoerk, *Zur Methodik des öffentlichen Rechts*, 34.

263. Stoerk, 34.

264. Stoerk, 34.

265. Stoerk, 35.

266. Stoerk, 35.

267. Stoerk, 35.

268. Stoerk, 36.

269. Stoerk, 39–42 and generally.

270. Tezner, *Die Wandlungen der österreichisch-ungarischen Reichsidee*, 47 (emphasis in original).

271. Tezner, 48.

272. Tezner, 45.

273. Tezner, 50.

274. Tezner, 50.

275. Tezner, 49 (emphasis in original).

Chapter Three: Fictional States

1. Georg Jellinek, *Allgemeine Staatslehre*, 3rd ed. (1900; Berlin: O. Häring, 1914), 286.

2. Clifford Geertz, "What Is a State If It Is Not a Sovereign? Reflections on Politics in Complicated Places," *Current Anthropology* 45, no. 5 (2004): 579.

3. Sheldon Pollock, *The Language of the Gods in the World of Men: Sanskrit, Culture, and Power in Premodern India* (Berkeley: University of California Press, 2006).

4. Georg Jellinek, *Ueber Staatsfragmente* (Heidelberg: Gustav Koester, 1896), 11.

5. Jellinek, 27–28.

6. Jellinek, 29–30.

7. Jellinek, 55.

8. For Canada (for example), see Jellinek, 25.

9. Robert Redslob, *Abhängige Länder. Eine Analyse des Begriffs von der ursprüngli-chen Herrschergewalt: Zugleich eine staatsrechtliche und politische Studie über Elsaß-Lothringen, die österreichischen Königreiche und Länder, Kroatien-Slavonien, Bosnien-Herzegowina, Finnland, Island, die Territorien der nordamerikanischen Union, Kanada, Australien, Südafrika* (Leipzig: Veit & Comp., 1914), 1–2.

10. Redslob, 143.

11. Redslob, 155.

12. Redslob, 155.

13. Redslob, 164.

14. Josef L. Kunz, *Die Staatenverbindungen*, Handbuch des Völkerrechts (Stuttgart: W. Kohlhammer, 1929), vol. 2, pt. 4, 149.

15. Geertz, "What Is a State If It Is Not a Sovereign?"; Makau wa Mutua, "Why Redraw the Map of Africa: A Moral and Legal Inquiry," *Michigan Journal of International Law* 16 (1994–19): 1113–76; Siba N'Zatioula Grovogui, *Sovereigns, Quasi Sovereigns, and Africans: Race and Self-Determination in International Law* (Minneapolis: University of Minnesota Press, 1996); Robert H. Jackson, *Quasi-States: Sovereignty, International Relations, and the Third World* (Cambridge: Cambridge University Press, 1990); Robert H. Jackson, "Juridical Statehood in Sub-Saharan Africa," *Journal of International Affairs* 46, no. 1 (1992): 1–16 (on regimes that lack many "essential requirements of empirical statehood" and are "far from credible realities," 1); Siba N. Grovogui, "Regimes of Sovereignty: International Morality and the African Condition," *European Journal of International Relations* 8, no. 3 (2002): 315–38; Zubairu Wai, "Neo-patrimonialism and the Discourse of State Failure in Africa," *Review of African Political Economy* 39 (2012): 27–43.

16. *Protokolle des Verfassungs-Ausschusses im Österreichischen Reichstag 1848–1849*, ed. Anton Springer (Leipzig: G. Hirzel, 1885), 117ff.

17. For the latter: *Protokolle des Verfassungs-Ausschusses*, 347.

18. At Kremsier, Franz von Hein referred to the lands as "persons" (*Personen*) on January 22. See also Mayer on February 6: "If one has first recognized the provinces as persons in their autonomy, then one must grant them equal rights." *Protokolle des Verfassungs-Ausschusses*, 21, 122. But the formal terminology of moral and legal persons, with its background in Roman private law and its connection to corporations and associations, never really took hold as a standard description of these once-were-states. (Though see Robert Redslob's discussion "Sind die österreichischen Länder Körperschäften?," in Redslob, *Abhängige Länder*, 171). After all, the question of whether states themselves should be understood as juridical persons still aroused some controversy in German-language jurisprudence; other organic or patrimonial models of the state remained attractive to many. See, for example, Friedrich Carl von Savigny, *System des heutigen römischen Rechts* (Berlin: Veit und Comp., 1840), 2:236–41.

19. *Protokolle des Verfassungs-Ausschusses*, 42.

20. Kais. Patent vom 5. Marz 1860, RGBl. Nr. 56, text in Edmund Bernatzik, *Die österreichischen Verfassungsgesetze mit Erläuterung*, 2nd ed. (Vienna: Manzsche, 1911), 217–20.

21. See Stefan Malfèr, "Der Kampf um eine Verfassung 1859–1861," in *Der österreichische Neoabsolutismus als Verfassungs- und Verwaltungsproblem: Diskussionen über einen strittigen Epochenbegriff*, ed. Harm-Hinrich Brandt (Vienna: Böhlau Verlag, 2014), 428–29; Thomas Olechowski, "Das Oktoberdiplom 1860: Ende des Neoabsolutismus und Wiederaufstehung des Föderalismus in Österreich," *Jogtörténeti Tanulmányok* 10 (2010): 150–52.

22. In his conservative agenda, "historical-political individuality" worked against the centralist absolutism he opposed but also against a more bourgeois form of constitutionalism (and of course against any sort of national self-determination). See György Szabad, *Hungarian Political Trends between the Revolution and the Compromise (1848–1867)* (Budapest: Akadémiai Kiadó, 1977), 39ff., 82; Josef Redlich, *Das Österreichische Staats- und Reichsproblem: Geschichtliche Darstellung der inneren Politik der habsburgischen Monarchie von 1848 bis zum Untergang des Reiches* (Leipzig: Der Neue Geist Verlag, 1920), 1:500–547.

23. *Verhandlungen des österreichischen verstärkten Reichsrates 1860, nach den stenographischen Berichten* (Vienna: Friedrich Manz, 1860), 2:40.

24. "geheimnissvolles Zauberwort." Malfèr, "Der Kampf um eine Verfassung 1859–1861," 429.

25. *Verhandlungen des österreichischen verstärkten Reichsrates 1860*, 2:46–47.

26. *Verhandlungen des österreichischen verstärkten Reichsrates 1860*, 2:47.

27. *Verhandlungen des österreichischen verstärkten Reichsrates 1860*, 2:47.

28. *Verhandlungen des österreichischen verstärkten Reichsrates 1860*, 2:63.

29. *Verhandlungen des österreichischen verstärkten Reichsrates 1860*, 2:68.

30. Kais. Diplom vom 20. Oktober 1860, RGBl. Nr. 226, zur Reglung der inneren staatsrechtlichen Verhältnisse der Monarchie, in Bernatzik, *Die österreichischen Verfassungsgesetze*, 223–27.

31. Olechowski, "Das Oktoberdiplom 1860," 157. See also Ludwig Gumplowicz, *Einleitung in das Staatsrecht* (Berlin: Carl Heymanns, 1889), 217–18; Franz Hauke, "Verfassungsgeschichte," in *Österreichisches Staatswörterbuch: Handbuch des gesamten österreichischen öffentlichen Rechtes*, 2nd ed., ed. Ernst Mischler and Josef Ulbrich (Vienna: Alfred Hölder, 1909), 4:727; Gerald Stourzh, *Die Gleichberechtigung der Nationalitäten in der Verfassung und Verwaltung Österreichs, 1848–1918* (Vienna: Verlag der Österreichischen Akademie der Wissenschaften, 1985), 46, 52; Szabad, *Hungarian Political Trends between the Revolution and the Compromise*, 85.

32. Ludwig Gumplowicz, *Das Oesterreichische Staatsrecht (Verfassungs- und Verwaltungsrecht): Ein Lehr- und Handbuch* (Vienna: Manzsche, 1891), 77.

33. Gumplowicz, *Das Oesterreichische Staatsrecht*, 77.

34. The distinction between subjective and objective law was quite crucial in nineteenth-century German-language jurisprudence.

35. For an introduction to Bohemian claims to historical state rights, see Valentin Urfus, "Das Programm des sog. Böhmischen 'Historischen Staatsrechtes' in den Sechziger Jahren des 19. Jahrhunderts," in Andor Csizmadia, ed., *Die Freiheitsrechte und die Staatstheorien im Zeitalter des Dualismus: Materialien der VII. Ungarisch-tschechoslowakischen Rechtshistorikerkonferenz in Pécs (23–25 September, 1965)* (Budapest: Tankönyvkiadó, 1966), 103–9.

36. See Pieter Judson, *Exclusive Revolutionaries: Liberal Politics, Social Experience, and National Identity in the Austrian Empire, 1848–1914* (Ann Arbor: University of Michigan Press, 1996), 74–83.

37. *Beschlüße des Landtages der Markgrafschaft Mähren in den Sessionen der Jahre 1861–1868* (Brünn: Breza, Winiker & Co., 1869), 310.

38. *Verhandlungs-Protokoll aus der Sitzung des böhmischen Landtages vom ... April 1861* (Prague: Staathalterei-Druckerei, n.d. [1861?]), 53. Also available online at http://www.psp.cz/eknih/1861skc/1/stenprot/index.htm. This declaration, dated April 5 (but tabled on April 10), was brought by thirty-one delegates from the noble great landowners (*Grossgrundbesitz*), led by Friedrich Fürst Schwarzenberg, and posited the Renewed Land Order of 1627 as the legitimate legal foundation of further development. See Otto Urban, "Der Böhmische Landtag," in *Die Habsburgermonarchie 1848–1918*, vol. 7, *Verfassung und Paralamentarismus*, pt. 2, ed. Helmut Rumpler and Peter Urbanitsch (Vienna: Verlag der Österreichischen Akademie der Wissenschaften, 2000), 2004.

39. *Beschlüße des Landtages der Markgrafschaft Mähren in den Sessionen der Jahre 1861–1868*, 310.

40. *Verhandlungs-Protokoll aus der Sitzung des böhmischen Landtages vom ... April 1861*, 53.

41. *Verhandlungs-Protokoll aus der Sitzung des böhmischen Landtages vom ... April 1861*, 114. Czech into German translation from Joseph Alexander von Helfert, *Die Böhmische Frage in ihrer jüngsten Phase* (Prague: F. Tempsky, 1873), Urkunde 13b (second pagination), 51.

42. The "abstinence explanation" of June 17, 1863, that laid out the reasons for their withdrawal is another classic statement of "historical rights" and "constitutional individuality." See 4. Sitzung der 2. Session am 25 Juni 1863, *Stenographische Protokolle über die Sitzungen des Hauses des Abgeordneten in der II. Reichsratssession (vom 17. Juni 1863 bis 15. Februar 1864)* (Vienna: Kaiserlich-königlichen Hof- und Staatsdruckerei, 1864), 1:16–17.

See further Stanley Z. Pech, "Passive Resistance of the Czechs, 1863–1879," *Slavonic and East European Review* 36, no. 87 (1958): 434–52.

43. Otto Brunner, "Moderner Verfassungsbegriff und mittelalterlichen Verfassungsgeschichte," *Mitteilungen des Instituts für Österreichische Geschichtsforschung*, erg. bd. 14 (1939): 513–28; Brunner, *Land und Herrschaft: Grundlagen der Territorialen Verfassungsgeschichte Südostdeutschlands im Mittelalter* (Baden bei Wien: Rudolf M. Rohrer, 1939), 132–94.

44. From a protest directed to the emperor as the Settlement looked ever more likely in early 1867: V. Sitzung der ersten Session des böhmischen Landtages vom Jahre 1867, am 25 Februar 1867, *Stenographische Berichte des böhmischen Landtages* (Prague: Statthalterei-Buchdruckerei, 1867), 7.

45. "Declaration der böhmischen Abgeordneten vom 22 August 1868," reproduced in Gustav Kolmer, *Parlament und Verfassung in Oesterreich*, vol. 1 *1848–1869* (Vienna: Carl Fromme, 1902), 347–50; in Bernatzik, *Die österreichischen Verfassungsgesetze*, 1087–91; and in Helfert, *Die Böhmische Frage in ihrer jüngsten Phase*, Urkunde 18, 67–76 (second pagination). As Helfert includes the long preamble in addition to the declaration's programmatic ten points, I cite henceforth his edition for the German. On the declaration and its significance, see Valentin Urfus, "Die Ausprägung der Idee des historischen böhmischen Staatsrechtes in den sechziger Jahren des 19. Jahrhundert und der österreichisch-ungarische Dualismus," in *Der österreichisch-ungarische Ausgleich 1867: Materialien (Referate und Diskussion) der internationalen Konferenz in Bratislava 28.8–1.9 1967*, ed. Ľudovít Holotík (Bratislava: Verlag der Slowakischen Akademie der Wissenschaften, 1971), 545, 553–54; Urban, "Der Böhmische Landtag," 2014; Karel Schelle and Renata Veselá, "On the Traditions of Czech State Right Thinking: Parliamentarianism and the Struggle for Czech State Right during the Second Half of the Nineteenth Century," *Parliaments, Estates and Representation* 25, no. 1 (2005): 121.

46. Declaration, text in Helfert, *Die Böhmische Frage in ihrer jüngsten Phase*, 73 (second pagination).

47. Declaration, text in Helfert, 71 (second pagination).

48. [Ferenc Deák], *Die Rede Franz Deak's bei Gelegenheit der Adreßdebatte im Unterhause des ungarischen Landtages* (Vienna: Friedrich Förster & Brüder, n.d. [1861]), 8.

49. Helmut Slapnicka, "Der Weg der tschechischen Rechtswissenschaft von Wien nach Moskau," *Der Donauraum* 2, no. 1 (1957): 190. On the history of *Staatsrecht* claims, see Jana Osterkamp, "Geschichte als Argument: Das Böhmische Staatsrecht als politischer Leitbegriff im 19. Jahrhundert," *Střed* 1 (2016): 9–27; Luboš Velek, "Böhmisches Staatsrecht auf 'weichem Papier': Tatsache, Mythos und ihre symbolische Bedeutung in der tschechischen politischen Kultur," *Bohemia* 47 (2007): 103–18; Peter Haslinger, "Staatsrecht oder Staatsgebiet? Böhmisches Staatsrecht, territoriales Denken und tschechische Emanzipationsbestrebungen 1890–1914," in *Reiche und Territorien in Ostmitteleuropa: Historische Beziehungen und politische Herrschaftslegitimation*, ed. Dietmar Willoweit und Hans Lemberg (Munich: Oldenbourg, 2006), 345–58; Peter Haslinger, *Nation und Territorium im tschechischen politischen Diskurs 1880–1938* (Munich: Oldenbourg, 2010), 41–207.

50. See Richard Georg Plaschka, "Das böhmische Staatsrecht in tschechischer Sicht," collected in his *Nationalismus Staatsgewalt Widerstand: Aspekte nationaler und sozialer Entwicklung in Ostmittel- und Südosteuropa* (Vienna: Verlag für Geschichte und Politik, 1985), 59–72.

51. Josef Kalousek, *Einige Grundlagen des böhmischen Staatsrechtes* (Prague: J. S. Skrejšovský'schen Buchdruckerei, 1871), 5. For the Czech version of Kalousek's book, see Josef Kalousek, *České státní právo* (Prague: Skrejšovský, 1871; revised edition published by Bursík a Kohout, 1892).

52. Kalousek, *Einige Grundlagen des böhmischen Staatsrechtes*, 5.

53. David Graeber and Marshall Sahlins, *On Kings* (Chicago: HAU Books, 2017); Marshall Sahlins, "Stranger-Kings in General: The Cosmo-logics of Power," in *Framing Cosmologies: The Anthropology of Worlds*, ed. Allen Abramson and Martin Holbraad (Manchester: Manchester University Press, 2014), 137–63.

54. Kalousek, *Einige Grundlagen des böhmischen Staatsrechtes*, 25ff.

55. Hugo Toman, *Das böhmische Staatsrecht und die Entwicklung der österreichischen Reichsidee vom Jahre 1527 bis 1848: Eine rechtsgeschichtliche Studie* (Prague: J. G. Calve'sche k. k. Univers.-Buchhandlung, 1872), 3.

56. Kalousek, *Einige Grundlagen des böhmischen Staatsrechtes*, 59.

57. Kalousek, 48.

58. Kalousek, 53.

59. For an enormous, near-comprehensive compendium account of current Czech research on Kramář, running to almost eight hundred pages (with abstracts in English), see Jan Bílek and Luboš Velek, eds., *Karel Kramář (1860–1937): Život a dílo* (Prague: Masarykův ústav a Archiv AV ČR: Historický ústav AV ČR, 2009). See also Martina Winkler, *Karel Kramář (1860–1937): Selbstbild, Fremdwahrnehmungen und Modernisierungsverständnis eines tschechischen Politikers* (Munich: Oldenbourg Verlag, 2002).

60. Karel Kramář, *Das böhmische Staatsrecht* (Vienna: Verlag "Die Zeit," 1896), 3.

61. Kramář, 3.

62. Kramář, 6.

63. Kramář, 5.

64. Kramář, 6.

65. Kramář, 7.

66. Kramář, 8 (emphasis added).

67. Kramář, 8.

68. Kramář, 9.

69. Kramář, 17.

70. Kramář, 18.

71. Kramář, 19.

72. Kramář, 34.

73. Kramář, 25.

74. Karel Kramář, *Anmerkungen zur Böhmischen Politik*, trans. Josef Penížek (Vienna: Carl Konegen, 1906), 4.

75. Kramář, 72.

76. Kramář, 72.

77. Kramář, 74.

78. Kramář, 136.

79. Kramář, 137.

80. Kramář, *Das böhmische Staatsrecht*, 20 (emphasis added).

81. Kramář, 22.

82. Kramář, 34.

83. Toman, *Das böhmische Staatsrecht*, 226, 218; Kalousek, *Einige Grundlagen des böhmischen Staatsrechtes*, 65, 74. For an example from the Hungarian side: Heinrich [Henrik] Marczali, *Ungarisches Verfassungsrecht* (Tübingen: J. C. B. Mohr, 1911), 175.

84. Albert Apponyi, "The Army Question in Austria and Hungary," *Monthly Review* 16 (July 1904): 7.

85. Albert Apponyi, *Lectures on the Peace Problem and on the Constitutional Growth of Hungary Delivered in the United States and Canada* (Budapest: St. Stephen's Printing Press, 1911), 56–57 (emphasis added).

86. Friedrich Tezner, "Böhmisches Staatsrecht," *Die Zeit* 12, no. 148 (1897): 65.

87. Friedrich Tezner, *Technik und Geist des ständisch-monarchischen Staatsrechts* (Leipzig: Duncker und Humblot, 1901), 51, 53.

88. Tezner, 47, 49, 53 (quotation on 53).

89. *Verhandlungen des österreichischen verstärkten Reichsrates 1860*, 2:46 (per Szécsen) (emphasis added).

90. For a balanced appraisal of these sorts of claims of the continuity of Hungarian law, see László Péter, "Die Verfassungsentwicklung in Ungarn," in *Die Habsburgermonarchie 1848–1918*, vol. 7 *Verfassung und Parlamentarismus*, pt. 1, *Verfassungsrecht, Verfassungswirklichkeit, Zentrale Repräsentativkörperschaften*, ed. Helmut Rumpler and Peter Urbanitsch (Vienna: Verlag der Österreichischen Akademie der Wissenschaften, 2000), 239–40.

91. Edouard [Edvard] Beneš, *Bohemia's Case for Independence* (London: George Allen and Unwin, 1917), 18.

92. Beneš, 23.

93. Beneš, 23.

94. František Palacký, *Politisches Vermächtniss*, 2nd ed. (Prague: Theodor Mourek, 1872), 15.

95. František Palacký, *Oesterreichs Staatsidee* (Prague: J. L. Kober, 1866), 14.

96. Palacký, 14.

97. Kaiserl. Patent vom 2. Dezember 1848, RGBl. Nr. 1 ex 1849, text in Bernatzik, *Die österreichischen* Verfassungsgesetze, 113.

98. Ludwig Gumplowicz, *Das Recht der Nationalitäten und Sprachen in Oesterreich-Ungarn* (Innsbruck: Verlag der Wagner'schen Universitäts-Buchhandlung, 1879), 101.

99. Gumplowicz, 101.

100. Gumplowicz, 103, 105.

101. Gumplowicz, 29.

102. Edmund Bernatzik, *Die jurisrische Persönlichkeit der Behörden; Zugleich ein Beitrag zur Theorie der juristischen Personen* (Freiburg: J. C. B. Mohr, 1890), 100n259.

103. Rudolf von Herrnritt, *Nationalität und Recht: Dargestellt nach der österreichischen und ausländischen Gesetzgebung* (Vienna: Manzsche, 1899), 51–53.

104. Georg Jellinek, *System der subjektiven öffentlichen Rechte* (Freiburg: J. C. B. Mohr, 1892), 94.

105. Adolf Exner, "Subjektive Rechte aus Artikel 19 des Staatsgrundgesetzes über die allgemeinen Rechte der Staatsbürger," *Juristische Blätter* 49 (1892): 583.

106. Exner, "Subjective Rechte aus Artikel 19 des Staatsgrundgesetzes," 584.

107. The memorandum is reproduced as Beilage 15 in Eugen Brote, *Die rumänische Frage in Siebenbürgen und Ungarn: Eine politische Denkschrift* (Berlin: Puttkammer & Mühlbrecht, 1895), 177–81 (here 177).

108. Brote, 181.

109. Brote, 179.

110. N. N. [József Eötvös], *Über die Gleichberechtigung der Nationalitäten in Oesterreich* (Pest: Hartleben's Verlag, 1850), 100. For Eötvös's place in the region's intellectual history, see Balázs Trencsényi, Maciej Janowski, Monika Baár, Maria Falina, and Michal Kopeček, *A History of Modern Political Thought in East Central Europe* (Oxford: Oxford University Press, 2016), 1:292–93.

111. [Eötvös], *Über die Gleichberechtigung der Nationalitäten*, 83.

112. [Eötvös], 82.

113. See, for example, Gunther Teubner, "Globale Bukowina: Zur Emergenz eines transnationalen Rechtspluralismus," *Rechtshistorisches Journal* 15 (1996): 255–90; Michael Stolleis, "Vormodernes und Postmodernes Recht," *Quaderni Fiorentini per la storia del pensiero giuridico moderno* 37 (2008): 543–51.

114. Pieter Judson, *The Habsburg Empire: A New History* (Cambridge, MA: Harvard University Press, 2016); see also Tara Zahra, *Kidnapped Souls: National Indifference and the Battle for Children in the Bohemian Lands, 1900–1948* (Ithaca, NY: Cornell University Press, 2008).

115. Gerald Stourzh has thus argued that the binary between individual citizens and organized nationalities fitted out with representative organs does not capture the political reality of old Austria. See Gerald Stourzh, "Die Gleichberechtigung der Volkstämme als Verfassungsprinzip 1848–1918," in *Die Habsburgermonarchie 1848–1918*, vol. 3, *Die Völker des Reiches*, pt. 2, ed. Adam Wandruszka and Peter Urbanitsch (Vienna: Verlag der Österreichischen Akademie der Wissenschaften, 1980), 1149–57. On the municipalities as significant sites of nationalist activity, see Jeremy King, "The Municipal and the National in the Bohemian Lands, 1848–1914," *Austrian History Yearbook* 42 (2011): 89–109.

116. See Zahra, *Kidnapped Souls*, 32–39; Börries Kuzmany, "Habsburg Austria: Experiments in Non-territorial Autonomy," *Ethnopolitics* 15, no. 1 (2016): 43–65.

117. Hans von Frisch, contribution to "Die Stellung der Krönländer im Gefüge der österreichischen Verfassung: Eine Rundfrage," in *Länderautonomie*, Sonderheft of the Österreichische Zeitschrift für öffentliches Recht, ed. Edmund Bernatzik, Max Freiherr, Hussarek von Heinlein, Heinrich Lammasch, and Adolf Menzel, with Hans Kelsen (Vienna: Manzsche, 1916), 36.

118. Otto Bauer, *Die Nationalitätenfrage und die Sozialdemokratie* (Vienna: Wiener Volksbuchhandlung Ignaz Brand, 1907); Karl Renner, *Staat und Nation: Zur österreichischen Nationalitätenfrage* (Vienna: Dietl, 1899).

119. Karl Renner, *Das Selbstbestimmungsrecht der Nationen in besonderer Anwendung auf Oesterreich* (Leipzig: Franz Deuticke, 1918), unpaginated preface (*Vorrede*). This text was a much-revised and retitled second edition of his earlier work; Rudolf Springer [Karl Renner], *Der Kampf der österreichischen Nationen um den Staat* (Leipzig: Deuticke, 1902).

120. Renner, *Das Selbstbestimmungsrecht der Nationen*.

121. Renner, 29ff.

122. Renner, 36.

123. Renner, 38–39.

124. Renner, 40–41.

125. Renner, 67.

126. Renner, 69.

127. Renner, 74.

128. See Josef Lukas, "Territorialitäts- und Personalitätsprinzip im österreichischen Nationalitätenrecht," *Jahrbuch des öffentlichen Recht der Gegenwart* 2 (1908): 349 and passim.

129. Renner, *Das Selbstbestimmungsrecht der Nationen*, 78.

130. Joseph Maria Baernreither, *Zur böhmischen Frage: Eine politische Studie* (Vienna: Manzsche, 1910), 13–14.

131. Baernreither, 13–14. In Baerenreither's assessment, this idea possessed utility for administrative law, even if it was not possible to implement it fully.

132. Renner, *Das Selbstbestimmungsrecht der Nationen*, 115.

133. The Czech national movement was from the start suspended between two different genres of claim that corresponded to differing conceptions of the nation: on the one hand, the historical-constitutional (*historisch-staatsrechtliche*) idea with its *Landespatriotismus* for the (multiethnic) lands of the Bohemian crown, and, on the other, the natural law/liberal tradition that understood the nation in ethnic terms. The ethnic-national position became associated with the Young Czechs, who broke away from the National Party in the early 1870s, rejecting the inflexible, passive program of their elders who had unwaveringly held to their *Staatsrecht* position and their boycott of the imperial parliament.

These divisions were not fixed: someone like Palacký fluctuated between positions. See Jiří Kořalka, *Tschechen im Habsburgerreich und in Europa, 1815–1914: Sozialgeschichtliche Zusammenhänge der neuzeitlichen Nationsbildung und der Nationalitätenfrage in den böhmischen Ländern* (Vienna: Verlag für Geschichte und Politik, 1991); Haslinger, *Nation und Territorium im tschechischen politischen Diskurs*, 41–207; Stanley B. Winters, "The Young Czech Party (1874–1914): An Appraisal," *Slavic Review* 28, no. 3 (1969): 426–44; Bruce M. Garver, *The Young Czech Party 1874–1901 and the Emergence of a Multi-party System* (New Haven, CT: Yale University Press, 1978); Anna M. Drabek, "Tschechen und Deutsche in den böhmischen Ländern: Vom nationalen Erwachen der Tschechen bis zum Vorabend des Ersten Weltkrieges," in *Volk, Land und Staat: Landesbewußtsein, Staatsidee und nationale Fragen in der Geschichte Österreichs*, ed. Erich Zöllner (Vienna: Österreichischer Bundesverlag, 1984), 54–82; Schelle and Veselá, "On the Traditions of Czech State Right Thinking." For a subtle analysis that eschews a simple characterization of these programs as "backward looking" and "forward looking" respectively, and that shows how the historical-constitutional tradition (whose slow emergence from the late eighteenth century had been fundamentally shaped by the concomitant rise of historicism and new historical methods) had deeper roots in the Czech national revival than the ethnic or Austroslavist tradition, see Urfus, "Das Programm des sog. Böhmischen 'Historischen Staatsrechtes,'" 103–9. See further Eagle Glassheim, *Noble Nationalists: The Transformation of the Bohemian Aristocracy* (Cambridge, MA: Harvard University Press, 2005), 23–33.

134. Renner, *Das Selbstbestimmungsrecht der Nationen*, 118.

135. Renner, 118. As he summed up on 136: "die Nation als freie Einheit, als juristische Person des privaten und als Körperschaft des öffentlichen Rechtes organisiert werden muss, wenn ihr in Wahrheit die Rechte zukommen sollen, die ihr vermeint sind."

136. Renner, 123.

137. Renner, 146.

138. Renner, 150.

139. See Arno Mayer, *Wilson vs. Lenin: The Political Origins of the New Diplomacy, 1917–1918* (Cleveland: World, 1964); Erez Manela, *The Wilsonian Moment: Self-Determination and the International Origins of Anticolonial Nationalism* (Oxford: Oxford University Press, 2007); Eric Weitz, "Self-Determination: How a German Enlightenment Idea Became the Slogan of National Liberation and a Human Right," *American Historical Review* 120, no. 2 (2015): 462–96; Hussein Omar, "The Arab Spring of 1919," LRB Blog, April 4, 2019, https://www.lrb.co.uk/blog/2019/april/the-arab-spring-of-1919; Adom Getachew, *Worldmaking after Empire: The Rise and Fall of Self-Determination* (Princeton, NJ: Princeton University Press, 2019), chap. 2.

140. See further Natasha Wheatley, "Spectral Legal Personality in Interwar International Law: On New Ways of Not Being a State," *Law and History Review* 35, no. 3 (2017): 753–87; Wheatley, "New Subjects in International Law and Order," in *Internationalisms: A Twentieth-Century History*, ed. Patricia Clavin and Glenda Sluga (Cambridge: Cambridge University Press, 2017), 265–86; Wheatley, "Making Nations into Legal Persons between Imperial and International Law: Scenes from a Central European History of Group Rights," *Duke Journal of Comparative and International Law* 28 (2018): 481–94; Börries Kuzmany, "Non-Territorial Autonomy in Interwar European Minority Protection and its Habsburg Legacies," in *Remaking Central Europe: The League of Nations and the Former Habsburg Lands*, ed. Peter Becker and Natasha Wheatley (Oxford: Oxford University Press, 2020), 315–42; Anna Adorjáni and László Bence Bari, "National Minority: The Emergence of the Concept in the Habsburg and International Legal Thought," *Acta Universitatis Sapientiae, European and Regional Studies* 16, no. 1 (2019): 7–37.

141. Point two of the "Programme-minimum" ran: "Les Etats garantiront aux nationalités comprises dans leur territoire l'égalité civile, la liberté religieuse et le libre usage de

leur langue." The nine points are reproduced in full in the frontispiece of each volume of the *Recueil de Rapports* cited in the following note.

142. Organisation Centrale pour une Paix durable, ed., *Recueil de Rapports sur les différents points du programme-minimum*, 4 vols. (The Hague: Martinus Nijhoff, 1916–18).

143. Franz Oppenheimer, "Nationale Autonomie," in *Recueil de Rapports sur les différents points du programme-minimum*, ed. Organisation Centrale pour une Paix durable (The Hague: Martinus Nijhoff, 1918), 4:74–103. Oppenheimer's sociological work was also deeply influenced by Ludwig Gumplowicz.

144. Halvdan Koht, *Avant-project d'un traité général relatif aux droits des minorités nationales* (The Hague: Organisation Centrale pour une Paix durable, 1917), 20 and passim. Koht was not the only foreigner to come to this conclusion. See, for example, the work of the French diplomat Jacques Fouques-Duparc, *La protection des minorités de race, de langue et de religion: Étude de droit des gens* (Paris: Librairie Dalloz, 1922).

145. Koht, *Avant-project d'un traité général*, 20–28 (with section 19 on page 28). Erwin Viefhaus places this moment within the context of the broader development toward international minority protection in his *Die Minderheitenfrage und die Entstehung der Minderheitenschutzverträge auf der Pariser Friedenskonferenz 1919: Eine Studie zur Geschichte des Nationalitätenproblems im 19. und 20. Jahrhundert* (Frankfurt am Main: Textor Verlag, 2008), 43–45.

146. Lammasch's essay "Das österreichische Nationalitätenrecht," dated 1917, is included in Heinrich Lammasch, *Europas elfte Stunde* (Munich: Verlag für Kulturpolitik, 1919), 120.

147. Charles Roden Buxton, "Nationality," in *Recueil de Rapports sur les différents points du programme-minimum*, ed. Organisation Centrale pour une Paix durable (The Hague: Martinus Nijhoff, 1916), 1:49–66.

148. Charles Roden Buxton, "Nationality," in *Towards a Lasting Settlement*, ed. Charles Roden Buxton (New York: Macmillan, 1916), 55–56.

149. Eugen Ehrlich, *The National Problems in Austria*, International Congress for the Study of the Principles of a Durable Peace (The Hague: Martinus Nijhoff, 1917), 4, 6.

150. Ehrlich, 7.

151. "den Spieß umzudrehen, den Gegnern ihre eigenen politischen Sünden und Schwächen vorzuhalten." Rudolf Laun, *Das Nationalitätenrecht als internationales Problem*, Sonderabdruck aus der *Österreichischen Zeitschrift für öffentliches Recht* (Vienna: Manzsche, 1917), 17.

152. Laun, 19.

153. Laun, 20.

154. For similar skepticism: Lammasch, *Europas elfte Stunde*, 123.

155. Laun, *Das Nationalitätenrecht als internationales Problem*, 6.

156. Laun, 7.

157. Laun, 7.

158. Laun, 7.

159. Laun, 11.

160. See Rudolf Laun, *Entwurf eine Internationalen Vertrages über den Schutz nationaler Minderheiten* (Berlin: Heymann, 1920).

161. This latter phase of his career has been the subject of new research; see especially Lora Wildenthal, "Rudolf Laun and the Human Rights of Germans in Occupied and Early West Germany," in *Human Rights in the Twentieth Century*, ed. Stefan-Ludwig Hoffmann (Cambridge: Cambridge University Press, 2011), 125–44; Wildenthal, *The Language of Human Rights in West Germany* (Philadelphia: University of Pennsylvania Press, 2012). More generally, see Rainer Biskup, *Rudolf Laun: Staatsrechtslehrer zwischen Republik und Diktatur* (Hamburg: ConferencePoint Verlag, 2010).

162. Rudolf Laun, *Der Wandel der Ideen Staat und Volk als Äusserung des Weltgewissens: Eine völkerrechtliche und staatsrechtliche Untersuchung auf philosophischer Grundlagen* (Berlin: Bruno Cassirer, 1933), 279.

163. Rudolf Laun at the Siebente Jahreversammlung of the Deutschen Gesellschaft für Völkerrecht, in the discussion on May 27, 1926, following G[odehard J]. Ebers, "Sind im Völkerrecht allein die Staaten parteifähig?," *Mitteilungen der Deutschen Gesellschaft für Völkerrecht* 7 (1926): 33.

164. See, for example, Jean André Eichhoff to Arthur Salter, 19 June 1926, League of Nations Archive, Geneva (hereafter LNA), R1616, 41/54546/609, and the subsequent correspondence in the same file.

165. Edouard de Haller, "Etude sur les conditions d'avant-guerre en Autriche en vue d'en tirer des donnée utilisables pour l'examen des problèmes de minorités," 2 April 1927, LNA, R1616, 41/58578/609. De Haller cited Josef Redlich and many others from the cohort of Austrian jurists discussed in this book.

166. See, for example, the literature cited in the long, programmatic, 1932 article by Austrian jurist Josef Kunz (on whom, see chapter 6), published on the cusp of his emigration to the United States: Josef L. Kunz, "Prolegomena zur einer allgemeinen Theorie des internationalen Rechtes nationaler Minderheiten," *Zeitschrift für öffentliches Recht* 12 (1932): 221–2. See also Kunz, *Der Revision der Pariser Friedensverträge: Eine Völkerrechtliche Untersuchung* (Vienna: Julius Springer, 1932), 260. These theoretical and administrative spheres also overlapped: Kunz, acting on behalf of the Austrian League of Nations Society, submitted a memorandum on Austrian minorities protection to the league in 1921: Josef Kunz for the Austrian League of Nations Union to Eric Drummond, 5 January 1921, LNA, R1615, 41/10217/609, and the subsequent correspondence in the same file.

167. Hans Kelsen considered rights guaranteed in the new Austria through the *Minderheitenschutz* norms of the Treaty of Saint-Germain and observed that they did not go further than article 19 and in fact remained a little behind, "als die Einführung einer Staatssprache ausdrücklich zugelassen wird." Hans Kelsen, *Österreichisches Staatsrecht: Ein Grundriss Entwicklungsgeschichtlich Dargestellt* (Tübingen: J. C. B. Mohr, 1923), 63.

168. Alfred Verdross, *Völkerrecht* (Berlin: Julius Springer, 1937), 226 (emphasis in original).

169. Verdross, 230.

170. Verdross, 230.

171. Verdross, 230–31 (emphasis in original). For a survey of the jurisprudence of *Volksgruppenrecht* in the 1920s and 1930s, see Samuel Salzborn, "'Volksgruppenrecht': Zum Transfer(versuch) eines politischen Paradigmas in das Europäische Minderheitenrecht," in *Rechtstransfer in der Geschichte / Legal Transfer in History*, ed. Vanessa Duss, Nikolaus Linder, Katrin Kastl, Christina Börner, Fabienne Hirt, and Felix Züsli (Munich: Martin Meidenbauer, 2006), 44–63.

172. Resolutions to the XII Nationalities Congress, held in Geneva in September 1936. Quoted in Verdross, *Völkerrecht*, 231. A wide spectrum of groups and individuals produced varied proposals to reform the regime so that minorities could be parties to proceedings and thereby have a standing and personality of their own. For a survey of these proposals, see, for example, Otto Junghann, *Das Minderheitenschutzverfahren vor dem Völkerbund* (Tübingen: J. C. B. Mohr, 1934), 33–35.

173. Seventh Meeting (October 6, 1932), Minutes of the Sixth Committee, Records of the Thirteenth Ordinary Session of the Assembly, *League of Nations Official Journal*, special supplement No. 109 (1932): 44.

174. Mark Mazower, "Minorities and the League of Nations in Interwar Europe," *Daedalus* 126, no. 2 (1997): 55–56; and see Virginia L. Gott, "The National Socialist Theory of International Law," *American Journal of International Law* 32, no. 4 (1938): 714.

175. Fifth Meeting (October 3, 1933), Minutes of the Sixth Committee (Political Questions), Records of the Fourteenth Ordinary Session of the Assembly, *League of Nations Official Journal*, special supplement No. 120 (1933): 23.

176. Sixth Meeting (October 4, 1933), Minutes of the Sixth Committee, Records of the Fourteenth Ordinary Session of the Assembly, *League of Nations Official Journal*, special supplement No. 120 (1933): 35.

177. Sixth Meeting (October 4, 1933), Minutes of the Sixth Committee, 39.

Chapter Four: Pure Theory

1. Hans Kelsen, "The Conception of the State and Social Psychology: With Special Reference to Freud's Group Theory," *International Journal of Psychoanalysis* 5 (January 1924): 1 (emphasis added).

2. It is hard to overstate Kelsen's significance for legal philosophy. As Albert A. Ehrenzweig reflected on the occasion of Kelsen's ninetieth birthday in 1971, "For half a century, there have hardly been publications in legal philosophy anywhere, books or articles, that have not praised or opposed the Pure Theory of Law." Albert A. Ehrenzweig, "Preface," *California Law Review* 59, no. 3 (1971): 609.

3. For a comprehensive treatment of Kelsen's life, see Thomas Olechowski's monumental thousand-page biography: Olechowski, *Hans Kelsen: Biographie eines Rechtswissenschaftlers* (Tübingen: Mohr Siebeck, 2020). For a clear and succinct overview of Kelsen's legal theory, see Olechowski, "Kelsens Rechtslehre im Überblick," in *Hans Kelsen: Eine politikwissenschaftliche Einführung*, ed. Tamara Ehs (Vienna: Nomos, 2009), 47–65. A comprehensive, chronological edition of Kelsen's immense oeuvre—encompassing some eighteen thousand pages of published work in addition to unpublished material—is gradually appearing under the editorship of Matthias Jestaedt with the cooperation of the Hans Kelsen Institute in Vienna: *Hans Kelsen Werke*, ed. Matthias Jestaedt (Tübingen: Mohr Siebeck, 2007–). While the legal-philosophical literature on Kelsen is enormous, the historical literature on Kelsen is still modest. An impression of the landscape of Kelsen scholarship is given by the *Schriftenreihe*/book series published by the Hans Kelsen Institute, currently running to forty-one volumes: see https://www.univie.ac.at/staatsrecht-kelsen/schriftenreihe.php. On the constitutional court he helped design, see Stanley L. Paulson, "Constitutional Review in the United States and Austria: Notes on the Beginnings," *Ratio Juris* 16, no. 2 (2003): 223–39. Kelsen contributed significantly not only to legal theory but also to political theory, writing extensively on democracy as well as the Marxist theory of the state. On the nonreception of his political theory in the English-speaking world, see Nadia Urbanati and Carlo Invernizzi Accetti, "Editors' Introduction," in Hans Kelsen, *The Essence and Value of Democracy*, trans. Brian Graf (Lanham, MD: Rowman and Littlefield, 2013), 1–24.

4. Hans Kelsen, "Autobiographie (1947)," in *Hans Kelsen Werke*, ed. Matthias Jestaedt (Tübingen: Mohr Siebeck, 2007), 1:59.

5. Kelsen, 1:59–60.

6. Kelsen, 1:60. On Kelsen in the Habsburg context, see Christoph Schönberger, "Hans Kelsen's *Main Problems in the Theory of Public Law*: Transition from the State as Substance to the State as Function," trans. Bonnie Litschewski and Stanley L. Paulson, in *Hans Kelsen Werke*, vol. 2, *Veröffentlichte Schriften 1911*, pt. 1, ed. Matthias Jestaedt (Tübingen: Mohr Siebeck, 2008), especially 42; Manfred Baldus, "Hapsburgian Multiethnicity and the 'Unity of the State'—On the Structural Setting of Kelsen's Legal Thought," in *Hans Kelsen and Carl Schmitt: A Juxtaposition*, ed. Dan Diner and Michael Stolleis (Gerlingen: Bleicher, 1999), 13–25; Johannes Feichtinger, *Wissenschaft als reflexives Projekt. Von Bolzano über Freud zu Kelsen: Österreichische Wissenschaftsgeschichte 1848–1938* (Bielefeld: Transcript

NOTES TO CHAPTER 4 [335]

Verlag, 2010); Franz Leander Fillafer, "Imperial Diversity, Fractured Sovereignty, and Legal Universals: Hans Kelsen and Eugen Ehrlich in Their Habsburg Context," *Modern Intellectual History* 19, no. 2 (2022): 421–43.

7. For an introduction to organic theories of the state, see Michael Stolleis, *Public Law in Germany, 1800–1914* (New York: Berghahn Books, 2001), 90–115; and to the historical school, see John E. Toews, *Becoming Historical: Cultural Reformation and Public Memory in Early-Nineteenth Century Berlin* (Cambridge: Cambridge University Press, 2004).

8. Rudolf Laun, "Naturrecht und Völkerrecht," *Jahrbuch für internationales Recht* 4 (1954): 25.

9. Alfred Verdross, "Österreich—Heimat der Rechtstheorie," in *Philosophie huldigt dem Recht. Hans Kelsen, Adolf J. Merkl, Alfred Verdross, Ehrendoktoren der Universität Salzburg: Erinnerungsband zum 1. June 1967* [pamphlet] (Europa Verlag, 1967), 51. Christoph Scönberger notes how so many of the major critics of mainstream (Labandian) German constitutional legal thought stemmed from the Habsburg lands: there could be no simple "will of the state" in these multinational circumstances. Christoph Schönberger, "Ein Liberaler zwischen Staatswille und Volkswille: Georg Jellinek und die Krise des staatsrechtlichen Positivismus um die Jahrhundertwende," in *Georg Jellinek: Beiträge zu Leben und Werk*, ed. Stanley L. Paulson and Martin Schulte (Tübingen: Mohr Siebeck, 2000), 15–17.

10. Discussions of the fact/norm distinction in Kelsen tend to refer simply to its neo-Kantian derivation. As Kelsen himself recounted in the preface to the second edition (1923) of *Hauptprobleme der Staatsrechtslehre*, he only belatedly learned of the parallel between his work and that of the prominent neo-Kantian Hermann Cohen, especially regarding the "purity of method." He had reached a similar conclusion "more instinctually," he wrote in his "Autobiographie" (36–37). Scholars often repeat this framing—so conducive to the Kelsen mystique—rather than point out that the (neo-Kantian) project of cleanly separating fact and norm lay at the core of Jellinek's late methodology. When Kelsen's first major work, *Hauptprobleme der Staatsrechtslehre*, was published in 1911, he acknowledged that "every page" bore the trace of Jellinek's influence—which a thorough engagement with Jellinek can only confirm. The genealogy runs not from Cohen but from neo-Kantian Wilhelm Windelband over Jellinek. In this I agree with Olechowski's observations in Thomas Olechowski, "Von Georg Jellinek zu Hans Kelsen: Ein Beitrag zur Geschichte der Staatsrechtslehre an der Universität Wien um 1900," in *Migration und Innovation um 1900: Perspektiven auf das Wien der Jahrhundertwende*, ed. Elisabeth Röhrlich (Vienna: Böhlau, 2016), 375, 395–96 and Olechowski, *Hans Kelsen*, 921. Part of the confusion stems from doubts about Jellinek's own neo-Kantianism amid the breadth of his methodological inspirations. On all these topics, see further in this chapter. Note Kelsen later crediting Rudolf Stammler with the introduction of "Kantian transcendental philosophy" into legal science: Hans Kelsen, *Das Problem der Souveränität und die Theorie des Völkerrechts: Beitrag zu einer reinen Rechtslehre* (Tübingen: C. B. Mohr, 1920), vi. Stammler wrote after Jellinek's *System der subjektiven öffentlichen Rechte* (1892), discussed below.

11. While there are many discussions of Jellinek's deployment of the *Sein/Sollen* distinction, no one seems to have noticed that Jellinek was, apparently, the first to introduce this terminology as a holistic framework for legal science. The history reconstructed in this chapter, especially regarding Jellinek's relationship to the neo-Kantian philosopher Wilhelm Windelband, shows why it is highly explicable that this departure would originate with him. In his book-length treatment of Jellinek, Jens Kersten refers in passing to Jellinek's 1892 deployment of the neo-Kantian framework as a more superficial question of terminology. In light of the way Jellinek painstakingly elaborated a new legal methodology on that basis (see below), this assessment is puzzling. Jens Kersten, *Georg Jellinek und die klassische Staatslehre* (Tübingen: Mohr Siebeck, 2000), 145, 150.

12. Jellinek to Ehrenberg, 16 January 1891, in Christian Keller, ed. *Victor Ehrenberg und Georg Jellinek: Briefwechsel 1872-1911* (Frankfurt: Vittorio Klostermann, 2005) (hereafter *Briefwechsel*), 369-70.

13. "Zur Verjudung der Wiener Universität," *Das Vaterland*, no. 127 (May 10, 1883): 5 (emphasis in original). See also Camilla Jellinek, "Georg Jellinek: Ein Lebensbild," in Georg Jellinek, *Ausgewählte Schriften und Reden* (Aalen: Scientia Verlag, 1970), 1:34* (the asterisk distinguishes two paginations in this text). The community of international law was long understood as a community of Christian states; it was only in the nineteenth century that "civilization" comprehensively replaced Christianity as the ostensible qualification for participation. For an introduction, see Gerrit Gong, *The Standard of 'Civilization' in International Society* (New York: Oxford University Press, 1984); and Ntina Tzouvala, *Capitalism as Civilisation: A History of International Law* (Cambridge: Cambridge University Press, 2020).

14. As observed by Olechowski, "Von Georg Jellinek zu Hans Kelsen," 381.

15. Paul, born May 1884; Walter, born July 1885; and Clara Dorothea, born January 1888.

16. Report and resolutions in *Das Vaterland*, no. 119 (May 2, 1889): 3-5 (quotation on 5).

17. Lammasch would become a significant international lawyer and serve the empire's last minister president in October and November 1918. See Gerhard Oberkofler and Eduard Rabofsky, *Heinrich Lammasch (1853-1920): Notizen zur akademischen Laufbahn des großen österreichischen Völker-und Strafrechtsgelehrten* (Innsbruck: Archiv der Leopold-Franzens-Universität, 1993); and Markus P. Beham, "A Forgotten Lighthouse of International Law: Heinrich Lammasch and the League of Nations," *German Yearbook of International Law* 62 (2019): 245-74.

18. It was reported widely in newspapers in Germany and Austria. See also Georg Jellinek to Victor Ehrenberg, 3 October 1889, in *Briefwechsel*, 360-61.

19. On this period, see C. Jellinek, "Georg Jellinek: Ein Lebensbild," 55*-60*; Klaus Kempter, *Die Jellineks 1820-1955: Eine familienbiographische Studie zum deutschjüdischen Bildungsbürgertum* (Düsseldorf: Droste Verlag, 1998), 244-45.

20. Jellinek to Ehrenberg, 4 July 1890, in *Briefwechsel*, 366.

21. Georg Jellinek to Rosalie Jellinek, 22 October 1890, in C. Jellinek, "Georg Jellinek: Ein Lebensbild," 75*-77* (quotation on 77).

22. Camilla would become an important writer, lawyer, and activist for women's rights.

23. C. Jellinek, "Georg Jellinek: Ein Lebensbild," 82*-85*.

24. On this period in Georg and Camilla's lives (including the Eranos Circle), see Kempter, *Die Jellineks*, 261-91. Religion was central to Jellinek's widely influential essay on the rights of man; see Duncan Kelly, "Revisiting the Rights of Man: Georg Jellinek on Right and the State," *Law and History Review* 22, no. 3 (2004): 493-529. On Jellinek's significant influence on Weber, see Stefan Breuer, *Georg Jellinek und Max Weber: Von der sozialen zur soziologischen Staatslehre* (Baden-Baden: Nomos, 1999); Peter Ghosh, "Max Weber und Georg Jellinek: Two Divergent Conceptions of Law," *Saeculum* 50 (2008): 299-347; Andreas Anter, "Max Weber und Georg Jellinek: Wissenschaftliche Beziehungen, Affinitäten und Divergenzen," in *Georg Jellinek: Beiträge zu Leben und Werk*, ed. Stanley L. Paulson and Martin Schulte (Tübingen: Mohr Siebeck, 2000), 67-86.

25. George Jellinek to Victor Ehrenberg, 9 June 1873, in *Briefwechsel*, 190-91.

26. Wilhelm Windelband, "Zum Geleit," in Georg Jellinek, *Ausgewählte Schriften und Reden* (1911; Aalen: Scientia Verlag, 1970), 1:v, vi.

27. Georg Jellinek to Ludwig Felix, 21 November 1890, Nachlass Georg Jellinek, Bundesarchiv Koblenz (hereafter NGJ, BArch), N 1136/43; also extracted in C. Jellinek, "Georg Jellinek: Ein Lebensbild," 77*-79*.

28. Wilhelm Dilthey, *Einleitung in die Geisteswissenschaften: Versuch einer Grundlegung für das Studium der Gesellschaft und der Geschichte* (Leipzig: Duncker und Humblot, 1883). See Georg G. Iggers, *German Conception of History: The National Tradition of Historical Thought from Herder to the Present* (Middletown, CT: Wesleyan University Press, 1968); Iggers, "Historicism: The History and Meaning of the Term," *Journal of the History of Ideas* 56, no. 1 (1995): 129–52; Charles Bambach, *Heidegger, Dilthey, and the Crisis of Historicism* (Ithaca, NY: Cornell University Press, 1995); Thomas E. Willey, *Back to Kant: The Revival of Kantianism in German Social and Historical Thought, 1860–1914* (Detroit: Wayne State University Press, 1978); Thomas Duve, *Normativität und Empirie im öffentlichen Recht und der Politikwissenschaft um 1900: Historisch-systematische Untersuchung des Lebens und Werks von Richard Schmidt (1862–1944) und der Methodenentwicklung seiner Zeit* (Edelsback: Aktiv Druck & Verlag, 1998).

29. The juxtaposition of rational and psychological man is from Carl E. Schorske, *Fin-de-Siècle Vienna: Politics and Culture* (New York: Vintage Books, 1981), especially chap. 1. On the pressure these transformations placed on the German academy, and the social and institutional setting, see Fritz K. Ringer, *The Decline of the German Mandarins: The German Academic Community, 1890–1933* (Cambridge, MA: Harvard University Press, 1969).

30. If law is absent from the English-language classics like Schorske, *Fin-de-Siècle Vienna*, and Allan Janik and Stephen Toulmin, *Wittgenstein's Vienna* (New York: Simon and Schuster, 1973)—though note the many jurists in the sprawling family portrait at the heart of Deborah R. Coen's *Vienna in the Age of Uncertainty: Science, Liberalism, and Private Life* (Chicago: University of Chicago Press, 2007)—the German historiography differs here. See, for example, Otto Gerhard Oexle, ed., *Krise des Historismus—Krise der Wirklichkeit: Wissenschaft, Kunst und Literatur 1880–1932* (Göttingen: Vandenhoeck & Ruprecht, 2007), which includes a chapter by Oliver Lepsius on law. For a close contextualization of the jurist Richard Schmitt within this epistemological moment, see Duve, *Normativität und Empirie*. For an overview of the fin de siècle grappling with industrial society in legal scholarship, see Stolleis, *Public Law in Germany*, 438–49. For an internalist account of the crisis of legal positivism that backdates the Weimar crisis of jurisprudence to the first decade of the twentieth century, see Stefan Korioth's important article, "Erschütterung des staatsrechtlichen Positivismus im ausgehenden Kaiserreich: Anmerkungen zu frühen Arbeiten von Carl Schmitt, Rudolf Smend und Erich Kaufmann," *Archiv des öffentlichen Rechts* 117, no. 2 (1992): 212–38.

31. He is generally cast as a (simple) positivist, an impression aided by of some of his most famous ideas, including the "normative power of the factual"; on which see more below. For an excellent corrective on this point, see Oliver Lepsius, "Georg Jellineks Methodenlehre im Spiegel der zeitgenössischen Erkenntnistheorie," in *Georg Jellinek: Beiträge zu Leben und Werk*, ed. Stanley L. Paulson and Martin Schulte (Tübingen: Mohr Siebeck, 2000), 309–43. See also Christoph Schönberger, "Ein Liberaler zwischen Staatswille und Volkswille: Georg Jellinek und die Krise des staatsrechtlichen Positivismus um die Jahrhundertwende," in the same volume, 1–32. Note Schönberger's perception that Jellinek's background in the multinational Habsburg Empire gave him a "certain distance" from Prussian *Staatlichkeit* and shaped his more reflective approach (15–16).

32. Georg Jellinek, *System der subjektiven öffentlichen Rechte* (Freiburg: J. C. B. Mohr, 1892), 11.

33. Jellinek, 11.

34. Jellinek, 11.

35. Jellinek, 11.

36. Jellinek, 12. For his later development of this point, see Georg Jellinek, *Allgemeine Staatslehre*, 3rd ed. (Berlin: O. Häring, 1914), 25–27.

37. Jellinek, *System der subjektiven öffentlichen Rechte*, 12.

38. "Anyone who does not thoroughly know this argument over methods, and has not taken a position on it, lacks the scholarly basis that alone entitles them to work on the solution of these fundamental questions," he commented in the second edition of the same work. Georg Jellinek, *System der subjektiven öffentlichen Rechte*, 2nd ed. (Tübingen: J. C. B. Mohr, 1905), 20n2, carried over from the previous page. All other references to this text are to the original 1892 edition.

39. Jellinek, *System der subjektiven öffentlichen Rechte*, 12, 13.

40. Jellinek, 14.

41. Jellinek, 14–15.

42. "Eigenthum und Besitz, Servitut und Pfandrecht, Kauf und Miethe, Ehe und Erbschaft sind nicht greif- oder sichtbare Dinge oder Eigenschaften." Jellinek, 15.

43. Jellinek, 15.

44. Jellinek, 15.

45. Jellinek, *Allgemeine Staatslehre*, 138.

46. See Lepsius, "Georg Jellinek's Methodenlehre," 309–43, and (especially on Laband's lack of methodological reflection) Schönberger, "Ein Liberaler zwischen Staatswille und Volkswille," 1–32. But compare the treatment in Walter Pauly, *Der Methodenwandel im deutschen Spätkonstitutionalismus: Ein Beitrag zu Entwicklung und Gestalt der Wissenschaft vom Öffentlichen Recht im 19. Jahrhundert* (Tübingen: J. C. B. Mohr, 1993), 211–23.

47. Jellinek, *System der subjektiven öffentlichen Rechte*, 16 (question marks added for clarity).

48. Jellinek, 16.

49. Jellinek, 16 (emphasis added).

50. Jellinek, 16–17n2.

51. Jellinek, 20.

52. With characteristic philosophical seriousness, Jellinek actually reached "back" even further to first explore the nature of *Einheiten*—unities or entities—in general. Despite the importance of the problem, we lack a comprehensive philosophical treatment, he wrote. Are there *objective* entities in the external world—that is, something with a natural/necessary spatial delimitation and indivisibility? Seemingly only the atom would qualify. But the human world is full of *subjective* entities—that is, entities that are executed by our minds by cleaving off and distinguishing things from the flowing continuities of time and space. We describe as entities things that appear to us as distinct delimitations within continuously flowing time (the lecture, the drive, the kick, the lightning, the storm) and within continuous space (the apartment, the floor, the building, the street, the city). The conception of the delimited as an entity was founded in Aristotle's categories, he observed. Jellinek, 20–21.

53. Jellinek, 21.

54. Jellinek, 22–23.

55. Jellinek, *Allgemeine Staatslehre*, 143, 169–72.

56. Jellinek, *System der subjektiven öffentlichen Rechte*, 26–27.

57. Jellinek, 25.

58. See Emil Lingg, *Empirische Untersuchungen zur Allgemeinen Staatslehre* (Vienna: Alfred Hölder, 1890). See page 116 for Lingg's discussion of continuity as a "fiction."

59. Jellinek, *System der subjektiven öffentlichen Rechte*, 25, 32–33; see also Jellinek, *Allgemeine Staatslehre*, 143, 147, 167.

60. Jellinek, *Allgemeine Staatslehre*, 147.

61. Jellinek, *System der subjektiven öffentlichen Rechte*, 25, 36–38; see also Jellinek, *Allgemeine Staatslehre*, 163.

62. Jellinek, *Allgemeine Staatslehre*, 163.

63. Jellinek, 163; see also 177. Michael Stolleis and Martti Koskenniemi have presented Jellinek's *Allgemeine Staatslehre* as a great "synthesis" (on which, more below): Stolleis,

Public Law in Germany, 440–44; Martti Koskenniemi, *The Gentle Civilizer of Nations: The Rise and Fall of International Law, 1870–1960* (Cambridge: Cambridge University Press, 2004), 198–204; the argument here is that this interpretation can be taken further. It is not just his treatment of the state that synthesizes: the notion and process of synthesis is integral to his characterization of legal concepts and legal thought more broadly.

64. See chapter 2, as well as Pauly, *Methodenwandel*; Peter von Oertzen, *Die soziale Funktion des staatsrechtlichen Positivismus: Eine wissenssoziologische Studie über die Entstehung des formalistischen Positivismus in der deutschen Staatsrechtswissenschaft* (Frankfurt am Main: Suhrkamp Verlag, 1974); on what Jellinek owed Laband and Gerber see also Kersten, *Georg Jellinek und die klassische Staatslehre*, 50–68; Andrew Spadafora, "Georg Jellinek on Values and Objectivity in the Legal and Political Sciences," *Modern Intellectual History* 14, no. 3 (2017): 747–76. Note that unlike Laband and Gerber, Jellinek did not believe in the gaplessness of the legal order. Jellinek, *Allgemeine Staatslehre*, 353.

65. Jellinek, *Allgemeine Staatslehre*, 163–64.

66. Nicoletta Bersier Ladavac, Christoph Bezemek, and Frederick Schauer, eds., *The Normative Force of the Factual: Legal Philosophy between Is and Ought* (Cham, Switzerland: Springer, 2019).

67. In Beiser's phrasing, neo-Kantianism offered a compelling solution to the "identity crisis" of philosophy. Frederick C. Beiser, *The Genesis of Neo-Kantianism, 1796–1880* (Oxford: Oxford University Press, 2015), see 11–22, 455–524.

68. Lepsius, "Georg Jellinek's Methodenlehre," 310–12, 337–38.

69. See the excellent discussion in Lepsius, 340–41 and generally.

70. Jellinek, *System der subjektiven öffentlichen Rechte*, 13.

71. See Troeltsch's penetrating intellectual profile of Jellinek published in the form of a review of Jellinek's selected essays in the wake of Jellinek's death: Ernst Troeltsch, review of *Ausgewählte Schriften und Reden*, by Georg Jellinek, *Zeitschrift für das Privat- und Öffentliche Recht der Gegenwart* 39 (1912): 278.

72. Take, for example, widespread debate and disagreement among neo-Kantian philosophers about the place of empirical psychology in the study of cognition. See generally Beiser, *Genesis of Neo-Kantianism*.

73. Georg Jellinek, "Aus einem Notizbuche" [n.d., 1877?], in Jellinek, *Ausgewählte Schriften und Reden* (1911; Aalen: Scientia Verlag, 1970), 1:173. These notebooks are also filled with reflections on the relationship between different sorts of knowledge, such as philosophy, natural science, and art.

74. Georg Jellinek, "Die deutsche Philosophie in Österreich," *Im neuen Reich* 4, no. 2 (1874): 327–36; Georg Jellinek, "Smith und Kant," *Wiener Abendpost*, no. 174, Beilage 31 July 1877, p. 649, continued in *Wiener Abendpost*, no. 175, Beilage 1 August 1877, 698–99. See chapter 2.

75. George Jellinek to Victor Ehrenberg, 20 October 1872, in *Briefwechsel*, 157. For other Kant banter, see Jellinek to Ehrenberg, 9 September 1872; Ehrenberg to Jellinek, 12 May 1873; Jellinek to Ehrenberg, 9 June 1873; in *Briefwechsel*, 153, 182, 191–92.

76. See Beiser, *Genesis of Neo-Kantianism*, especially chap. 13, "Wilhelm Windelband and Normativity," 492–529; Willey, *Back to Kant*, especially chap. 6, "The Southwestern School," 131–52.

77. Wilhelm Windelband, *Ueber die Gewissheit der Erkenntnis: Eine psychologisch-erkenntnisstheoretische Studie* (Berlin: F. Henschel, 1873). See Jellinek to Ehrenberg, 29 April 1873, in *Briefwechsel*, 180. For Windelband's side of the correspondence, see his letters collected in NGJ, BArch, N 1136/32 and N 1136/56.

78. There is scarcely a letter that fails to mention Windelband: even no news of or from Windelband was news for these two. For some examples, see Jellinek to Ehrenberg, 9 September 1872; Jellinek to Ehrenberg, 9 November 1872; Jellinek to Ehrenberg, 1 December 1872; Jellinek to Ehrenberg, 16 April 1873; Jellinek to Ehrenberg, 11 November 1873;

Jellinek to Ehrenberg, 8 August 1876; Jellinek to Ehrenberg, 17 July 1883; in *Briefwechsel*, 152–53, 161, 165–66, 178, 205, 258–59, 318.

79. Jellinek to Ehrenberg, 16 May 1874, in *Briefwechsel*, 219.

80. "Die letzte Schranke, das conventionelle 'Sie' ist nun auch zwischen uns gefallen und so besitze ich ihn als Freund und Bruder." Jellinek to Ehrenberg, 6 June 1874, in *Briefwechsel*, 221.

81. Jellinek to Ehrenberg, 6 June 1874, in *Briefwechsel*, 221.

82. Jellinek to Ehrenberg, 27 June 1874, in *Briefwechsel*, 222–23.

83. Jellinek to Adolf Jellinek, 13 June 1874, NGJ, BArch, N 1136/46 (also in C. Jellinek, "Georg Jellinek: Ein Lebensbild," 20*).

84. Spending time with these "older, finished people" sometimes made him aware of his own unripened immaturity: Jellinek to Ehrenberg, 27 June 1874, in *Briefwechsel*, 222.

85. Jellinek to Ehrenberg, 15 July 1874, in *Briefwechsel*, 223.

86. On Lotze, see Beiser, *Genesis of Neo-Kantianism*, 462.

87. Beiser, 518.

88. Windelband, *Ueber die Gewissheit der Erkenntnis*.

89. Though his habilitation encompassed both these natural-psychological laws and logical ones, over the course of the 1870s he moved to an exclusively logical understanding of epistemology focused on the rules according to which judgments were recognized as true. Beiser, *Genesis of Neo-Kantianism*, 499–503, 520.

90. As we recall, the neo-Kantians maintained that humans could have no direct experience of things in themselves but only of our perception of them.

91. Wilhelm Windelband, "Normen und Naturgesetze" (1882), in his *Präludien: Aufsätze und Reden zur Philosophie und ihrer Geschichte*, 5th ed. (1883; Tübingen: J. C. B. Mohr, 1915), 2:59–98; Beiser, *Genesis of Neo-Kantianism*, 503; Willey, *Back to Kant*, 108–13, 131–39.

92. George Jellinek to Victor Ehrenberg, 8 August 1876, in *Briefwechsel*, 259.

93. Troeltsch observed that Jellinek's lifelong love of philosophy produced the oft-repeated conviction that the "jurist needed a philosophical foundation and a philosophical integration into the system of knowledge." Troeltsch, review of *Ausgewählte Schriften und Reden*, 275; see also 274.

94. Windelband, "Zum Geleit," vii.

95. Windelband, *Ueber die Gewissheit der Erkenntniss*, iv.

96. Troeltsch, review of *Ausgewählte Schriften und Reden*, 275; see also 278.

97. Jellinek, *System der subjektiven öffentlichen Rechte*, vi.

98. Victor Ehrenberg to Georg Jellinek, 3 July 1892, in *Briefwechsel*, 374; original in NGJ, BArch, N 1136/6.

99. Georg Jellinek to Adolf Jellinek, 2 July 1892, in C. Jellinek, "Georg Jellinek: Ein Lebensbild," 94.

100. Otto Mayer, review of *System der subjektiven öffentlichen Rechte*, by Georg Jellinek, *Archiv für Öffentliches Recht* 9, vol. 2 (1894): 281.

101. Mayer, 288.

102. A. M., "Jellineks System der subjektiven öffentlichen Rechte," *Neue Freie Presse*, no. 14882 (January 28, 1906): 32.

103. A. M., 33.

104. This, too, had been a preoccupation of Windelband's. See Windelband, "Normen und Naturgesetze"; Beiser, *Genesis of Neo-Kantianism*, 503–10.

105. Jellinek, *System der subjektiven öffentlichen Rechte*, 18n1.

106. I am grateful to Christian Neumeier for helpful conversation on this point.

107. Jellinek, *Allgemeine Staatslehre*, 27. See Kempter, *Die Jellineks*, 180–82.

108. Jellinek, *Allgemeine Staatslehre*, 5, 16–17, 50.

109. Jellinek, 19–21, 50–51, 138. "Kunst der Abstraktion" on 51. "Die Rechtswissenschaft ist daher eine Normwissenschaft, ähnlich wie die Logik, die uns nicht lehrt, was die Dinge sind, sondern wie sie gedacht werden müssen, um eine in sich widerspruchslose Erkenntnis hervorzurefen" (138).

110. Jellinek, 138.

111. Jellinek, 139.

112. "Wie wird Nichtrecht zu Recht?" Jellinek, 350.

113. Jellinek anchored law emphatically in our psyches: it was not an objective reality or metaphysical truth but a psychological fact. "Also rein innerlich, in den Köpfen der Menschen vollzieht sich dieser Prozeß" (342). Law has its location, its base, "in us, not outside us" (343). Jellinek, 337–39. Michael Stolleis terms this Jellinek's "psychological positivism": Stolleis, *Public Law in Germany*, 442.

114. Also because invocations of natural law worked to stabilize moments of rupture and transition. Jellinek, *Allgemeine Staatslehre*, 340–54.

115. In Troeltsch's sharp, affectionate appraisal, the tension between the normative and the factual ran through the heart of Jellinek's whole oeuvre but was never properly tamed or resolved. Troeltsch, review of *Ausgewählte Schriften und Reden*, especially 276.

116. On Jellinek's reach for synthesis and attempt to bring the disciplines together, see also Stolleis, *Public Law in Germany*, 440–44.

117. "Aus der Welt des Judentums: Georg Jellinek," Abschrift einer NWDR-Sendung, 1 April 1955, NGJ, BArch, N 1136/64.

118. Jellinek, *Allgemeine Staatslehre*, vii.

119. Koskenniemi, *Gentle Civilizer of Nations*, 198–204; Stolleis, *Public Law in Germany*, 440–44.

120. The long list of Americans included the likes of James Brown Scott. The two kept in extensive touch; Scott angled for Jellinek's involvement in his Classics of International Law series. James Brown Scott to Georg Jellinek, 16 April 1907, NGJ, BArch, N 1136/26. See also, for example, the ongoing contact with former students from Japan: S. Uyesugi to Georg Jellinek, 23 July 1909, NGJ, BArch, N 1136/30. See also Kempter, *Die Jellineks*, 374–79.

121. Karl Samuel Grünhut to Georg Jellinek, 29 December 1907, NGJ, BArch, N 1136/9.

122. Guido Leser, Georg Jellinek: Ein Gedenkblatt, 16 January 1911, NGJ, BArch, N 1136/38; Hans von Frisch, "Georg Jellinek, †11 Januar 1911," Sonderabdruck aus dem *Juristischen Literaturblatt* 222, 15 Febuary 1911, NGJ, BArch, N 1136/38.

123. Princeton awarded him an honorary degree, inviting him to partake in the ceremony celebrating the institution's 150th birthday (and change of name), as one of Europe's "eminent men of science and letters" and with the "esteem" of Professor Woodrow Wilson. See Henry B. Fine to Georg Jellinek, 21 March 1896, NGJ, BArch, N1136/7; College of New Jersey/Princeton University to Georg Jellinek, n.d. 1896, NGJ, BArch, N 1136/30. See too Columbia's Henry Alfred Todd to Georg Jellinek, 1 December 1903, NGJ, BArch, N 1136/30, and Harvard's Albert Bushnell Hart to Georg Jellinek, 6 July 1892, NGJ, BArch, N 1136/10 (the latter also introducing his student W. E. B. Du Bois). The Austrian press was especially eager for articles: see the *Neue Freie Presse*'s constant requests for articles from "our famous compatriot," including more than one invitation to reflect on his "Viennese past." Neue Freie Presse to Georg Jellinek, 5 May 1909; 16 March 1908; 12 December 1907; 16 November 1906, NGJ, BArch, N 1136/20. See also Österreichische Rundschau to Georg Jellinek, 17 June 1905, NGJ, BArch, N 1136/21; Pester Lloyd to Georg Jellinek, 17 November 1907, NGJ, BArch, N 1136/22.

124. See Lepsius, "Georg Jellineks Methodenlehre," 331, as well as Kersten, *Georg Jellinek und die klassische Staatslehre*, 171.

125. See Olechowski, "Von Georg Jellinek zu Hans Kelsen," 375–98, where Olechowski is interested in the "parallels" in their lives.

126. Georg Jellinek, "Unsere Mutter: Ein Familiengedenkblatt" (1893), NGJ, BArch, N 1136/36; Kelsen, "Autobiographie," 31.

127. Kelsen, "Autobiographie," 30–31; Olechowski, "Von Georg Jellinek zu Hans Kelsen"; Olechowski, *Hans Kelsen*, 30–32, 36–43. The two-towered, Gothic-style synagogue (known as Synagoge Neudeggergasse or Josefstädter Tempel) stood at Neudeggergasse 10–12.

128. Kelsen, "Autobiographie," 33.

129. Kelsen, 32–33.

130. Kelsen, 33.

131. Kelsen, 34–35.

132. This footnote from Sigmund Freud's *Analyse der Phobie eines fünfjährigen Knaben* (1909) is quoted in multiple places, such as Olechowski, *Hans Kelsen*, 79, as well as Robert S. Wistrich, *The Jews of Vienna in the Age of Franz Joseph* (Oxford: Littman Library of Jewish Civilization, 1990), 535–36. For Schopenhauer here, see Kelsen, "Autobiographie," 33.

133. Hans Kelsen, Interview with Kurt Eissler, 19 December 1953, Sigmund Freud Papers: Interviews and Recollections, 1914–1998, box 117, mss39990, Library of Congress (digital ID: http://hdl.loc.gov/loc.mss/ms004017.mss39990.01500). Quotations from pp. 21–22, then 20, of the interview transcript.

134. Among a vast Weininger literature, see Chandak Sengoopta, *Otto Weininger: Sex, Science, and Self in Imperial Vienna* (Chicago: University of Chicago Press, 2000); David S. Luft, *Eros and Inwardness in Vienna: Weininger, Musil, Doderer* (Chicago: University of Chicago Press, 2003); William M. Johnston, *The Austrian Mind: An Intellectual and Social History 1848–1938* (Berkeley: University of California Press, 1972), 158–62; Janik and Toulmin, *Wittgenstein's Vienna*, 71–74; for Weininger's influence on the Prague writers, see Scott Spector, *Prague Territories: National Conflict and Cultural Innovation in Franz Kafka's Fin de Siècle* (Berkeley: University of California Press, 2000), 118–22, 182–85; and for his influence on Adolf Hitler, see Brigitte Hamann, *Hitler's Vienna: A Dictator's Apprenticeship*, trans. Thomas Thornton (New York: Oxford University Press, 1999), 227–30.

135. Hamann, *Hitler's Vienna*, 227; and, for a different version of the same idea, Janik and Toulmin, *Wittgenstein's Vienna*, 73.

136. Kelsen, "Autobiographie," 35. On Kelsen and Weininger, see Olechowski, *Hans Kelsen*, 75–80; Mónica García-Salmones Rovira, *The Project of Positivism in International Law* (Oxford: Oxford University Press, 2013), 160–64.

137. Hans Kelsen, *Die Staatslehre Dante Alighieri* (Vienna: F. Deuticke, 1905); Kelsen, "Autobiographie," 35–36. See further Olechowski, *Hans Kelsen*, 80–85.

138. Not that Bernatzik himself liked theory! See Kelsen, "Autobiographie," 37; Olechowski, *Hans Kelsen*, 70–73.

139. Kelsen, "Autobiographie," 37.

140. Kelsen, 40. On the ambiguity of the date of the travel scholarship, see Olechowski, *Hans Kelsen*, 101, who surmises there might have been two grants that funded Kelsen's consecutive winters in Heidelberg.

141. Kelsen, "Autobiographie," 40.

142. Kelsen, 40. Kelsen's account of Jellinek's teaching style diverges sharply from that of other students who commented precisely on being roused toward their own education. See, for example, Guido Leser, "Georg Jellinek: Ein Gedenkblatt," 16 January 1911, NGJ, BArch, N 1136/38.

143. Hans Kelsen, *Hauptprobleme der Staatsrechtslehre entwickelt aus der Lehre vom Rechtssatze* (Tübingen: J. C. B. Mohr, 1911), xiii.

144. See the voluminous collection of obituaries and tributes collected in NGJ, BArch, N 1136/38; Kempter, *Die Jellineks*, 379–81.

145. As Thomas Olechowski observes: Olechowski, *Hans Kelsen*, 921.

146. The last sentence here reads in the original: "Möge es meiner Arbeit vergönnt sein, dem Andenken dieses Großen ein Weniges beizutragen." Kelsen, *Hauptprobleme*, xii–xiii. Even in the thick of his substantive critique later in the book, Jellinek is described as the scholar "to whom the modern theory of state owes more than anyone else" (172). The contrast between this tribute from the time and the dismissive attitude decades later in Kelsen's autobiography is noteworthy.

147. On occasion, literally: Kelsen, *Hauptprobleme*, 184.

148. Hans Kelsen, *Über Grenzen zwischen juristischer und soziologischer Methode: Vortrag gehalten in der Soziologischen Gesellschaft zu Wien* (Tübingen: J. C. B. Mohr, 1911), 6–7, 10–11 (unüberbrückbare on 6). Kelsen employed the theft example on multiple occasions; see, for example, Hans Kelsen, *Der soziologische und der juristische Staatsbegriff: Kritische Untersuchungen des Verhältnisses von Staat und Recht* (Tübingen: J. C. B. Mohr, 1922), 76.

149. It was an example Kelsen liked. See Kelsen, *Das Problem der Souveränität und die Theorie des Völkerrechts*, 6–7; Kelsen, *Der soziologische und der juristische Staatsbegriff*, 84, 128–29. (Note that Carl Schmitt also made this point in his *Political Theology* though without citing Kelsen, despite engaging repeatedly with his work. See Schmitt, *Political Theology*, 17: "From the standpoint of reality, which is governed by the law of causality, no single factor can be picked out and accorded such a superlative. In political reality there is no irresistible highest or greatest power that operates according to the certainty of natural law.") Hence his important idea of the state as simply the "end point of legal imputation": *we* impute the state to be the ultimate source of legal norms—that ascription or imputation, that juridical idea of causation or source, does not exist outside our judgment of it. See Kelsen, *Hauptprobleme*, 184–89; for his shorter overview, see Kelsen, *Über Grenzen zwischen juristischer und soziologischer Methode*, 86.

150. What scholars were really reaching for in referring to the will of the state, Kelsen argued, was its formal legal unity, its singularity, not some mystical, collective mind or meta-consciousness willing things in a psychological sense. Kelsen, *Hauptprobleme*, 174, 183–89. On *Zweck*/purpose and will as inherently nonlegal or metajuridical concepts, see Kelsen, *Hauptprobleme*, 86 (especially note 4), 89, 91–93, 172–79, 184–86, 398, 400–401, 411–12.

151. Kelsen, *Hauptprobleme*, viii; see also 176–81.

152. Kelsen, v. Kelsen already uses the adjective *pure* in this first major work, though not yet invoking/naming a "pure theory of law" as such. See, for example, vi, ix. The "pure theory of law" is named as such from 1920. As we see here, and as many have noted, the "purity" is a *methodological* purity.

153. Kelsen, vi–vii.

154. Kelsen, vi–vii, 181–83.

155. Hence Kelsen's framing of the state as simply the "end point of legal imputation." Kelsen, *Hauptprobleme*, 183–89. For subsequent, systematic expositions of *ought* as an "imputation" (*Zurechnung*) and a "linking" (*Verknüpfung*) of condition and consequence (including a return to the thief example), see Hans Kelsen, *Reine Rechtslehre: Einleitung in die Rechtswissenschaftliche Problematik* (Leipzig: Franz Deuticke, 1934), § 11, § 16 (pp. 21–23, 35–37); also available in English translation: Hans Kelsen, *Introduction to the Problems of Legal Theory: A Translation of the First Edition of the* Reine Rechtslehre *or* Pure Theory of Law, trans. Bonnie Litschewski Paulson and Stanley L. Paulson (Oxford: Clarendon Press, 1992), 23–24, 34. See also the late essay "Causality and Accounting," in Hans Kelsen, *Essays in Legal and Moral Philosophy*, ed. Ota Weinberger, trans. Peter Heath (Dordrecht: D. Reidel, 1973), 154–64.

156. Kelsen, *Hauptprobleme*, 176–81, 184. For subsequent elaboration of this point—namely, that "abstract" in the usual sense was not in fact the opposite of the "empirical," but

rather its condensation or reduction into a simpler form—see also Kelsen, *Der soziologische und der juristische Staatsbegriff*, 65, 120.

157. Kelsen, *Hauptprobleme*, 181–83.

158. Kelsen, 93.

159. Indeed, geometry "delivered proof that one could achieve 'form without content' without delivering 'results without worth.'" Kelsen, 93.

160. "Eine Geometrie der totalen Rechtserscheinung." Kelsen, *Hauptprobleme*, 93.

161. Kelsen, vii.

162. Kelsen, viii.

163. Kelsen, ix (italics added for clarity in the place of capitalization in the German).

164. In this it resembles philosophy as a "spiritual exercise": see most famously Pierre Hadot, *Philosophy as a Way of Life: Spiritual Exercises from Socrates to Foucault*, trans. Michael Chase (Oxford: Blackwell, 1995).

165. Kelsen, *Hauptprobleme*, xii.

166. Kelsen, xii.

167. Kelsen, vi (emphasis in original).

168. Kelsen, *Das Problem der Souveränität und die Theorie des Völkerrechts*, iii. Though published only after the war, substantial parts of the book were written in 1915 and 1916. On this work, see further in chapter 6.

169. For an introduction to the philosophical conjuncture of 1919 and beyond, see Wolfram Eilenberger, *Time of the Magicians: Wittgenstein, Benjamin, Cassirer, Heidegger, and the Decade That Reinvented Philosophy*, trans. Shaun Whiteside (New York: Penguin, 2020).

170. Kelsen, *Der soziologische und der juristische Staatsbegriff*, 4–45.

171. Kelsen, 75–83, 86, 122.

172. Kelsen, 76, 83; see also 206.

173. Kelsen, 89.

174. Kelsen, 89–90; see also 96–97.

175. Kelsen, 90n1. The "Gorki" title Kelsen gives is "Nachtasyl"—"Night Asylum"—a text rendered in English variously as "The Lower Depths," "A Night's Lodging," and "At the Bottom."

176. Kelsen, 92; also 86–89, 91, 104.

177. Kelsen, 123; see also 85–86.

178. Kelsen, "Autobiographie," 59–60.

179. Kelsen, *Der soziologische und der juristische Staatsbegriff*, 106.

180. Kelsen, 106, 114–32. This is generally understood as Kelsen's "neo-Kantian" critique of Jellinek: the fact that Jellinek seemed to accept the existence of the "state as such," existing prior to cognition and distinct from either methodological approach, is presented as evidence of his "incomplete" or faulty neo-Kantianism. We might note that neo-Kantian philosophy comprised a broad range of themes and that one of Windelband's central, unresolved preoccupations (for example) was the relationship between norms and (natural/causal) laws. In trying to understand how norms become facts and facts become norms, Jellinek's "two sides" theory can also be seen as an attempt to address this question for law, in direct continuity with this strand of neo-Kantian philosophy. See Windelband's 1882 essay "Normen und Naturgesetze," 59–98; Beiser, *Genesis of Neo-Kantianism*, 503–10, 520.

181. Kelsen, *Der soziologische und der juristische Staatsbegriff*, 116–17.

182. Kelsen, 3; "metarechtlich" on 1.

183. Kelsen, 205.

184. Kelsen, 206, drawing on Hans Vaihinger, *Die Philosophie des Als Ob: System der theoretischen, praktischen und religiösen Fiktionen der Menschheit auf Grund eines idealistischen Positivismus* (Berlin: Reuther und Reichard, 1911).

185. Kelsen, *Der soziologische und der juristische Staatsbegriff,* 206; drawing on Ernst Cassirer, *Das Erkenntnisproblem in der Philosophie und Wissenschaft der neueren Zeit* (Berlin: Bruno Casirer, 1907), 2:588.

186. Kelsen, *Der soziologische und der juristische Staatsbegriff,* 206. Kelsen applied this epistemological critique to the notion of legal personality as a whole—that is, the foundational notion of a rights-bearing legal subject (whether an individual, or the state, or a corporation)—which in truth was only an "anthropomorphic personification of a complex of legal norms produced for the purpose of visualization" (134). As he expounded in his *Allgemeine Staatslehre* three years later, law reproduced the linguistic structure of subject and predicate in positing "subjects" that possessed or carried rights: but that "legal person" was simply a way of grouping and visualizing a particular cluster of norms. "The thing that has properties is made from a mere incarnation of these properties into their substantive double. There is no such thing as a leaf and next to it the qualities: green, smooth, round, etc.": the leaf was simply the "unified aggregation" (*einheitliche Zusammenfassung*) of those qualities. Hans Kelsen, *Allgemeine Staatslehre* (Berlin: Julius Springer, 1925), 62; see also Kelsen, *Reine Rechtslehre,* § 25, English in Kelsen, *Introduction to the Problems of Legal Theory,* 46–53.

187. Kelsen, *Der soziologische und der juristische Staatsbegriff,* 137–39, "Staatsfetischismus" on 250; Kelsen, *Allgemeine Staatslehre,* 67, 210, 250. This applied also at the level of individual legal personality and subjective right, doctrines that posited things like property rights as somehow prior to the general legal order rather than mere (changeable) norms inside it, with regrettable political consequences. See, for example, Kelsen, *Reine Rechtslehre,* §§ 19–21; English in Kelsen, *Introduction to the Problems of Legal Theory,* 38–41.

188. Kelsen, *Der soziologische und der juristische Staatsbegriff,* 250.

189. Kelsen, 133.

190. See chapter 2.

191. Kelsen, *Der soziologische und der juristische Staatsbegriff,* 206; see also 135.

192. Kelsen, 211–14.

193. Kelsen, 206–7. This powerful argument in fact drew substantially on the work of Kelsen's student Fritz Sander. As Kelsen acknowledged in a long footnote (207n1), Sander had first argued the state was a "substance concept" akin to the natural science equivalents; he likened it to "energy" for theoretical physics. For a rich analysis of these broader commonalities between different branches of natural and humanistic enquiry, see Johannes Feichtinger, "Intellectual Affinities: Ernst Mach, Sigmund Freud, Hans Kelsen and the Austrian Anti-essentialist Approach to Science and Scholarship," in *The Foundation of the Juridico-Political: Concept Formation in Hans Kelsen and Max Weber,* ed. Ian Bryan, Peter Langford, and John McGarry (New York: Routledge, 2016), 117–39; Feichtinger, *Wissenschaft als reflexives Projekt.*

194. Kelsen, *Der soziologische und der juristische Staatsbegriff,* 207–8.

195. Kelsen, 207.

196. Kelsen, 207–8. On this theory, see further Alexander Somek, "Stateless Law: Kelsen's Conception and Its Limits," *Oxford Journal of Legal Studies* 26, no. 4 (2006): 753–74.

197. Hans Kelsen, Interview with Kurt Eissler, 19 December 1953.

198. Kelsen first attended as a guest for his friend Hans Sachs's presentation on December 13, 1911: Vortragsabend am 13. Dezember 1911, in *Protokolle der Wiener Psychoanalytischen Vereinigung,* ed. Herman Nunberg and Ernst Federn, vol. 3, 1910–1911 (Frankfurt am Main: S. Fischer, 1979), 331. For subsequent visits on January 3, January 31, May 8, May 15 (Freud's "Über das Tabu"), and October 30, 1912, see *Protokolle der Wiener Psychoanalytischen Vereinigung,* ed. Herman Nunberg and Ernst Federn, vol. 4, 1912–1918 (Frankfurt am Main: S. Fischer, 1981), 1, 26, 94, 95, 104; and Olechowski, *Hans Kelsen,* 371.

199. Sigmund Freud, *Totem and Taboo: Some Points of Agreement between the Mental Lives of Savages and Neurotics*, trans. and ed. James Strachey (New York: Norton, 1950), 3 (indeed, the language of traces: "the relics of his mode of thought which survive in our own manners and customs").

200. Freud, 4.

201. Freud, 5. Freud was especially interested in the relationship between totemism and the seemingly most intense taboo, that against incest. "In almost every place where we find totems we also find a law against persons of the same totem having sexual relations with one another and consequently against their marrying. This, then, is 'exogamy,' an institution related to totemism" (6). Freud sought psychohistorical reasons for their linking.

202. Freud, 176. The brothers felt—really, inaugurated—the "same contradictory feelings which we can see at work in the ambivalent father-complexes of our children and our neurotic patients" (177).

203. Freud, especially the final of the four essays, "The Return of Totemism in Childhood" (125–200); "father-surrogate" on 183.

204. Kelsen reported to Freud the perplexing dream of a colleague and was astounded by the power and insight of Freud's immediate interpretation. Hans Kelsen, Interview with Kurt Eissler, 19 December 1953.

205. Hans Kelsen, "Der Begriff des Staates und die Sozialpsychologie: Mit besonderer Berücksichtigung von Freuds Theorie der Masse," *Imago: Zeitschrift für Anwendung der Psychoanlyse auf die Geisteswissenschaften* 8, no. 2 (1922): 97–141; Hans Kelsen, "The Conception of the State and Social Psychology: With Special Reference to Freud's Group Theory," *International Journal of Psycho-analysis* 5 (January 1924): 1–38; subsequent citations given from the English version. Regarding Kelsen's work in English, see Olechowski, *Hans Kelsen*, 375n816, 590.

206. Working closely with *Freud's Group Psychology and the Analysis of the Ego* (1921), Kelsen offered a long critical appraisal of the social-psychological idea of a group mind, praising Freud for (at least partially) avoiding this erroneous hypostatization in favor of an exclusively individual psychology, though warning of creeping hypostatizations in his approach, too. Kelsen also experimented with Freud's account of the "libidinal structure of the group" and adapted his analysis of the role of the leader and the ego ideal, arguing that the state was the "*guiding idea*" that individuals "put in the place of their ego-ideal in order thereby to identify themselves with one another." Kelsen, "The Conception of the State and Social Psychology," quotation on 23 (emphasis in original). The secondary literature has focused its attention on these questions of group psychology/the collective mind, making far less of Kelsen's use of *Totem and Taboo* in the latter parts of the article. Olechowski, *Hans Kelsen*, 372–75; Feichtinger, *Wissenschaft als reflexives Projekt*, 312–24; Ludwig Adamovich, "Kelsen und die Tiefenpsychologie: Staatsgefundene und nicht staatsgefundene Begegnungen," in *Hans Kelsens Wege sozialphilosophischer Forschung: Ergebnisse eines Internationalen Symposiums in Wien (14.-15. Oktober 1996)*, ed. Robert Walter and Clemens Jabloner (Vienna: Manzsche Verlags- und Universitätsbuchhandlung, 1997), 129–41. But note the engagement with the totemic material in Alina Avscharova and Martina Huttar, "Ohne Seele, ohne Staat: Hans Kelsen und Sigmund Freud," in *Hans Kelsen: Eine politikwissenschaftliche Einführung*, ed. Tamara Ehs (Vienna: Nomos, 2009), 171–91. Étienne Balibar moots Kelsen's reciprocal influence on Freud, especially regarding Freud's invention of the "superego" (das *Über-Ich*), which occurred in the immediate wake of this 1922 encounter. See his suggestive essay "The Invention of the Superego: Freud and Kelsen, 1922," in Étienne Balibar, *Citizen Subject: Foundations for a Philosophical Anthropology*, trans. Steven Miller (New York: Fordham University Press, 2017), 227–55.

207. Kelsen, "The Conception of the State and Social Psychology," 33.

208. Kelsen, 37.

209. Hans Kelsen, "Gott und Staat," *Logos* 11 (1922–23): 261–84; translated as Hans Kelsen, "God and the State," in Hans Kelsen, *Essays in Legal and Moral Philosophy*, ed. Ota Weinberger, trans. Peter Heath (Dordrecht: D. Reidel, 1973), 61–82. Subsequent references given to the English version.

210. Kelsen, "God and the State," 73.

211. Kelsen, 73. "by means of mysticism" comes from the elucidation of this same point in Kelsen, "The Conception of the State and Social Psychology," 37.

212. Kelsen, "The Conception of the State and Social Psychology," 37; see also Kelsen, "God and the State," 73–74.

213. Kelsen, "God and the State," 73.

214. Kelsen, 74.

215. Kelsen, "The Conception of the State and Social Psychology," 38; Kelsen, "God and the State," 68, 69, 73.

216. Kelsen, "The Conception of the State and Social Psychology," 32.

217. Kelsen, 33.

218. Kelsen, 33.

219. Kelsen, "God and the State," 65, see also 66.

220. Kelsen, "The Conception of the State and Social Psychology," 33, footnote 37.

221. Quoted passage from Kelsen, "The Conception of the State and Social Psychology," 33.

222. So Kelsen quotes Freud and adds emphasis at "The Conception of the State and Social Psychology," 34. The relevant passage in the here-used translation of *Totem and Taboo* reads: "the participation in the same substance establishes a sacred bond between those who consume it when it has entered their bodies." Freud, *Totem and Taboo*, 170. Freud is here drawing on William Robertson Smith's *Religion of the Semites*, first published 1889.

223. Freud, *Totem and Taboo*, 170–71.

224. Kelsen, "The Conception of the State and Social Psychology," 34.

225. Kelsen, 34. He would resurrect these arguments almost verbatim in the short piece published by the Internationaler Psychoanalytischer Verlag in 1927: Hans Kelsen, "Der Staatsbegriff und die Psychoanalyse," *Almanach* (1927): 135–41.

226. Kelsen, "The Conception of the State and Social Psychology," 36.

227. Kelsen, 36, 38.

228. Kelsen, 36.

229. Kelsen, 36, 37.

230. Kelsen, "God and the State," 66–67. Kelsen also used this argument and analogy in his *The Essence and Value of Democracy*, referring to the idea of popular sovereignty as an (albeit "more refined") "totemic mask." Hans Kelsen, *Vom Wesen und Wert der Demokratie*, 2nd ed. (1920; Tübingen: J. C. B. Mohr, 1929), 86; Kelsen, *The Essence and Value of Democracy*, trans. Brian Graf (Lanham: Rowman and Littlefield, 2013), 92.

231. Kelsen, "The Conception of the State and Social Psychology," 38; "masks" at Kelsen, "God and the State," 66, 67.

232. Kelsen, "God and the State," 67.

233. Kelsen, "The Conception of the State and Social Psychology," 37. Here I have deviated from the published English translation, which gives "politics" for "Staatstheorie" in the German; the more precise/literal rendering of Staatstheorie is relevant here. See Kelsen, "Der Begriff des Staates und die Sozialpsychologie," 139.

234. "Thus the connection between matters religious and social indicated by social psychology is confirmed from the point of view of the critique of knowledge" (that he had undertaken). Kelsen, "The Conception of the State and Social Psychology," 38.

235. Kelsen, *Der soziologische und der juristische Staatsbegriff*, 208.

236. Kelsen, "God and the State," 82.

237. Kelsen, "The Conception of the State and Social Psychology," 38.

238. This should not be confused with the idea that jurists made the law/legal norms themselves; on the contrary, Kelsen saw the creation of law as entirely beyond the pale of legal scholarship, which could seek only to construe existing positive law into logical systems. But that logical system was itself the state . . .

239. Focused on the few essays in which Kelsen explicitly engages Freud, there has been a tendency in the secondary literature to see this encounter as fleeting and insubstantial. But echoes of Freud's work—or, perhaps more accurately, of the set of assumptions and approaches Kelsen and Freud shared—resound through Kelsen's oeuvre. See, for example, in his essay "The Soul and the Law": "It must never be forgotten that modern thought is the outcome of primitive mentality, and that the difference between the civilized and the primitive man is only a difference of degree. Th[e] striking analogy existing between the mental life of primitives and that of children, or certain modern neuroses, proves this." Kelsen offered no footnote for the idea. Hans Kelsen, "The Soul and the Law," *Review of Religion* 1, no. 4 (1937): 340.

240. Quoted phrases from Hans Kelsen, Interview with Kurt Eissler, 19 December 1953, pp. 24–25. On this variety of themes and beyond, see for example: Kelsen, "The Soul and the Law"; Hans Kelsen, *Society and Nature: A Sociological Inquiry* (Chicago: University of Chicago Press, 1943); Hans Kelsen, "Die platonische Liebe," *Imago* 19 (1933): 225–55, in English as Hans Kelsen, "Platonic Love," trans. George B. Wilbur, *American Imago* 3, no. 1/2 (1942): 3–110; Hans Kelsen, "Die platonische Gerechtigkeit," *Kant-Studien* 38 (1933): 91–117, in English as "Platonic Justice," trans. Glenn Negley, *Ethics* 48, no. 3 (1938): 367–400; Hans Kelsen, "The Idea of Justice in the Holy Scriptures," *Revista Juridica de la Universidad de Puerto Rico* 22, nos. 1–4 (1952–53): 1–63.

241. Stated clearly already in Kelsen, *Hauptprobleme*, 91–92. As he would emphasize, the normative-logical approach asked not if a norm was true or false, but if it was valid or invalid. For systematic treatment of this distinction, see Kelsen's later essays "Causality and Accounting" and "The Foundation of the Theory of Natural Law," both in Hans Kelsen, *Essays in Legal and Moral Philosophy*, ed. Ota Weinberger, trans. Peter Heath (Dordrecht: D. Reidel, 1973).

242. See the preface to Kelsen, *Hauptprobleme*, vi–ix, xii, discussed above.

243. Kelsen, "The Conception of the State and Social Psychology"; Kelsen, "God and the State."

244. Kelsen, "The Soul and the Law"; Kelsen, *Society and Nature.*

245. Carl E. Schorske, *Fin-de-Siècle Vienna*, especially chap. 1.

246. For an especially clear and suggestive account of these themes, see Hans Kelsen, "State-Form and World Outlook," in Kelsen, *Essays in Legal and Moral Philosophy*, ed. Ota Weinberger, trans. Peter Heath (Dordrecht: D. Reidel Publishing Company 1973), 95–113.

247. Friedrich Tezner, *Rechtslogik und Rechtswirklichkeit: Eine empirisch-realistische Studie* (Vienna: Österreichischen Staatsdruckerei, 1925), 9. This text was first published as the first part of Tezner's 1922 book *Das österreichische Administrativverfahren* before appearing thus as a stand-alone methodological intervention (following the prompting of colleagues) in 1925.

248. Even in the midst of his critique, Tezner emphasized the enormous importance of Kelsen's approach: he had ripped all idols from the altar, and old opinions could no longer rest on their laurels; everything needed to be re-researched and resurrected on new foundations if it wished to be considered scientific. "Kelsen's work thus forms the central point of modern legal science . . . and we Austrians can be proud of our compatriot." Tezner, *Rechtslogik und Rechtswirklichkeit*, 21. This combination of praise and critique was present all the way from Tezner's review of Kelsen's 1911 *Main Problems*: Friedrich Tezner, "Betrachtung über Kelsens Lehre vom Rechtssatz," *Archiv des öffentlichen Rechts*

28, no. 2/3 (1912): 325–44. The high regard and affection were mutual. In the preface to *Main Problems*, Kelsen reserved his warmest thanks for Tezner ("I owe more than I can express with words to Hofrat Professor Dr. Friedrich Tezner in Vienna, whose energetic assistance and warm sympathy helped me over things that lay in the way of my work": Kelsen, *Hauptprobleme*, xiii), a regard that remained evident in the obituary he wrote for Tezner in the *Neues Wiener Tagblat*, June 14, 1925.

249. Tezner, *Rechtslogik und Rechtswirklichkeit*, 11, 20.

250. Tezner, 9–11.

251. Tezner, 10, 17.

252. Tezner, 12.

253. Tezner, 12.

254. Tezner, 15.

255. Tezner, 45–46.

256. Carl Schmitt, *Political Theology: Four Chapters on the Concept of Sovereignty*, trans. George Schwab (1922, 1934; Cambridge, MA: MIT Press, 1985), 36.

257. Schmitt, 36, and on 40: "Kelsen has the merit of having stressed since 1920 the methodological relationship of theology and jurisprudence." Indeed, many of Schmitt's points echoed Kelsen's directly; for example: "To the conception of God in the seventeenth and eighteenth centuries belongs the idea of his transcendence vis-à-vis the world, just as to that period's philosophy of state belongs the notion of the transcendence of the sovereign vis-à-vis the state. Everything in the nineteenth century was increasingly governed by conceptions of immanence" (49).

258. Schmitt, 7, 18–22, 29, 36, 40–42, 49–50.

259. Tezner, *Rechtslogik und Rechtswirklichkeit*, 23.

260. Tezner, 23 (quotation in previous sentence—"selbst ohne menschliches Zutun bewirken"—also on 23). Indeed, the broader parallels between Tezner's and Schmitt's critiques—the latter legendary, the former all but forgotten—are striking. If Schmitt rejected the idea of a gapless legal order by focusing on the exception and the arbitrary, especially in relation to the figure of the sovereign and the judge, Tezner's similar insistence that one could not simply seal out the arbitrary took its orientation and examples from Austro-Hungarian constitutional law.

261. Tezner, 17.

262. Tezner, 17–18.

Chapter Five: What Is a New State?

1. Hans Kelsen, "Autobiographie (1947)," in Hans Kelsen, *Werke*, ed. Matthias Jestaedt (Tübingen: Mohr Siebeck, 2007), 1:49–50. On Kelsen during the war, see further chapter 6. On Kelsen's wartime service, see Thomas Olechowski, *Hans Kelsen: Biographie eines Rechtswissenschaftlers* (Tübingen: Mohr Siebeck, 2020), 171–78, 195–202, 219–20; Jürgen Busch, "Hans Kelsen im Ersten Weltkrieg: Achsenzeit einer Weltkarriere," in *Hans Kelsen: Leben—Werk—Wirksamkeit*, ed. Robert Walter, Werner Ogris, and Thomas Olechowski (Vienna: Manz, 2009), 57–80.

2. Kelsen, "Autobiographie," 50.

3. Pieter Judson, *The Habsburg Empire: A New History* (Cambridge, MA: Harvard University Press, 2016). If history writing more broadly long took nations as its natural protagonists, that assumption was particularly pronounced in the historiography of Central and Eastern Europe. Its undoing has been equally zealous. A new generation of historians, including Tara Zahra, Alison Frank Johnson, Jeremy King, Eagle Glassheim, and John Deak, have unearthed "nonnational" histories in a variety of forms. This turn has gone hand in hand with a new emphasis on the many contingencies surrounding the empire's

collapse. See Judson, *The Habsburg Empire*; Maureen Healy, *Vienna and the Fall of the Habsburg Empire: Total War and Everyday Life in World War I* (Cambridge: Cambridge University Press, 2004); and Aviel Roshwald, *Ethnic Nationalism and the Fall of Empires: Central Europe, Russia and the Middle East, 1914–1923* (London: Routledge, 2001). But note, too, contrasting perspectives: John Connelly, *Peoples into Nations: A History of Eastern Europe* (Princeton, NJ: Princeton University Press, 2020); R. J. W. Evans, "Remembering the Fall of the Habsburg Monarchy One Hundred Years on: Three Master Interpretations," *Austrian History Yearbook* 51 (2020): 269–91. A burgeoning new literature excavates the different pieces of the imperial order—from personnel and mentalities to infrastructure and bureaucracy—that persisted in the successor states. See Dominique Kirchner Reill, *The Fiume Crisis: Life in the Wake of the Habsburg Empire* (Cambridge, MA: Harvard University Press, 2020); Gábor Egry, "The Empire's New Clothes: How Austria-Hungary's Legacy Kept the Successor States Running," Foundation for Austrian Studies, Leiden, Annual Lecture 2020, http://real.mtak.hu/id/eprint/141411, last accessed June 1, 2022; Dominique Kirchner Reill, Ivan Jeličić, and Francesca Rolandi, "Redefining Citizenship after Empire: The Rights to Welfare, to Work, and to Remain in a Post-Habsburg World," *Journal of Modern History* 94, no. 2 (2022): 326–62; Paul Miller and Clare Morelon, eds., *Embers of Empire: Continuity and Rupture in the Habsburg Successor States after 1918* (New York: Berghahn Books, 2018); Franz Adlgasser and Fredrik Lindström, eds., *The Habsburg Civil Service and Beyond: Bureaucracy and Civil Servants from the Vormärz to the Inter-war Years* (Vienna: Verlag der Österreichischen Akademie der Wissenschaften, 2018); Tomasz Pudłocki and Kamil Ruszała, eds., *Postwar Continuity and New Challenges in Central and Eastern Europe, 1918–1923: The War That Never Ended* (Abingdon: Routledge, 2022); Peter Becker and Natasha Wheatley, eds., *Remaking Central Europe: The League of Nations and the Former Habsburg Lands* (Oxford: Oxford University Press, 2020); Iryna Vushko, *The Lost Fatherland: Europeans between Empire and Nation States, 1867–1939* (New Haven, CT: Yale University Press, forthcoming).

4. This is true in systems and theories of positive law but not, of course, for natural law, which derives its legitimacy from God or nature or reason rather than the state.

5. Akin to the process Lauren Benton describes unfolding within imperial formations: "The internal dynamics of challenges to legal authority and changing political schemes to craft a stable plural legal order were crucial in moulding the character and reach of political authority and in making it intelligible to outsiders." Lauren Benton, *Law and Colonial Cultures: Legal Regimes in World History* (New York: Cambridge University Press, 2002), 25. For an important parallel story about the unwinding of the Ottoman imperial order into international law, see Aimee Genell, *Empire by Law: The Ottoman Origins of the Mandates System* (New York: Columbia University Press, forthcoming).

6. The focus is on questions of state and sovereignty. On the continuing validity of Habsburg statutes and codes in the postwar successor states and ongoing practices of differentiated rule, see Helmut Slapnicka, *Österreichs Recht ausserhalb Österreichs: Der Untergang des österreichischen Rechtsraums* (Vienna: Verlag für Geschichte und Politik, 1973), and Egry, "The Empire's New Clothes."

7. In this area, see Erez Manela, *The Wilsonian Moment: Self-Determination and the International Origins of Anticolonial Nationalism* (Oxford: Oxford University Press, 2007); Eric Weitz, "Self-Determination: How a German Enlightenment Idea Became the Slogan of National Liberation and a Human Right," *American Historical Review* 120, no. 2 (2015): 462–96; Hussein Omar, "The Arab Spring of 1919," LRB Blog, April 4, 2019, https://www.lrb.co.uk/blog/2019/april/the-arab-spring-of-1919; Adom Getachew, *Worldmaking after Empire: The Rise and Fall of Self-Determination* (Princeton, NJ: Princeton University Press, 2019), chap. 2; Leonard Smith, *Sovereignty at the Paris Peace Conference of 1919* (Oxford: Oxford University Press, 2018); Larry Wolff, *Woodrow Wilson*

and the Reimagining of Eastern Europe (Stanford, CA: Stanford University Press, 2020); Marcus M. Payk and Roberta Pergher, eds., *Beyond Versailles: Sovereignty, Legitimacy, and the Formation of New Polities after the Great War* (Bloomington: Indiana University Press, 2019); Marcus Payk, *Frieden durch Recht? Der Aufstieg des modernen Völkerrechts und der Friedenschluss nach dem Ersten Weltkrieg* (Oldenbourg: De Gruyter, 2018).

8. Law's philosophical difficulty with the creation of states is discussed further in chapter 6.

9. On postwar border-drawing in the region more broadly, see Volker Prott, *The Politics of Self-Determination: Remaking Territories and National Identities in Europe, 1917–1923* (Oxford: Oxford University Press, 2016); Machteld Venken and Steen Bo Frandsen, eds., "The Dissolution of Austria-Hungary: Border-Making and its Consequences," special issue, *European Review of History: Revue européenne d'histoire* 27, no. 6 (2020): 679–865; Béatrice von Hirschhausen, Hannes Grandits, Claudia Kraft, Dietmar Müller, and Thomas Serrier, eds., *Phantomgrenzen: Räume und Akteure in der Zeit neu denken* (Göttingen: Wallstein Verlag, 2015); Hans Lemberg, ed., *Grenzen in Ostmitteleuropa im 19. und 20. Jahrhundert: Aktuelle Forschungsprobleme* (Marburg: Verlag Herder Institut, 2000), especially chapters by Peter Haslinger and Robert Luft.

10. As Hans Peter Hye has written, the lands were not originally territorial entities but rather estates endowed with political rights and composed largely of lords exercising patrimonial jurisdiction over their lands. Hans Peter Hye, "Die Länder im Gefüge der Habsburgermonarchie," in *Die Habsburgermonarchie 1848–1918*, vol. 7, *Verfassung und Parlamentarismus*, ed. Helmut Rumpler und Peter Urbanitsch, pt. 2: *Die regionalen und Repräsentativkörperschaften* (Vienna: Verlag der österreichischen Akademie der Wissenschaften, 2000), 2429.

11. Philip Marshall Brown, "Self-Determination in Central Europe," *American Journal of International Law* 14, no. 1–2 (1920): 237.

12. Holly Case, *Between States: The Transylvanian Question and the European Idea during World War II* (Stanford, CA: Stanford University Press, 2009), 226 and passim. On the effects of the 1918 moment on understandings of political community in the region, see further Gábor Egry, "New Horizons from Prague to Bucharest: Ethnonational Stereotypes and Regionalist Self-Perceptions in Interwar Slovakia and Transylvania," *Historie—Otázky—Problémy* 8, no. 2 (2016): 47–58.

13. See chapter 2.

14. On the manifesto, see Helmut Rumpler, *Das Völkermanifest Kaiser Karls vom 16. Oktober 1918* (Munich: Oldenbourg, 1966). Despite Charles's preemptory concessions, the Hungarian premier, Dr. Werkele, rejected the manifesto anyway. See Joseph Redlich, *Austrian War Government* (New Haven, CT: Yale University Press, 1929), 173.

15. For neat sketches of Beneš's and Masaryk's backgrounds and personalities, see Robert J. Kerner, "Two Architects of New Europe: Masaryk and Beneš," *Journal of International Relations* 12, no. 1 (1921): 27–43; Andrea Orzoff, *Battle for the Castle: The Myth of Czechoslovakia in Europe, 1914–1948* (New York: Oxford University Press, 2009), 25–42.

16. See the catalog of their crimes published after the war: Deutschnationalen Geschäftsstelle, ed., *Das Verhalten der Tschechen im Weltkrieg* (Vienna: Im Selbstverlage des Reichsratsabgeordneten Dr. Hans Schürff, 1918); and Judson, *Habsburg Empire*.

17. See Pascale Cassanova, *The World Republic of Letters*, trans. M. B. DeBevoise (Cambridge, MA: Harvard University Press, 2004), esp. 30–32; Tyler Stoval, *Paris and the Spirit of 1919: Consumer Struggles, Transnationalism and Revolution* (Cambridge: Cambridge University Press, 2012); and for the next chapter of that story: Michael Goebel, *Anti-imperial Metropolis: Interwar Paris and the Seeds of Third World Nationalism* (Cambridge: Cambridge University Press, 2015).

18. E. Denis, "Notre Programme," *La Nation Tchèque* 1, no. 1 (May 1, 1915): 3.

19. Josef Dürich (a deputy in the imperial parliament for the Agrarian Party who had joined Masaryk in Paris) and Milan Rastislav Štefánik (a Slovak serving in the French army) were named vice presidents. There is a complex story, less relevant for our purposes, about the different national committees and councils: the more pro-Russian Dürich established one in Kiev in 1916 in opposition to the one in Paris, though the Russian Revolution cut short its life. See Thomas Garrigue Masaryk, *The Making of a State: Memories and Observations, 1914–1918* (London: George Allen and Unwin, 1927), 88–89; Edvard Beneš, *Der Aufstand der Nationen: Der Weltkrieg und die Tschechoslowakische Revolution* (Berlin: Bruno Cassirer Verlag, 1928), 63ff.; Ladislav Cabada, "Czech Statehood and the Birth of Czechoslovakia," in Ladislav Cabada and Šárka Waisová, *Czechoslovakia and the Czech Republic in World Politics* (Washington, DC: Lexington Books, 2011), 4–9.

20. "Manifeste du Comité d'action tchèque à l'étranger," *La Nation Tchèque* 1, no. 14 (November 15, 1915): 215–18 (signed by Masaryk, Dürich, and others).

21. "Erste Pariser Proklamation" (1915), in Leo Epstein, *Studien-Ausgabe der Verfassungsgesetze der Tschechoslowakischen Republik* (Reichenberg: Gebrüder Stiepel, 1923), 15.

22. "Dreikönigs-Deklaration vom 6. Jänner 1918," in Epstein, *Studien-Ausgabe der Verfassungsgesetze der Tschechoslowakischen Republik*, 48.

23. *Declaration of Independence of the Czechoslovak Nation by Its Provisional Government* (New York: Marchbanks Press for the Czechoslovak Arts Club of New York City, 1918), 3. On the relationship of the Declaration of October 18 to that of October 28 in Prague (that formally announced the existence of the state), and to the constitutional order that followed, see Peter Burian, "Der Neue Staat und Seine Verfassung," in *Das Jahr 1919 in der Tschechoslowakei und in Ostmitteleuropa: Vorträge der Tagung des Collegium Carolinum in Bad Wiessee vom 24. bis 26. November 1989*, ed. Hans Lemberg and Peter Heumos (Munich: Oldenbourg, 1993), 203–14.

24. *Declaration of Independence of the Czechoslovak Nation*, 4

25. *Declaration of Independence of the Czechoslovak Nation*, 5.

26. *Declaration of Independence of the Czechoslovak Nation*, 6.

27. See David Graeber and Marshall Sahlins, *On Kings* (Chicago: HAU Books, 2017); and Marshall Sahlins, "Stranger-Kings in General: The Cosmo-logics of Power," in *Framing Cosmologies: The Anthropology of Worlds*, ed. Allen Abramson and Martin Holbraad (Manchester: Manchester University Press, 2014), 137–63, and the discussion in chapters 2 and 3 of this book.

28. Masaryk, *Making of a State*, 340.

29. Masaryk, 340 (emphasis added).

30. President Masaryk, "The Germans in the Czechoslovak Lands, Especially in Bohemia," December 9, 1918, Archives of the School for Slavonic and East European Studies, University College London (hereafter SSEES), SEW 6/1/2.

31. The memorandums were drawn up hastily by Beneš, largely without resources at hand. They were then edited as required by the other members of the delegation when they arrived in Paris. See Beneš, *Der Aufstand der Nationen*, 687–88.

32. Czechoslovak Delegation, Peace Conference, *Mémoires*, Mémoire No. 2: Territorial claims of the Czecho-Slovak Republic (n.p., n.d. [1919]), 6–7, viewed at the Hoover Institution Library, Stanford University.

33. Czechoslovak Delegation, Peace Conference, *Mémoires*, Mémoire No. 2, 7.

34. Interestingly (and in keeping with faultlines of constitutional debate), he dated the disappearance of factual Czech independence later than the Battle of the White Mountain. "In 1526, the Hapsburgs had been elected Kings of Bohemia, and, though, up to the present time they had *de jure* recognized Czech institutions, they had begun from that date to centralize power," he recounted. "Czech independence might be said to have lasted until 1747. Since then, though the juridical existence of the State continued to be acknowledged,

it had no practical significance." Secretary's Notes of a Conversation Held in M. Pichon's Room at the Quai d'Orsay, Paris, on Wednesday, 5th February, 1919, at 3:00 p.m. in David Hunter Miller, *My Diary at the Conference of Paris, with Documents*, vol. 14 (New York: Appeal Printing Company, 1924), 212 (per Beneš).

35. On the centrality of democracy to Czech self-understanding and self-presentation, see Orzoff, *Battle for the Castle.*

36. "Verbal exposé of Count Albert Apponyi, president of the Hungarian Delegation at the Peace Conference, addressed to the Supreme Council at the sitting of January 16, 1920 at Paris," in *The Hungarian Peace Negotiations: An Account of the Work of the Hungarian Peace Delegation at Neuilly s/S, from January to March, 1920* (Budapest: Royal Hungarian Ministry of Foreign Affairs, 1921), 1:310–17.

37. While in St. Louis for a meeting of the Inter-Parliamentary Union—where he was described as "one of the foremost statesmen in Europe"—Apponyi gave the lecture at the Congress of Arts and Science, an extensive international symposium organized alongside the world's fair held that year in the same city. For the latter quotation, see "Proceedings of the Interparliamentary Conference at St. Louis," *Advocate of Peace* 66, no. 10 (1904): 188.

38. Albert Apponyi, *The Juridical Nature of the Relations between Austria and Hungary* (Budapest: St.-Stephens-Printing Press, 1907), 4. A number of versions of the address were published; see, for example, the shorter version: Albert Apponyi, "The Juridical Nature of the Relations between Austria and Hungary," *North American Review* 180, no. 582 (1905): 735–45. Both publications identify the text as the address delivered at the 1904 Arts and Science Congress of St. Louis.

39. Note II ("Presentation Note"), Neuilly, January 14, 1920, Annex I: "Memorandum concerning the evolution of relations between Austria and Hungary, from the point of view of public law," in *The Hungarian Peace Negotiations*, 1:34.

40. Ernő Ludwigh made this precise comparison: E. Ludwigh, *A Plea in Support of Hungary's Territorial Integrity* (Budapest: Hungarian Territorial Integrity League, 1919).

41. The late date had much to do with the short-lived Hungarian Soviet Republic under Bela Kun (March–August, 1919) which the Allies did not recognize. See Alfred D. Low, "The Soviet Hungarian Republic and the Paris Peace Conference," *Transactions of the American Philosophical Society* 53, no. 10 (1963): 1–91; and for a general overview of diplomatic efforts in this period, see Peter Pastor, "Major Trends in Hungarian Foreign Policy from the Collapse of the Monarchy to the Peace Treaty of Trianon," *Hungarian Studies* 17, no. 1 (2003): 3–11; Gyula Juhász, *Hungarian Foreign Policy, 1919-1945* (Budapest: Akadémiai Kiadó, 1979), 7–67.

42. Teleki and Bethlen did the majority of the work. A geography professor in Budapest, Teleki's knowledge of history, geography, and demography formed the backbone of the delegation's work. Both were relative "newcomers" (though Teleki had served as minister of foreign affairs in the provisional Hungarian government set up in Szeged in 1919 to combat Bela Kun's regime), but both would go on to serve as Hungarian prime ministers in the 1920s. Francis Deák, *Hungary at the Peace Conference: The Diplomatic History of the Treaty of Trianon* (New York: Columbia University Press, 1942), 173–82. See further Steven Seegel, *Map Men: Transnational Lives and Deaths of Geographers in the Making of East Central Europe* (Chicago: University of Chicago Press, 2018).

43. Note II ("Presentation Note"), Annex I: "Memorandum concerning the evolution of relations between Austria and Hungary, from the point of view of public law," 1:34.

44. Note II ("Presentation Note"), Annex I: "Memorandum concerning the evolution of relations between Austria and Hungary, from the point of view of public law," 1:34.

45. Note II ("Presentation Note"), Annex I: "Memorandum concerning the evolution of relations between Austria and Hungary, from the point of view of public law," 1:34.

46. Note II ("Presentation Note"), Annex I: "Memorandum concerning the evolution of relations between Austria and Hungary, from the point of view of public law," 1:35.

47. Note II ("Presentation Note"), Annex I: "Memorandum concerning the evolution of relations between Austria and Hungary, from the point of view of public law," 1:35.

48. Note II ("Presentation Note"), Annex I: "Memorandum concerning the evolution of relations between Austria and Hungary, from the point of view of public law," 1:35.

49. Note II ("Presentation Note"), Annex I: "Memorandum concerning the evolution of relations between Austria and Hungary, from the point of view of public law," 1:36.

50. Note II ("Presentation Note"), Neuilly, January 14, 1920, Annex 26, "The relationship of Hungary and Austria in public law till the dissolution of the Austro-Hungarian Monarchy," in *The Hungarian Peace Negotiations*, 1:68.

51. Note II ("Presentation Note"), Neuilly, January 14, 1920, *The Hungarian Peace Negotiations* 1:4.

52. Application by Hungary, Report of the First Sub-committee of the Sixth Committee: Admission of New Members to the League of Nations, September 14th, 1922, League of Nations, *Records of the Third Assembly*, Minutes of the Sixth Committee (Geneva, 1922), 55 (Annex 4).

53. The Mission to Austria-Hungary, Report by General Smuts, April 9, 1919, The National Archives, London (hereafter TNA), FO 608/16/29. See also Quincy Wright, *Mandates under the League of Nations* (Chicago: University of Chicago Press, 1930), 33–34.

54. See the report prepared by the intelligence section (January 1919), document 246, in David Hunter Miller, *My Diary at the Conference of Paris, with Documents* (New York: Appeal Printing Company, 1924), 4:231.

55. The latter provinces would ostensibly serve as a counterweight to Vienna's socialist-industrialist leanings. Memorandum by Professor Lammasch (n.d. [March?] 1919), forwarded to Curzon by Acton, March 28, 1919, TNA, FO 608/11/10.

56. Gerald Stourzh, "Erschütterung und Konsolidierung des Österreichbewusstseins— Vom Zussamenbruch der Monarchie zur Zweiten Republik," in *Was heißt Österreich? Inhalt und Umfang des Österreichbegriffs vom 10. Jahrhundert bis Heute*, ed. Richard Plaschka, Gerald Stourzh, and Jan Paul Niederkorn (Vienna: Verlag der Österreichischen Akademie der Wissenschaften, 1995), 289–311.

57. See Stourzh, 289–311.

58. Otto Bauer, *Die österreichische Revolution* (Vienna: Wiener Volksbuchhandlung, 1923), 113.

59. Bauer, 114. That view of the new Austria was very widespread; see, for example, Chroust, *Die Österreichische Frage* (Würzburg: Kabitzsch & Mönnich, 1920).

60. Karl Renner, "Austria: Key for War and Peace," *Foreign Affairs* 26, no. 4 (1948): 595.

61. Renner, 595.

62. Of course, the symbiotic relationship between Austria and the League of Nations would only be deepened after the Austrian financial crisis of the early 1920s and the subsequent bailout by the league. If the league saved Austria, Austria was also a crucial early test for the new international organization. John Deak has argued that the crisis and bailout drove the real transition "from core lands of an empire to a republic. It was largely a result of the financial crisis . . . that the administrative structures of the Habsburg Empire were finally dismantled, clearing the path for a new republic." John Deak, "Dismantling Empire: Ignaz Seipel and Austria's Financial Crisis, 1922–1925," in *From Empire to Republic: Post–World War I Austria*, ed. Günter Bischof and Fritz Plasser (New Orleans: University of New Orleans Press, 2010), 123–41. See also Patricia Clavin, *Securing the World Economy: The Reinvention of the League of Nations, 1920–1946* (Oxford: Oxford University Press, 2013); Becker and Wheatley, *Remaking Central Europe*, especially the chapter by Nathan Marcus. On the place of these interventions in the emergence of projects to govern

global capitalism, see Jamie Martin, *The Meddlers: Sovereignty, Empire, and the Birth of Global Economic Governance* (Cambridge, MA: Harvard University Press, 2022).

63. Bevollmächtige Vertretung des Deutsch-Österreichischen Staates in der Schweiz to the Schweizerische Politische Department (Bern), February 3, 1919, TNA, FO 608/9/6.

64. Bevollmächtige Vertretung des Deutsch-Österreichischen Staates in der Schweiz to the Schweizerische Politische Department (Bern).

65. Minute by Leeper (February 20, 1919) on docket; Minute by Crowe; Bevollmächtige Vertretung des Des Deutsch-Österreichischen Staates in der Schweiz to the Schweizerische Politische Department (Bern).

66. Rede des Staatskanzlers vom 2. Juni, in *Bericht über die Tätigkeit der Deutschösterreichischen Friedensdelegation in St. Germain-en-Laye* (Vienna: Staatsdruckerei, 1919), 40.

67. Deutschösterreichiche Delegation, Note über die internationale Rechtspersönlichkeit Deutschösterreichs, June 16, 1919, Beilage 29, in *Bericht über die Tätigkeit der Deutsch-österreichischen Friedensdelegation*, 164ff.: the treaty's articles "lassen nämlich das internationale Subjekt, mit dem der Vertrag abgeschlossen werden soll, unsicher erscheinen."

68. See Olechowski, *Hans Kelsen*, 230–32.

69. Deutschösterreichiche Delegation, Note über die internationale Rechtspersönlichkeit Deutschösterreichs, 165.

70. Deutschösterreichiche Delegation, Note über die internationale Rechtspersönlichkeit Deutschösterreichs, 165.

71. Deutschösterreichiche Delegation, Note über die internationale Rechtspersönlichkeit Deutschösterreichs, J 168.

72. J. W. Headlam-Morley, Note on the Draft Austrian Treaty, May 26, 1919, TNA, FO 608/19/10.

73. J. W. Headlam-Morley, Note on the Draft Austrian Treaty.

74. J. W. Headlam-Morley, Note on the Draft Austrian Treaty.

75. J. W. Headlam-Morley, Note on the Draft Austrian Treaty.

76. Mr. Namier, Reference to Mr. Headlam-Morley's "Note on the Draft Austrian Treaty," May 31, 1919, TNA, FO 608/19/10.

77. Recall (from chapter 3) Robert Redslob's argument that the empire only existed through its various autonomous lands, wirh no "empire" on top or beside them. See Robert Redslob, *Abhängige Länder: Eine Analyse des Begriffs von der ursprünglichen Herrschergewalt: Zugleich eine staatsrechtliche und politische Studie über Elsaß-Lothringen, die österreichischen Königreiche und Länder, Kroatien-Slavonien, Bosnien-Herzegowina, Finnland, Island, die Territorien der nordamerikanischen Union, Kanada, Australien, Südafrika* (Leipzig: Veit & Comp., 1914), 155–64.

78. Scholars like Pieter Judson have argued that, broadly speaking, Austria had no imperial master race, that it was not a "German empire," as against those who have argued for the applicability of postcolonial theory. See Pieter Judson, "L'Autriche-Hongrie était-elle un empire?," *Annales* 63, no. 3 (2008): 563–96; see also Jana Osterkamp's powerful article "Cooperative Empires: Provincial Initiatives in Imperial Austria," trans. Jaime Hyland, *Austrian History Yearbook* 47 (2016): 128–146; cf. Johannes Feichtinger, Ursula Prutsch, and Moritz Csaky, eds., *Habsburg Postcolonial: Machtstrukturen und Kollektives Gedächtnis* (Innsbruck: StudienVerlag, 2003); Clemens Ruthner, "Central Europe Goes Post-colonial: New Approaches to the Habsburg Empire around 1900," *Cultural Studies* 16, no. 6 (2002): 877–83.

79. ". . . and though the United Kingdom eo ipso [*sic*] would cease to exist, no one could deny that Great Britain would be the heir to its personality especially were the Union to be dissolved against her will." Mr. Namier, Reference to Mr. Headlam-Morley's "Note

on the Draft Austrian Treaty." Strikingly, a version of this debate was revived in relation to Scotland's possible succession. See Anthony Caty and Mairianna Clyde, "Scotland and England from a Union of Parliaments to Two Independent Kingdoms," *London Review of International Law* 2, no. 2 (2014): 299–328.

80. Mr. Namier, Reference to Mr. Headlam-Morley's "Note on the Draft Austrian Treaty."

81. Minute by Headlam-Morley, June 30, 1919, TNA, FO 608/19/10.

82. Minute by Headlam-Morley, June 30, 1919. Interestingly, he here reasoned from an imperial "periphery" to assert a comparable legal status for the imperial "metropole."

83. For a sample of some of these domains, see Edwin M. Borchard, "Austrian and Hungarian 'Debt' Claims," *American Journal of International Law* 22, no. 1 (1928): 142–46; Ernst H. Feilchenfeld, *Public Debts and State Succession* (New York: Macmillan, 1931); A. N. Sack, "Die Verteilung der Schulden der österreichisch-ungarischen Monarchie," *Weltwirtschaftliches Archiv* 23 (1926): 369–90; Alfred Kramer, *Die Staatsangehörigkeit der Altösterreicher und Ungarn nach den Friedensverträgen* (Vienna: Staatsdruckerei, 1926); Ludwig Bittner, "Die zwischenstaatlichen Verhandlungen über das Schicksal der österreichschen Archive nach dem Zusammenbruch Österreich-Ungarns," *Archiv für Politik und Geschichte* 3 (1925): 58–96.

84. H. W. V. Temperley, *A History of the Peace Conference of Paris*, vol. 5 (London: Henry Frowde and Hodder & Stoughton, 1921), 5:142–43.

85. Alfred Verdross, *Die Verfassung der Völkerrechtsgemeinschaft* (Vienna: Julius Springer, 1926), 151; Josef L. Kunz, *Der Revision der Pariser Friedensverträge: Eine Völkerrechtliche Untersuchung* (Vienna: Julius Springer, 1932), 9–10; Franz Klein, *Die Revision des Friedensvertrages von St. Germain: Ein Leitfaden für die Aufklärungsarbeit* (Vienna: Verlag der Internationalen Frauenlige, 1920).

86. Krystyna Marek, *Identity and Continuity of States in Public International Law*, 2nd ed. (1954; Geneva: Librairie Droz, 1968), 199–236.

87. The *Austrian Pensions (State Succession) Case* (1925) involved a woman who claimed a pension owed by the former Austrian empire to her husband, who had been killed while working on state railways. The Austrian Supreme Court in Civil and Administrative Matters held that there was no continuity between old and new Austria and that article 177 of the Treaty of Saint-Germain did not contradict this. In an interesting interpretation of the treaty, the court maintained that article 177 in effect held that "the Allied and Associated Powers intended to burden only one part of the inhabitants of the former monarchy, namely the inhabitants of the Austrian Republic, with the responsibility for the war conducted by the monarchy as a whole; this is all that was intended by the Peace Treaty, and not universal succession proper." *Austrian Pensions (State Succession) Case*, Austrian Supreme Court in Civil and Administrative Matters, 23 June 1925, Case 25, in *Annual Digest of Public International Law Cases, Years 1925–1926*, ed. Arnold D. McNair and Hersch Lauterpacht (London: Longmans, Green, 1929), 34. So debts and liabilities were seemingly transferred onto a segment of the population but *not* directly from state to state. See also *Military Decoration Pension Case*, Austrian Constitutional Court, 15 March 1926, Case 58, in *Annual Digest of Public International Law Cases, Years 1925–1926*, 79ff.; and *Austrian Empire (Succession) Case*, Austria, Constitutional Court, 11 March 1919 (No. 18), Case 39, in *Annual Digest of Public International Law Cases, Years 1919–1922*, ed. John Fischer Williams and Hersch Lauterpacht (London: Longmans, Green, 1932), 67–68.

88. Third Meeting (December 1, 1920), Minutes of the Fifth Committee (Admission of New Members into the League), League of Nations, *Records of the First Assembly*, 166.

89. H. Duncan Hall, *Mandates, Dependencies and Trusteeship* (Washington, DC: Carnegie Endowment for International Peace, 1948), 3, 8, and passim.

90. Kunz, *Der Revision der Pariser Friedensverträge*, 25, 35.

91. Alfred Verdross, *Völkerrecht* (Berlin: Julius Springer, 1937), 14.

92. M. Pachitch to M. Clemenceau, July 24, 1919, Annex C to the Thirty-Ninth Meeting of the New States Committee, in *La Paix de Versailles: Commission des nouveaux États et des Minorités* (Paris: Les Éditions Internationales, 1932), 245.

93. Pachitch to the President of the Committee on New States, August 1, 1919, Annex G to the Forty-First Meeting of the New States Committee, in *La Paix de Versailles: Commission des nouveaux États et des Minorités*, 262. The New States Committee, for its part, would not be drawn into these sorts of arguments. In its report for the Supreme Council, it explained that "no distinction is drawn between the old and new provinces." "While it does not seem necessary to discuss the technical legal point whether the new Kingdom is legally identical with the old Kingdom of Serbia," the transformation of the last six years was so great (especially through a huge increase in population) that it was now a very different state. See Report to the Supreme Council from the Committee on New States Enclosing the Treaty for Presentation to the Serb-Croat-Slovene Delegation, August 29, 1919, Forty-Seventh Meeting, in *La Paix de Versailles: Commission des nouveaux États et des Minorités*, 305.

94. Albert Apponyi, *The American Peace and Hungary*, 2nd ed. (Budapest: Hungarian Territorial Integrity League, 1919), 4–5.

95. Apponyi, 5–6.

96. Apponyi, 6.

97. Apponyi, 8–9.

98. Apponyi, 12 (emphasis added).

99. Apponyi, 13 (emphasis added). Apponyi was not the only one to suggest a deterritorialized federal solution to the national problem in order to preserve Hungary's historic frontiers (oh the curious fate of Austro-Marxism!): see, for example, Eugene [Jenő] Horváth, *The Independence and Integrity of Hungary: Appeal of the Academy of Laws and Politics at Nagyvárad to the Western Universities* (Nagyvárad: Academy of Laws and Politics, 1919), 12; E. [Ernő] Ludwigh, *A Plea in Support of Hungarian Territorial Integrity: Advocating an United States of Hungary* (Geneva: Printed by Albert Kundig under the auspices of the Hungarian Territorial Integrity League, 1919).

100. Julius [Gyula] Wlassics, *The Right of Self-Determination. The Protection of the National Minorities: Reply Given in 1919 to the Questions of the "Central Organisation for Durable Peace"* (Budapest: Ferdinand Pfeifer [Zeidler Brothers], 1922), 3.

101. Wlassics, 4–5.

102. Wlassics, 7.

103. Wlassics, 7, 12.

104. Wlassics, 13.

105. Wlassics, 13.

106. Wlassics, 14.

107. Wlassics, 20.

108. "The assertion that only a people speaking the same language can build nation States, is just as false as the assertion that Peoples speaking the same language can form, under all conditions, only one State. Natural development may lead to both results." Wlassics, 20. For the wider context of these questions of defining the Hungarian political community, see Egry, "New Horizons from Prague to Bucharest."

109. Wlassics, *The Right of Self-Determination*, 20–21, 25.

110. Wlassics, 28.

111. Wlassics, 29.

112. Wlassics, 29–30. Hungarian politicians and publicists of this period routinely contrasted the contours of the settlement with what Wilson had ostensibly intended. See, for example, Emeric Radványi, "Ungarn und Trianon," in *Die tragödie Ungarns: Die grösste*

Ungerechtigkeit der Weltgeschichte, ed. Emeric Radványi (Budapest: Druckerei Viktor Hornyánszky A.-G., 1920?), [no page numbers; third page]; Louis [Lajos] Steier, *There Is No Czech Culture in Upper Hungary*, illustrations by Joseph de Makoldy (Budapest: printed by Wodianer & Sons, 1920), 78; and, later, Hungarian Frontier Readjustment League, *Facts* (Budapest: Victor Hornyánszky Co., 1928); Albert Apponyi, Albert Berzeviczy, Oliver Eöttevenyi, Francis Fodor, Béla Földes, Eugene Horváth, George Lukács, Emil Nagy, and Baron Julius Wlassics, *Justice for Hungary: Review and Criticism of the Effect of the Treaty of Trianon* (London: Longmans, Green, 1928), especially 133. Hungarian jurists also pursued this line of argumentation through the interwar years. See, for example, the richly argued pamphlet put out by the Society of Hungarian Lawyers in 1931: Magyar Jogászegylet, Budapest [The Society of Hungarian Lawyers], *The Peace-Treaty of Trianon from the View-Point of International Peace, Security and the Co-operation of Nations: An Appeal by the Lawyers, Judges, and Professors of Law of Hungary to the Lawyers of all Civilised Nations* (Budapest: Printed by Stephaneum Co., 1931), 19–20. On Hungarian propaganda in this period more generally, see Cintia Gunda, "The Hungarian Nation: Post-World War I Propaganda Abroad for Protecting Hungary's Territorial Integrity," *Hungarian Studies Review* 40, no. 2 (2013): 97–122. This interpretation of self-determination also appeared in activism abroad; see, for example, the publication *Chains*, intended to be the "Organ of the Oxford League for Hungarian Self-Determination," edited by R. Denne Waterhouse and J. R. Adams. See, for example, D. D. A. Lockhart, "Transylvania and the Roumanian Blight," *Chains*, March 16 1922, 14–15. *Chains* viewed at SSEES, SEW 11/1/1.

113. Note XXII ("Concerning the frontiers of Hungary"), [Neuilly, 12 February 1920], in *The Hungarian Peace Negotiations*, 2:12.

114. Julius [Gyula] Wlassics, *The Territorial Integrity of Hungary and the League of Nations* (Budapest: Hungarian Territorial Integrity League, 1919), 11.

115. Report of Commission of Jurists (Larnaude, Huber, Struycken), *League of Nations Official Journal*, special supplement No. 3 (October 1920), 5–6; quoted at length in James Crawford, *The Creation of States in International Law*, 2nd ed. (Oxford: Clarendon Press, 2006), 109–10.

116. "To concede to minorities, either of language or religion, or to any fraction of the population the right of withdrawing from the community to which they belong, because it is their good wish or their good pleasure, would be to destroy order and stability within states and to inaugurate anarchy in international life." Report of the Committee of Rapporteurs (Beyens, Calonder, Elkens), April 16, 1921: League of Nations Council Doct. B7/21/68/106 [VII], 22–23; quoted in Crawford, *Creation of States in International Law*, 111.

117. See Crawford, *The Creation of States in International Law*, 59–60.

118. Note II ("Presentation Note"), Neuilly, January 14, 1920, in *The Hungarian Peace Negotiations*, 1:5.

119. "Verbal exposé of Count Albert Apponyi, president of the Hungarian Delegation at the Peace Conference, addressed to the Supreme Council at the sitting of January 16, 1920 at Paris," in *The Hungarian Peace Negotiations*, 1:314–15.

120. Apponyi, *American Peace and Hungary*, 4–5. See further peace conference propaganda like *La Hongrie; cartes et notions géographiques, historiques, etnographiques, économiques et intellectuelles* (Paris [?]: n.p., 1919 [?]), 5; as well as Steier, *There Is No Czech Culture in Upper Hungary*, 41.

121. See Deák, *Hungary at the Peace Conference*, 206ff.

122. Note C ("Introductory Note"), Neuilly, 12 February 1920, in *The Hungarian Peace Negotiations*, 2:2. Emphasis is found in the (Hungarian) original—i.e., presumably added to the internal quotation by the Hungarian delegation, which is quoting the Allied powers' response to the Austrian delegation (Note II of 2 September 1919).

123. Note XXII ("Concerning the frontiers of Hungary"), 2:13.

124. Note XXII ("Concerning the frontiers of Hungary"), 2:15. See also page 18.

125. Following the work of the committees, Hungary's frontiers were essentially decided in a single meeting of the Council of Foreign Ministers on May 8. For an account of the unfolding of the determination of Hungary's frontiers, see Deák, *Hungary at the Peace Conference*, 27–90.

126. Secretary's Notes of a Conversation Held in M. Pichon's Room at the Quai d'Orsay, Paris, 212 (per Beneš).

127. Czechoslovak Delegation, Peace Conference, *Mémoires*, Mémoire No. 2, 7.

128. Czechoslovak Delegation, Peace Conference, *Mémoires*, Mémoire No. 2, 7–8.

129. Czechoslovak Delegation, Peace Conference, *Mémoires*, Mémoire No. 2, 8.

130. See, generally, D. Perman, *The Shaping of the Czechoslovak State: Diplomatic History of the Boundaries of Czechoslovakia, 1914–1920* (Leiden: E. J. Brill, 1962); Robert Luft, "'Alte Grenzen' und Kulturgeographie: Zur historischen Konstanz der Grenzen Böhmens und der böhmischen Länder," in *Grenzen in Ostmitteleuropa im 19. und 20. Jahrhundert: Aktuelle Forschungsprobleme*, ed. Hans Lemberg (Marburg: Verlag Herder-Institut, 2000), 95–135.

131. For the Kremsier debates, see chapter 1. On this relationship over the longue durée, see Václav Houžvička, *Czechs and Germans 1848–2004: The Sudeten Question and the Transformation of Central Europe* (Chicago: University of Chicago Press, 2013).

132. Masaryk, *Making of a State*, 385–86. See also his 1918 memorandum: President Masaryk, "The Germans in the Czechoslovak Lands, Especially in Bohemia."

133. Rudolf Lodgman von Auen, *Für die Selbstbestimmung Deutschböhmens*, Flugblätter für Deutschösterreichs Recht, No. 7 (Vienna: Alfred Hölder, 1919). The publication identifies the text as a speech he presented on December 28, 1918, at the meeting of the Deutschböhmischen Landesversammlung in Vienna.

134. "Information Concerning the Situation of the Germans in the Czecho-Slovak State," Memorandum submitted to (Prof) Herron [intended for Peace Conference] by Rudolf Ritter Lodgman von Auen, Landeshauptmann in Deutschböhmen, and Robert Freissler, Landeshauptmann der Provinz Sudetenland, February 17, 1919, TNA, FO 608/5/16.

135. Rudolf Laun, *Die tschechoslowakischen Ansprüche auf deutsches Land*, Flugblätter für Deutschösterreichs Recht, No. 4 (Vienna: Alfred Hölder, 1919), 6.

136. Laun, 6.

137. Laun, 10.

138. "Das deutsche Sudetenland will sein Schicksal selbst bestimmen." Erwin Barta, *Die Ansprüche der Tschechen auf das Sudetenland*, Flugblätter für Deutschösterreichs Recht, No. 9 (Vienna: Alfred Hölder, 1919), 6. See also *Deutschsüdmähren an Wilson*, Flugblätter für Deutschösterreichs Recht, No. 21 (Vienna: Alfred Hölder, 1919).

139. Case, *Between States*, 11. See also, for the case at hand, Kurt Rabl, "'Historisches Staatsrecht' und Selbstbestimmungsrecht bei der Staatsgründung der Tschechoslowakei 1918/19," in *Das böhmische Staatsrecht in den deutsch-tschechische Auseinandersetzungen des 19. und 20. Jahrhunderts*, ed. Ernst Birke und Kurt Oberdorffer (Marburg: N. G. Elwert-Verlag, 1960), 79–99.

140. Masaryk, *Making of a State*, 386.

141. Edvard Beneš, Rapport sur la situation generale, December 24, 1918, Masaryk Institute and Archives of the ASCR, Prague (hereafter MUA), EB1, 549, k. 114.

142. Czecho-Slovak Government, Memorandum on the Affairs in Silesia, January 21, 1919 [signed by Svehla, m.p., Minister of the Interior, for the Prime Minister and the Minister of Foreign Affairs], transmitted in Prague Dispatch No. 8, January 26, 1919, TNA, FO 608/6/7.

143. Political Intelligence Department [P.I.D.], Minute by Lewis Namier, February 15, 1919, TNA, FO 608/7/1. On American reservations, see also Margaret MacMillan, *Paris 1919: Six Months That Changed the World* (New York: Random House, 2001), 236–37.

144. Headlam-Morley, Minute on German Territories in the Tyrol and Northern Bohemia, January 21, 1919, TNA, FO 608/6/8.

145. See also the formulation of the peace conference committees dealing with the Teschen question: Note presented to the Supreme Council of the Allies by the Commission on Polish Affairs and the Committee on Tchecho-Slovak Questions, Frontier between Poland and Tchecho-Slovakia, April 6, 1919 (collected under the docket heading: Frontiers between Polish and Czecho-Slovak States), TNA, FO 608/6/7. On the unfolding of the Teschen question, see MacMillan, *Paris 1919*, 225ff.

146. For background, see Orzoff, *Battle for the Castle*; Judson, *Habsburg Empire*, 407.

147. Czechoslovak Delegation, Peace Conference, *Mémoires*, Mémoire No. 2, 1.

148. *Declaration of Independence of the Czechoslovak Nation by Its Provisional Government*, 4.

149. Masaryk, *Making of a State*, 361.

150. On this union, its ambivalences, and its consequences, see Nadya Nedelsky, *Defining the Sovereign Community: The Czech and Slovak Republics* (Philadelphia: University of Pennsylvania Press, 2009), 65ff.; Carol Skalnik Leff, *National Conflict in Czechoslovakia: The Making and Remaking of a State, 1918–1987* (Princeton, NJ: Princeton University Press, 1988); Alexander Maxwell, *Choosing Slovakia: Slavic Hungary, the Czechoslovak Language and Accidental Nationalism* (London: I. B. Tauris, 2009), 166ff.; Hugh LeCaine Agnew, "New States, Old Identities? The Czech Republic, Slovakia, and Historical Understandings of Statehood," *Nationalities Papers* 28, no. 4 (2000): 620–29.

151. Aide-Memoir by Victor Dworcak [n.b., the docket reads: Victor Wborcadki], Président du Conseil National Slovaque, August 21, 1919, forwarded by Percy Wyndham (British legation, Warsaw) to Curzon (FO), September 6, 1919, TNA, FO 608/8/2. Dvorčák, who had represented Slovakia in the Hungarian parliament before the war, was a complicated figure who later became a paid agent of Hungary. I thank Gábor Egry for notes on this point.

152. Masaryk, *Making of a State*, 338.

153. Masaryk, 338.

154. Masaryk, 361.

155. Nicole M. Phelps, *U.S.-Habsburg Relations from 1815 to the Paris Peace Conference: Sovereignty Transformed* (New York: Cambridge University Press, 2013), 163.

156. E. Ludwigh, *A Plea in Support of Hungary's Territorial Integrity* (Budapest: Hungarian Territorial Integrity League, 1919), 15.

157. Some were reminded of dualism in the more literal sense: "'Czecho-Slovak unit'—a phrase similar to the former national state idea of Austria!" wrote Lajos Steier, who agitated for the Slovak cause throughout the interwar period. Steier, *There Is No Czech Culture in Upper Hungary*, 45.

158. Laun, *Die tschechoslowakischen Ansprüche auf deutsches Land*, 7.

159. Friedrich F. G. Kleinwaechter, *Der Untergang der Oesterrichisch-Ungarischen Monarchie* (Leipzig: K. F. Koehler, 1920), 55.

160. Kleinwaechter, 54–55 (emphasis added for clarity).

161. *Establishment of Czechoslovak State Case*, Supreme Administrative Court of Czechoslovakia, No. 11224, 29 May 1925, Case 8, in *Annual Digest of Public International Law Cases, Years 1925-1926*, 13–14.

162. *Payment of War Tax (Czechoslovakia) Case*, Czechoslovakia Supreme Administrative Court, 21 January 1921 (No. 580), Case 4, in *Annual Digest of Public International Law Cases, Years 1919-1922*, 11–12.

163. See *Foreign Bills Decree (Establishment of Czechoslovakia) Case*, Supreme Administrative Court of Czechoslovakia, No. 5142, 14 May 1925, Case 9, in *Annual Digest of Public International Law Cases, Years 1925-1926*, 14 (see footnote 1 from the editors).

164. *Foreign Bills Decree (Establishment of Czechoslovakia) Case*, 14–15 (see footnote 1 from the editors).

165. Baron J. von Szilassy, *Der Untergang der Donau-Monarchie: Diplomatische Erinnerungen* (Berlin: Verlag Neues Vaterland, 1921), 370.

166. Note XII ("Concerning Southern Hungary"), Annex 6, "Three Nationality States instead of One," in *The Hungarian Peace Negotiations*, 1:427.

167. Oscar Jászi, "War Germs in the Danube Basin, II: Constitutional Problems in the Victor States," *The Nation* 139, no. 3620 (1934): 583–84.

168. See Orzoff, *Battle for the Castle*.

169. Slovak Council, *Should Great Britain Go to War—for Czechoslovakia? An Appeal to British Common Sense for the Sake of World Peace* (London: Slovak Council, 1937), 25–26. See also Slovak Council, *Shall Millions Die for "This Czechoslovakia . . ."?* (London: Slovak Council, 1938).

170. See Michael Yuhasz, *Wilson's Principles in Czechoslovak Practice: The Situation of the Carpatho-Russian People under the Czech Yoke* (Homestead, PA: [n.p.], 1929).

Chapter Six: State Birth at the Frontier of Knowledge

1. Hans Kelsen, *Der soziologische und der juristische Staatsbegriff: Kritische Untersuchungen des Verhältnisses von Staat und Recht* (Tübingen: J. C. B. Mohr, 1922), 85 (emphasis added).

2. Kelsen, 85.

3. Kelsen, 85.

4. Note an existing literature on state *succession*—treating the transfer of rights and obligations between states, rather than the temporal dimensions of the state *as such* (like identity, continuity, and creation). For the most prominent example of the succession literature, see Max Huber, *Die Staatensuccession: Völkerrechtliche und staatsrechtlcihe Praxis im XIX. Jahrhundert* (Leipzig: Duncker & Humblot, 1898).

5. "Sie tritt mit dem Anspruch auf, *ewig* zu gelten." Hans Kelsen, *Allgemeine Staatslehre* (Berlin: Julius Springer, 1925), 148 (emphasis in original).

6. Kelsen, 148.

7. Last phrase here from Ernst Kantorowicz, *The King's Two Bodies: A Study in Mediaeval Political Theology* (1957; Princeton, NJ: Princeton University Press, 1997), 284.

8. See Matthew Craven, *The Decolonization of International Law: State Succession and the Law of Treaties* (Oxford: Oxford University Press, 2007); Sundhya Pahuja, *Decolonising International Law: Development, Economic Growth and the Politics of Universality* (Cambridge: Cambridge University Press, 2011); Jochen von Bernstoff and Philipp Dann, eds., *The Battle for International Law: South-North Perspectives on the Decolonization Era* (Oxford: Oxford University Press, 2019); Rose Parfitt, *The Process of International Legal Reproduction: Inequality, Historiography, Resistance* (Cambridge: Cambridge University Press, 2019); "Towards a History of the Decolonization of International Law," special issue edited by Natasha Wheatley and Samuel Moyn, *Journal of the History of International Law* 23, no. 1 (2021): 1–228.

9. Note that this framing of the problem also represented a rejection by late nineteenth-century positivist jurists of the "standard of civilization" as the benchmark for the recognition of sovereign states. By positing statehood as something determined by objective matters of fact, they sought to overcome the subjectivity of the "standard of

civilization" test that structured this area of law earlier in the nineteenth century (and, of course, found ever new mutations afterward). I am grateful to Martti Koskenniemi for conversation on this point.

10. "Erst an die fertige Tatsache des Staates knüpfe das Recht an." Alfred Verdross, *Die Verfassung der Völkerrechtsgemeinschaft* (Vienna: Julius Springer, 1926), 125.

11. Charles de Visscher, *Theory and Reality in Public International Law*, trans. P. E. Corbett (Princeton, NJ: Princeton University Press, 1957), 166.

12. For an overview of the landscape that includes the other international jurists working in Vienna at the time, see Sebastian M. Spitra, "After the Great War: International Law in Austria's First Republic, 1918–mid 1920s," *Clio Themis* 18 (2020): 1–22. For a different sort of genealogy of Kelsen's thought, see Mónica García-Salmones Rovira, *The Project of Positivism in International Law* (Oxford: Oxford University Press, 2013); and for a reconstruction of Kelsen's international legal thought more broadly, see Jochen von Bernstorff, *The Public International Law Theory of Hans Kelsen: Believing in Universal Law* (Cambridge: Cambridge University Press, 2010).

13. Stefan Zweig, *The World of Yesterday*, trans. Anthea Bell (1942; Lincoln: University of Nebraska Press, 2009), 61–62. See further William M. Johnston, *The Austrian Mind: An Intellectual and Social History, 1848–1938* (Berkeley: University of California Press, 1972), 120.

14. Zweig, *World of Yesterday*, 34, 38, 40.

15. Quoted phrase from Carl E. Schorske, *Fin-de-siècle Vienna: Politics and Culture* (New York: Vintage Books, 1981), 182.

16. For old and new work on fin de siècle Vienna in the wake of Carl Schorske's field-shaping study, see Allan Janik and Stephen Toulmin, *Wittgenstein's Vienna* (Chicago: Elephant Paperbacks, 1996); Deborah R. Coen, *Vienna in the Age of Uncertainty: Science, Liberalism, and Private Life* (Chicago: University of Chicago Press, 2007); Steven Beller, ed., *Rethinking Vienna 1900* (New York: Berghahn Books, 2001); Jürgen Nautz and Richard Vahrenkamp, *Die Wiener Jahrhundertwende: Einflüsse, Umwelt, Wirkungen*, 2nd ed. (Vienna: Böhlau Verlag, 1996); Peter Galison, "Aufbau/Bauhaus: Logical Positivism and Architectural Modernism," *Critical Inquiry* 16, no. 4 (1990): 709–52; Malachi H. Hacohen, "Karl Popper, the Vienna Circle, and Red Vienna," *Journal of the History of Ideas* 59, no. 4 (1998): 711–34.

17. Zweig, *World of Yesterday*, 65, 80; and for the existing culture that revered age and experience, especially 54–56.

18. Schorske, *Fin-de-siècle Vienna* (especially "Politics in a New Key," 116–80), but see also Coen, *Vienna in the Age of Uncertainty*, for a more nuanced reflection on the liberal subject and Schorske's juxtaposition of "rational man" and "psychological man." On this history of liberalism in the Habsburg Monarchy, see Pieter Judson, *Exclusive Revolutionaries: Liberal Politics, Social Experience, and National Identity in the Austrian Empire, 1848–1914* (Ann Arbor: University of Michigan Press, 1996).

19. On the phenomenon of the *Kreis*, see especially Edward Timms, "Die Wiener Kreise: Schöpferische Interaktionen in der Wiener Moderne," in *Die Wiener Jahrhundertwende: Einflüsse, Umwelt, Wirkungen*, 2nd ed., ed. Jürgen Nautz and Richard Vahrenkamp (Vienna: Böhlau Verlag, 1996), 128–43; Edward Timms, *Karl Kraus—Apocalyptic Satirist: Culture and Catastrophe in Habsburg Vienna* (New Haven, CT: Yale University Press, 1986); Erwin Dekker, "The Vienna Circles: Cultivating Economic Knowledge Outside Academia," *Erasmus Journal for Philosophy and Economics* 7, no. 2 (2014): 30–53; Ohad Reiss-Sorokin, "Thinking outside the Circle: The *Geistkreis* and the Viennese 'Kreis Culture'" in America," *Modern Intellectual History*, December 21, 2021, 1–27. For a recent popular history of the Vienna circle of logical empiricism, see David Edmonds, *The Murder of Professor Schlick: The Rise and Fall of the Vienna Circle* (Princeton, NJ: Princeton University Press,

2020); on Ludwig von Mises's *Privatseminar* and its place in the intellectual history of neoliberalism, see Quinn Slobodian, *Globalists: The End of Empire and the Birth of Neoliberalism* (Cambridge, MA: Harvard University Press, 2018).

20. Deborah Holmes, *Langeweile ist Gift: Das Leben der Eugenie Schwarzwald* (St. Pölten: Residenz Verlag, 2012), 132–33, 280–86; Deborah Holmes, "Die Schwarzwaldschule und Hans Kelsen," in *Hans Kelsen: Leben—Werk—Wirksamkeit*, ed. Robert Walter, Werner Ogris, and Thomas Olechowski (Vienna: Manzsche, 2009), 98–109; Thomas Olechowski, *Hans Kelsen: Biographie eines Rechtswissenschaftlers* (Tübingen: Mohr Siebeck, 2020), 119–23.

21. It was not Kelsen's first change of religion: he had first converted from Judaism to Catholicism in 1905 while a student. Thomas Olechowski speculates that the more liberal marriage laws for those outside the Catholic Church may have made the evangelical option attractive to the young couple. Olechowski, *Hans Kelsen*, 87–88, 116–19.

22. Hans Kelsen, "Autobiographie (1947)," in Hans Kelsen, *Werke*, ed. Matthias Jestaedt (Tübingen: Mohr Siebeck, 2007), 1:46; Rudolf Aladár Métall, *Hans Kelsen: Leben und Werk* (Vienna: Franz Deuticke, 1969), 79; Olechowski, *Hans Kelsen*, 113–19, 377–80; Holmes, *Langeweile ist Gift*, 280–86.

23. On Kelsen and Freud, see chapter 4. For his friendships with the Austro-Marxists, stretching back to student days, see Olechowski, *Hans Kelsen*, 178–84.

24. On *Main Problems*, and the theory of the state it launched, see chapter 4. On the passage of his habilitation and early teaching, see Kelsen, "Autobiogaphie," 44; Olechowski, *Hans Kelsen*, 141–45.

25. As Verdross tells the story: Alfred Verdross, "Österreich—Heimat der Rechtstheorie," in *Philosophie huldigt dem Recht. Hans Kelsen, Adolf J. Merkl, Alfred Verdross, Ehrendoktoren der Universität Salzburg: Erinnerungsband zum 1. June 1967* (Vienna: Europa Verlag, 1967), 50. See also Friedrich Engel-Jánosi, *... aber ein stolzer Bettler: Erinnerungen aus einer verlorenen Generation* (Graz: Verlag Styria, 1974), 38.

26. Adolf Julius Merkl, [Selbstdarstellung/self presentation], in *Österreichische Rechts- und Staatswissenschaften der Gegenwart in Selbstdarstellung*, ed. Nikolaus Grass (Innsbruck: Universitätsverlag Wagner, 1952), 137; Wolf-Dietrich Grussmann, *Adolf Julius Merkl: Leben und Werk* (Vienna: Manzsche, 1989), 15.

27. Verdross, "Österreich—Heimat der Rechtstheorie," 50.

28. Kelsen, "Autobiogaphie," 55–56.

29. Merkl himself referred to the "'jungösterreichischen' Juristenschule" in his newspaper review of Kelsen's *Allgemeine Staatslehre*: Adolf Merkl, "Eine allgemeine Staatslehre: Zum neuesten Werk Hans Kelsens," *Neue Freie Presse*, October 17, 1925 (Morgenblatt), 2. See, earlier, and critically, Bernhard Stark, "Die jungösterreichische Schule der Rechtswissenschaft und die naturwissenschaftliche Methode," *Juristische Blätter*, no. 26 (June 30, 1918): 301–4.

30. The architect Anton Krones Jr. designed the 1907 building. The Kelsens would remain in the apartment until Kelsen was pushed out of Austria in 1930. Olechowski, *Hans Kelsen*, 118–19.

31. Helen Silving [known then as Henda Silberpfennig], *Memoirs* (New York: Vantage Press, 1988), 90. In keeping with their milieu, the Kelsens had *Dienstpersonal* and a *Kindermädchen*. Olechowski, *Hans Kelsen*, 376–77.

32. Verdross, "Österreich—Heimat der Rechtstheorie," 50; Silving *Memoirs*, 90.

33. Verdross, "Österreich—Heimat der Rechtstheorie," 49.

34. See Christoph Kletzer, "Fritz Sander," in *Der Kreis um Hans Kelsen: Die Anfangsjahre der Reinen Rechtslehre*, ed. Robert Walter, Clemens Jabloner, and Klaus Zeleny (Vienna: Manzsche, 2008), 445–70; and Thomas Olechowski's detailed reconstruction of the Sander affair: Olechowski, *Hans Kelsen*, 148–49, 317–41.

35. See Olechowski, *Hans Kelsen*, 321–22, 342–44. On more than one occasion, Verdross pointedly reconstructed the sequence of publications to establish the priority of his arguments. See, for example, Alfred Verdross, *Die Einheit des rechtlichen Weltbildes auf Grundlage der Völkerrechtsverfassung* (Tübingen: J. C. B. Mohr, 1923), vii.

36. Hans Kelsen, *Hauptprobleme der Staatsrechtslehre entwickelt aus der Lehre vom Rechtssatze*, 2nd ed. (Tübingen: J. C. B. Mohr, 1923), dedication page in frontmatter, and xv–xvi of the "Vorrede zur zweiten Auflage."

37. Kelsen gives these examples in Hans Kelsen, *Das Problem der Souveränität und die Theorie des Völkerrechts: Beitrag zu einer reinen Rechtslehre* (Tübingen: J. C. B. Mohr, 1920), 97n1; see also Kelsen, *Der soziologische und der juristische Staatsbegriff*, 94.

38. Alfred Verdross, "Zur Konstruktion des Völkerrechts," *Zeitschrift für Völkerrecht* 8 (1914): 355 (first emphasis in original, second emphasis added).

39. Kelsen, *Der soziologische und der juristische Staatsbegriff*, 94–95; "metajuristische Annahme" already in Verdross, "Zur Konstruktion des Völkerrechts," 355.

40. For a chronological sequence of different formulations, see Robert Walter, "Entstehung und Entwicklung des Gedankens der Grundnorm," in *Schwerpunkte der Reinen Rechtslehre*, ed. Robert Walter (Vienna: Manzsche, 1992), 47–59; and for a typological account of its different iterations, see Stanley Paulson, "Die unterschiedlichen Formulierungen der 'Grundnorm,'" in *Rechtsnorm und Rechtswirklichkeit: Festschrift für Werner Krawietz zum 60. Geburtstag*, ed. Aulis Aarnio, Stanley L. Paulson, Ota Weinberger, Georg Henrik von Wright, Dieter Wyduckel (Berlin: Duncker & Humblot, 1993), 53–74.

41. Hans Kelsen, *Reine Rechtslehre: Einleitung in die rechtswissenschaftliche Problematik* (Leipzig: Franz Deuticke, 1934), §29, 67; English from Hans Kelsen, *Introduction to the Problems of Legal Theory: A Translation of the First Edition of the* Reine Rechtslehre *or Pure Theory of Law*, trans. Bonnie Litschewski Paulson and Stanley L. Paulson (Oxford: Clarendon Press, 1992), § 29, 58. (I will cite both the German and English editions going forward; the English is taken from the published translation.) Or as he put it later, "The basic norm is only the necessary presupposition of any positivistic interpretation of the legal material." Hans Kelsen, *General Theory of Law and State*, trans. Anders Wedberg (Cambridge, MA: Harvard University Press, 1945), 116.

42. Kelsen, *Reine Rechtslehre*, § 29, 67/Kelsen, *Introduction to the Problems of Legal Theory*, § 29, 58 (emphasis added). Very similar formulation in Kelsen, *General Theory of Law and State*, 116.

43. Kelsen, *Das Problem der Souveränität*, vi.

44. Kelsen, *Reine Rechtslehre*, § 29, 66/Kelsen, *Introduction to the Problems of Legal Theory*, § 29, 58.

45. "Ursprungshypothese." Kelsen, *Der soziologische und der juristische Staatsbegriff*, 102, in footnote carried over from the previous page.

46. For explicit reference to the Kantian foundations of the basic norm, see Kelsen, *Das Problem der Souveränität*, v–vi. On Kelsen and neo-Kantianism more broadly, including further citations, see chapter 4.

47. Kelsen, *Allgemeine Staatslehre*, 250.

48. The notion of a contract, as Kelsen saw it, rested on the prior idea that "you only have to do what you want" (*du sollst nur, was du willst*). Kelsen, *Allgemeine Staatslehre*, 251.

49. Kelsen, 251; Kelsen, *Der soziologische und der juristische Staatsbegriff*, 102, in footnote carried over from the previous page.

50. Kelsen, *Allgemeine Staatslehre*, 251.

51. Kelsen, "The Idea of Natural Law," in Hans Kelsen, *Essays in Legal and Moral Philosophy*, ed. Ota Weinberger, trans. Peter Heath (Dordrecht: D. Reidel, 1973), 37.

52. "The norms of positive law are 'valid'... not because, like those of natural law, they derive from nature, God or reason, and thus from a principle of the *absolutely good*, right or just, from an *absolutely supreme value*, but because they are created in a certain way"—made in accordance with that system's presupposed basic norm. Kelsen, "The Idea of Natural Law," 37. Critics decried law's formalism, Kelsen wrote, but formalism simply meant that law was law because of its formal qualities, because it was made in a particular way, rather than deduced from a substantive value or source.

53. Kelsen, *Das Problem der Souveränität*, 96 (emphasis added).

54. It is quite possible that Kelsen had the idea for the Münchhausen swamp parable from the Hungarian politician Albert Apponyi, beautifully highlighting the imperial-political context of the pure theory. As mentioned in chapter 2, Apponyi used the image in an article on the legal nature of Austria-Hungary and did so to capture the same problem, namely that "the empire could not possibly have been independent before its creation, before it possessed its own source of law; only a Münchhausen managed to pull himself out of the swamp by his own hair." Albert Apponyi, "Die rechtliche Natur der Beziehung zwischen Österreich und Ungarn," *Österreichische Rundschau* 28 (1911): 168. Apponyi's article appeared in a major Austrian journal in the same year that Kelsen started teaching at the University of Vienna, and one of his first classes focused on the law of the Austro-Hungarian Settlement, so he would have been closely following new publications on the topic.

55. "den letzten Grenzen des juristischen Erkenntnisgebietes": Hans Kelsen, "Reichsgesetz und Landesgesetz nach österreichischer Verfassung," *Archiv des öffentlichen Rechts* 32 (1914): 397.

56. Eric Voegelin, Review of *General Theory of Law and State* by Hans Kelsen, *Louisiana Law Review* 6 (1945): 491.

57. See chapter 4.

58. Walter, "Entstehung und Entwicklung des Gedankens der Grundnorm," 47–59; Manfred Baldus, "Hapsburgian Multiethnicity and the 'Unity of the State'—On the Structural Setting of Kelsen's Legal Thought," in *Hans Kelsen and Carl Schmitt: A Juxtaposition*, ed. Dan Diner and Michael Stolleis (Gerlingen: Bleicher, 1999), 13–25; Olechowski, *Hans Kelsen*, 155–59.

59. Ludwig Spiegel, "Autonomie und Selbstverwaltung in der Gegenwart," as part of the entry for "Länder" in *Öesterreichisches Staatswörterbuch: Handbuch des gesammten österreichischen öffentlichen Rechtes*, 2nd ed., ed. Ernst Mischler and Josef Ulbrich (Vienna: Alfred Hölder, 1907), 3:419 and generally (3:395–430).

60. Hans Kelsen, "Reichsgesetz und Landesgesetz," *Archiv des öffentlichen Rechts* 32 (1914): 213, 229–30, 400, 411–12.

61. Baldus emphasizes the conflict of laws problem in "Hapsburgian Multiethnicity and the 'Unity of the State,'" 16–18. In the 1880s, Jellinek famously proposed a constitutional court capable of resolving conflicts of this sort. Georg Jellinek, *Ein Verfassungsgerichtshof für Österreich* (Vienna: A. Hölder, 1885). This idea would eventually be realized by Kelsen in the constitution of the postwar Republic of Austria; its groundbreaking constitutional court was the component of which he was proudest. On the court, see Clemens Jabloner, "Hans Kelsen und die Entwicklung des B-VG 1920," in *Die Verfassungsentwicklung 1918–1920 und Hans Kelsen*, ed. Clemens Jabloner, Thomas Olechowski, and Klaus Zeleny (Vienna: Manz, 2020), 143–55.

62. Kelsen, "Reichsgesetz und Landesgesetz," 202–45, 390–438.

63. Kelsen, 213, 231.

64. Kelsen, 203, 207, 213–14, 398, 400, 412.

65. Kelsen, 221–25, 231, 400, 411.

66. Kelsen, 220–31, 244, 411–12 ("standpoint" on 225; "choice" on 231).

67. Kelsen, 417 ("Doppelstandpunkt").

68. Kelsen, 414–15. If one took 1861 as the basis for legitimacy, then the competence of the lands could not be changed without their involvement and consent, making the 1867 competence provisions invalid.

69. Kelsen, 413–14 ("arbitrary" also on 413).

70. Kelsen, 217.

71. Kelsen, 217.

72. Verdross, "Zur Konstruktion des Völkerrechts," 355. See also 337: "Der Normerfasser muss aber irgendwo haltmachen und irgendeine Norm as die oberste annehmen." Curiously, this piece is left out of Robert Walter's genealogy of the basic norm: Walter, "Entstehung und Entwicklung des Gedankens der Grundnorm."

73. This was another two-part piece: Alfred Verdross, "Die Neuordnung der gemeinsamen Wappen und Fahnen in ihrer Bedeutung für die rechtlich Gestalt der österreichisch-ungarischen Monarchie," *Juristische Blätter* 45, no. 11 (March 12, 1916): 121–23; and *Juristische Blätter* 45, no. 12 (March 19, 1916): 134–37. First subtitle ("Die Rechtskonstruktion des österreichisch-ungarischen Verbandes und die Grenzen der juristischen Erkenntnis") on 121.

74. Verdross, 122.

75. Verdross, 122–23 (quotation on 122).

76. Verdross, 123 (emphasis in original). Last sentence: "So offenbaren sich hier die Grenzen der juristischen . . . Erkenntnis."

77. Note the parallel (and simultaneous) lines of thought of František Weyr in Prague; but also, further afield, Walter Jellinek—Georg's son—in Germany, surveyed in Walter, "Entstehung und Entwicklung des Gedankens der Grundnorm," 48–50.

78. Verdross, "Die Neuordnung der gemeinsamen Wappen und Fahnen," 121.

79. Verdross, 123.

80. Rudolf Aladár Métall, *Hans Kelsen: Leben und Werk* (Vienna: Deutike, 1969), 18–19; Jürgen Busch, "Hans Kelsen im Ersten Weltkrieg: Achsenzeit einer Weltkarriere," in *Hans Kelsen: Leben—Werk—Wirksamkeit*, ed. Robert Walter, Werner Ogris, and Thomas Olechowski (Vienna: Manz, 2009), 63–64; Olechowski, *Hans Kelsen*, 173–77.

81. Kelsen, "Autobiographie," 47–55; Olechowski, *Hans Kelsen*, 171–78; Busch, "Hans Kelsen im Ersten Weltkrieg," 69–70.

82. Verdross, [Selbstdarstellung/self presentation], 201–2; "Alfred Verdross (1890–1980): Biographical Note with Bibliography," *European Journal of International Law* 6, no. 1 (1995): 103; Olechowski, *Hans Kelsen*, 173.

83. Grussmann, *Adolf Julius Merkl*, 17, 21–25.

84. Kelsen, "Autobiographie," 46–49; Busch, "Hans Kelsen im Ersten Weltkrieg," 67–69; Olechowski, *Hans Kelsen*, 195–200; Christoph Schmetterer, "Hans Kelsens Vorschläge zur Reform der österreichisch-ungarischen Wehrverfassung," *Beiträge zur Rechtsgeschichte Österreichs* 6, no. 1 (2016): 129–55.

85. A course on the Austro-Hungarian Settlement was among those he offered in his very first semester teaching in 1911. See Kelsen, "Autobiographie," 44, and for subsequent offerings of this class, Olechowski, *Hans Kelsen*, 145, 186.

86. Kelsen, "Autobiographie," 50–54; Christoph Schmetterer, "Hans Kelsens Überlegungen zur Reform der Österreichisch-Ungarischen Monarchie," in *Das internationale Wirken Hans Kelsen*, ed. Clemens Jabloner, Thomas Olechowski, and Klaus Zelany (Vienna: Manz, 2016), 1–24, which also reprints Kelsen's 1917 and 1918 memorandums (11–24); Olechowski, *Hans Kelsen*, 214–19; Grussmann, *Adolf Julius Merkl*, 25.

87. He renounced participation in state business on November 11, though never formally abdicated. For a legal analysis, see Hans Kelsen, *Österreichisches Staatsrecht: Ein Grundriss Entwicklungsgeschichtlich Dargestellt* (Tübingen: J. C. B. Mohr, 1923), 76–79.

88. Busch, "Hans Kelsen im Ersten Weltkrieg," 74; Olechowski, *Hans Kelsen*, 188.

89. Olechowski, *Hans Kelsen*, 177.

90. Among his voluminous writings on the legal protection of the environment, see the early pieces Adolf Merkl, "Ein Walderhaltungsgesetz," *Österreichische Zeitschrift für Verwaltung* 54 (1921): 250–51; Merkl, "Die Neuordnung der Bundesforstverwaltung und die Intressen des Naturschutz," *Blätter für Naturkunde und Naturschutz* 12 (1925): 61–67; Merkl, "Das Naturschutzgesetz: Eine Entgegnung," *Juristische Blätter* 54, no. 9–10 (May 3, 1925): 86–89; Merkl, "Erreichtes und Erstrebtes in Naturschutz," *Blätter für Naturkunde und Naturschutz* 16 (1929): 45–50. See also Grussmann, *Adolf Julius Merkl*, 31–32.

91. Especially his language and imagery. See Grussmann, *Adolf Julius Merkl*, 15–16 (also drawing on Rene Marcic).

92. See chapter 4.

93. See his 1917 two-part essay, in part responding to the aforementioned Verdross article from 1916: Adolf Merkl, "Die Unveränderlichkeit von Gesetzen—ein normlogisches Prinzip," *Juristische Blätter* 46, no. 9 (March 4, 1917): 97–98, and *Juristische Blätter* 46, no. 10 (March 11, 1917): 109–11. Carl Schmitt refers to this piece in *Political Theology* with an incorrect citation; the translator of the English edition was unable to locate the correct one. Carl Schmitt, *Political Theology: Four Chapters on the Concept of Sovereignty*, trans. George Schwab (Cambridge, MA: MIT Press, 1985), 32.

94. See Adolf Merkl, "Das Doppelte Rechtsantlitz: Eine Betrachtung aus der Erkenntnistheorie des Rechtes," *Juristische Blätter* 47, no. 41–42 (October 20, 1918): 425–27, 444–47, 463–65; and his most complete statement of the *Stufenbau* theory: Adolf Merkl, "Prolegomena einer Theorie des rechtlichen Stufenbaues," in *Gesellschaft, Staat, und Recht: Festschrift für Hans Kelsen zum 50. Geburtstag*, ed. Alfred Verdross (Vienna: Springer, 1931), 252–94.

95. Adolf Julius Merk, "Das Recht im Lichte seiner Anwendung" (1917), in Merkl, *Gesammelte Schriften*, vol. 1, *Grundlagen des Rechts*, pt. 1, ed. Dorothea Mayer-Maly, Herbert Schambeck, and Wolf-Dietrich Grussmann (Berlin: Humblot & Duncker, 1993), 115. This important text was first published as a series of essays in the *Deutsche Richterzeitung* in 1916, 1917, and 1919 under the title "Das Recht im Spiegel seiner Auslegung," the first two of which were published as a stand-alone special printing in 1917. For ease of reader reference amid this complex publication history, I cite here the version from his collected works. He returned to the "cataracts of a watercourse" image; see Merkl, [Selbstdarstellung], 141.

96. Kelsen, "Vorrede zur zweiten Auflage," in *Hauptprobleme der Staatsrechtslehre*, xvi. In the first edition, he had argued that the creation of law lay outside the domain of legal analysis; now, having accepted the idea that law needed to govern its own creation, he saw only the basic norm as metajuridical (xiv–xv).

97. On the separation of *is* and *ought* and the identity thesis, see chapter 4.

98. In the preface, Kelsen wrote that he had largely completed it in 1916: Kelsen, *Das Problem der Souveränität*, vi. But it seems clear that several sections, including those most relevant for this chapter (on the primacy of international law and the creation and demise of states) took shape under the influence of the empire's collapse and Verdross's writing on the same themes at the war's end.

99. Kelsen, v, 115n1.

100. "Nicht als die einem realen, physischen order psychischen Naturojekt anhaftende reale und daher empirisch induktiv beobachtbare Eigenschaft in der Außenwelt wahrnembarer Tatsachen ist Souveränität zu erkennen, sondern als eine Annahme, eine Voraussetzung im Denken des Staat und Recht erfassenden Betrachters." Kelsen, *Das Problem der Souveränität*, 14.

101. Adolf Merkl, "Die Rechtseinheit des österreichischen Staates: Eine staatsrechtliche Untersuchung auf Grund der Lehre von der lex posterior," *Archiv des öffentlichen Rechts* 37 (1918): 57 (emphasis in original).

102. Merkl, 60.

103. Merkl, 58–59 (quotation on 59).

104. Merkl, 65.

105. Merkl, 66 (emphasis in original).

106. Merkl, 67 (emphasis added).

107. Merkl, 91.

108. Merkl, 92–93.

109. "darüber hinaus in die Vergangenheit zurück im Rechtssinn Fremdland, Ausland liegt." Merkl, 104.

110. Merkl, 104.

111. Adolf Merkl, *Die Verfassung der Republik Deutschösterreich: Ein kritisch-systematischer Grundriß* (Vienna: Franz Deuticke, 1919), vi.

112. Merkl, [Selbstdarstellung], 138; Grussmann, *Adolf Julius Merkl*, 25–26.

113. Grussmann, *Adolf Julius Merkl*, 25–29.

114. Kelsen, "Autobiographie," 65–67; Merkl, [Selbstdarstellung], 138; Olechowski, *Hans Kelsen*, 271–79, 288–95; Grussmann, *Adolf Julius Merkl*, 27; Clemens Jabloner, Thomas Olechowski, and Klaus Zeleny, eds., *Die Verfassungsentwicklung 1918–1920 und Hans Kelsen* (Vienna: Manz, 2020).

115. See Olechowski, *Hans Kelsen*, 230–32.

116. Grussmann, *Adolf Julius Merkl*, 27–29.

117. Verdross, [Selbstdarstellung], 202–3.

118. Abschrift eines Berichtes der d.ö. Gesandschaft in Berlin Z!. 9426, ddo. 4. Juli 1919, betreffend: Schutz nationaler Minderheiten, an das Staatsamt für Aeusseres in Wien, enclosed within: Staatssekretär Bauer (Deutschöst. Staatsamt für Äußeres) to die deutschösterreichische Friedensdelegation, 9 July 1919 (Prot. No. 730), Österreichisches Staatsarchiv, Archiv der Republik, Karton 1, Fasz. I/Fr./c.

119. Merkl, *Die Verfassung der Republik Deutschösterreich*.

120. Fritz Sander, "Das Faktum der Revolution und die Kontinuität der Rechtsordnung," *Zeitschrift für öffentliches Recht* 1 (1919): 132.

121. Sander, 134 (emphasis in original).

122. Sander, 134–35.

123. Sander, 154; see also 156.

124. Sander, 134 (emphasis in original).

125. Josef L. Kunz, *Völkerrechtswissenschaft und reine Rechtslehre* (Leipzig: Franz Deuticke, 1923), 64.

126. Sander, "Das Faktum der Revolution," 141.

127. Sander, 153–54.

128. For Headlam-Morley and the discussions on this point at the Paris Peace Conference, see chapter 5.

129. Sander, "Das Faktum der Revolution," 154.

130. Sander, 154.

131. Sander, 154.

132. Verdross, "Zur Konstruktion des Völkerrechts," 337.

133. Alfred Verdross, *Die völkerrechtswidrige Kriegshandlung und der Strafanspruch der Staaten* (Berlin: Verlag Hans Robert Engelmann, 1920), 42.

134. Verdross, *Die völkerrechtswidrige Kriegshandlung*, 42 (emphasis added). See also Alfred Verdross, "Die Souveränität der Staaten und das Völkerrecht," *Die Friedens-Warte* 22, no. 9 (1920): 261.

135. Verdross, *Die völkerrechtswidrige Kriegshandlung*, 42.

136. Alfred Verdross, "Grundlagen und Grundlegungen des Völkerrechts: Ein Beitrag zu den Hypothesen des Völkerrechtspositivismus," *Niemeyers Zeitschrift für Völkerrecht* 29 (1921): 69–72.

137. Verdross, 72.

138. "die Brücke des Rechtes" in Kelsen, *Das Problem der Souveränität*, 238.

139. Verdross, *Die Einheit des rechtlichen Weltbildes*, vi.

140. Josef L. Kunz, "On the Theoretical Basis of the Law of Nations," *Transactions of the Grotius Society* 10 (1924): 140.

141. Verdross, "Grundlagen und Grundlegungen des Völkerrechts," 72; Kunz, "On the Theoretical Basis of the Law of Nations," 140.

142. Verdross, "Grundlagen und Grundlegungen des Völkerrechts," 86.

143. Verdross, 86; Kunz, "On the Theoretical Basis of the Law of Nations," 140; also already in Sander, "Das Faktum der Revolution," 160–61.

144. He described it as the "most important result" of his 1920 book: Kelsen, *Das Problem der Souveränität*, iii.

145. Kelsen, 103–5, 120–21.

146. Kelsen, 108, 152.

147. Kelsen, 113, 115 (see especially note 1), 117, 123.

148. "Erkenntnistheoretische Hypothesen": Kelsen, 314 (emphasis in original).

149. Kelsen, 190.

150. Kelsen, 224–27, 238.

151. Kelsen, 224–27 (especially 225).

152. Kelsen, 204–5.

153. Kelsen, 229.

154. Kelsen, 314.

155. Kelsen devoted copious pages to a thorough demonstration of this point: see Kelsen, 138–39, 152–55, 170, 184–200, 315.

156. Kelsen, 315.

157. Kelsen, 315.

158. Kelsen, 316.

159. Kelsen, 316.

160. Kelsen, 317–18.

161. Kelsen, 317 (emphasis in original).

162. Kelsen, 317 (emphasis in original).

163. Kelsen, 236.

164. Kelsen himself developed that connection in subtle ways. If one transferred the notion of the basic norm to international law, then it actually stopped being a merely "hypothetical" or "epistemological" proposition, stopped being merely implied or imputed, and appeared as an actual legal norm. See Kelsen, *Das Problem der Souveränität*, 240–41.

165. Kelsen, 236.

166. Constitutional example at Kelsen, 239.

167. "Im rechtsleeren Raum gibt es keine juristische Erkenntnis." Kelsen, 236.

168. Kelsen, 238.

169. Kelsen, *Reine Rechtslehre*, § 50(g), 149; English translation from Kelsen, *Introduction to the Problems of Legal Theory*, § 50(g), 121. Also Kelsen, *Allgemeine Staatslehre*, 127.

170. "The creation of a state can only be conceptualized as an object of juridical knowledge from the perspective of international law [*Die Entstehung eines Staates kann als Gegenstand juristiscer Erkenntnis nur vom Standpunkte des Völkerrechtes aus begriffen werden*]." Hans Kelsen, "Gutachten: Über die Frage der Entstehung des Čchoslovakischen Staates und der Čechoslovakischen Staatsbürgerschaft," 1 November 1927, *Permanent Court of International Justice, Series C*, No. 68 (1933): 71.

171. Josef L. Kunz, "The 'Vienna School' and International Law," *New York University Law Quarterly Review* 11, no. 3 (1934): 408 (emphasis added).

172. First two quotations from Kunz, "The 'Vienna School' and International Law," 409; "bridge of law" in Kelsen, *Das Problem der Souveränität*, 238.

173. Josef L. Kunz, *Die Anerkennung der Staaten und Regierungen im Völkerrecht* (Stuttgart: Kohlhammer, 1928), 89 ("völkerrechtlichen Nichts"; "sogenannten 'Wilden'").

174. See, broadly, Antony Anghie, *Imperialism, Sovereignty and the Making of International Law* (Cambridge: Cambridge University Press, 2005); Jennifer Pitts, *Boundaries of the International: Law and Empire* (Cambridge, MA: Harvard University Press, 2018); and for an introduction to the uneven application of the laws of war to "uncivilized" peoples, see Samuel Moyn, *Humane: How the United States Abandoned Peace and Reinvented War* (New York: Farrar, Straus and Giroux, 2021), chap. 3; Kim A. Wagner, "Savage Warfare: Violence and the Rule of Colonial Difference in Early British Counterinsurgency," *History Workshop Journal* 85 (2018): 217–37. Note, too, the varied ways in which the extra-European world was *not* conceived of as a legal vacuum by many European jurists and colonial actors: see for example Lauren Benton, *Law and Colonial Cultures: Legal Regimes in World History* (New York: Cambridge University Press, 2002); Lauren Benton and Lisa Ford, *Rage for Order: The British Empire and the Origins of International Law* (Cambridge, MA: Harvard University Press, 2016); Andrew Fitzmaurice, *Sovereignty, Property and Empire, 1500–2000* (Cambridge: Cambridge University Press, 2014).

175. Kunz, *Die Anerkennung der Staaten und Regierungen*, 1.

176. Kelsen, *Reine Rechtslehre*, § 50(a), 135–36/Kelsen, *Introduction to the Problems of Legal Theory*, § 50(a), 111–12. See also Kelsen, *Das Problem der Souveränität*, 108.

177. Kelsen, *Reine Rechtslehre*, § 50(a), 135/Kelsen, *Introduction to the Problems of Legal Theory*, § 50(a), 111.

178. Kunz, "On the Theoretical Basis of the Law of Nations," 140.

179. Sander, "Das Faktum der Revolution," first phrase on 154, second on 136.

180. Sander, 136.

181. Sander, 137, here critiquing Merkl's 1918 essay.

182. Sander, 155.

183. Sander, 156.

184. Carl Schmitt (reading not only Kelsen but Merkl, too) would make this observation, tying it to his theory of exception: Schmitt, *Political Theology*, 36.

185. Sander, "Das Faktum der Revolution," 139.

186. Verdross, *Die Einheit des rechtlichen Weltbildes*, ix.

187. Adolf Merkl, "Das Problem der Rechtskontinuität und die Forderung des einheitlichen rechtlichen Weltbildes," *Zeitschrift für öffentliches Recht* 5 (1926): 497.

188. Verdross, *Die Einheit des rechtlichen Weltbildes*, 128.

189. Kunz, "The 'Vienna School' and International Law," 402 (emphasis in original).

190. Kunz, "On the Theoretical Basis of the Law of Nations," 140.

191. Kelsen, *Reine Rechtslehre*, § 49(a), 130/Kelsen, *Introduction to the Problems of Legal Theory*, § 49(a), 108.

192. Verdross, *Die Einheit des rechtlichen Weltbildes*, 128.

193. Kunz, "The 'Vienna School' and International Law," 404.

194. Kelsen, "Autobiographie," 64–65.

195. Sander, "Das Faktum der Revolution," 163.

196. Sander, 154.

197. Kelsen, *Reine Rechtslehre*.

198. Quoted phrases from Hans Blumenberg, *Paradigms for a Metaphorology*, trans. Robert Savage (1960; Ithaca, NY: Cornell University Press, 2010), 3, 4.

199. For the complicated publication history, see Olechowski, *Hans Kelsen*, 587–93.

200. Compare here also Franz Leander Fillafer, "Imperial Diversity, Fractured Sovereignty, and Legal Universals: Hans Kelsen and Eugen Ehrlich in their Habsburg Context," *Modern Intellectual History* 19, no. 2 (2022): 421–43.

201. See Kelsen, "Autobiographie," 59–60, and chapter 4.

202. Kelsen, "Reichsgesetz und Landesgesetz nach österreichischer Verfassung," 217.

203. Kelsen, *Reine Rechtslehre*, § 50(h), 153/Kelsen, *Introduction to the Problems of Legal Theory*, § 50(h), 124.

204. Kelsen, *Reine Rechtslehre*, § 50(h), 153/Kelsen, *Introduction to the Problems of Legal Theory*, § 50(h), 124.

205. Kelsen, *Reine Rechtslehre*, § 50(i), 153/Kelsen, *Introduction to the Problems of Legal Theory*, § 50(i), 124.

206. Bernstoff sees the wrestle between methodological purity and political conviction as the central tension of Kelsen's engagement with international law. Bernstorff, *The Public International Law Theory of Hans Kelsen*.

207. Kelsen, *Reine Rechtslehre*, § 50(i), 154/Kelsen, *Introduction to the Problems of Legal Theory*, § 50(i), 124–25.

208. On the French jurists, see Martti Koskenniemi, *The Gentle Civilizer of Nations: The Rise and Fall of International Law, 1870–1960* (Cambridge: Cambridge University Press, 2001), 266–352 (quotation on 298). For a contemporary view of this moment in international legal thinking by another of its protagonists, see Nicolas Politis, *The New Aspects of International Law* (Washington, DC: Carnegie Endowment for International Peace, 1928); for an enormously rich analysis of its avant-garde "modernism" see Nathaniel Berman, "'But the Alternative Is Despair': European Nationalism and the Modernist Renewal of International Law," *Harvard Law Review* 106, no. 8 (1993): 1792–1903; and Nathaniel Berman, "Modernism, Nationalism, and the Rhetoric of Reconstruction," *Yale Journal of Law and the Humanities* 4 (1992): 351–80; and for its reconfiguration of relations between state and citizen, see Mira L. Siegelberg, *Statelessness: A Modern History* (Cambridge, MA: Harvard University Press, 2020). For a study of prominent Jewish international lawyers in this moment, which places Kelsen alongside Hans Morgenthau, Hersch Lauterpacht, and Erich Kaufmann, see Reut Paz, *A Gateway between a Distant God and a Cruel World: The Contribution of Jewish German-Speaking Scholars to International Law* (Leiden: Martinus Nijhoff, 2013).

209. See Benton and Ford, *Rage for Order*; Lauren Benton, *A Search for Sovereignty: Law and Geography in European Empires, 1400–1900* (Cambridge: Cambridge University Press, 2010).

210. Slobodian, *Globalists*, 52, 50.

211. Olechowski, *Hans Kelsen*, 50.

212. Olechowski, 315–16.

213. The second witness was Gottfried von Haberler. Wilhelm Röpke and William Rappard and their wives joined the wedding party for lunch afterward at the Hôtel des Bergues. Olechowski suggests that William Rappard first approached Mises for the Geneva job on the basis of Kelsen's recommendation. Olechowski, 581–82.

214. Slobodian, *Globalists*, chap. 1.

215. Kelsen, "Autobiographie," 58.

216. Kelsen, 58–59.

217. Kelsen, 59. On Kelsen, Austro-Marxism, and socialism, see further Olechowski, *Hans Kelsen*, 178–84, 296–302. For some of Kelsen's own substantial writing on Marxism, socialism, and the state, see Hans Kelsen, *Sozialismus und Staat: Eine Untersuchung der Politischen Theorie des Marxismus*, 2nd ed. (Leipzig: Hirschfeld, 1923); Hans Kelsen, "Allgemeine Rechtslehre im Lichte materialistischer Geschichtsauffassung," *Archiv für Sozialwissenschaft und Sozialpolitik* 66 (1931): 449–521.

218. Kelsen, *Reine Rechtslehre*, § 20–21, 41–44/Kelsen, *Introduction to the Problems of Legal Theory*, § 20–21, 39–41.

219. See Slobodian, *Globalists*, 10–11 and generally.

220. See especially the recently translated Hans Kelsen, *The Essence and Value of Democracy*, ed. Nadia Urbanati and Carlo Invernizzi Accetti, trans. Brian Graf (Lanham, MD: Rowman and Littlefield, 2013), including the introduction by the editors (1–24); and Tamara Ehs, ed., *Hans Kelsen: Eine politikwissenschaftliche Einführung* (Vienna: Nomos, 2009).

221. Adom Getachew, *Worldmaking after Empire: The Rise and Fall of Self-Determination* (Princeton, NJ: Princeton University Press, 2019).

222. Natasha Wheatley, "Central Europe as Ground Zero of the New International Order," *Slavic Review* 78, no. 4 (2019): 900–911; Patricia Clavin, "The Austrian Hunger Crisis and the Genesis of International Organization after the First World War," *International Affairs* 90, no. 2 (2014): 265–78; and for a synoptic account of Austria in the history of internationalism, see Glenda Sluga, "Habsburg Histories of Internationalism," in *Remaking Central Europe: The League of Nations and the Former Habsburg Lands*, ed. Peter Becker and Natasha Wheatley (Oxford: Oxford University Press, 2021), 17–36.

223. See, for example, David Petruccelli, "Fighting the Scourge of International Crime: The Internationalization of Policing and Criminal Law in Interwar Europe"; Sara Silverstein, "Reinventing International Health in East Central Europe"; and Madeleine Dungy, "International Commerce in the Wake of Empire," all in *Remaking Central Europe: The League of Nations and the Former Habsburg Lands*, ed. Peter Becker and Natasha Wheatley (Oxford: Oxford University Press, 2021), 241–58, 71–98, 213–40.

224. Patricia Clavin, *Securing the World Economy: The Reinvention of the League of Nations, 1920–1946* (Oxford: Oxford University Press, 2013); Jamie Martin, *The Meddlers: Sovereignty, Empire, and the Birth of Global Economic Governance* (Cambridge, MA: Harvard University Press, 2022); Nathan Marcus, "Austria, the League of Nations, and the Birth of Multilateral Financial Control," in *Remaking Central Europe: The League of Nations and the Former Habsburg Lands*, ed. Peter Becker and Natasha Wheatley (Oxford: Oxford University Press, 2021), 127–44; Mark Mazower, "Minorities and the League of Nations in Interwar Europe," *Daedalus* 126, no. 2 (1997): 47–63; Carole Fink, *Defending the Rights of Others: The Great Powers, the Jews, and International Minority Protection* (Cambridge: Cambridge University Press, 2004); Laura Robson, "Capitulations Redux: The Imperial Genealogy of the Post–World War I 'Minority' Regimes," *American Historical Review* 126, no. 3 (2021): 978–1000.

225. Wheatley, "Central Europe as Ground Zero of the New International Order"; see also Keith Watenpaugh, "The League of Nations' Rescue of Armenian Genocide Survivors and the Making of Modern Humanitarianism, 1920–1927," *American Historical Review* 115, no. 5 (2010): 1315–39. See more broadly Anghie, *Imperialism, Sovereignty*; Anne Orford, *International Authority and the Responsibility to Protect* (Cambridge: Cambridge University Press, 2011).

Chapter Seven: Sovereignty in Sequence

1. Hans Kelsen, *Der soziologische und der juristische Staatsbegriff: Kritische Untersuchungen des Verhältnisses von Staat und Recht* (Tübingen: J. C. B. Mohr, 1922), 85.

2. "Sie tritt mit dem Anspruch auf, *ewig zu gelten*." Hans Kelsen, *Allgemeine Staatslehre* (Berlin: Julius Springer, 1925), 148. See chapter 6.

3. Hans Kelsen, *Principles of International Law* (New York: Rinehart and Company, 1952), 257–58.

4. Kelsen, 258.

5. See Thomas Olechowski, "Kelsens Debellatio-These: Rechtshistorische und rechtstheoretische Überlegungen zur Kontinuität von Staaten," in *Hans Kelsen in seiner Zeit*, ed. Clemens Jabloner, Thomas Olechowski, and Klaus Zeleny (Vienna: Manz'sche, 2019), 275–96. Even before World War II (and before Hitler's rise to power), the Permanent Court of International Justice had been asked to consider whether a proposed customs union between Germany and Austria would "alienate" the latter's independence in contravention of the Treaty of Saint Germain. See Customs Regime between Germany and Austria, Advisory Opinion of 5 September 1931, *Permanent Court of International Justice, Series A/B*, No. 41 (1931): 37ff. Kelsen was involved with many aspects of the international legal reckoning with defeated Germany, arguing against Germany's legal continuity as well as the immunity of its war criminals from prosecution. Hans Kelsen, "The Legal Status of Germany According to the Declaration of Berlin," *American Journal of International Law* 39, no. 3 (1945): 518–26; Hans Kelsen, "Is a Peace Treaty with Germany Legally Possible and Politically Desirable?," *American Political Science Review* 41, no. 6 (1947): 1188–93; Hans Kelsen, "The Rule against Ex Post Facto Laws and the Prosecution of the Axis War Criminals," *Judge Advocate Journal* (1945): 8–12. On his involvement with the Nuremberg Trial and postwar deliberation about the law(s) of war, see Oona A. Hathaway and Scott J. Shapiro, *The Internationalists: How a Radical Plan to Outlaw War Remade the World* (New York: Simon and Schuster, 2017), chaps. 10–12. On the ways in which ambiguities about sovereignty continued to shape divided postwar Germany, see Sebastian Gehrig, *Legal Entanglements: Law, Rights, and the Battle for Legitimacy in Divided Germany, 1945–1989* (New York: Berghahn Books, 2021).

6. Kunz was invited to join the editorial committee of the *American Journal of International Law* in 1944. Among the fruit of his Latin American immersion, see Josef Kunz, *Latin American Philosophy of Law in the Twentieth Century* (New York: Inter-American Law Institute, 1950). On Kunz, see Jörg Kammerhofer, "Josef Laurenz Kunz," in *Der Kreis um Hans Kelsen: Die Anfangsjahre der Reinen Rechtslehre*, ed. Robert Walter, Clemens Jabloner, and Klaus Zeleny (Vienna: Manzsche, 2008), 243–59.

7. Josef L. Kunz, "Identity of States under International Law," *American Journal of International Law* 49, no. 1 (1955): 68–69 (emphasis added).

8. R. P. Anand, "Editor's Introduction," *Asian States and the Development of Universal International Law*, ed. R. P. Anand (Delhi: Vikas Publications, 1972), xvii (emphasis in original). Similar passages in earlier pieces such as R. P. Anand, "Attitude of the Asian-African States toward Certain Problems of International Law," *International and Comparative Law Quarterly* 15, no. 1 (1966): 55.

9. For a sample: J. J. G. Syatauw, *Some Newly Established Asian States and the Development of International Law* (The Hague: Martinus Nijhoff, 1961); R. P. Anand, "Role of the 'New' Asian-African Countries in the Present International Legal Order," *American Journal of International Law* 56, no. 2 (1962): 383–406; Georges M. Abi-Saab, "The Newly Independent States and the Rules of International Law," *Howard Law Journal* 8 (1962): 95–121; Quincy Wright, "The Influence of the New Nations of Asia and Africa upon International Law," *Foreign Affairs Reports* 7, no. 3 (1958): 33–39; William Vincent O'Brien, ed., *The New Nations in International Law and Diplomacy* (New York: Institute of World Polity, 1965).

10. Gerry Simpson, "Something to Do with States," in *The Oxford Handbook of the Theory of International Law*, ed. Anne Orford and Florian Hoffmann (Oxford: Oxford University Press, 2016), 576, paraphrasing Mikhail Gorbachev (!).

11. Wendy Brown, *Walled States, Waning Sovereignty* (New York: Zone Books, 2010), 66. Here she cites Jean Bodin, *On Sovereignty: Four Chapters from the Six Books of the Commonwealth*, trans. Julian H. Franklin (Cambridge: Cambridge University Press, 1992), 2, 3, 12–13, 71.

12. Rose Parfitt, *The Process of International Legal Reproduction: Inequality, Historiography, Resistance* (Cambridge: Cambridge University Press, 2019), 13. On the "unique type of sovereignty that was inherited by the Third World," see, foundationally, Antony Anghie, *Imperialism, Sovereignty and the Making of International Law* (Cambridge: Cambridge University Press, 2005), chaps. 4 and 5 (quotation on 199).

13. J. J. G. Syatauw, "The Relationship between the Newness of States and Their Practices of International Law," in *Asian States and the Development of Universal International Law*, ed. R. P. Anand (Delhi: Vikas Publications, 1972), 19.

14. Syatauw, 19.

15. Anghie, *Imperialism, Sovereignty*; Anghie, "The Standard of Civilization," as part of the program, *Now Is the Time of Monsters: What Comes after Nations?*, Haus der Kulturen der Welt, Berlin, March 2017, online at https://journal.hkw.de/en/das-mass-der-zivilisation/. See also Susan Pedersen, "Getting Out of Iraq—in 1932: The League of Nations and the Road to Normative Statehood," *American Historical Review* 115, no. 4 (2010): 974–1000; Pedersen, *The Guardians: The League of Nations and the Crisis of Empire* (New York: Oxford University Press, 2015); Sundhya Pahuja, *Decolonising International Law: Development, Economic Growth and the Politics of Universality* (Cambridge: Cambridge University Press, 2011). On the Responsibility to Protect, see Anne Orford, *International Authority and the Responsibility to Protect* (Cambridge: Cambridge University Press, 2011).

16. Quinn Slobodian, *Globalists: The End of Empire and the Birth of Neoliberalism* (Cambridge, MA: Harvard University Press, 2018); Jamie Martin, *The Meddlers* (Cambridge, MA: Harvard University Press, 2022).

17. As Hungary's chief representative at the Paris Peace Conference, Albert Apponyi, liked to phrase it. Here from Albert Apponyi, *The Juridical Nature of the Relations between Austria and Hungary* (Budapest: St.-Stephens Printing Press, 1907), 4.

18. A/C.6/SR.1036, Sixth Committee, 1036th Meeting, Friday, 11 October 1968, United Nations General Assembly, Twenty-Third Session, Official Records, 4.

19. Ahmed Banyamina, "Un Itinéraire exemplaire—An Exemplary Career," in *Liber Amicorum: Judge Mohammed Bedjaoui*, ed. Emile Yakp and Thar Boumedra (The Hague: Kluwer Law International, 1999), 12.

20. Fatsah Ouguergouz and Tahar Boumedra, "Il était une fois—A Charmed Life," in *Liber Amicorum: Judge Mohammed Bedjaoui*, ed. Emile Yakp and Thar Boumedra (The Hague: Kluwer Law International, 1999), 2.

21. Banyamina, "Un Itinéraire exemplaire," 11.

22. On Bedjaoui, see Umut Özsu, "Determining New Selves: Mohammed Bedjaoui on Algeria, Western Sahara, and Post-classical International Law," in *The Battle for International Law: South-North Perspectives on the Decolonization Era*, ed. Jochen von Bernstoff and Philipp Dann (Oxford: Oxford University Press, 2019), 341–57; Özsu, "'In the Interests of Mankind as a Whole': Mohammed Bedjaoui's New International Economic Order," *Humanity* 6, no. 1 (2015): 129–43.

23. Mohammed Bedjaoui, *Law and the Algerian Revolution* (Brussels: Publications of the International Association of Democratic Lawyers, 1961), 15.

24. Bedjaoui, 17.

25. *Case Concerning Right of Passage over Indian Territory (Portugal v. India)*, Judgment of 12 April 1960, I.C.J. Reports 1960, 6 (at 95).

26. Bedjaoui argued that resurrection was not the sole basis for statehood: "It is obvious that even if no Algerian State had existed in the past, this would be no reason against its creation now, not an argument against its existence." Bedjaoui, *Law and the Algerian Revolution*, 17. For the Czechs, see Thomas Garrigue Masaryk, *The Making of a State: Memories and Observations, 1914–1918* (London: George Allen and Unwin, 1927), 340, as well as chapter 5.

27. David Armitage and Jennifer Pitts have done an extraordinary job of piecing together Alexandrowicz's biography from globe-spanning archival fragments. See David Armitage and Jennifer Pitts, "'This Modern Grotius': An Introduction to the Life and Thought of C. H. Alexandrowicz," in C. H. Alexandrowicz, *The Law of Nations in Global History*, ed. David Armitage and Jennifer Pitts (Oxford: Oxford University Press, 2017), 3–4.

28. Armitage and Pitts, 6–7.

29. T. S. Ramu Rao, "Prof. C. H. Alexandrowicz: A Tribute," *Indian Yearbook for International Affairs* 18 (1980): viii.

30. See Kalyani Ramnath, "Intertwined Itineraries: Debt, Decolonization, and International Law in Post–World War II South Asia," *Law and History Review* 38, no. 1 (2020): 16–19; Armitage and Pitts, "'This Modern Grotius,'" 8–10. At the end of the 1950s, Madras was slowly replaced by New Delhi as the central locus of Indian international legal thought, and Alexandrowicz's journal, the *Indian Yearbook of International Affairs*, was correspondingly overtaken by a new publication, the *Indian Journal of International Law*, edited by Radhabinod Pal. On the latter, see Prabhakar Singh, "Reading RP Anand in the Post-colony: Between Resistance and Appropriation," in *The Battle for International Law: South-North Perspectives on the Decolonization Era*, ed. Jochen von Bernstoff and Philipp Dann (Oxford: Oxford University Press, 2019), 302–3 (including note 34).

31. Rao, "Prof. C. H. Alexandrowicz," ix.

32. C. H. Alexandrowicz, "Grotius and India," *Indian Yearbook of International Affairs* 3 (1954): 357.

33. Jennifer Pitts works closely with Alexandrowicz's schema in *Boundaries of the International: Law and Empire* (Cambridge, MA: Harvard University Press, 2018).

34. C. H. Alexandrowicz, "Mogul Sovereignty and the Law of Nations," *Indian Yearbook of International Affairs* 4 (1955): 316–24; Alexandrowicz, "'Jus Gentium' and the Law of Nature in Asia," *Aryan Path* 27 (1956): 13–19.

35. B. S. Chimni, "The Past, Present and Future of International Law: A Critical Third World Approach," *Melbourne Journal of International Law* 8, no. 2 (2007): 500–501. In Baxi's account, he was something of an unwitting or accidental theorist: "Charles had the courage of his conviction, in a wholly pre-postmodern era, that defiantly legitimated the telling of the stories of the making of modern international law from non-European perspectives." Upendra Baxi, "New Approaches to the History of International Law," *Leiden Journal of International Law* 19 (2006): 555.

36. Anand, "Role of the 'New' Asian-African Countries in the Present International Legal Order," 386–87 (quotation on 386).

37. R. P. Anand, "Attitude of the Asian-African States toward Certain Problems of International Law," *International and Comparative Law Quarterly* 15, no. 1 (1966): 58.

38. Anand puts this phrase in quotation marks, though it is not to be found in the Alexandrowicz citation he gives in the next sentence. Anand, 58.

39. Alexandrowicz, "Mogul Sovereignty and the Law of Nations," 318, and quoted in Anand, "Attitude of the Asian-African States toward Certain Problems of International Law," 58.

40. Anand, "Role of the 'New' Asian-African Countries in the Present International Legal Order," 383–406; Anand, "Attitude of the Asian-African States toward Certain Problems of International Law," 55–75.

41. Anand, "Editor's Introduction," xvii (emphasis in original).

42. Upendra Baxi, "Some Remarks on Eurocentrism and the Law of Nations," in *Asian States and the Development of Universal International Law*, ed. R. P. Anand (Delhi: Vikas Publications, 1972), 4 (emphasis in original).

43. See Armitage and Pitts, "'This Modern Grotius,'" 11–12.

44. Upendra Baxi in Sundhya Pahuja and Adil Hasan Khan, "The Southern Jurist as a Teacher of Laws: An Interview with Upendra Baxi," *Jindal Global Law Review* 9 (2018): 363.

45. Upendra Baxi to Kaka [Vishnuprasad Venilal Baxi], 24 October 1964, reproduced in Pratiksha Baxi and Viplav Baxi, "Letters to Kaka: Postcard-Images of Upendra Baxi," *Jindal Global Law Review* 9 (2018): 245.

46. Baxi and Baxi, "Letters to Kaka," 245; Baxi recollections in Pahuja and Khan, "The Southern Jurist as a Teacher of Laws," 363.

47. Upendra Baxi, "Charles Henry Alexandrowicz: A Memorial," *Tamil Nadu National Law University Law Review* 2, no. 1 (2019): 2.

48. Baxi, 3.

49. Charles H. Alexandrowicz, "New and Original States: The Issue of Reversion to Sovereignty," *International Affairs* 45, no. 3 (1969): 465; also 471.

50. Alexandrowicz, 474.

51. Alexandrowicz, 474.

52. C. H. Alexandrowicz, "The New States and International Law," *Millennium* 4 (1974): 226.

53. Rao, "Prof. C. H. Alexandrowicz," xi.

54. Alexandrowicz, "New and Original States," 475.

55. Alexandrowicz, 478, including note 35.

56. See Miranda Johnson, "Indigenizing Self-Determination at the United Nations: Reparative Progress in the Declaration on the Rights of Indigenous Peoples," *Journal of the History of International Law* 23, no. 1 (2021): 206–28.

57. Irene Watson, "The Future Is Our Past: We Once Were Sovereign and We Still Are," *Indigenous Law Bulletin* 8, no. 3 (2012): 14.

58. Watson, 14.

59. United Nations, Economic and Social Council, Commission on Human Rights, "Human Rights of Indigenous Peoples: Study on Treaties, Agreements and Other Constructive Arrangements between States and Indigenous Populations," Final Report by Miguel Alfonso Martínez, Special Rapporteur, 22 June 1999, E/CN.4/Sub.2/1999/20, at paragraph 288. See also 286.

60. The Uluru Statement from the Heart, 2017, https://ulurustatement.org/the -statement.

61. C. H. Alexandrowicz to Hedley Bull, 22 October 1971, Records of the Australian Institute of International Affairs, National Library of Australia, MS 2821, Research Committee Chairman's Correspondence Files, 1969–1982, Box 93 (Prof. C. H. Alexandrowicz, 1972–73). Alexandrowicz was inquiring about the possibility of a research grant from an Australian institution to continue this research in Canberra.

62. James Crawford, *The Creation of States in International Law* (Oxford: Clarendon Press, 1979), based on Crawford's 1977 degree, supervised by Ian Brownlie, whom Alexandrowicz cited on reversion to sovereignty ("New and Original States," 475, 479). A much revised and expanded new edition, running close to nine hundred pages, was published in 2006: James Crawford, *The Creation of States in International Law*, 2nd ed. (Oxford: Clarendon Press, 2006). Citations below continue to refer to the first edition. The quoted passage about Crawford's standing, expressing a widely held sentiment, is from Philippe Sands, "James Crawford Obituary," *The Guardian*, June 13, 2021, https://www.theguardian.com /law/2021/jun/13/james-crawford-obituary.

63. Crawford, *Creation of States*, 5.

64. As Alexandrowicz had been at pains to point out, prepositivist international law (Grotius, Pufendorf, and so forth), with its naturalistic universalism, had none of the same problems with topic. Crawford too surveyed that earlier tradition, noting that they also

spent far less time thinking about the state in an external sense. Crawford, *Creation of States*, 5–11.

65. The two major theories of recognition—the declarative and the constitutive—were characterized by substantial disagreement and ambiguity such that they no longer seemed a viable way of handling the problem in international law. See Crawford, *Creation of States*, 15–25.

66. Matthew Craven, "Statehood, Self-Determination, and Recognition," in *International Law*, 3rd ed., ed. Malcolm D. Evans (Oxford: Oxford University Press, 2010), 205 (emphasis added).

67. Nathaniel Berman, "Sovereignty in Abeyance: Self-Determination and International Law," *Wisconsin International Law Journal* 7, no. 1 (1988): 63.

68. To adapt a phrase from David Armitage, *The Declaration of Independence: A Global History* (Cambridge, MA: Harvard University Press, 2007).

69. Crawford, *Creation of States*, 3.

70. Crawford, 5.

71. Crawford, vii.

72. Krystyna Marek, *Identity and Continuity of States in Public International Law* (Geneva: Librairie E. Droz, 1954), 1.

73. Alfred Verdross, Review of *Identity and Continuity of States in Public International Law* by Krystyna Marek, *Österreichische Zeitschrift für öffentliches Recht*, no. 1 (1955): 107–8.

74. See Natasha Wheatley, "What Can We (She) Know about Sovereignty? Krystyna Marek and the Worldedness of International Law," in *Women's International Thought: A New History*, ed. Patricia Owens and Katharina Rietzler (Cambridge: Cambridge University Press, 2021), 327–44.

75. Much of the following biographical information is taken from the extended curriculum vitae and dossier (written in part by Pierre Pagneux) contained in map 19 at the Krystyna Marek Papers, Polish Museum, Rapperswil, Switzerland (hereafter KMP). I provide a fuller account in Wheatley, "What Can We (She) Know About Sovereignty?" See also Bogumił Termiński, "Krystyna Marek (1914–1993): Polish Lawyer and Patriot," *Revista europea de derecho de la navegación marítima y aeronáutica* (December 2013), http://rednma.eumed.net/krystyna-marek-1914-1993/.

76. Mrs A. Deacon, Adminstrative Office (Political Intelligence Department of the Foreign Office) to Krystyna Marek, 26 November 1943, KMP, map 43.

77. Certification of Marek passing Diplomatic-Consular Examination signed by Minister Tadeusz Romer, Republic of Poland, Ministry of Foreign Affairs, 5 May 1944, KMP, map 18.

78. R. Dunbar (Foreign Office) to Count Edward Raczyński (Ambassador), 7 December 1944, KMP, map 54.

79. Most of Marek's subsequent adult life was spent in Switzerland in refugee status. This only changed with the end of the Cold War and the collapse of the Soviet Union. On July 31, 1992, the Swiss Federal Office for Refugees wrote to Marek seeking confirmation that she was in possession of a Polish passport and stating that once the reason underpinning refugee status was removed, that status, too, was revoked. Marek replied on August 6 and affirmed that, yes, she would now be taking up her Polish passport once again, with all the consequences of that act, renounced her right of asylum in Switzerland, and thanked them for providing the juridical foundation for her existence over these long decades. She died the following year, having lived Hobsbawm's "short twentieth century" almost to the day, and in more ways than one. Bundesamt für Fluchtlinger to Krystyna Marek, 31 July 1992, KMP, map 42; Krystyna Marek to Office fédéraldes réfugiés, 6 August 1992, KMP, map 42.

80. Université de Genève, École d'Interprètes, Examens, Diplome, 1949, KMP, map 18; l'Union internationale des télécommunications, Certificate, 20 April 1953, KMP, map 18; World Meteorological Organization, Certificate of Service, 2 June 1954, KMP, map 18.

81. Marek, *Identity and Continuity of States*, 1.

82. Marek, 2.

83. See chapter 6.

84. For a gorgeous, irreverent discussion of these philosophical problems, see Miguel Tamen, *Friends of Interpretable Objects* (Cambridge, MA: Harvard University Press, 2001), 85–86, and generally chapters 4 and 5 on "Persons" and "Rights," respectively.

85. Marek, *Identity and Continuity of States*, 2.

86. See chapter 6.

87. Marek, *Identity and Continuity of States*, 2.

88. Marek, 548 and generally.

89. Marek, Part 1.

90. Marek, 581–82 (emphasis added).

91. He also quoted Justice Holmes: Were these states "ghosts that are seen in the law but that are elusive to the grasp"? Philip Jessup, Review of *Identity and Continuity of States in Public International Law* by Krystyna Marek, *University of Pennsylvania Law Review* 104, no. 4 (1956): 574.

92. Roughly half the book was devoted to more formal legal argument; the second half comprised a more empirical tour through all the major cases of the modern period up to that point.

93. See John Forrester, *Thinking in Cases* (Cambridge: Polity, 2017).

94. Martti Koskenniemi, *The Gentle Civilizer of Nations: The Rise and Fall of International Law, 1870–1960* (Cambridge: Cambridge University Press, 2001), chap. 6. See, more generally, Matthew Specter, *The Atlantic Realists* (Stanford, CA: Stanford University Press, 2022).

95. In the final pages of his landmark book, Koskenniemi celebrated something he called "the culture of formalism," which "tries to induce every particularity to bring about the universality hidden within it," and argued that it is the only thing that gives the history of international law any "coherence." Koskenniemi, *The Gentle Civilizer of Nations*, 500–509. For a discussion of the critical potential of this renewed formalism, see Justin Desautels-Stein, "Chiastic Law in the Crystal Ball: Exploring Legal Formalism and Its Alternatives," *London Review of International Law* 2, no. 2 (2014): 263–96.

96. A raft of new scholarship explores some of these links: see, for example, Malgorzata Mazurek, "Polish Economists in Nehru's India: Making Science for the Third World in an Era of De-Stalinization and Decolonization," *Slavic Review* 77, no. 3 (2019): 588–610; Slobodian, *Globalists*; James Mark and Paul Betts, coord., *Socialism Goes Global: The Soviet Union and Eastern Europe in the Age of Decolonization* (Oxford: Oxford University Press, 2022).

97. Abi-Saab, "The Newly Independent States," 100.

98. Syatauw, "The Relationship between the Newness of States and Their Practices of International Law," 11.

99. Abi-Saab, "The Newly Independent States," 113.

100. In determining to what extent a postcolonial state could start with a clean slate, the law of succession indexed, in Matthew Craven's words, "either the profundity or superficiality of decolonization." Matthew Craven, *The Decolonization of International Law: State Succession and the Law of Treaties* (Oxford: Oxford University Press, 2007), 5.

101. Mohammed Bedjaoui, *Towards a New International Economic Order* (Paris: UNESCO, 1979), 81.

102. For studies of this process and the history of the law of succession more broadly, see Santiago Torres Bernardez, "Succession of States," in *International Law: Achievements*

and Prospects, ed. Mohammed Bedjaoui (Paris: UNESCO, 1991), 381–404; Craven, *The Decolonization of International Law*; Michael Waibel, "Decolonization and Sovereign Debt: A Quagmire," in *Sovereign Debt Diplomacies: Rethinking Sovereign Debt from Colonial Empires to Hegemony*, ed. Pierre Pénet and Juan Flores Zendejas (Oxford: Oxford University Press, 2021), 313–31.

103. Mohammed Bedjaoui, First Report on Succession of States in respect of rights and duties resulting from sources other than treaties, by Mr. Mohammed Bedjaoui, Special Rapporteur, Document A/CN.4/204, extract from the *Yearbook of the International Law Commission* vol. 2 (1968): 98 (hereafter Bedjaoui, First Report on Succession of States).

104. Bedjaoui, *Towards a New International Economic Order*, 134.

105. Bedjaoui, First Report on Succession of States, 100, 101.

106. Bedjaoui, 134. On Kelsen and totems, see chap. 4 of this book.

107. Bedjaoui, First Report on Succession of States, 134.

108. Bedjaoui, 98, 99.

109. Bedjaoui, 100.

110. Bedjaoui, 100.

111. Bedjaoui, 100 (emphasis in original).

112. Bedjaoui, 100–101 (emphasis in original).

113. Bedjaoui, 101 (emphasis in original).

114. Bedjaoui, 101.

115. Bedjaoui, 101.

116. Bedjaoui, 101.

117. Bedjaoui, 101.

118. Bedjaoui, 101.

119. See especially Adom Getachew, *Worldmaking after Empire: The Rise and Fall of Self-Determination* (Princeton, NJ: Princeton University Press, 2019).

120. Declaration on the Establishment of a New International Economic Order, General Assembly Resolution 3201 (S-VI), May 1, 1974; Bedjaoui, *Towards a New International Economic Order*. See further Özsu, "'In the Interests of Mankind as a Whole.'"

121. "Texts of Declarations by 3 Republic Leaders," *New York Times*, December 9, 1991, A8. See further the subsequent declaration of eleven republics with a parallel formulation: "Text of Declaration: 'Mutual Recognition' and 'an Equal Basis,'" *New York Times*, December 22, 1991, 12.

122. *New York Times*, December 9, 1991, A1.

123. For a study of longer-term structural malaise, see Stephen Kotkin, *Armageddon Averted: The Soviet Collapse, 1970–2000* (Oxford: Oxford University Press, 2008).

124. László Lengyel, "Europe through Hungarian Eyes," *International Affairs* 66, no. 2 (1990): 291, 296.

125. Lengyel, "Europe through Hungarian Eyes," 296.

126. See Holm Sundhaussen, "Der Gegensatz zwischen historischen Rechten und Selbstbestimmungsrechten als Ursache von Konflikten: Kosovo und Krajina im Vergleich," in *Nationalitätenkonflikte im 20. Jahrhundert: Ursachen von inter-ethnischer Gewalt im Vergleich*, ed. Philipp Ther and Holm Sundhaussen (Wiesbaden: Harrassowitz, 2001), 19–33.

127. Report of the Austrian Federal Ministry for Foreign Affairs for the year 1992, *Austrian Foreign Policy Yearbook* (1992): 30.

128. Martti Koskenniemi, "Report of the Director of Studies of the English-speaking Section of the Centre," in *La succession d'Etats: la codification à l'épreuve des faits / State Succession: Codification Tested against the Facts*, ed. Pierre Michel Eisemann and Martti Koskenniemi (The Hague: Martinus Nijhoff, 2000), 65.

129. "Dumbfounded analysts" in Kotkin, *Armageddon Averted*, 3.

130. Norman Davies, *Vanished Kingdoms: The Rise and Fall of States and Nations* (New York: Penguin 2011), 729. See also Timothy Snyder, *The Reconstruction of Nations: Poland, Ukraine, Lithuania, Belarus, 1569–1999* (New Haven, CT: Yale University Press, 2003).

131. Alexei Yurchak, *Everything Was Forever Until It Was No More* (Princeton, NJ: Princeton University Press, 2005).

132. Figure from Koskenniemi, "Report of the Director of Studies," 75.

133. Martti Koskenniemi in manuscript workshop, March 1, 2022, recording on file with author; Martti Koskenniemi email to Natasha Wheatley, September 7, 2022, on file with author.

134. Martti Koskenniemi in manuscript workshop, March 1, 2022, recording on file with author.

135. Koskenniemi, "Report of the Director of Studies," 119. See further Craven, *The Decolonization of International Law*, 208–58.

136. Perhaps the most vocal critic was succession expert Daniel Patrick O'Connell (1924–1979). Born in New Zealand, O'Connell pursued a PhD at Cambridge where his supervisor, Hersch Lauterpacht—one of Kelsen's students—suggested the topic of succession. O'Connell then taught for some twenty years at the University of Adelaide, where a young James Crawford was among his students, before election as Chichele professor at Oxford. A devout Catholic and social conservative, O'Connell thought succession resisted all codification and decried "preoccupation with the special problem of decolonization, around which myth and emotion have accumulated like mists in the marsh, so that the whole context became intellectually distorted." D. P. O'Connell, "Reflections on the State Succession Convention," *Zeitschrift für ausländisches öffentliches Recht und Völkerrecht* 39 (1979): 726. See further I. A. Shearer, "O'Connell, Daniel Patrick (1924–1979)," *Australian Dictionary of Biography* (Melbourne: Melbourne University Press, 2000), 15:514–15; James Crawford, "International Law and the Rule of Law," *Adelaide Law Review* 24 (2003): 3–12; and the extensive discussion in Craven, *The Decolonization of International Law*.

137. Craven, *The Decolonization of International Law*, 2; O'Connell, "Reflections on the State Succession Convention"; Wilfried Fiedler, "Die Konventionen zum Recht der Staatensukzession: Ein Beitrag der ILC zur Entwicklung eines 'modern international law'?," *German Yearbook of International Law* 24 (1981): 9–62; Stefan Oeter, "German Unification and State Succession," *Zeitschrift für ausländisches öffentliches Recht und Völkerrecht* 51 (1991): 352–59; Malcolm N. Shaw, "State Succession Revisited," *Finnish Yearbook of International Law* 5 (1994): 34–40; Gerhard Hafner and Elisabeth Kornfeind, "The Recent Austrian Practice of State Succession: Does the Clean Slate Rule Still Exist?," *Austrian Review of International and European Law* 1 (1996): 2.

138. Quoted in Yehuda Z. Blum, "Russia Takes Over the Soviet Union's Seat at the United Nations," *European Journal of International Law* 3 (1992): 356.

139. Blum, "Russia Takes Over the Soviet Union's Seat"; Malcolm N. Shaw, "State Succession Revisited," *Finnish Yearbook of International Law* 5 (1994): 47–50; discussion of the term *continuator* in Guido Acquaviva, "Russia as the State Continuing the Legal Personality of the USSR—An Inquiry into State Identity or Succession," *Journal of the History of International Law* 23, no. 2 (2021): 311, 316–17, 320.

140. For figures, see Acquaviva, "Russia as the State Continuing the Legal Personality of the USSR," 312.

141. Quoted in Lesia Dubenko, "Ukraine Doubts Russia's UN Security Council Membership," *Kyiv Post*, February 10, 2022, https://www.kyivpost.com/world/ukraine-doubts -russias-un-security-council-membership.html. See further Hayes Brown, "Why Ukraine Thinks Russia Doesn't Belong at the United Nations," *MSNBC*, February 25, 2022,

https://www.msnbc.com/opinion/msnbc-opinion/ukraine-s-u-n-ambassador-calls-russia-s-veto-question-n1289826.

142. Quoted in "Ukraine Believes Russia's UN, UNSC Membership Illegitimate," *Euromaidan Press*, 25 February 2022, https://euromaidanpress.com/2022/02/25/ukraine-questions-legality-of-russias-un-unsc-membership/.

143. Slovenia, Croatia, and Bosnia-Herzegovina joined the UN as new states on May 22, 1992.

144. For an overview, see Shaw, "State Succession Revisited," 50–54.

145. United Nations Security Council Resolution 777, 19 September 1992, UN Doc. S/RES/777 (1992). It was a major issue for financial institutions, too, where the outstanding obligations of Yugoslavia and Czechoslovakia combined tallied over 3.5 billion dollars. The IMF and the World Bank similarly judged that the former Yugoslavia no longer existed. Paul R. Williams, "State Succession and the International Financial Institutions: Political Criteria v. Protection of Outstanding Financial Obligations," *International and Comparative Law Quarterly* 43, no. 4 (1994): 776–808.

146. The special status of Ukraine and Byelorussia/Belarus is also worth noting. Though components of the USSR, they already enjoyed some form of international legal personality as founding members of the UN in their own names. Their UN membership was the result of Stalin's angling for more seats in the UN General Assembly (a parallel to the separate membership of multiple British colonies in the League of Nations). Thus, between 1945 and 1990, Ukraine and Byelorussia were UN members alongside the USSR, while "Russia" was not. Their membership continued through the collapse of the USSR uninterrupted. Many scholars have likened this to the status of India and the Philippines, "which became members of the UN as dependent units and preserved this status after declaring independence." Lech Antonowicz, "The Disintegration of the USSR from the Point of View of International Law," *Polish Yearbook of International Law* 19 (1991–92): 12. On the checkered history of the international standing of the USSR's constituent republics, see John N. Hazard, "Soviet Republics in International Law," in *Encyclopedia of Public International Law*, Installment 10, ed. Rudolf Bernhardt (Amsterdam: North-Holland, 1987), 418–23.

147. Resolution of the Supreme Soviet of the Estonian SSR on the State Status of Estonia, Tallinn, March 30, 1990, *Finnish Yearbook of International Law* 2 (1991): 523.

148. Declaration on the National Independence of Estonia, Tallinn, February 2, 1990, *Finnish Yearbook of International Law* 2 (1991): 519.

149. The Republic of Estonia Supreme Council Resolution on the National Independence of Estonia, Tallinn, August 20, 1991, *Finnish Yearbook of International Law* 2 (1991): 525.

150. Lauri Mälksoo, *Illegal Annexation and State Continuity: The Case of the Incorporation of the Baltic States by the USSR*, 2nd rev. ed. (Leiden: Brill Nijhoff, 2022), 1.

151. Martti Koskenniemi, "National Self-Determination Today: Problems of Legal Theory and Practice," *International and Comparative Law Quarterly* 43, no. 2 (1994): 244, 258n63.

152. Statement by an extraordinary EPC Ministerial Meeting concerning the Baltic States, Brussels, 27 August 1991, *European Political Cooperation Documentation Bulletin* 7 (1991): 388.

153. Rein Müllerson, "The Continuity and Succession of States, by Reference to the Former USSR and Yugoslavia," *International and Comparative Law Quarterly* 42, no. 3 (1993): 482.

154. Antonowicz, "The Disintegration of the USSR," 14.

155. Antonowicz, 14.

156. Koskenniemi, "Report of the Director of Studies," 67; see further 68.

157. Müllerson, "The Continuity and Succession of States," 483. Müllerson, who served as deputy foreign minister of Estonia in 1991–92, conceded that "in practice it was very difficult to neglect legal norms and juridical facts that had occurred during the period since 1940," making it "often more a legal fiction than a reality."

158. Craven, *The Decolonization of International Law*, 223–25; Shaw, "State Succession Revisited," 58; Hafner and Kornfeind, "The Recent Austrian Practice of State Succession," 18; Arman Sarvarian, "Codifying the Law of State Succession: A Futile Endeavor?," *European Journal of International Law* 27, no. 3 (2016): 789–812; and for a thorough treatment, Mälksoo, *Illegal Annexation and State Continuity*.

159. Pierre Michel Eisenmann and Martti Koskenniemi, ed., *La succession d'Etats: la codification à l'épreuve des faits / State Succession: Codification Tested against the Facts* (The Hague: Martinus Nijhoff, 2000).

160. Koskenniemi, "Report of the Director of Studies," 124.

161. Koskenniemi, 131–32.

Conclusion

1. In the phrasing of international lawyer James Crawford, authority on the creation of states (and character in chapter 7 of this book). He added that states are "one of the few secure transmission mechanisms we have." James Crawford, *Chance, Order, Change: The Course of International Law* ([The Hague]: The Hague Academy of International Law, 2014), 113. See also James Crawford and Jeremy Watkins, "International Responsibility," in *The Philosophy of International Law*, ed. Samantha Besson and John Tasioulas (Oxford: Oxford University Press, 2010), 291–92, where they highlighted the need for transmission mechanisms in "a world in which long-term planning is important."

2. Miguel Tamen, *Friends of Interpretable Objects* (Cambridge, MA: Harvard University Press, 2001), 101, 102.

3. To paraphrase Ernst Kantorowicz, *The King's Two Bodies: A Study in Mediaeval Political Theology* (1957; Princeton, NJ: Princeton University Press, 1997), 281.

4. Christopher Clark, *Time and Power: Visions of History in German Politics, from the Thirty Years' War to the Third Reich* (Princeton, NJ: Princeton University Press, 2019), chap. 1 ("The History Machine").

5. Matthew Craven, "Statehood, Self-Determination, and Recognition," in *International Law*, 4th ed., ed. Malcolm D. Evans (Oxford: Oxford University Press, 2014), 201.

6. For work in political science that attempts a general theory valid across the modern period, see Tanisha M. Fazal, *State Death: The Politics and Geography of Conquest, Occupation, and Annexation* (Princeton, NJ: Princeton University Press, 2007).

7. For an alternative way of doing so, see Alison Frank, "The Children of the Desert and the Laws of the Sea: Austria, Great Britain, the Ottoman Empire, and the Mediterranean Slave Trade in the Nineteenth Century," *American Historical Review* 117, no. 2 (2012): 410–44.

8. Nicholas B. Dirks, *The Hollow Crown: Ethnohistory of an Indian Kingdom* (Cambridge: Cambridge University Press, 1987): "theatre state," a phrase he borrowed from Clifford Geertz, is the title of chapter 13. On the Indian princely states through and beyond empire, see Priyasha Saksena, "Jousting over Jurisdiction: Sovereignty and International Law in Late Nineteenth-Century South Asia," *Law and History Review* 38, no. 2 (2020): 409–57 (including a survey of challenges to Dirks's characterization in footnote 12); and Lauren Benton, "From International Law to Imperial Constitutions: The Problem of Quasi-Sovereignty, 1870–1900," *Law and History Review* 26, no. 3 (2008): 595–619. On the Ottoman provinces, see especially Aimee Genell, "Autonomous Provinces and the Problem of 'Semi-Sovereignty' in European International Law," *Journal of Balkan and Near Eastern*

Studies 18, no. 6 (2016): 533–49, and Aimee Genell, *Empire by Law: The Ottoman Origins of the Mandates System in the Middle East* (New York: Columbia University Press, forthcoming). See further Lauren Benton and Adam Clulow, "Protection Shopping among Empires: Suspended Sovereignty in the Cocos-Keeling Islands," *Past and Present* (forthcoming).

9. See, for example, Ben Silverstein, "Submerged Sovereignty: Native Title within a History of Incorporation," in *Sovereignty: Frontiers of Possibility*, ed. Julie Evans, Ann Genovese, Alexander Reilly, and Patrick Wolfe (Honolulu: University of Hawai'i Press, 2013), 60–85; as well as Elizabeth A. Povinelli, "The Governance of the Prior," *Interventions* 13, no. 1 (2011): 13–30; Natasha Wheatley, "Legal Pluralism as Temporal Pluralism: Historical Rights, Legal Vitalism, and Non-Synchronous Sovereignty," in *Power and Time: Temporalities in Conflict and the Making of History*, ed. Dan Edelstein, Stefanos Geroulanos, and Natasha Wheatley (Chicago: University of Chicago Press, 2020), 53–79.

10. Duncan Bell, *The Idea of Greater Britain: Empire and the Future of World Order, 1860–1900* (Princeton, NJ: Princeton University Press, 2007); Mark Mazower, *No Enchanted Palace: The End of Empire and the Ideological Origins of the United Nations* (Princeton, NJ: Princeton University Press, 2009); Mark Mazower, *Governing the World: The History of an Idea, 1815 to the Present* (New York: Penguin Books, 2013); Susan Pedersen, *The Guardians: The League of Nations and the Crisis of Empire* (Oxford: Oxford University Press, 2015).

11. Peter Holquist, "The Laws of War," *Berlin Journal* 32 (2018): 68–70; Peter Holquist, "By Right of War: The Discipline and Practice of International Law in Imperial Russia, 1868–1917," manuscript in preparation; Philippa Hetherington, "International Criminology and the Russian Fight against Transnational Obscenity, 1885–1925," *Russian History* 43, no. 3–4 (2016): 275–310; Philippa Hetherington, "Victims of the Social Temperament: Prostitution, Migration and the Traffic in Women from Imperial Russia and the Soviet Union, 1885–1935," PhD diss. (Harvard University, 2014); Will Smiley, *From Slaves to Prisoners of War: The Ottoman Empire, Russia, and International Law* (Oxford: Oxford University Press, 2018); Francine Hirsch, *Soviet Judgement at Nuremberg: A New History of the International Military Tribunal after World War II* (Oxford: Oxford University Press, 2020). On the Ottoman empire, see further Lâle Can, Michael Christopher Low, Kent F. Schull, and Robert Zens, eds., *The Subjects of Ottoman International Law* (Bloomington: Indiana University Press, 2020), as well as work by Aimee Genell, cited above.

12. Peter Becker, "Von *Listen* und anderen Stolpersteinen auf dem Weg zur Globalisierung: Die Habsburgermonarchie und der Internationalismus des 'langen' 19. Jahrhunderts," in *Internationale Geschichte in Theorie und Praxis*, ed. Barbara Haider-Wilson, William D. Godsey, and Wolfgang Mueller (Vienna: Verlag der Österreichischen Akademie der Wissenschaften, 2017), 665–93.

13. Benton, "From International Law to Imperial Constitutions"; Lauren Benton and Lisa Ford, *Rage for Order: The British Empire and the Origins of International Law* (Cambridge, MA: Harvard University Press, 2016).

14. Hans Kelsen, *Der soziologische und der juristische Staatsbegriff: Kritische Untersuchungen des Verhältnisses von Staat und Recht* (Tübingen: J. C. B. Mohr, 1922), 90n1.

15. On Tezner, see chapters 2 and 4. On Ehrlich, see the work cited in the introduction to this book (at note 30). For research on empirical-sociological conceptions of the state in Austria-Hungary, see Thomas R. Prendergast, "The Sociological Idea of the State: Legal Education, Austrian Multinationalism, and the Future of Continental Empire," *Comparative Studies in Society and History* 62, no. 2 (2020): 327–58.

16. David Kennedy, "The International Style in Postwar Law and Policy," *Utah Law Review* 1 (1994): 21.

17. Judith N. Shklar, *Legalism: Law, Morals, and Political Trials* (Cambridge, MA: Harvard University Press, 1964), 38.

18. "Is the Basic Norm the people of Ghana who supported the armed forces and the police or is the Basic Norm to be detected from the armoured cars at Burma Camp?," asked a Ghanaian court, critical of this approach, in 1970. On all these cases, see Tayyab Mahmud, "Jurisprudence of Successful Treason: Coup d'Etat & Common Law," *Cornell International Law Journal* 27, no. 1 (1994): 49–140; Ghanaian case *Sallah v. Attorney-General* is quoted on 67. Mahmud argued that Kelsen's theory was "out of step with the reality of coups in post-colonial societies that do not aim at destruction of the entire legal order, but only at usurpation of political offices" (107). See, further, brilliantly, Samuel Fury Childs Daly, "The Portable Coup: The Jurisprudence of 'Revolution' in Uganda and Nigeria," *Law and History Review* 39, no. 4 (2021): 737–64, especially 751–58 on Kelsen and the *Grundnorm* as "an unlikely buzzword in 1970s Nigeria" (756).

19. For one resurrection that uses Kelsen's framework to argue that the formal abstraction of the state is precisely what enables us to mediate society's competing appeals to authenticity, see Martti Koskenniemi, "The Wonderful Artificiality of States," *Proceedings of the Annual Meeting (American Society of International Law)* 88 (1994): 22–9.

20. For an introduction to this influential subfield of historical epistemology, see Lorraine Daston, "Historical Epistemology," in *Questions of Evidence: Proof, Practice, and Persuasion across the Disciplines*, ed. James Chandler, Arnold I. Davidson, and Harry Harootunian (Chicago: University of Chicago Press, 1994), 282–89; Lorraine Daston and Peter Galison, *Objectivity* (New York: Zone Books, 2007); and Paul Veyne, "Foucault Revolutionizes History," in *Foucault and His Interlocutors*, ed. Arnold I. Davidson (Chicago: University of Chicago Press, 1997), 146–82.

281; Raczyński and, 269; as refugee, 377n79
Marek, Zygmunt, 269
Maria Theresa, 9; dual sovereignty and, 62, 65; fictional states and, 117–24
Marikar, Naina, 260
Marx, Karl, 17
Marxism: Austro-Marxism 16, 17, 129–33, 252–3, 286, 299n65, 357n99, 363n23, 371n217; Bauer and, 129, 131, 286; Bloch and, 305n63; Engels and, 299n64; Renner and, 129, 286; Rosdolsky and, 299n64
Masaryk, T. G., 116; background of, 186, 351n15; fictional states and, 116; new international order and, 184–90, 197, 208–12, 351n15, 352n19
Máthé, Gábor, 67
May Day, 222
Mayer, Arno, 16
Mayer, Kajetan, 33–38, 41–43, 107
Mayer, Otto, 158
Mazower, Mark, 285
Merkl, Adolf: Bernatzik and, 60; constitutional issues and, 232, 234–37; discontinuity and, 236, 239; juridical cognition and, 237–41; "The Legal Unity of the Austrian State," 234–35; pluralism and, 236–37; pure theory of law and, 223–25, 232–41, 245, 248, 251, 271; Stufenbau (pyramid of the legal order) of, 224, 233–35, 239, 241, 249, 367n94
Metternich, 32, 40–43, 85
Mexico, 98, 292n16
Mischler, Ernst, 91
Mises, Ludwig von, 16, 162, 222, 252, 298n56, 362n19, 371n213
modernism: avant-garde, 371n208; fiction, 56; legal, 4, 56, 58, 288; pure theory of law and, 4; Young Vienna and, 221
"Mogul Sovereignty and the Law of Nations" (Alexandrowicz), 262
Moldau, 109
monarchy: composite, 7–8, 12–13, 19, 30, 55, 57, 62, 64, 67, 78, 81, 111, 113, 124, 183, 199, 232; constitutional issues and, 7–8, 12–13, 19, 30, 36, 44, 47, 55–59, 62–69, 76–83, 100, 102, 111, 113,

122, 124, 183, 189, 192, 206, 232, 235–36; divine right and, 12, 14, 20, 22–24, 142, 288; dual sovereignty and, 56–59, 62–69, 76–83, 100, 102, 194, 232, 235; elective kingship, 62–64, 115, 187; new international order and, 183, 189, 192, 195, 199, 206; pure theory of law and, 142, 152, 164, 174, 225, 235–36, 287; stranger kings, 63, 115, 187–88.
Montenegro, 201, 280, 292n8
Moravia, 92, 162; constitutional issues and, 8–9, 34–42, 57, 107, 110–12, 129, 134, 139; dual sovereignty and, 57, 92; new international order and, 187, 189, 193, 196, 208, 211–13
Moravian Compromise, 134, 139
Morgenthau, Hans, 273
Morocco, 269
Mudalair, A. L., 261
multiculturalism, 16
Musil, Robert: dual sovereignty and, 56, 58, 60, 70, 75, 80, 86, 308n5; Kakania humor of, 58; language game of, 58; The Man without Qualities, 56, 58, 60, 223, 308n5; pure theory of law and, 178, 222–23
mythological methodology, 172–76

Namier, Lewis, 198–99, 210
National Liberation Front (FLN), 260
national questions: Austro-Marxism and, 129–33, 299n65; constitutional issues and, 16–18, 31, 32, 35–43, 45, 48–50, 68, 85, 91, 106–7, 124–38, 142, 181, 232, 285–86, 298n56, 317n146, 325n22, 330n115, 330n133, 333n166–67, 357n99; new international order and, 132–40, 142, 181–82, 184–86, 189, 201–5, 207, 209–13, 215, 232, 333n166–67, 333n172, 357n99; pure theory of law and, 143, 177–78, 227–28, 232, 287
national rights, 16–18, 35, 37–38, 42–43, 49, 124–40, 184, 188, 202, 204, 208, 209, 211; Bauer and, 137; Renner and, 132–34, 137
nationalities as legal entities, 26, 124–40
Nationalities Congress, 333n172